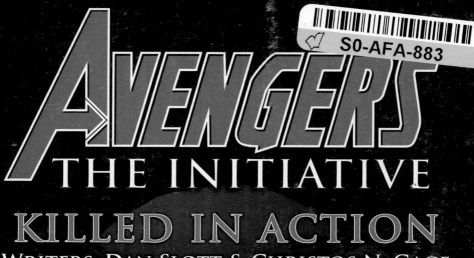

AVENGERS
THE INITIATIVE

KILLED IN ACTION

WRITERS: DAN SLOTT & CHRISTOS N. GAGE
ARTIST: STEFANO CASELLI
WITH STEVE UY (ISSUE #12-13)
COLOR ART: DANIELE RUDONI WITH STEVE UY (ISSUE #12-13)
COVER ART: STEFANO CASELLI & STEVE UY

ANNUAL #1

WRITERS: DAN SLOTT WITH CHRISTOS N. GAGE
ARTISTS: SALVADOR LARROCA, CLAYTON HENRY
& PAUL NEARY, STEVE UY, TOM FEISTER
& CARMINE DI GIANDOMENICO AND
PATRICK SCHERBERGER & DAVE MEIKIS
COLOR ART: STEPHANE PERU, DANIELE RUDONI, STEVE UY,
JOSE VILLARRUBIA & WIL QUINTANA
COVER ART: JIM CHEUNG

LETTERER: VIRTUAL CALLIGRAPHY'S JOE CARAMAGNA
ASSISTANT EDITOR: MOLLY LAZER
EDITOR: TOM BREVOORT

COLLECTION EDITOR: JENNIFER GRÜNWALD
ASSISTANT EDITORS: CORY LEVINE & JOHN DENNING
EDITOR, SPECIAL PROJECTS: MARK D. BEAZLEY
SENIOR EDITOR, SPECIAL PROJECTS: JEFF YOUNGQUIST
SENIOR VICE PRESIDENT OF SALES: DAVID GABRIEL
PRODUCTION: NELSON RIBEIRO
VICE PRESIDENT OF CREATIVE: TOM MARVELLI

EDITOR IN CHIEF: JOE QUESADA
PUBLISHER: DAN BUCKLEY

AVENGERS: THE INITIATIVE VOL. 2 — KILLED IN ACTION. Contains material originally published in magazine form as AVENGERS: THE INITIATIVE #7-13 and ANNUAL #1. First printing 2008. Hardcover ISBN# 978-0-7851-2868-7. Softcover ISBN# 978-0-7851-2861-8. Published by MARVEL PUBLISHING, INC., a subsidiary of MARVEL ENTERTAINMENT, INC. OFFICE OF PUBLICATION: 417 5th Avenue, New York, NY 10016. Copyright © 2007 and 2008 Marvel Characters, Inc. All rights reserved. Hardcover: $24.99 per copy in the U.S. and $26.50 in Canada (GST #R127032852). Softcover: $19.99 per copy in the U.S. and $21.00 in Canada (GST #R127032852). Canadian Agreement #40668537. All characters featured in this issue and the distinctive names and likenesses thereof, and all related indicia are trademarks of Marvel Characters, Inc. No similarity between any of the names, characters, persons, and/or institutions in this magazine with those of any living or dead person or institution is intended, and any such similarity which may exist is purely coincidental. **Printed in the U.S.A.** ALAN FINE, CEO Marvel Toys & Publishing Divisions and CMO Marvel Entertainment, Inc.; DAVID GABRIEL, SVP of Publishing Sales & Circulation; DAVID BOGART, SVP of Business Affairs & Talent.Management; MICHAEL PASCIULLO, VP of Merchandising & Communications; JIM O'KEEFE, VP of Operations & Logistics; DAN CARR, Executive Director of Publishing Technology; JUSTIN F. GABRIE, Director of Editorial Operations; SUSAN CRESPI, Editorial Operations Manager; OMAR OTIEKU, Production Manager; STAN LEE, Chairman Emeritus. For information regarding advertising in Marvel Comics or on Marvel.com, please contact Mitch Dane, Advertising Director, at mdane@marvel.com. For Marvel subscription inquiries, please call 800-217-9158.

10 9 8 7 6 5 4 3 2 1

AVENGERS THE INITIATIVE

AFTER STAMFORD, CONNECTICUT WAS DESTROYED DURING A TELEVISED FIGHT BETWEEN THE NEW WARRIORS AND A GROUP OF DANGEROUS VILLAINS, A FEDERAL SUPERHUMAN REGISTRATION ACT WAS PASSED. ALL INDIVIDUALS POSSESSING PARANORMAL ABILITIES MUST NOW REGISTER WITH THE GOVERNMENT. TONY STARK, A.K.A. IRON MAN, HAS BEEN APPOINTED DIRECTOR OF S.H.I.E.L.D., THE INTERNATIONAL PEACEKEEPING FORCE. HE HAS SET IN MOTION THE INITIATIVE, A PLAN FOR TRAINING AND POLICING SUPER HEROES IN THIS BRAVE NEW WORLD, INTENDED TO POSITION A LOCAL SUPER HERO TEAM IN EACH OF AMERICA'S FIFTY STATES.

STAFF

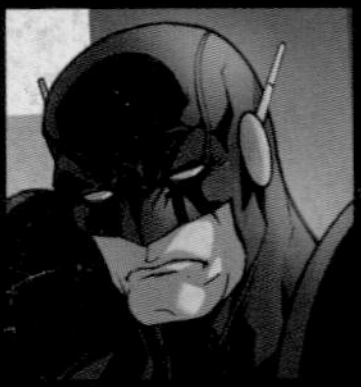
YELLOW JACKET

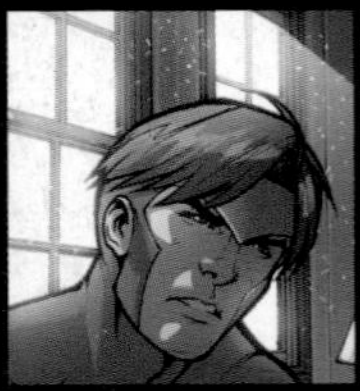
JUSTICE

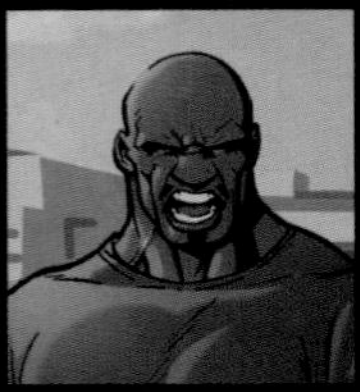
THE GAUNTLET

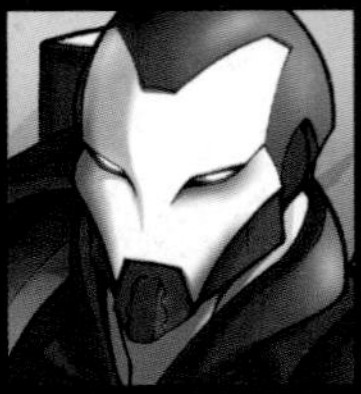
WAR MACHINE

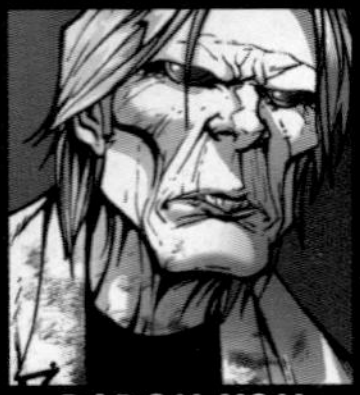
BARON VON BLITZSCHLAG

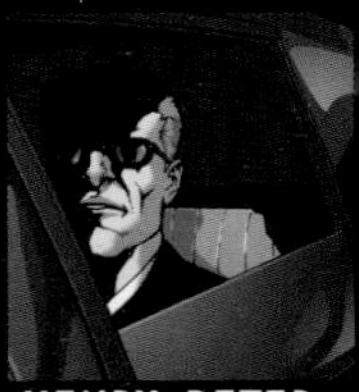
HENRY PETER GYRICH

TRAINEES

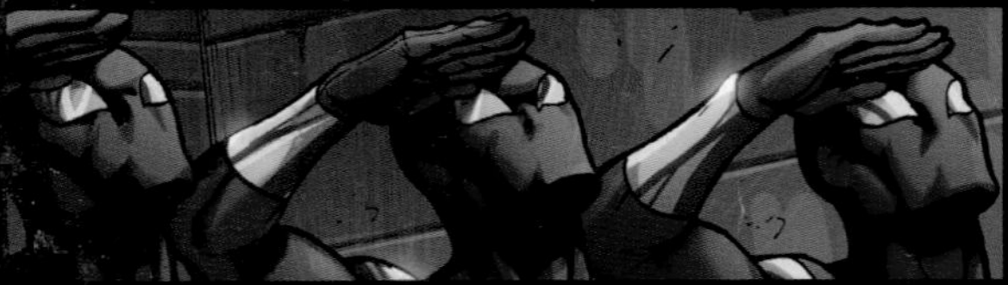
SCARLET SPIDERS

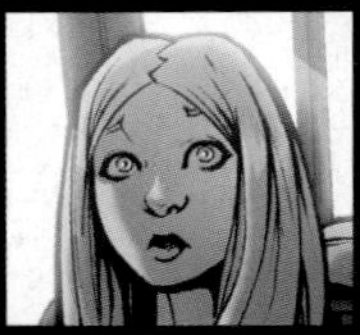
CLOUD 9

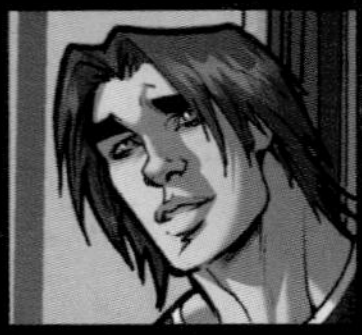
MVP (DECEASED?)

CIVILIANS

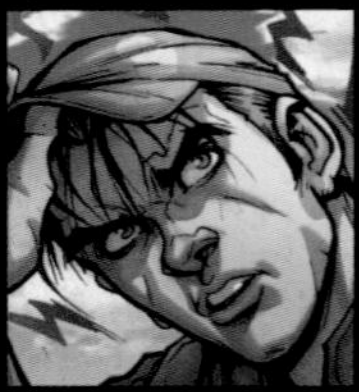
PETER PARKER/SPIDER-MAN

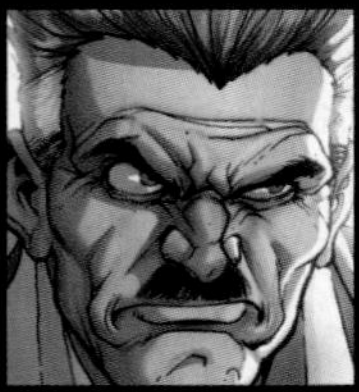
J. JONAH JAMESON

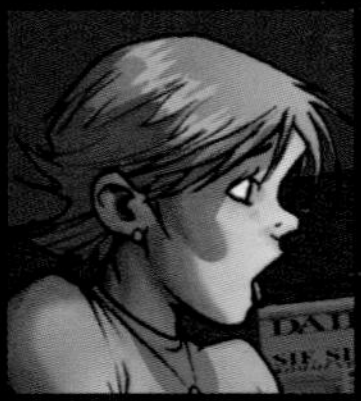
BETTY BRANT

When a training exercise goes awry, MVP — the most promising trainee in the Initiative — is killed. All those present in the room during the accident are told the incident never happened. However, on a visit to MVP's home in Kentucky, Justice and Cloud 9 discover Michael Van Patrick, very much alive!

When the Hulk threatened New York City and a group of Initiative members were captured, Gyrich sent in the Shadow Initiative, a black ops team that included the three mysterious Scarlet Spiders, to rescue them. Hulk destroyed much of Manhattan — including Stark Tower, headquarters of the Avengers — but the Initiative trainees came out relatively unharmed.

Meanwhile, apart from the destruction wrought by the Hulk, May Parker, aunt of Peter Parker (a.k.a. Spider-Man), lies in a Manhattan hospital on life support after being shot by a sniper.

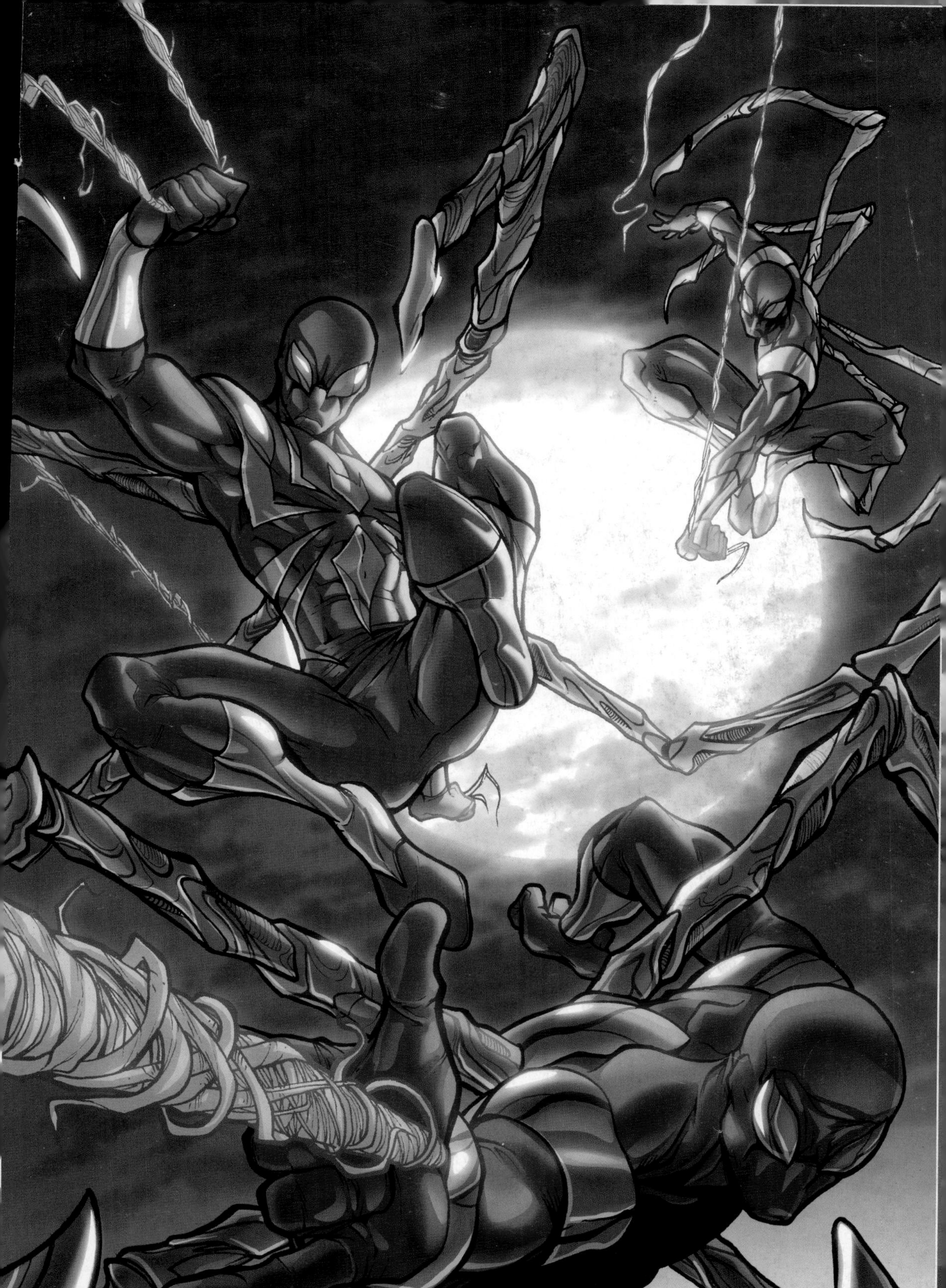

#7

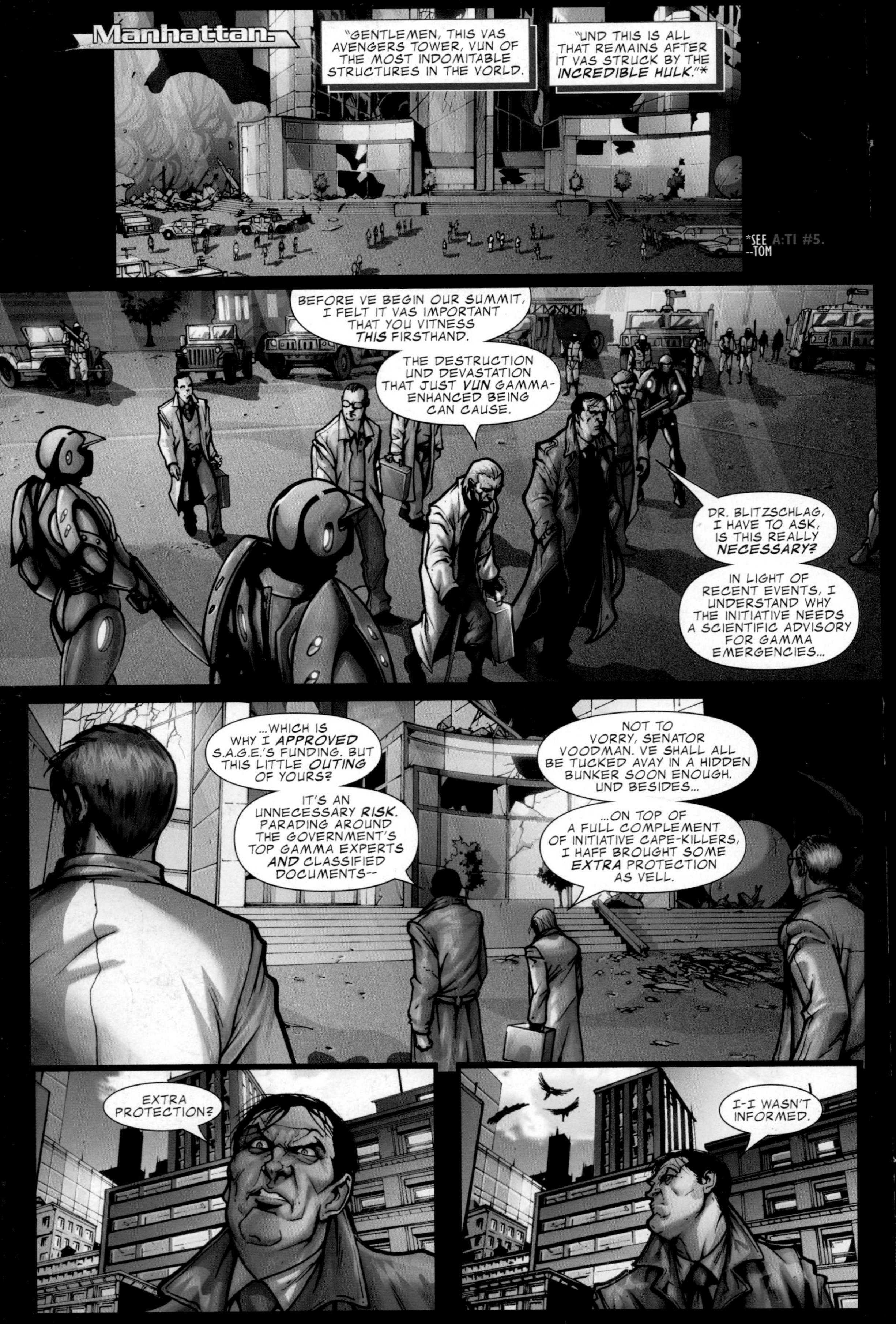
Manhattan.
"GENTLEMEN, THIS VAS AVENGERS TOWER, VUN OF THE MOST INDOMITABLE STRUCTURES IN THE VORLD.
"UND THIS IS ALL THAT REMAINS AFTER IT VAS STRUCK BY THE INCREDIBLE HULK."*
*SEE A:TI #5. --TOM
BEFORE VE BEGIN OUR SUMMIT, I FELT IT VAS IMPORTANT THAT YOU VITNESS THIS FIRSTHAND.
THE DESTRUCTION UND DEVASTATION THAT JUST VUN GAMMA-ENHANCED BEING CAN CAUSE.
DR. BLITZSCHLAG, I HAVE TO ASK, IS THIS REALLY NECESSARY?
IN LIGHT OF RECENT EVENTS, I UNDERSTAND WHY THE INITIATIVE NEEDS A SCIENTIFIC ADVISORY FOR GAMMA EMERGENCIES...
...WHICH IS WHY I APPROVED S.A.G.E.'S FUNDING. BUT THIS LITTLE OUTING OF YOURS?
IT'S AN UNNECESSARY RISK. PARADING AROUND THE GOVERNMENT'S TOP GAMMA EXPERTS AND CLASSIFIED DOCUMENTS--
NOT TO VORRY, SENATOR VOODMAN. VE SHALL ALL BE TUCKED AVAY IN A HIDDEN BUNKER SOON ENOUGH. UND BESIDES...
...ON TOP OF A FULL COMPLEMENT OF INITIATIVE CAPE-KILLERS, I HAFF BROUGHT SOME EXTRA PROTECTION AS VELL.
EXTRA PROTECTION?
I-I WASN'T INFORMED.

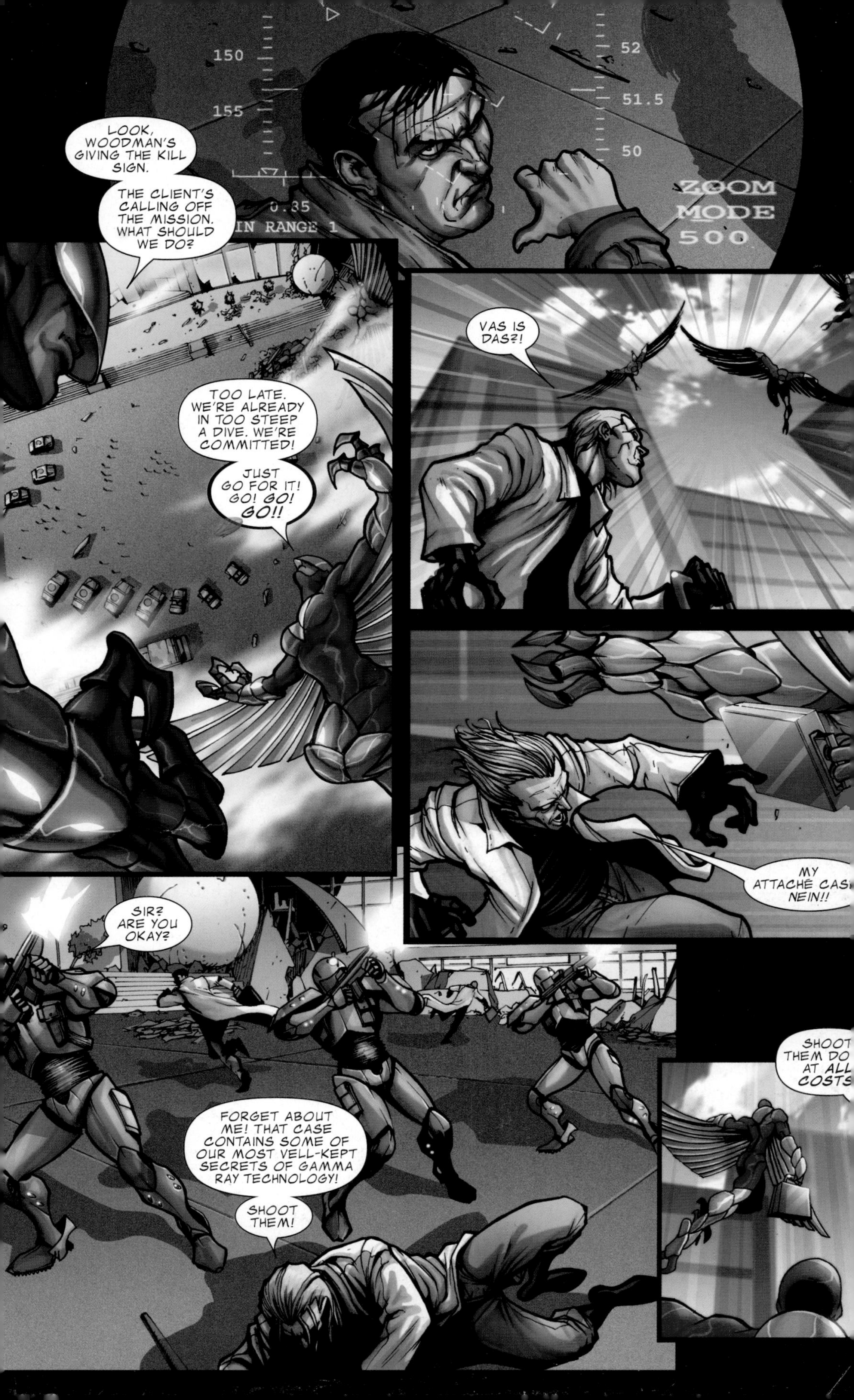
150
155
52
51.5
50
0.85
IN RANGE 1
ZOOM
MODE
500
LOOK, WOODMAN'S GIVING THE KILL SIGN.
THE CLIENT'S CALLING OFF THE MISSION. WHAT SHOULD WE DO?
TOO LATE. WE'RE ALREADY IN TOO STEEP A DIVE. WE'RE COMMITTED!
JUST GO FOR IT! GO! GO! GO!!
VAS IS DAS?!
MY ATTACHÉ CAS NEIN!!
SIR? ARE YOU OKAY?
FORGET ABOUT ME! THAT CASE CONTAINS SOME OF OUR MOST VELL-KEPT SECRETS OF GAMMA RAY TECHNOLOGY!
SHOOT THEM!
SHOOT THEM DO AT ALL COSTS

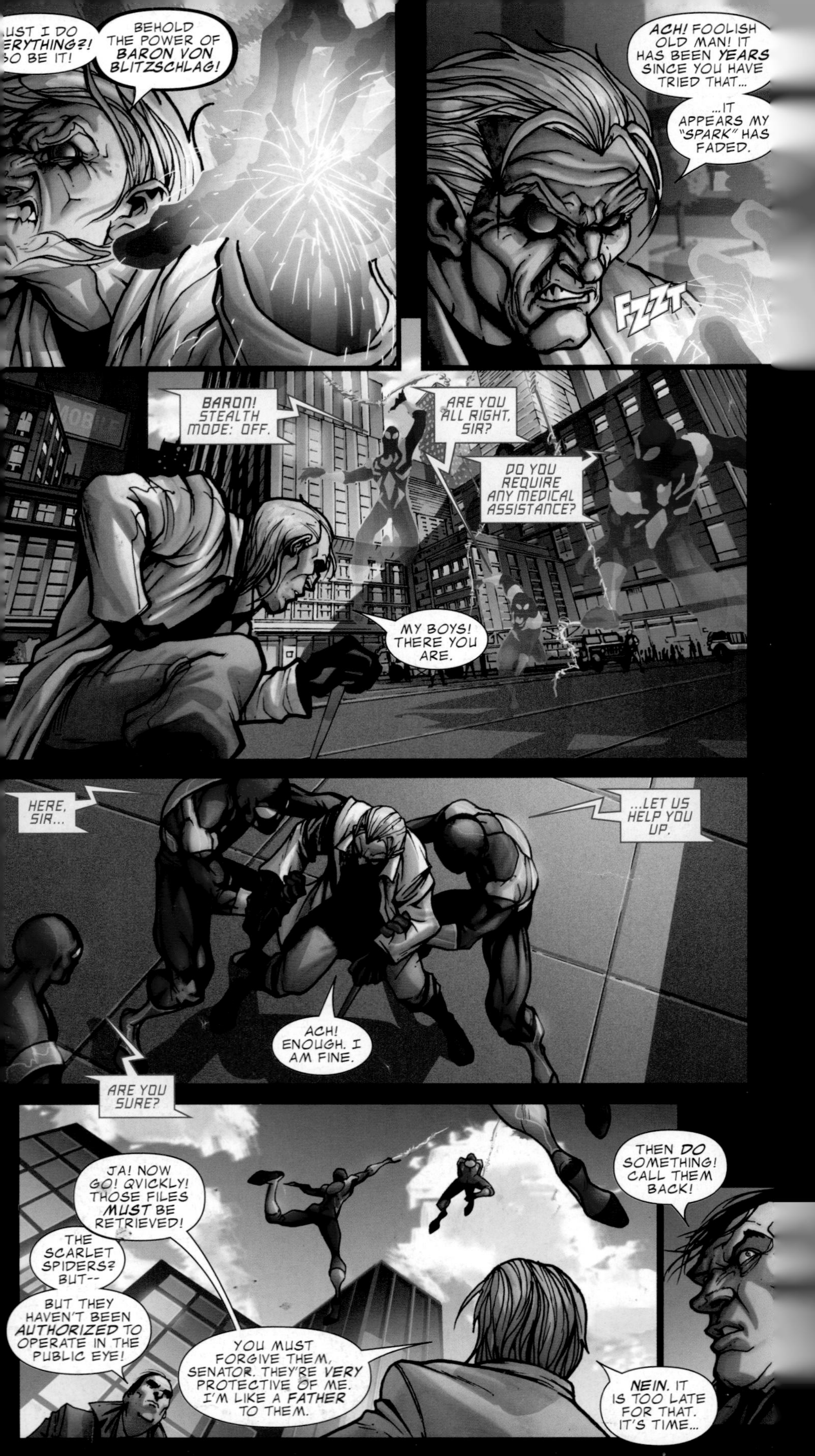
UST I DO ERYTHING?! SO BE IT!
BEHOLD THE POWER OF BARON VON BLITZSCHLAG!
ACH! FOOLISH OLD MAN! IT HAS BEEN YEARS SINCE YOU HAVE TRIED THAT...
...IT APPEARS MY "SPARK" HAS FADED.
FZZZT
BARON! STEALTH MODE: OFF.
ARE YOU ALL RIGHT, SIR?
DO YOU REQUIRE ANY MEDICAL ASSISTANCE?
MY BOYS! THERE YOU ARE.
HERE, SIR...
...LET US HELP YOU UP.
ACH! ENOUGH. I AM FINE.
ARE YOU SURE?
JA! NOW GO! QVICKLY! THOSE FILES MUST BE RETRIEVED!
THE SCARLET SPIDERS? BUT--
BUT THEY HAVEN'T BEEN AUTHORIZED TO OPERATE IN THE PUBLIC EYE!
YOU MUST FORGIVE THEM, SENATOR. THEY'RE VERY PROTECTIVE OF ME. I'M LIKE A FATHER TO THEM.
THEN DO SOMETHING! CALL THEM BACK!
NEIN. IT IS TOO LATE FOR THAT. IT'S TIME...

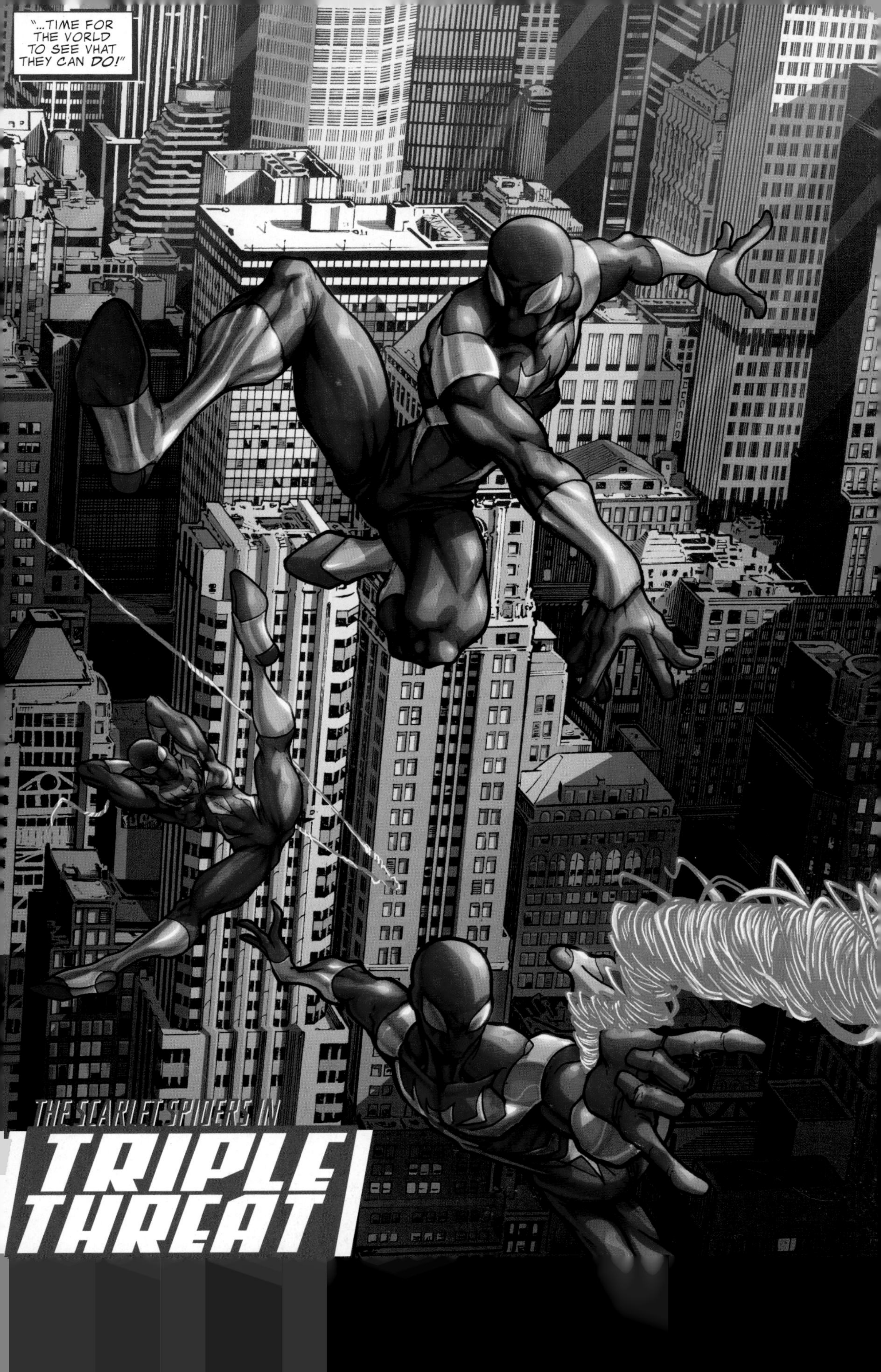
"...TIME FOR THE VORLD TO SEE VHAT THEY CAN DO!"
THE SCARLET SPIDERS IN
TRIPLE THREAT

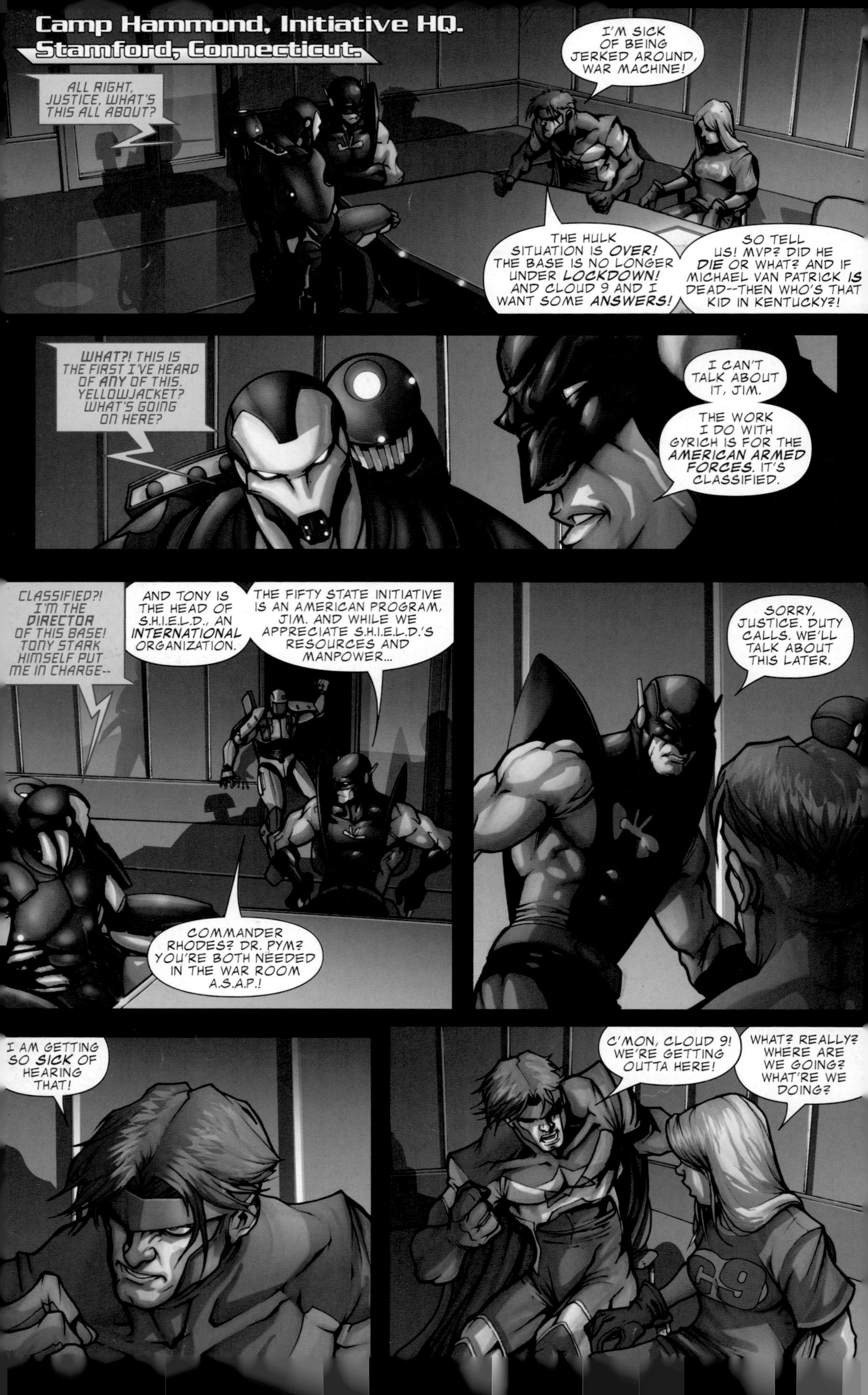
Camp Hammond, Initiative HQ.
Stamford, Connecticut.
ALL RIGHT, JUSTICE, WHAT'S THIS ALL ABOUT?
I'M SICK OF BEING JERKED AROUND, WAR MACHINE!
THE HULK SITUATION IS OVER! THE BASE IS NO LONGER UNDER LOCKDOWN! AND CLOUD 9 AND I WANT SOME ANSWERS!
SO TELL US! MVP? DID HE DIE OR WHAT? AND IF MICHAEL VAN PATRICK IS DEAD--THEN WHO'S THAT KID IN KENTUCKY?!
WHAT?! THIS IS THE FIRST I'VE HEARD OF ANY OF THIS. YELLOWJACKET? WHAT'S GOING ON HERE?
I CAN'T TALK ABOUT IT, JIM.
THE WORK I DO WITH GYRICH IS FOR THE AMERICAN ARMED FORCES. IT'S CLASSIFIED.
CLASSIFIED?! I'M THE DIRECTOR OF THIS BASE! TONY STARK HIMSELF PUT ME IN CHARGE--
AND TONY IS THE HEAD OF S.H.I.E.L.D., AN INTERNATIONAL ORGANIZATION.
THE FIFTY STATE INITIATIVE IS AN AMERICAN PROGRAM, JIM. AND WHILE WE APPRECIATE S.H.I.E.L.D.'S RESOURCES AND MANPOWER...
COMMANDER RHODES? DR. PYM? YOU'RE BOTH NEEDED IN THE WAR ROOM A.S.A.P.!
SORRY, JUSTICE. DUTY CALLS. WE'LL TALK ABOUT THIS LATER.
I AM GETTING SO SICK OF HEARING THAT!
C'MON, CLOUD 9! WE'RE GETTING OUTTA HERE!
WHAT? REALLY? WHERE ARE WE GOING? WHAT'RE WE DOING?

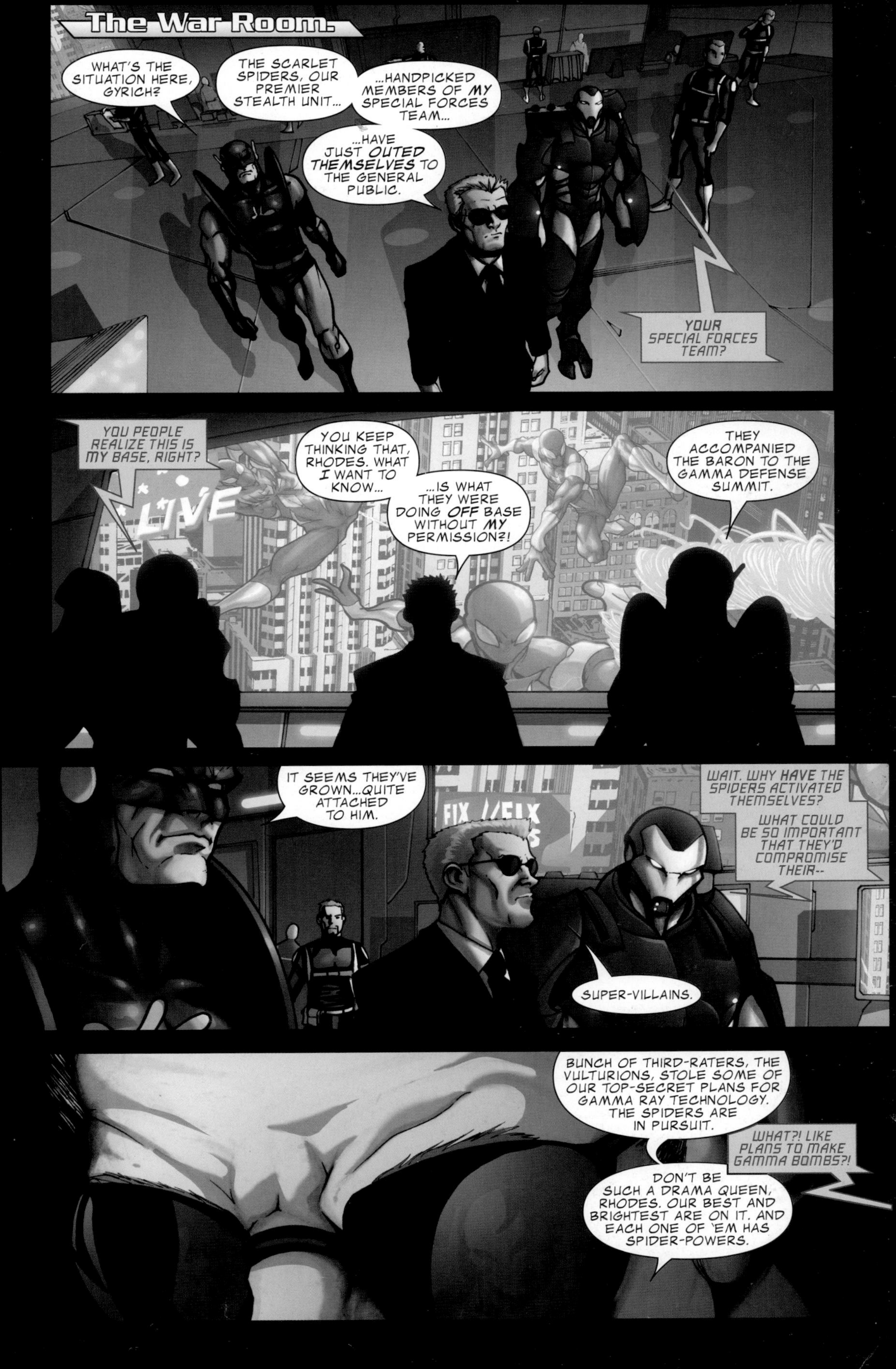
The War Room.
WHAT'S THE SITUATION HERE, GYRICH?
THE SCARLET SPIDERS, OUR PREMIER STEALTH UNIT...
...HANDPICKED MEMBERS OF MY SPECIAL FORCES TEAM...
...HAVE JUST OUTED THEMSELVES TO THE GENERAL PUBLIC.
YOUR SPECIAL FORCES TEAM?
YOU PEOPLE REALIZE THIS IS MY BASE, RIGHT?
LIVE
YOU KEEP THINKING THAT, RHODES. WHAT I WANT TO KNOW...
...IS WHAT THEY WERE DOING OFF BASE WITHOUT MY PERMISSION?!
THEY ACCOMPANIED THE BARON TO THE GAMMA DEFENSE SUMMIT.
IT SEEMS THEY'VE GROWN...QUITE ATTACHED TO HIM.
WAIT. WHY HAVE THE SPIDERS ACTIVATED THEMSELVES?
WHAT COULD BE SO IMPORTANT THAT THEY'D COMPROMISE THEIR--
SUPER-VILLAINS.
BUNCH OF THIRD-RATERS, THE VULTURIONS, STOLE SOME OF OUR TOP-SECRET PLANS FOR GAMMA RAY TECHNOLOGY. THE SPIDERS ARE IN PURSUIT.
WHAT?! LIKE PLANS TO MAKE GAMMA BOMBS?!
DON'T BE SUCH A DRAMA QUEEN, RHODES. OUR BEST AND BRIGHTEST ARE ON IT. AND EACH ONE OF 'EM HAS SPIDER-POWERS.

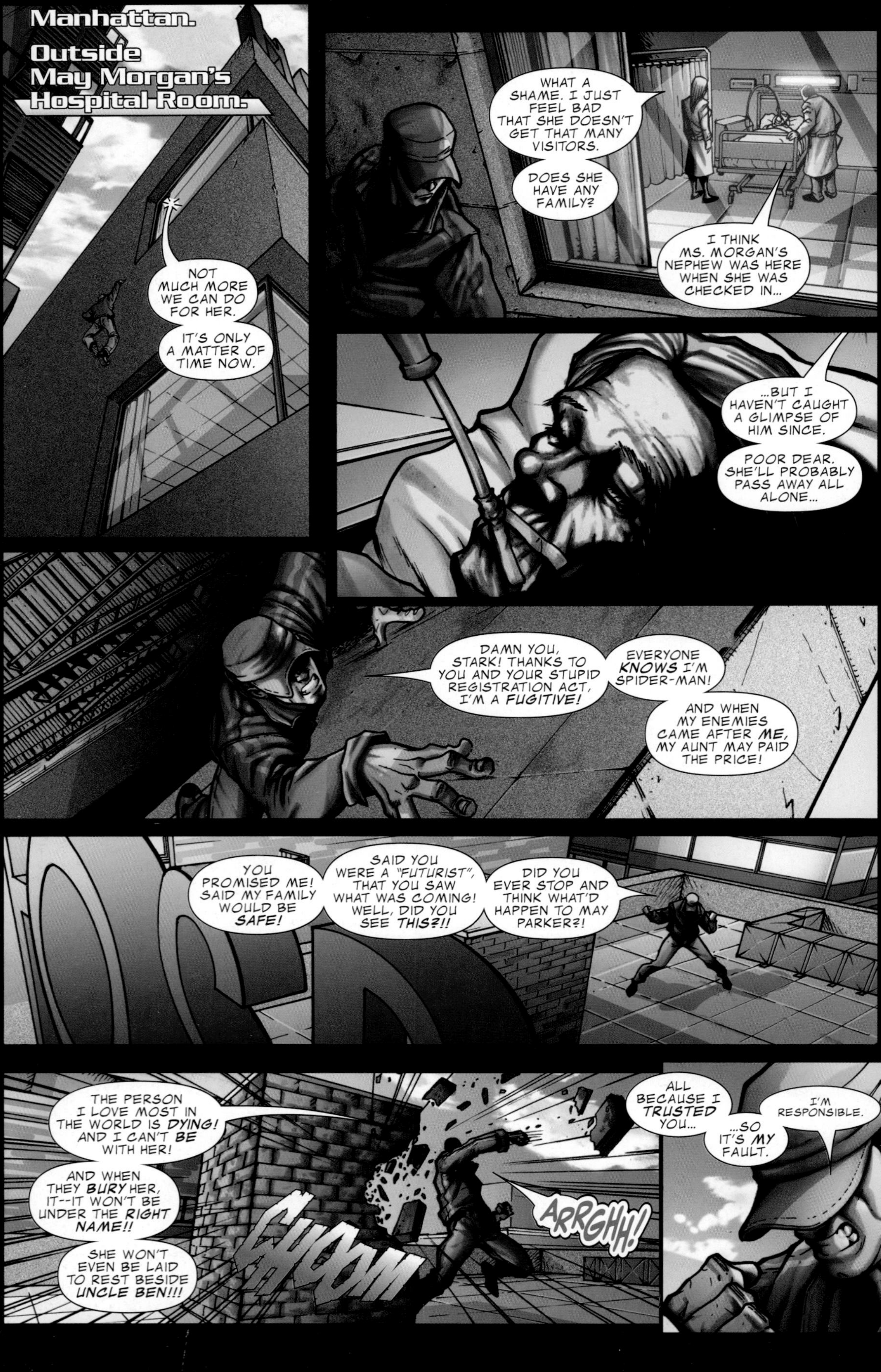
Manhattan.
Outside May Morgan's Hospital Room.
NOT MUCH MORE WE CAN DO FOR HER.
IT'S ONLY A MATTER OF TIME NOW.
WHAT A SHAME. I JUST FEEL BAD THAT SHE DOESN'T GET THAT MANY VISITORS.
DOES SHE HAVE ANY FAMILY?
I THINK MS. MORGAN'S NEPHEW WAS HERE WHEN SHE WAS CHECKED IN...
...BUT I HAVEN'T CAUGHT A GLIMPSE OF HIM SINCE.
POOR DEAR. SHE'LL PROBABLY PASS AWAY ALL ALONE...
DAMN YOU, STARK! THANKS TO YOU AND YOUR STUPID REGISTRATION ACT, I'M A FUGITIVE!
EVERYONE KNOWS I'M SPIDER-MAN!
AND WHEN MY ENEMIES CAME AFTER ME, MY AUNT MAY PAID THE PRICE!
YOU PROMISED ME! SAID MY FAMILY WOULD BE SAFE!
SAID YOU WERE A "FUTURIST", THAT YOU SAW WHAT WAS COMING! WELL, DID YOU SEE THIS?!!
DID YOU EVER STOP AND THINK WHAT'D HAPPEN TO MAY PARKER?!
THE PERSON I LOVE MOST IN THE WORLD IS DYING! AND I CAN'T BE WITH HER!
AND WHEN THEY BURY HER, IT--IT WON'T BE UNDER THE RIGHT NAME!!
SHE WON'T EVEN BE LAID TO REST BESIDE UNCLE BEN!!!
GHOOM
ARRGHH!
ALL BECAUSE I TRUSTED YOU...
...SO IT'S MY FAULT.
I'M RESPONSIBLE.

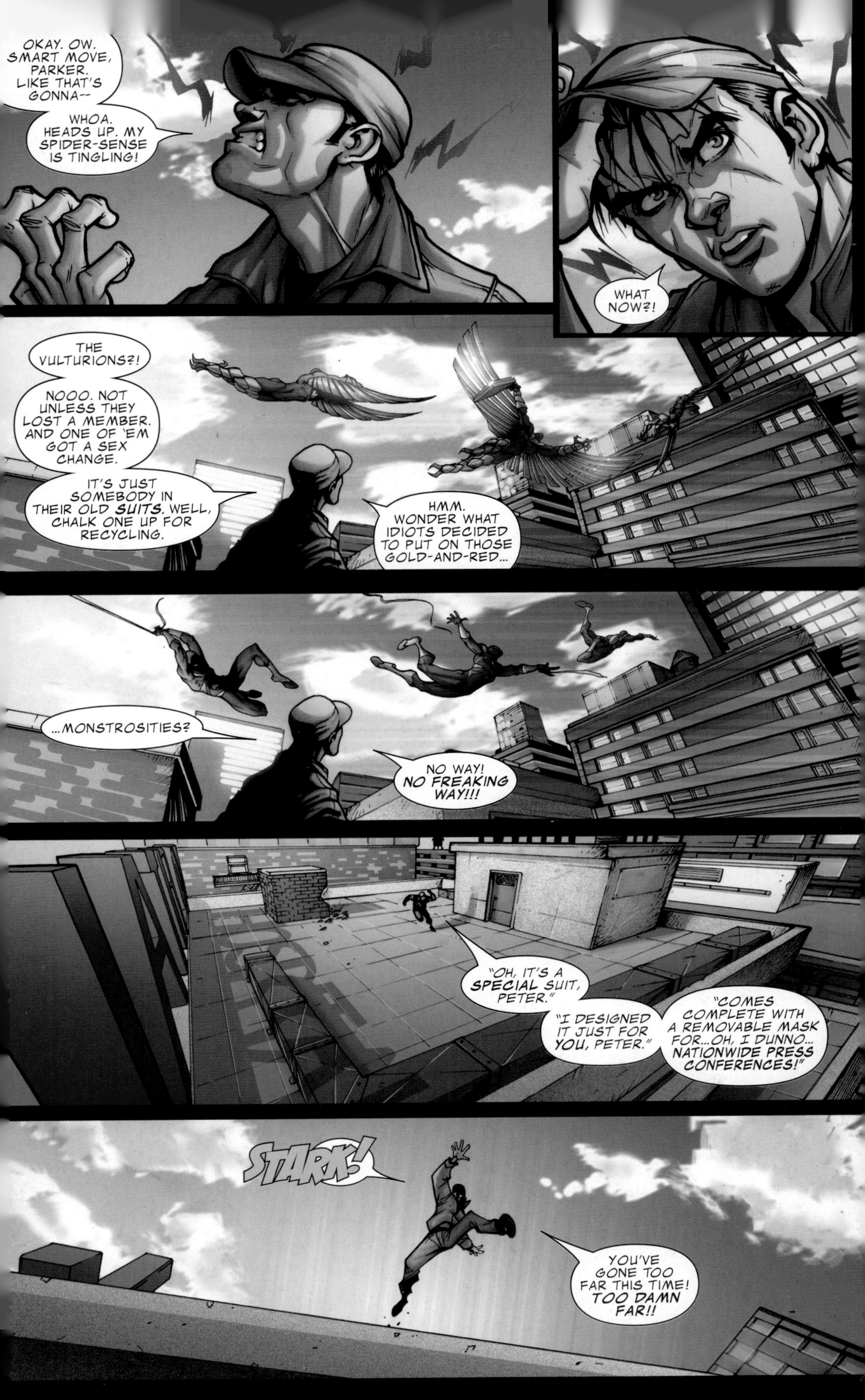
OKAY. OW. SMART MOVE, PARKER. LIKE THAT'S GONNA--
WHOA. HEADS UP. MY SPIDER-SENSE IS TINGLING!
WHAT NOW?!
THE VULTURIONS?!
NOOO. NOT UNLESS THEY LOST A MEMBER. AND ONE OF 'EM GOT A SEX CHANGE.
IT'S JUST SOMEBODY IN THEIR OLD SUITS. WELL, CHALK ONE UP FOR RECYCLING.
HMM. WONDER WHAT IDIOTS DECIDED TO PUT ON THOSE GOLD-AND-RED...
...MONSTROSITIES?
NO WAY! NO FREAKING WAY!!!
"OH, IT'S A SPECIAL SUIT, PETER."
"I DESIGNED IT JUST FOR YOU, PETER."
"COMES COMPLETE WITH A REMOVABLE MASK FOR...OH, I DUNNO... NATIONWIDE PRESS CONFERENCES!"
STARK!
YOU'VE GONE TOO FAR THIS TIME! TOO DAMN FAR!!

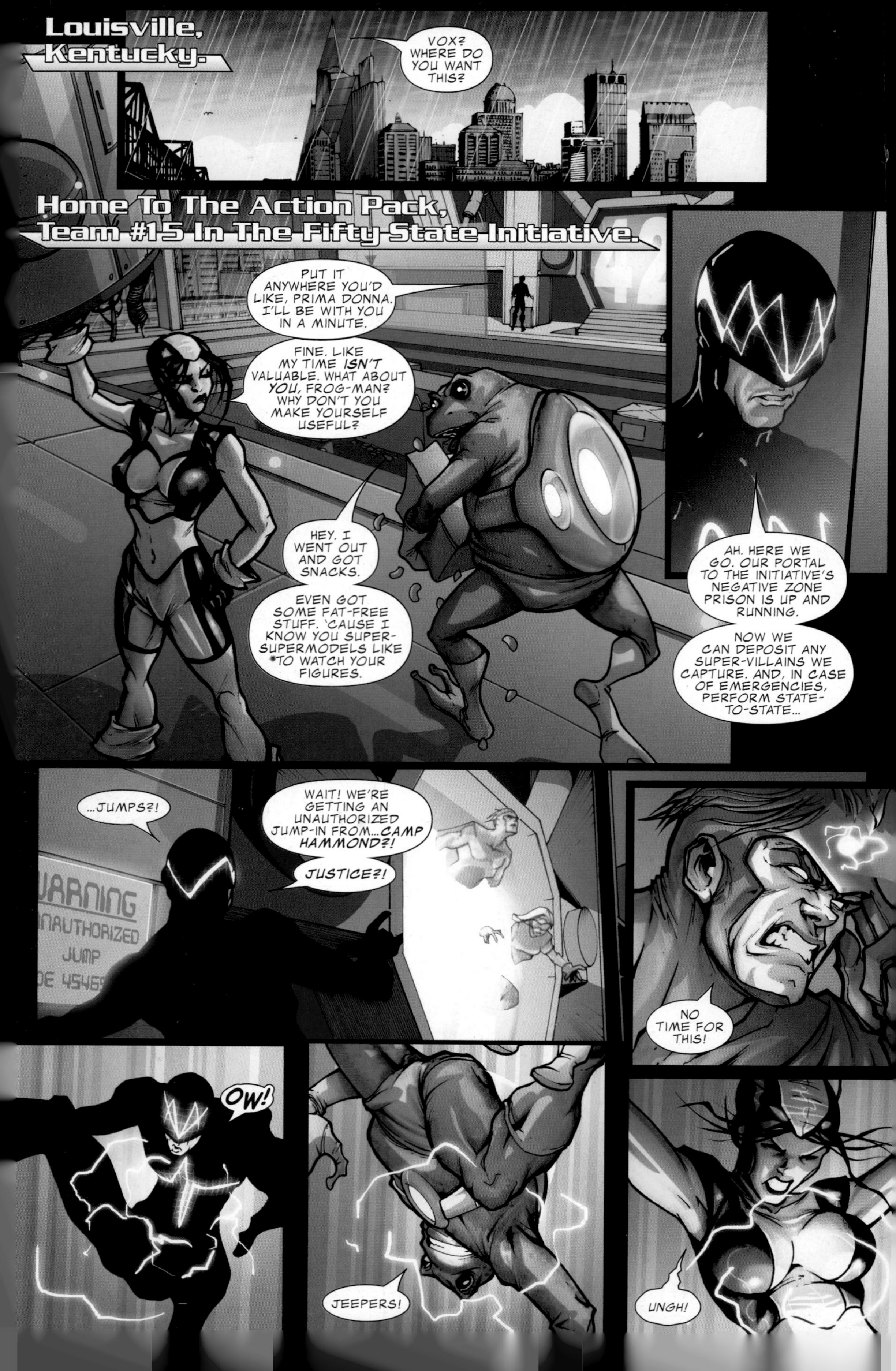
Louisville, Kentucky.
VOX? WHERE DO YOU WANT THIS?
Home To The Action Pack, Team #15 In The Fifty State Initiative.
PUT IT ANYWHERE YOU'D LIKE, PRIMA DONNA. I'LL BE WITH YOU IN A MINUTE.
FINE. LIKE MY TIME ISN'T VALUABLE. WHAT ABOUT YOU, FROG-MAN? WHY DON'T YOU MAKE YOURSELF USEFUL?
HEY. I WENT OUT AND GOT SNACKS.
EVEN GOT SOME FAT-FREE STUFF. 'CAUSE I KNOW YOU SUPER-SUPERMODELS LIKE TO WATCH YOUR FIGURES.
AH. HERE WE GO. OUR PORTAL TO THE INITIATIVE'S NEGATIVE ZONE PRISON IS UP AND RUNNING.
NOW WE CAN DEPOSIT ANY SUPER-VILLAINS WE CAPTURE. AND, IN CASE OF EMERGENCIES, PERFORM STATE-TO-STATE...
...JUMPS?!
WAIT! WE'RE GETTING AN UNAUTHORIZED JUMP-IN FROM...CAMP HAMMOND?!
JUSTICE?!
WARNING
NAUTHORIZED
JUMP
DE 4546
NO TIME FOR THIS!
OW!
JEEPERS!
UNGH!

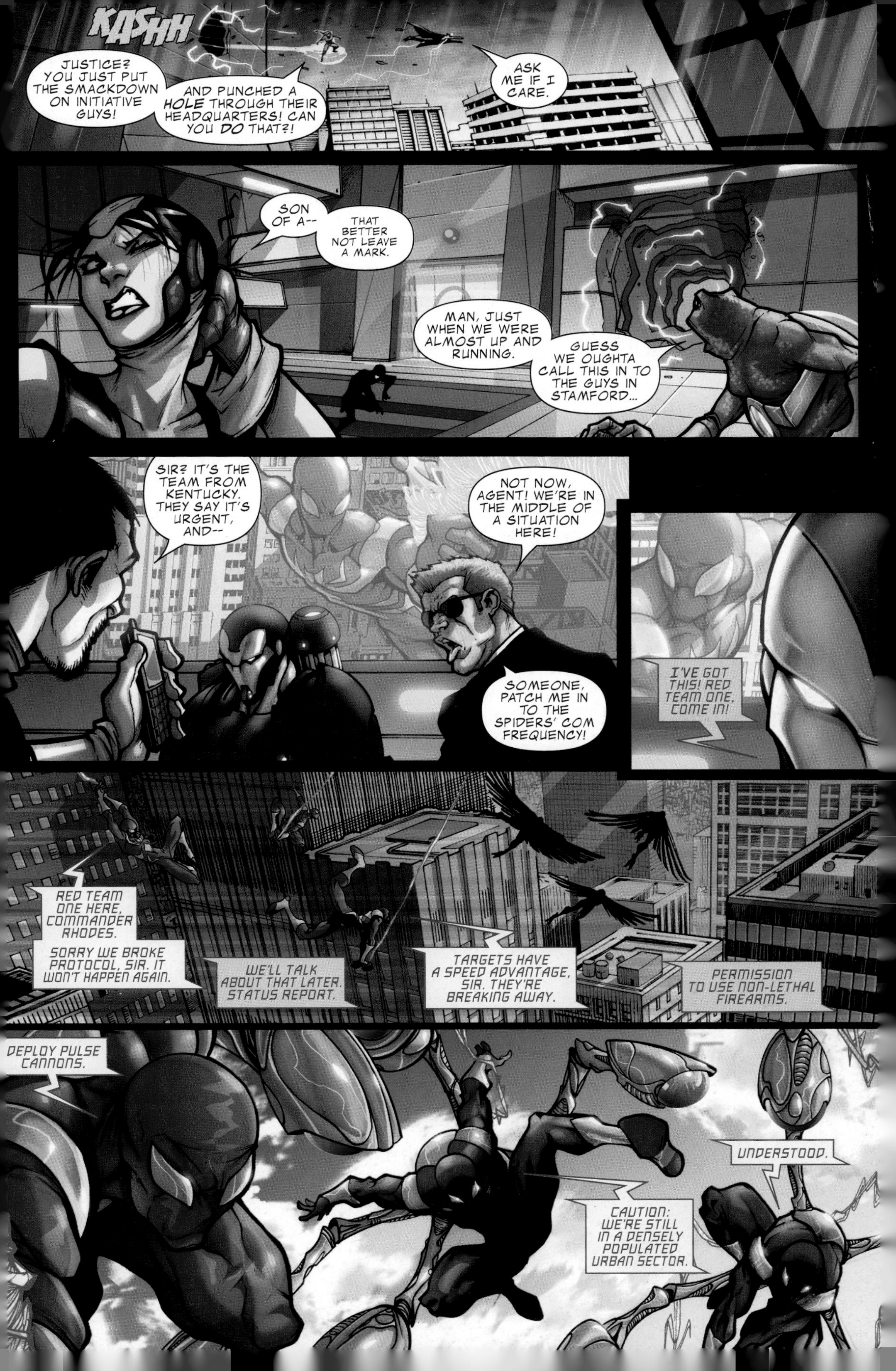
KASHH
JUSTICE? YOU JUST PUT THE SMACKDOWN ON INITIATIVE GUYS!
AND PUNCHED A HOLE THROUGH THEIR HEADQUARTERS! CAN YOU DO THAT?!
ASK ME IF I CARE.
SON OF A--
THAT BETTER NOT LEAVE A MARK.
MAN, JUST WHEN WE WERE ALMOST UP AND RUNNING.
GUESS WE OUGHTA CALL THIS IN TO THE GUYS IN STAMFORD...
SIR? IT'S THE TEAM FROM KENTUCKY. THEY SAY IT'S URGENT, AND--
NOT NOW, AGENT! WE'RE IN THE MIDDLE OF A SITUATION HERE!
SOMEONE, PATCH ME IN TO THE SPIDERS' COM FREQUENCY!
I'VE GOT THIS! RED TEAM ONE, COME IN!
RED TEAM ONE HERE, COMMANDER RHODES.
SORRY WE BROKE PROTOCOL, SIR. IT WON'T HAPPEN AGAIN.
WE'LL TALK ABOUT THAT LATER. STATUS REPORT.
TARGETS HAVE A SPEED ADVANTAGE, SIR. THEY'RE BREAKING AWAY.
PERMISSION TO USE NON-LETHAL FIREARMS.
DEPLOY PULSE CANNONS.
UNDERSTOOD.
CAUTION: WE'RE STILL IN A DENSELY POPULATED URBAN SECTOR.

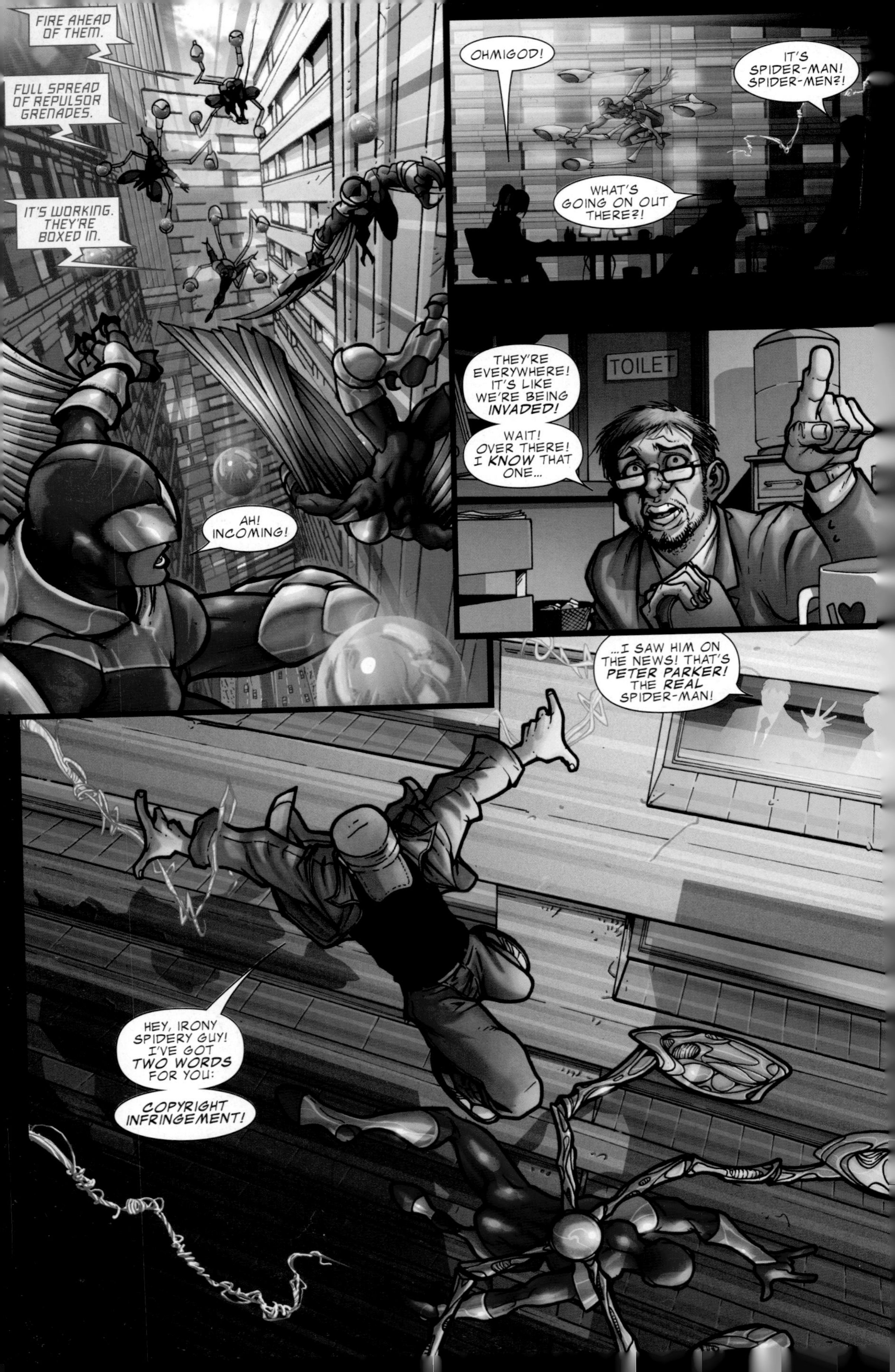
FIRE AHEAD OF THEM.
FULL SPREAD OF REPULSOR GRENADES.
IT'S WORKING. THEY'RE BOXED IN.
AH! INCOMING!
OHMIGOD!
IT'S SPIDER-MAN! SPIDER-MEN?!
WHAT'S GOING ON OUT THERE?!
TOILET
THEY'RE EVERYWHERE! IT'S LIKE WE'RE BEING INVADED!
WAIT! OVER THERE! I KNOW THAT ONE...
...I SAW HIM ON THE NEWS! THAT'S PETER PARKER! THE REAL SPIDER-MAN!
HEY, IRONY SPIDERY GUY! I'VE GOT TWO WORDS FOR YOU:
COPYRIGHT INFRINGEMENT!

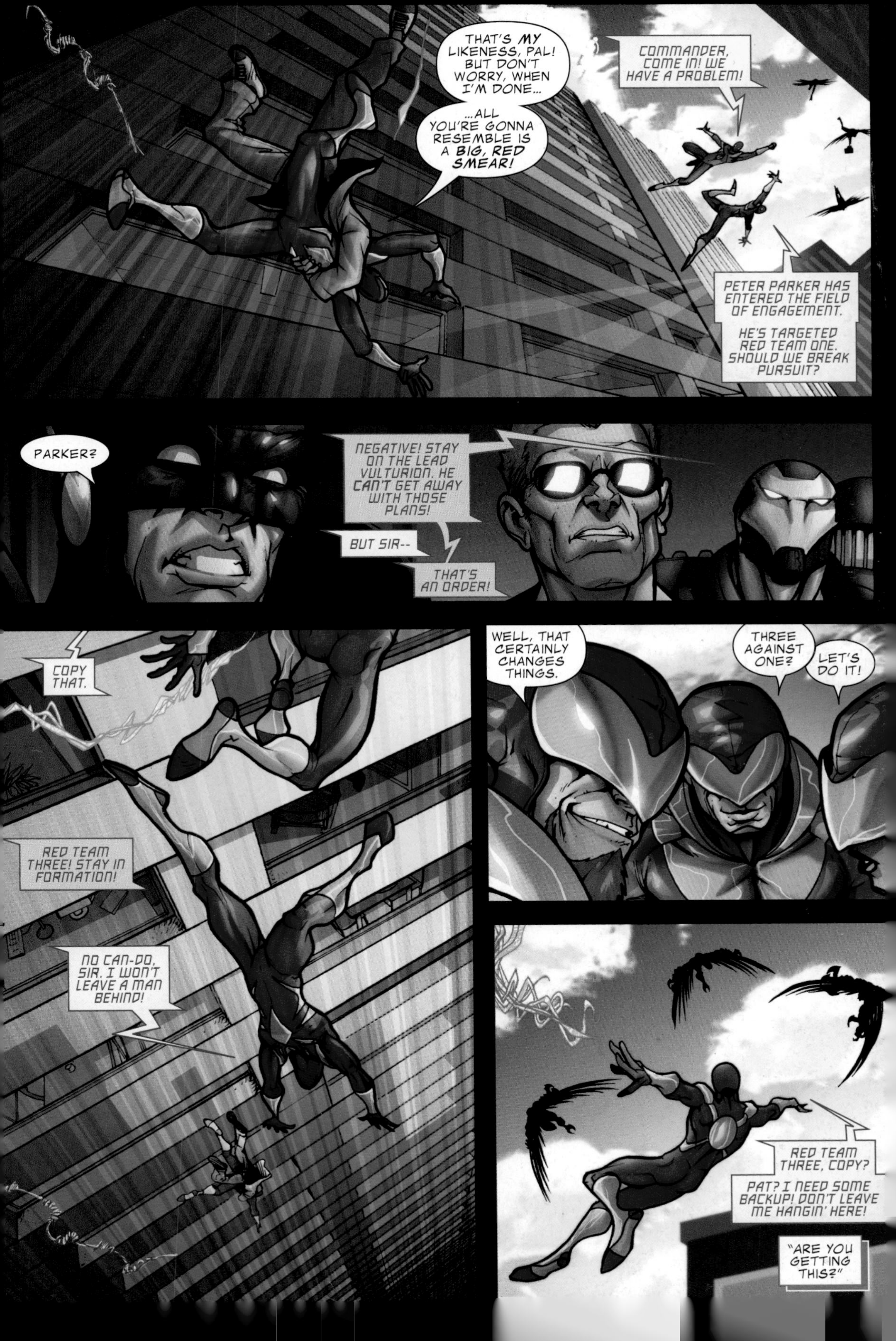
THAT'S MY LIKENESS, PAL! BUT DON'T WORRY, WHEN I'M DONE...
...ALL YOU'RE GONNA RESEMBLE IS A BIG, RED SMEAR!
COMMANDER, COME IN! WE HAVE A PROBLEM!
PETER PARKER HAS ENTERED THE FIELD OF ENGAGEMENT.
HE'S TARGETED RED TEAM ONE. SHOULD WE BREAK PURSUIT?
PARKER?
NEGATIVE! STAY ON THE LEAD VULTURION. HE CAN'T GET AWAY WITH THOSE PLANS!
BUT SIR--
THAT'S AN ORDER!
COPY THAT.
RED TEAM THREE! STAY IN FORMATION!
NO CAN-DO, SIR. I WON'T LEAVE A MAN BEHIND!
WELL, THAT CERTAINLY CHANGES THINGS.
THREE AGAINST ONE?
LET'S DO IT!
RED TEAM THREE, COPY?
PAT? I NEED SOME BACKUP! DON'T LEAVE ME HANGIN' HERE!
"ARE YOU GETTING THIS?"

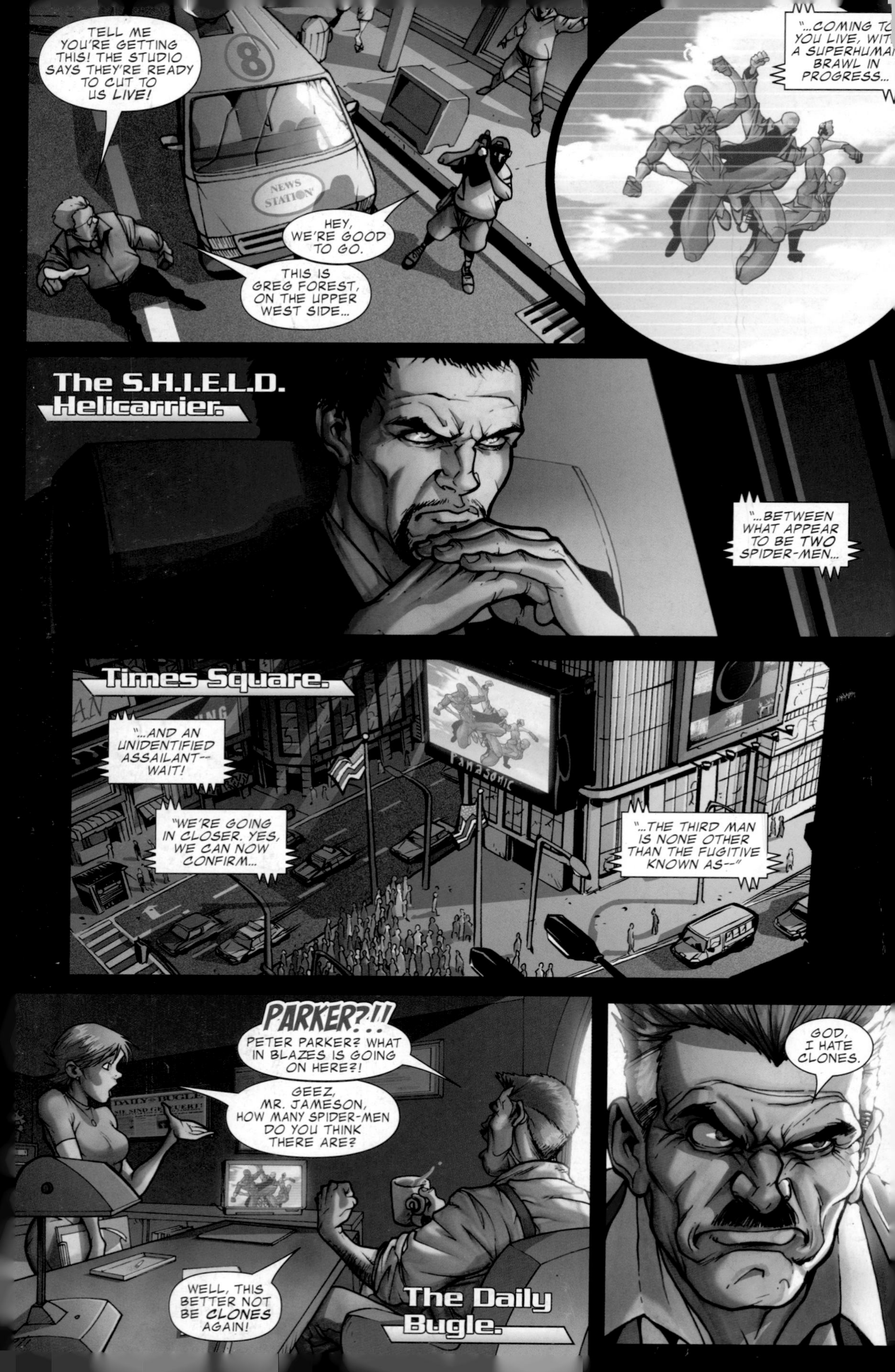
TELL ME YOU'RE GETTING THIS! THE STUDIO SAYS THEY'RE READY TO CUT TO US LIVE!
NEWS STATION
HEY, WE'RE GOOD TO GO.
THIS IS GREG FOREST, ON THE UPPER WEST SIDE...
"...COMING TO YOU LIVE, WIT A SUPERHUMAN BRAWL IN PROGRESS...
The S.H.I.E.L.D. Helicarrier.
"...BETWEEN WHAT APPEAR TO BE TWO SPIDER-MEN...
Times Square.
"...AND AN UNIDENTIFIED ASSAILANT-- WAIT!
"WE'RE GOING IN CLOSER. YES, WE CAN NOW CONFIRM...
"...THE THIRD MAN IS NONE OTHER THAN THE FUGITIVE KNOWN AS--"
PARKER?!!... PETER PARKER? WHAT IN BLAZES IS GOING ON HERE?!
GEEZ, MR. JAMESON, HOW MANY SPIDER-MEN DO YOU THINK THERE ARE?
WELL, THIS BETTER NOT BE CLONES AGAIN!
The Daily Bugle.
GOD, I HATE CLONES.

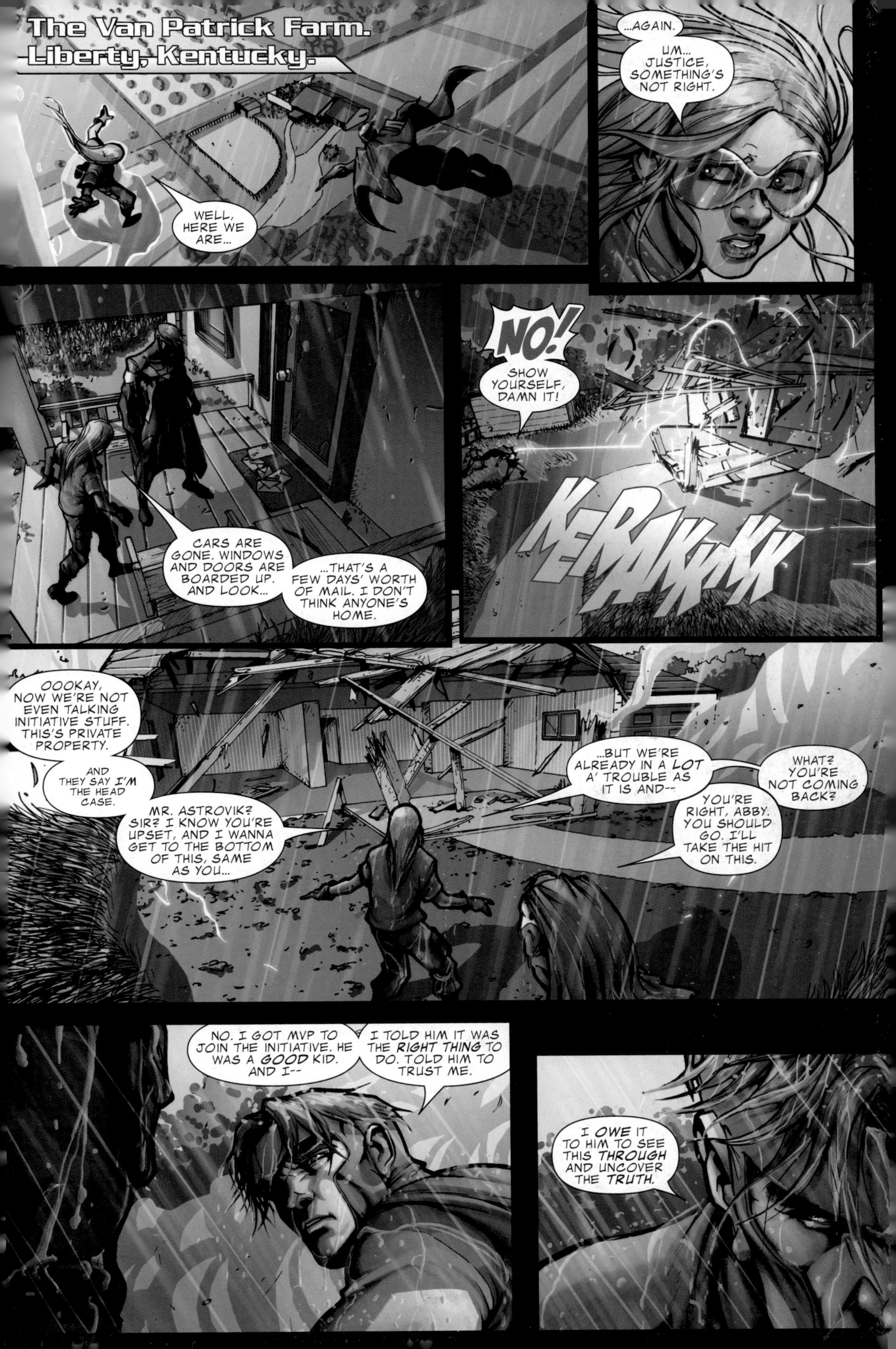
The Van Patrick Farm.
Liberty, Kentucky.
WELL, HERE WE ARE...
...AGAIN.
UM... JUSTICE, SOMETHING'S NOT RIGHT.
CARS ARE GONE. WINDOWS AND DOORS ARE BOARDED UP. AND LOOK...
...THAT'S A FEW DAYS' WORTH OF MAIL. I DON'T THINK ANYONE'S HOME.
NO!
SHOW YOURSELF, DAMN IT!
KERAKKKK
OOOKAY, NOW WE'RE NOT EVEN TALKING INITIATIVE STUFF. THIS'S PRIVATE PROPERTY.
AND THEY SAY I'M THE HEAD CASE.
MR. ASTROVIK? SIR? I KNOW YOU'RE UPSET, AND I WANNA GET TO THE BOTTOM OF THIS, SAME AS YOU...
...BUT WE'RE ALREADY IN A LOT A' TROUBLE AS IT IS AND--
WHAT? YOU'RE NOT COMING BACK?
YOU'RE RIGHT, ABBY. YOU SHOULD GO. I'LL TAKE THE HIT ON THIS.
NO. I GOT MVP TO JOIN THE INITIATIVE. HE WAS A GOOD KID. AND I--
I TOLD HIM IT WAS THE RIGHT THING TO DO. TOLD HIM TO TRUST ME.
I OWE IT TO HIM TO SEE THIS THROUGH AND UNCOVER THE TRUTH.

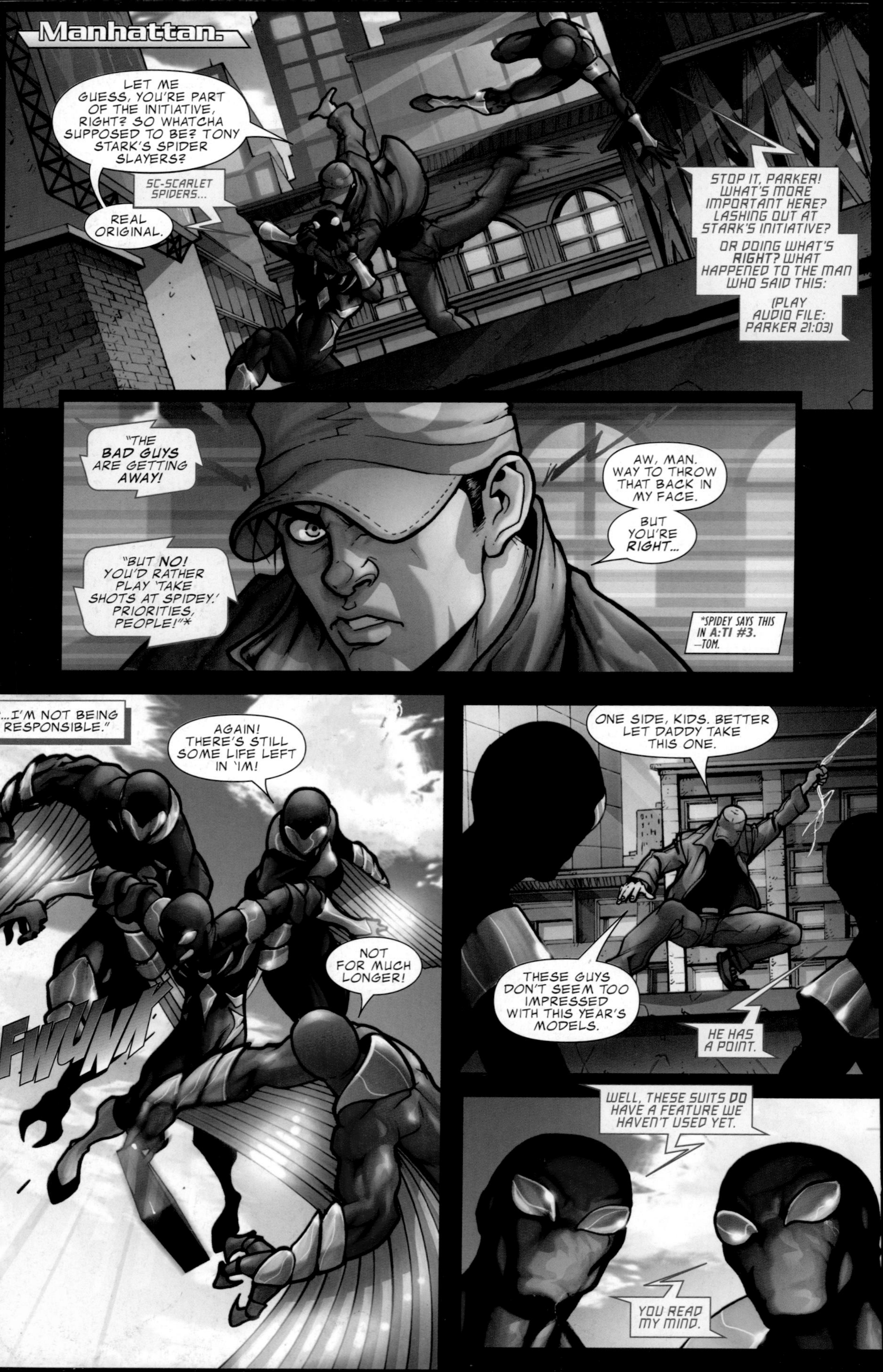
Manhattan.
LET ME GUESS, YOU'RE PART OF THE INITIATIVE, RIGHT? SO WHATCHA SUPPOSED TO BE? TONY STARK'S SPIDER SLAYERS?
SC-SCARLET SPIDERS...
REAL ORIGINAL.
STOP IT, PARKER! WHAT'S MORE IMPORTANT HERE? LASHING OUT AT STARK'S INITIATIVE?
OR DOING WHAT'S RIGHT? WHAT HAPPENED TO THE MAN WHO SAID THIS:
(PLAY AUDIO FILE: PARKER 21:03)
"THE BAD GUYS ARE GETTING AWAY!
"BUT NO! YOU'D RATHER PLAY 'TAKE SHOTS AT SPIDEY.' PRIORITIES, PEOPLE!"*
AW, MAN. WAY TO THROW THAT BACK IN MY FACE.
BUT YOU'RE RIGHT...
*SPIDEY SAYS THIS IN A:TI #3. —TOM.
"...I'M NOT BEING RESPONSIBLE."
AGAIN! THERE'S STILL SOME LIFE LEFT IN 'IM!
NOT FOR MUCH LONGER!
FWUNK
ONE SIDE, KIDS. BETTER LET DADDY TAKE THIS ONE.
THESE GUYS DON'T SEEM TOO IMPRESSED WITH THIS YEAR'S MODELS.
HE HAS A POINT.
WELL, THESE SUITS DO HAVE A FEATURE WE HAVEN'T USED YET.
YOU READ MY MIND.

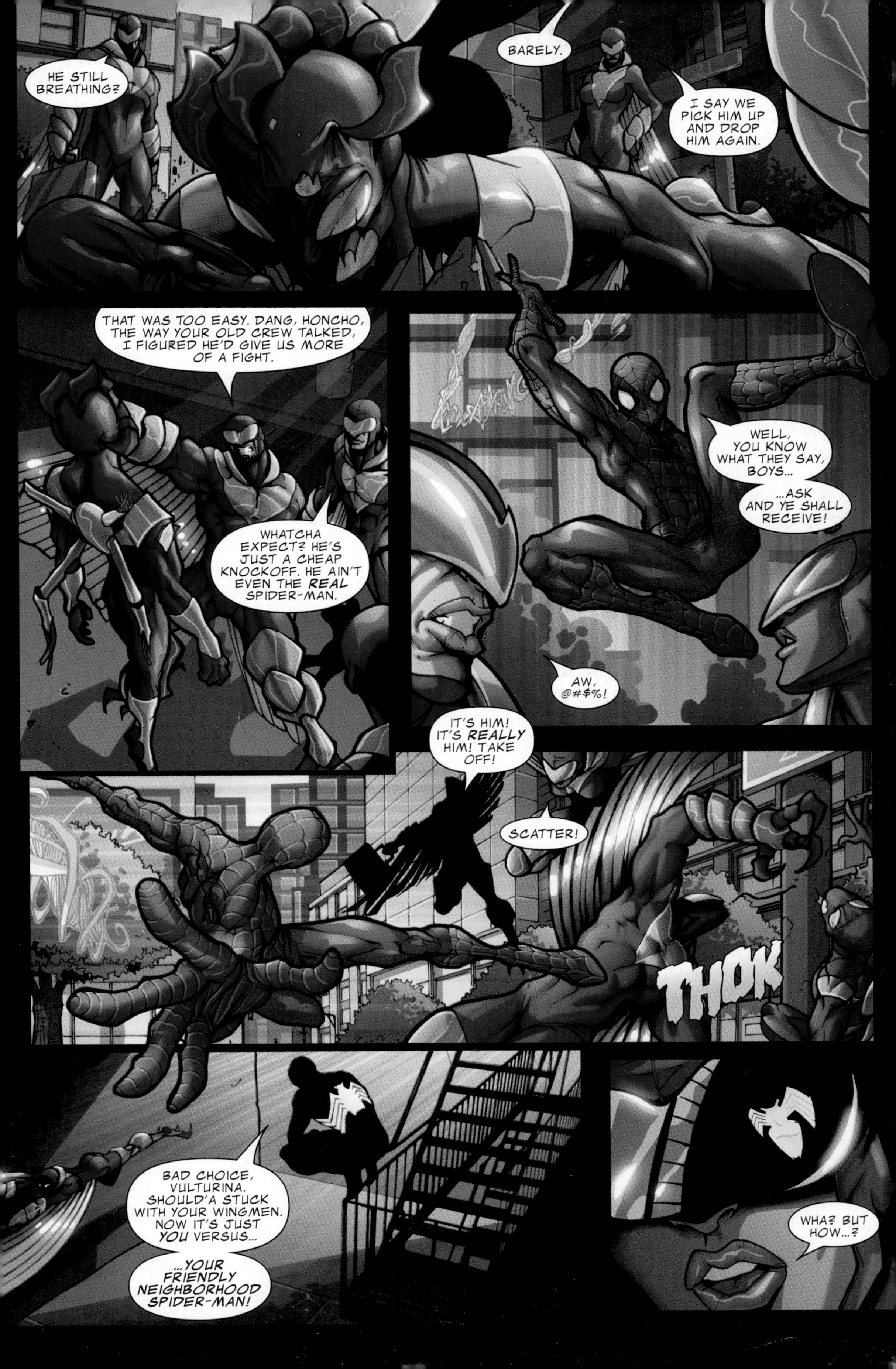
HE STILL BREATHING?
BARELY.
I SAY WE PICK HIM UP AND DROP HIM AGAIN.
THAT WAS TOO EASY. DANG, HONCHO, THE WAY YOUR OLD CREW TALKED, I FIGURED HE'D GIVE US MORE OF A FIGHT.
WHATCHA EXPECT? HE'S JUST A CHEAP KNOCKOFF. HE AIN'T EVEN THE REAL SPIDER-MAN.
WELL, YOU KNOW WHAT THEY SAY, BOYS...
...ASK AND YE SHALL RECEIVE!
AW, @#$%!
IT'S HIM! IT'S REALLY HIM! TAKE OFF!
SCATTER!
THOK
BAD CHOICE, VULTURINA. SHOULD'A STUCK WITH YOUR WINGMEN. NOW IT'S JUST YOU VERSUS...
...YOUR FRIENDLY NEIGHBORHOOD SPIDER-MAN!
WHA? BUT HOW...?

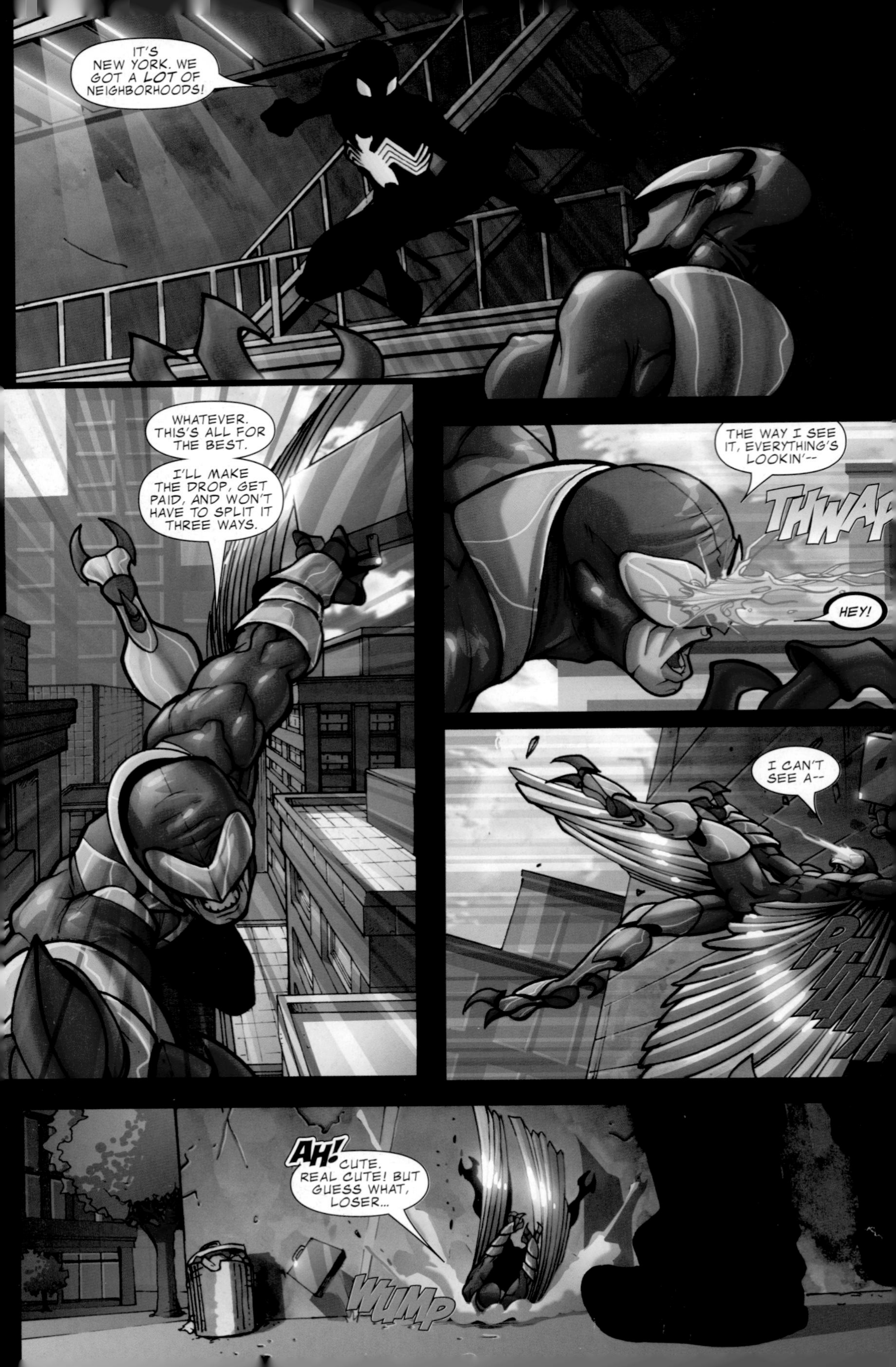
IT'S NEW YORK. WE GOT A LOT OF NEIGHBORHOODS!
WHATEVER. THIS'S ALL FOR THE BEST.
I'LL MAKE THE DROP, GET PAID, AND WON'T HAVE TO SPLIT IT THREE WAYS.
THE WAY I SEE IT, EVERYTHING'S LOOKIN'--
THWAP
HEY!
I CAN'T SEE A--
AH!
CUTE. REAL CUTE! BUT GUESS WHAT, LOSER...
WUMP

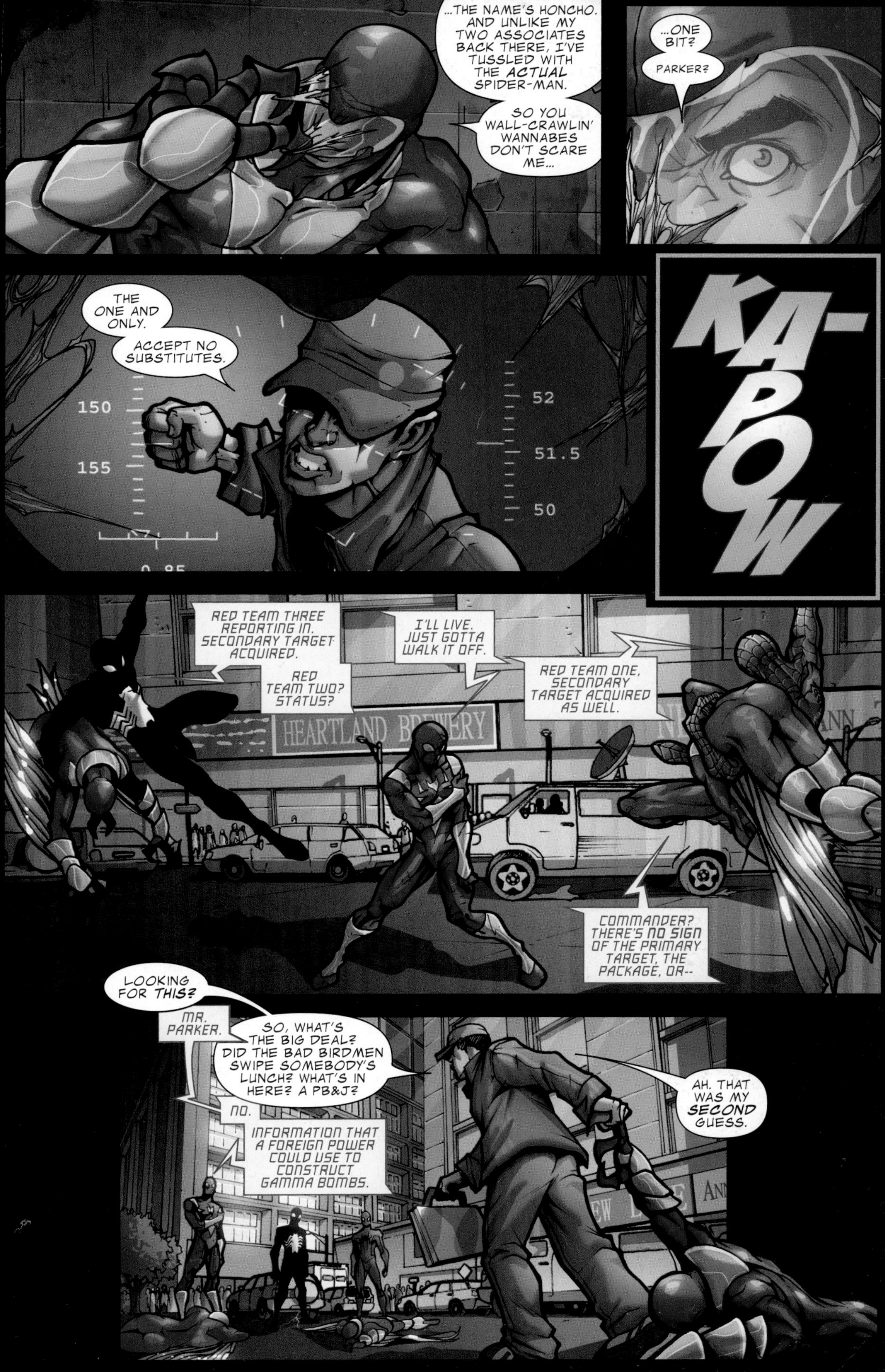
...THE NAME'S HONCHO. AND UNLIKE MY TWO ASSOCIATES BACK THERE, I'VE TUSSLED WITH THE ACTUAL SPIDER-MAN.
SO YOU WALL-CRAWLIN' WANNABES DON'T SCARE ME...
...ONE BIT?
PARKER?
THE ONE AND ONLY.
ACCEPT NO SUBSTITUTES.
150
155
52
51.5
50
KA-POW
RED TEAM THREE REPORTING IN. SECONDARY TARGET ACQUIRED.
RED TEAM TWO? STATUS?
I'LL LIVE. JUST GOTTA WALK IT OFF.
RED TEAM ONE, SECONDARY TARGET ACQUIRED AS WELL.
HEARTLAND BREWERY
COMMANDER? THERE'S NO SIGN OF THE PRIMARY TARGET, THE PACKAGE, OR--
LOOKING FOR THIS?
MR. PARKER.
SO, WHAT'S THE BIG DEAL? DID THE BAD BIRDMEN SWIPE SOMEBODY'S LUNCH? WHAT'S IN HERE? A PB&J?
NO.
INFORMATION THAT A FOREIGN POWER COULD USE TO CONSTRUCT GAMMA BOMBS.
AH. THAT WAS MY SECOND GUESS.

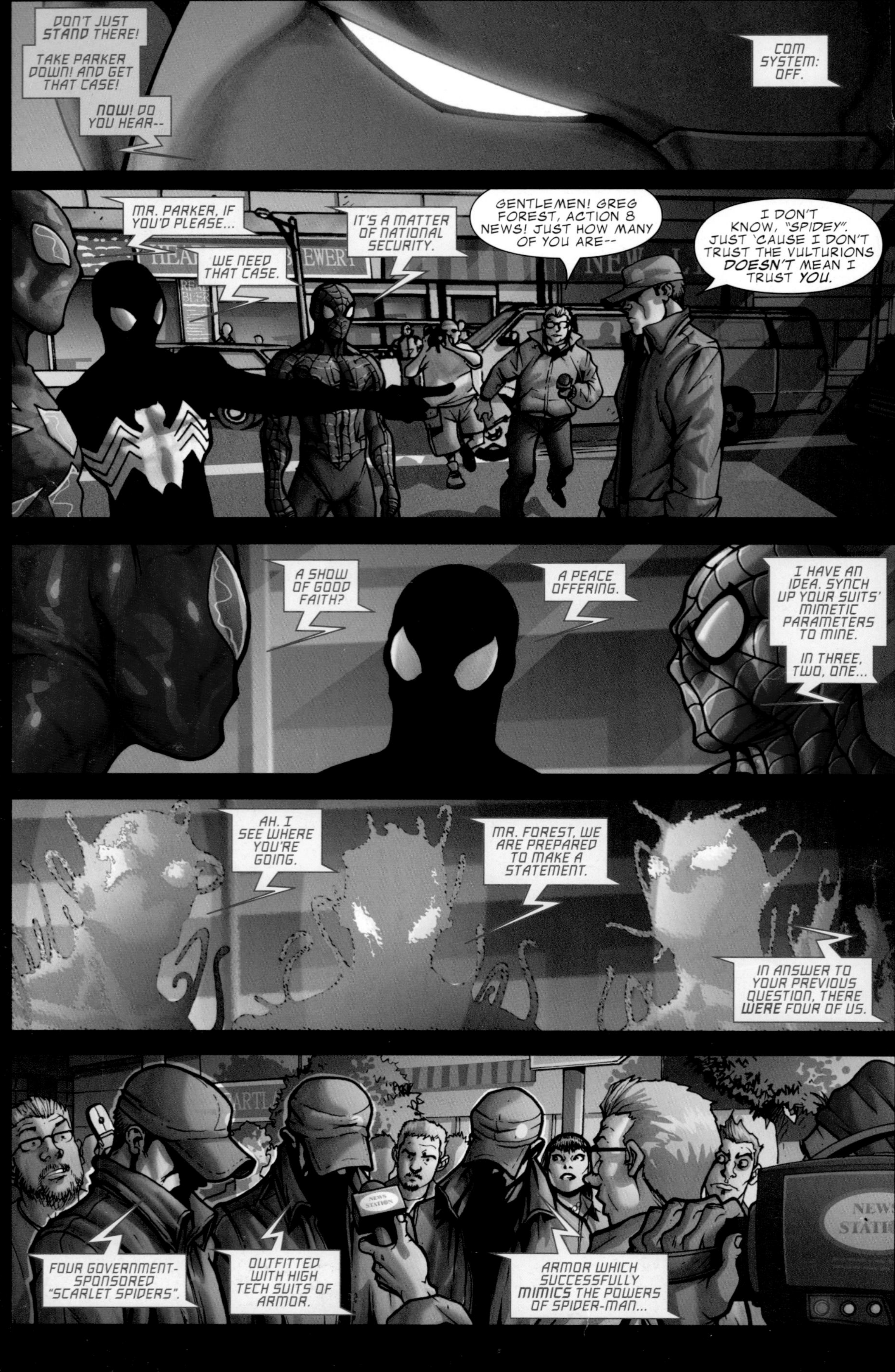

DON'T JUST STAND THERE!
TAKE PARKER DOWN! AND GET THAT CASE!
NOW! DO YOU HEAR--
COM SYSTEM: OFF.
MR. PARKER, IF YOU'D PLEASE...
WE NEED THAT CASE.
IT'S A MATTER OF NATIONAL SECURITY.
GENTLEMEN! GREG FOREST, ACTION 8 NEWS! JUST HOW MANY OF YOU ARE--
I DON'T KNOW, "SPIDEY". JUST 'CAUSE I DON'T TRUST THE VULTURIONS DOESN'T MEAN I TRUST YOU.
A SHOW OF GOOD FAITH?
A PEACE OFFERING.
I HAVE AN IDEA. SYNCH UP YOUR SUITS' MIMETIC PARAMETERS TO MINE.
IN THREE, TWO, ONE...
AH. I SEE WHERE YOU'RE GOING.
MR. FOREST, WE ARE PREPARED TO MAKE A STATEMENT.
IN ANSWER TO YOUR PREVIOUS QUESTION, THERE WERE FOUR OF US.
FOUR GOVERNMENT-SPONSORED "SCARLET SPIDERS".
OUTFITTED WITH HIGH TECH SUITS OF ARMOR.
ARMOR WHICH SUCCESSFULLY MIMICS THE POWERS OF SPIDER-MAN...

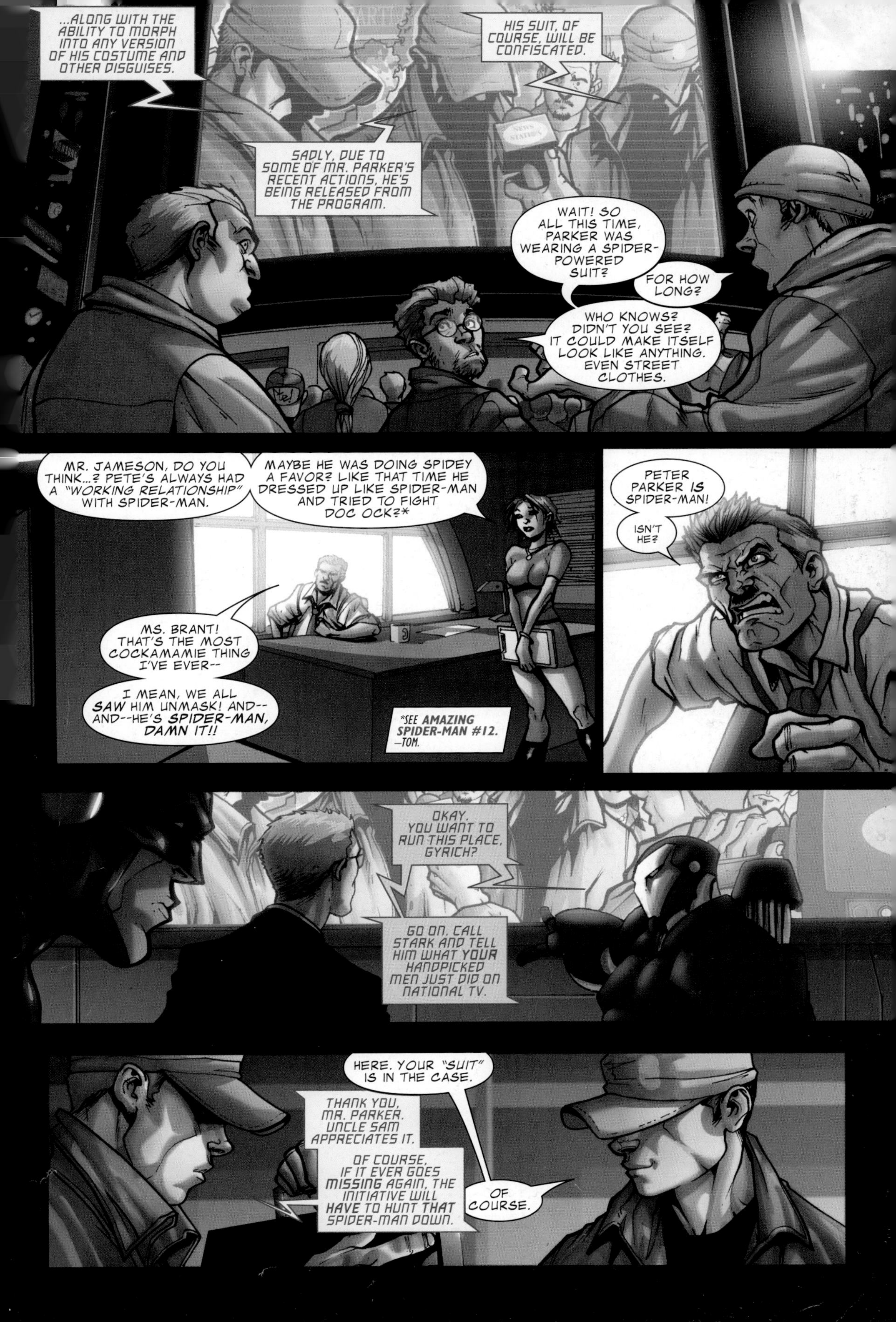
...ALONG WITH THE ABILITY TO MORPH INTO ANY VERSION OF HIS COSTUME AND OTHER DISGUISES.
HIS SUIT, OF COURSE, WILL BE CONFISCATED.
SADLY, DUE TO SOME OF MR. PARKER'S RECENT ACTIONS, HE'S BEING RELEASED FROM THE PROGRAM.
WAIT! SO ALL THIS TIME, PARKER WAS WEARING A SPIDER-POWERED SUIT?
FOR HOW LONG?
WHO KNOWS? DIDN'T YOU SEE? IT COULD MAKE ITSELF LOOK LIKE ANYTHING. EVEN STREET CLOTHES.
MR. JAMESON, DO YOU THINK...? PETE'S ALWAYS HAD A "WORKING RELATIONSHIP" WITH SPIDER-MAN.
MAYBE HE WAS DOING SPIDEY A FAVOR? LIKE THAT TIME HE DRESSED UP LIKE SPIDER-MAN AND TRIED TO FIGHT DOC OCK?*
MS. BRANT! THAT'S THE MOST COCKAMAMIE THING I'VE EVER--
I MEAN, WE ALL **SAW** HIM UNMASK! AND--AND--HE'S **SPIDER-MAN, DAMN IT!!**
*SEE **AMAZING SPIDER-MAN #12.** —TOM.
PETER PARKER **IS** SPIDER-MAN!
ISN'T HE?
OKAY. YOU WANT TO RUN THIS PLACE, GYRICH?
GO ON. CALL STARK AND TELL HIM WHAT **YOUR** HANDPICKED MEN JUST DID ON NATIONAL TV.
HERE. YOUR "SUIT" IS IN THE CASE.
THANK YOU, MR. PARKER. UNCLE SAM APPRECIATES IT.
OF COURSE, IF IT EVER GOES **MISSING** AGAIN, THE INITIATIVE WILL **HAVE** TO HUNT **THAT** SPIDER-MAN DOWN.
OF COURSE.

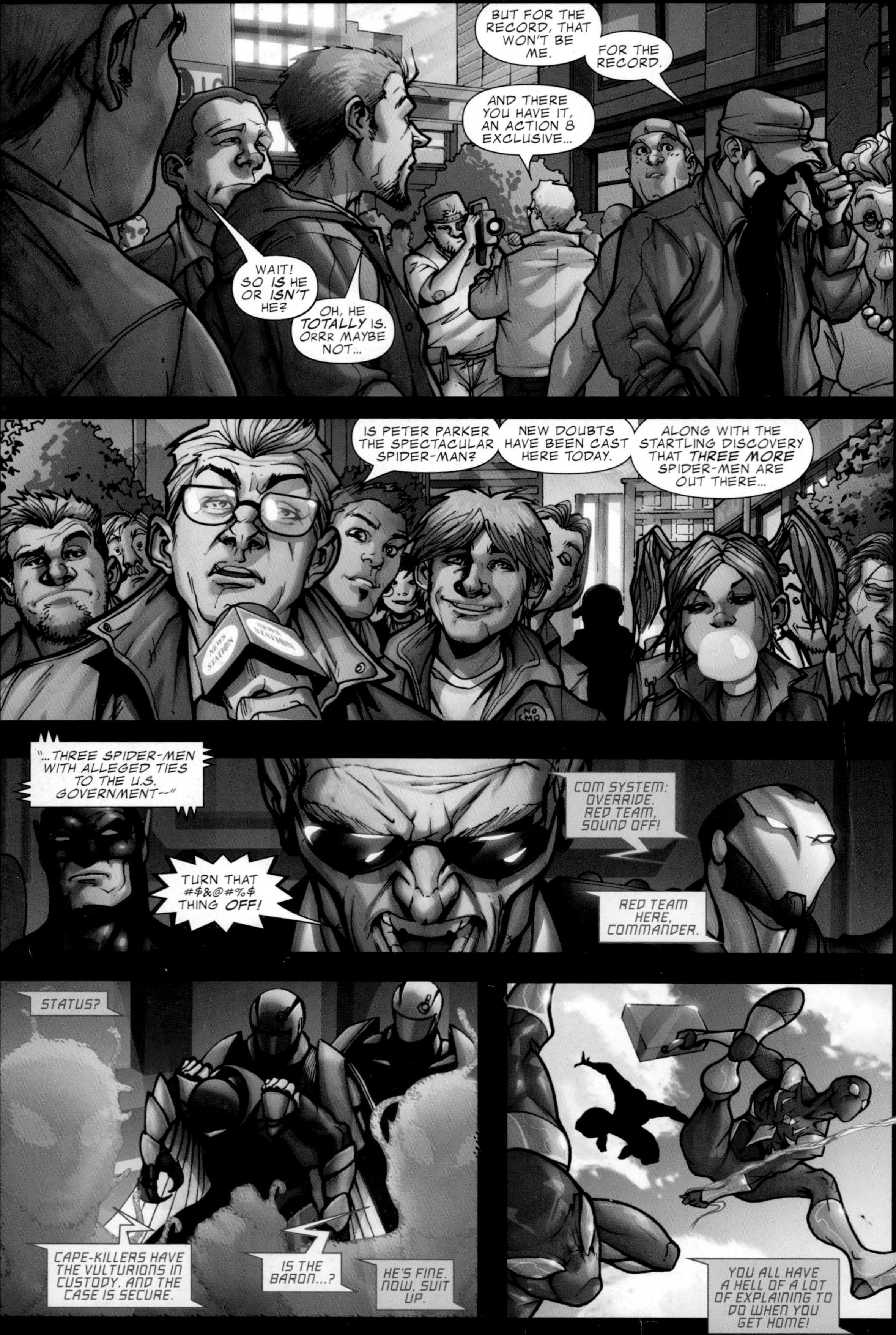

BUT FOR THE RECORD, THAT WON'T BE ME.
FOR THE RECORD.
AND THERE YOU HAVE IT, AN ACTION 8 EXCLUSIVE...
WAIT! SO IS HE OR ISN'T HE?
OH, HE TOTALLY IS. ORRR MAYBE NOT...
IS PETER PARKER THE SPECTACULAR SPIDER-MAN?
NEW DOUBTS HAVE BEEN CAST HERE TODAY.
ALONG WITH THE STARTLING DISCOVERY THAT THREE MORE SPIDER-MEN ARE OUT THERE...
"...THREE SPIDER-MEN WITH ALLEGED TIES TO THE U.S. GOVERNMENT--"
TURN THAT #$&@#%$ THING OFF!
COM SYSTEM: OVERRIDE. RED TEAM, SOUND OFF!
RED TEAM HERE, COMMANDER.
STATUS?
CAPE-KILLERS HAVE THE VULTURIONS IN CUSTODY. AND THE CASE IS SECURE.
IS THE BARON...?
HE'S FINE. NOW, SUIT UP.
YOU ALL HAVE A HELL OF A LOT OF EXPLAINING TO DO WHEN YOU GET HOME!

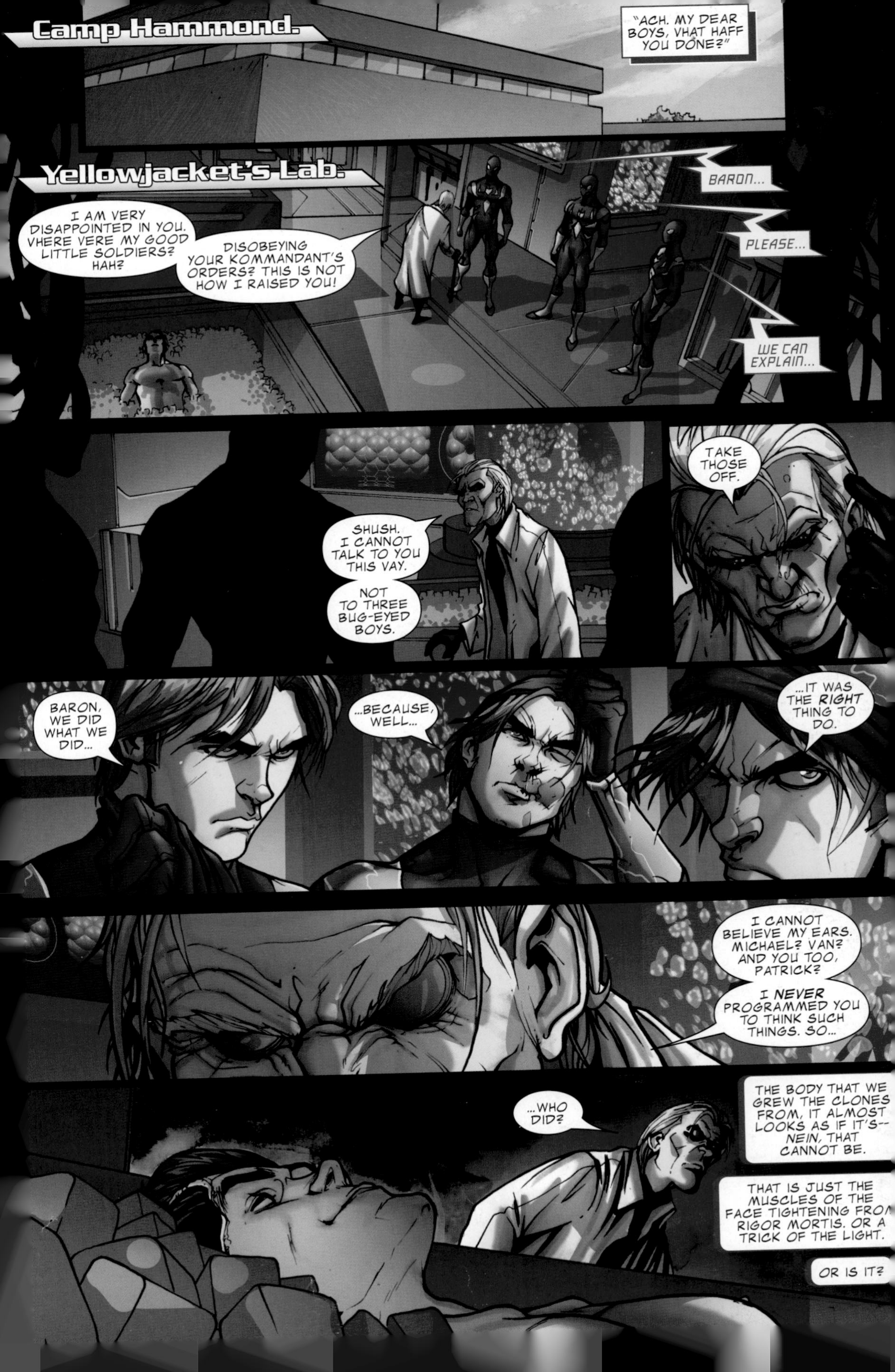
Camp Hammond.
"ACH. MY DEAR BOYS, VHAT HAFF YOU DONE?"
Yellowjacket's Lab.
I AM VERY DISAPPOINTED IN YOU. VHERE VERE MY GOOD LITTLE SOLDIERS? HAH?
DISOBEYING YOUR KOMMANDANT'S ORDERS? THIS IS NOT HOW I RAISED YOU!
BARON...
PLEASE...
WE CAN EXPLAIN...
SHUSH. I CANNOT TALK TO YOU THIS VAY.
NOT TO THREE BUG-EYED BOYS.
TAKE THOSE OFF.
BARON, WE DID WHAT WE DID...
...BECAUSE, WELL...
...IT WAS THE RIGHT THING TO DO.
I CANNOT BELIEVE MY EARS. MICHAEL? VAN? AND YOU TOO, PATRICK?
I NEVER PROGRAMMED YOU TO THINK SUCH THINGS. SO...
...WHO DID?
THE BODY THAT WE GREW THE CLONES FROM, IT ALMOST LOOKS AS IF IT'S-- NEIN, THAT CANNOT BE.
THAT IS JUST THE MUSCLES OF THE FACE TIGHTENING FROM RIGOR MORTIS. OR A TRICK OF THE LIGHT.
OR IS IT?

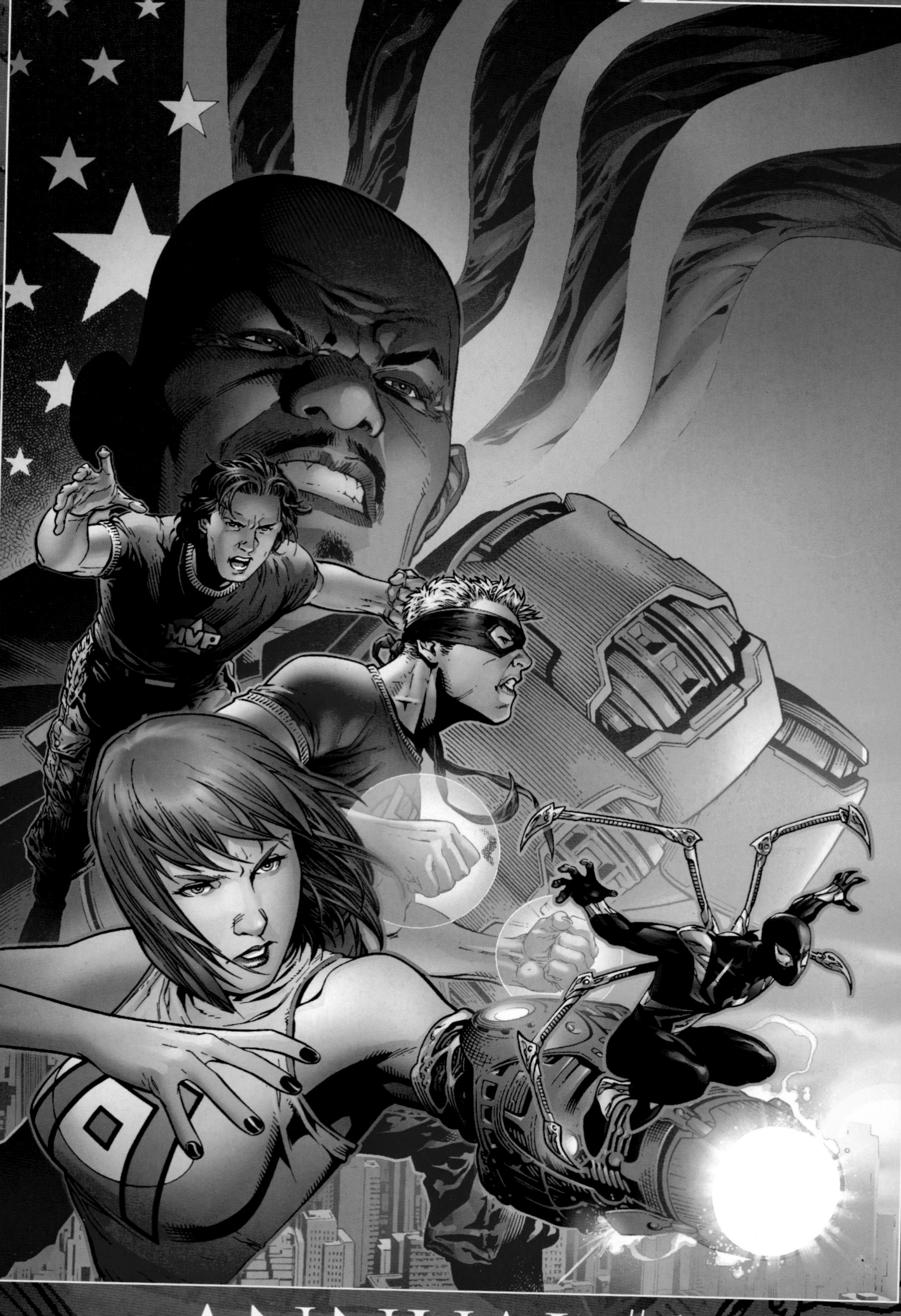
MVP

ANNUAL #1

FIFTY STATE INITIATIVE

Dan Slott with Christos Gage - Writers

"SECOND BEST"
Salvador Larroca - Artist
Stephane Peru - Color Art

"REASON FOR BEING"
Clayton Henry - Penciler
Paul Neary - Inker
Daniele Rudoni - Colorist

"BE ALL THAT YOU CAN BE"
Steve Uy - Artist

"BORN TO SERVE"
Tom Feister & Carmine Di Giandomenico - Artists
Jose Villarrubia - Color Art

"STATE OF READINESS"
Patrick Scherberger - Penciler
David Meikis - Inker
Wil Quintana - Colorist

VC's Joe Caramagna - Letterer

Molly Lazer - Assistant Editor
Tom Brevoort - Editor
Joe Quesada - Editor in Chief
Dan Buckley - Publisher

THE LIBERTEENS

GAUNTLET
ST. JOSEPH GREEN

ARMORY
VIOLET LIGHTNER

MVP
MICHAEL VAN PATRICK

HARDBALL
ROGER BROKERIDGE

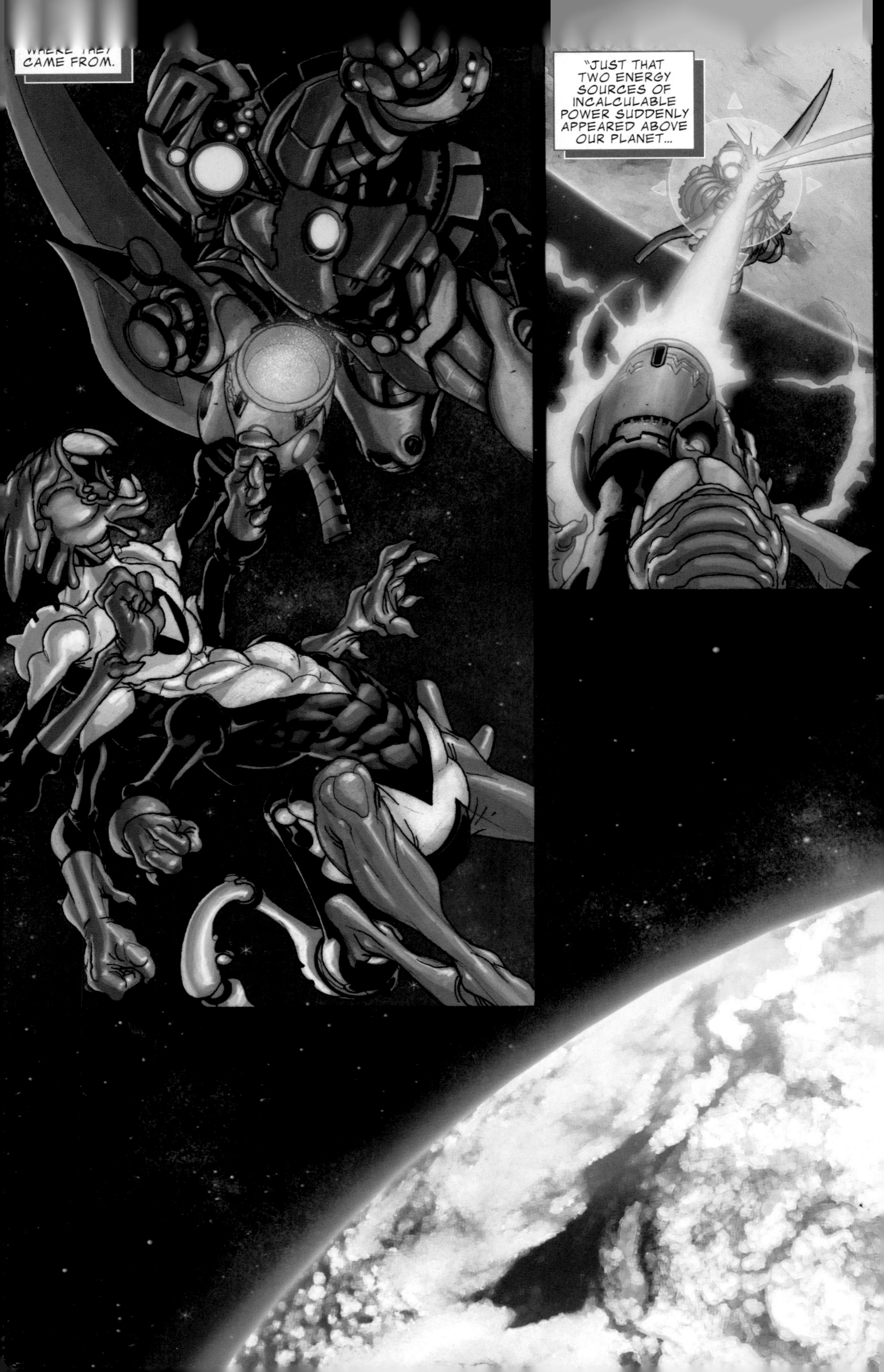
CAME FROM.
"JUST THAT TWO ENERGY SOURCES OF INCALCULABLE POWER SUDDENLY APPEARED ABOVE OUR PLANET...

"...COLLIDED WITH ONE ANOTHER...

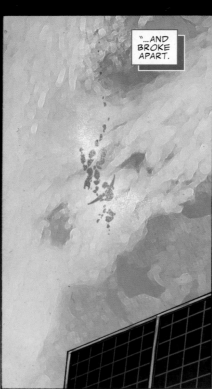

"...AND BROKE APART.

"AS THEY FELL INTO THE ATMOSPHERE, THE FRAGMENTS WERE THROWN IN MULTIPLE DIRECTIONS, TOWARD DIFFERENT PARTS OF THE GLOBE.

"OUR SATELLITES TRACKED THEM AS BEST THEY COULD...

THE GAUNTLET IN "SECOND BEST"

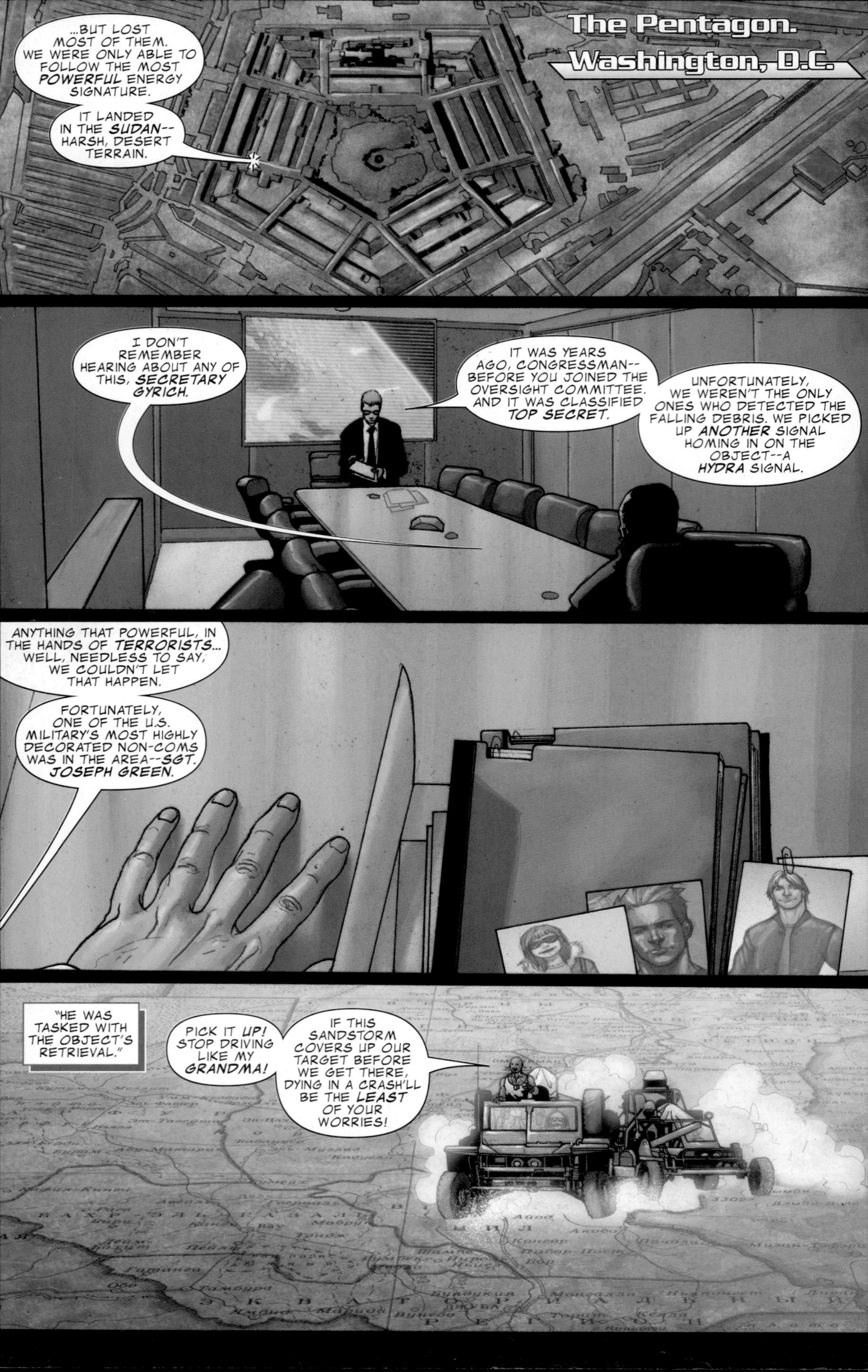

The Pentagon. Washington, D.C.
...BUT LOST MOST OF THEM. WE WERE ONLY ABLE TO FOLLOW THE MOST POWERFUL ENERGY SIGNATURE.
IT LANDED IN THE SUDAN-- HARSH, DESERT TERRAIN.
I DON'T REMEMBER HEARING ABOUT ANY OF THIS, SECRETARY GYRICH.
IT WAS YEARS AGO, CONGRESSMAN-- BEFORE YOU JOINED THE OVERSIGHT COMMITTEE. AND IT WAS CLASSIFIED TOP SECRET.
UNFORTUNATELY, WE WEREN'T THE ONLY ONES WHO DETECTED THE FALLING DEBRIS. WE PICKED UP ANOTHER SIGNAL HOMING IN ON THE OBJECT--A HYDRA SIGNAL.
ANYTHING THAT POWERFUL, IN THE HANDS OF TERRORISTS... WELL, NEEDLESS TO SAY, WE COULDN'T LET THAT HAPPEN.
FORTUNATELY, ONE OF THE U.S. MILITARY'S MOST HIGHLY DECORATED NON-COMS WAS IN THE AREA--SGT. JOSEPH GREEN.
"HE WAS TASKED WITH THE OBJECT'S RETRIEVAL."
PICK IT UP! STOP DRIVING LIKE MY GRANDMA!
IF THIS SANDSTORM COVERS UP OUR TARGET BEFORE WE GET THERE, DYING IN A CRASH'LL BE THE LEAST OF YOUR WORRIES!

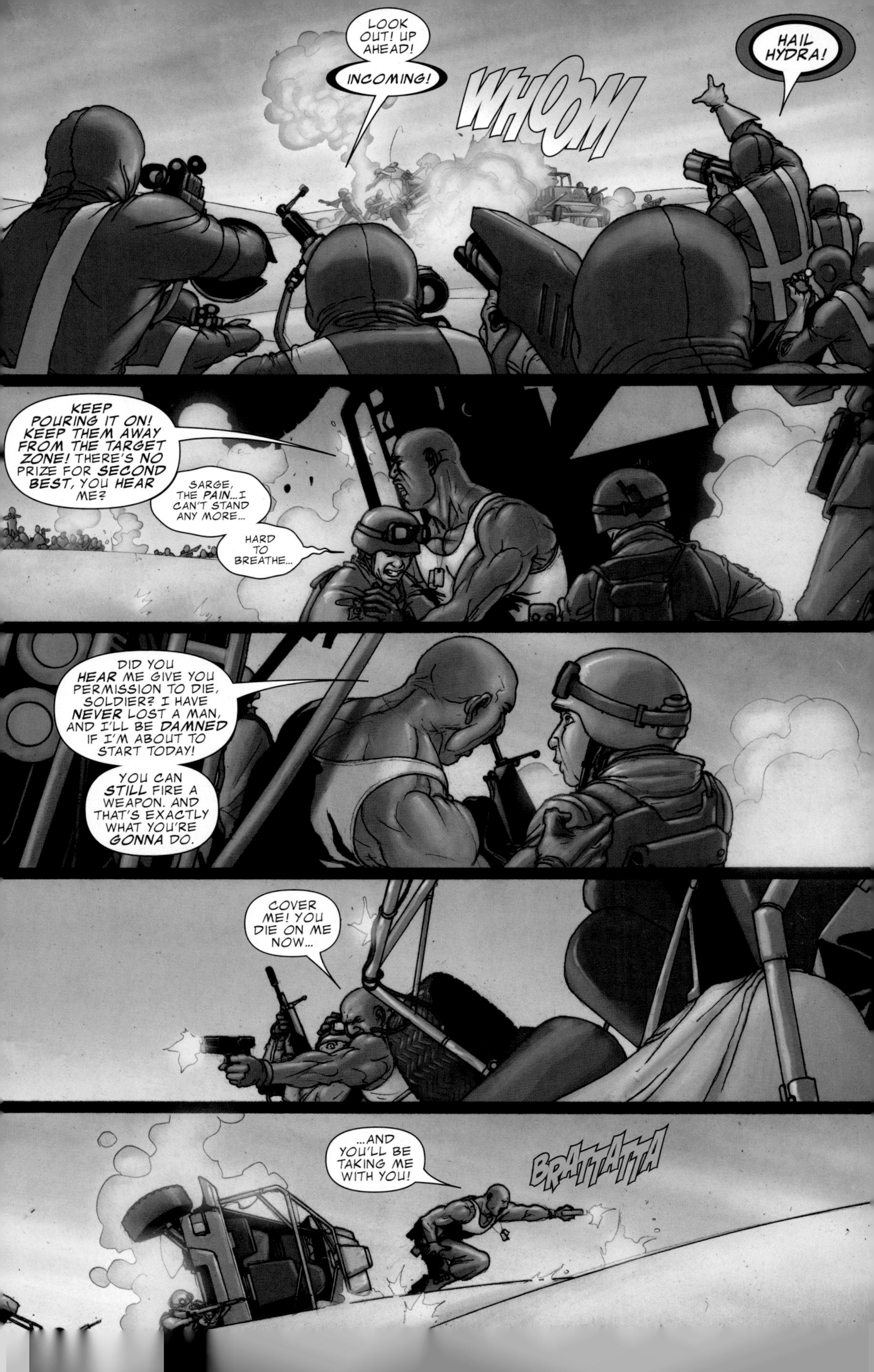
LOOK OUT! UP AHEAD!
INCOMING!
WHOOM
HAIL HYDRA!
KEEP POURING IT ON! KEEP THEM AWAY FROM THE TARGET ZONE! THERE'S NO PRIZE FOR SECOND BEST, YOU HEAR ME?
SARGE, THE PAIN...I CAN'T STAND ANY MORE...
HARD TO BREATHE...
DID YOU HEAR ME GIVE YOU PERMISSION TO DIE, SOLDIER? I HAVE NEVER LOST A MAN, AND I'LL BE DAMNED IF I'M ABOUT TO START TODAY!
YOU CAN STILL FIRE A WEAPON. AND THAT'S EXACTLY WHAT YOU'RE GONNA DO.
COVER ME! YOU DIE ON ME NOW...
...AND YOU'LL BE TAKING ME WITH YOU!
BRATTATTA

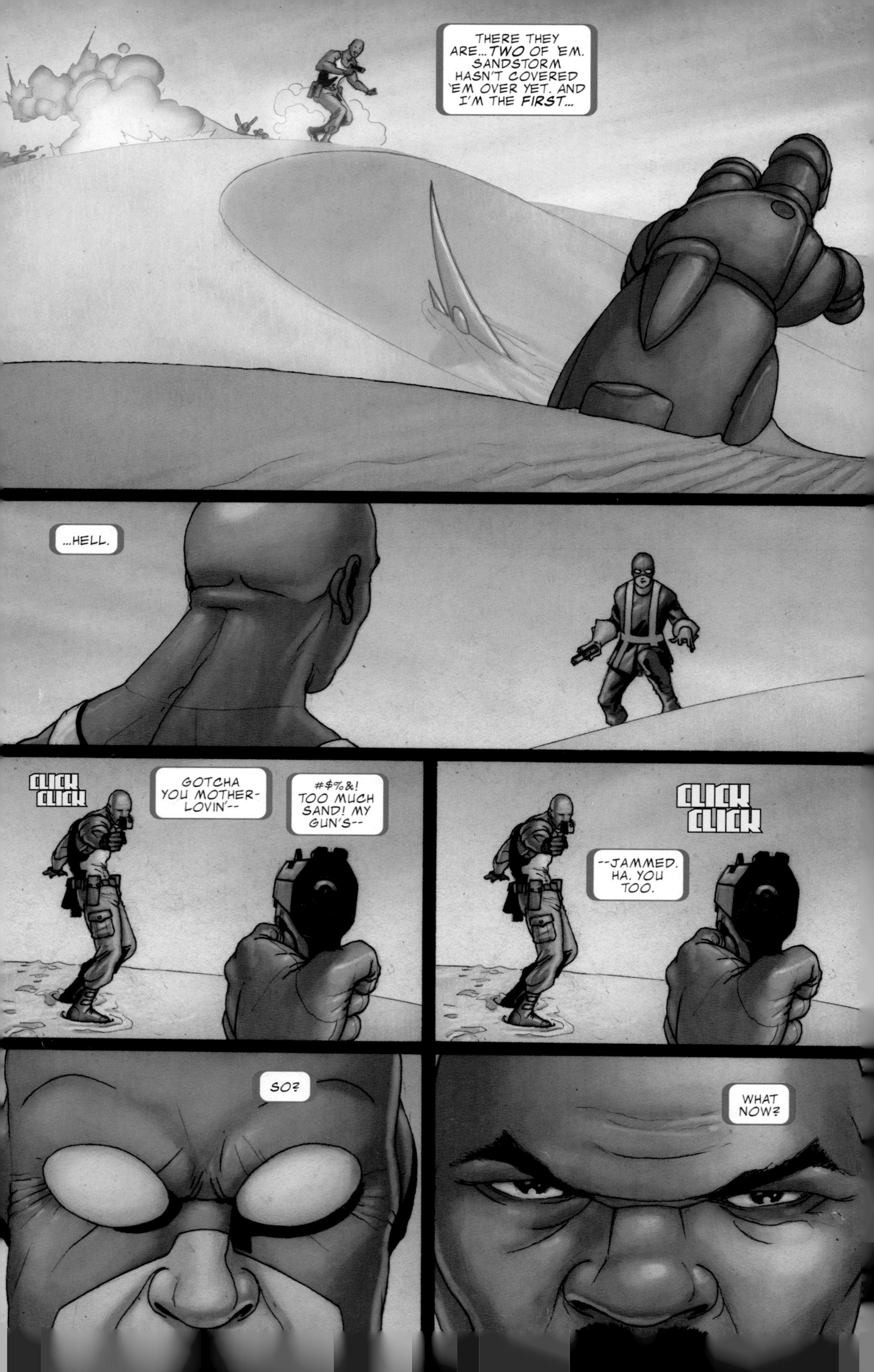
THERE THEY ARE...TWO OF 'EM. SANDSTORM HASN'T COVERED 'EM OVER YET. AND I'M THE FIRST...
...HELL.
CLICK CLICK
GOTCHA YOU MOTHER-LOVIN'--
#$%&! TOO MUCH SAND! MY GUN'S--
CLICK CLICK
--JAMMED. HA. YOU TOO.
SO?
WHAT NOW?

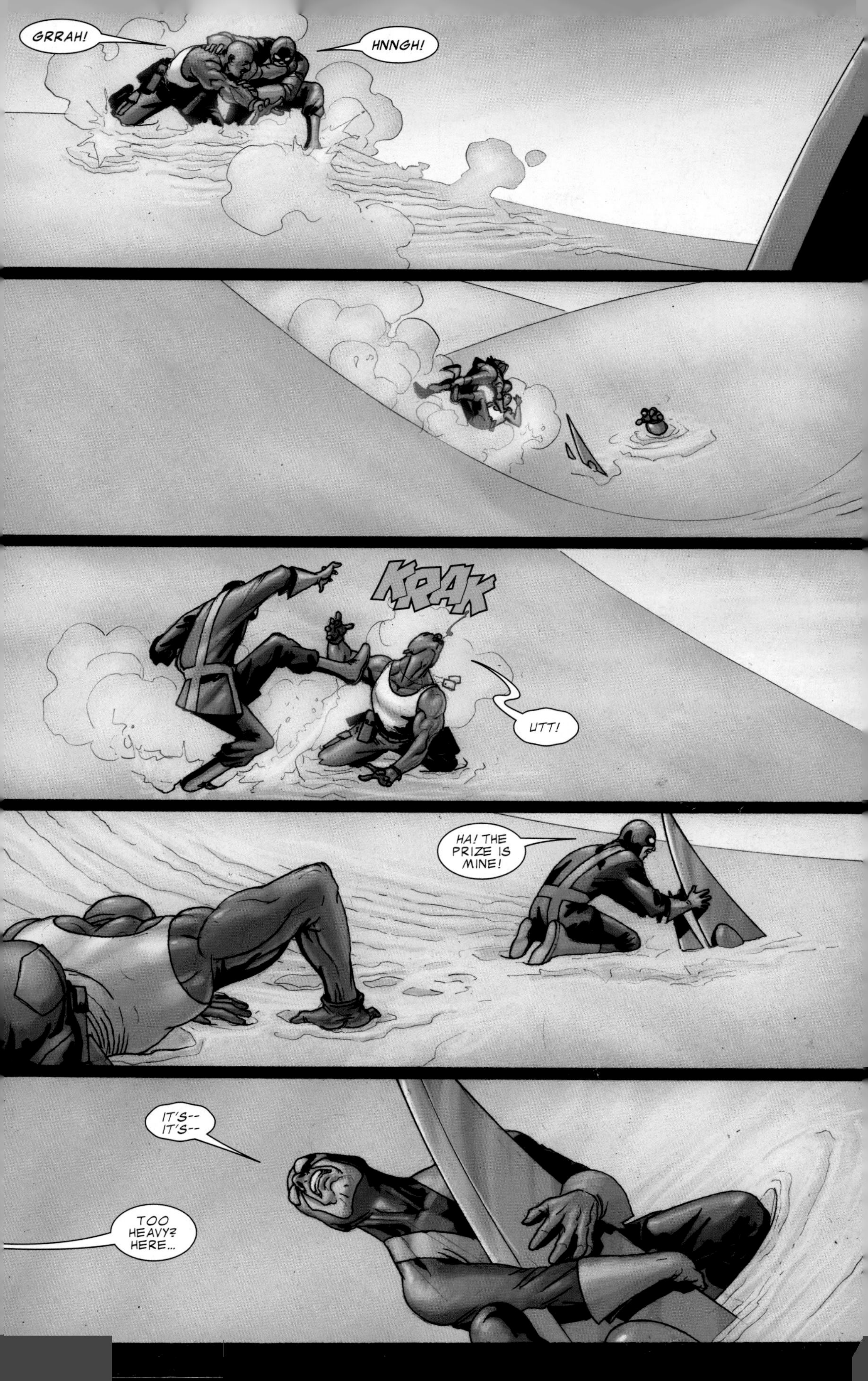
GRRAH!
HNNGH!
KRAK
UTT!
HA! THE PRIZE IS MINE!
IT'S-- IT'S--
TOO HEAVY? HERE...

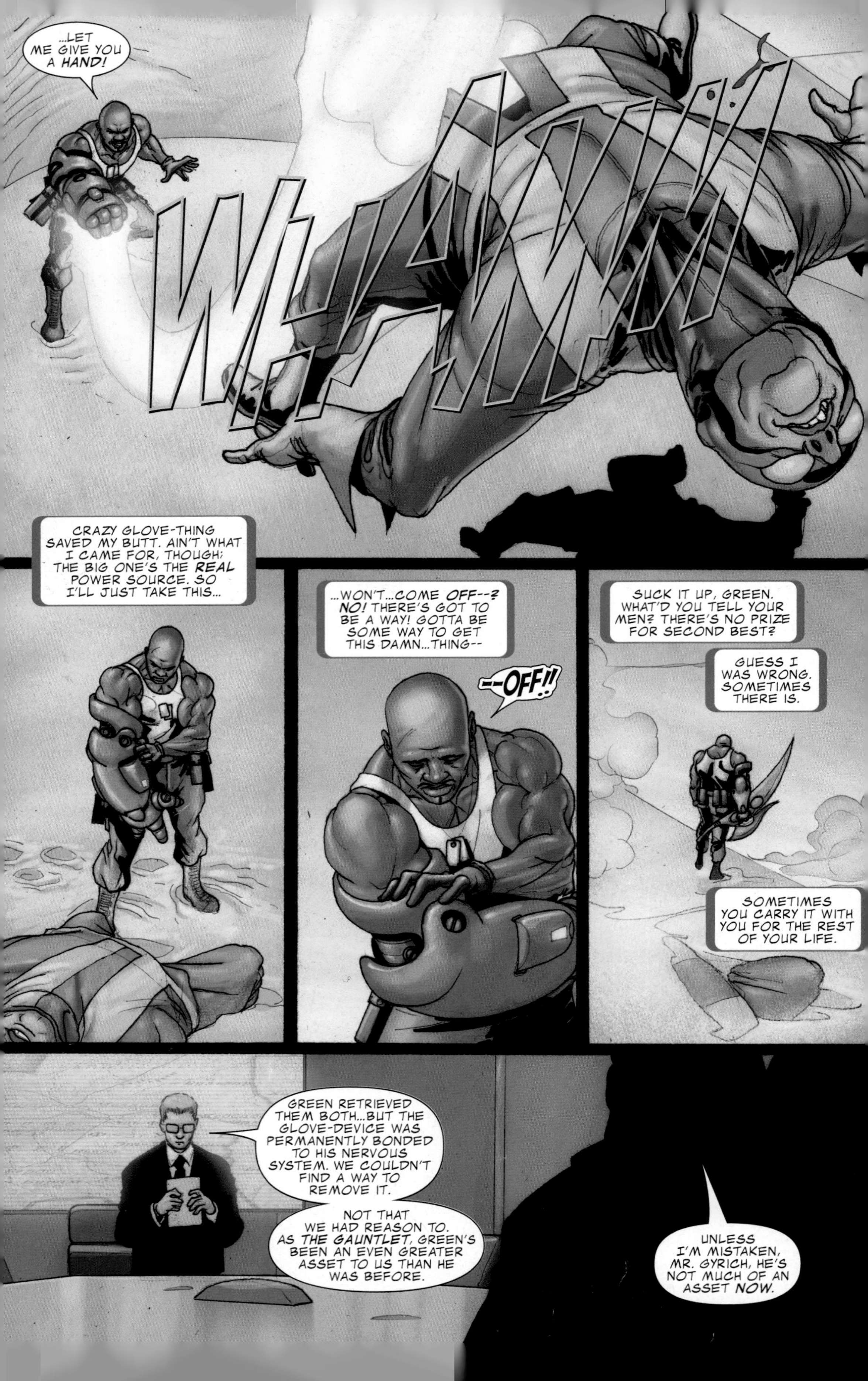

...LET ME GIVE YOU A *HAND!*
WHAAAM
CRAZY GLOVE-THING SAVED MY BUTT. AIN'T WHAT I CAME FOR, THOUGH; THE BIG ONE'S THE *REAL* POWER SOURCE. SO I'LL JUST TAKE THIS...
...WON'T...COME *OFF*--? *NO!* THERE'S GOT TO BE A WAY! GOTTA BE SOME WAY TO GET THIS DAMN...THING--
--OFF!!
SUCK IT UP, GREEN. WHAT'D YOU TELL YOUR MEN? THERE'S NO PRIZE FOR SECOND BEST?
GUESS I WAS WRONG. SOMETIMES THERE IS.
SOMETIMES YOU CARRY IT WITH YOU FOR THE REST OF YOUR LIFE.
GREEN RETRIEVED THEM BOTH...BUT THE GLOVE-DEVICE WAS PERMANENTLY BONDED TO HIS NERVOUS SYSTEM. WE COULDN'T FIND A WAY TO REMOVE IT.
NOT THAT WE HAD REASON TO. AS *THE GAUNTLET*, GREEN'S BEEN AN EVEN GREATER ASSET TO US THAN HE WAS BEFORE.
UNLESS I'M MISTAKEN, MR. GYRICH, HE'S NOT MUCH OF AN ASSET *NOW*.

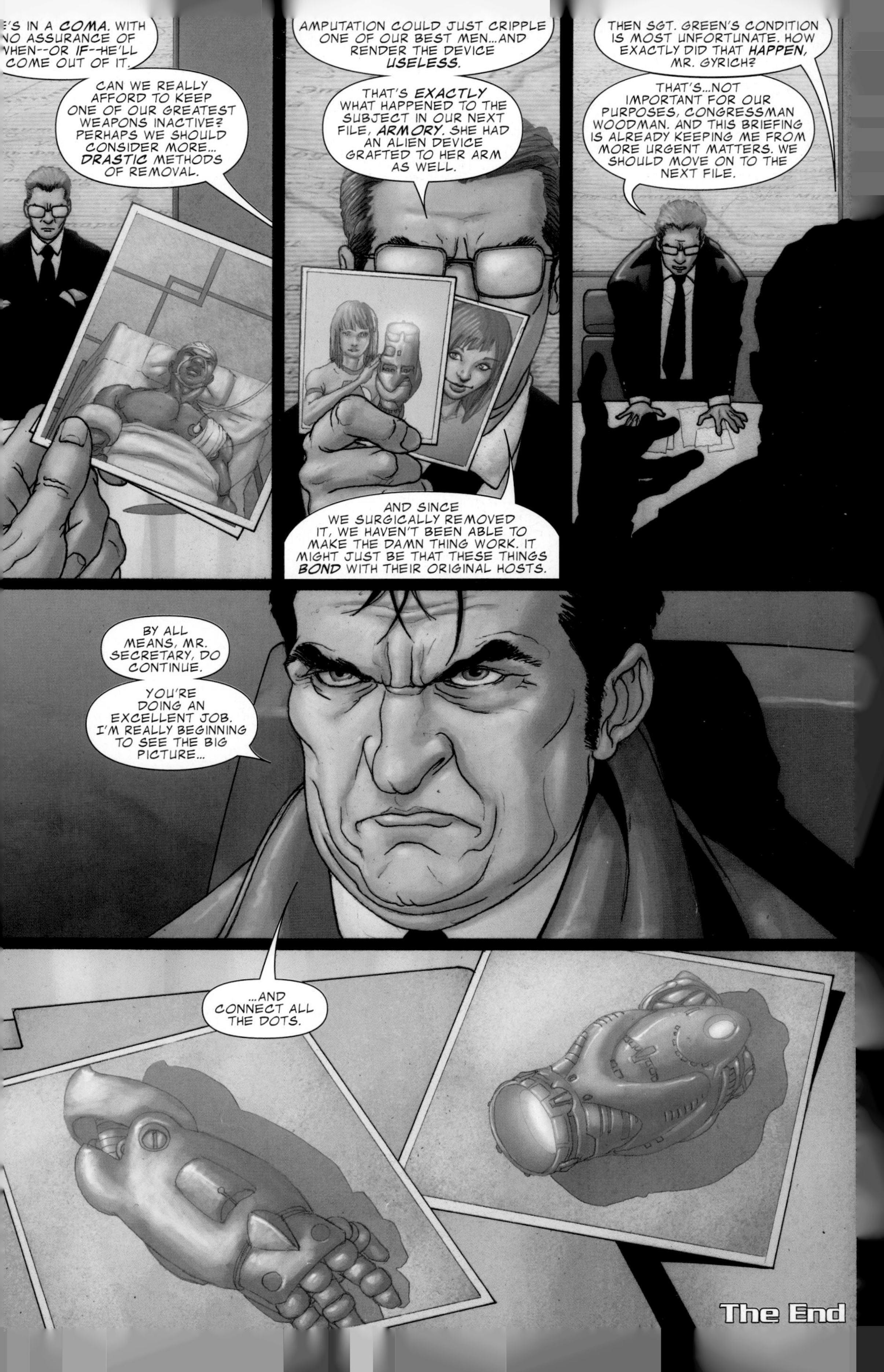

'S IN A COMA. WITH NO ASSURANCE OF WHEN--OR IF--HE'LL COME OUT OF IT.
CAN WE REALLY AFFORD TO KEEP ONE OF OUR GREATEST WEAPONS INACTIVE? PERHAPS WE SHOULD CONSIDER MORE... DRASTIC METHODS OF REMOVAL.
AMPUTATION COULD JUST CRIPPLE ONE OF OUR BEST MEN...AND RENDER THE DEVICE USELESS.
THAT'S EXACTLY WHAT HAPPENED TO THE SUBJECT IN OUR NEXT FILE, ARMORY. SHE HAD AN ALIEN DEVICE GRAFTED TO HER ARM AS WELL.
AND SINCE WE SURGICALLY REMOVED IT, WE HAVEN'T BEEN ABLE TO MAKE THE DAMN THING WORK. IT MIGHT JUST BE THAT THESE THINGS BOND WITH THEIR ORIGINAL HOSTS.
THEN SGT. GREEN'S CONDITION IS MOST UNFORTUNATE. HOW EXACTLY DID THAT HAPPEN, MR. GYRICH?
THAT'S...NOT IMPORTANT FOR OUR PURPOSES, CONGRESSMAN WOODMAN. AND THIS BRIEFING IS ALREADY KEEPING ME FROM MORE URGENT MATTERS. WE SHOULD MOVE ON TO THE NEXT FILE.
BY ALL MEANS, MR. SECRETARY, DO CONTINUE.
YOU'RE DOING AN EXCELLENT JOB. I'M REALLY BEGINNING TO SEE THE BIG PICTURE...
...AND CONNECT ALL THE DOTS.
The End

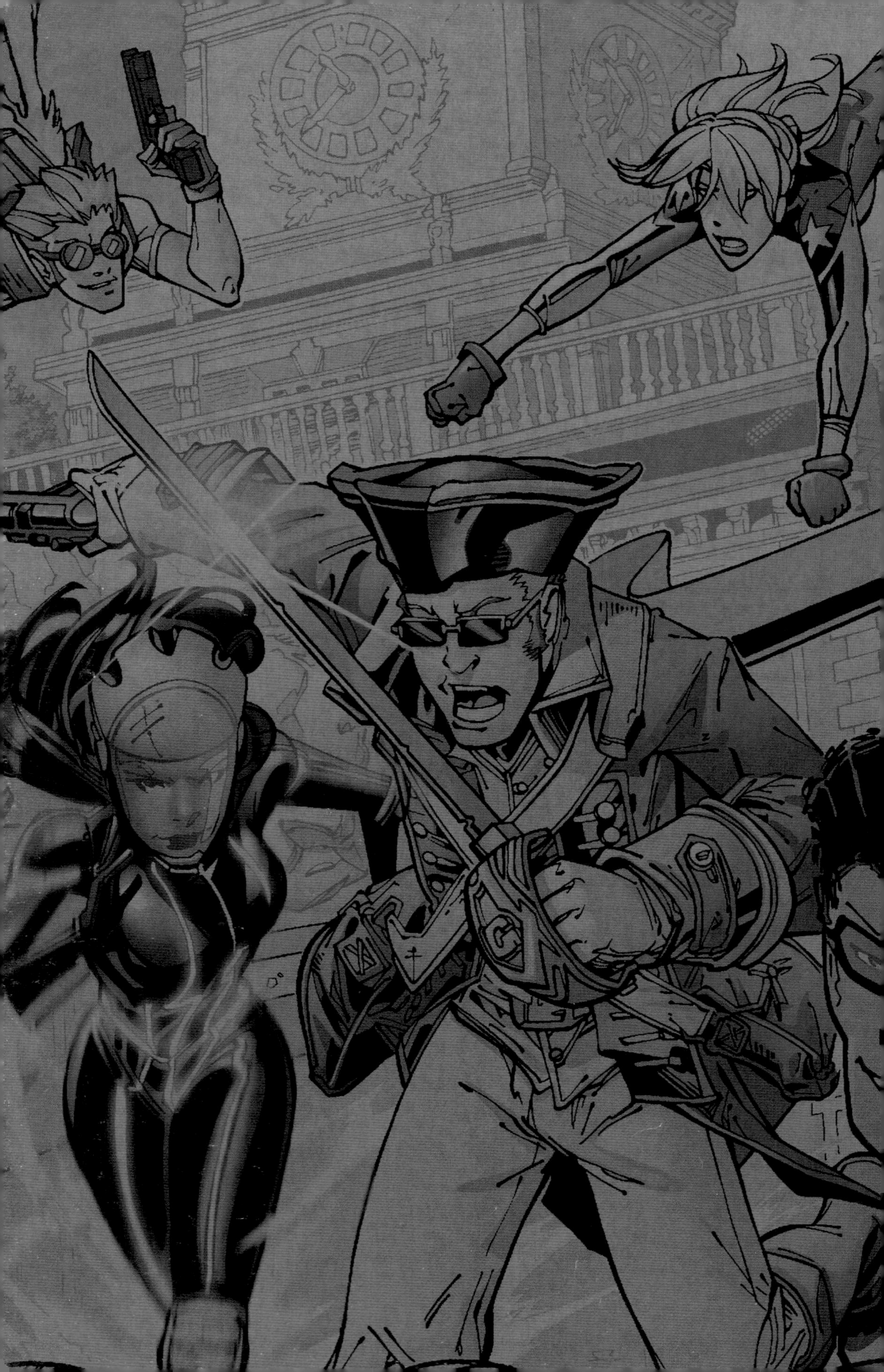

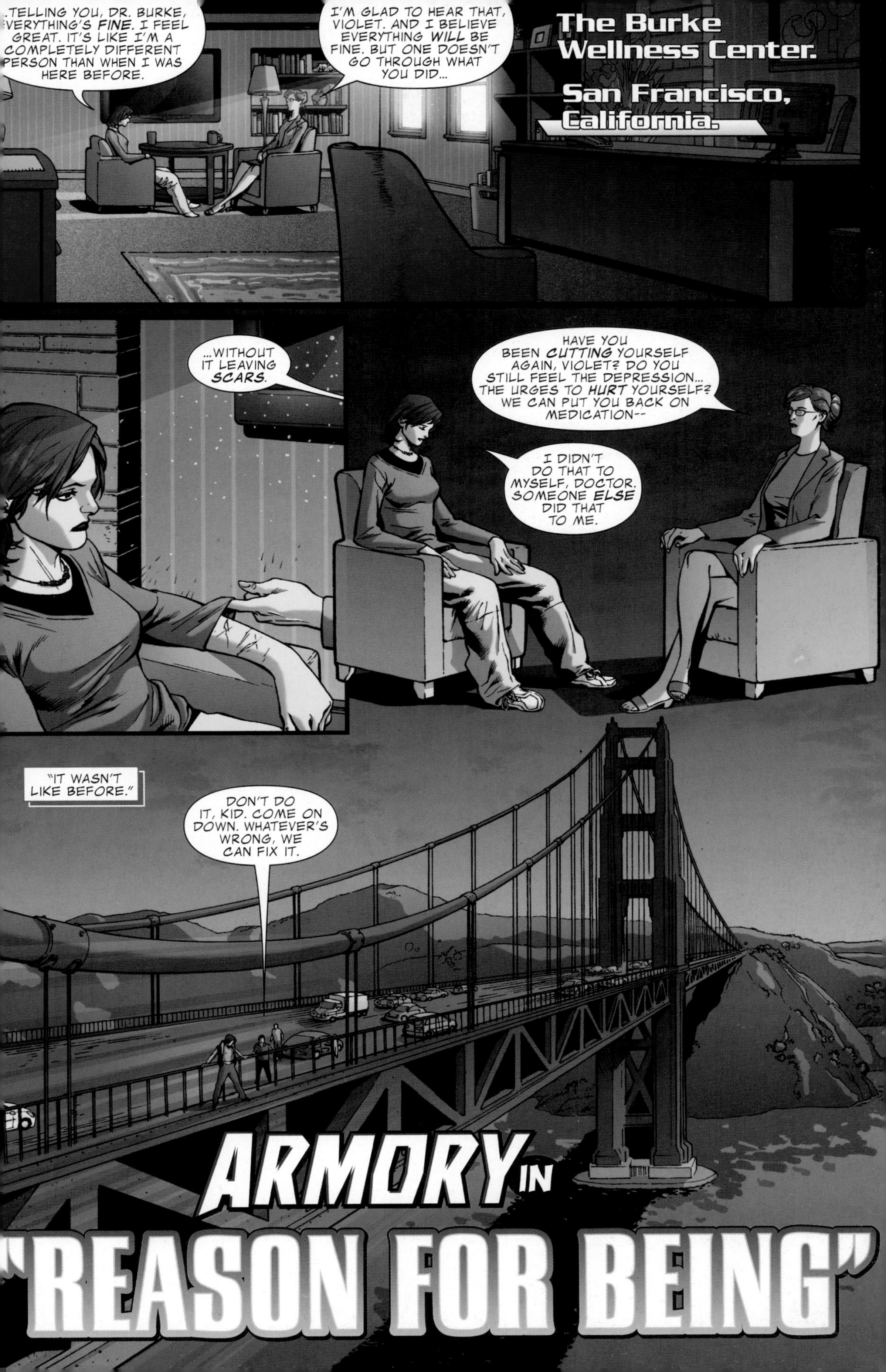
...TELLING YOU, DR. BURKE, EVERYTHING'S FINE. I FEEL GREAT. IT'S LIKE I'M A COMPLETELY DIFFERENT PERSON THAN WHEN I WAS HERE BEFORE.
I'M GLAD TO HEAR THAT, VIOLET. AND I BELIEVE EVERYTHING WILL BE FINE. BUT ONE DOESN'T GO THROUGH WHAT YOU DID...
The Burke Wellness Center.
San Francisco, California.
...WITHOUT IT LEAVING SCARS.
HAVE YOU BEEN CUTTING YOURSELF AGAIN, VIOLET? DO YOU STILL FEEL THE DEPRESSION... THE URGES TO HURT YOURSELF? WE CAN PUT YOU BACK ON MEDICATION--
I DIDN'T DO THAT TO MYSELF, DOCTOR. SOMEONE ELSE DID THAT TO ME.
"IT WASN'T LIKE BEFORE."
DON'T DO IT, KID. COME ON DOWN. WHATEVER'S WRONG, WE CAN FIX IT.
ARMORY IN
"REASON FOR BEING"

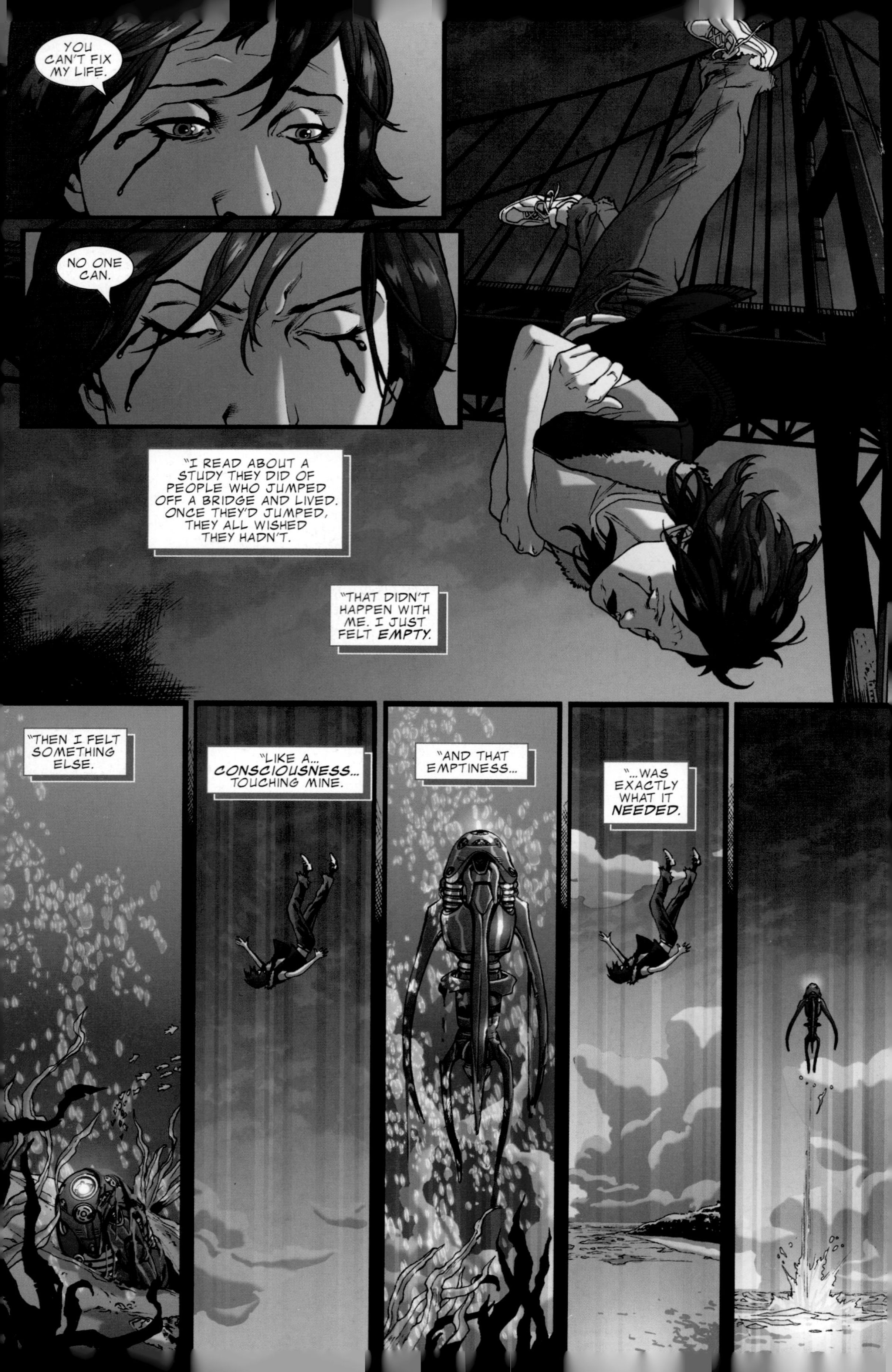
YOU CAN'T FIX MY LIFE.
NO ONE CAN.
"I READ ABOUT A STUDY THEY DID OF PEOPLE WHO JUMPED OFF A BRIDGE AND LIVED. ONCE THEY'D JUMPED, THEY ALL WISHED THEY HADN'T.
"THAT DIDN'T HAPPEN WITH ME. I JUST FELT EMPTY.
"THEN I FELT SOMETHING ELSE.
"LIKE A... CONSCIOUSNESS... TOUCHING MINE.
"AND THAT EMPTINESS...
"...WAS EXACTLY WHAT IT NEEDED.

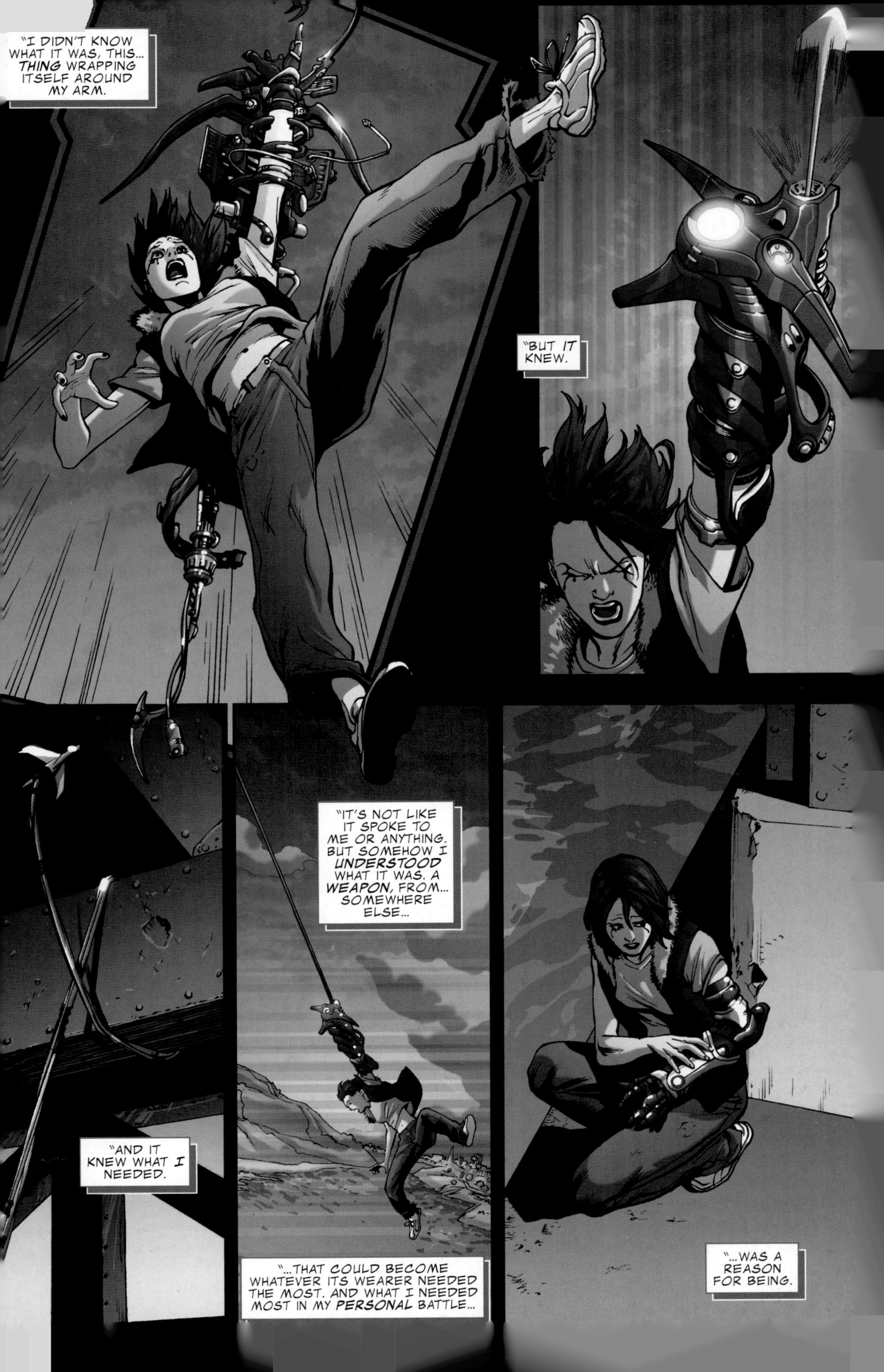
"I DIDN'T KNOW WHAT IT WAS, THIS... *THING* WRAPPING ITSELF AROUND MY ARM.
"BUT *IT* KNEW.
"AND IT KNEW WHAT *I* NEEDED.
"IT'S NOT LIKE IT SPOKE TO ME OR ANYTHING. BUT SOMEHOW I *UNDERSTOOD* WHAT IT WAS. A *WEAPON*, FROM... SOMEWHERE ELSE...
"...THAT COULD BECOME WHATEVER ITS WEARER NEEDED THE MOST. AND WHAT I NEEDED MOST IN MY *PERSONAL* BATTLE...
"...WAS A REASON FOR BEING.

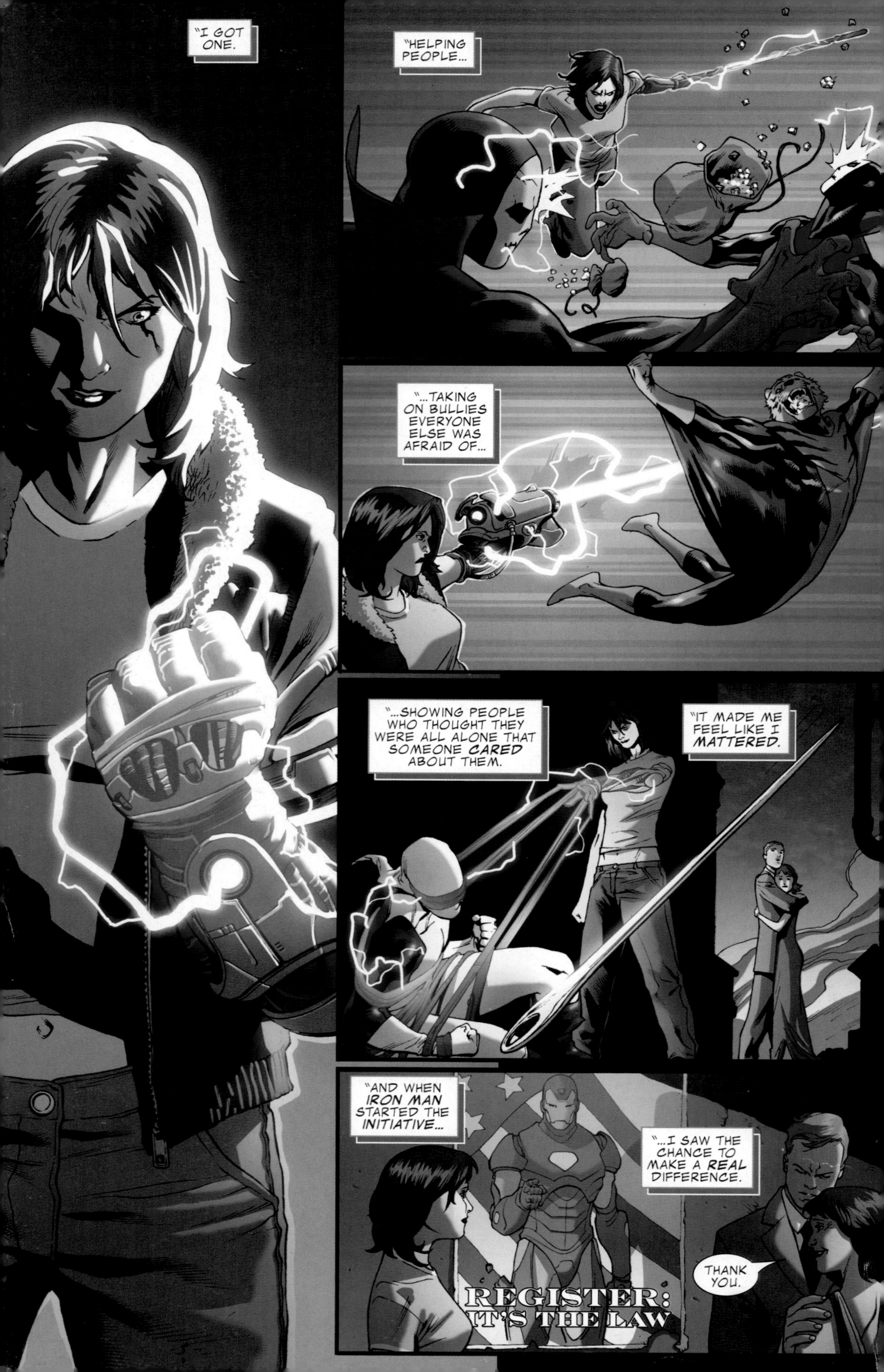
"I GOT ONE.
"HELPING PEOPLE...
"...TAKING ON BULLIES EVERYONE ELSE WAS AFRAID OF...
"...SHOWING PEOPLE WHO THOUGHT THEY WERE ALL ALONE THAT SOMEONE CARED ABOUT THEM.
"IT MADE ME FEEL LIKE I MATTERED.
"AND WHEN IRON MAN STARTED THE INITIATIVE...
"...I SAW THE CHANCE TO MAKE A REAL DIFFERENCE.
THANK YOU.
REGISTER: IT'S THE LAW

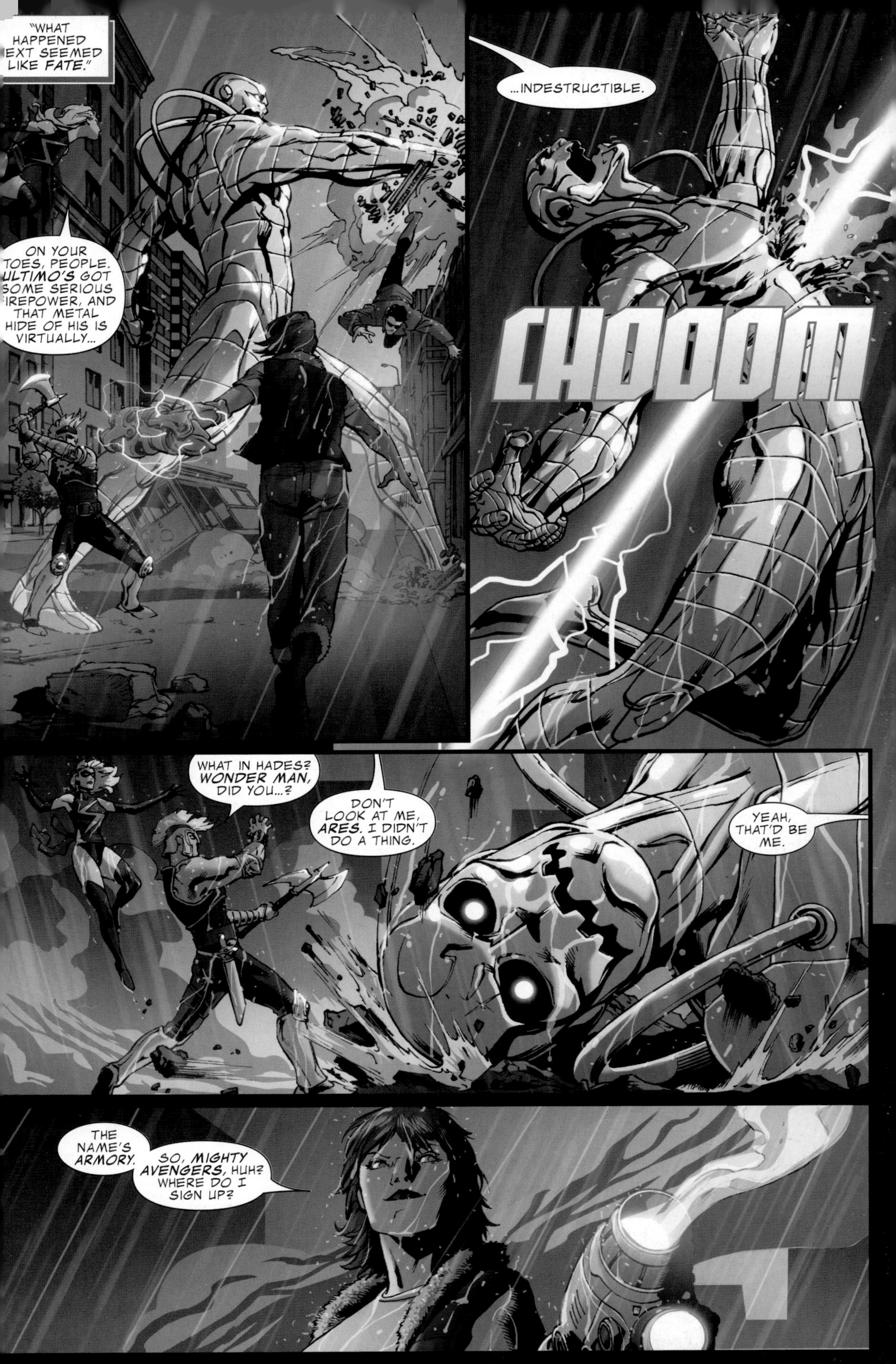
"WHAT HAPPENED NEXT SEEMED LIKE FATE."
ON YOUR TOES, PEOPLE. ULTIMO'S GOT SOME SERIOUS FIREPOWER, AND THAT METAL HIDE OF HIS IS VIRTUALLY...
...INDESTRUCTIBLE.
CHOOOM
WHAT IN HADES? WONDER MAN, DID YOU...?
DON'T LOOK AT ME, ARES. I DIDN'T DO A THING.
YEAH, THAT'D BE ME.
THE NAME'S ARMORY.
SO, MIGHTY AVENGERS, HUH? WHERE DO I SIGN UP?

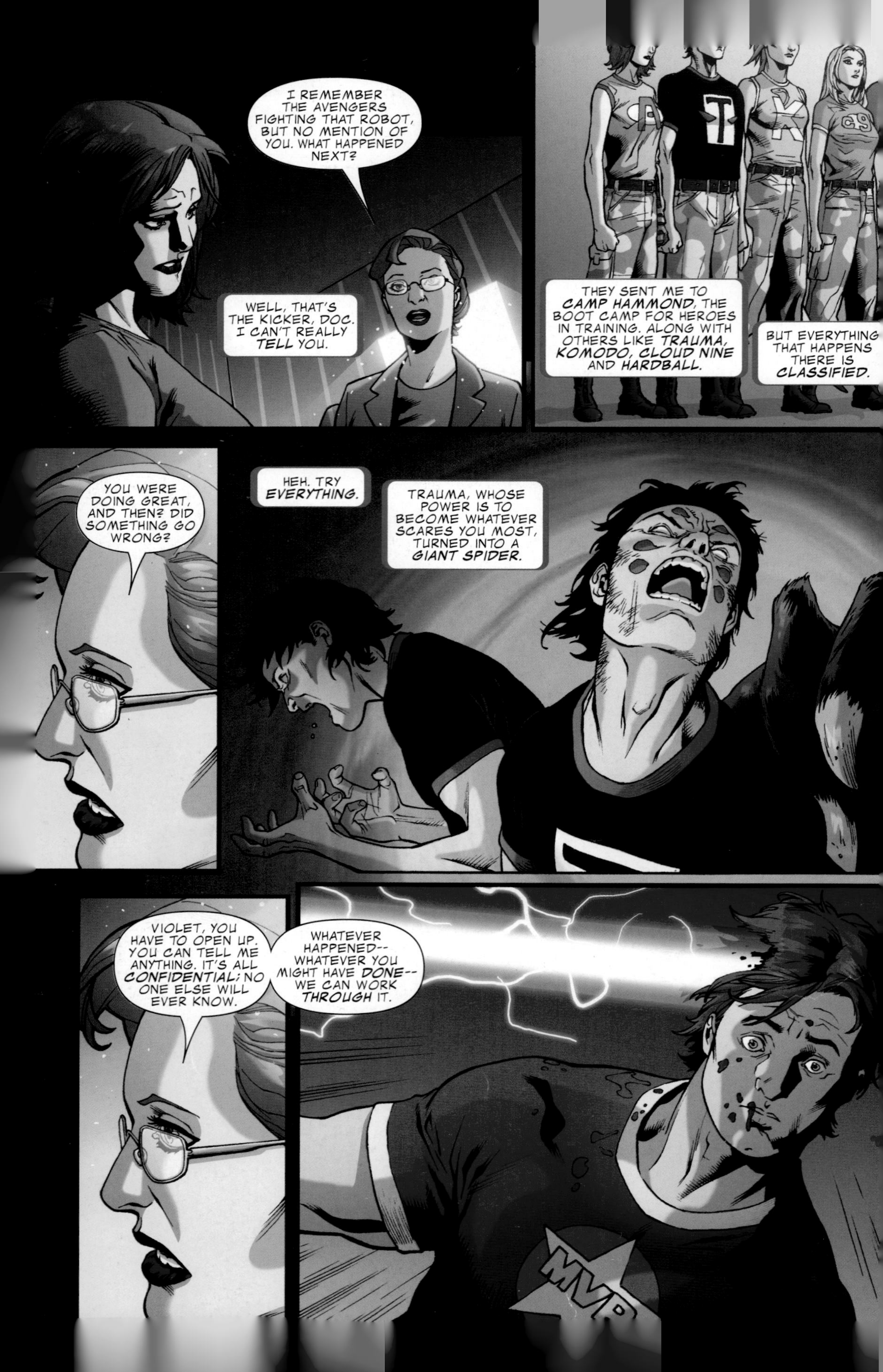
I REMEMBER THE AVENGERS FIGHTING THAT ROBOT, BUT NO MENTION OF YOU. WHAT HAPPENED NEXT?
WELL, THAT'S THE KICKER, DOC. I CAN'T REALLY TELL YOU.
THEY SENT ME TO CAMP HAMMOND, THE BOOT CAMP FOR HEROES IN TRAINING. ALONG WITH OTHERS LIKE TRAUMA, KOMODO, CLOUD NINE AND HARDBALL.
BUT EVERYTHING THAT HAPPENS THERE IS CLASSIFIED.
YOU WERE DOING GREAT, AND THEN? DID SOMETHING GO WRONG?
HEH. TRY EVERYTHING.
TRAUMA, WHOSE POWER IS TO BECOME WHATEVER SCARES YOU MOST, TURNED INTO A GIANT SPIDER.
VIOLET, YOU HAVE TO OPEN UP. YOU CAN TELL ME ANYTHING. IT'S ALL CONFIDENTIAL; NO ONE ELSE WILL EVER KNOW.
WHATEVER HAPPENED-- WHATEVER YOU MIGHT HAVE DONE-- WE CAN WORK THROUGH IT.

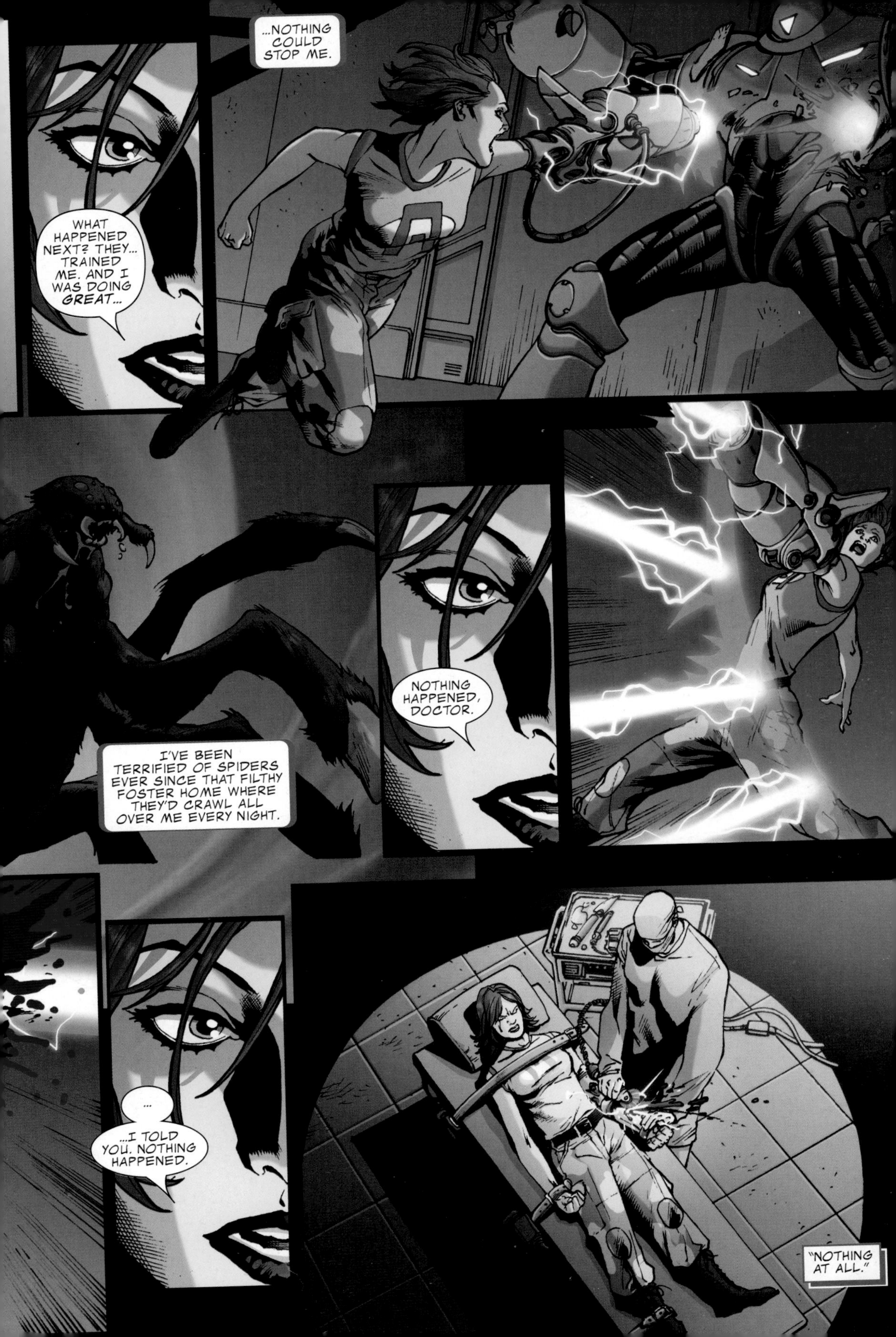
...NOTHING COULD STOP ME.
WHAT HAPPENED NEXT? THEY... TRAINED ME. AND I WAS DOING GREAT...
NOTHING HAPPENED, DOCTOR.
I'VE BEEN TERRIFIED OF SPIDERS EVER SINCE THAT FILTHY FOSTER HOME WHERE THEY'D CRAWL ALL OVER ME EVERY NIGHT.
...
...I TOLD YOU. NOTHING HAPPENED.
"NOTHING AT ALL."

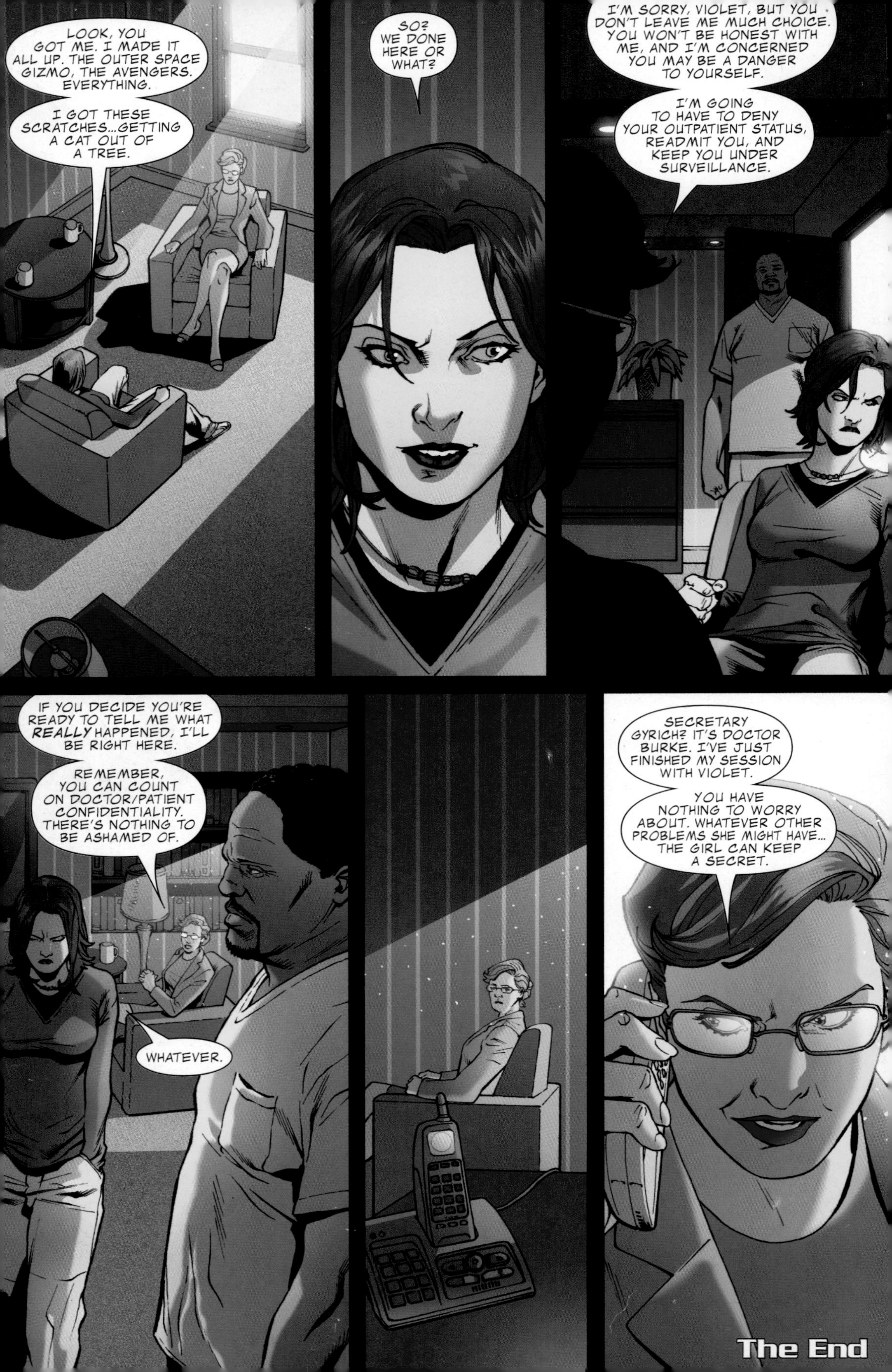
LOOK, YOU GOT ME. I MADE IT ALL UP. THE OUTER SPACE GIZMO, THE AVENGERS. EVERYTHING.
I GOT THESE SCRATCHES...GETTING A CAT OUT OF A TREE.
SO? WE DONE HERE OR WHAT?
I'M SORRY, VIOLET, BUT YOU DON'T LEAVE ME MUCH CHOICE. YOU WON'T BE HONEST WITH ME, AND I'M CONCERNED YOU MAY BE A DANGER TO YOURSELF.
I'M GOING TO HAVE TO DENY YOUR OUTPATIENT STATUS, READMIT YOU, AND KEEP YOU UNDER SURVEILLANCE.
IF YOU DECIDE YOU'RE READY TO TELL ME WHAT REALLY HAPPENED, I'LL BE RIGHT HERE.
REMEMBER, YOU CAN COUNT ON DOCTOR/PATIENT CONFIDENTIALITY. THERE'S NOTHING TO BE ASHAMED OF.
WHATEVER.
SECRETARY GYRICH? IT'S DOCTOR BURKE. I'VE JUST FINISHED MY SESSION WITH VIOLET.
YOU HAVE NOTHING TO WORRY ABOUT. WHATEVER OTHER PROBLEMS SHE MIGHT HAVE... THE GIRL CAN KEEP A SECRET.
The End

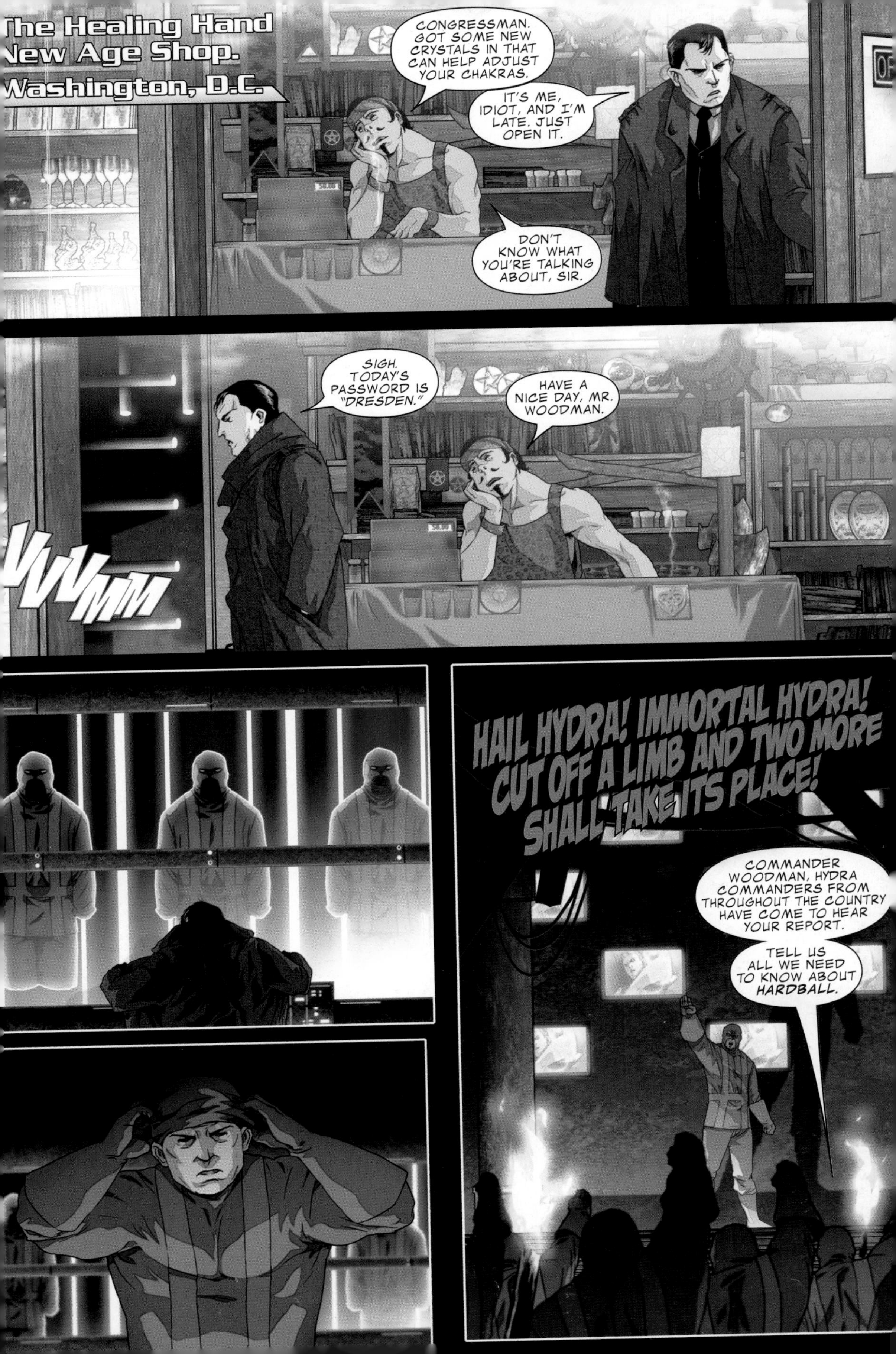
The Healing Hand New Age Shop. Washington, D.C.
CONGRESSMAN. GOT SOME NEW CRYSTALS IN THAT CAN HELP ADJUST YOUR CHAKRAS.
IT'S ME, IDIOT, AND I'M LATE. JUST OPEN IT.
DON'T KNOW WHAT YOU'RE TALKING ABOUT, SIR.
SIGH. TODAY'S PASSWORD IS "DRESDEN."
HAVE A NICE DAY, MR. WOODMAN.
VVVMMM
HAIL HYDRA! IMMORTAL HYDRA! CUT OFF A LIMB AND TWO MORE SHALL TAKE ITS PLACE!
COMMANDER WOODMAN, HYDRA COMMANDERS FROM THROUGHOUT THE COUNTRY HAVE COME TO HEAR YOUR REPORT.
TELL US ALL WE NEED TO KNOW ABOUT HARDBALL.

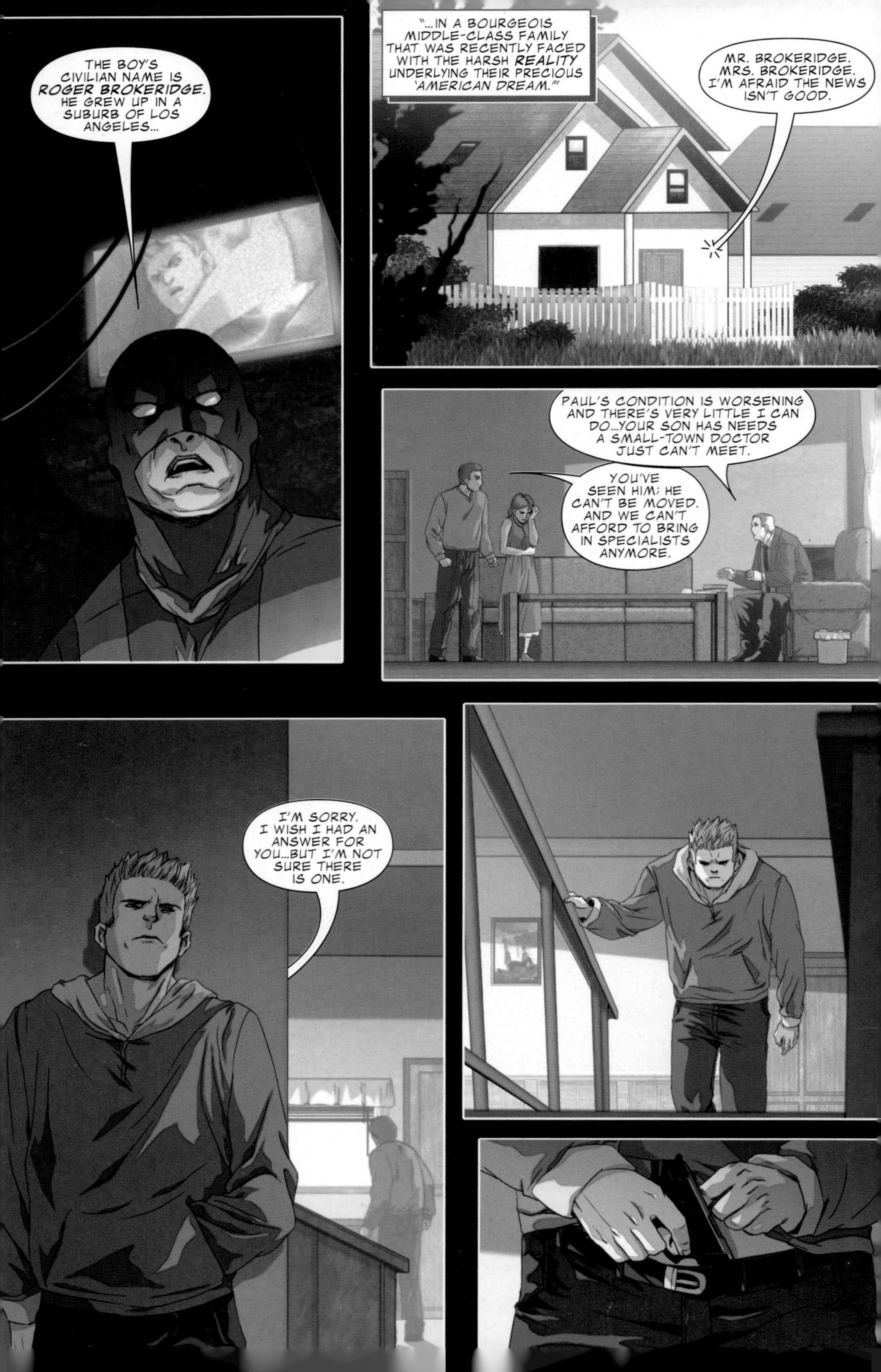
THE BOY'S CIVILIAN NAME IS ROGER BROKERIDGE. HE GREW UP IN A SUBURB OF LOS ANGELES...
"...IN A BOURGEOIS MIDDLE-CLASS FAMILY THAT WAS RECENTLY FACED WITH THE HARSH REALITY UNDERLYING THEIR PRECIOUS 'AMERICAN DREAM.'"
MR. BROKERIDGE. MRS. BROKERIDGE. I'M AFRAID THE NEWS ISN'T GOOD.
PAUL'S CONDITION IS WORSENING AND THERE'S VERY LITTLE I CAN DO...YOUR SON HAS NEEDS A SMALL-TOWN DOCTOR JUST CAN'T MEET.
YOU'VE SEEN HIM; HE CAN'T BE MOVED. AND WE CAN'T AFFORD TO BRING IN SPECIALISTS ANYMORE.
I'M SORRY. I WISH I HAD AN ANSWER FOR YOU...BUT I'M NOT SURE THERE IS ONE.

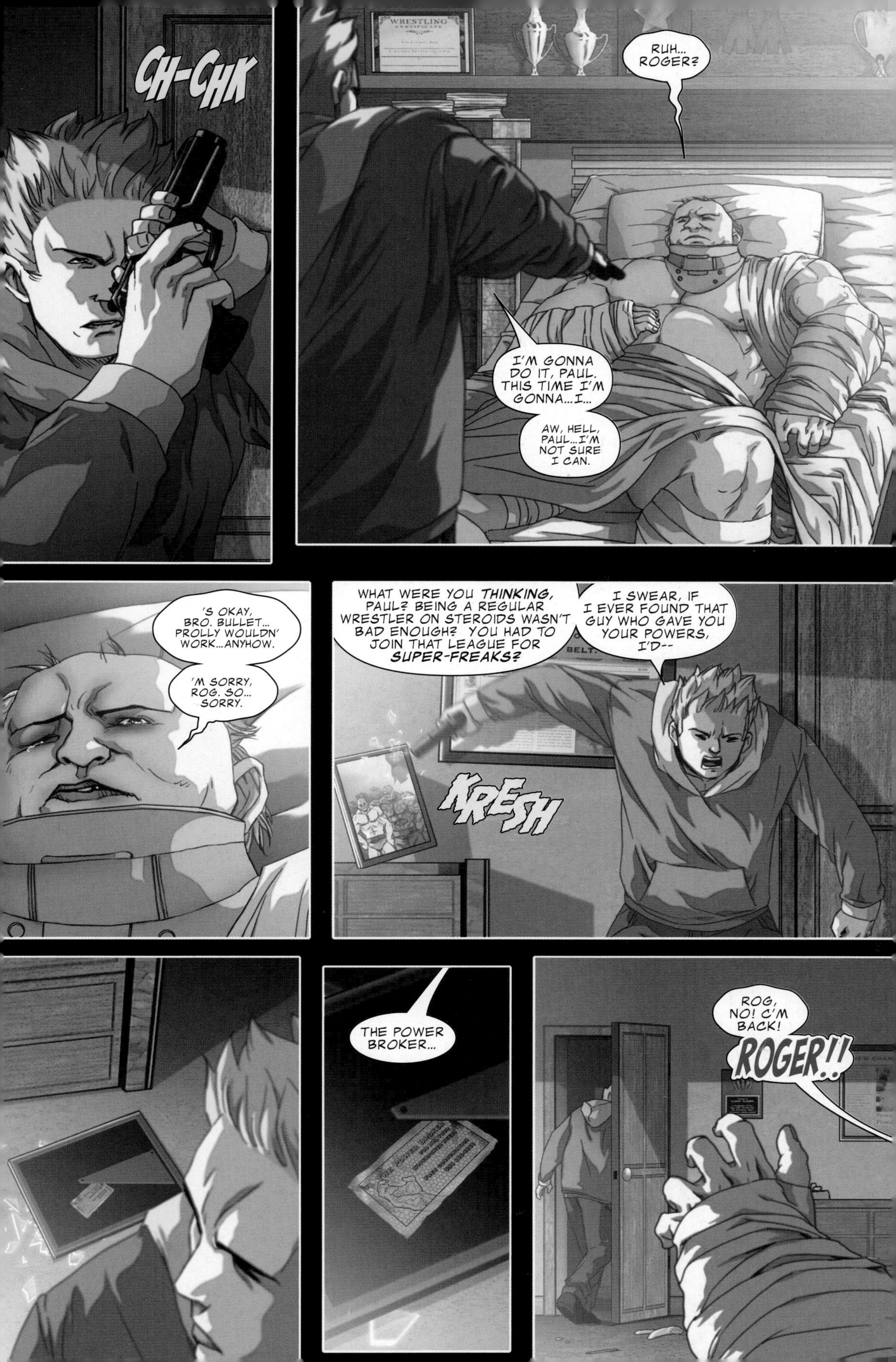
CH-CHK
RUH... ROGER?
I'M GONNA DO IT, PAUL. THIS TIME I'M GONNA...I...
AW, HELL, PAUL...I'M NOT SURE I CAN.
'S OKAY, BRO. BULLET... PROLLY WOULDN' WORK...ANYHOW.
'M SORRY, ROG. SO... SORRY.
WHAT WERE YOU THINKING, PAUL? BEING A REGULAR WRESTLER ON STEROIDS WASN'T BAD ENOUGH? YOU HAD TO JOIN THAT LEAGUE FOR SUPER-FREAKS?
I SWEAR, IF I EVER FOUND THAT GUY WHO GAVE YOU YOUR POWERS, I'D--
KRESH
THE POWER BROKER...
ROG, NO! C'M BACK!
ROGER!!

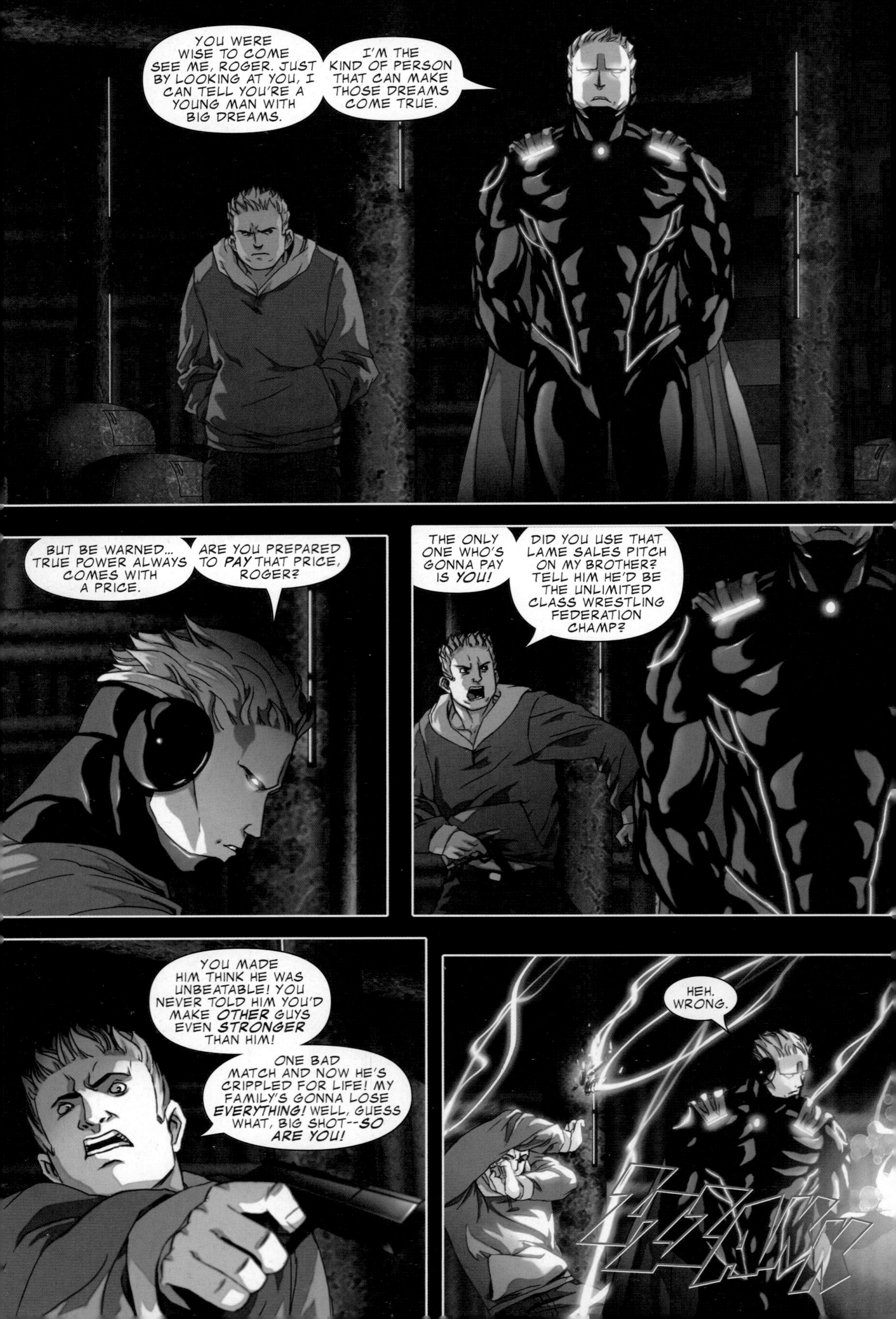
YOU WERE WISE TO COME SEE ME, ROGER. JUST BY LOOKING AT YOU, I CAN TELL YOU'RE A YOUNG MAN WITH BIG DREAMS.
I'M THE KIND OF PERSON THAT CAN MAKE THOSE DREAMS COME TRUE.
BUT BE WARNED... TRUE POWER ALWAYS COMES WITH A PRICE.
ARE YOU PREPARED TO PAY THAT PRICE, ROGER?
THE ONLY ONE WHO'S GONNA PAY IS YOU!
DID YOU USE THAT LAME SALES PITCH ON MY BROTHER? TELL HIM HE'D BE THE UNLIMITED CLASS WRESTLING FEDERATION CHAMP?
YOU MADE HIM THINK HE WAS UNBEATABLE! YOU NEVER TOLD HIM YOU'D MAKE OTHER GUYS EVEN STRONGER THAN HIM!
ONE BAD MATCH AND NOW HE'S CRIPPLED FOR LIFE! MY FAMILY'S GONNA LOSE EVERYTHING! WELL, GUESS WHAT, BIG SHOT--SO ARE YOU!
HEH. WRONG.

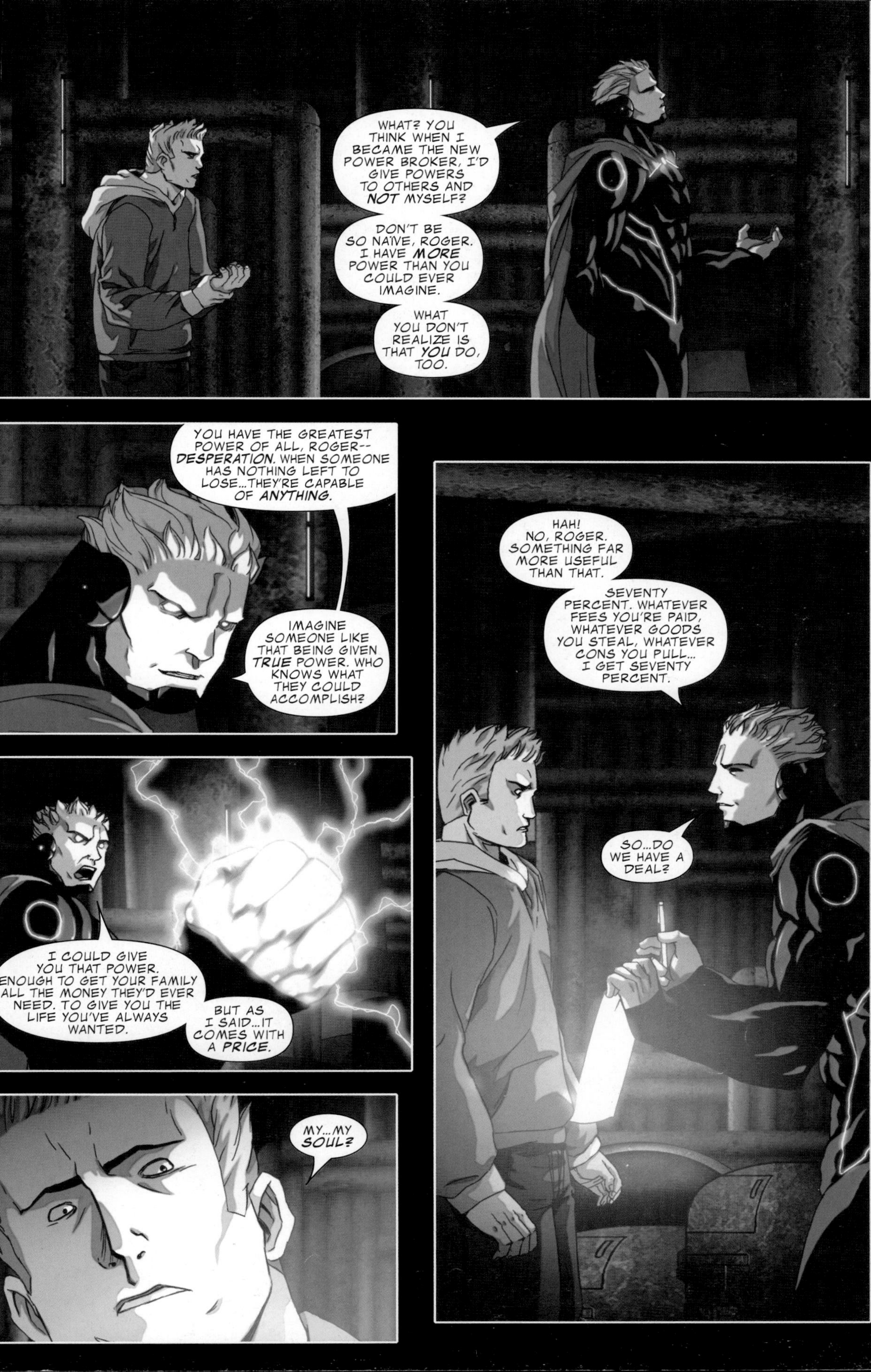
WHAT? YOU THINK WHEN I BECAME THE NEW POWER BROKER, I'D GIVE POWERS TO OTHERS AND NOT MYSELF?
DON'T BE SO NAÏVE, ROGER. I HAVE MORE POWER THAN YOU COULD EVER IMAGINE.
WHAT YOU DON'T REALIZE IS THAT YOU DO, TOO.
YOU HAVE THE GREATEST POWER OF ALL, ROGER-- DESPERATION. WHEN SOMEONE HAS NOTHING LEFT TO LOSE...THEY'RE CAPABLE OF ANYTHING.
IMAGINE SOMEONE LIKE THAT BEING GIVEN TRUE POWER. WHO KNOWS WHAT THEY COULD ACCOMPLISH?
I COULD GIVE YOU THAT POWER. ENOUGH TO GET YOUR FAMILY ALL THE MONEY THEY'D EVER NEED. TO GIVE YOU THE LIFE YOU'VE ALWAYS WANTED.
BUT AS I SAID...IT COMES WITH A PRICE.
MY...MY SOUL?
HAH! NO, ROGER. SOMETHING FAR MORE USEFUL THAN THAT.
SEVENTY PERCENT. WHATEVER FEES YOU'RE PAID, WHATEVER GOODS YOU STEAL, WHATEVER CONS YOU PULL... I GET SEVENTY PERCENT.
SO...DO WE HAVE A DEAL?

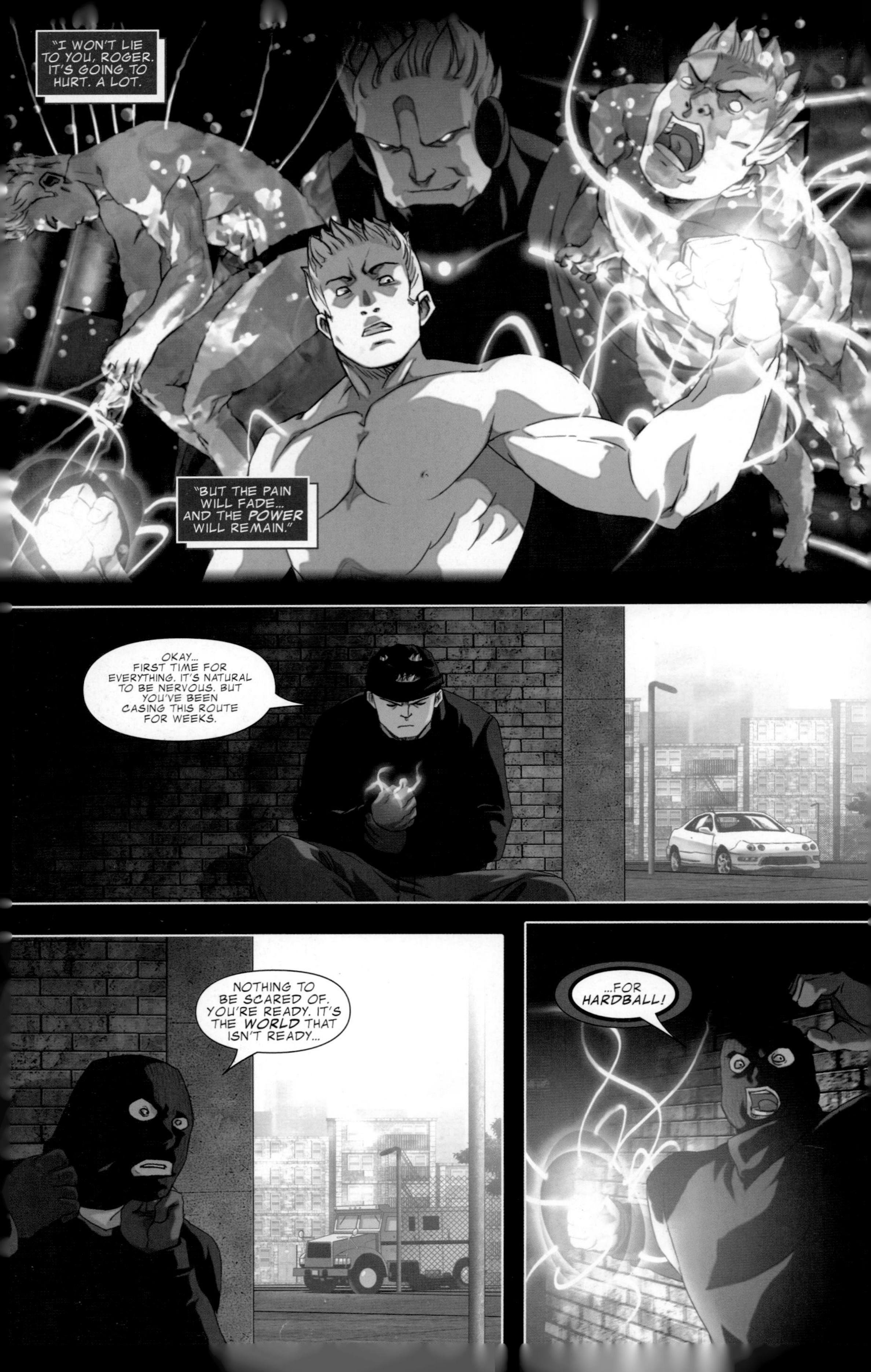
"I WON'T LIE TO YOU, ROGER. IT'S GOING TO HURT. A LOT.
"BUT THE PAIN WILL FADE... AND THE POWER WILL REMAIN."
OKAY... FIRST TIME FOR EVERYTHING. IT'S NATURAL TO BE NERVOUS. BUT YOU'VE BEEN CASING THIS ROUTE FOR WEEKS.
NOTHING TO BE SCARED OF. YOU'RE READY. IT'S THE WORLD THAT ISN'T READY...
...FOR HARDBALL!

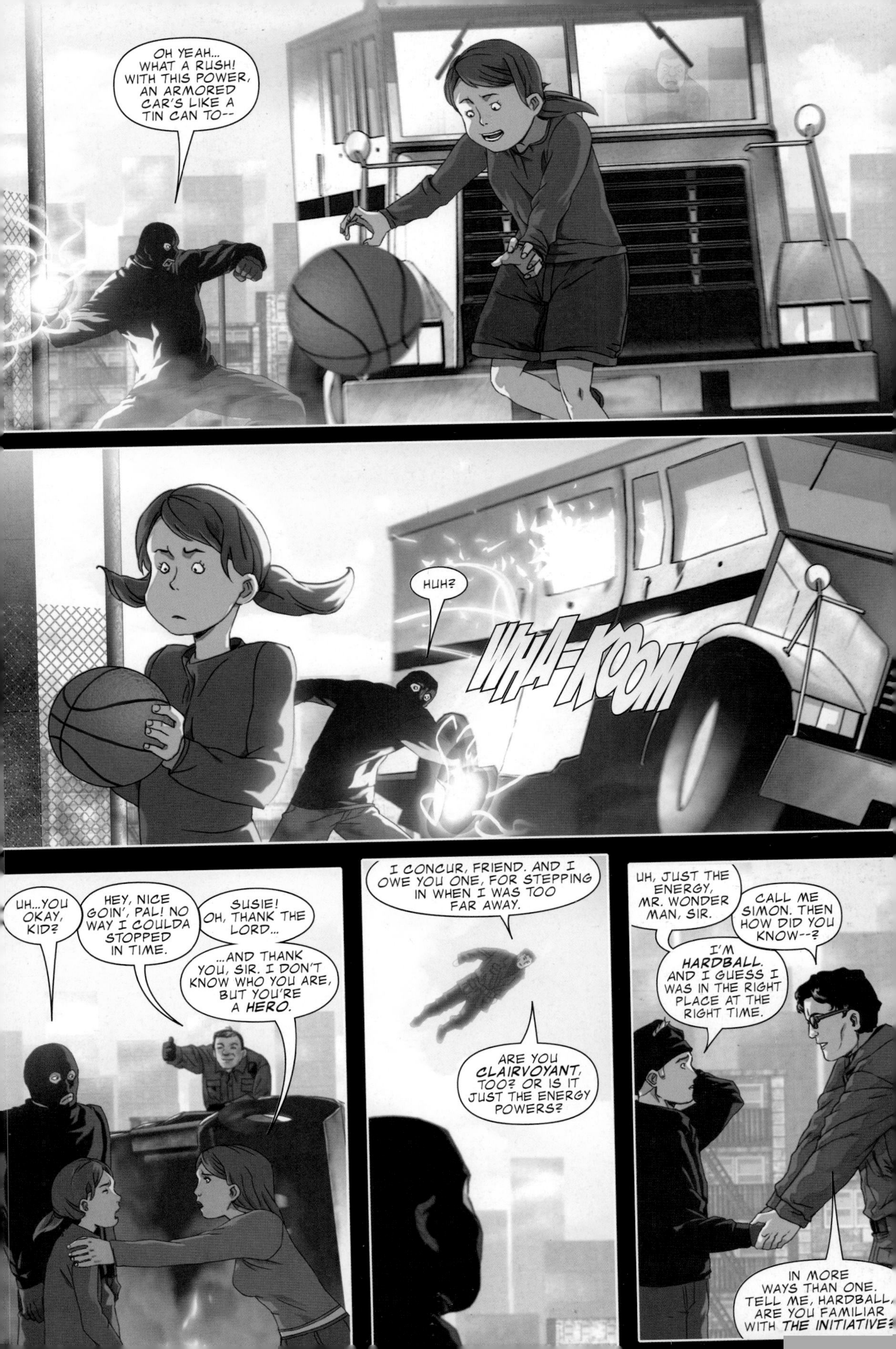
OH YEAH... WHAT A RUSH! WITH THIS POWER, AN ARMORED CAR'S LIKE A TIN CAN TO--
HUH?
WHA-KOOM
UH...YOU OKAY, KID?
HEY, NICE GOIN', PAL! NO WAY I COULDA STOPPED IN TIME.
SUSIE! OH, THANK THE LORD...
...AND THANK YOU, SIR. I DON'T KNOW WHO YOU ARE, BUT YOU'RE A HERO.
I CONCUR, FRIEND. AND I OWE YOU ONE, FOR STEPPING IN WHEN I WAS TOO FAR AWAY.
ARE YOU CLAIRVOYANT, TOO? OR IS IT JUST THE ENERGY POWERS?
UH, JUST THE ENERGY, MR. WONDER MAN, SIR.
CALL ME SIMON. THEN HOW DID YOU KNOW--?
I'M HARDBALL. AND I GUESS I WAS IN THE RIGHT PLACE AT THE RIGHT TIME.
IN MORE WAYS THAN ONE. TELL ME, HARDBALL, ARE YOU FAMILIAR WITH THE INITIATIVE?

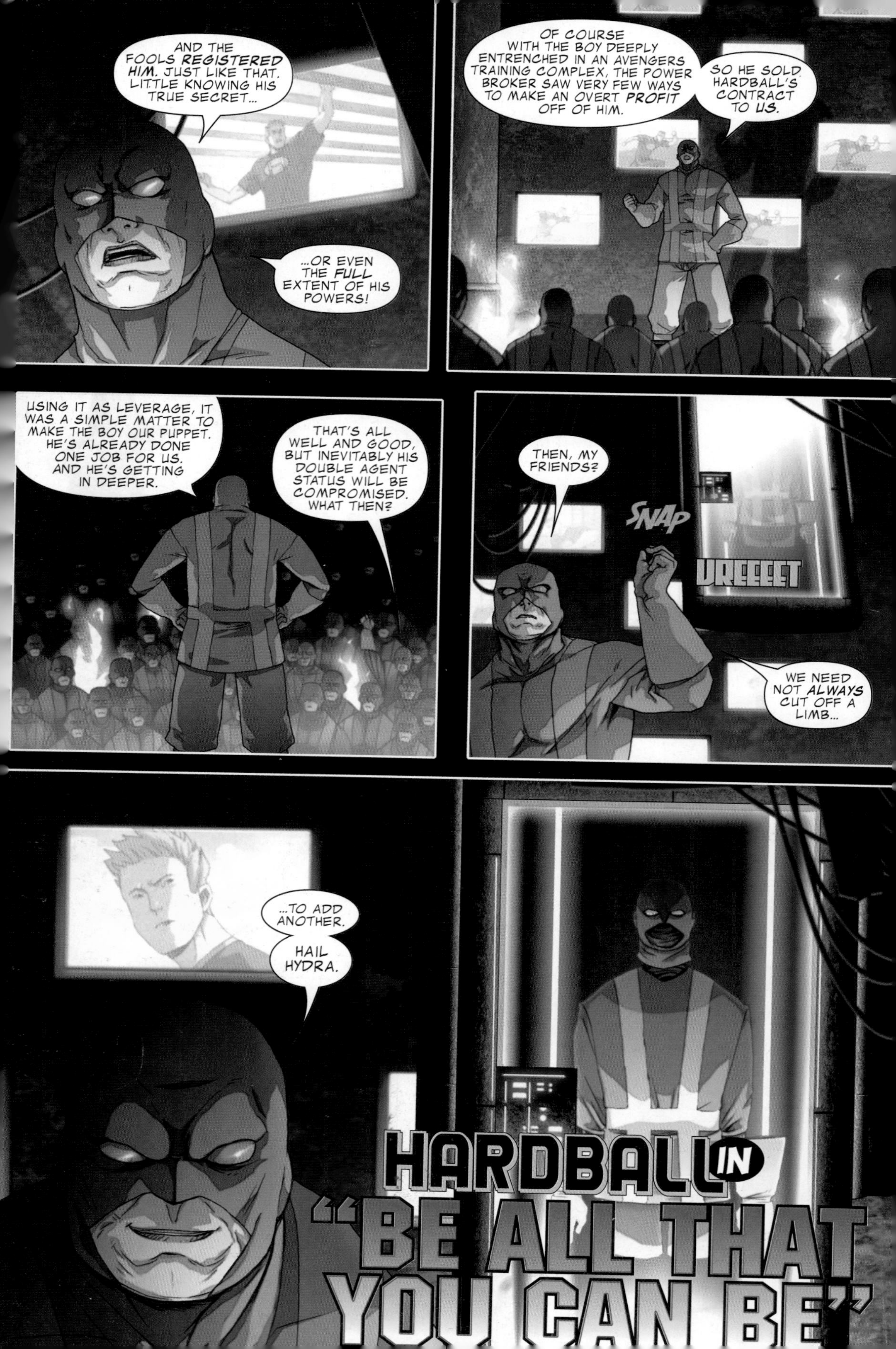
AND THE FOOLS REGISTERED HIM. JUST LIKE THAT. LITTLE KNOWING HIS TRUE SECRET...
...OR EVEN THE FULL EXTENT OF HIS POWERS!
OF COURSE WITH THE BOY DEEPLY ENTRENCHED IN AN AVENGERS TRAINING COMPLEX, THE POWER BROKER SAW VERY FEW WAYS TO MAKE AN OVERT PROFIT OFF OF HIM.
SO HE SOLD HARDBALL'S CONTRACT TO US.
USING IT AS LEVERAGE, IT WAS A SIMPLE MATTER TO MAKE THE BOY OUR PUPPET. HE'S ALREADY DONE ONE JOB FOR US. AND HE'S GETTING IN DEEPER.
THAT'S ALL WELL AND GOOD, BUT INEVITABLY HIS DOUBLE AGENT STATUS WILL BE COMPROMISED. WHAT THEN?
THEN, MY FRIENDS?
SNAP
VREEEET
WE NEED NOT ALWAYS CUT OFF A LIMB...
...TO ADD ANOTHER.
HAIL HYDRA.
HARDBALL IN
"BE ALL THAT YOU CAN BE"

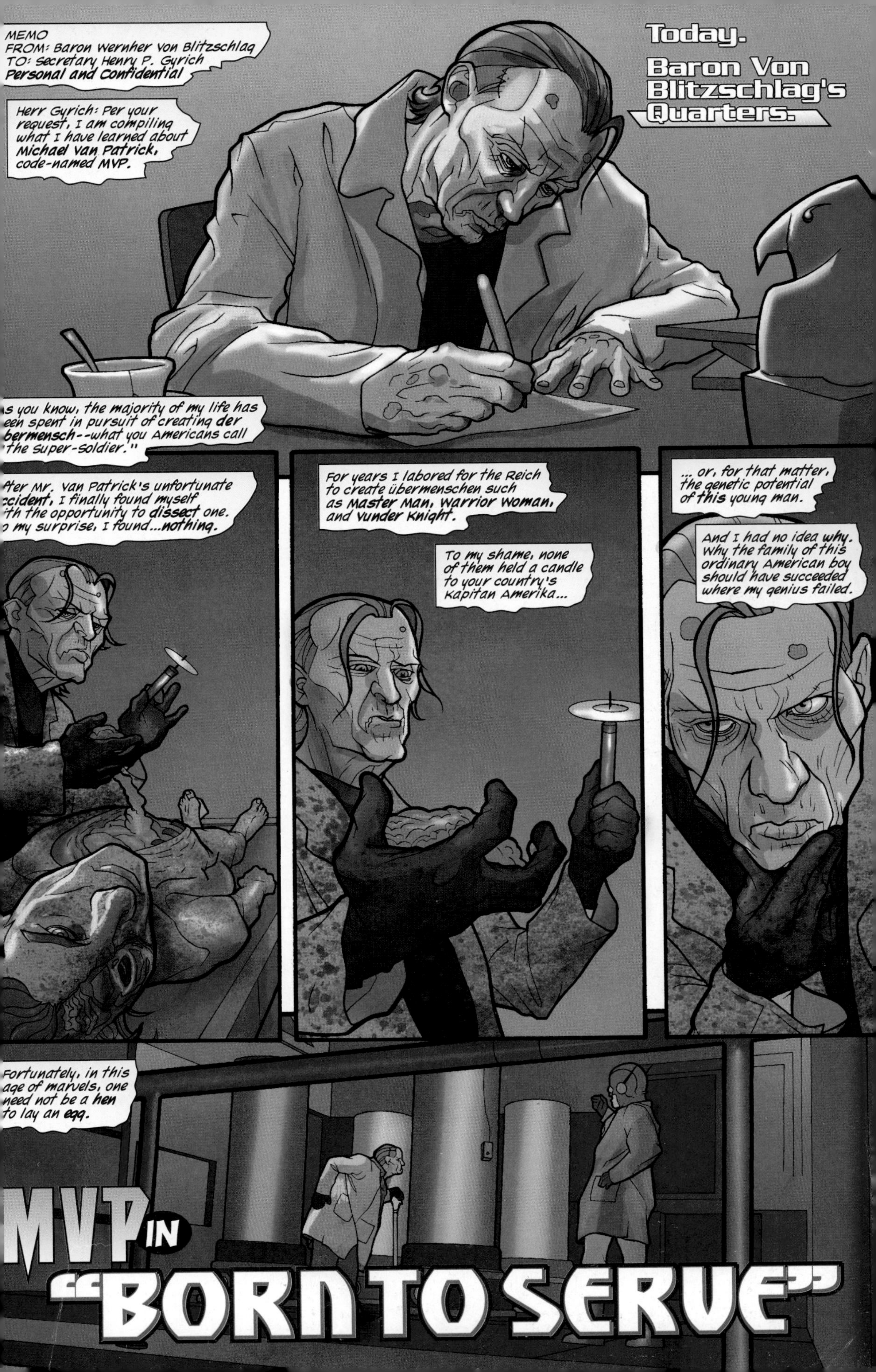
MEMO
FROM: Baron Wernher Von Blitzschlaq
TO: Secretary Henry P. Gyrich
Personal and Confidential
Today.
Baron Von Blitzschlag's Quarters.
Herr Gyrich: Per your request, I am compiling what I have learned about Michael van Patrick, code-named MVP.
s you know, the majority of my life has een spent in pursuit of creating der bermensch--what you Americans call "the super-soldier."
fter Mr. van Patrick's unfortunate ccident, I finally found myself ith the opportunity to dissect one. o my surprise, I found...nothing.
For years I labored for the Reich to create übermenschen such as Master Man, Warrior Woman, and Vunder Knight.
To my shame, none of them held a candle to your country's Kapitan Amerika...
... or, for that matter, the genetic potential of this young man.
And I had no idea why. Why the family of this ordinary American boy should have succeeded where my genius failed.
Fortunately, in this age of marvels, one need not be a hen to lay an egg.
MVP IN
"BORN TO SERVE"

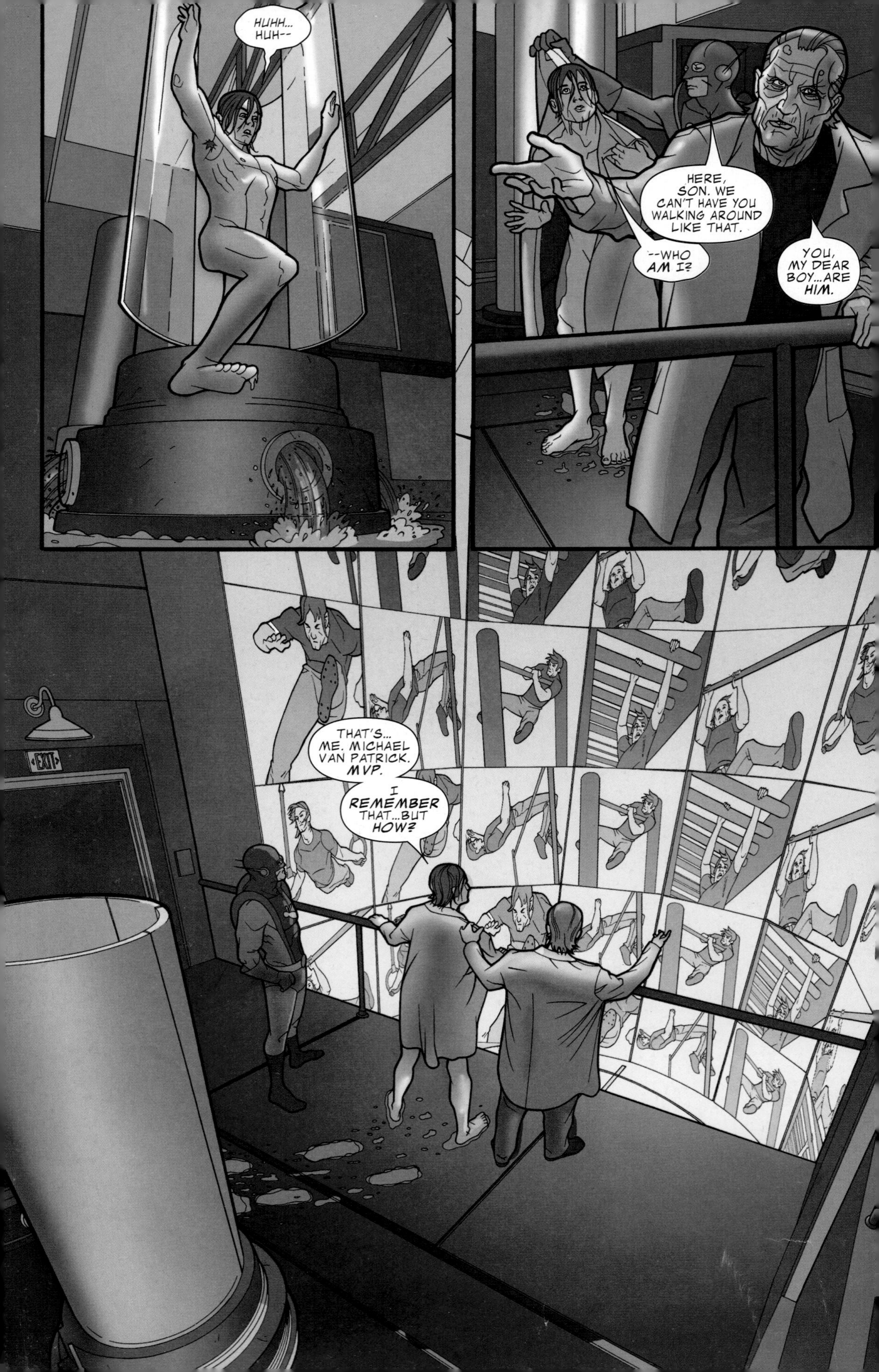
HUHH...
HUH--
HERE, SON. WE CAN'T HAVE YOU WALKING AROUND LIKE THAT.
--WHO AM I?
YOU, MY DEAR BOY...ARE HIM.
EXIT
THAT'S... ME. MICHAEL VAN PATRICK. MVP.
I REMEMBER THAT...BUT HOW?

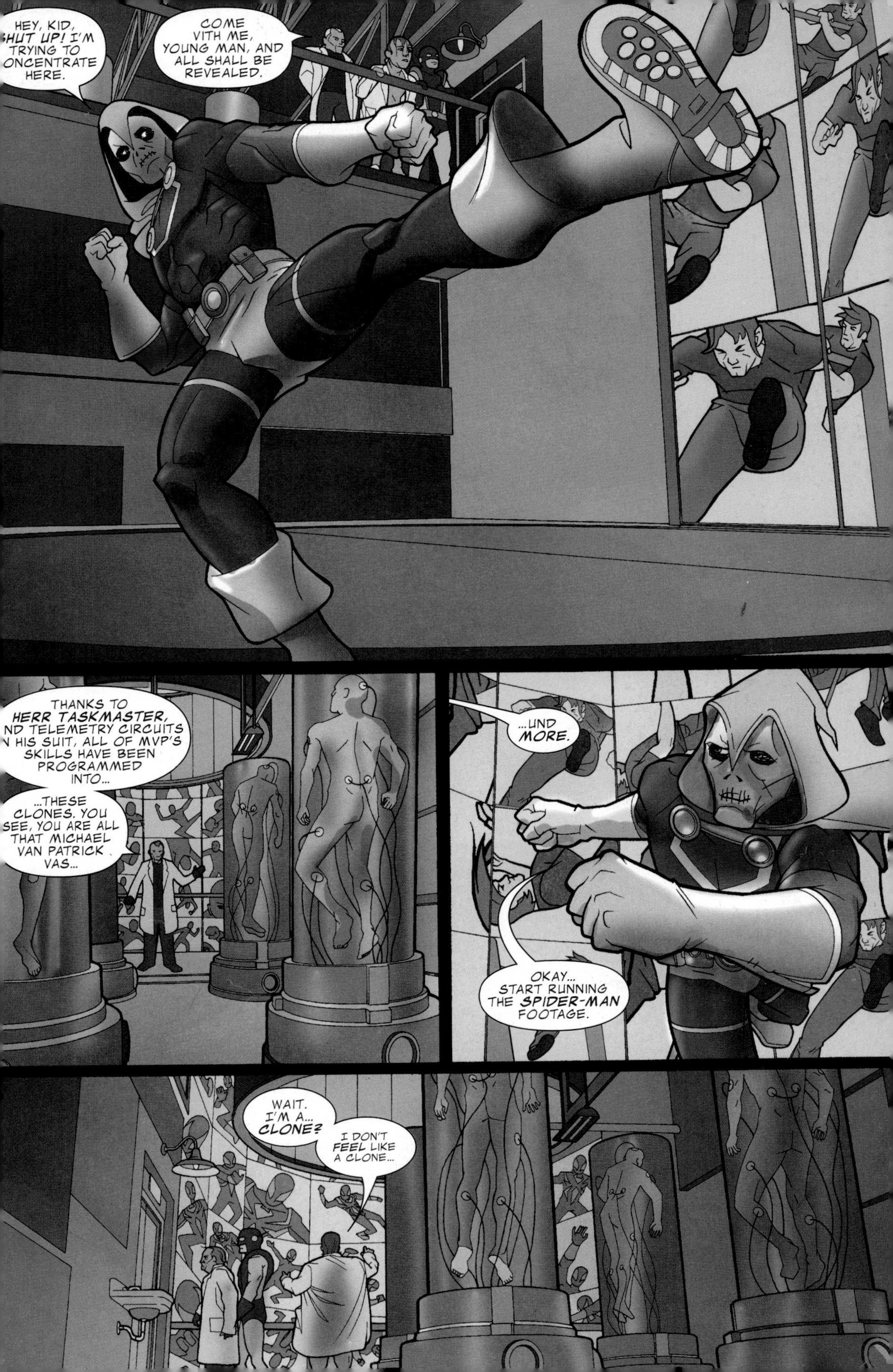
HEY, KID, SHUT UP! I'M TRYING TO CONCENTRATE HERE.
COME VITH ME, YOUNG MAN, AND ALL SHALL BE REVEALED.
THANKS TO HERR TASKMASTER, AND TELEMETRY CIRCUITS IN HIS SUIT, ALL OF MVP'S SKILLS HAVE BEEN PROGRAMMED INTO...
...THESE CLONES. YOU SEE, YOU ARE ALL THAT MICHAEL VAN PATRICK VAS...
...UND MORE.
OKAY... START RUNNING THE SPIDER-MAN FOOTAGE.
WAIT. I'M A... CLONE?
I DON'T FEEL LIKE A CLONE...

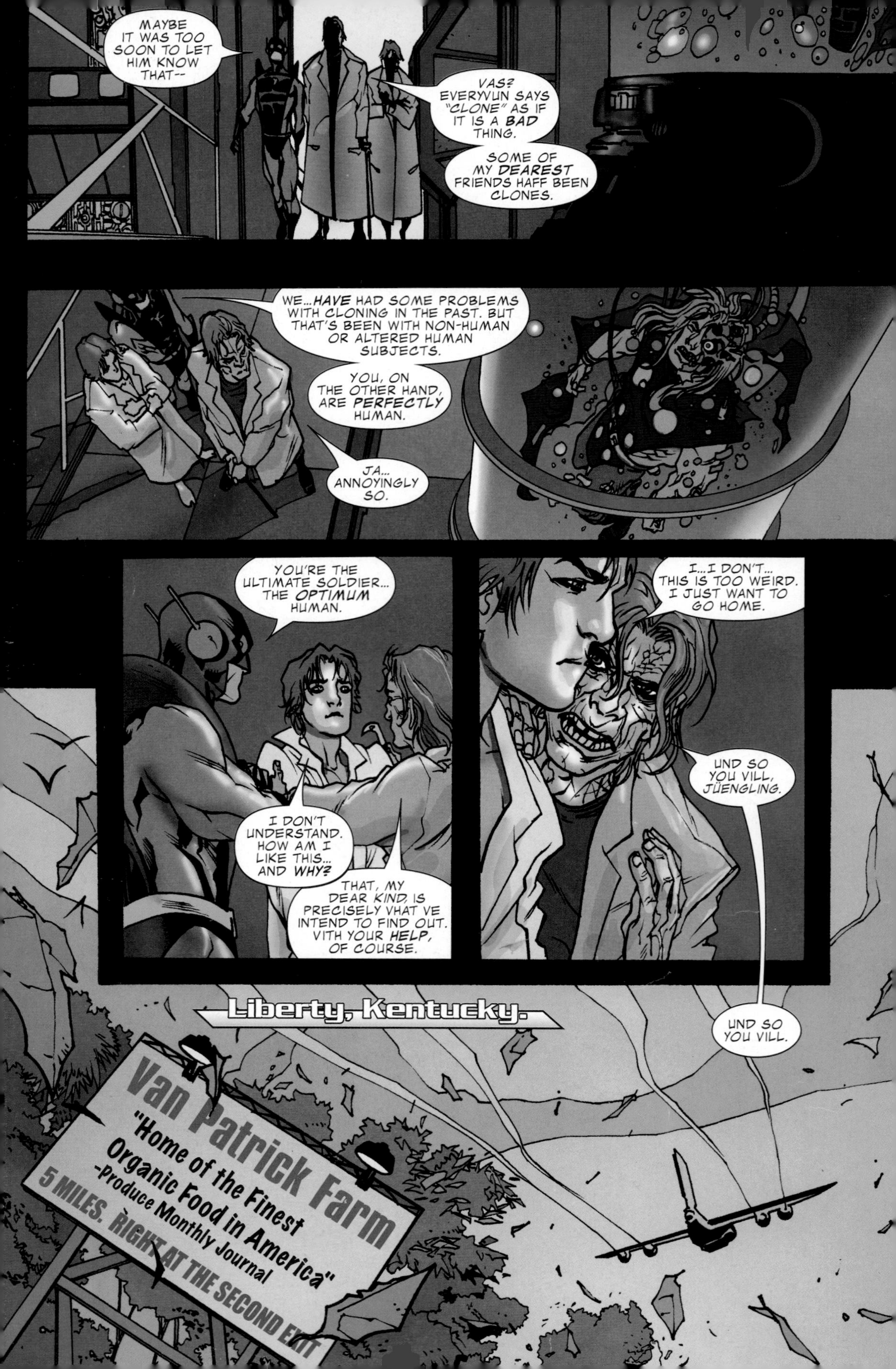
MAYBE IT WAS TOO SOON TO LET HIM KNOW THAT--
VAS? EVERYVUN SAYS "CLONE" AS IF IT IS A BAD THING.
SOME OF MY DEAREST FRIENDS HAFF BEEN CLONES.
WE...HAVE HAD SOME PROBLEMS WITH CLONING IN THE PAST. BUT THAT'S BEEN WITH NON-HUMAN OR ALTERED HUMAN SUBJECTS.
YOU, ON THE OTHER HAND, ARE PERFECTLY HUMAN.
JA... ANNOYINGLY SO.
YOU'RE THE ULTIMATE SOLDIER... THE OPTIMUM HUMAN.
I DON'T UNDERSTAND. HOW AM I LIKE THIS... AND WHY?
THAT, MY DEAR KIND, IS PRECISELY VHAT VE INTEND TO FIND OUT. VITH YOUR HELP, OF COURSE.
I...I DON'T... THIS IS TOO WEIRD. I JUST WANT TO GO HOME.
UND SO YOU VILL, JÜENGLING.
Liberty, Kentucky.
UND SO YOU VILL.
Van Patrick Farm
"Home of the Finest Organic Food in America"
-Produce Monthly Journal
5 MILES. RIGHT AT THE SECOND EXIT

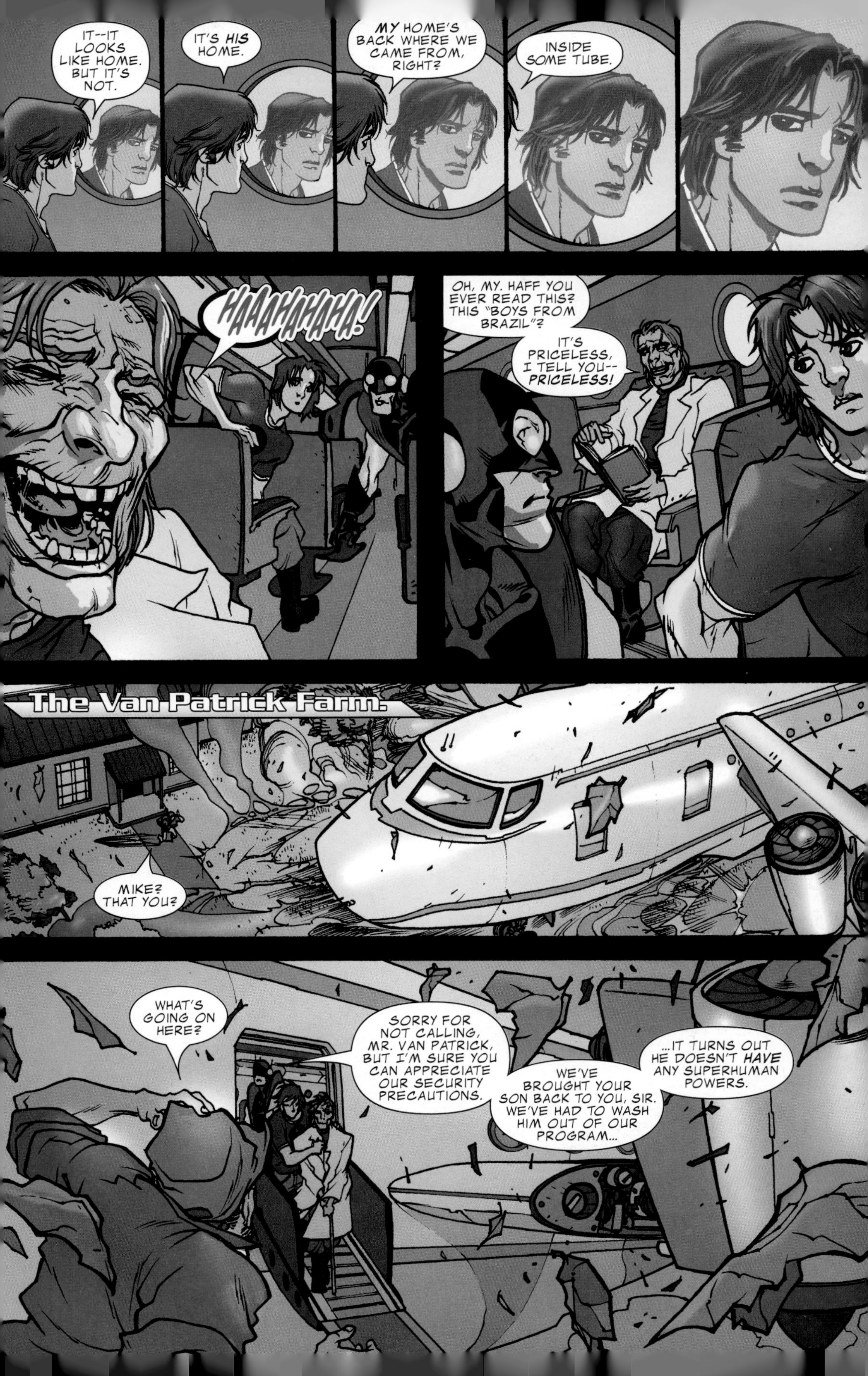

IT--IT LOOKS LIKE HOME. BUT IT'S NOT.
IT'S **HIS** HOME.
MY HOME'S BACK WHERE WE CAME FROM, RIGHT?
INSIDE SOME TUBE.
HAAAAHAHAHA!
OH, MY. HAFF YOU EVER READ THIS? THIS "BOYS FROM BRAZIL"?
IT'S PRICELESS, I TELL YOU-- ***PRICELESS!***
The Van Patrick Farm.
MIKE? THAT YOU?
WHAT'S GOING ON HERE?
SORRY FOR NOT CALLING, MR. VAN PATRICK, BUT I'M SURE YOU CAN APPRECIATE OUR SECURITY PRECAUTIONS.
WE'VE BROUGHT YOUR SON BACK TO YOU, SIR. WE'VE HAD TO WASH HIM OUT OF OUR PROGRAM...
...IT TURNS OUT HE DOESN'T ***HAVE*** ANY SUPERHUMAN POWERS.

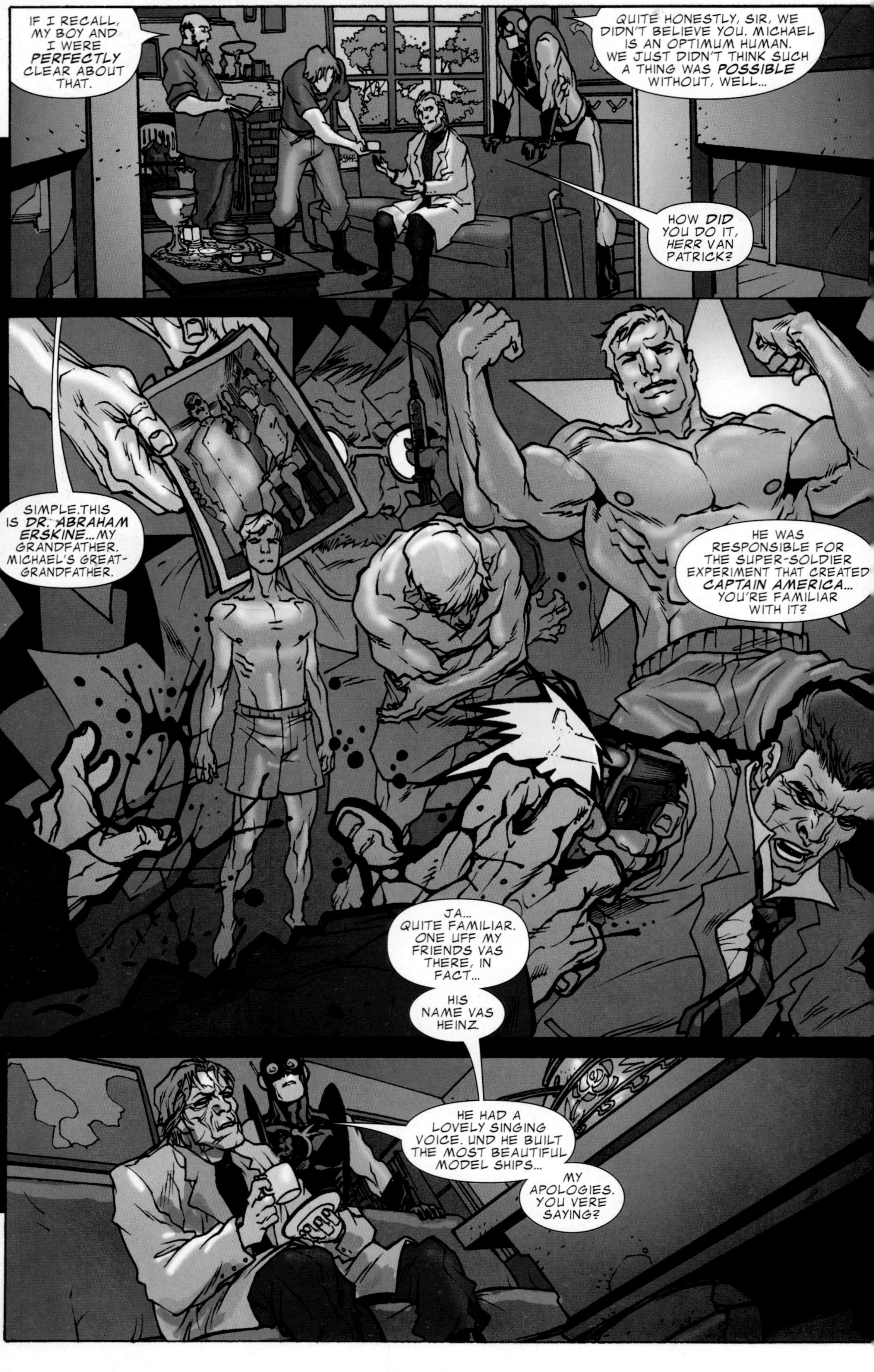

IF I RECALL, MY BOY AND I WERE PERFECTLY CLEAR ABOUT THAT.
QUITE HONESTLY, SIR, WE DIDN'T BELIEVE YOU. MICHAEL IS AN OPTIMUM HUMAN. WE JUST DIDN'T THINK SUCH A THING WAS POSSIBLE WITHOUT, WELL...
HOW DID YOU DO IT, HERR VAN PATRICK?
SIMPLE. THIS IS DR. ABRAHAM ERSKINE...MY GRANDFATHER. MICHAEL'S GREAT-GRANDFATHER.
HE WAS RESPONSIBLE FOR THE SUPER-SOLDIER EXPERIMENT THAT CREATED CAPTAIN AMERICA... YOU'RE FAMILIAR WITH IT?
JA... QUITE FAMILIAR. ONE UFF MY FRIENDS VAS THERE, IN FACT...
HIS NAME VAS HEINZ.
HE HAD A LOVELY SINGING VOICE. UND HE BUILT THE MOST BEAUTIFUL MODEL SHIPS...
MY APOLOGIES. YOU VERE SAYING?

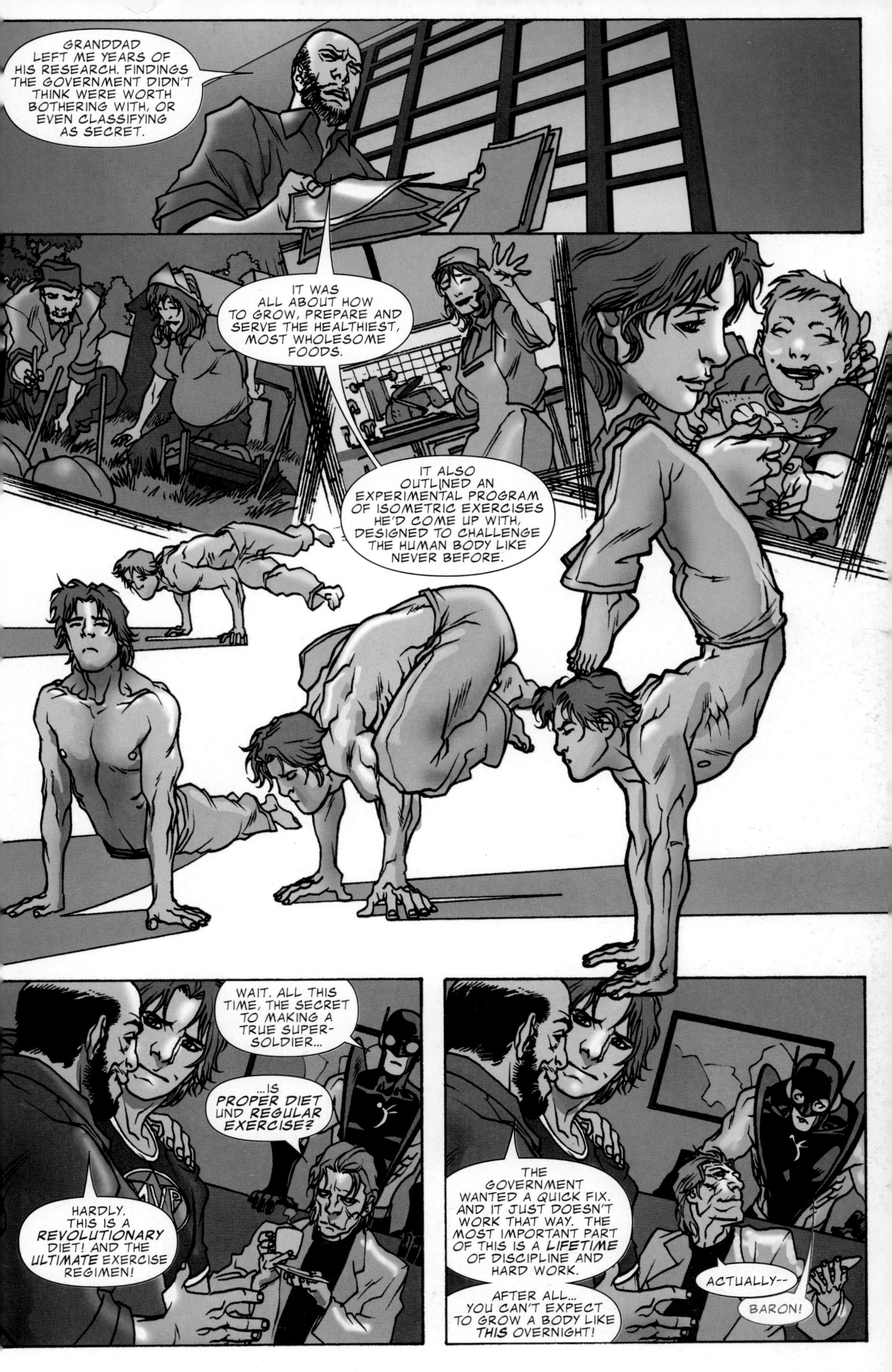
GRANDDAD LEFT ME YEARS OF HIS RESEARCH. FINDINGS THE GOVERNMENT DIDN'T THINK WERE WORTH BOTHERING WITH, OR EVEN CLASSIFYING AS SECRET.
IT WAS ALL ABOUT HOW TO GROW, PREPARE AND SERVE THE HEALTHIEST, MOST WHOLESOME FOODS.
IT ALSO OUTLINED AN EXPERIMENTAL PROGRAM OF ISOMETRIC EXERCISES HE'D COME UP WITH, DESIGNED TO CHALLENGE THE HUMAN BODY LIKE NEVER BEFORE.
WAIT. ALL THIS TIME, THE SECRET TO MAKING A TRUE SUPER-SOLDIER...
...IS PROPER DIET UND REGULAR EXERCISE?
HARDLY. THIS IS A REVOLUTIONARY DIET! AND THE ULTIMATE EXERCISE REGIMEN!
THE GOVERNMENT WANTED A QUICK FIX. AND IT JUST DOESN'T WORK THAT WAY. THE MOST IMPORTANT PART OF THIS IS A LIFETIME OF DISCIPLINE AND HARD WORK.
AFTER ALL... YOU CAN'T EXPECT TO GROW A BODY LIKE THIS OVERNIGHT!
ACTUALLY--
BARON!

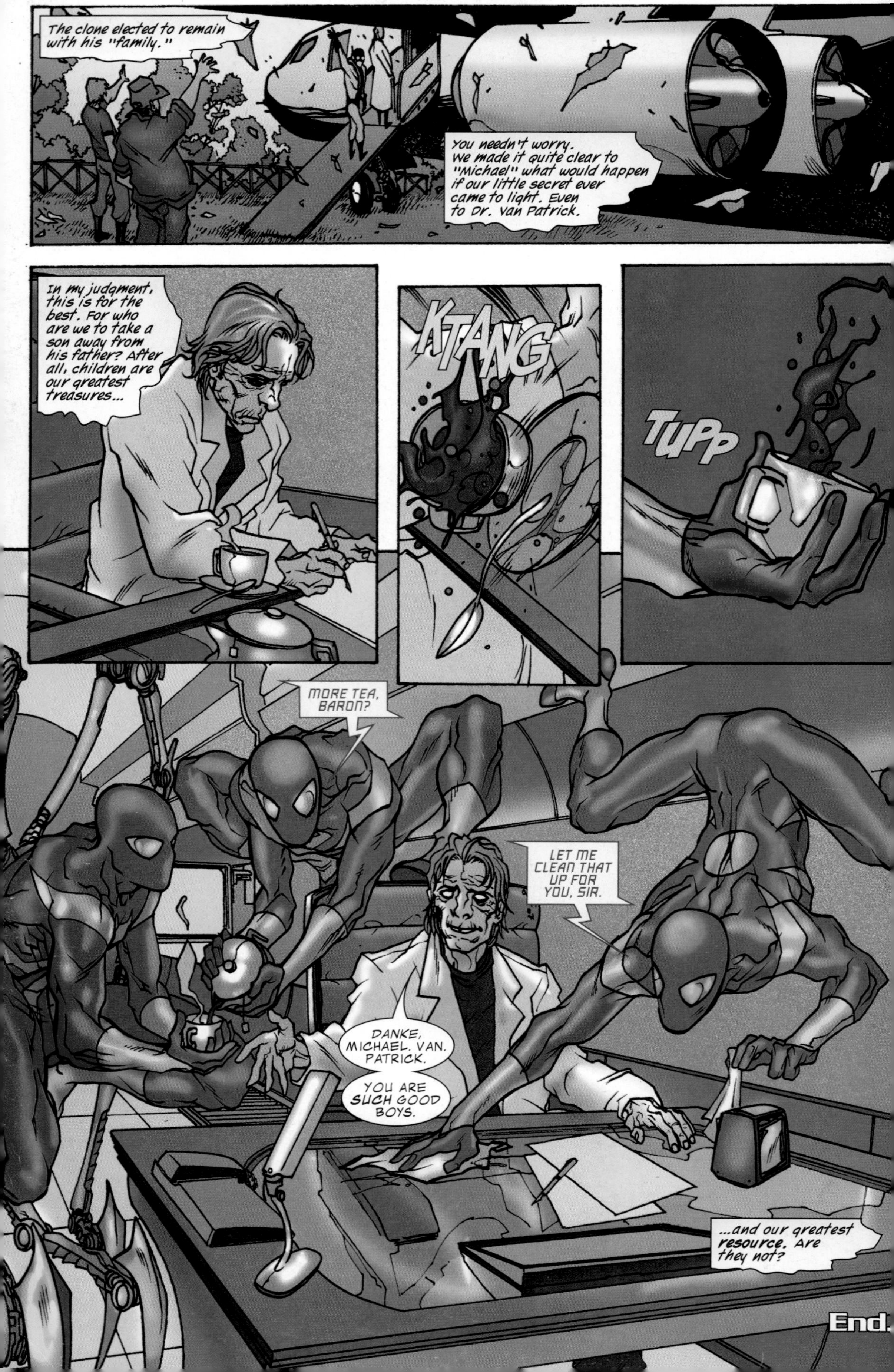
The clone elected to remain with his "family."
You needn't worry. We made it quite clear to "Michael" what would happen if our little secret ever came to light. Even to Dr. van Patrick.
In my judgment, this is for the best. For who are we to take a son away from his father? After all, children are our greatest treasures...
KTANG
TUPP
MORE TEA, BARON?
LET ME CLEAN THAT UP FOR YOU, SIR.
DANKE, MICHAEL. VAN. PATRICK.
YOU ARE SUCH GOOD BOYS.
...and our greatest resource. Are they not?
End.

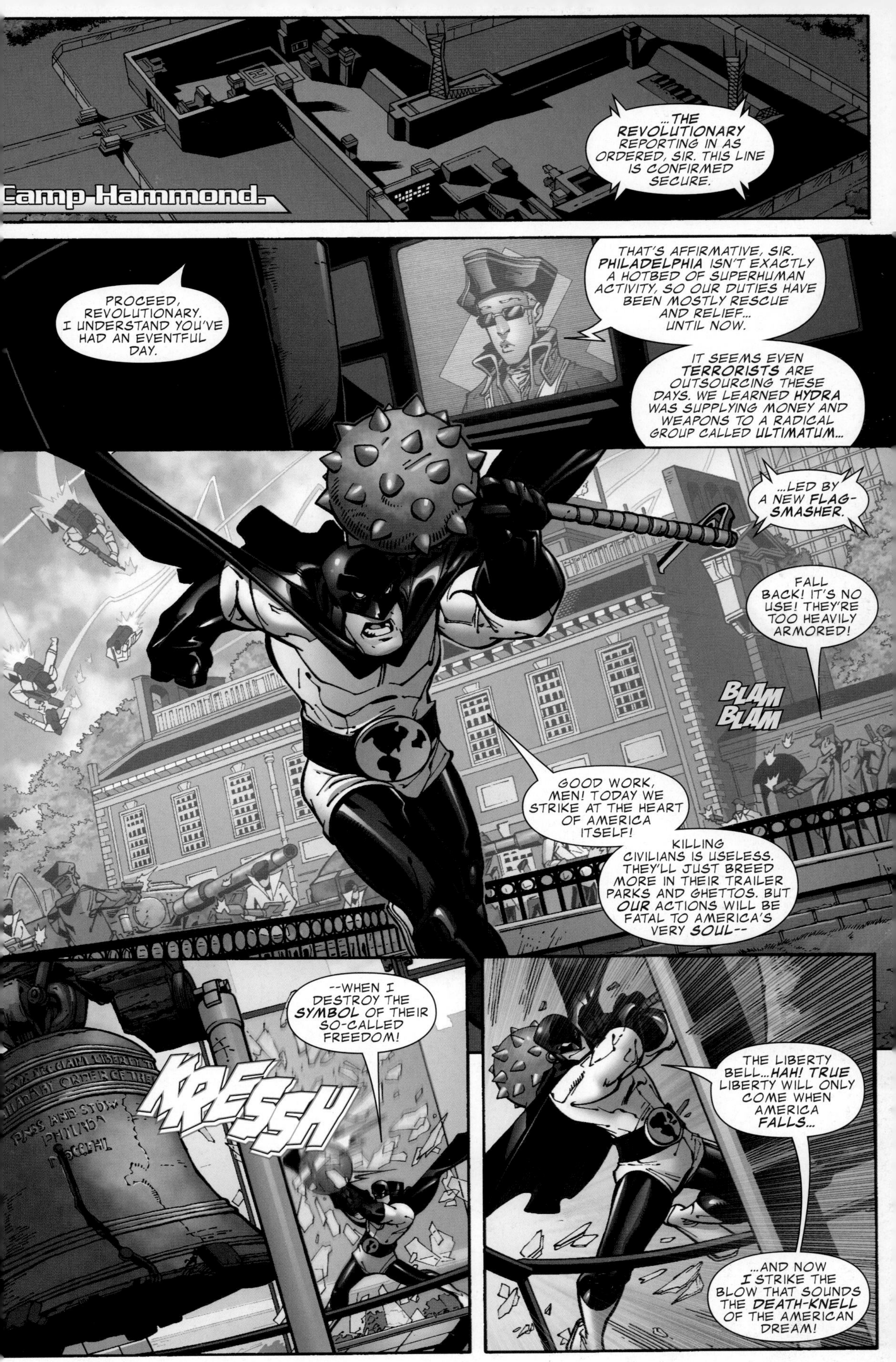
Camp Hammond.
...THE REVOLUTIONARY REPORTING IN AS ORDERED, SIR. THIS LINE IS CONFIRMED SECURE.
PROCEED, REVOLUTIONARY. I UNDERSTAND YOU'VE HAD AN EVENTFUL DAY.
THAT'S AFFIRMATIVE, SIR. PHILADELPHIA ISN'T EXACTLY A HOTBED OF SUPERHUMAN ACTIVITY, SO OUR DUTIES HAVE BEEN MOSTLY RESCUE AND RELIEF... UNTIL NOW.
IT SEEMS EVEN TERRORISTS ARE OUTSOURCING THESE DAYS. WE LEARNED HYDRA WAS SUPPLYING MONEY AND WEAPONS TO A RADICAL GROUP CALLED ULTIMATUM...
...LED BY A NEW FLAG-SMASHER.
FALL BACK! IT'S NO USE! THEY'RE TOO HEAVILY ARMORED!
BLAM BLAM
GOOD WORK, MEN! TODAY WE STRIKE AT THE HEART OF AMERICA ITSELF!
KILLING CIVILIANS IS USELESS. THEY'LL JUST BREED MORE IN THEIR TRAILER PARKS AND GHETTOS. BUT OUR ACTIONS WILL BE FATAL TO AMERICA'S VERY SOUL--
--WHEN I DESTROY THE SYMBOL OF THEIR SO-CALLED FREEDOM!
KRESSH
THE LIBERTY BELL...HAH! TRUE LIBERTY WILL ONLY COME WHEN AMERICA FALLS...
...AND NOW I STRIKE THE BLOW THAT SOUNDS THE DEATH-KNELL OF THE AMERICAN DREAM!

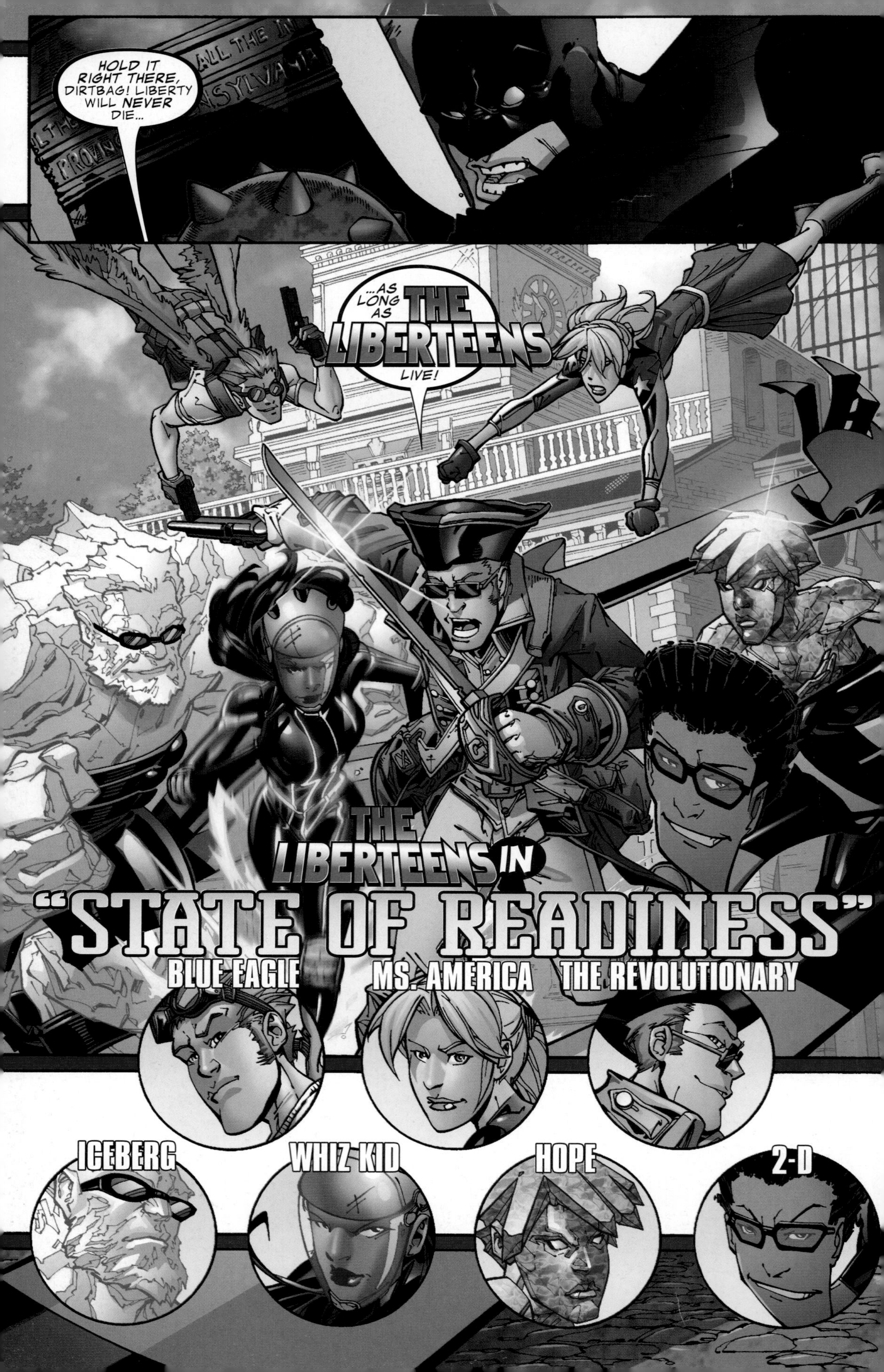
HOLD IT RIGHT THERE, DIRTBAG! LIBERTY WILL NEVER DIE...
...AS LONG AS THE LIBERTEENS LIVE!
THE LIBERTEENS IN
"STATE OF READINESS"
BLUE EAGLE
MS. AMERICA
THE REVOLUTIONARY
ICEBERG
WHIZ KID
HOPE
2-D

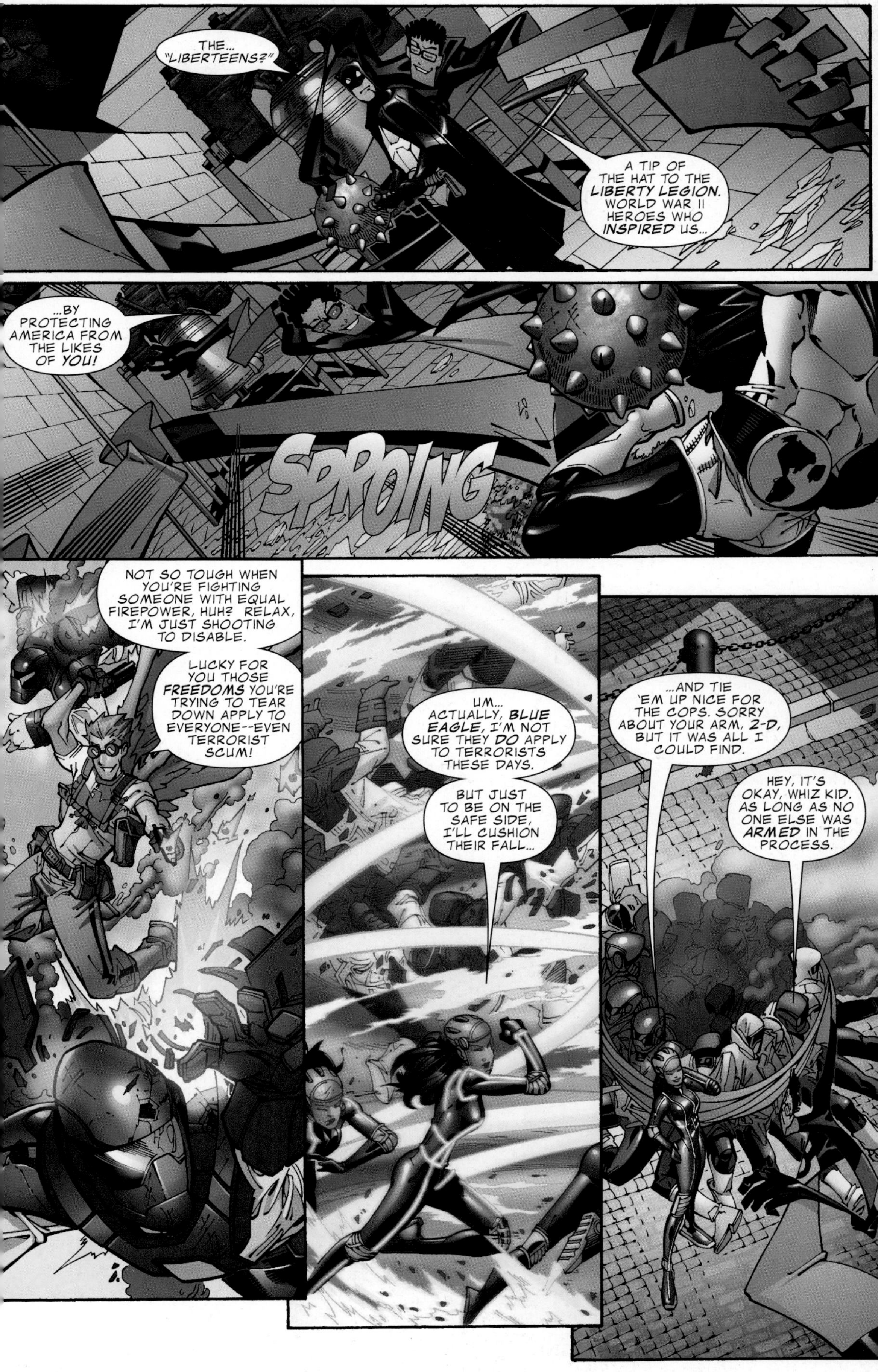
THE... "LIBERTEENS?"
A TIP OF THE HAT TO THE LIBERTY LEGION. WORLD WAR II HEROES WHO INSPIRED US...
...BY PROTECTING AMERICA FROM THE LIKES OF YOU!
SPROING
NOT SO TOUGH WHEN YOU'RE FIGHTING SOMEONE WITH EQUAL FIREPOWER, HUH? RELAX, I'M JUST SHOOTING TO DISABLE.
LUCKY FOR YOU THOSE FREEDOMS YOU'RE TRYING TO TEAR DOWN APPLY TO EVERYONE--EVEN TERRORIST SCUM!
UM... ACTUALLY, BLUE EAGLE, I'M NOT SURE THEY DO APPLY TO TERRORISTS THESE DAYS.
BUT JUST TO BE ON THE SAFE SIDE, I'LL CUSHION THEIR FALL...
...AND TIE 'EM UP NICE FOR THE COPS. SORRY ABOUT YOUR ARM, 2-D, BUT IT WAS ALL I COULD FIND.
HEY, IT'S OKAY, WHIZ KID. AS LONG AS NO ONE ELSE WAS ARMED IN THE PROCESS.

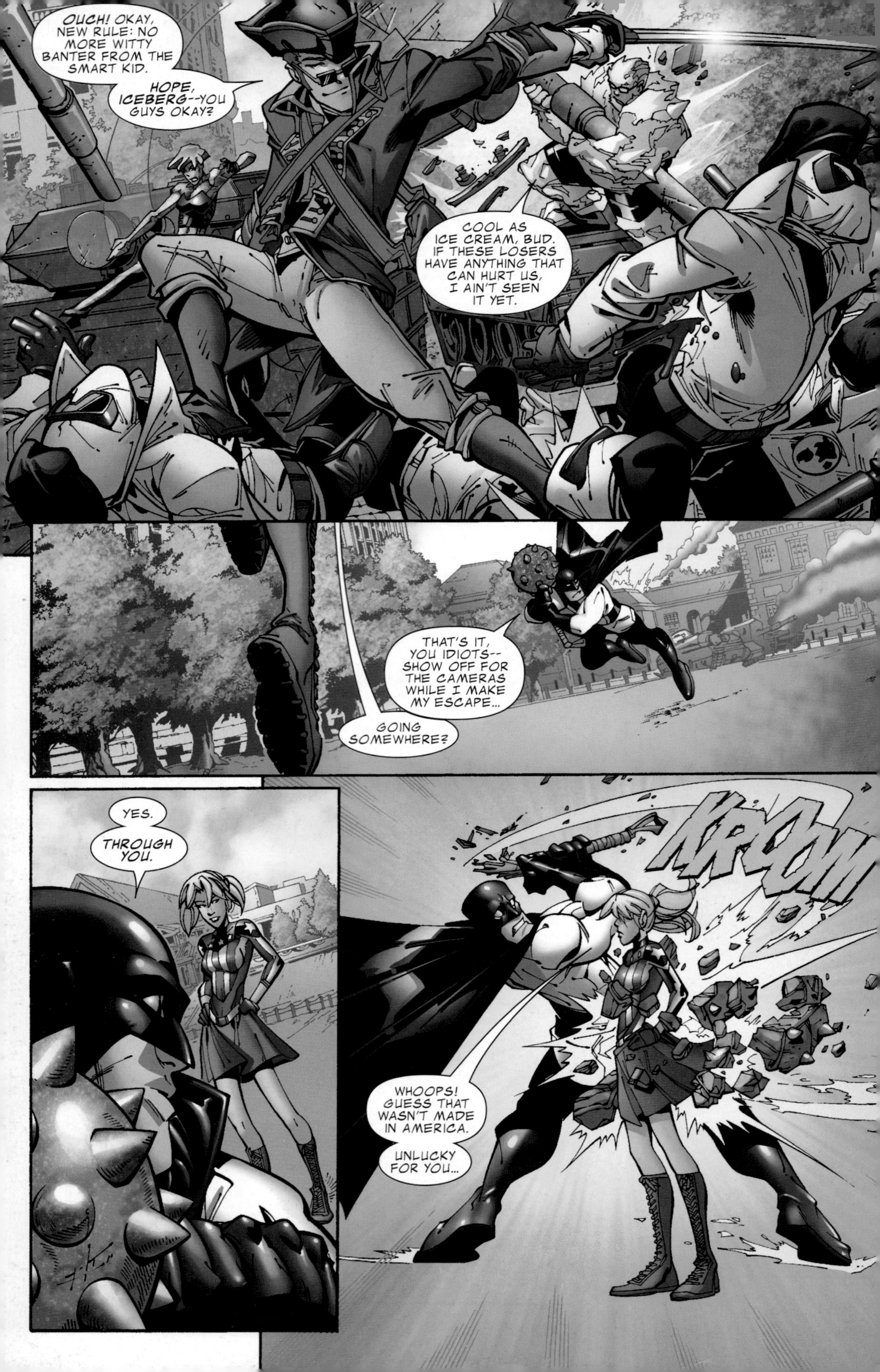
OUCH! OKAY, NEW RULE: NO MORE WITTY BANTER FROM THE SMART KID.
HOPE, ICEBERG--YOU GUYS OKAY?
COOL AS ICE CREAM, BUD. IF THESE LOSERS HAVE ANYTHING THAT CAN HURT US, I AIN'T SEEN IT YET.
THAT'S IT, YOU IDIOTS--SHOW OFF FOR THE CAMERAS WHILE I MAKE MY ESCAPE...
GOING SOMEWHERE?
YES.
THROUGH YOU.
KRUMM
WHOOPS! GUESS THAT WASN'T MADE IN AMERICA.
UNLUCKY FOR YOU...

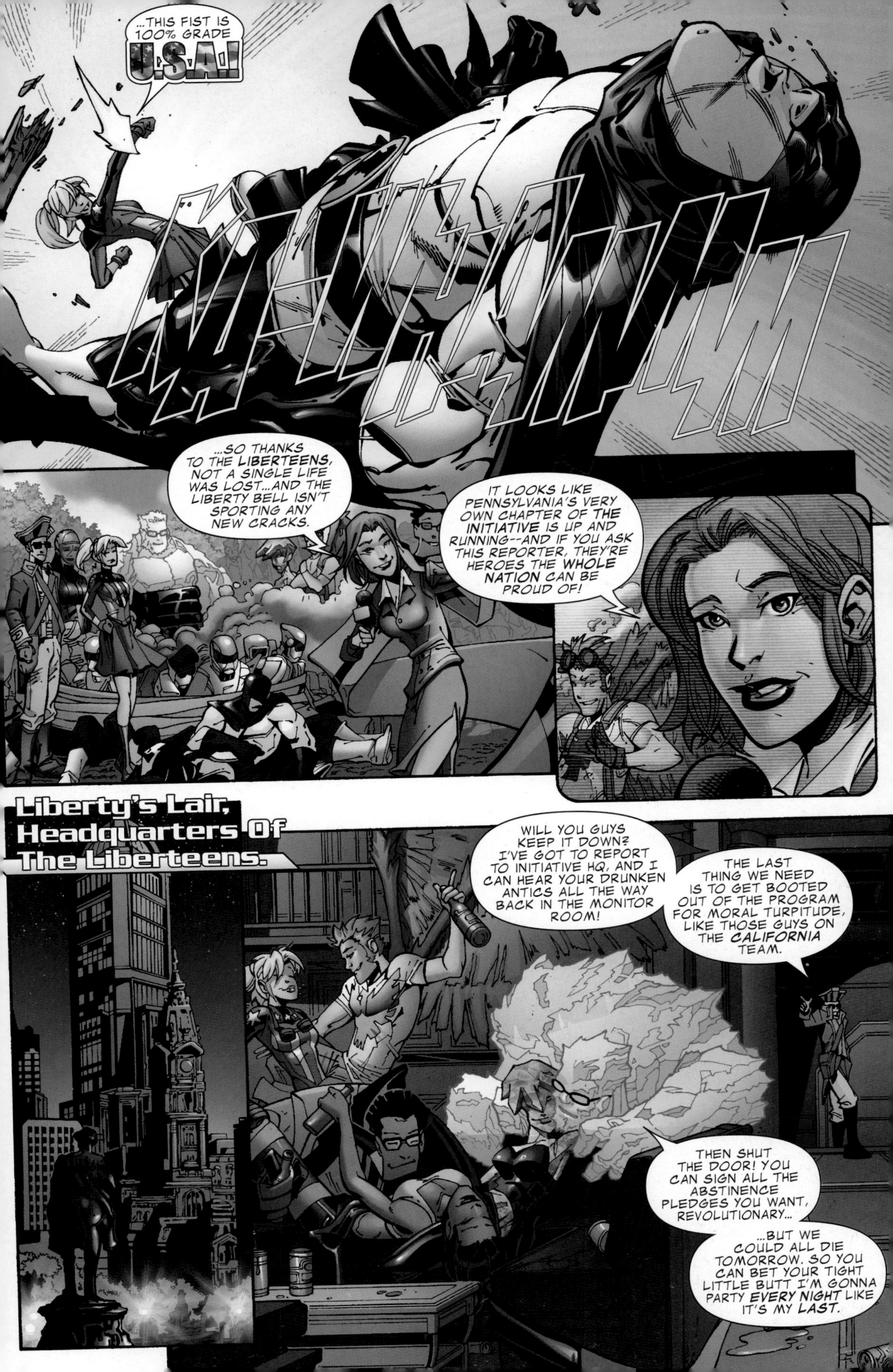
...THIS FIST IS 100% GRADE U.S.A.!
...SO THANKS TO THE LIBERTEENS, NOT A SINGLE LIFE WAS LOST...AND THE LIBERTY BELL ISN'T SPORTING ANY NEW CRACKS.
IT LOOKS LIKE PENNSYLVANIA'S VERY OWN CHAPTER OF THE INITIATIVE IS UP AND RUNNING--AND IF YOU ASK THIS REPORTER, THEY'RE HEROES THE WHOLE NATION CAN BE PROUD OF!
Liberty's Lair, Headquarters Of The Liberteens.
WILL YOU GUYS KEEP IT DOWN? I'VE GOT TO REPORT TO INITIATIVE HQ, AND I CAN HEAR YOUR DRUNKEN ANTICS ALL THE WAY BACK IN THE MONITOR ROOM!
THE LAST THING WE NEED IS TO GET BOOTED OUT OF THE PROGRAM FOR MORAL TURPITUDE, LIKE THOSE GUYS ON THE CALIFORNIA TEAM.
THEN SHUT THE DOOR! YOU CAN SIGN ALL THE ABSTINENCE PLEDGES YOU WANT, REVOLUTIONARY...
...BUT WE COULD ALL DIE TOMORROW. SO YOU CAN BET YOUR TIGHT LITTLE BUTT I'M GONNA PARTY EVERY NIGHT LIKE IT'S MY LAST.

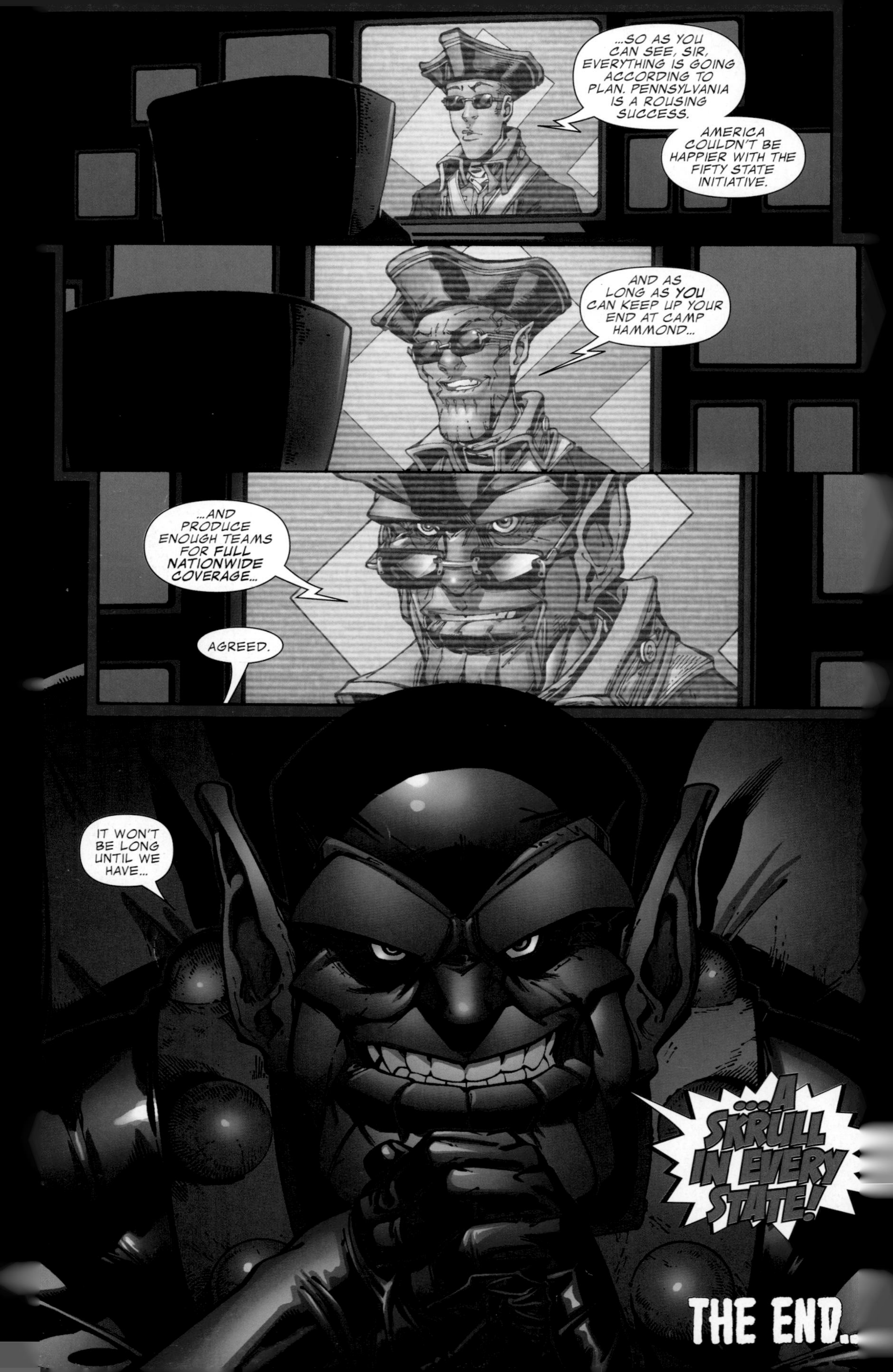
...SO AS YOU CAN SEE, SIR, EVERYTHING IS GOING ACCORDING TO PLAN. PENNSYLVANIA IS A ROUSING SUCCESS.
AMERICA COULDN'T BE HAPPIER WITH THE FIFTY STATE INITIATIVE.
AND AS LONG AS YOU CAN KEEP UP YOUR END AT CAMP HAMMOND...
...AND PRODUCE ENOUGH TEAMS FOR FULL NATIONWIDE COVERAGE...
AGREED.
IT WON'T BE LONG UNTIL WE HAVE...
...A SKRULL IN EVERY STATE!
THE END..

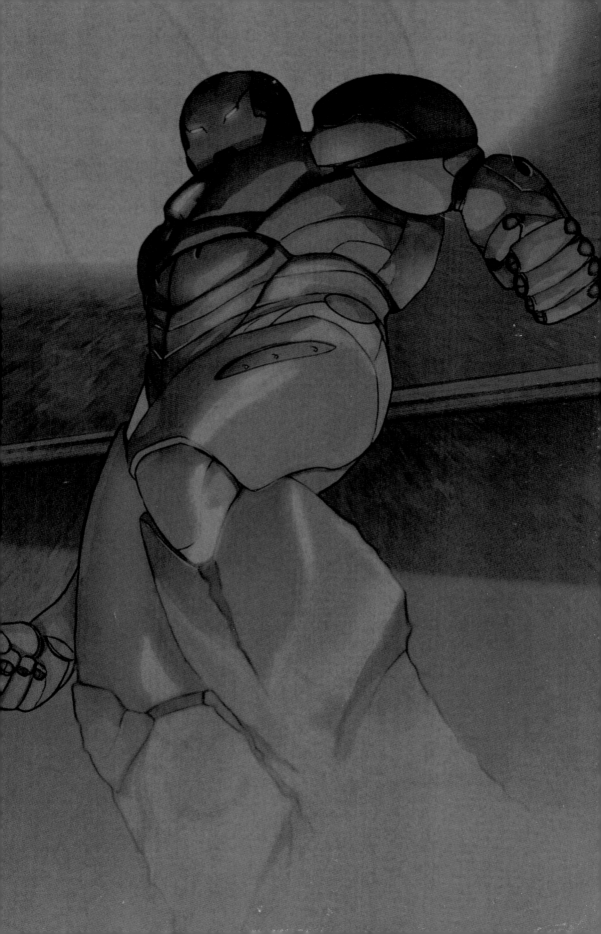

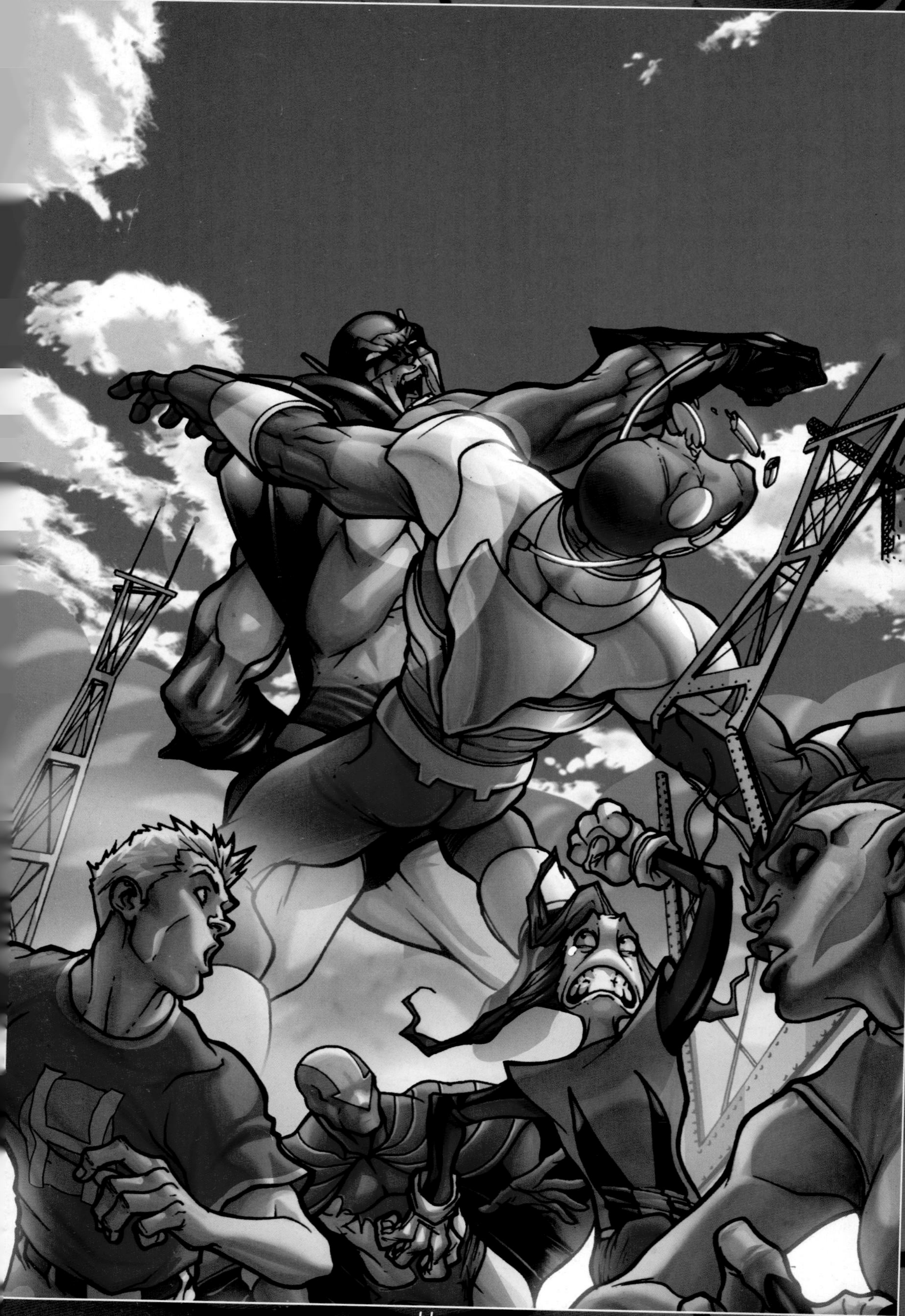

#8

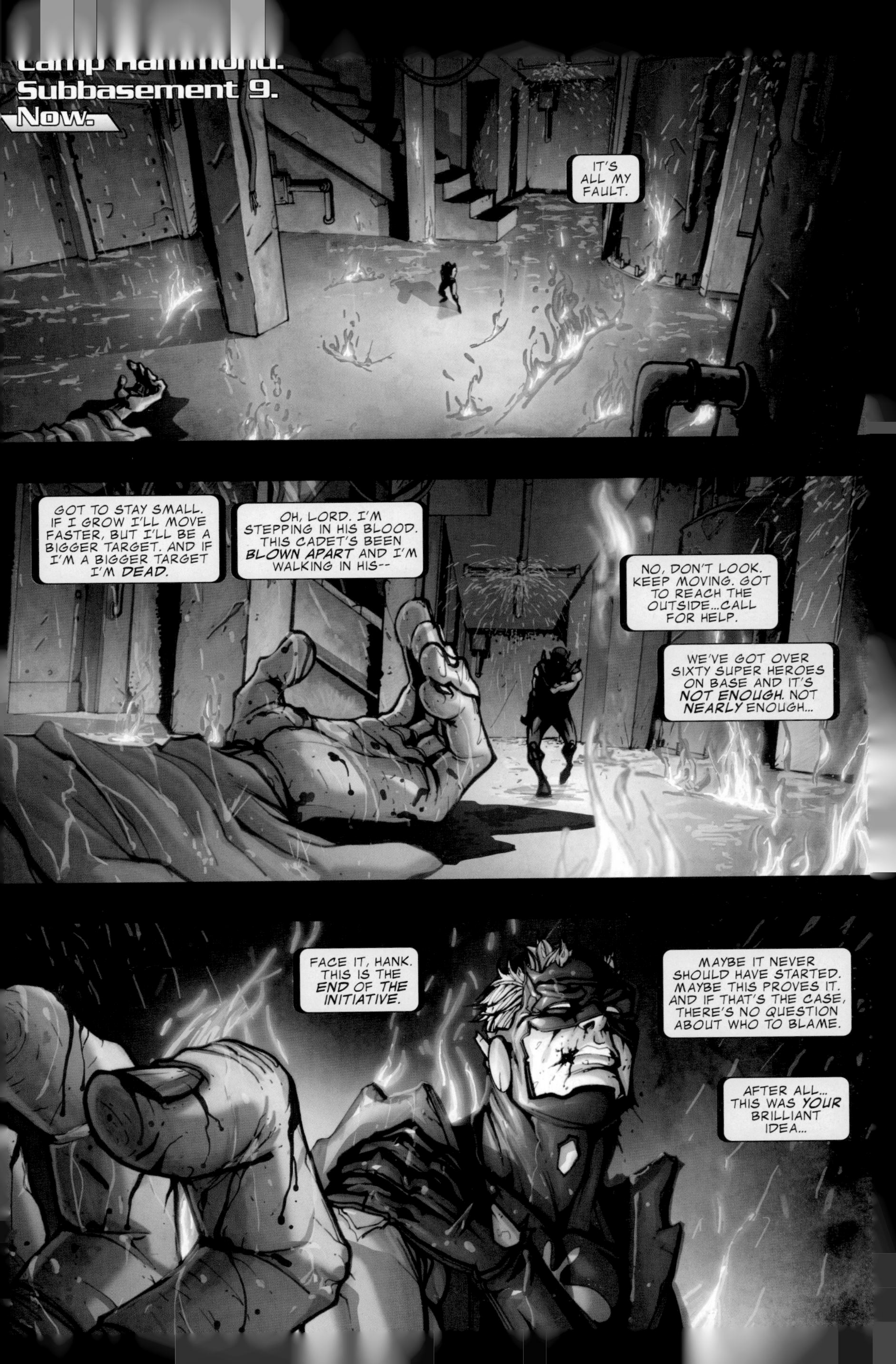
Subbasement 9.
Now.
IT'S ALL MY FAULT.
GOT TO STAY SMALL. IF I GROW I'LL MOVE FASTER, BUT I'LL BE A BIGGER TARGET. AND IF I'M A BIGGER TARGET I'M DEAD.
OH, LORD. I'M STEPPING IN HIS BLOOD. THIS CADET'S BEEN BLOWN APART AND I'M WALKING IN HIS--
NO, DON'T LOOK. KEEP MOVING. GOT TO REACH THE OUTSIDE...CALL FOR HELP.
WE'VE GOT OVER SIXTY SUPER HEROES ON BASE AND IT'S NOT ENOUGH. NOT NEARLY ENOUGH...
FACE IT, HANK. THIS IS THE END OF THE INITIATIVE.
MAYBE IT NEVER SHOULD HAVE STARTED. MAYBE THIS PROVES IT. AND IF THAT'S THE CASE, THERE'S NO QUESTION ABOUT WHO TO BLAME.
AFTER ALL... THIS WAS YOUR BRILLIANT IDEA...

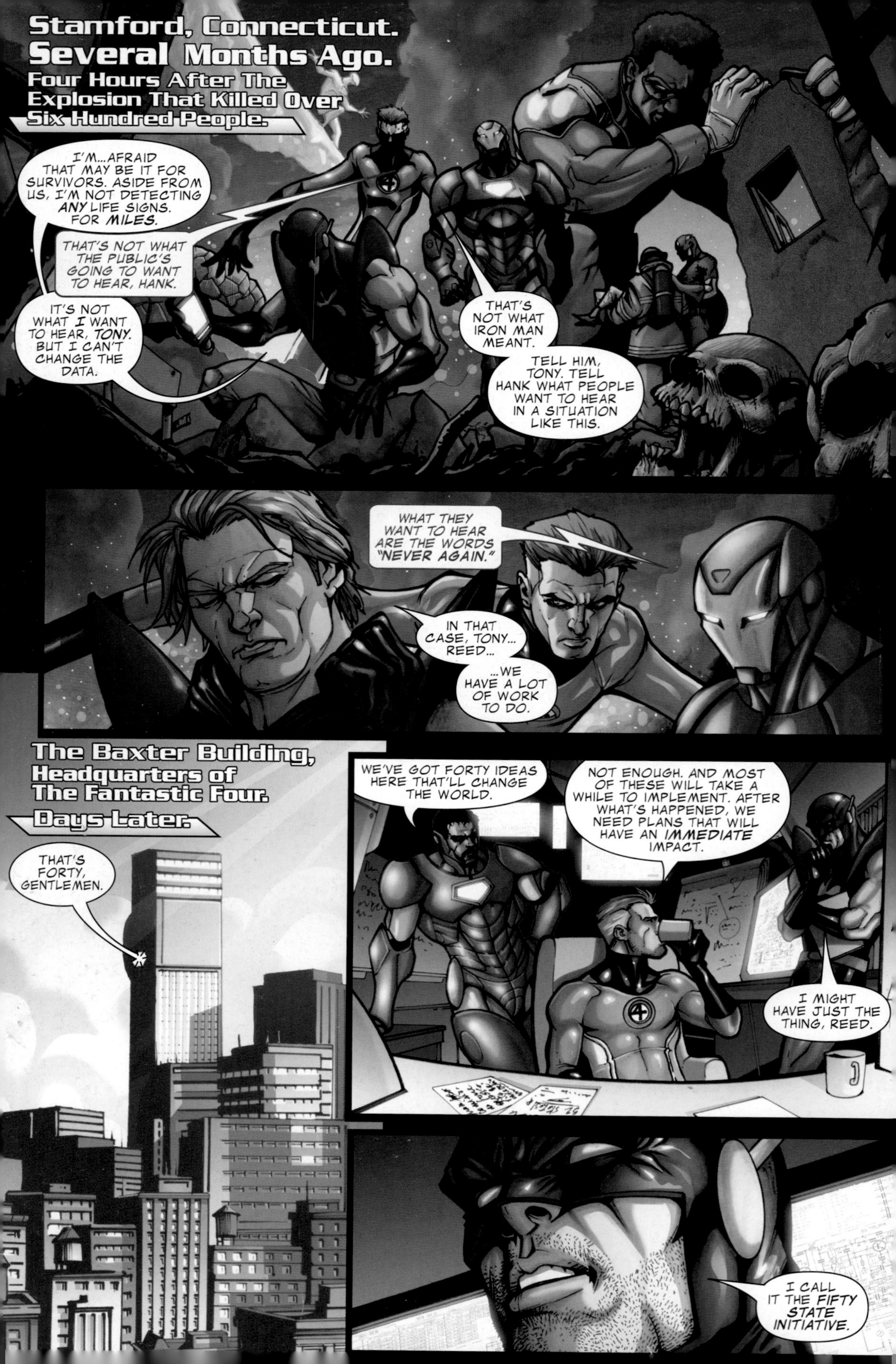
Stamford, Connecticut.
Several Months Ago.
Four Hours After The Explosion That Killed Over Six Hundred People.
I'M...AFRAID THAT MAY BE IT FOR SURVIVORS. ASIDE FROM US, I'M NOT DETECTING ANY LIFE SIGNS. FOR MILES.
THAT'S NOT WHAT THE PUBLIC'S GOING TO WANT TO HEAR, HANK.
IT'S NOT WHAT I WANT TO HEAR, TONY. BUT I CAN'T CHANGE THE DATA.
THAT'S NOT WHAT IRON MAN MEANT.
TELL HIM, TONY. TELL HANK WHAT PEOPLE WANT TO HEAR IN A SITUATION LIKE THIS.
WHAT THEY WANT TO HEAR ARE THE WORDS "NEVER AGAIN."
IN THAT CASE, TONY... REED...
...WE HAVE A LOT OF WORK TO DO.
The Baxter Building, Headquarters of The Fantastic Four.
Days Later.
THAT'S FORTY, GENTLEMEN.
WE'VE GOT FORTY IDEAS HERE THAT'LL CHANGE THE WORLD.
NOT ENOUGH. AND MOST OF THESE WILL TAKE A WHILE TO IMPLEMENT. AFTER WHAT'S HAPPENED, WE NEED PLANS THAT WILL HAVE AN IMMEDIATE IMPACT.
I MIGHT HAVE JUST THE THING, REED.
I CALL IT THE FIFTY STATE INITIATIVE.

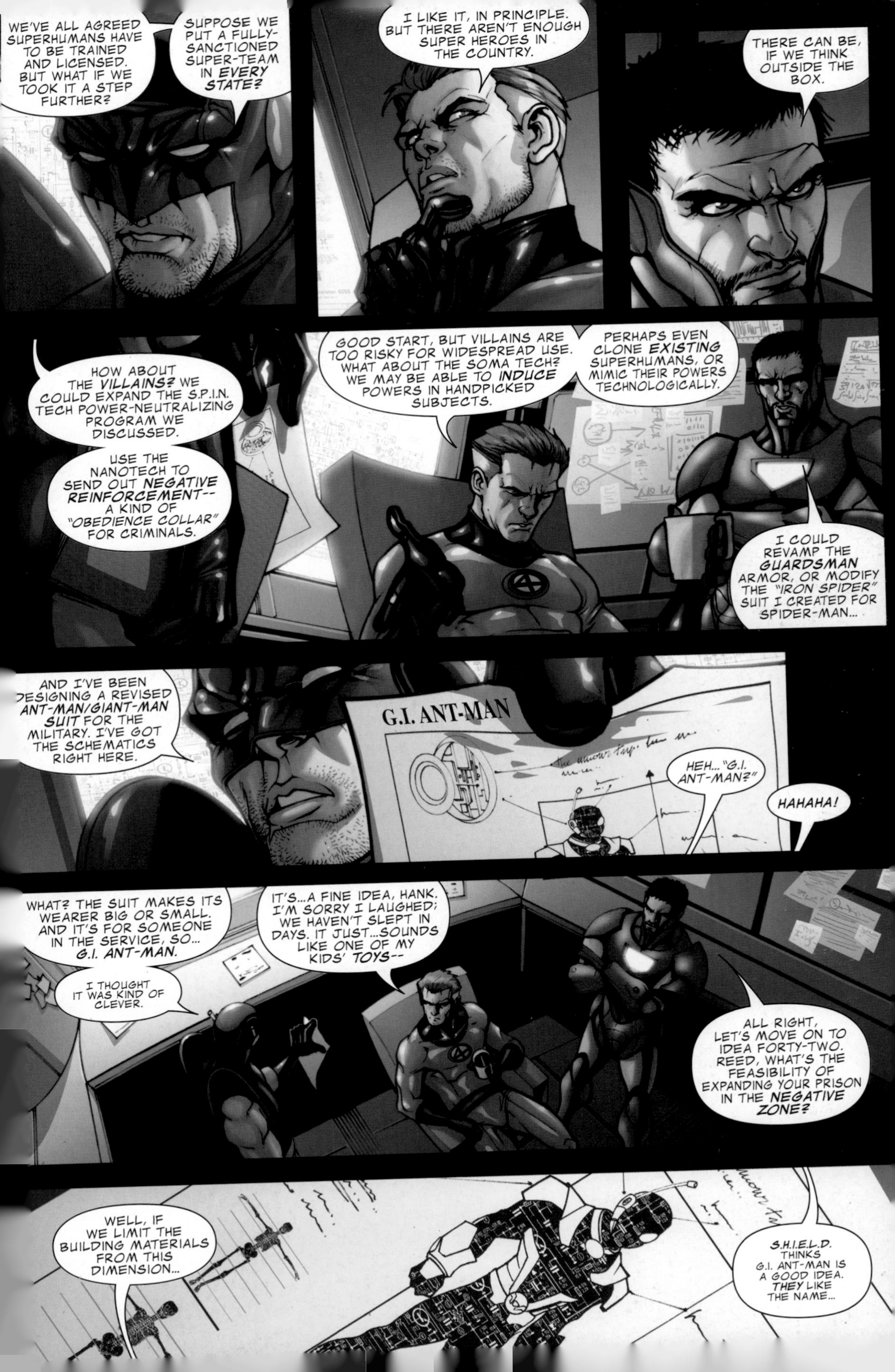
WE'VE ALL AGREED SUPERHUMANS HAVE TO BE TRAINED AND LICENSED. BUT WHAT IF WE TOOK IT A STEP FURTHER?
SUPPOSE WE PUT A FULLY-SANCTIONED SUPER-TEAM IN EVERY STATE?
I LIKE IT, IN PRINCIPLE. BUT THERE AREN'T ENOUGH SUPER HEROES IN THE COUNTRY.
THERE CAN BE, IF WE THINK OUTSIDE THE BOX.
HOW ABOUT THE VILLAINS? WE COULD EXPAND THE S.P.I.N. TECH POWER-NEUTRALIZING PROGRAM WE DISCUSSED.
USE THE NANOTECH TO SEND OUT NEGATIVE REINFORCEMENT-- A KIND OF "OBEDIENCE COLLAR" FOR CRIMINALS.
GOOD START, BUT VILLAINS ARE TOO RISKY FOR WIDESPREAD USE. WHAT ABOUT THE SOMA TECH? WE MAY BE ABLE TO INDUCE POWERS IN HANDPICKED SUBJECTS.
PERHAPS EVEN CLONE EXISTING SUPERHUMANS, OR MIMIC THEIR POWERS TECHNOLOGICALLY.
I COULD REVAMP THE GUARDSMAN ARMOR, OR MODIFY THE "IRON SPIDER" SUIT I CREATED FOR SPIDER-MAN...
AND I'VE BEEN DESIGNING A REVISED ANT-MAN/GIANT-MAN SUIT FOR THE MILITARY. I'VE GOT THE SCHEMATICS RIGHT HERE.
G.I. ANT-MAN
HEH... "G.I. ANT-MAN?"
HAHAHA!
WHAT? THE SUIT MAKES ITS WEARER BIG OR SMALL. AND IT'S FOR SOMEONE IN THE SERVICE, SO... G.I. ANT-MAN.
I THOUGHT IT WAS KIND OF CLEVER.
IT'S...A FINE IDEA, HANK. I'M SORRY I LAUGHED; WE HAVEN'T SLEPT IN DAYS. IT JUST...SOUNDS LIKE ONE OF MY KIDS' TOYS--
ALL RIGHT, LET'S MOVE ON TO IDEA FORTY-TWO. REED, WHAT'S THE FEASIBILITY OF EXPANDING YOUR PRISON IN THE NEGATIVE ZONE?
WELL, IF WE LIMIT THE BUILDING MATERIALS FROM THIS DIMENSION...
S.H.I.E.L.D. THINKS G.I. ANT-MAN IS A GOOD IDEA. THEY LIKE THE NAME...

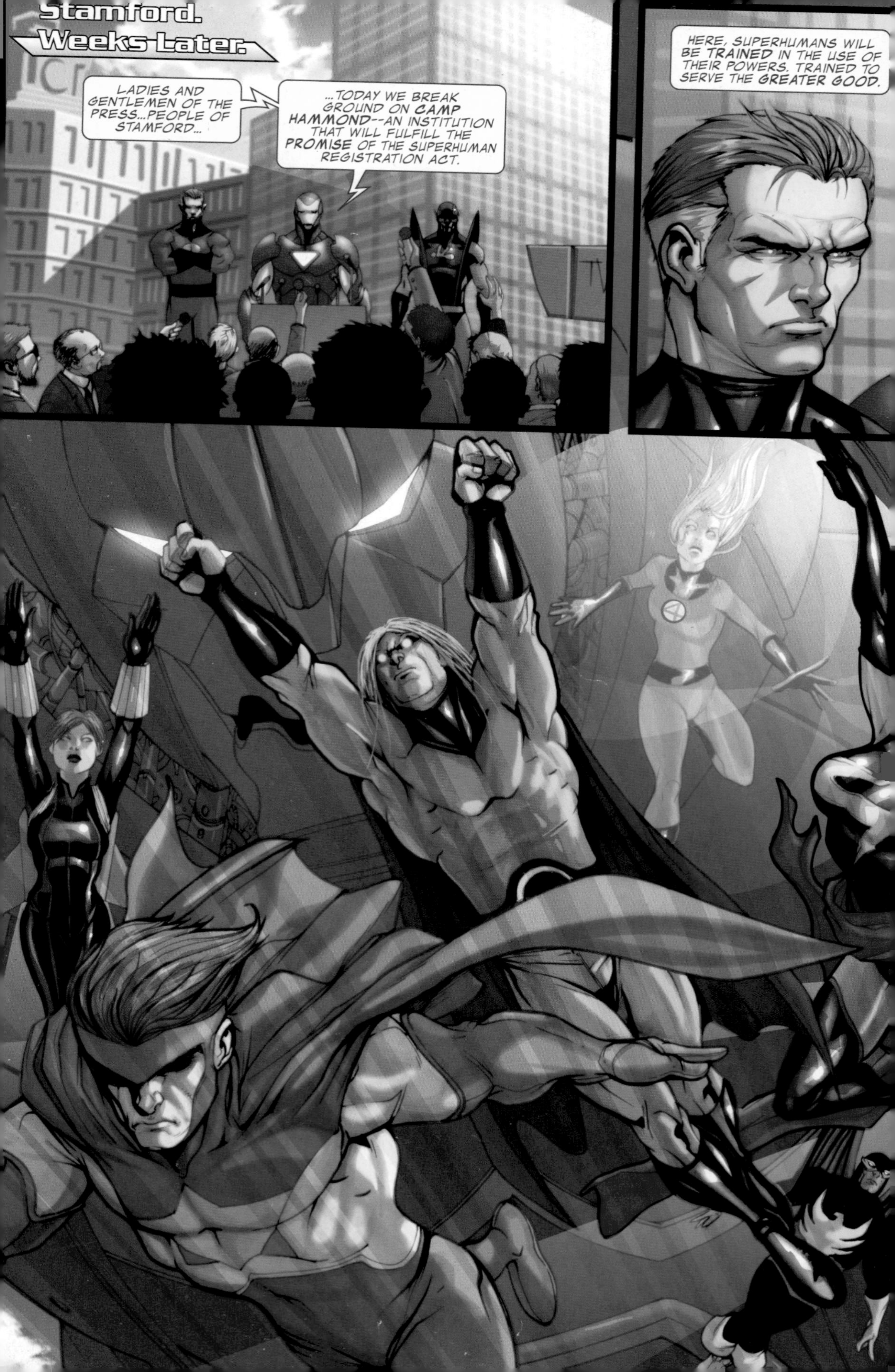
Stamford.
Weeks Later.
LADIES AND GENTLEMEN OF THE PRESS...PEOPLE OF STAMFORD...
...TODAY WE BREAK GROUND ON CAMP HAMMOND--AN INSTITUTION THAT WILL FULFILL THE PROMISE OF THE SUPERHUMAN REGISTRATION ACT.
HERE, SUPERHUMANS WILL BE TRAINED IN THE USE OF THEIR POWERS. TRAINED TO SERVE THE GREATER GOOD.

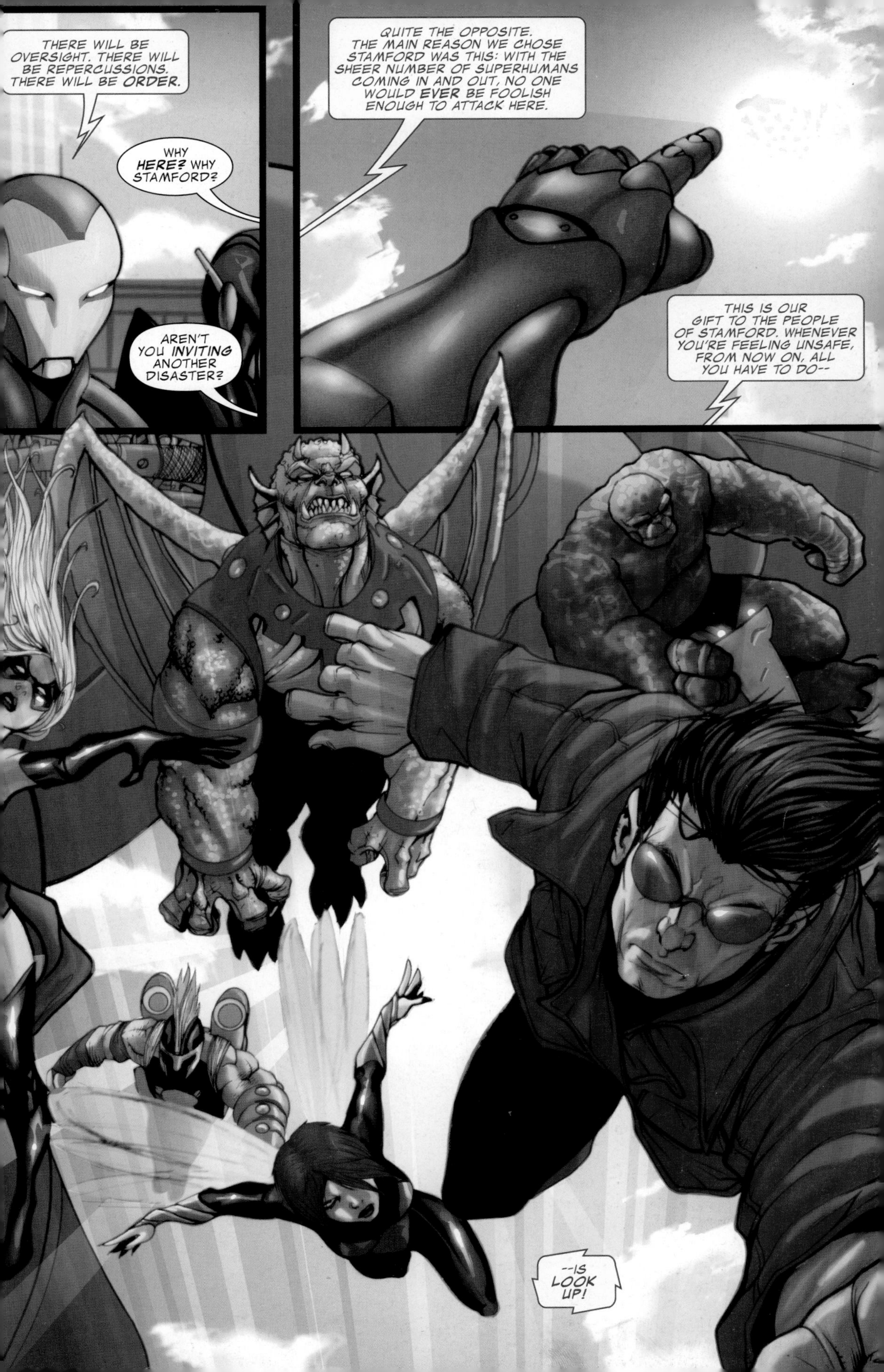

THERE WILL BE OVERSIGHT. THERE WILL BE REPERCUSSIONS. THERE WILL BE ORDER.
WHY HERE? WHY STAMFORD?
AREN'T YOU INVITING ANOTHER DISASTER?
QUITE THE OPPOSITE. THE MAIN REASON WE CHOSE STAMFORD WAS THIS: WITH THE SHEER NUMBER OF SUPERHUMANS COMING IN AND OUT, NO ONE WOULD EVER BE FOOLISH ENOUGH TO ATTACK HERE.
THIS IS OUR GIFT TO THE PEOPLE OF STAMFORD. WHENEVER YOU'RE FEELING UNSAFE, FROM NOW ON, ALL YOU HAVE TO DO--
--IS LOOK UP!

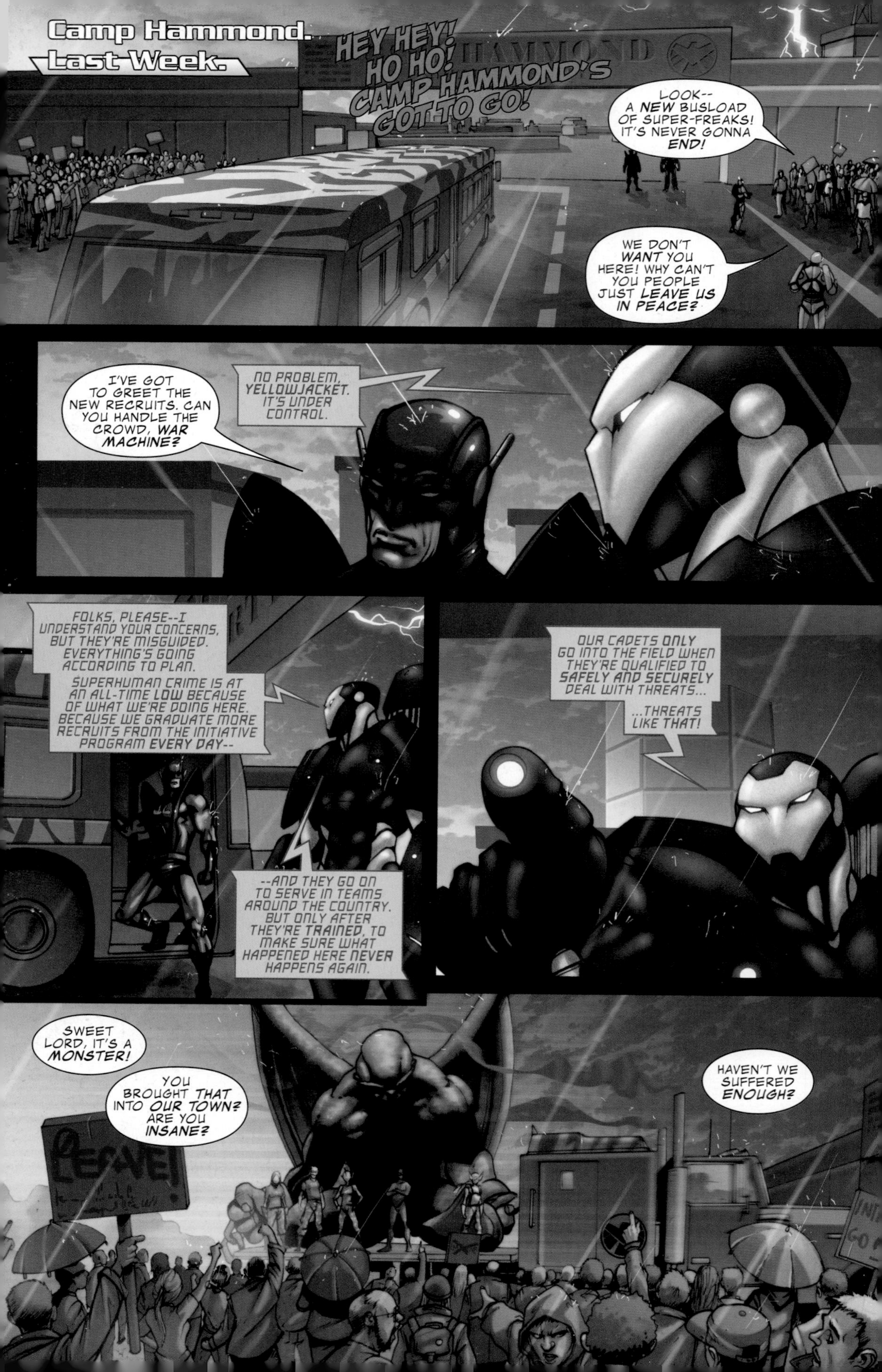
Camp Hammond.
Last Week.
HEY HEY! HO HO! CAMP HAMMOND'S GOT TO GO!
LOOK-- A NEW BUSLOAD OF SUPER-FREAKS! IT'S NEVER GONNA END!
WE DON'T WANT YOU HERE! WHY CAN'T YOU PEOPLE JUST LEAVE US IN PEACE?
I'VE GOT TO GREET THE NEW RECRUITS. CAN YOU HANDLE THE CROWD, WAR MACHINE?
NO PROBLEM, YELLOWJACKET. IT'S UNDER CONTROL.
FOLKS, PLEASE--I UNDERSTAND YOUR CONCERNS, BUT THEY'RE MISGUIDED. EVERYTHING'S GOING ACCORDING TO PLAN.
SUPERHUMAN CRIME IS AT AN ALL-TIME LOW BECAUSE OF WHAT WE'RE DOING HERE. BECAUSE WE GRADUATE MORE RECRUITS FROM THE INITIATIVE PROGRAM EVERY DAY--
--AND THEY GO ON TO SERVE IN TEAMS AROUND THE COUNTRY. BUT ONLY AFTER THEY'RE TRAINED, TO MAKE SURE WHAT HAPPENED HERE NEVER HAPPENS AGAIN.
OUR CADETS ONLY GO INTO THE FIELD WHEN THEY'RE QUALIFIED TO SAFELY AND SECURELY DEAL WITH THREATS...
...THREATS LIKE THAT!
SWEET LORD, IT'S A MONSTER!
YOU BROUGHT THAT INTO OUR TOWN? ARE YOU INSANE?
HAVEN'T WE SUFFERED ENOUGH?
LEAVE!

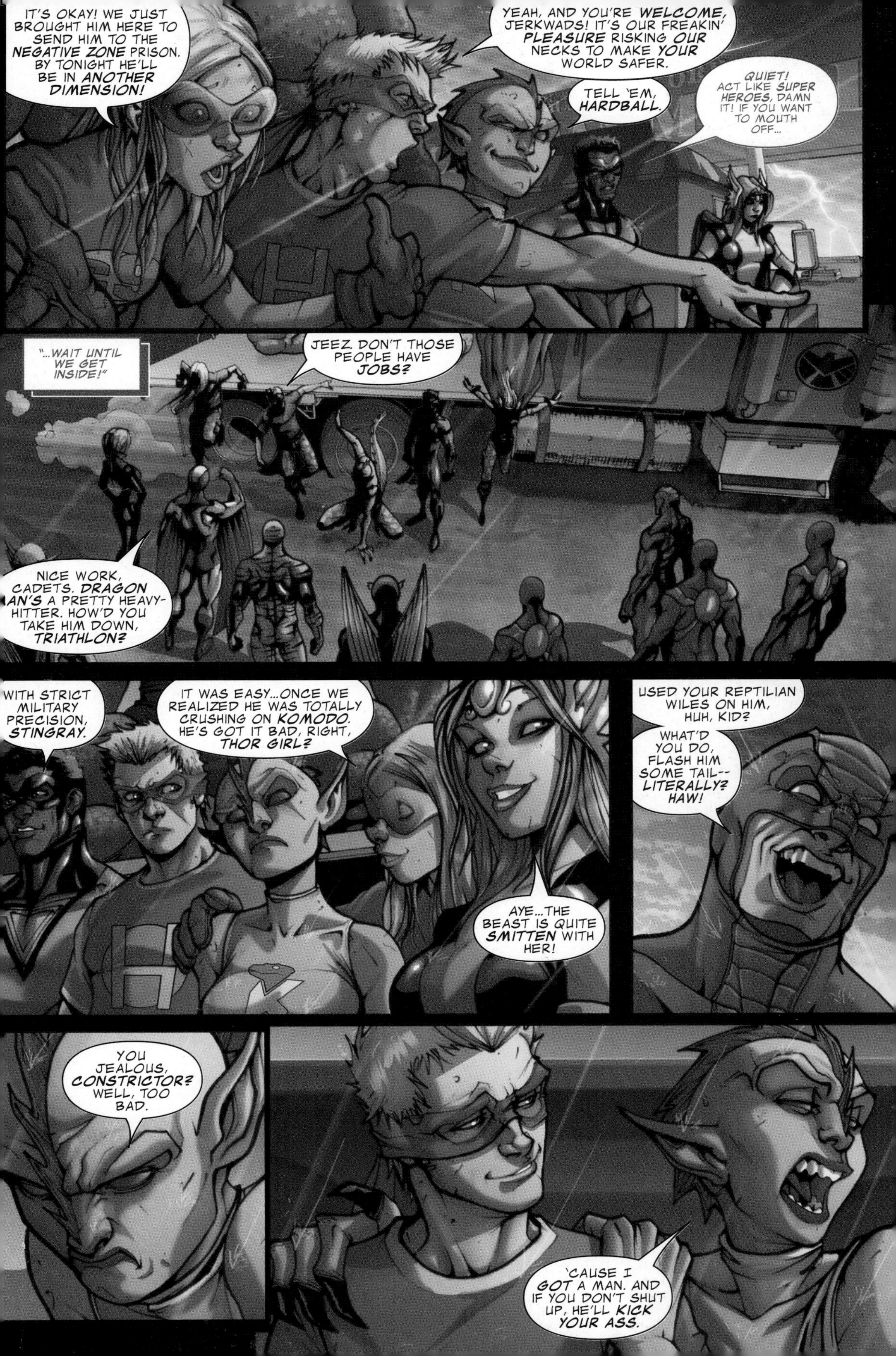
IT'S OKAY! WE JUST BROUGHT HIM HERE TO SEND HIM TO THE NEGATIVE ZONE PRISON. BY TONIGHT HE'LL BE IN ANOTHER DIMENSION!
YEAH, AND YOU'RE WELCOME, JERKWADS! IT'S OUR FREAKIN' PLEASURE RISKING OUR NECKS TO MAKE YOUR WORLD SAFER.
TELL 'EM, HARDBALL.
QUIET! ACT LIKE SUPER HEROES, DAMN IT! IF YOU WANT TO MOUTH OFF...
"...WAIT UNTIL WE GET INSIDE!"
JEEZ. DON'T THOSE PEOPLE HAVE JOBS?
NICE WORK, CADETS. DRAGON AN'S A PRETTY HEAVY-HITTER. HOW'D YOU TAKE HIM DOWN, TRIATHLON?
WITH STRICT MILITARY PRECISION, STINGRAY.
IT WAS EASY...ONCE WE REALIZED HE WAS TOTALLY CRUSHING ON KOMODO. HE'S GOT IT BAD, RIGHT, THOR GIRL?
AYE...THE BEAST IS QUITE SMITTEN WITH HER!
USED YOUR REPTILIAN WILES ON HIM, HUH, KID?
WHAT'D YOU DO, FLASH HIM SOME TAIL--LITERALLY? HAW!
YOU JEALOUS, CONSTRICTOR? WELL, TOO BAD.
'CAUSE I GOT A MAN. AND IF YOU DON'T SHUT UP, HE'LL KICK YOUR ASS.

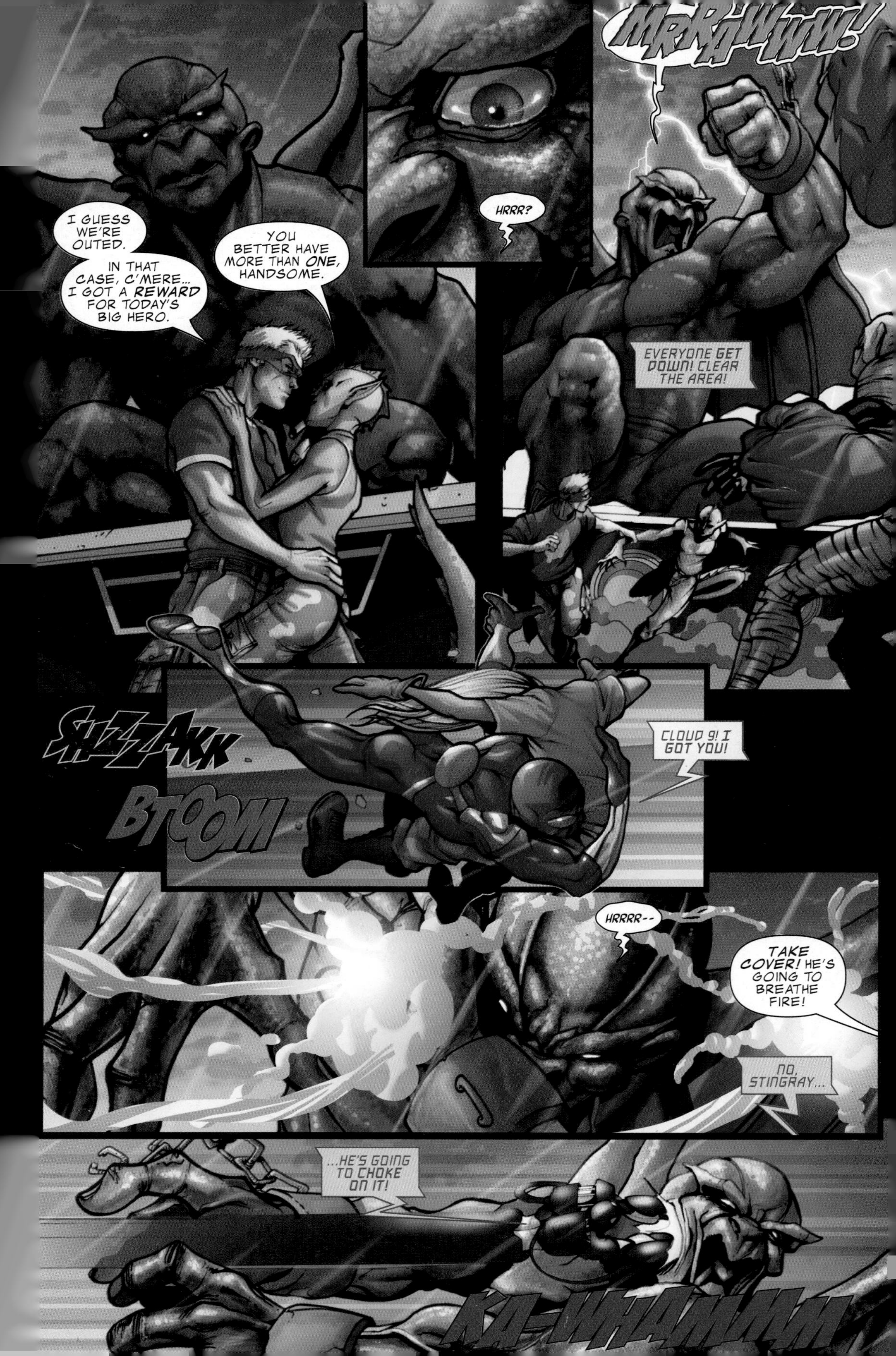
I GUESS WE'RE OUTED.
IN THAT CASE, C'MERE... I GOT A REWARD FOR TODAY'S BIG HERO.
YOU BETTER HAVE MORE THAN ONE, HANDSOME.
HRRR?
MRRAWWW!
EVERYONE GET DOWN! CLEAR THE AREA!
SHZZAKK
BTOOM
CLOUD 9! I GOT YOU!
HRRRR--
TAKE COVER! HE'S GOING TO BREATHE FIRE!
NO, STINGRAY...
...HE'S GOING TO CHOKE ON IT!
KA-WHAMMM

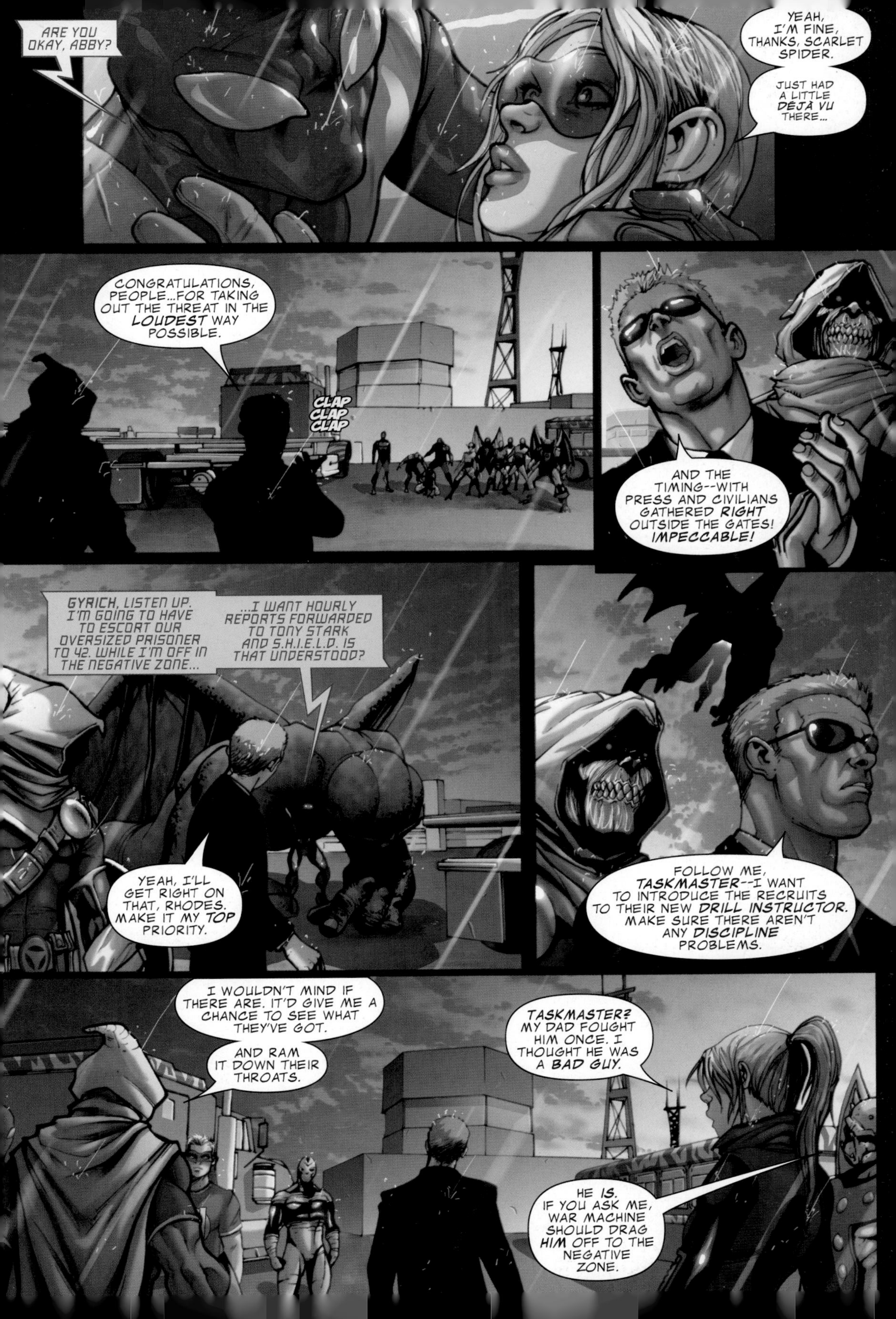
ARE YOU OKAY, ABBY?
YEAH, I'M FINE, THANKS, SCARLET SPIDER.
JUST HAD A LITTLE DÉJÀ VU THERE...
CONGRATULATIONS, PEOPLE...FOR TAKING OUT THE THREAT IN THE LOUDEST WAY POSSIBLE.
CLAP CLAP CLAP
AND THE TIMING--WITH PRESS AND CIVILIANS GATHERED RIGHT OUTSIDE THE GATES! IMPECCABLE!
GYRICH, LISTEN UP. I'M GOING TO HAVE TO ESCORT OUR OVERSIZED PRISONER TO 42. WHILE I'M OFF IN THE NEGATIVE ZONE...
...I WANT HOURLY REPORTS FORWARDED TO TONY STARK AND S.H.I.E.L.D. IS THAT UNDERSTOOD?
YEAH, I'LL GET RIGHT ON THAT, RHODES. MAKE IT MY TOP PRIORITY.
FOLLOW ME, TASKMASTER--I WANT TO INTRODUCE THE RECRUITS TO THEIR NEW DRILL INSTRUCTOR. MAKE SURE THERE AREN'T ANY DISCIPLINE PROBLEMS.
I WOULDN'T MIND IF THERE ARE. IT'D GIVE ME A CHANCE TO SEE WHAT THEY'VE GOT.
AND RAM IT DOWN THEIR THROATS.
TASKMASTER? MY DAD FOUGHT HIM ONCE. I THOUGHT HE WAS A BAD GUY.
HE IS. IF YOU ASK ME, WAR MACHINE SHOULD DRAG HIM OFF TO THE NEGATIVE ZONE.

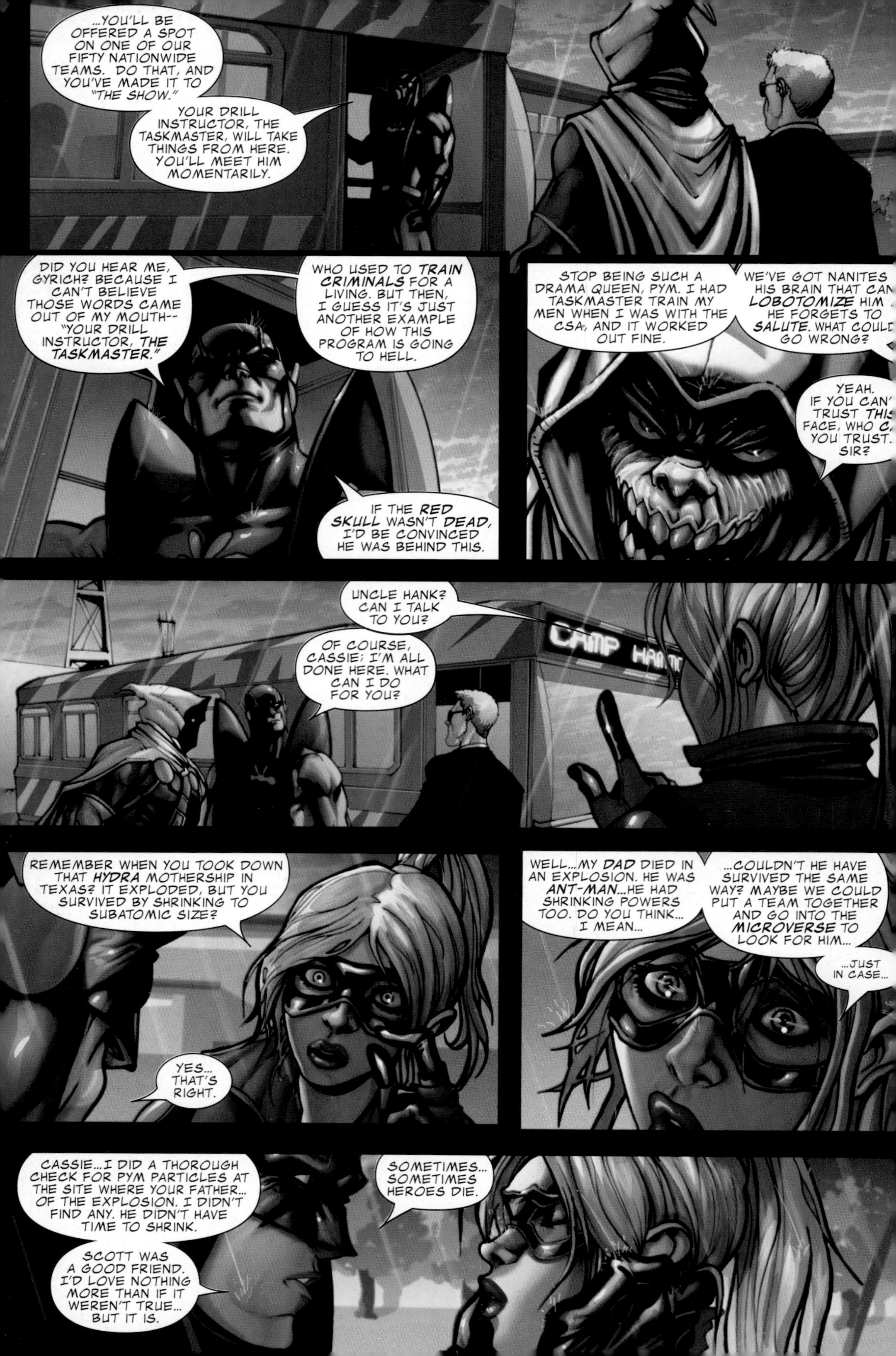
...YOU'LL BE OFFERED A SPOT ON ONE OF OUR FIFTY NATIONWIDE TEAMS. DO THAT, AND YOU'VE MADE IT TO "THE SHOW."
YOUR DRILL INSTRUCTOR, THE TASKMASTER, WILL TAKE THINGS FROM HERE. YOU'LL MEET HIM MOMENTARILY.
DID YOU HEAR ME, GYRICH? BECAUSE I CAN'T BELIEVE THOSE WORDS CAME OUT OF MY MOUTH-- "YOUR DRILL INSTRUCTOR, THE TASKMASTER."
WHO USED TO TRAIN CRIMINALS FOR A LIVING. BUT THEN, I GUESS IT'S JUST ANOTHER EXAMPLE OF HOW THIS PROGRAM IS GOING TO HELL.
IF THE RED SKULL WASN'T DEAD, I'D BE CONVINCED HE WAS BEHIND THIS.
STOP BEING SUCH A DRAMA QUEEN, PYM. I HAD TASKMASTER TRAIN MY MEN WHEN I WAS WITH THE CSA, AND IT WORKED OUT FINE.
WE'VE GOT NANITES HIS BRAIN THAT CAN LOBOTOMIZE HIM HE FORGETS TO SALUTE. WHAT COULD GO WRONG?
YEAH. IF YOU CAN' TRUST THIS FACE, WHO C YOU TRUST. SIR?
UNCLE HANK? CAN I TALK TO YOU?
CAMP HAMM
OF COURSE, CASSIE; I'M ALL DONE HERE. WHAT CAN I DO FOR YOU?
REMEMBER WHEN YOU TOOK DOWN THAT HYDRA MOTHERSHIP IN TEXAS? IT EXPLODED, BUT YOU SURVIVED BY SHRINKING TO SUBATOMIC SIZE?
YES... THAT'S RIGHT.
WELL...MY DAD DIED IN AN EXPLOSION. HE WAS ANT-MAN...HE HAD SHRINKING POWERS TOO. DO YOU THINK... I MEAN...
...COULDN'T HE HAVE SURVIVED THE SAME WAY? MAYBE WE COULD PUT A TEAM TOGETHER AND GO INTO THE MICROVERSE TO LOOK FOR HIM...
...JUST IN CASE...
CASSIE...I DID A THOROUGH CHECK FOR PYM PARTICLES AT THE SITE WHERE YOUR FATHER... OF THE EXPLOSION. I DIDN'T FIND ANY. HE DIDN'T HAVE TIME TO SHRINK.
SCOTT WAS A GOOD FRIEND. I'D LOVE NOTHING MORE THAN IF IT WEREN'T TRUE... BUT IT IS.
SOMETIMES... SOMETIMES HEROES DIE.

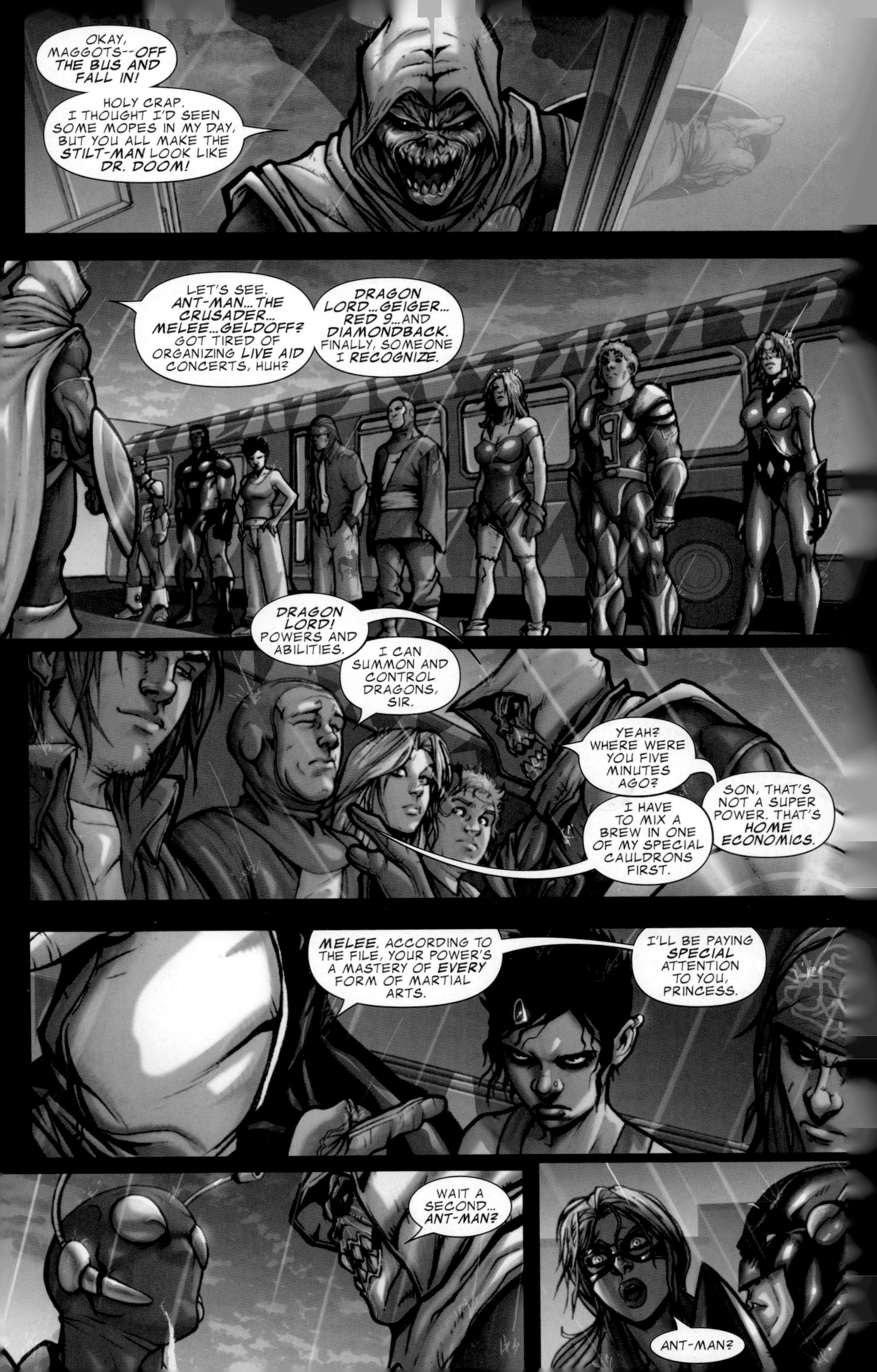
OKAY, MAGGOTS--OFF THE BUS AND FALL IN!
HOLY CRAP. I THOUGHT I'D SEEN SOME MOPES IN MY DAY, BUT YOU ALL MAKE THE STILT-MAN LOOK LIKE DR. DOOM!
LET'S SEE. ANT-MAN...THE CRUSADER... MELEE...GELDOFF? GOT TIRED OF ORGANIZING LIVE AID CONCERTS, HUH?
DRAGON LORD...GEIGER... RED 9...AND DIAMONDBACK. FINALLY, SOMEONE I RECOGNIZE.
DRAGON LORD! POWERS AND ABILITIES.
I CAN SUMMON AND CONTROL DRAGONS, SIR.
YEAH? WHERE WERE YOU FIVE MINUTES AGO?
I HAVE TO MIX A BREW IN ONE OF MY SPECIAL CAULDRONS FIRST.
SON, THAT'S NOT A SUPER POWER. THAT'S HOME ECONOMICS.
MELEE. ACCORDING TO THE FILE, YOUR POWER'S A MASTERY OF EVERY FORM OF MARTIAL ARTS.
I'LL BE PAYING SPECIAL ATTENTION TO YOU, PRINCESS.
WAIT A SECOND... ANT-MAN?
ANT-MAN?

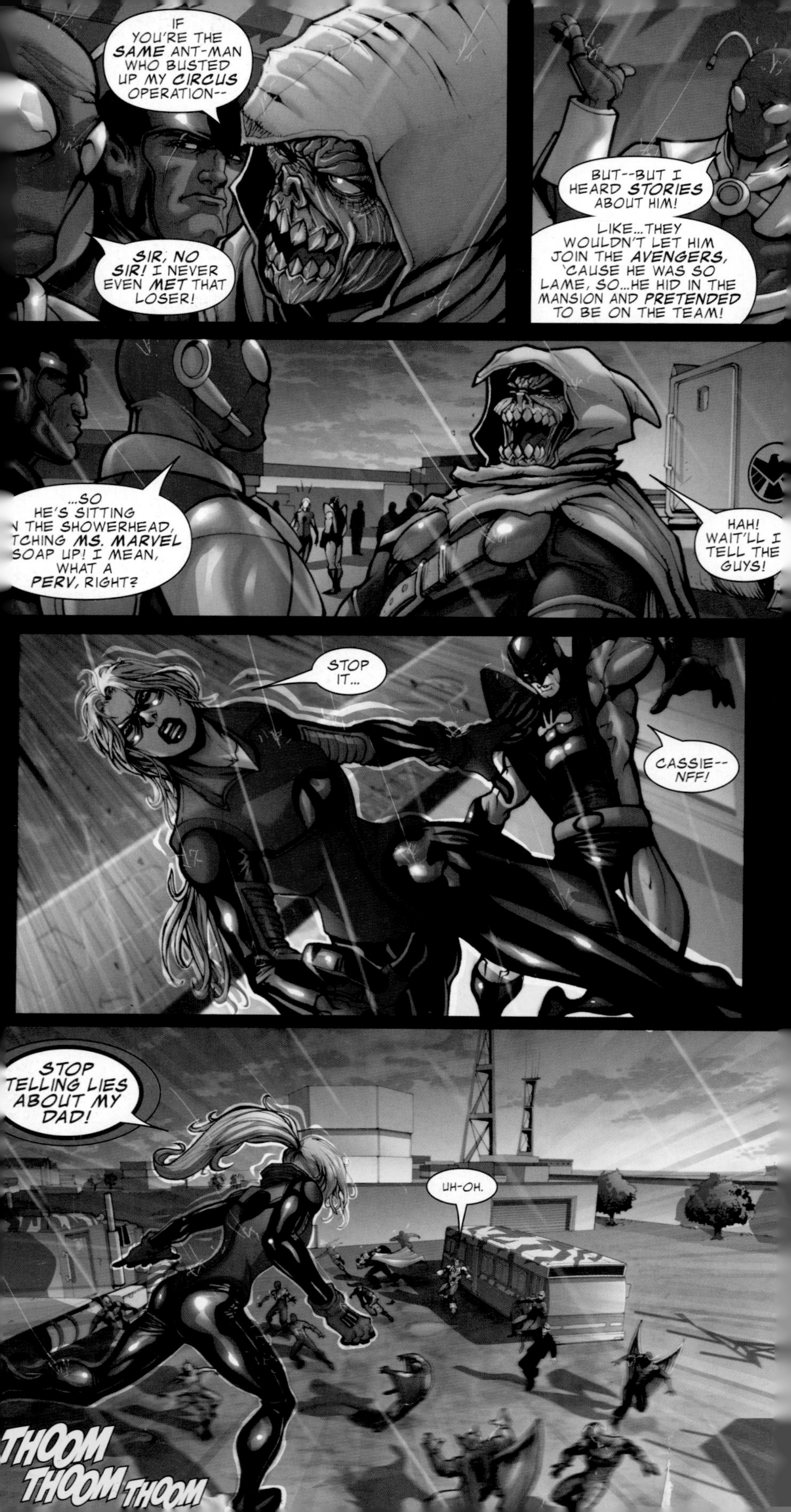
IF YOU'RE THE SAME ANT-MAN WHO BUSTED UP MY CIRCUS OPERATION--
SIR, NO SIR! I NEVER EVEN MET THAT LOSER!
BUT--BUT I HEARD STORIES ABOUT HIM!
LIKE...THEY WOULDN'T LET HIM JOIN THE AVENGERS, 'CAUSE HE WAS SO LAME, SO...HE HID IN THE MANSION AND PRETENDED TO BE ON THE TEAM!
...SO HE'S SITTING N THE SHOWERHEAD, TCHING MS. MARVEL SOAP UP! I MEAN, WHAT A PERV, RIGHT?
HAH! WAIT'LL I TELL THE GUYS!
STOP IT...
CASSIE--NFF!
STOP TELLING LIES ABOUT MY DAD!
UH-OH.
THOOM THOOM THOOM

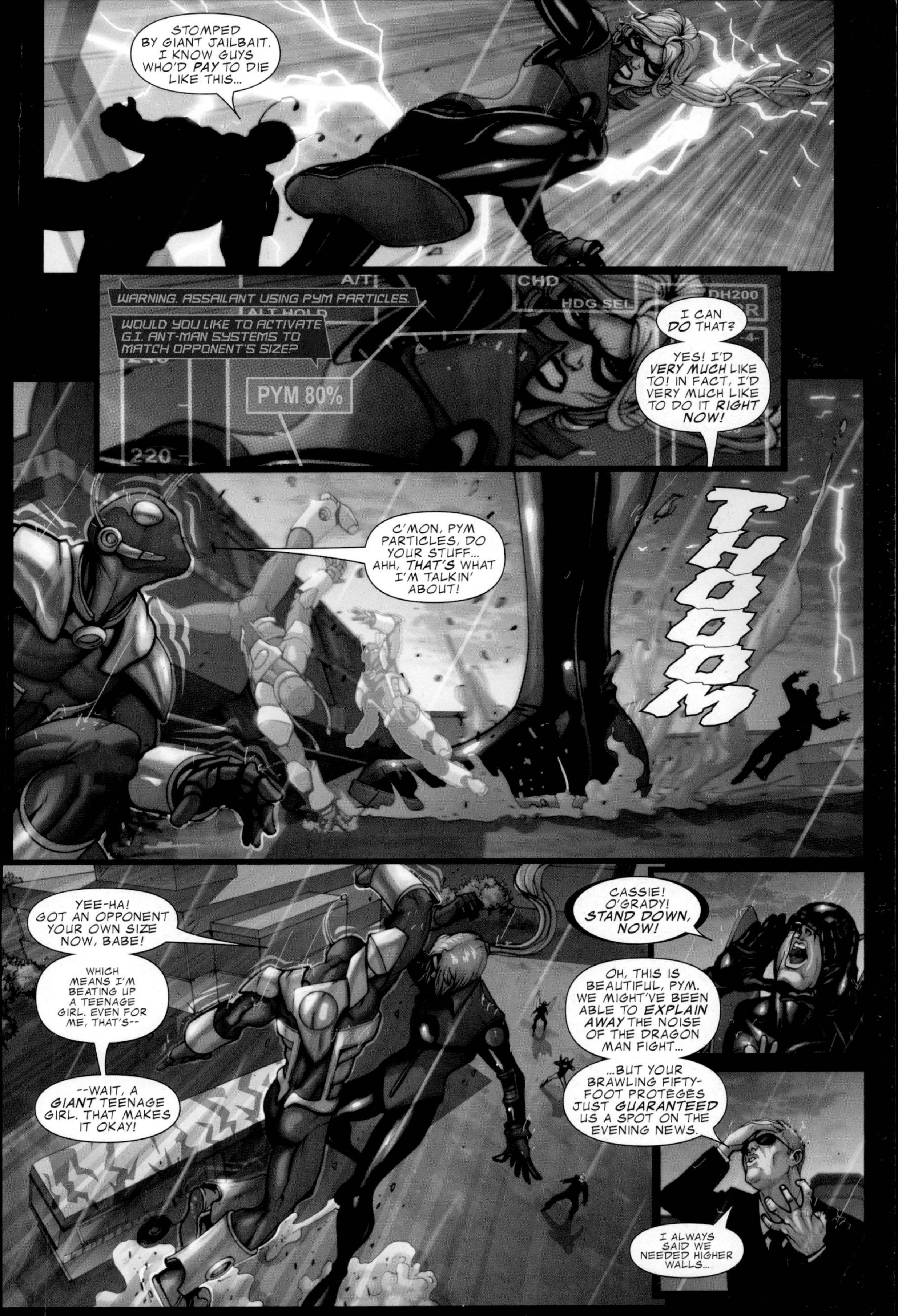
STOMPED BY GIANT JAILBAIT. I KNOW GUYS WHO'D PAY TO DIE LIKE THIS...
WARNING. ASSAILANT USING PYM PARTICLES.
WOULD YOU LIKE TO ACTIVATE G.I. ANT-MAN SYSTEMS TO MATCH OPPONENT'S SIZE?
PYM 80%
I CAN DO THAT?
YES! I'D VERY MUCH LIKE TO! IN FACT, I'D VERY MUCH LIKE TO DO IT RIGHT NOW!
C'MON, PYM PARTICLES, DO YOUR STUFF... AHH, THAT'S WHAT I'M TALKIN' ABOUT!
THOOOM
YEE-HA! GOT AN OPPONENT YOUR OWN SIZE NOW, BABE!
WHICH MEANS I'M BEATING UP A TEENAGE GIRL. EVEN FOR ME, THAT'S--
--WAIT, A GIANT TEENAGE GIRL. THAT MAKES IT OKAY!
CASSIE! O'GRADY! STAND DOWN, NOW!
OH, THIS IS BEAUTIFUL, PYM. WE MIGHT'VE BEEN ABLE TO EXPLAIN AWAY THE NOISE OF THE DRAGON MAN FIGHT...
...BUT YOUR BRAWLING FIFTY-FOOT PROTÉGÉS JUST GUARANTEED US A SPOT ON THE EVENING NEWS.
I ALWAYS SAID WE NEEDED HIGHER WALLS...

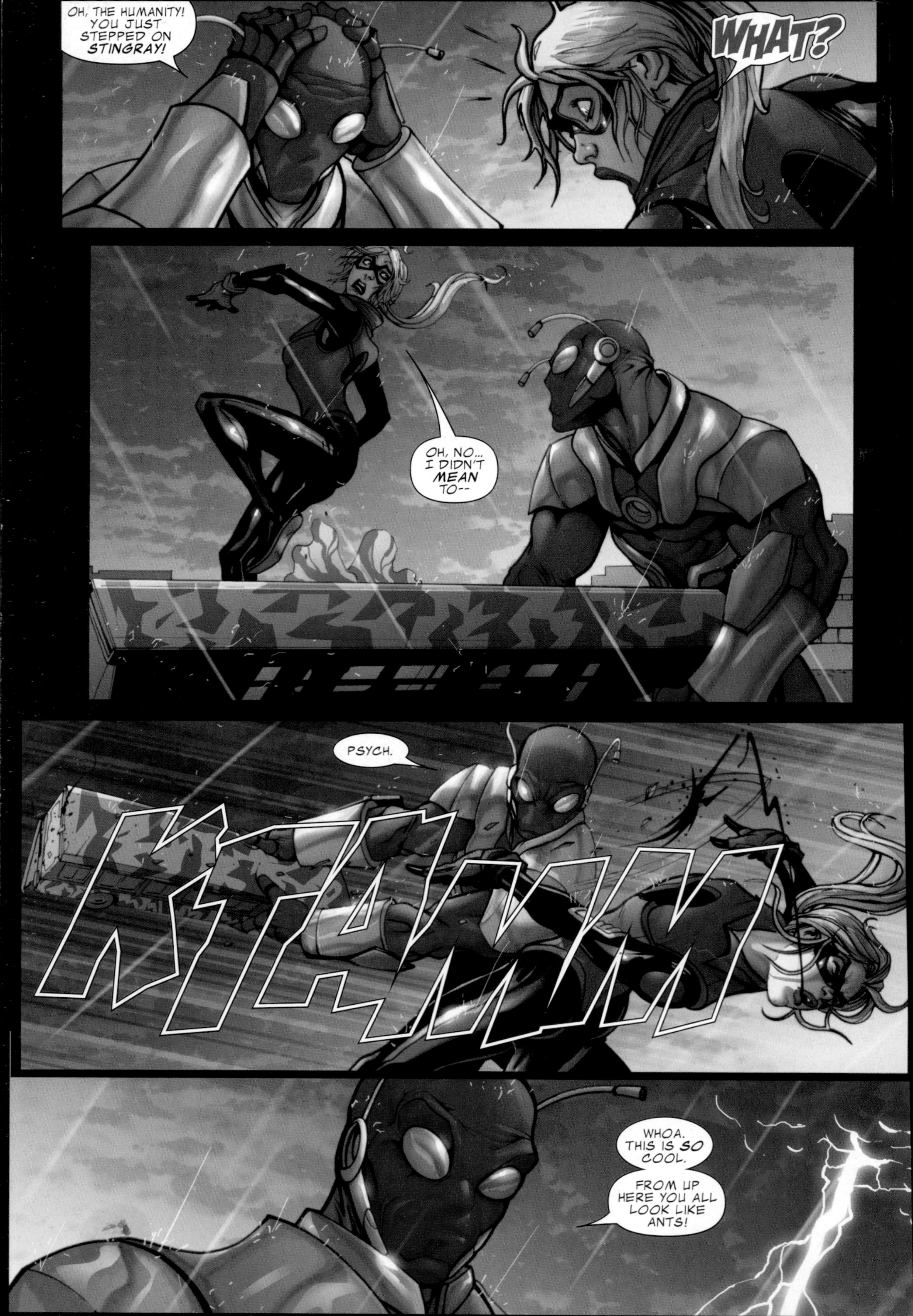
OH, THE HUMANITY! YOU JUST STEPPED ON STINGRAY!
WHAT?
OH, NO... I DIDN'T MEAN TO--
PSYCH.
WHOA. THIS IS SO COOL.
FROM UP HERE YOU ALL LOOK LIKE ANTS!

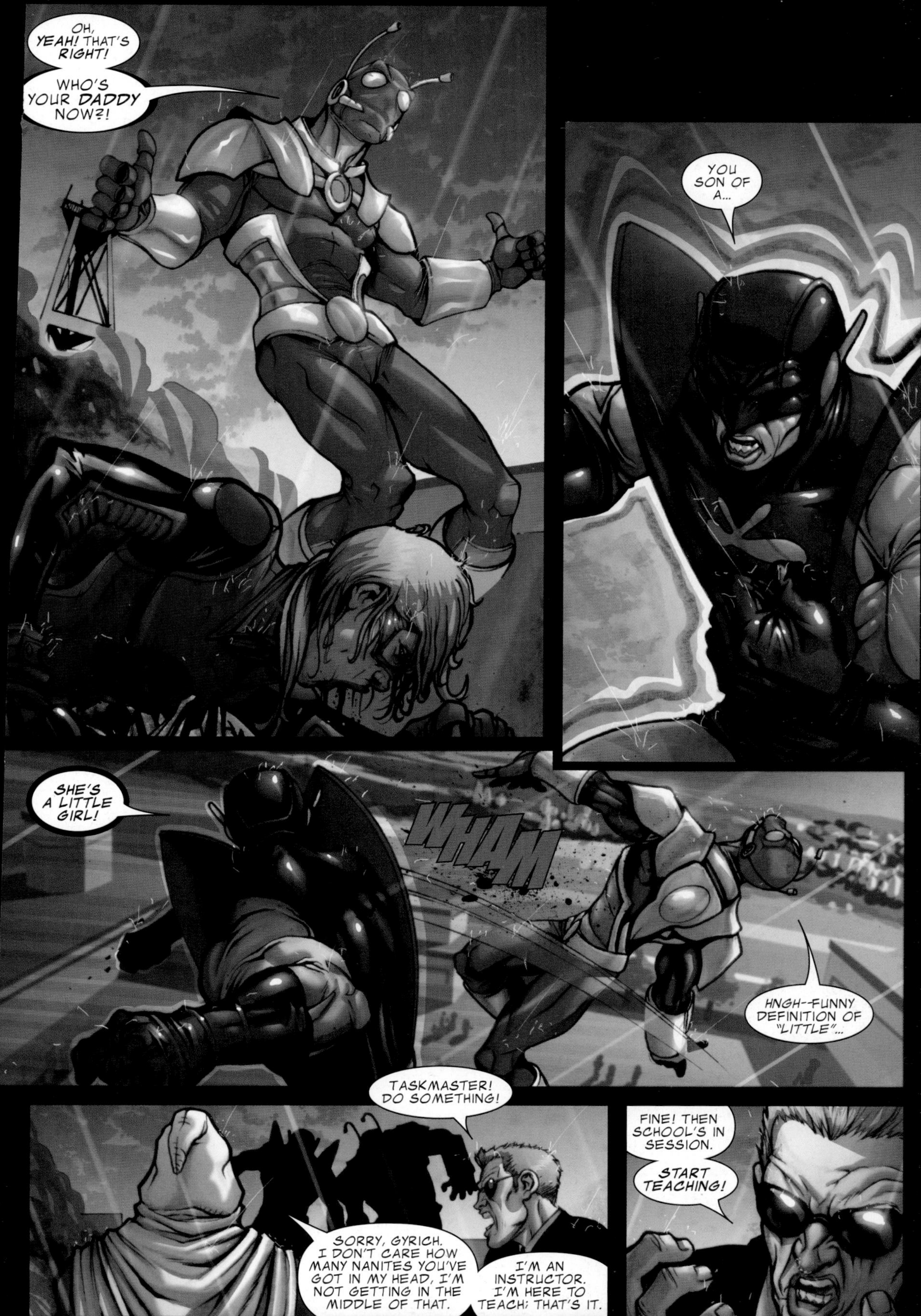
OH, YEAH! THAT'S RIGHT!
WHO'S YOUR DADDY NOW?!
YOU SON OF A...
SHE'S A LITTLE GIRL!
WHAM
HNGH--FUNNY DEFINITION OF "LITTLE"...
TASKMASTER! DO SOMETHING!
SORRY, GYRICH. I DON'T CARE HOW MANY NANITES YOU'VE GOT IN MY HEAD, I'M NOT GETTING IN THE MIDDLE OF THAT.
I'M AN INSTRUCTOR. I'M HERE TO TEACH; THAT'S IT.
FINE! THEN SCHOOL'S IN SESSION.
START TEACHING!

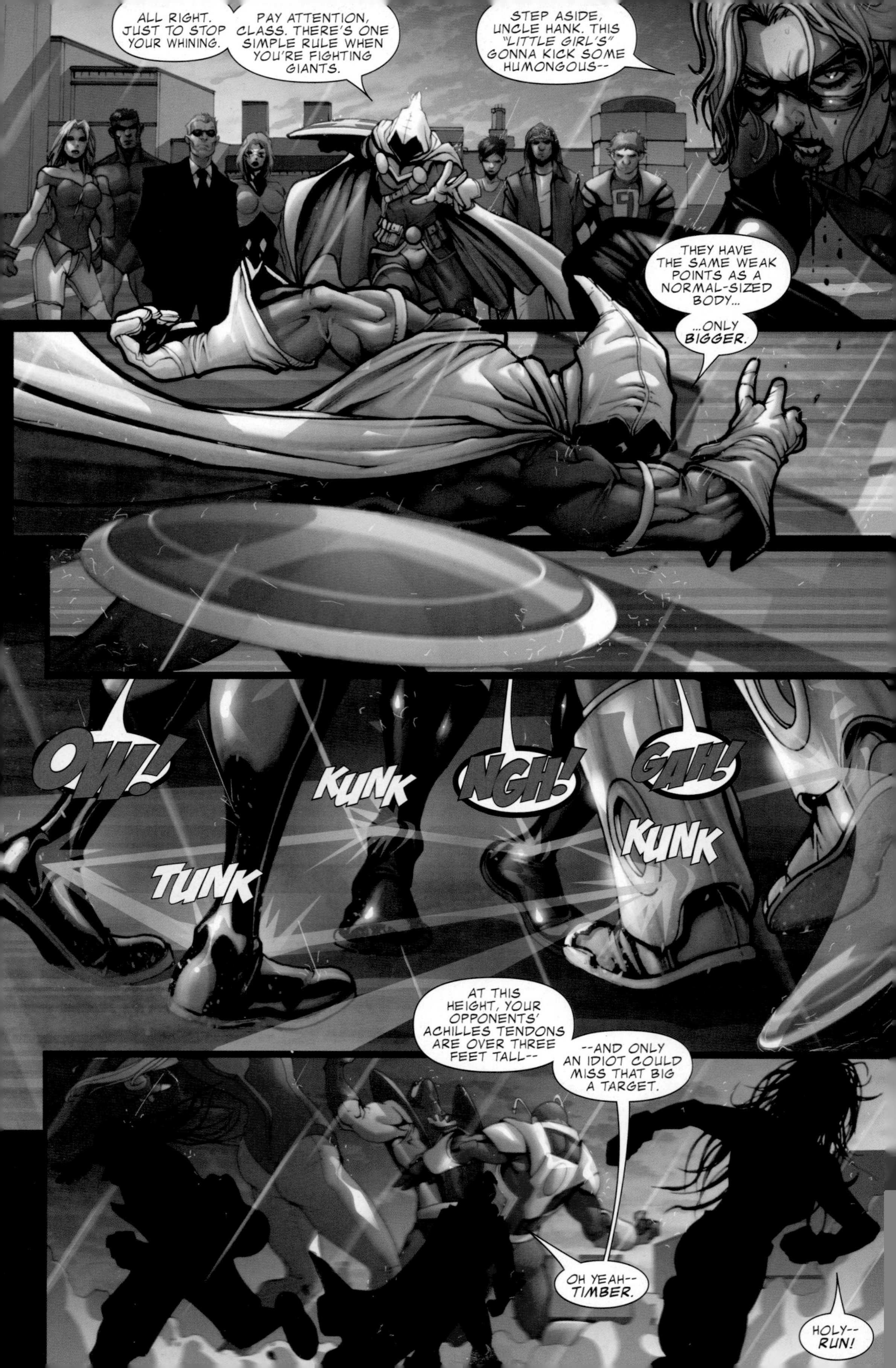
ALL RIGHT. JUST TO STOP YOUR WHINING.
PAY ATTENTION, CLASS. THERE'S ONE SIMPLE RULE WHEN YOU'RE FIGHTING GIANTS.
STEP ASIDE, UNCLE HANK. THIS "LITTLE GIRL'S" GONNA KICK SOME HUMONGOUS--
THEY HAVE THE SAME WEAK POINTS AS A NORMAL-SIZED BODY...
...ONLY BIGGER.
OW!
KUNK
NGH!
GAH!
KUNK
TUNK
AT THIS HEIGHT, YOUR OPPONENTS' ACHILLES TENDONS ARE OVER THREE FEET TALL--
--AND ONLY AN IDIOT COULD MISS THAT BIG A TARGET.
OH YEAH-- TIMBER.
HOLY-- RUN!

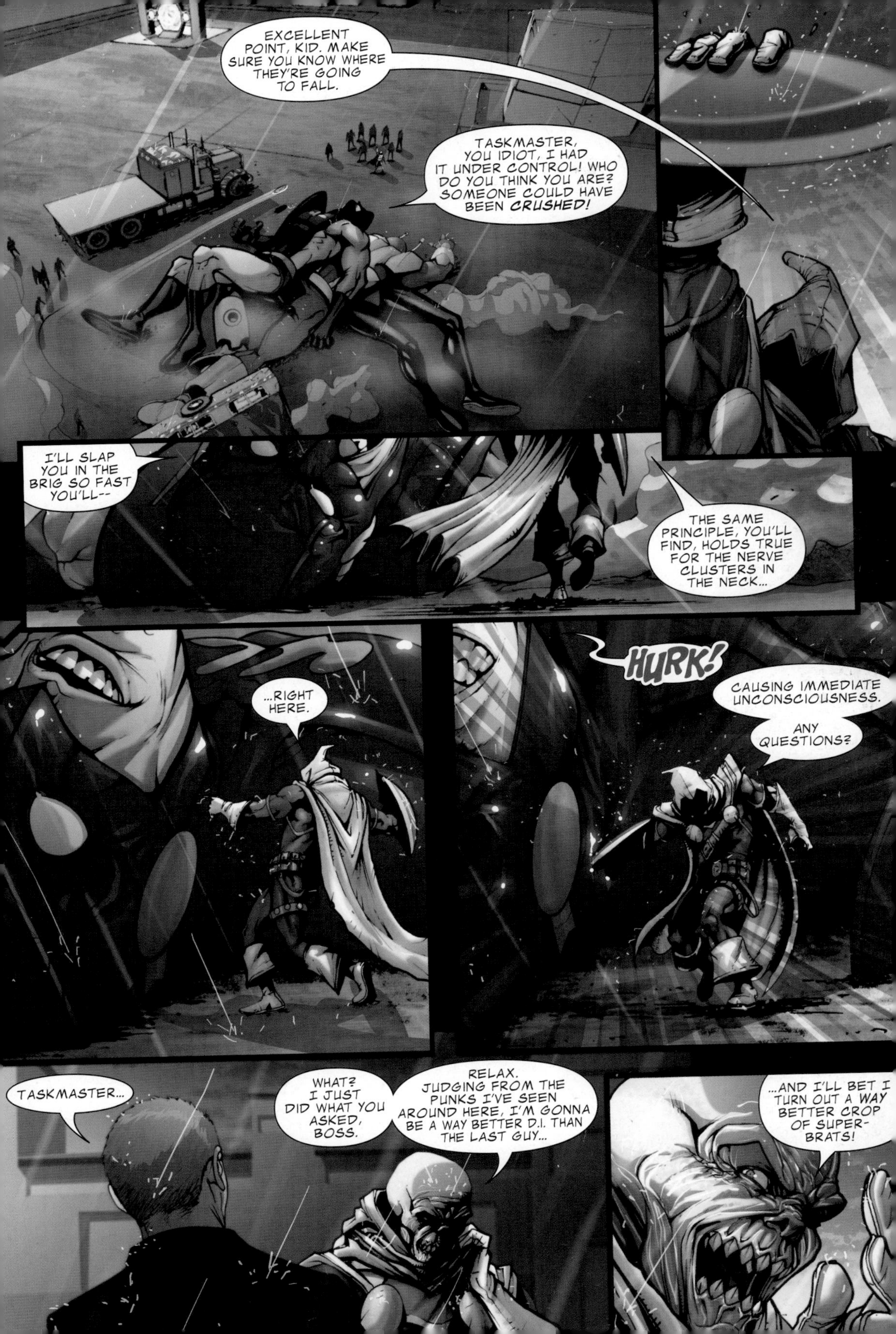
EXCELLENT POINT, KID. MAKE SURE YOU KNOW WHERE THEY'RE GOING TO FALL.
TASKMASTER, YOU IDIOT, I HAD IT UNDER CONTROL! WHO DO YOU THINK YOU ARE? SOMEONE COULD HAVE BEEN CRUSHED!
I'LL SLAP YOU IN THE BRIG SO FAST YOU'LL--
THE SAME PRINCIPLE, YOU'LL FIND, HOLDS TRUE FOR THE NERVE CLUSTERS IN THE NECK...
...RIGHT HERE.
HURK!
CAUSING IMMEDIATE UNCONSCIOUSNESS.
ANY QUESTIONS?
TASKMASTER...
WHAT? I JUST DID WHAT YOU ASKED, BOSS.
RELAX. JUDGING FROM THE PUNKS I'VE SEEN AROUND HERE, I'M GONNA BE A WAY BETTER D.I. THAN THE LAST GUY...
...AND I'LL BET I TURN OUT A WAY BETTER CROP OF SUPER-BRATS!

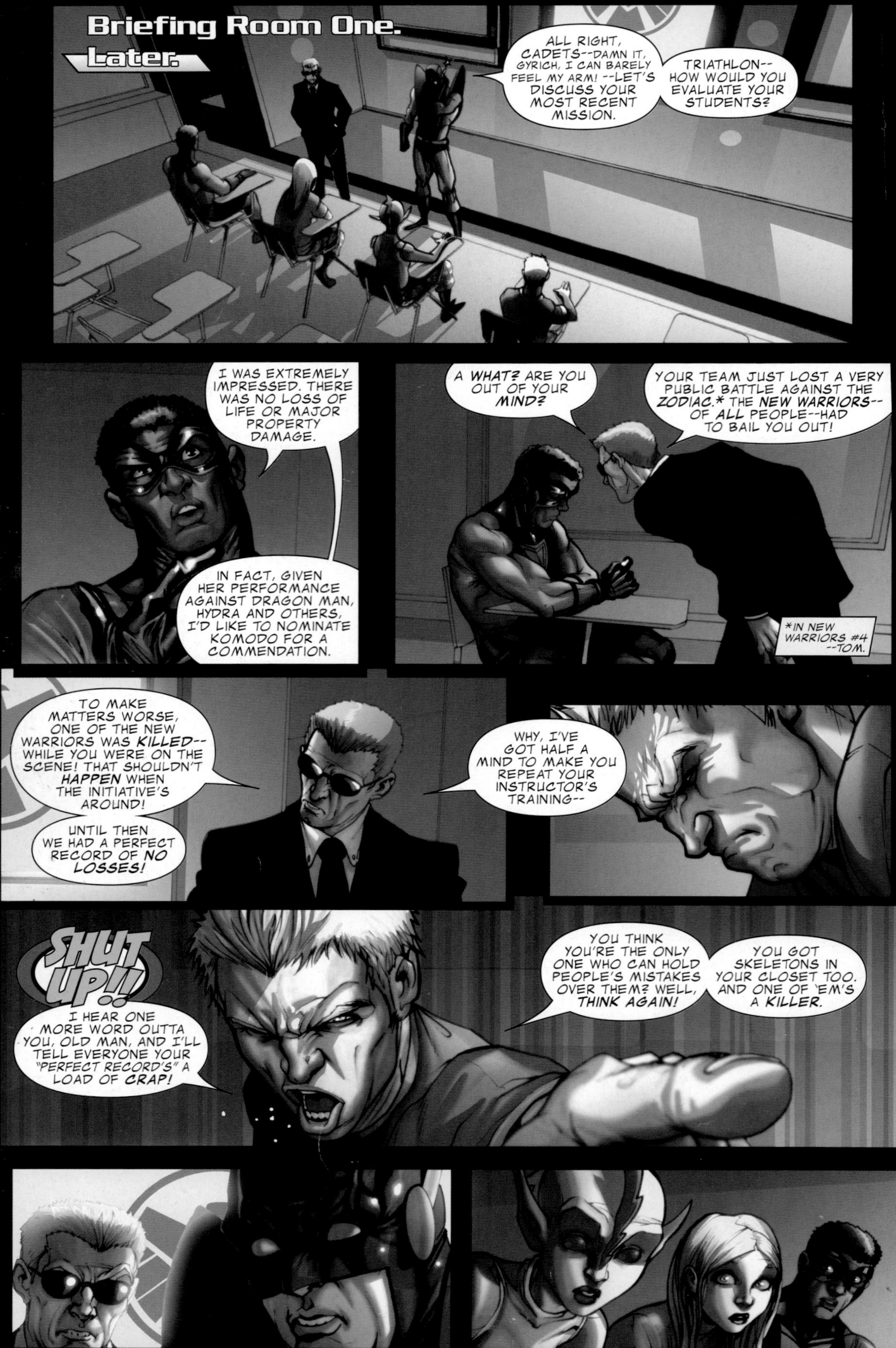

Briefing Room One.
Later.
ALL RIGHT, CADETS--DAMN IT, GYRICH, I CAN BARELY FEEL MY ARM! --LET'S DISCUSS YOUR MOST RECENT MISSION.
TRIATHLON--HOW WOULD YOU EVALUATE YOUR STUDENTS?
I WAS EXTREMELY IMPRESSED. THERE WAS NO LOSS OF LIFE OR MAJOR PROPERTY DAMAGE.
IN FACT, GIVEN HER PERFORMANCE AGAINST DRAGON MAN, HYDRA AND OTHERS, I'D LIKE TO NOMINATE KOMODO FOR A COMMENDATION.
A WHAT? ARE YOU OUT OF YOUR MIND?
YOUR TEAM JUST LOST A VERY PUBLIC BATTLE AGAINST THE ZODIAC.* THE NEW WARRIORS--OF ALL PEOPLE--HAD TO BAIL YOU OUT!
*IN NEW WARRIORS #4 --TOM.
TO MAKE MATTERS WORSE, ONE OF THE NEW WARRIORS WAS KILLED--WHILE YOU WERE ON THE SCENE! THAT SHOULDN'T HAPPEN WHEN THE INITIATIVE'S AROUND!
UNTIL THEN WE HAD A PERFECT RECORD OF NO LOSSES!
WHY, I'VE GOT HALF A MIND TO MAKE YOU REPEAT YOUR INSTRUCTOR'S TRAINING--
SHUT UP!!
I HEAR ONE MORE WORD OUTTA YOU, OLD MAN, AND I'LL TELL EVERYONE YOUR "PERFECT RECORD'S" A LOAD OF CRAP!
YOU THINK YOU'RE THE ONLY ONE WHO CAN HOLD PEOPLE'S MISTAKES OVER THEM? WELL, THINK AGAIN!
YOU GOT SKELETONS IN YOUR CLOSET TOO. AND ONE OF 'EM'S A KILLER.

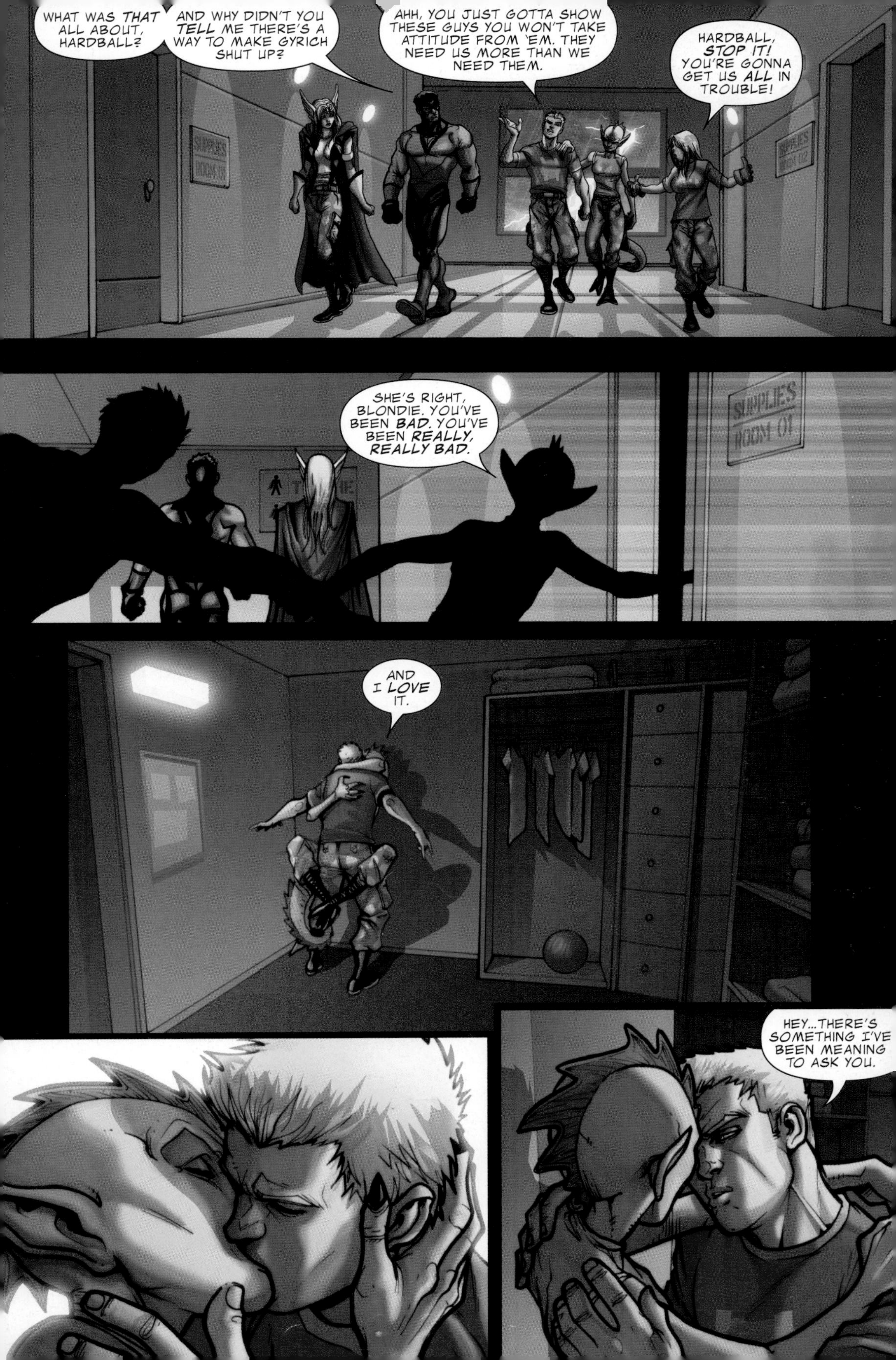
WHAT WAS THAT ALL ABOUT, HARDBALL?
AND WHY DIDN'T YOU TELL ME THERE'S A WAY TO MAKE GYRICH SHUT UP?
AHH, YOU JUST GOTTA SHOW THESE GUYS YOU WON'T TAKE ATTITUDE FROM 'EM. THEY NEED US MORE THAN WE NEED THEM.
HARDBALL, STOP IT! YOU'RE GONNA GET US ALL IN TROUBLE!
SUPPLIES ROOM 01
SUPPLIES ROOM 02
SHE'S RIGHT, BLONDIE. YOU'VE BEEN BAD. YOU'VE BEEN REALLY, REALLY BAD.
SUPPLIES ROOM 01
AND I LOVE IT.
HEY...THERE'S SOMETHING I'VE BEEN MEANING TO ASK YOU.

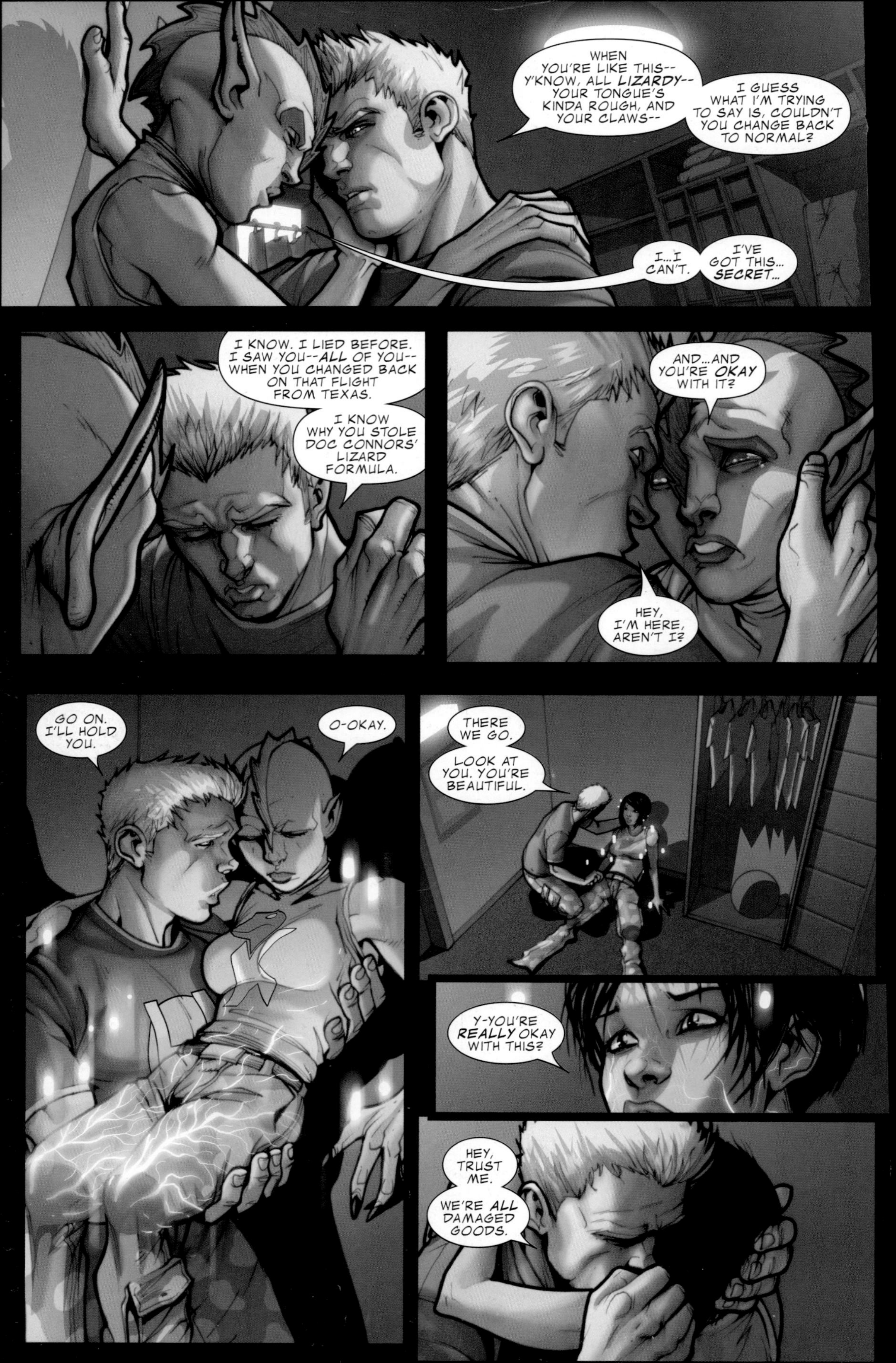
WHEN YOU'RE LIKE THIS-- Y'KNOW, ALL LIZARDY-- YOUR TONGUE'S KINDA ROUGH, AND YOUR CLAWS--
I GUESS WHAT I'M TRYING TO SAY IS, COULDN'T YOU CHANGE BACK TO NORMAL?
I...I CAN'T.
I'VE GOT THIS... SECRET...
I KNOW. I LIED BEFORE. I SAW YOU--ALL OF YOU-- WHEN YOU CHANGED BACK ON THAT FLIGHT FROM TEXAS.
I KNOW WHY YOU STOLE DOC CONNORS' LIZARD FORMULA.
AND...AND YOU'RE OKAY WITH IT?
HEY, I'M HERE, AREN'T I?
GO ON. I'LL HOLD YOU.
O-OKAY.
THERE WE GO.
LOOK AT YOU. YOU'RE BEAUTIFUL.
Y-YOU'RE REALLY OKAY WITH THIS?
HEY, TRUST ME.
WE'RE ALL DAMAGED GOODS.

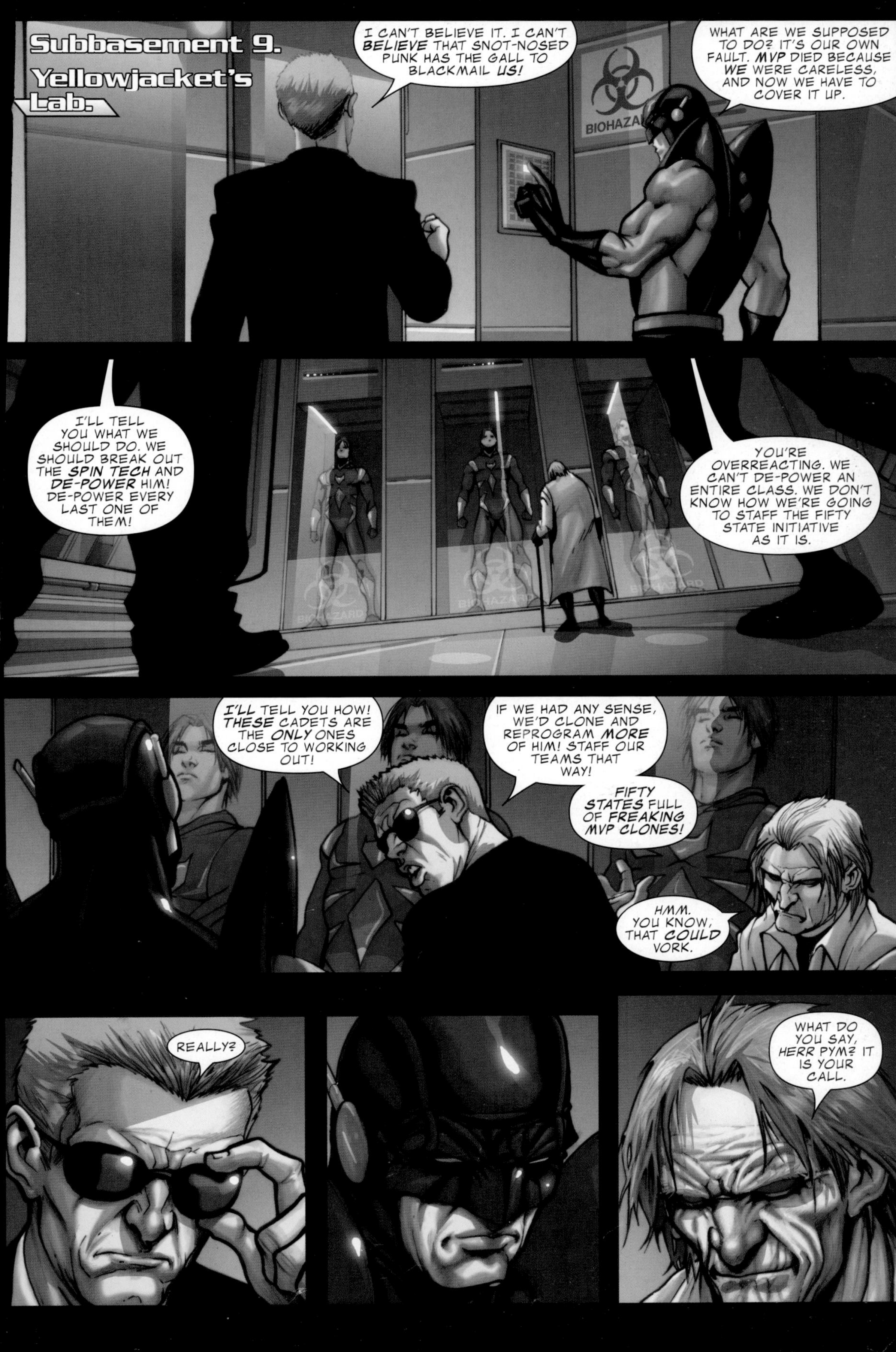
Subbasement 9.
Yellowjacket's Lab.
I CAN'T BELIEVE IT. I CAN'T BELIEVE THAT SNOT-NOSED PUNK HAS THE GALL TO BLACKMAIL US!
WHAT ARE WE SUPPOSED TO DO? IT'S OUR OWN FAULT. MVP DIED BECAUSE WE WERE CARELESS, AND NOW WE HAVE TO COVER IT UP.
BIOHAZARD
I'LL TELL YOU WHAT WE SHOULD DO. WE SHOULD BREAK OUT THE SPIN TECH AND DE-POWER HIM! DE-POWER EVERY LAST ONE OF THEM!
YOU'RE OVERREACTING. WE CAN'T DE-POWER AN ENTIRE CLASS. WE DON'T KNOW HOW WE'RE GOING TO STAFF THE FIFTY STATE INITIATIVE AS IT IS.
I'LL TELL YOU HOW! THESE CADETS ARE THE ONLY ONES CLOSE TO WORKING OUT!
IF WE HAD ANY SENSE, WE'D CLONE AND REPROGRAM MORE OF HIM! STAFF OUR TEAMS THAT WAY!
FIFTY STATES FULL OF FREAKING MVP CLONES!
HMM. YOU KNOW, THAT COULD VORK.
REALLY?
WHAT DO YOU SAY, HERR PYM? IT IS YOUR CALL.

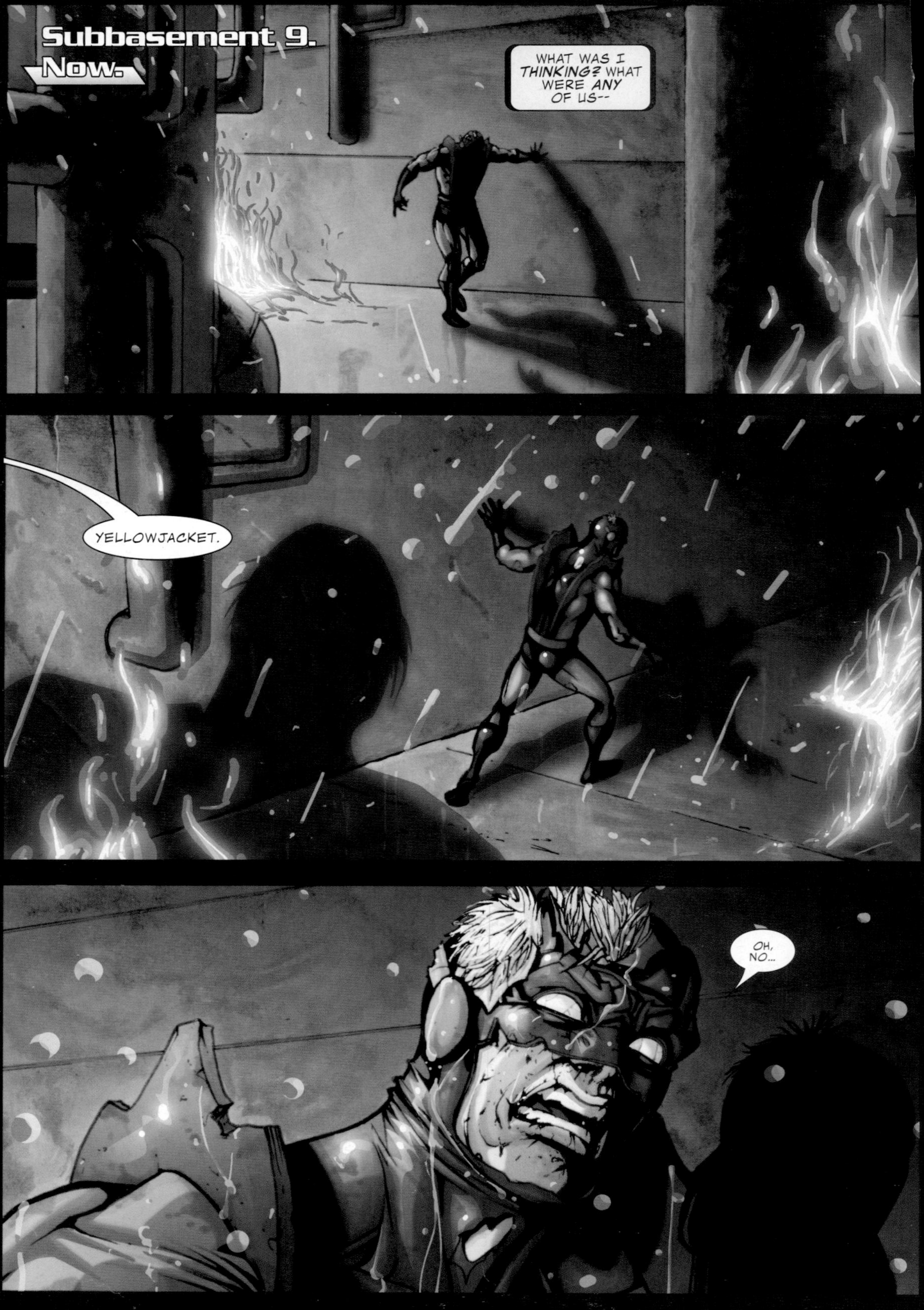
Subbasement 9.
Now.
WHAT WAS I THINKING? WHAT WERE ANY OF US--
YELLOWJACKET.
OH, NO...

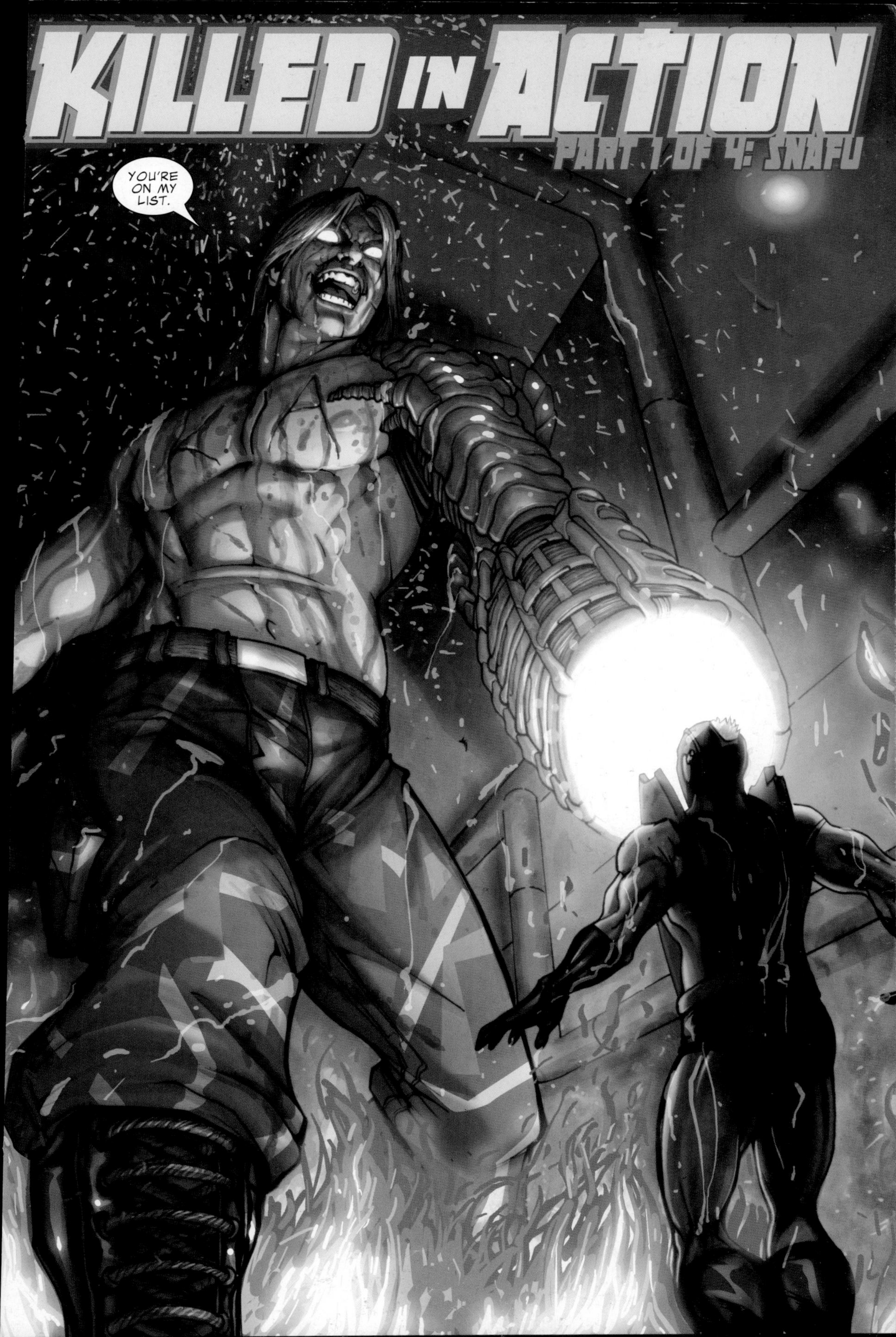
KILLED IN ACTION
PART 1 OF 4: SNAFU
YOU'RE ON MY LIST.

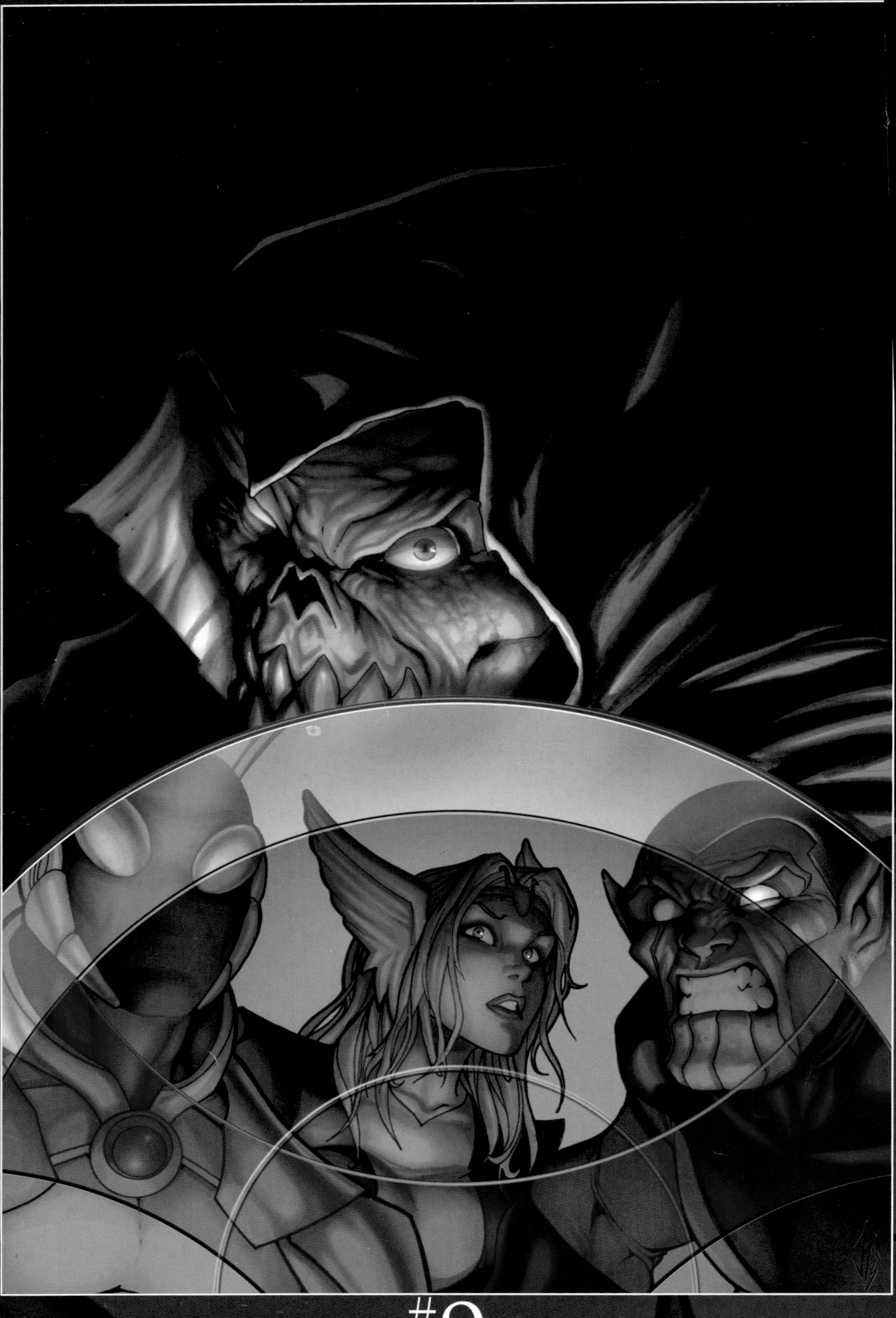

#9

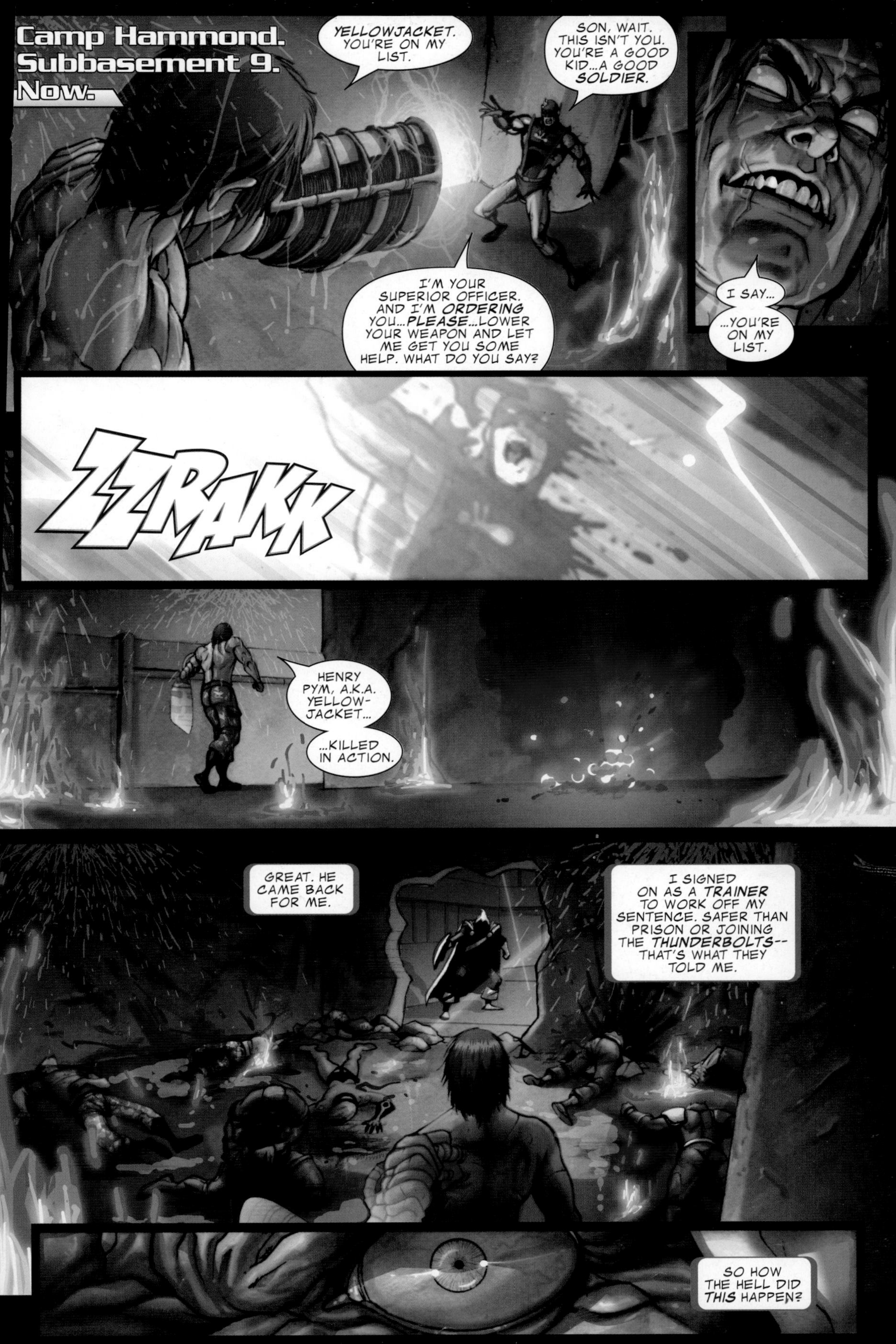
Camp Hammond. Subbasement 9. Now.
YELLOWJACKET. YOU'RE ON MY LIST.
SON, WAIT. THIS ISN'T YOU. YOU'RE A GOOD KID...A GOOD SOLDIER.
I'M YOUR SUPERIOR OFFICER. AND I'M ORDERING YOU...PLEASE...LOWER YOUR WEAPON AND LET ME GET YOU SOME HELP. WHAT DO YOU SAY?
I SAY...
...YOU'RE ON MY LIST.
ZZRAKK
HENRY PYM, A.K.A. YELLOW-JACKET...
...KILLED IN ACTION.
GREAT. HE CAME BACK FOR ME.
I SIGNED ON AS A TRAINER TO WORK OFF MY SENTENCE. SAFER THAN PRISON OR JOINING THE THUNDERBOLTS--THAT'S WHAT THEY TOLD ME.
SO HOW THE HELL DID THIS HAPPEN?

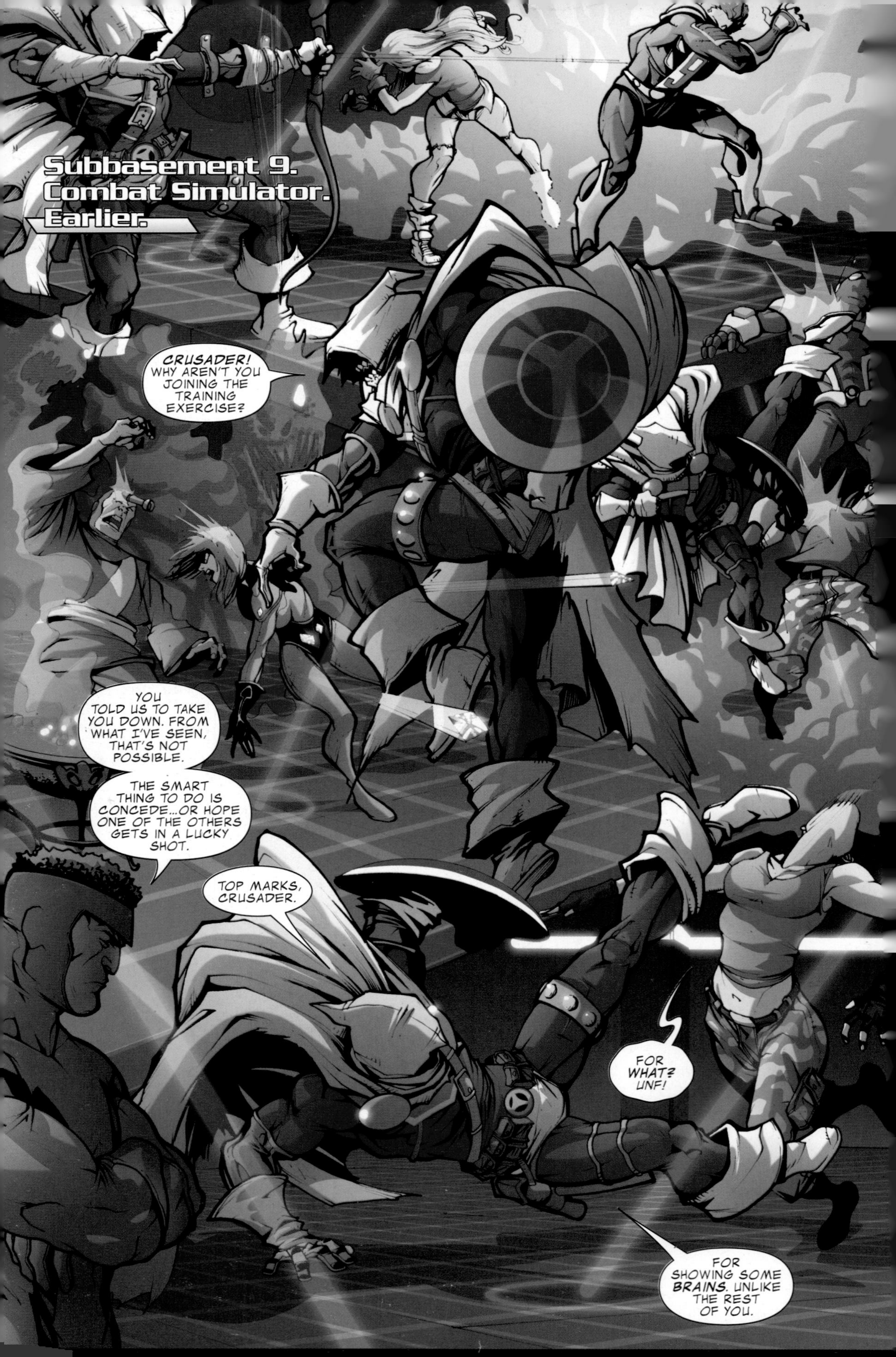
Subbasement 9. Combat Simulator. Earlier.
CRUSADER! WHY AREN'T YOU JOINING THE TRAINING EXERCISE?
YOU TOLD US TO TAKE YOU DOWN. FROM WHAT I'VE SEEN, THAT'S NOT POSSIBLE.
THE SMART THING TO DO IS CONCEDE...OR HOPE ONE OF THE OTHERS GETS IN A LUCKY SHOT.
TOP MARKS, CRUSADER.
FOR WHAT? UNF!
FOR SHOWING SOME BRAINS. UNLIKE THE REST OF YOU.

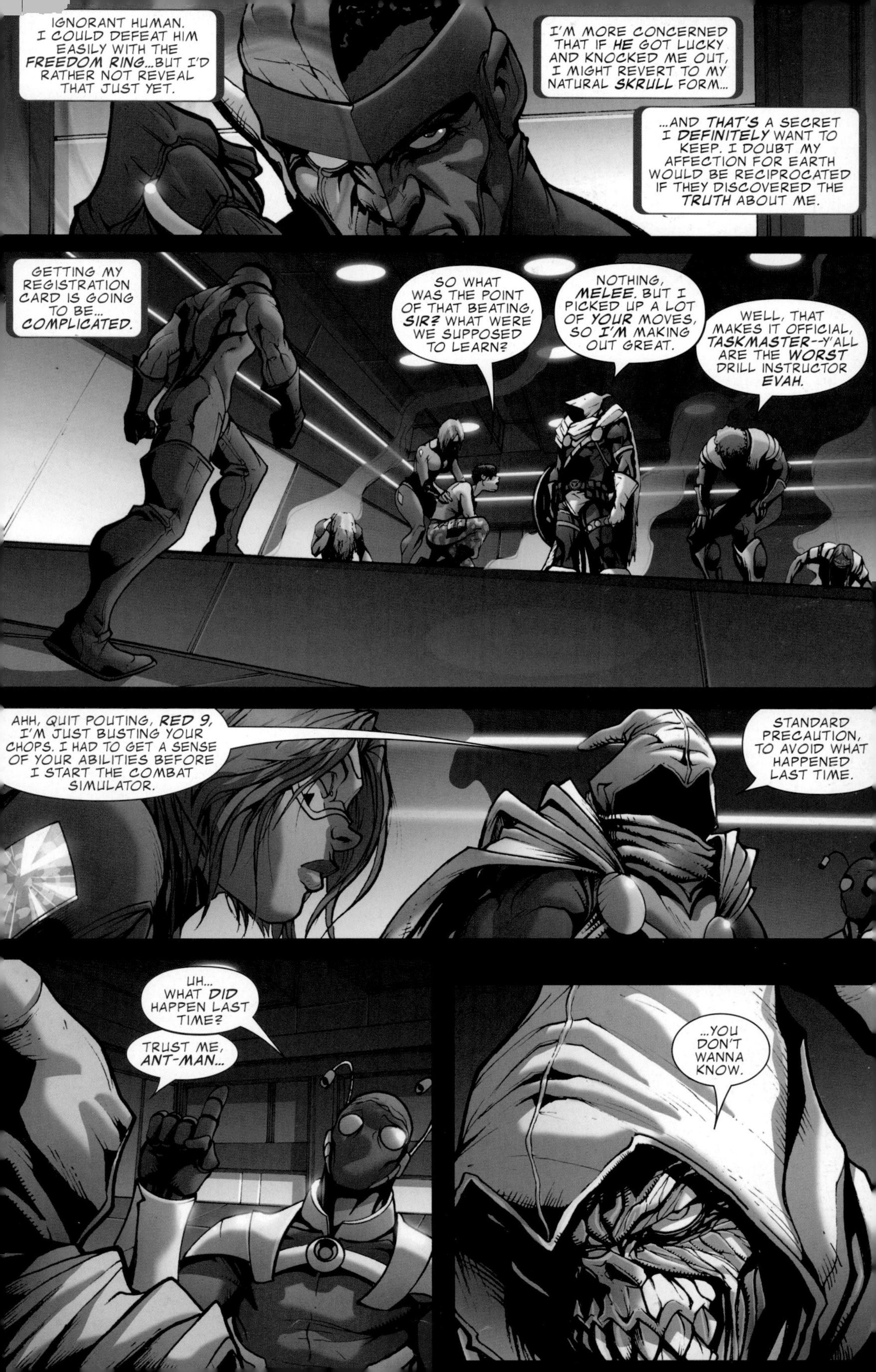
IGNORANT HUMAN. I COULD DEFEAT HIM EASILY WITH THE FREEDOM RING...BUT I'D RATHER NOT REVEAL THAT JUST YET.
I'M MORE CONCERNED THAT IF HE GOT LUCKY AND KNOCKED ME OUT, I MIGHT REVERT TO MY NATURAL SKRULL FORM...
...AND THAT'S A SECRET I DEFINITELY WANT TO KEEP. I DOUBT MY AFFECTION FOR EARTH WOULD BE RECIPROCATED IF THEY DISCOVERED THE TRUTH ABOUT ME.
GETTING MY REGISTRATION CARD IS GOING TO BE... COMPLICATED.
SO WHAT WAS THE POINT OF THAT BEATING, SIR? WHAT WERE WE SUPPOSED TO LEARN?
NOTHING, MELEE. BUT I PICKED UP A LOT OF YOUR MOVES, SO I'M MAKING OUT GREAT.
WELL, THAT MAKES IT OFFICIAL, TASKMASTER--Y'ALL ARE THE WORST DRILL INSTRUCTOR EVAH.
AHH, QUIT POUTING, RED 9, I'M JUST BUSTING YOUR CHOPS. I HAD TO GET A SENSE OF YOUR ABILITIES BEFORE I START THE COMBAT SIMULATOR.
STANDARD PRECAUTION, TO AVOID WHAT HAPPENED LAST TIME.
UH... WHAT DID HAPPEN LAST TIME?
TRUST ME, ANT-MAN...
...YOU DON'T WANNA KNOW.

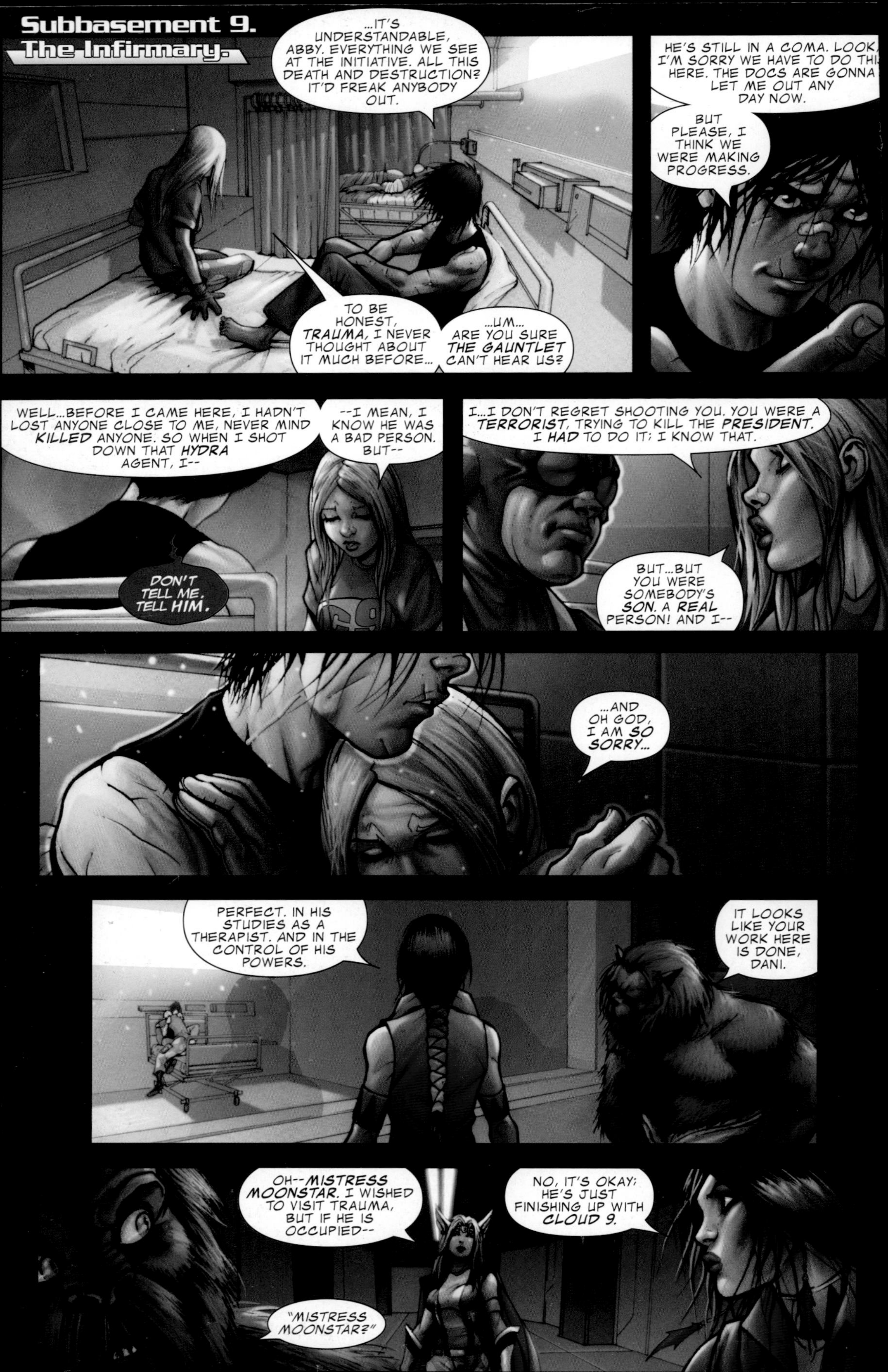
Subbasement 9.
The Infirmary.
...IT'S UNDERSTANDABLE, ABBY. EVERYTHING WE SEE AT THE INITIATIVE. ALL THIS DEATH AND DESTRUCTION? IT'D FREAK ANYBODY OUT.
TO BE HONEST, TRAUMA, I NEVER THOUGHT ABOUT IT MUCH BEFORE...
...UM... ARE YOU SURE THE GAUNTLET CAN'T HEAR US?
HE'S STILL IN A COMA. LOOK, I'M SORRY WE HAVE TO DO THIS HERE. THE DOCS ARE GONNA LET ME OUT ANY DAY NOW.
BUT PLEASE, I THINK WE WERE MAKING PROGRESS.
WELL...BEFORE I CAME HERE, I HADN'T LOST ANYONE CLOSE TO ME, NEVER MIND KILLED ANYONE. SO WHEN I SHOT DOWN THAT HYDRA AGENT, I--
--I MEAN, I KNOW HE WAS A BAD PERSON. BUT--
DON'T TELL ME. TELL HIM.
I...I DON'T REGRET SHOOTING YOU. YOU WERE A TERRORIST, TRYING TO KILL THE PRESIDENT. I HAD TO DO IT; I KNOW THAT.
BUT...BUT YOU WERE SOMEBODY'S SON. A REAL PERSON! AND I--
...AND OH GOD, I AM SO SORRY...
PERFECT. IN HIS STUDIES AS A THERAPIST. AND IN THE CONTROL OF HIS POWERS.
IT LOOKS LIKE YOUR WORK HERE IS DONE, DANI.
OH--MISTRESS MOONSTAR. I WISHED TO VISIT TRAUMA, BUT IF HE IS OCCUPIED--
NO, IT'S OKAY; HE'S JUST FINISHING UP WITH CLOUD 9.
"MISTRESS MOONSTAR?"

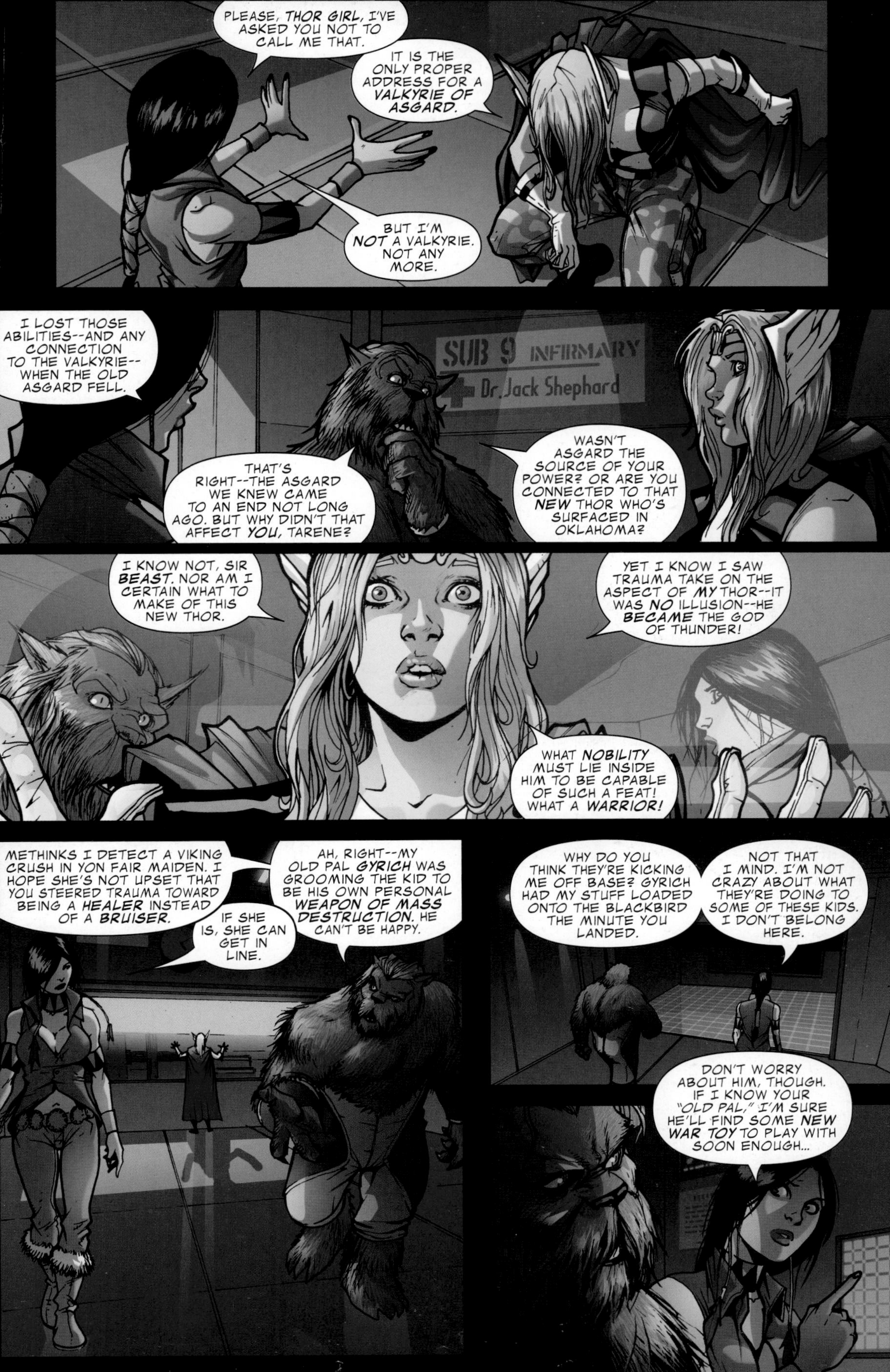
PLEASE, THOR GIRL, I'VE ASKED YOU NOT TO CALL ME THAT.
IT IS THE ONLY PROPER ADDRESS FOR A VALKYRIE OF ASGARD.
BUT I'M NOT A VALKYRIE. NOT ANY MORE.
I LOST THOSE ABILITIES--AND ANY CONNECTION TO THE VALKYRIE--WHEN THE OLD ASGARD FELL.
SUB 9 INFIRMARY
Dr. Jack Shephard
THAT'S RIGHT--THE ASGARD WE KNEW CAME TO AN END NOT LONG AGO. BUT WHY DIDN'T THAT AFFECT YOU, TARENE?
WASN'T ASGARD THE SOURCE OF YOUR POWER? OR ARE YOU CONNECTED TO THAT NEW THOR WHO'S SURFACED IN OKLAHOMA?
I KNOW NOT, SIR BEAST. NOR AM I CERTAIN WHAT TO MAKE OF THIS NEW THOR.
YET I KNOW I SAW TRAUMA TAKE ON THE ASPECT OF MY THOR--IT WAS NO ILLUSION--HE BECAME THE GOD OF THUNDER!
WHAT NOBILITY MUST LIE INSIDE HIM TO BE CAPABLE OF SUCH A FEAT! WHAT A WARRIOR!
METHINKS I DETECT A VIKING CRUSH IN YON FAIR MAIDEN. I HOPE SHE'S NOT UPSET THAT YOU STEERED TRAUMA TOWARD BEING A HEALER INSTEAD OF A BRUISER.
IF SHE IS, SHE CAN GET IN LINE.
AH, RIGHT--MY OLD PAL GYRICH WAS GROOMING THE KID TO BE HIS OWN PERSONAL WEAPON OF MASS DESTRUCTION. HE CAN'T BE HAPPY.
WHY DO YOU THINK THEY'RE KICKING ME OFF BASE? GYRICH HAD MY STUFF LOADED ONTO THE BLACKBIRD THE MINUTE YOU LANDED.
NOT THAT I MIND. I'M NOT CRAZY ABOUT WHAT THEY'RE DOING TO SOME OF THESE KIDS. I DON'T BELONG HERE.
DON'T WORRY ABOUT HIM, THOUGH. IF I KNOW YOUR "OLD PAL," I'M SURE HE'LL FIND SOME NEW WAR TOY TO PLAY WITH SOON ENOUGH...

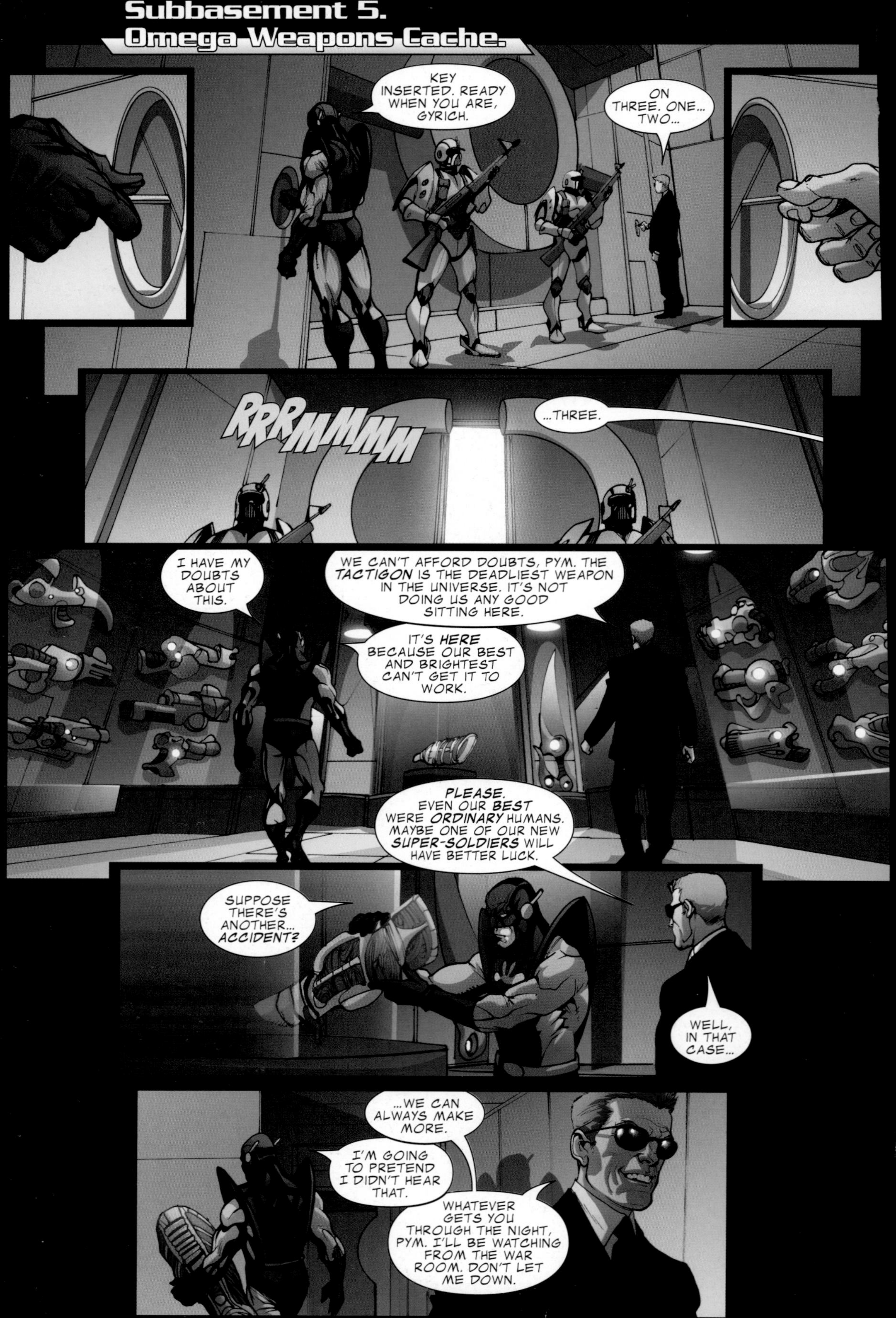

Subbasement 5.
Omega Weapons Cache.
KEY INSERTED. READY WHEN YOU ARE, GYRICH.
ON THREE. ONE... TWO...
RRRMMMMM
...THREE.
I HAVE MY DOUBTS ABOUT THIS.
WE CAN'T AFFORD DOUBTS, PYM. THE TACTIGON IS THE DEADLIEST WEAPON IN THE UNIVERSE. IT'S NOT DOING US ANY GOOD SITTING HERE.
IT'S HERE BECAUSE OUR BEST AND BRIGHTEST CAN'T GET IT TO WORK.
PLEASE. EVEN OUR BEST WERE ORDINARY HUMANS. MAYBE ONE OF OUR NEW SUPER-SOLDIERS WILL HAVE BETTER LUCK.
SUPPOSE THERE'S ANOTHER... ACCIDENT?
WELL, IN THAT CASE...
...WE CAN ALWAYS MAKE MORE.
I'M GOING TO PRETEND I DIDN'T HEAR THAT.
WHATEVER GETS YOU THROUGH THE NIGHT, PYM. I'LL BE WATCHING FROM THE WAR ROOM. DON'T LET ME DOWN.

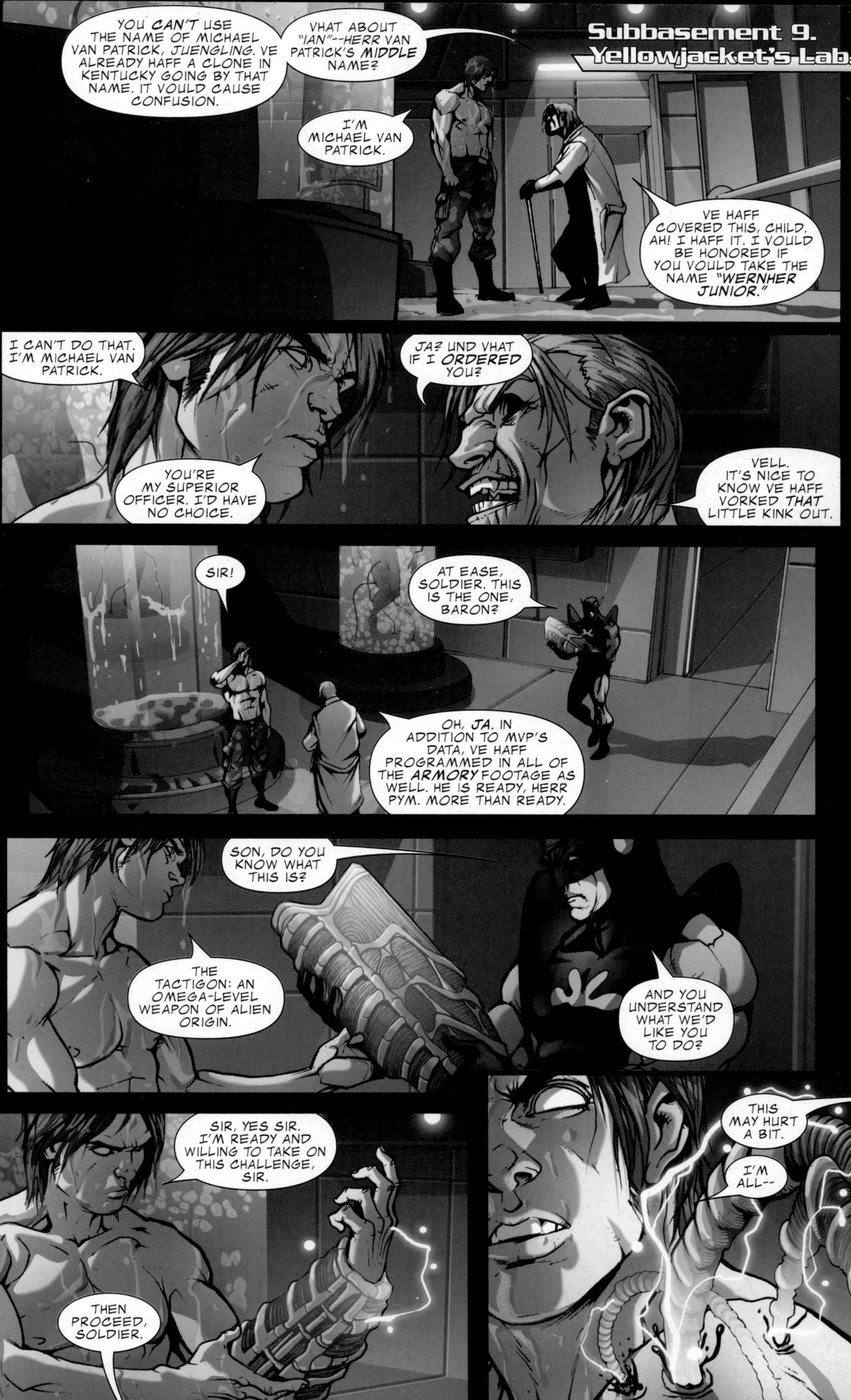

Subbasement 9. Yellowjacket's Lab.
YOU CAN'T USE THE NAME OF MICHAEL VAN PATRICK, JUENGLING. VE ALREADY HAFF A CLONE IN KENTUCKY GOING BY THAT NAME. IT VOULD CAUSE CONFUSION.
VHAT ABOUT "IAN"--HERR VAN PATRICK'S MIDDLE NAME?
I'M MICHAEL VAN PATRICK.
VE HAFF COVERED THIS, CHILD. AH! I HAFF IT. I VOULD BE HONORED IF YOU VOULD TAKE THE NAME "WERNHER JUNIOR."
I CAN'T DO THAT. I'M MICHAEL VAN PATRICK.
JA? UND VHAT IF I ORDERED YOU?
YOU'RE MY SUPERIOR OFFICER. I'D HAVE NO CHOICE.
VELL. IT'S NICE TO KNOW VE HAFF VORKED THAT LITTLE KINK OUT.
SIR!
AT EASE, SOLDIER. THIS IS THE ONE, BARON?
OH, JA. IN ADDITION TO MVP'S DATA, VE HAFF PROGRAMMED IN ALL OF THE ARMORY FOOTAGE AS WELL. HE IS READY, HERR PYM. MORE THAN READY.
SON, DO YOU KNOW WHAT THIS IS?
THE TACTIGON: AN OMEGA-LEVEL WEAPON OF ALIEN ORIGIN.
AND YOU UNDERSTAND WHAT WE'D LIKE YOU TO DO?
SIR, YES SIR. I'M READY AND WILLING TO TAKE ON THIS CHALLENGE, SIR.
THEN PROCEED, SOLDIER.
THIS MAY HURT A BIT.
I'M ALL--

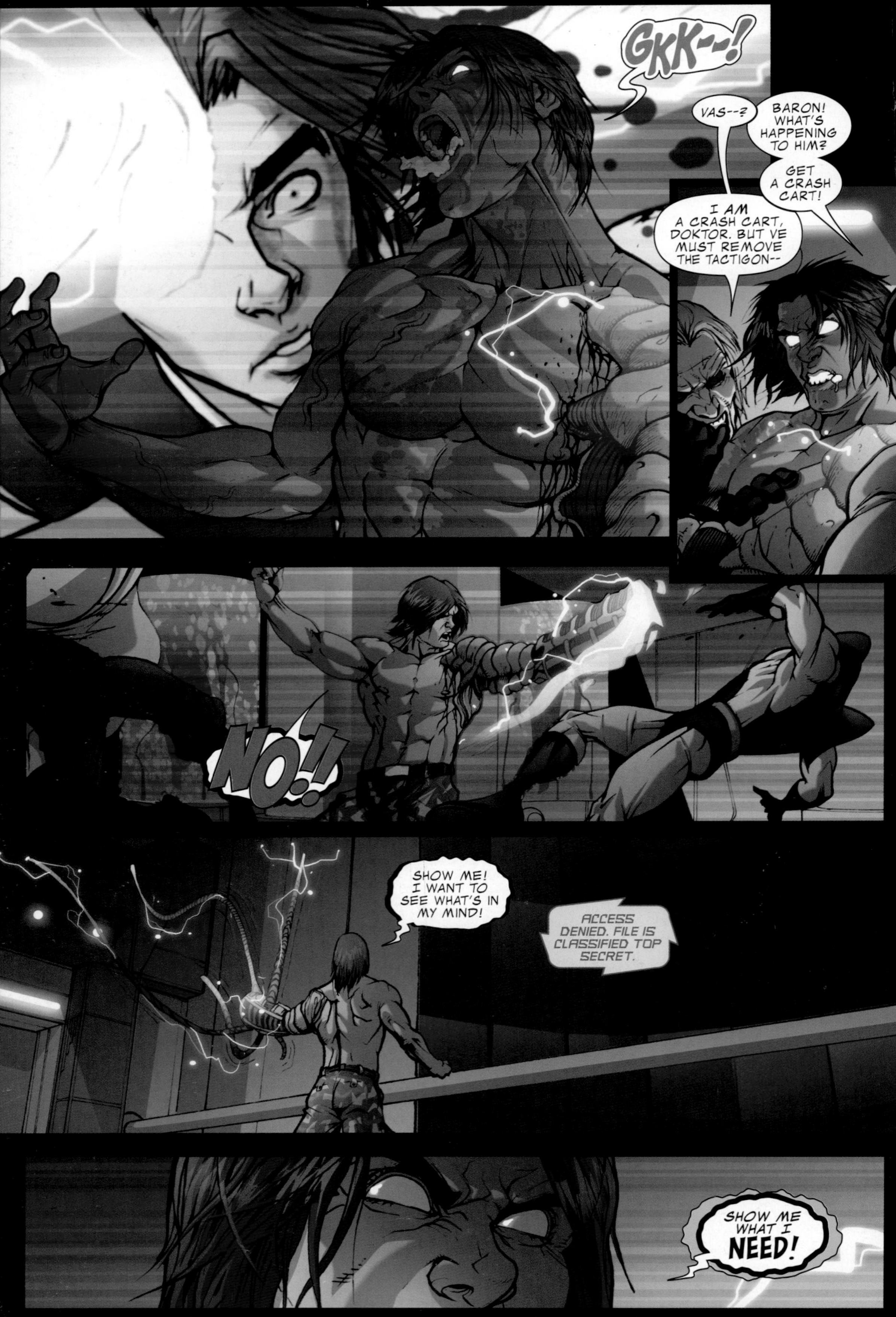
GKK--!
VAS--?
BARON! WHAT'S HAPPENING TO HIM?
GET A CRASH CART!
I AM A CRASH CART, DOKTOR. BUT VE MUST REMOVE THE TACTIGON--
NO!!
SHOW ME! I WANT TO SEE WHAT'S IN MY MIND!
ACCESS DENIED. FILE IS CLASSIFIED TOP SECRET.
SHOW ME WHAT I NEED!

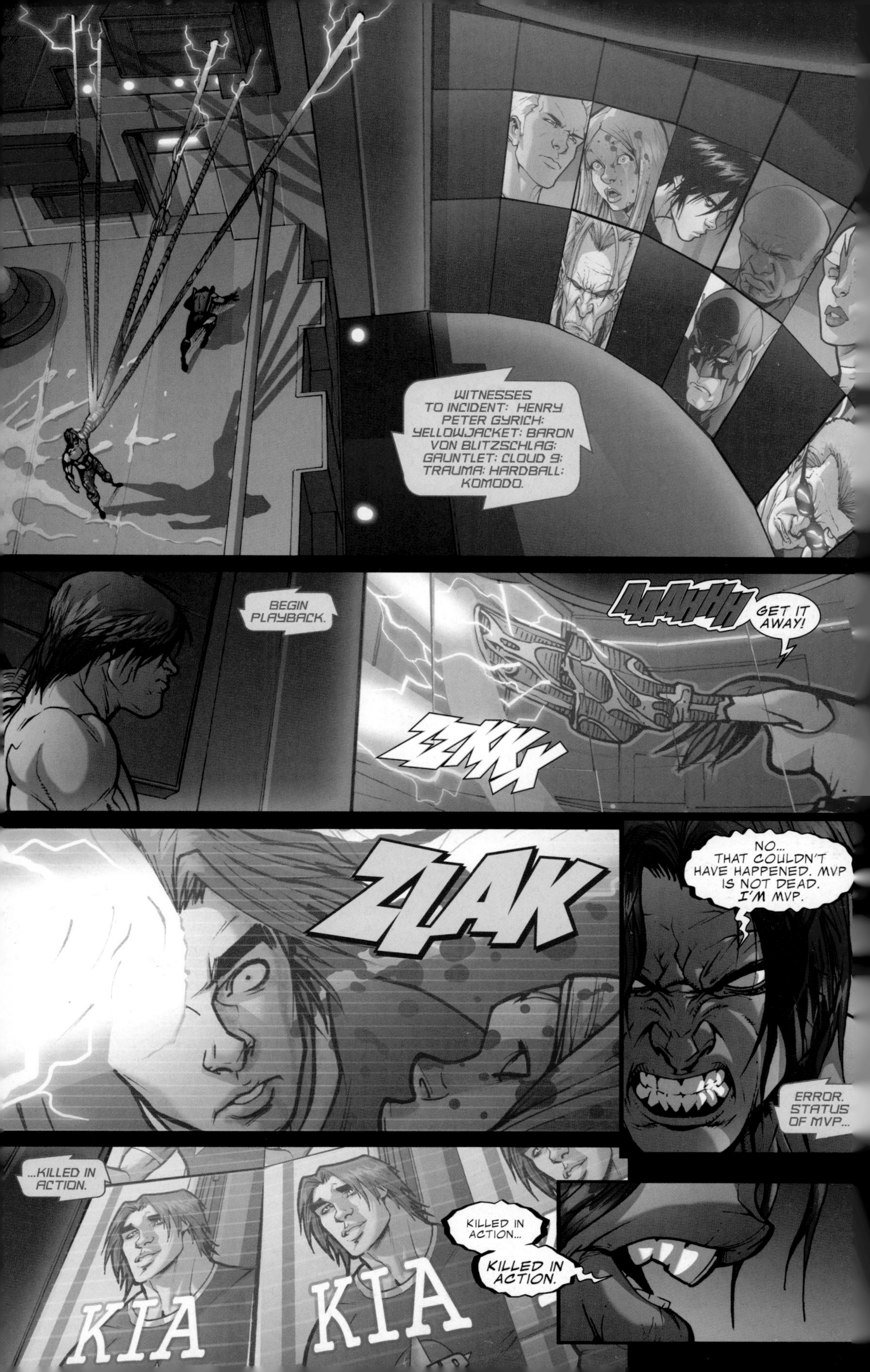
WITNESSES TO INCIDENT: HENRY PETER GYRICH; YELLOWJACKET; BARON VON BLITZSCHLAG; GAUNTLET; CLOUD 9; TRAUMA; HARDBALL; KOMODO.
BEGIN PLAYBACK.
AAAHHH
GET IT AWAY!
ZZZKKK
ZZAK
NO... THAT COULDN'T HAVE HAPPENED. MVP IS NOT DEAD. I'M MVP.
ERROR. STATUS OF MVP...
...KILLED IN ACTION.
KILLED IN ACTION...
KILLED IN ACTION.
KIA
KIA

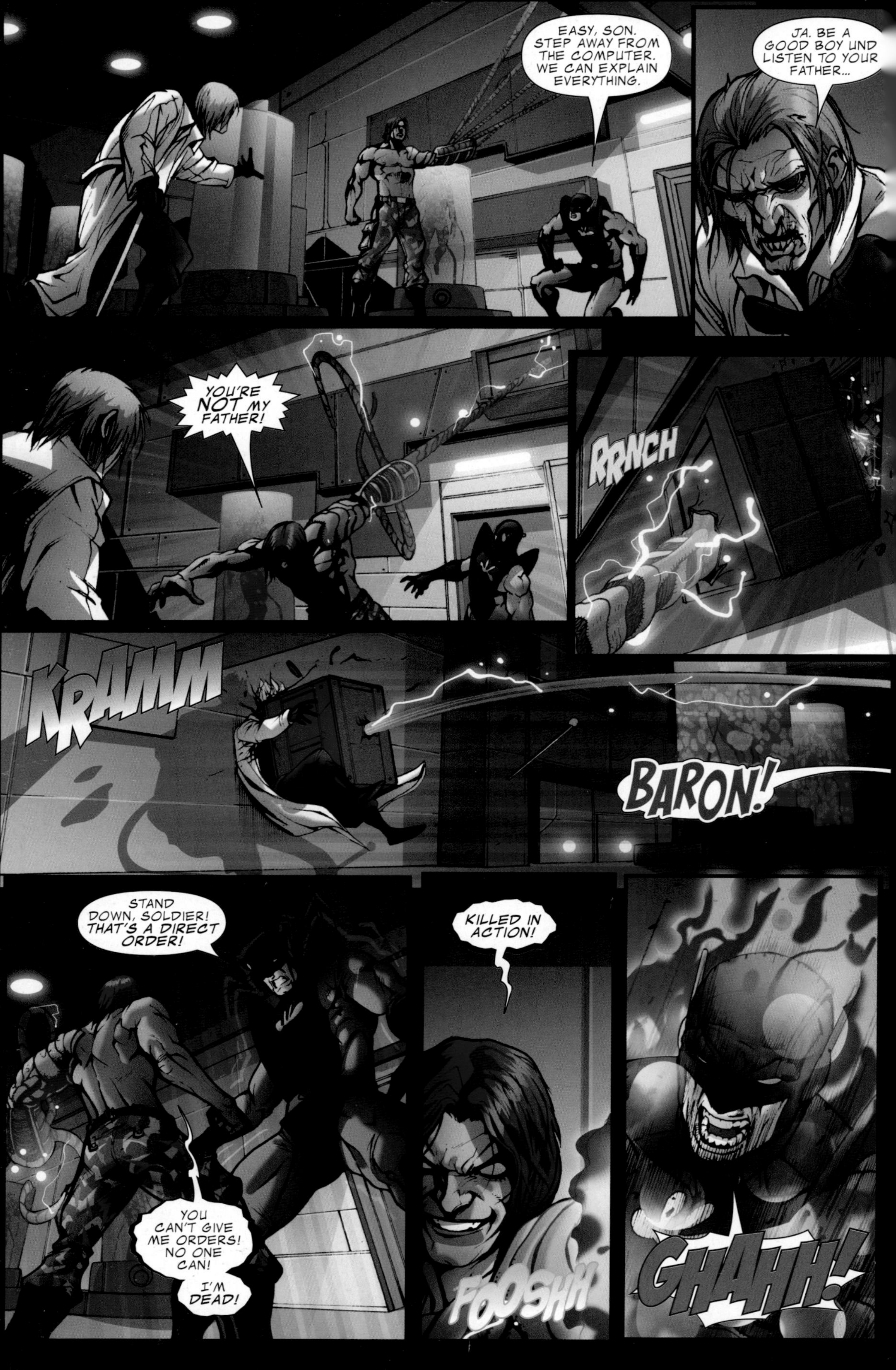
EASY, SON. STEP AWAY FROM THE COMPUTER. WE CAN EXPLAIN EVERYTHING.
JA. BE A GOOD BOY UND LISTEN TO YOUR FATHER...
YOU'RE NOT MY FATHER!
RRNCH
KRAMM
BARON!
STAND DOWN, SOLDIER! THAT'S A DIRECT ORDER!
YOU CAN'T GIVE ME ORDERS! NO ONE CAN!
I'M DEAD!
KILLED IN ACTION!
FOOSHH
GHAHH!

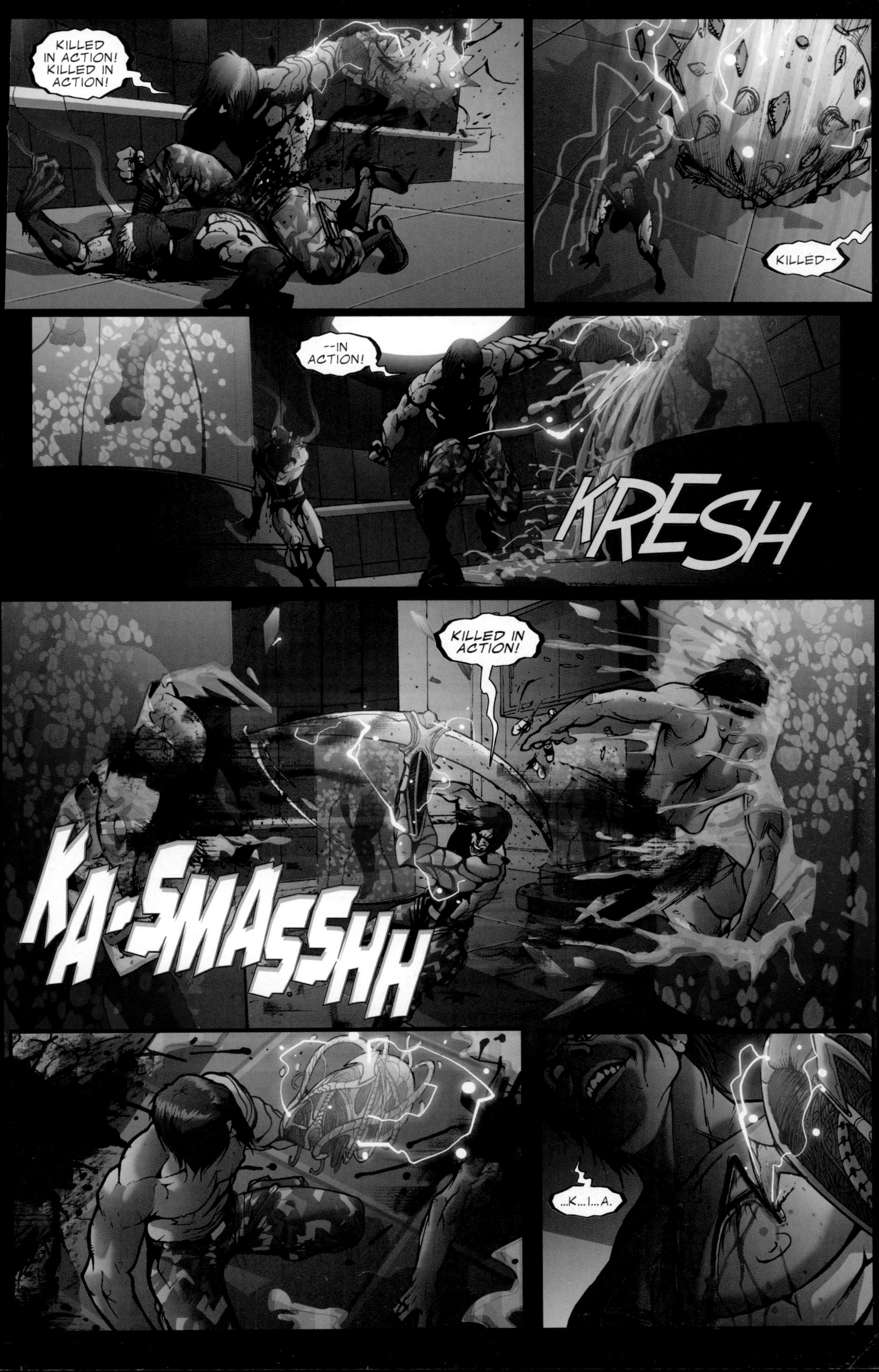
KILLED IN ACTION! KILLED IN ACTION!
KILLED--
--IN ACTION!
KRESH
KILLED IN ACTION!
KA-SMASSHH
...K...I...A.

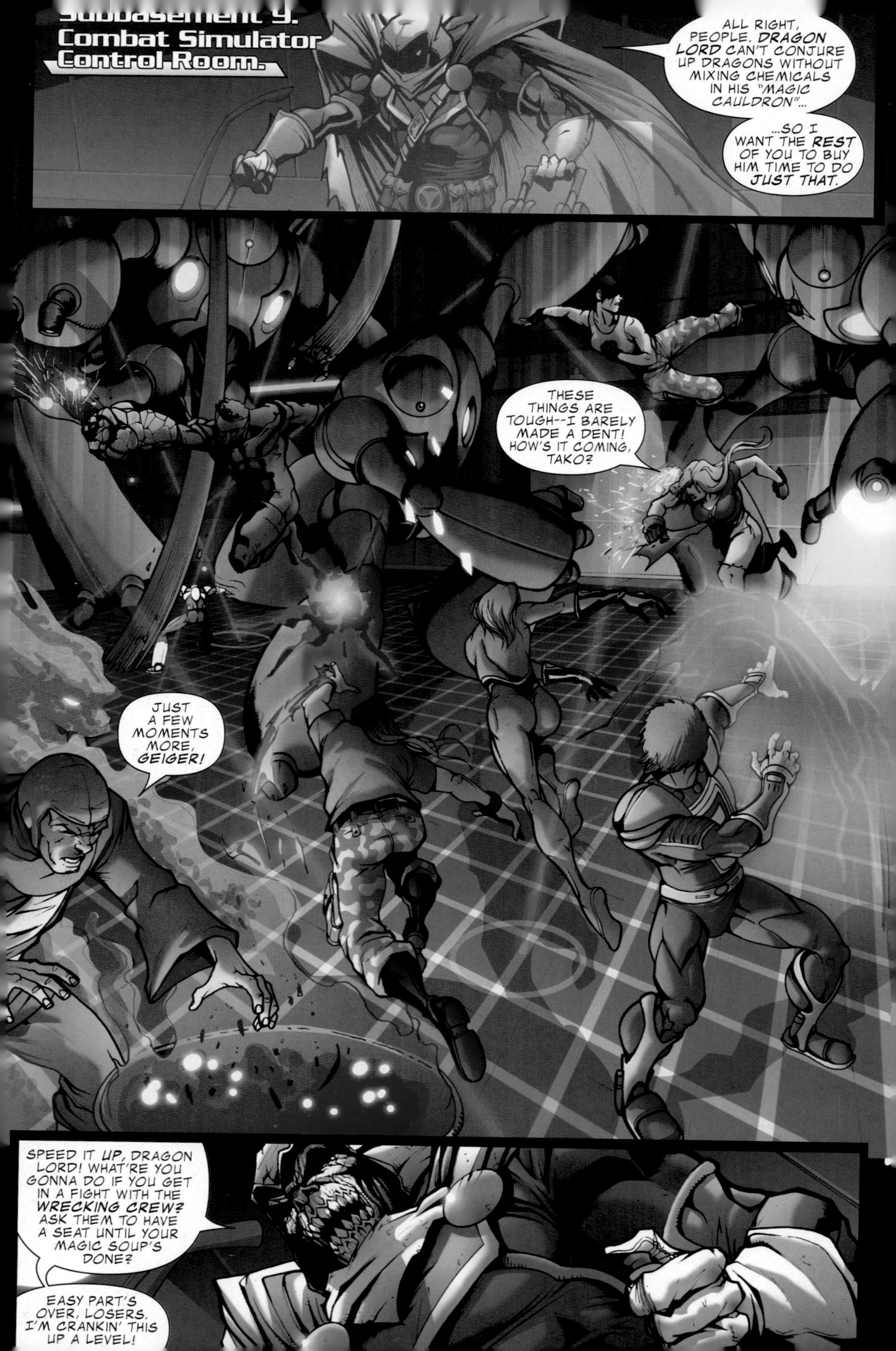
Subbasement 9. Combat Simulator Control Room.
ALL RIGHT, PEOPLE. DRAGON LORD CAN'T CONJURE UP DRAGONS WITHOUT MIXING CHEMICALS IN HIS "MAGIC CAULDRON"...
...SO I WANT THE REST OF YOU TO BUY HIM TIME TO DO JUST THAT.
THESE THINGS ARE TOUGH--I BARELY MADE A DENT! HOW'S IT COMING, TAKO?
JUST A FEW MOMENTS MORE, GEIGER!
SPEED IT UP, DRAGON LORD! WHAT'RE YOU GONNA DO IF YOU GET IN A FIGHT WITH THE WRECKING CREW? ASK THEM TO HAVE A SEAT UNTIL YOUR MAGIC SOUP'S DONE?
EASY PART'S OVER, LOSERS. I'M CRANKIN' THIS UP A LEVEL!

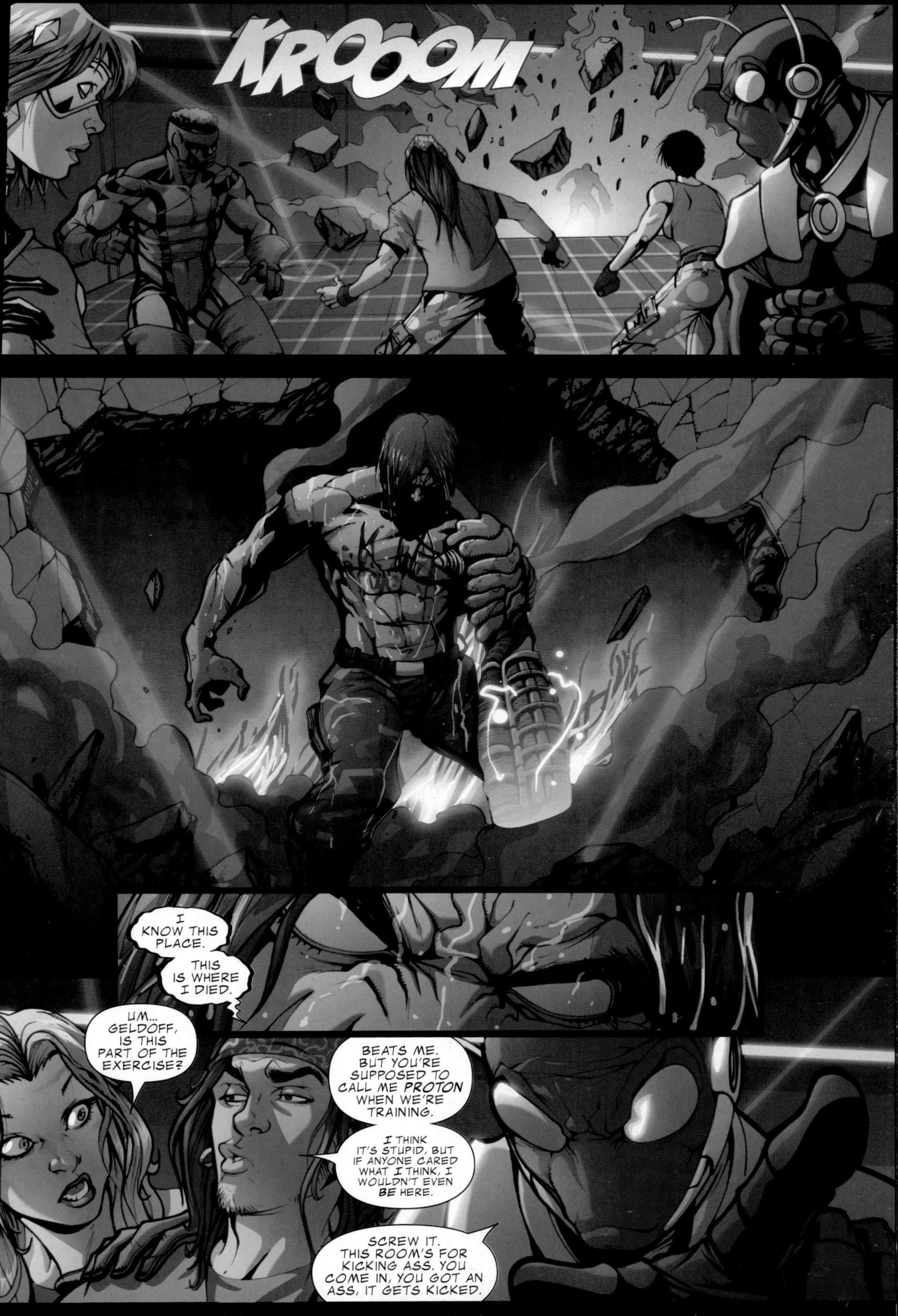
KROOOM
I KNOW THIS PLACE.
THIS IS WHERE I DIED.
UM... GELDOFF, IS THIS PART OF THE EXERCISE?
BEATS ME. BUT YOU'RE SUPPOSED TO CALL ME PROTON WHEN WE'RE TRAINING.
I THINK IT'S STUPID, BUT IF ANYONE CARED WHAT I THINK, I WOULDN'T EVEN BE HERE.
SCREW IT. THIS ROOM'S FOR KICKING ASS. YOU COME IN, YOU GOT AN ASS, IT GETS KICKED.

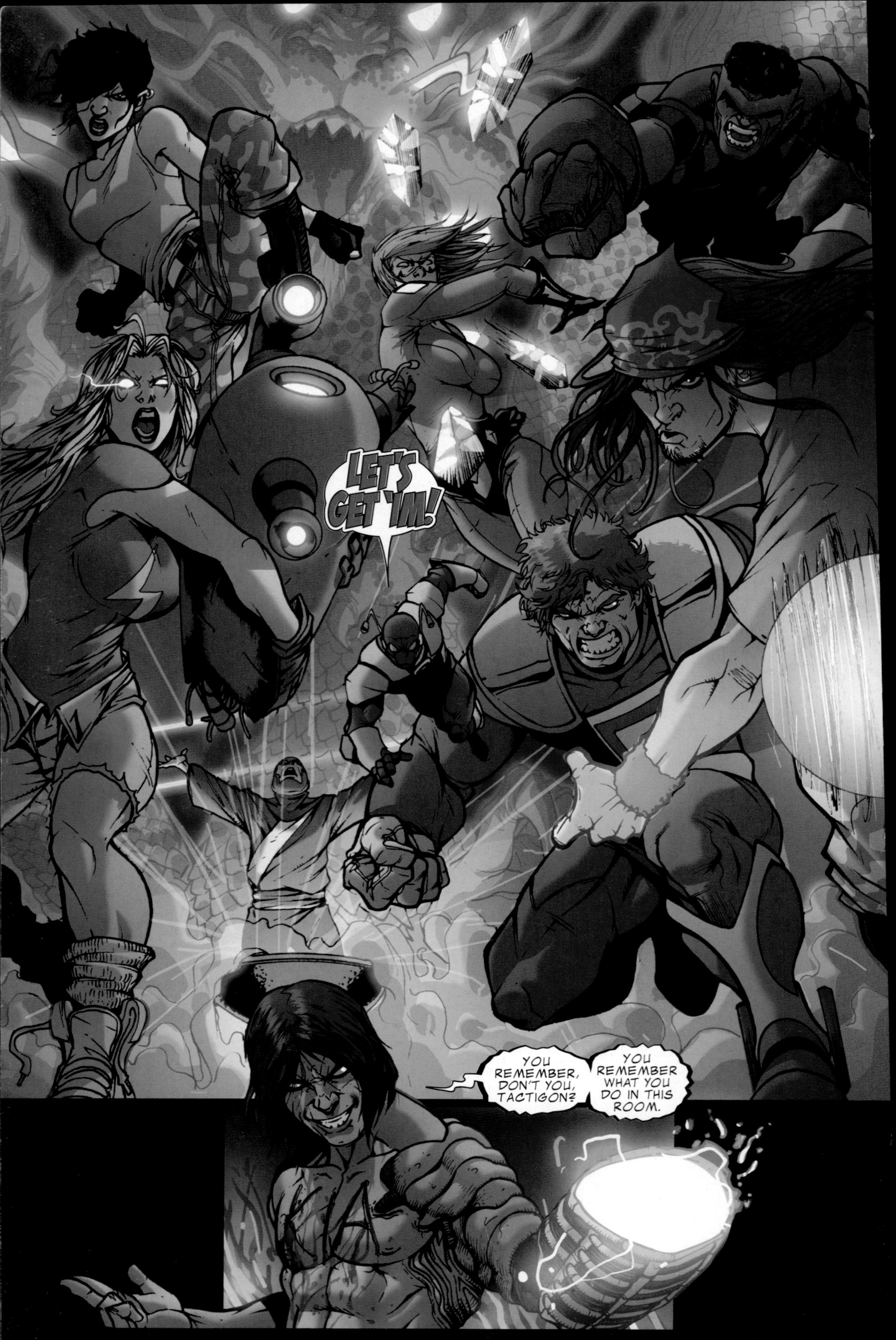
LET'S GET 'IM!
YOU REMEMBER, DON'T YOU, TACTIGON?
YOU REMEMBER WHAT YOU DO IN THIS ROOM.

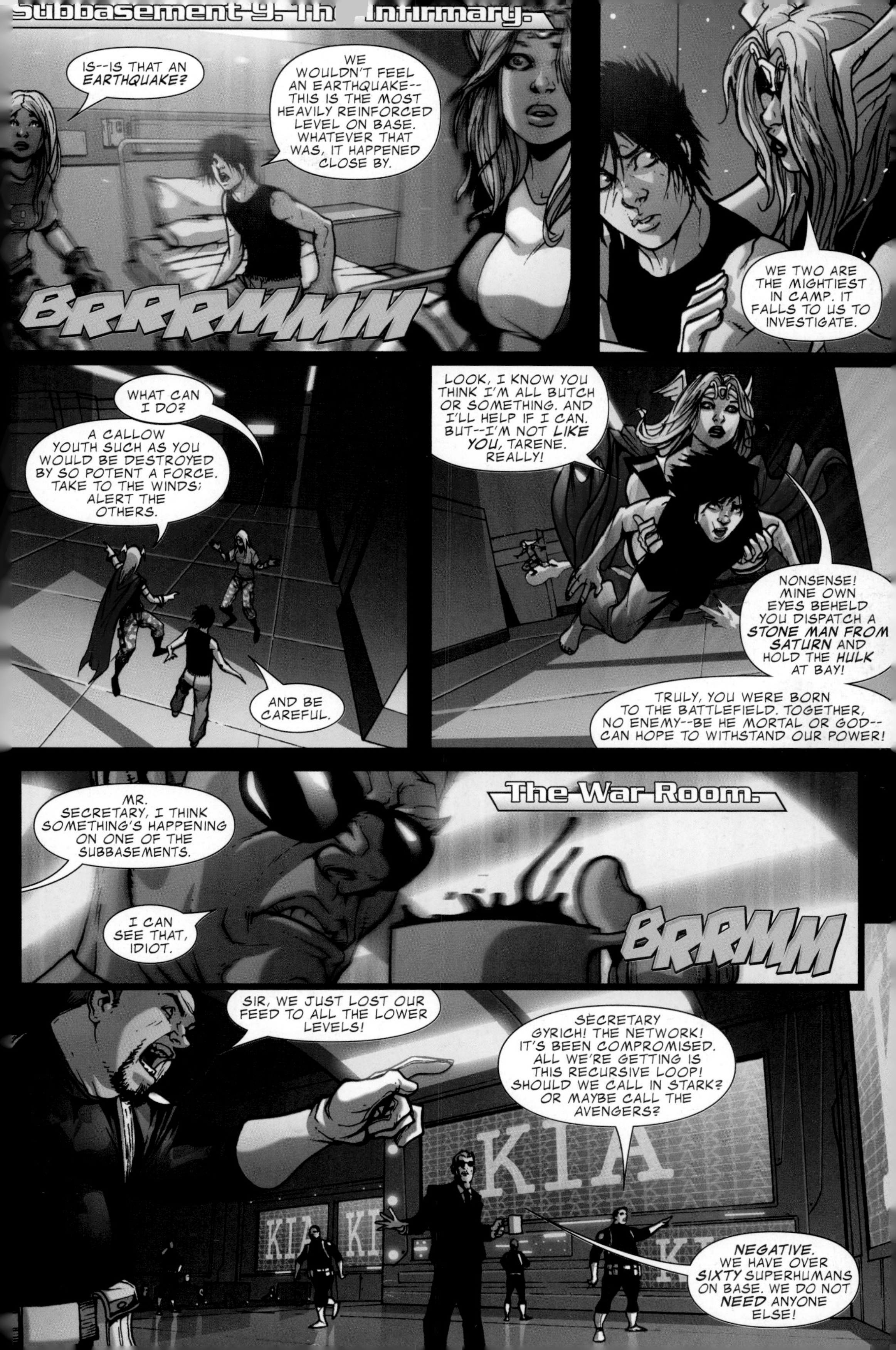
Subbasement 9: Th Infirmary.
IS--IS THAT AN EARTHQUAKE?
WE WOULDN'T FEEL AN EARTHQUAKE-- THIS IS THE MOST HEAVILY REINFORCED LEVEL ON BASE. WHATEVER THAT WAS, IT HAPPENED CLOSE BY.
BRRRMMMM
WE TWO ARE THE MIGHTIEST IN CAMP. IT FALLS TO US TO INVESTIGATE.
WHAT CAN I DO?
A CALLOW YOUTH SUCH AS YOU WOULD BE DESTROYED BY SO POTENT A FORCE. TAKE TO THE WINDS; ALERT THE OTHERS.
AND BE CAREFUL.
LOOK, I KNOW YOU THINK I'M ALL BUTCH OR SOMETHING. AND I'LL HELP IF I CAN. BUT--I'M NOT LIKE YOU, TARENE. REALLY!
NONSENSE! MINE OWN EYES BEHELD YOU DISPATCH A STONE MAN FROM SATURN AND HOLD THE HULK AT BAY!
TRULY, YOU WERE BORN TO THE BATTLEFIELD. TOGETHER, NO ENEMY--BE HE MORTAL OR GOD-- CAN HOPE TO WITHSTAND OUR POWER!
The War Room.
MR. SECRETARY, I THINK SOMETHING'S HAPPENING ON ONE OF THE SUBBASEMENTS.
I CAN SEE THAT, IDIOT.
BRRMMM
SIR, WE JUST LOST OUR FEED TO ALL THE LOWER LEVELS!
SECRETARY GYRICH! THE NETWORK! IT'S BEEN COMPROMISED. ALL WE'RE GETTING IS THIS RECURSIVE LOOP! SHOULD WE CALL IN STARK? OR MAYBE CALL THE AVENGERS?
KIA
NEGATIVE. WE HAVE OVER SIXTY SUPERHUMANS ON BASE. WE DO NOT NEED ANYONE ELSE!

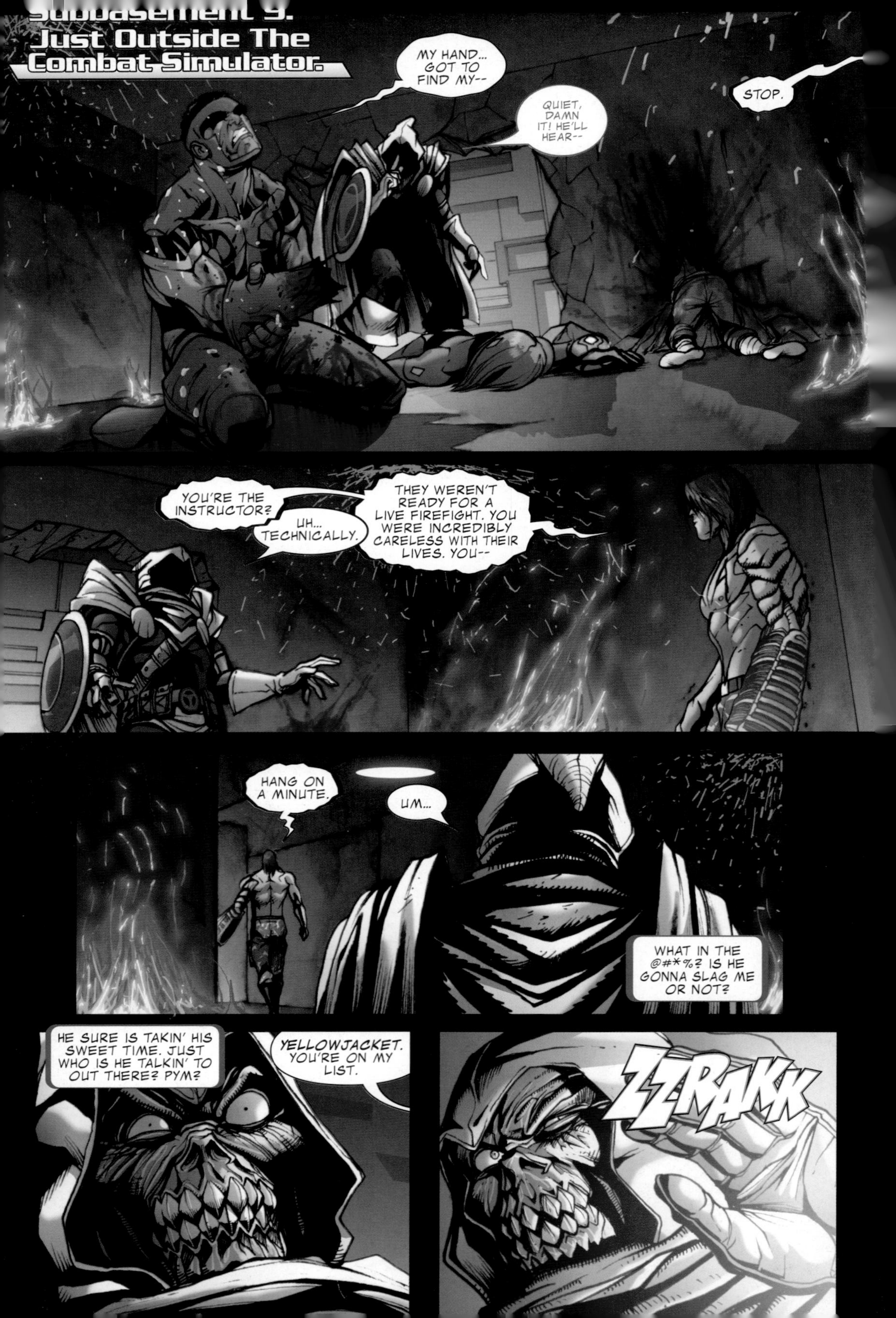

Subbasement 9. Just Outside The Combat Simulator.
MY HAND... GOT TO FIND MY--
QUIET, DAMN IT! HE'LL HEAR--
STOP.
YOU'RE THE INSTRUCTOR?
UH... TECHNICALLY.
THEY WEREN'T READY FOR A LIVE FIREFIGHT. YOU WERE INCREDIBLY CARELESS WITH THEIR LIVES. YOU--
HANG ON A MINUTE.
UM...
WHAT IN THE @#*%? IS HE GONNA SLAG ME OR NOT?
HE SURE IS TAKIN' HIS SWEET TIME. JUST WHO IS HE TALKIN' TO OUT THERE? PYM?
YELLOWJACKET. YOU'RE ON MY LIST.
ZZRAKK

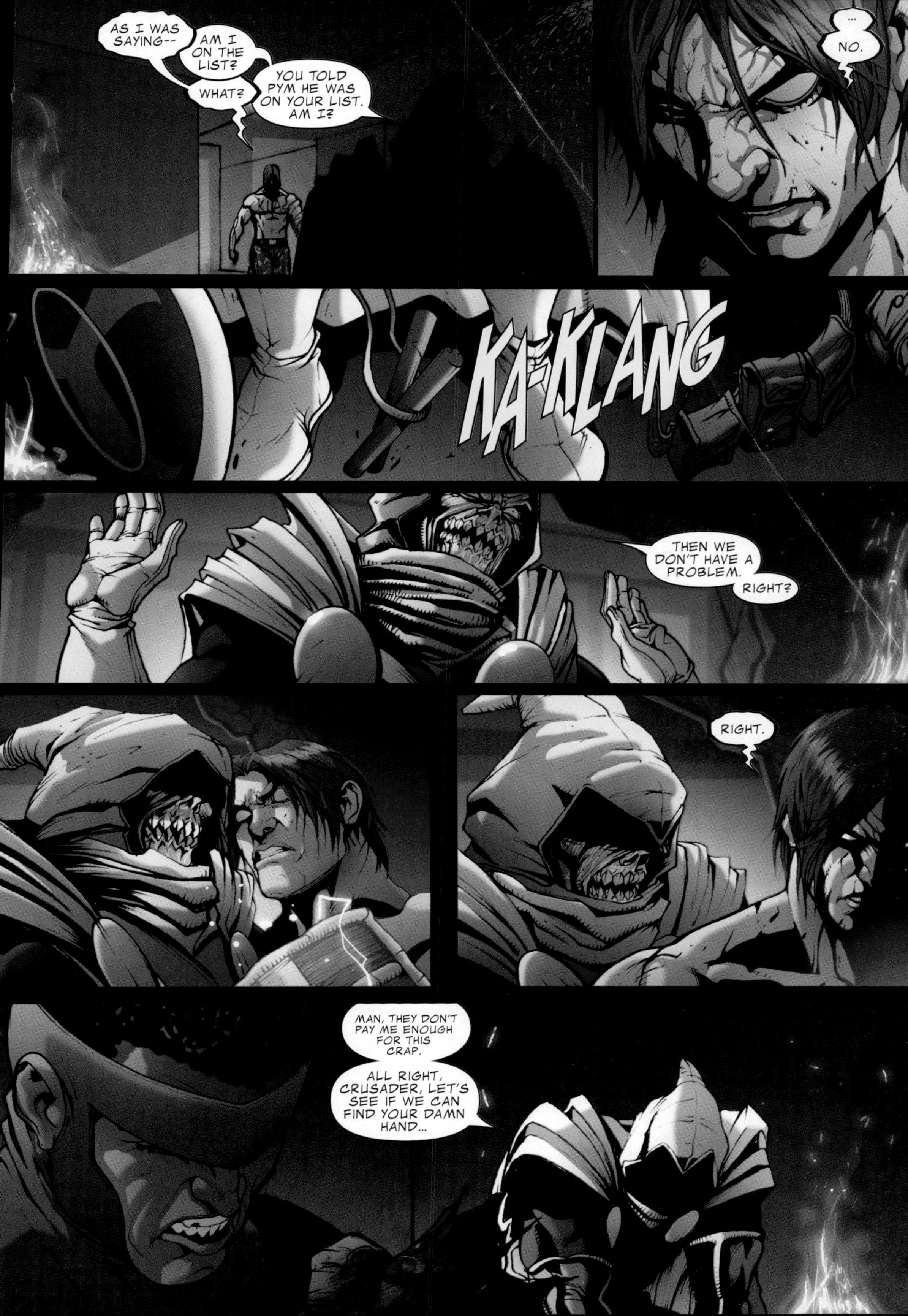
AS I WAS SAYING--
AM I ON THE LIST?
WHAT?
YOU TOLD PYM HE WAS ON YOUR LIST. AM I?
...
NO.
KA-KLANG
THEN WE DON'T HAVE A PROBLEM.
RIGHT?
RIGHT.
MAN, THEY DON'T PAY ME ENOUGH FOR THIS CRAP.
ALL RIGHT, CRUSADER, LET'S SEE IF WE CAN FIND YOUR DAMN HAND...

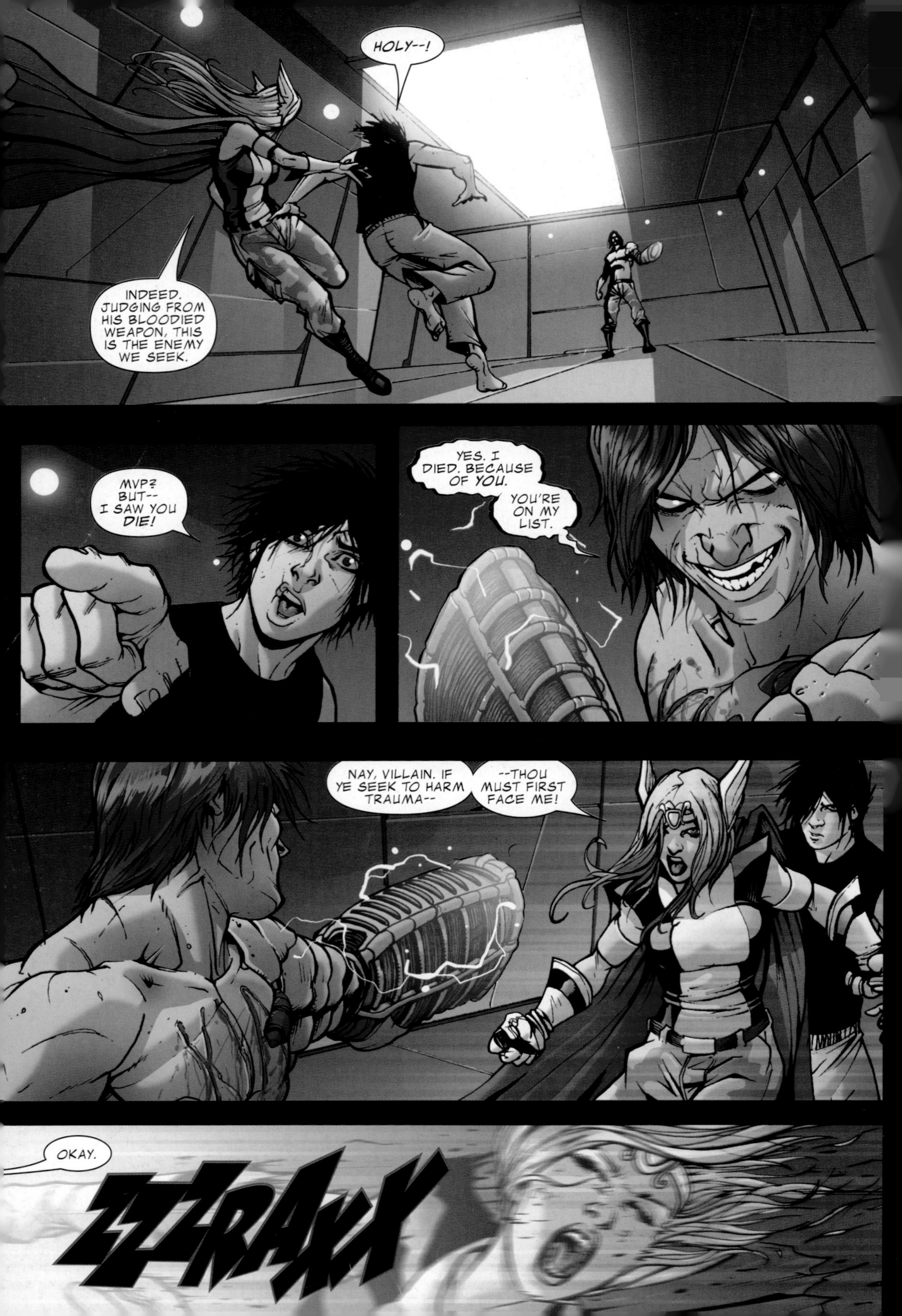
HOLY--!
INDEED. JUDGING FROM HIS BLOODIED WEAPON, THIS IS THE ENEMY WE SEEK.
MVP? BUT-- I SAW YOU DIE!
YES. I DIED. BECAUSE OF YOU.
YOU'RE ON MY LIST.
NAY, VILLAIN. IF YE SEEK TO HARM TRAUMA--
--THOU MUST FIRST FACE ME!
OKAY.
ZZZRAKX

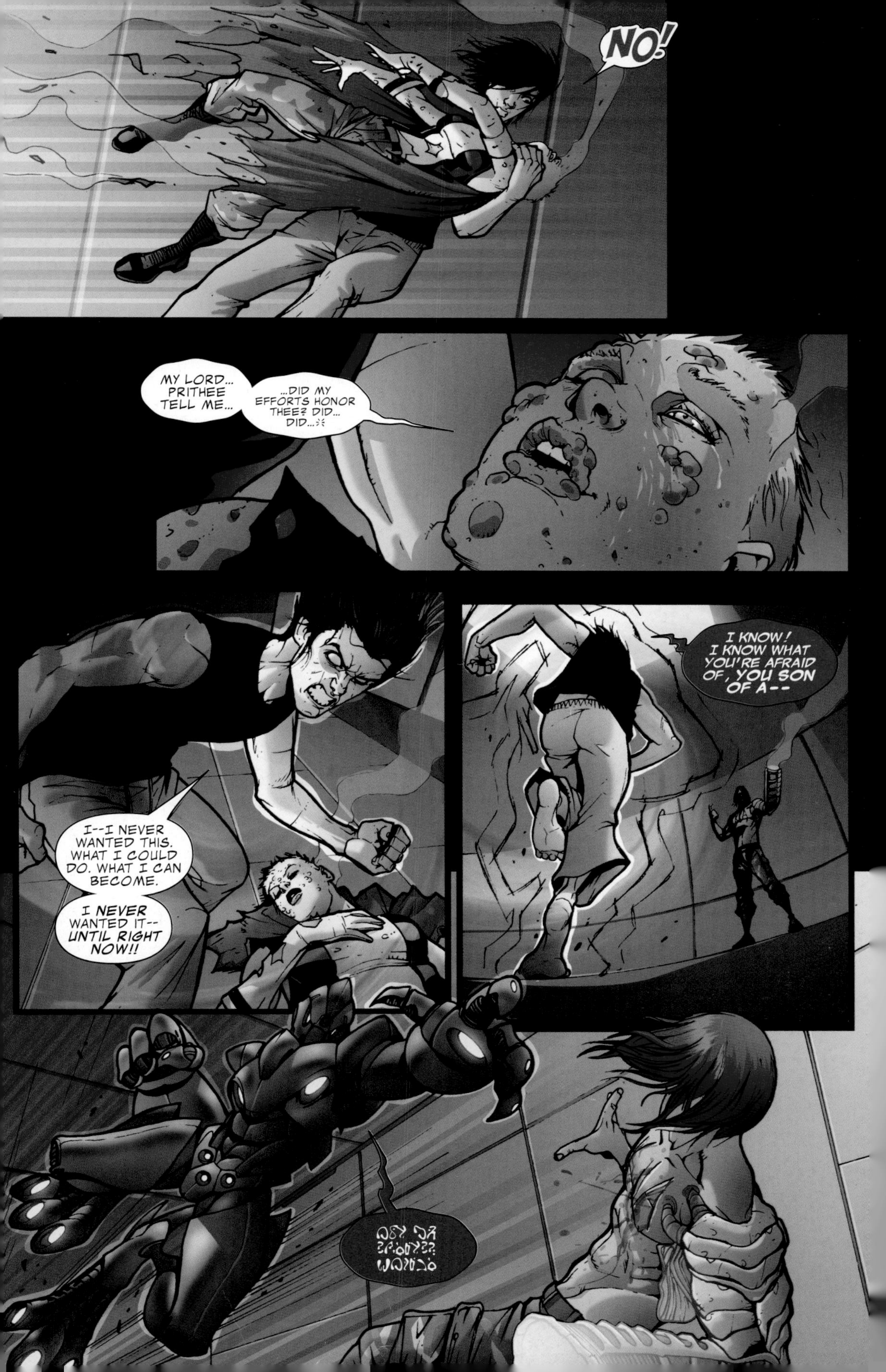
NO!
MY LORD... PRITHEE TELL ME...
...DID MY EFFORTS HONOR THEE? DID... DID...
I--I NEVER WANTED THIS. WHAT I COULD DO. WHAT I CAN BECOME.
I NEVER WANTED IT-- UNTIL RIGHT NOW!!
I KNOW! I KNOW WHAT YOU'RE AFRAID OF, YOU SON OF A--

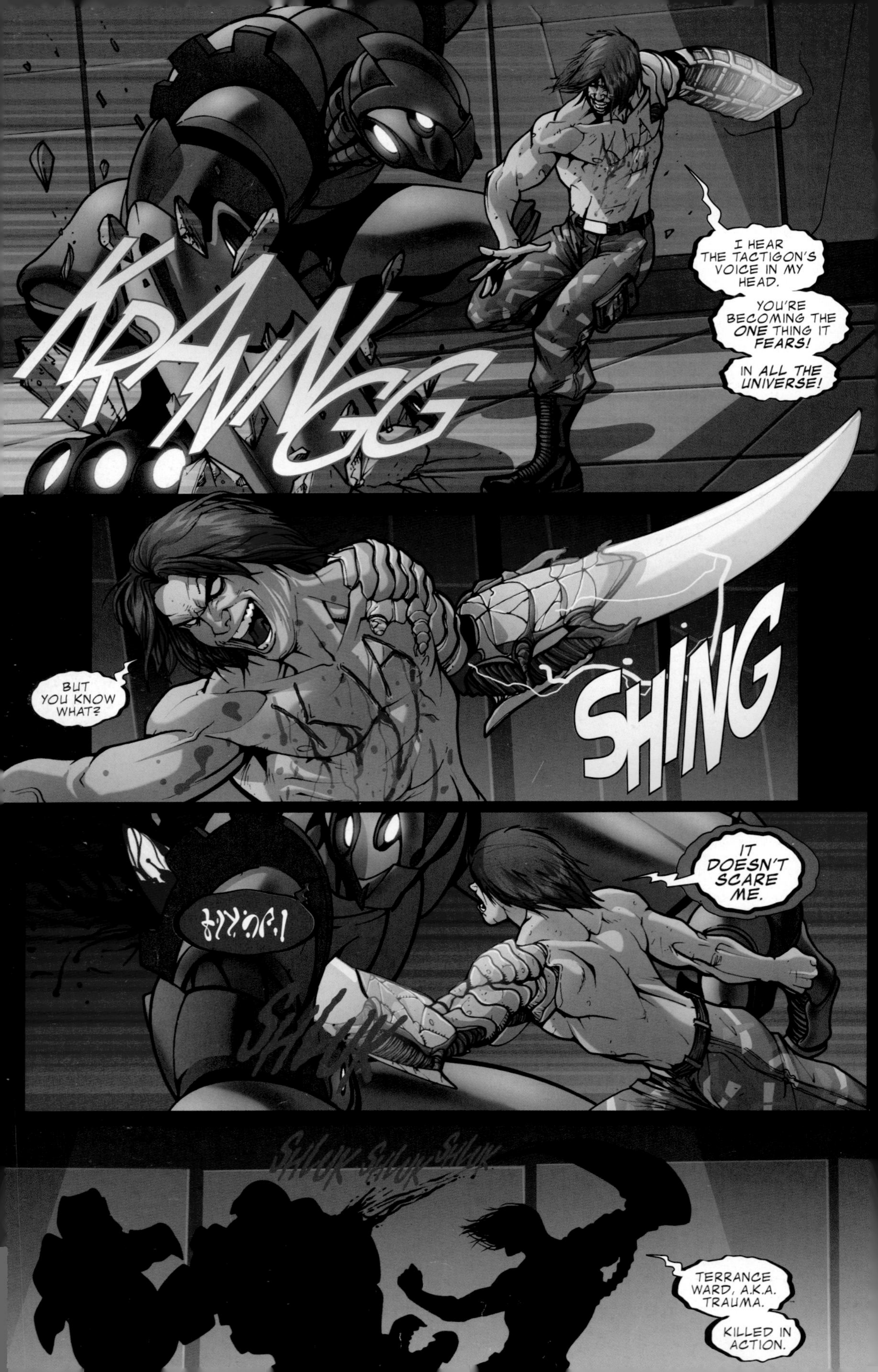
KRANNGG
I HEAR THE TACTIGON'S VOICE IN MY HEAD.
YOU'RE BECOMING THE ONE THING IT FEARS!
IN ALL THE UNIVERSE!
BUT YOU KNOW WHAT?
SHING
IT DOESN'T SCARE ME.
TERRANCE WARD, A.K.A. TRAUMA.
KILLED IN ACTION.

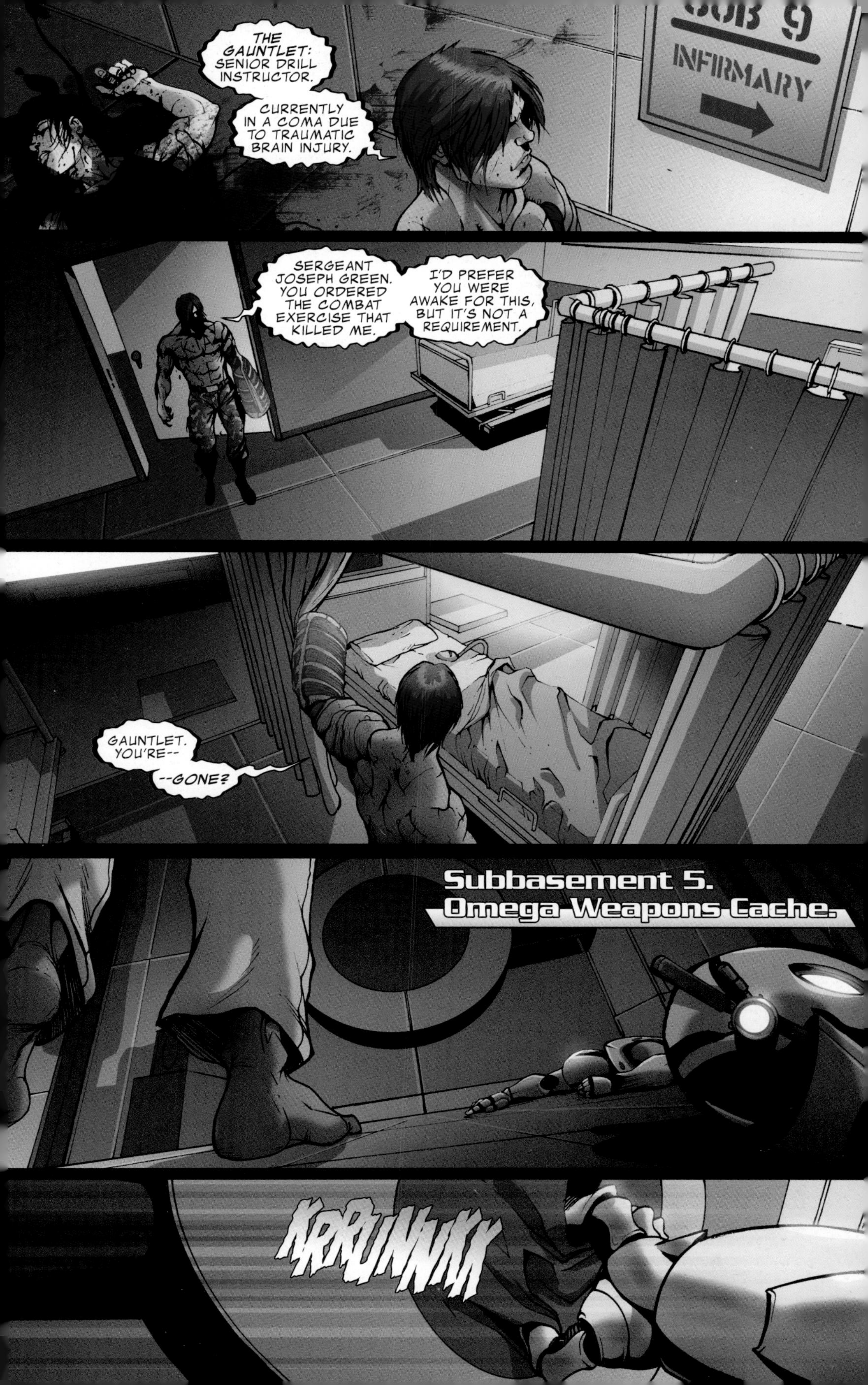
SUB 9
INFIRMARY
THE GAUNTLET: SENIOR DRILL INSTRUCTOR.
CURRENTLY IN A COMA DUE TO TRAUMATIC BRAIN INJURY.
SERGEANT JOSEPH GREEN. YOU ORDERED THE COMBAT EXERCISE THAT KILLED ME.
I'D PREFER YOU WERE AWAKE FOR THIS, BUT IT'S NOT A REQUIREMENT.
GAUNTLET. YOU'RE--
--GONE?
Subbasement 5.
Omega Weapons Cache.
KRRUNNKK

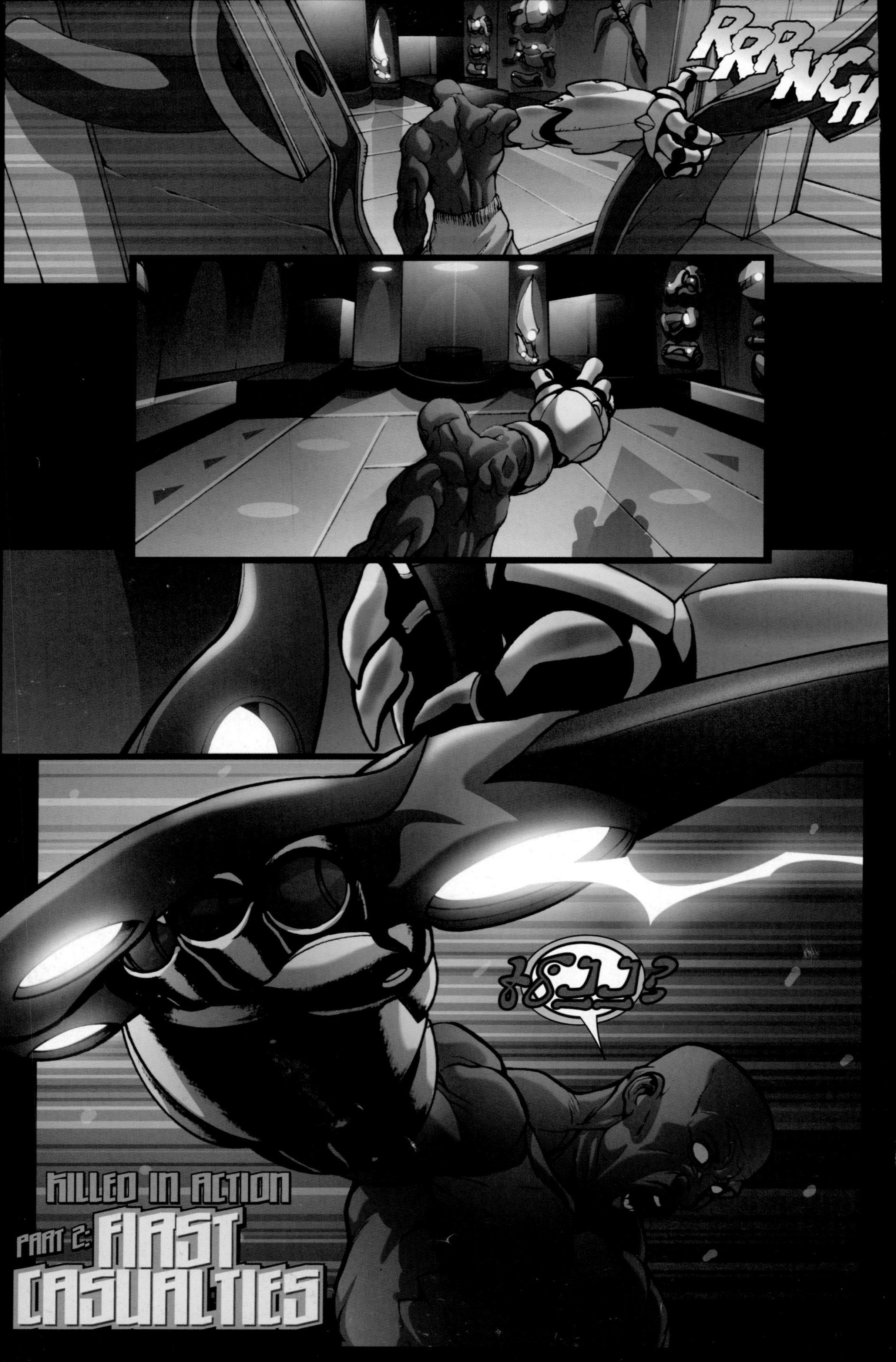
RRRNCH
KILLED IN ACTION
PART 2: FIRST CASUALTIES

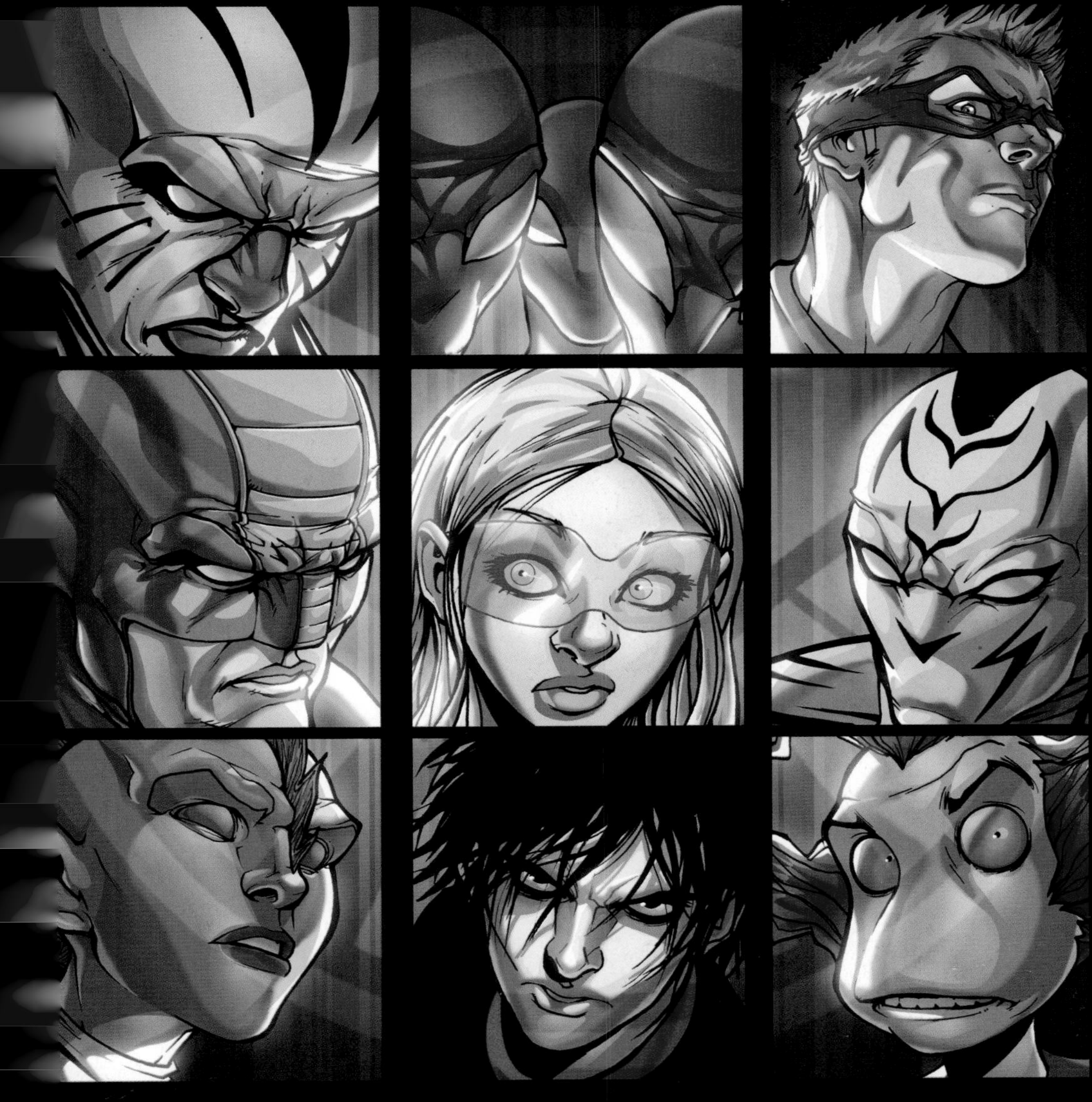

ONE WILL DIE!

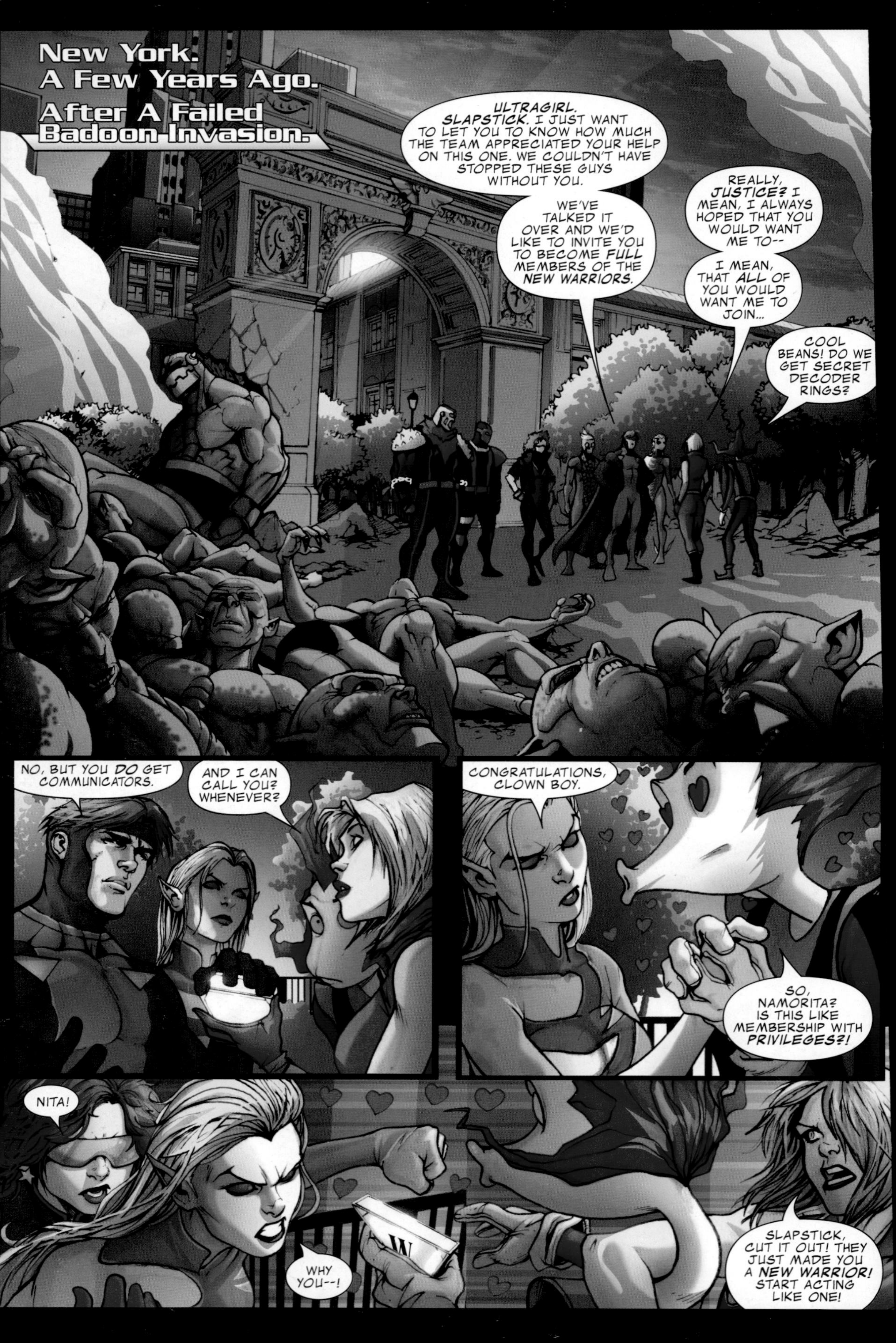
New York. A Few Years Ago.
After A Failed Badoon Invasion.
ULTRAGIRL. SLAPSTICK. I JUST WANT TO LET YOU TO KNOW HOW MUCH THE TEAM APPRECIATED YOUR HELP ON THIS ONE. WE COULDN'T HAVE STOPPED THESE GUYS WITHOUT YOU.
WE'VE TALKED IT OVER AND WE'D LIKE TO INVITE YOU TO BECOME FULL MEMBERS OF THE NEW WARRIORS.
REALLY, JUSTICE? I MEAN, I ALWAYS HOPED THAT YOU WOULD WANT ME TO--
I MEAN, THAT ALL OF YOU WOULD WANT ME TO JOIN...
COOL BEANS! DO WE GET SECRET DECODER RINGS?
NO, BUT YOU DO GET COMMUNICATORS.
AND I CAN CALL YOU? WHENEVER?
CONGRATULATIONS, CLOWN BOY.
SO, NAMORITA? IS THIS LIKE MEMBERSHIP WITH PRIVILEGES?!
NITA!
WHY YOU--!
SLAPSTICK, CUT IT OUT! THEY JUST MADE YOU A NEW WARRIOR! START ACTING LIKE ONE!

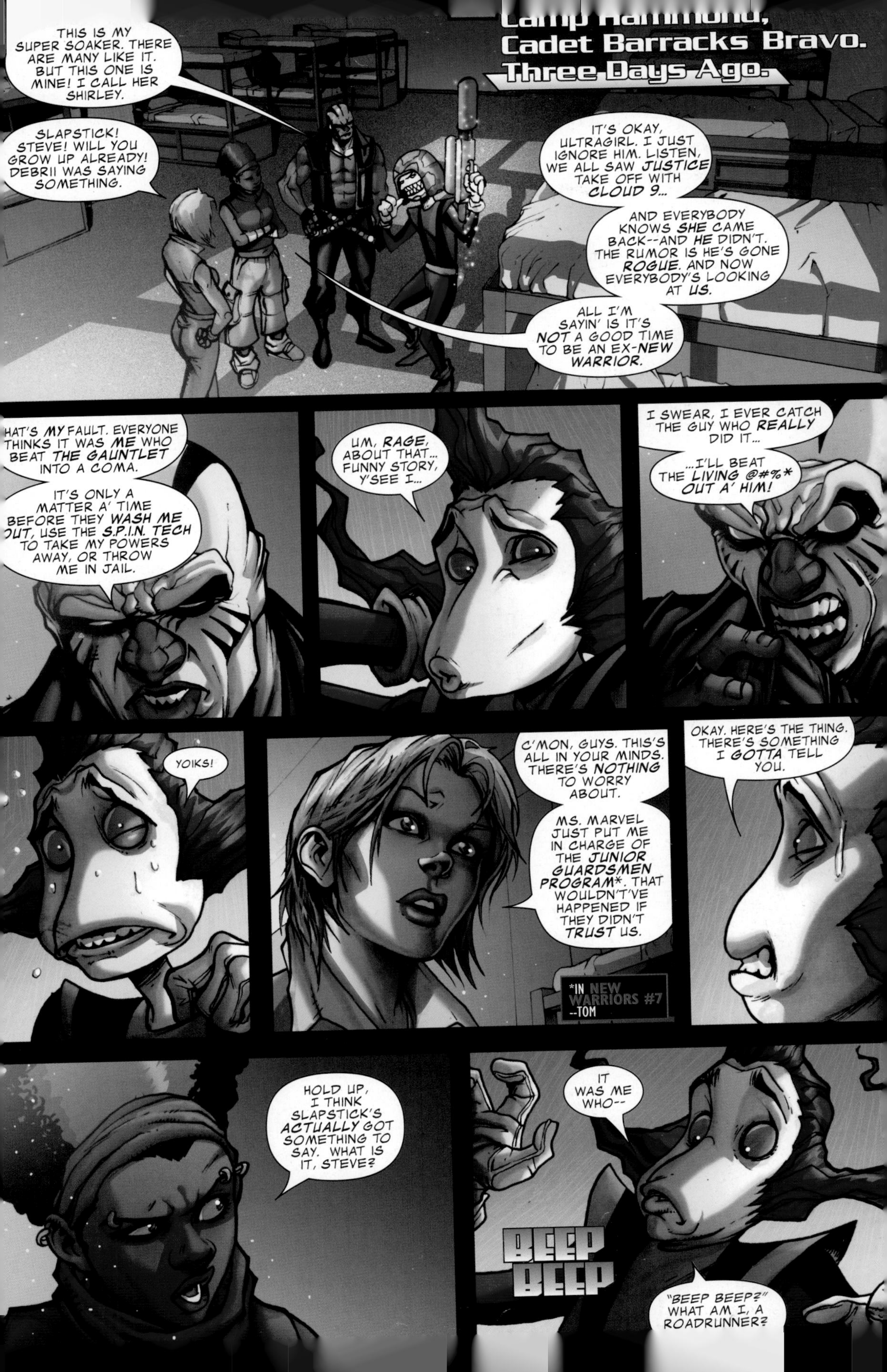

Camp Hammond,
Cadet Barracks Bravo.
Three Days Ago.
THIS IS MY SUPER SOAKER. THERE ARE MANY LIKE IT. BUT THIS ONE IS MINE! I CALL HER SHIRLEY.
SLAPSTICK! STEVE! WILL YOU GROW UP ALREADY! DEBRII WAS SAYING SOMETHING.
IT'S OKAY, ULTRAGIRL. I JUST IGNORE HIM. LISTEN, WE ALL SAW JUSTICE TAKE OFF WITH CLOUD 9...
AND EVERYBODY KNOWS SHE CAME BACK--AND HE DIDN'T. THE RUMOR IS HE'S GONE ROGUE. AND NOW EVERYBODY'S LOOKING AT US.
ALL I'M SAYIN' IS IT'S NOT A GOOD TIME TO BE AN EX-NEW WARRIOR.
HAT'S MY FAULT. EVERYONE THINKS IT WAS ME WHO BEAT THE GAUNTLET INTO A COMA.
IT'S ONLY A MATTER A' TIME BEFORE THEY WASH ME OUT, USE THE S.P.I.N. TECH TO TAKE MY POWERS AWAY, OR THROW ME IN JAIL.
UM, RAGE, ABOUT THAT... FUNNY STORY, Y'SEE I...
I SWEAR, I EVER CATCH THE GUY WHO REALLY DID IT...
...I'LL BEAT THE LIVING @#%* OUT A' HIM!
YOIKS!
C'MON, GUYS. THIS'S ALL IN YOUR MINDS. THERE'S NOTHING TO WORRY ABOUT.
MS. MARVEL JUST PUT ME IN CHARGE OF THE JUNIOR GUARDSMEN PROGRAM*. THAT WOULDN'T'VE HAPPENED IF THEY DIDN'T TRUST US.
*IN NEW WARRIORS #7 --TOM
OKAY. HERE'S THE THING. THERE'S SOMETHING I GOTTA TELL YOU.
HOLD UP, I THINK SLAPSTICK'S ACTUALLY GOT SOMETHING TO SAY. WHAT IS IT, STEVE?
IT WAS ME WHO--
BEEP BEEP
"BEEP BEEP?" WHAT AM I, A ROADRUNNER?

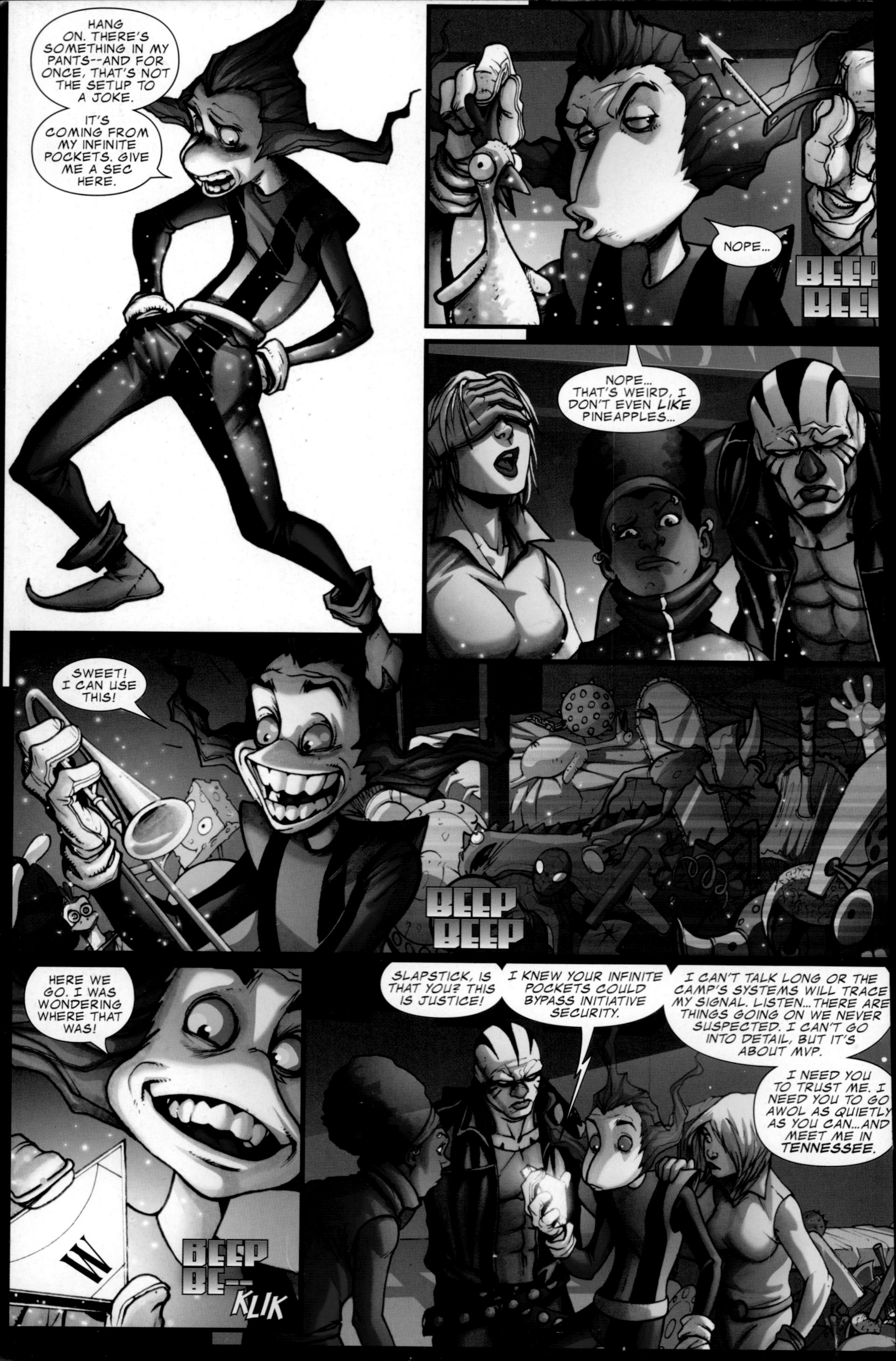
HANG ON. THERE'S SOMETHING IN MY PANTS--AND FOR ONCE, THAT'S NOT THE SETUP TO A JOKE.
IT'S COMING FROM MY INFINITE POCKETS. GIVE ME A SEC HERE.
NOPE...
BEEP BEEP
NOPE... THAT'S WEIRD, I DON'T EVEN LIKE PINEAPPLES...
SWEET! I CAN USE THIS!
BEEP BEEP
HERE WE GO. I WAS WONDERING WHERE THAT WAS!
BEEP BE--
KLIK
SLAPSTICK, IS THAT YOU? THIS IS JUSTICE!
I KNEW YOUR INFINITE POCKETS COULD BYPASS INITIATIVE SECURITY.
I CAN'T TALK LONG OR THE CAMP'S SYSTEMS WILL TRACE MY SIGNAL. LISTEN... THERE ARE THINGS GOING ON WE NEVER SUSPECTED. I CAN'T GO INTO DETAIL, BUT IT'S ABOUT MVP.
I NEED YOU TO TRUST ME. I NEED YOU TO GO AWOL AS QUIETLY AS YOU CAN... AND MEET ME IN TENNESSEE.

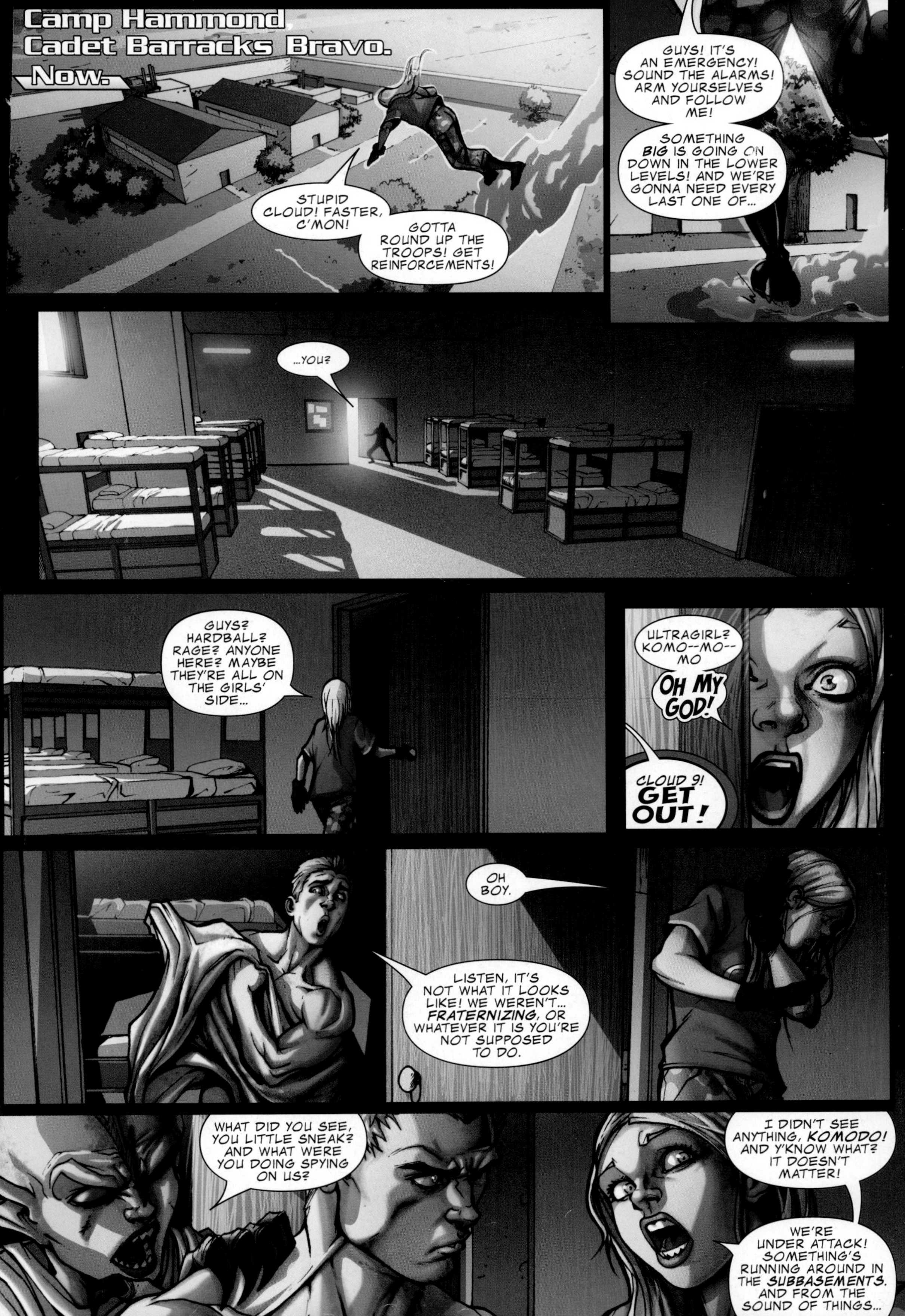
Camp Hammond, Cadet Barracks Bravo. Now.
STUPID CLOUD! FASTER, C'MON!
GOTTA ROUND UP THE TROOPS! GET REINFORCEMENTS!
GUYS! IT'S AN EMERGENCY! SOUND THE ALARMS! ARM YOURSELVES AND FOLLOW ME!
SOMETHING BIG IS GOING ON DOWN IN THE LOWER LEVELS! AND WE'RE GONNA NEED EVERY LAST ONE OF...
...YOU?
GUYS? HARDBALL? RAGE? ANYONE HERE? MAYBE THEY'RE ALL ON THE GIRLS' SIDE...
ULTRAGIRL? KOMO--MO--MO
OH MY GOD!
CLOUD 9! GET OUT!
OH BOY.
LISTEN, IT'S NOT WHAT IT LOOKS LIKE! WE WEREN'T... FRATERNIZING, OR WHATEVER IT IS YOU'RE NOT SUPPOSED TO DO.
WHAT DID YOU SEE, YOU LITTLE SNEAK? AND WHAT WERE YOU DOING SPYING ON US?
I DIDN'T SEE ANYTHING, KOMODO! AND Y'KNOW WHAT? IT DOESN'T MATTER!
WE'RE UNDER ATTACK! SOMETHING'S RUNNING AROUND IN THE SUBBASEMENTS. AND FROM THE SOUND OF THINGS...

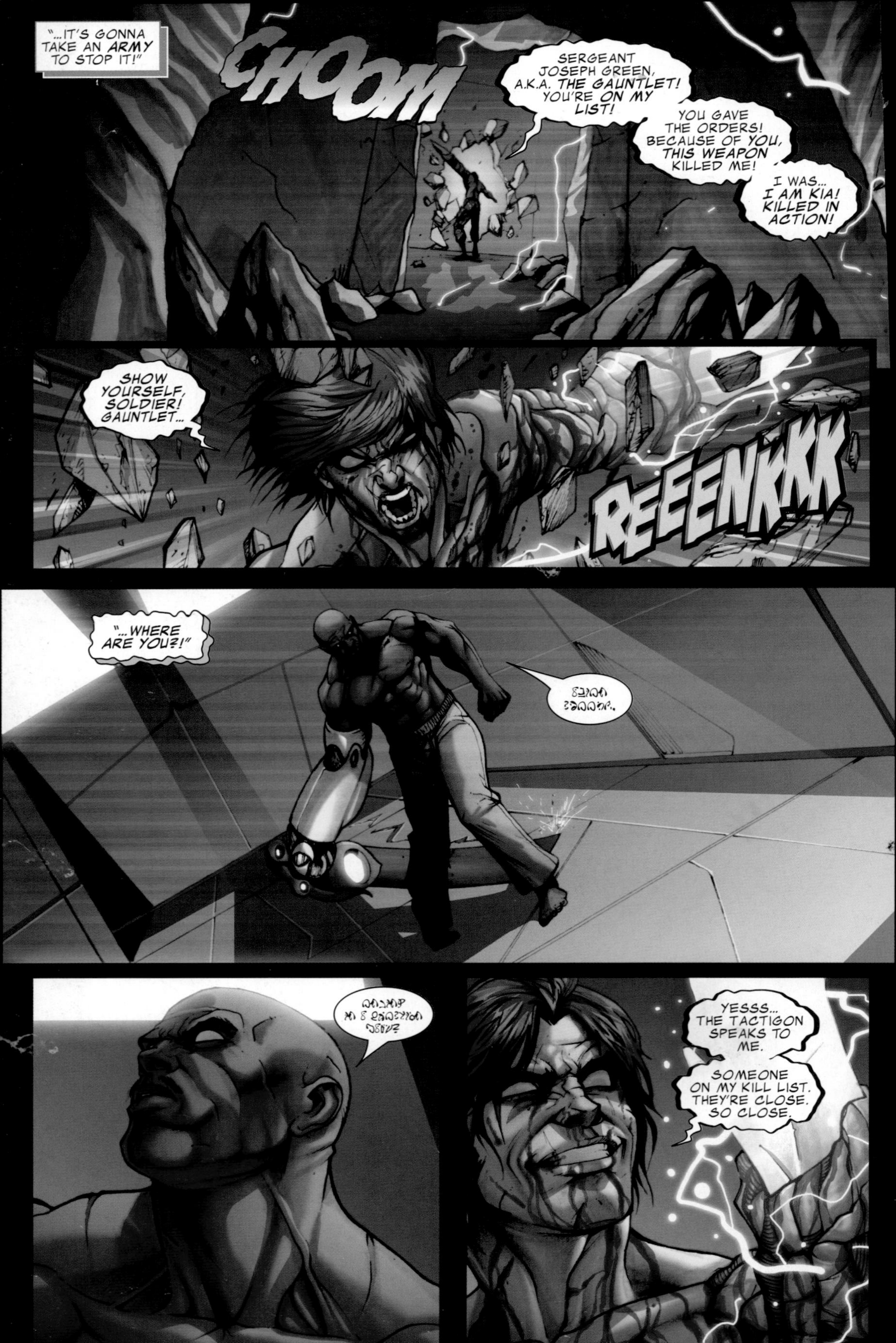
"...IT'S GONNA TAKE AN ARMY TO STOP IT!"
CHOOM
SERGEANT JOSEPH GREEN, A.K.A. THE GAUNTLET! YOU'RE ON MY LIST!
YOU GAVE THE ORDERS! BECAUSE OF YOU, THIS WEAPON KILLED ME!
I WAS... I AM KIA! KILLED IN ACTION!
SHOW YOURSELF, SOLDIER! GAUNTLET...
REEENKKK
"...WHERE ARE YOU?!"
YESSS... THE TACTIGON SPEAKS TO ME.
SOMEONE ON MY KILL LIST. THEY'RE CLOSE. SO CLOSE.

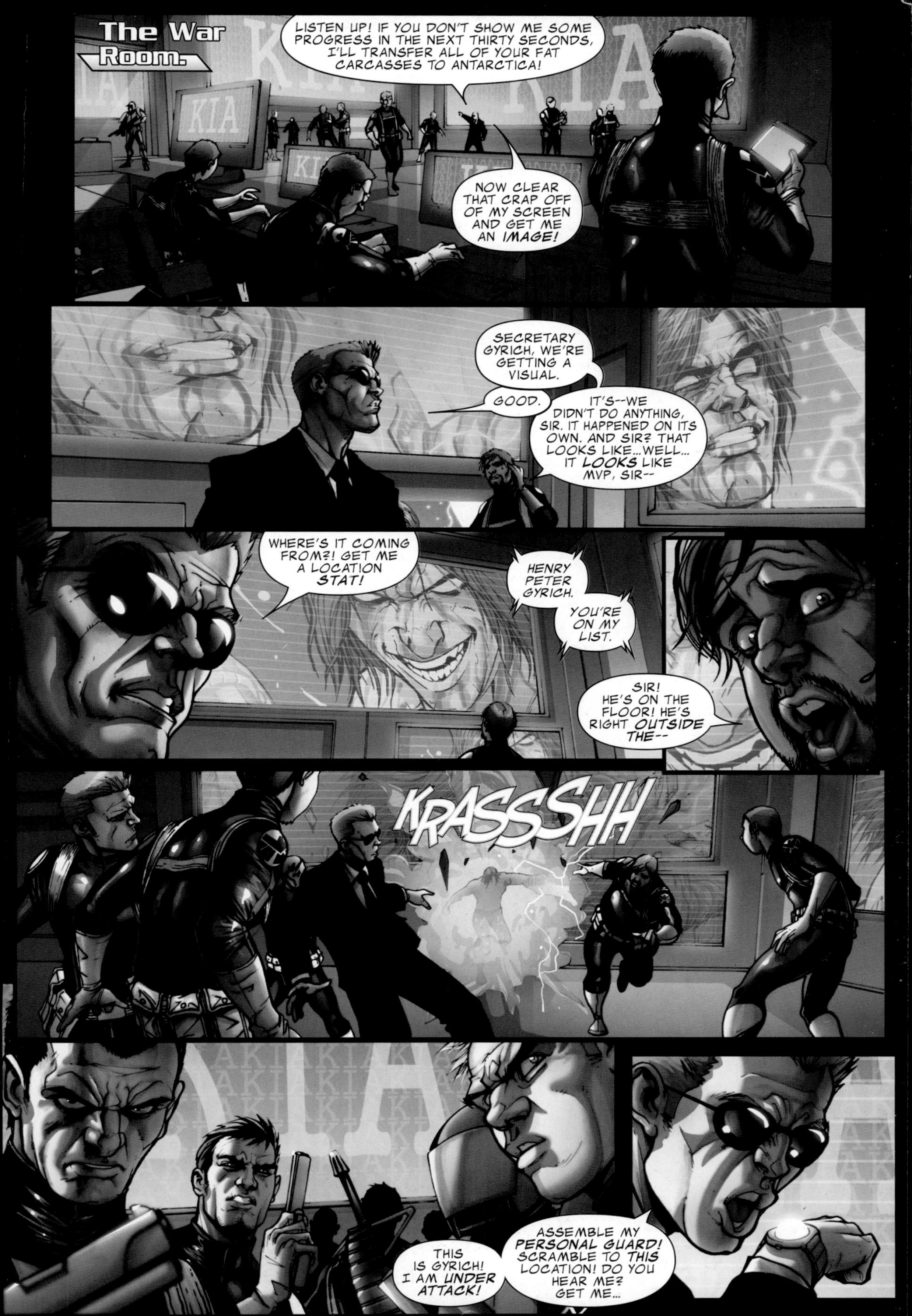
The War Room.
LISTEN UP! IF YOU DON'T SHOW ME SOME PROGRESS IN THE NEXT THIRTY SECONDS, I'LL TRANSFER ALL OF YOUR FAT CARCASSES TO ANTARCTICA!
NOW CLEAR THAT CRAP OFF OF MY SCREEN AND GET ME AN IMAGE!
SECRETARY GYRICH, WE'RE GETTING A VISUAL.
GOOD.
IT'S--WE DIDN'T DO ANYTHING, SIR. IT HAPPENED ON ITS OWN. AND SIR? THAT LOOKS LIKE...WELL... IT LOOKS LIKE MVP, SIR--
WHERE'S IT COMING FROM?! GET ME A LOCATION STAT!
HENRY PETER GYRICH.
YOU'RE ON MY LIST.
SIR! HE'S ON THE FLOOR! HE'S RIGHT OUTSIDE THE--
KRASSSHH
THIS IS GYRICH! I AM UNDER ATTACK!
ASSEMBLE MY PERSONAL GUARD! SCRAMBLE TO THIS LOCATION! DO YOU HEAR ME? GET ME...

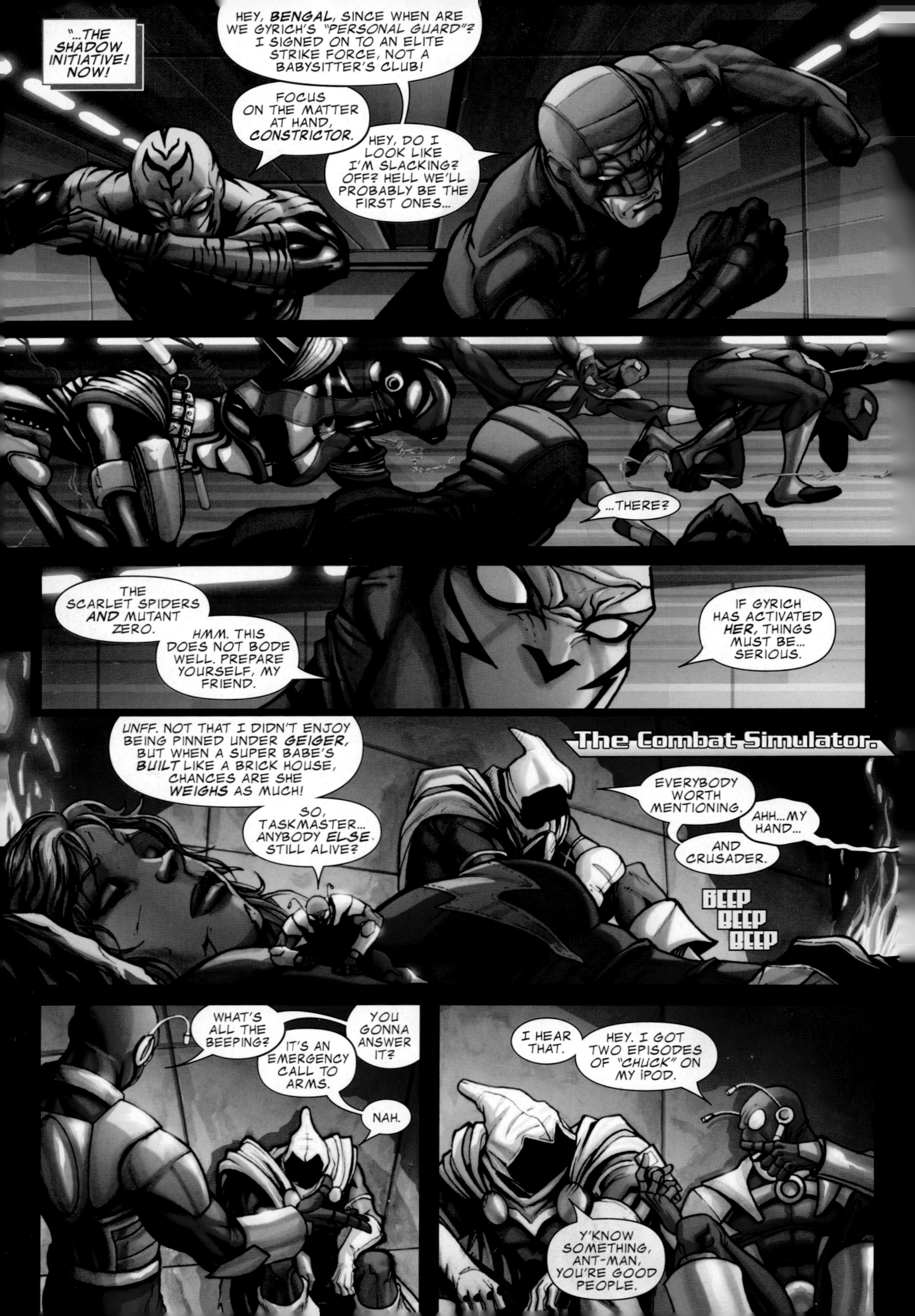
"...THE SHADOW INITIATIVE! NOW!
HEY, BENGAL, SINCE WHEN ARE WE GYRICH'S "PERSONAL GUARD"? I SIGNED ON TO AN ELITE STRIKE FORCE, NOT A BABYSITTER'S CLUB!
FOCUS ON THE MATTER AT HAND, CONSTRICTOR.
HEY, DO I LOOK LIKE I'M SLACKING? OFF? HELL WE'LL PROBABLY BE THE FIRST ONES...
...THERE?
THE SCARLET SPIDERS AND MUTANT ZERO.
HMM. THIS DOES NOT BODE WELL. PREPARE YOURSELF, MY FRIEND.
IF GYRICH HAS ACTIVATED HER, THINGS MUST BE... SERIOUS.
The Combat Simulator.
UNFF. NOT THAT I DIDN'T ENJOY BEING PINNED UNDER GEIGER, BUT WHEN A SUPER BABE'S BUILT LIKE A BRICK HOUSE, CHANCES ARE SHE WEIGHS AS MUCH!
SO, TASKMASTER... ANYBODY ELSE STILL ALIVE?
EVERYBODY WORTH MENTIONING.
AHH... MY HAND...
AND CRUSADER.
BEEP BEEP BEEP
WHAT'S ALL THE BEEPING?
IT'S AN EMERGENCY CALL TO ARMS.
YOU GONNA ANSWER IT?
NAH.
I HEAR THAT.
HEY. I GOT TWO EPISODES OF "CHUCK" ON MY iPOD.
Y'KNOW SOMETHING, ANT-MAN, YOU'RE GOOD PEOPLE.

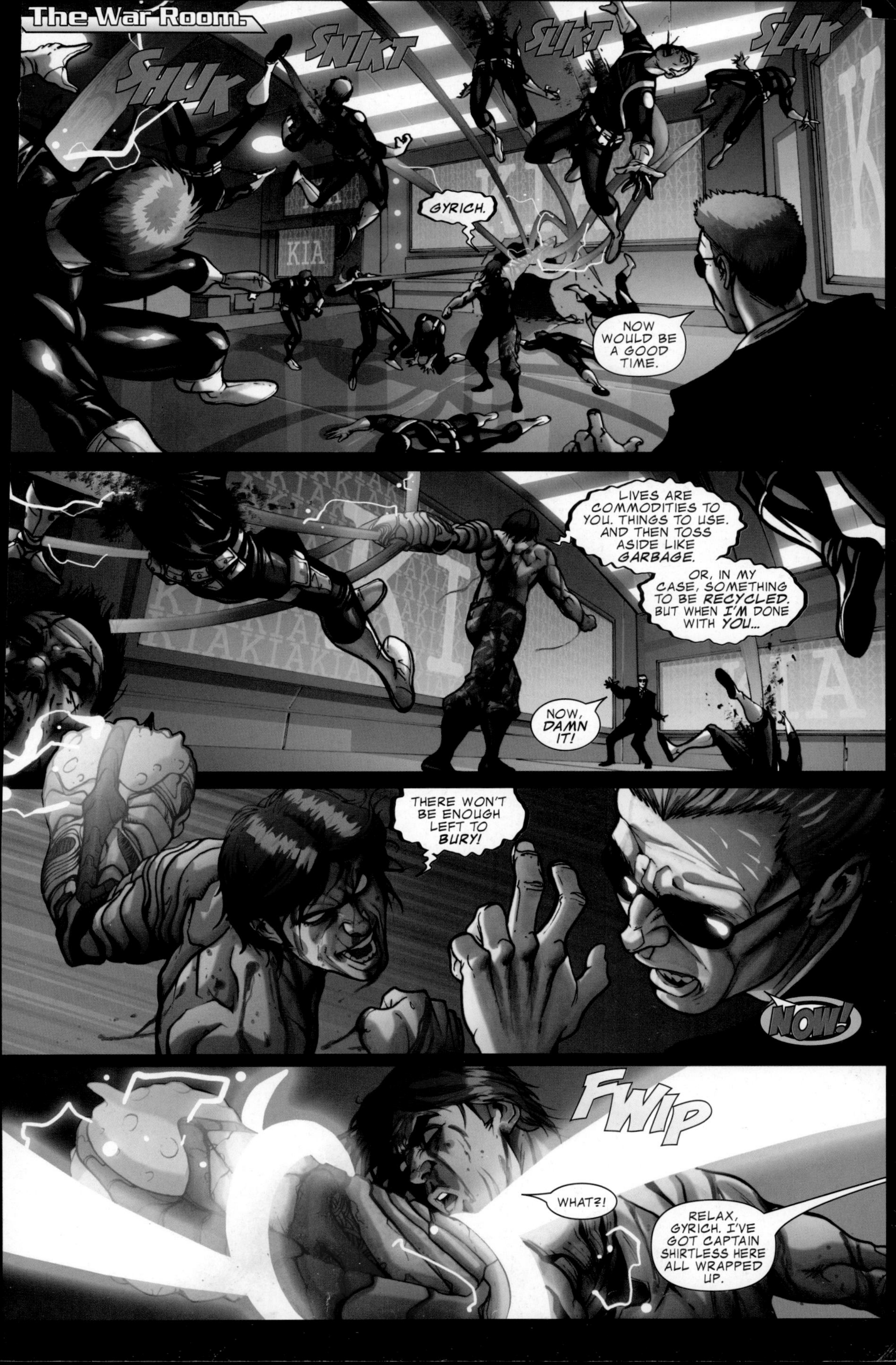
The War Room.
SHUK
SNIKT
SLIKT
SLAK
KIA
GYRICH.
NOW WOULD BE A GOOD TIME.
LIVES ARE COMMODITIES TO YOU. THINGS TO USE. AND THEN TOSS ASIDE LIKE GARBAGE.
OR, IN MY CASE, SOMETHING TO BE RECYCLED. BUT WHEN I'M DONE WITH YOU...
NOW, DAMN IT!
THERE WON'T BE ENOUGH LEFT TO BURY!
NOW!
FWIP
WHAT?!
RELAX, GYRICH. I'VE GOT CAPTAIN SHIRTLESS HERE ALL WRAPPED UP.

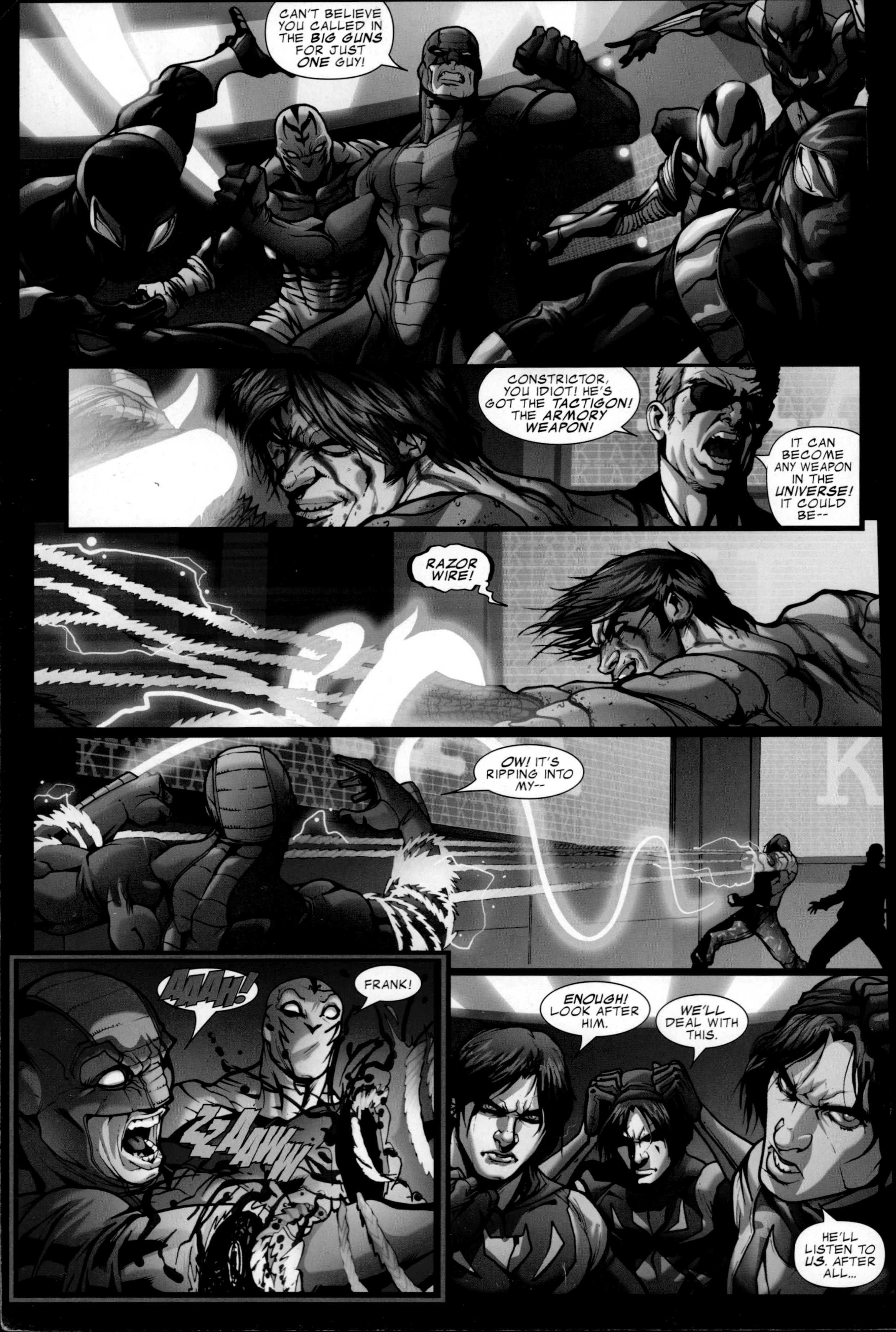
CAN'T BELIEVE YOU CALLED IN THE BIG GUNS FOR JUST ONE GUY!
CONSTRICTOR, YOU IDIOT! HE'S GOT THE TACTIGON! THE ARMORY WEAPON!
IT CAN BECOME ANY WEAPON IN THE UNIVERSE! IT COULD BE--
RAZOR WIRE!
OW! IT'S RIPPING INTO MY--
AAAH!
FRANK!
ZZAAWW
ENOUGH! LOOK AFTER HIM.
WE'LL DEAL WITH THIS.
HE'LL LISTEN TO US. AFTER ALL...

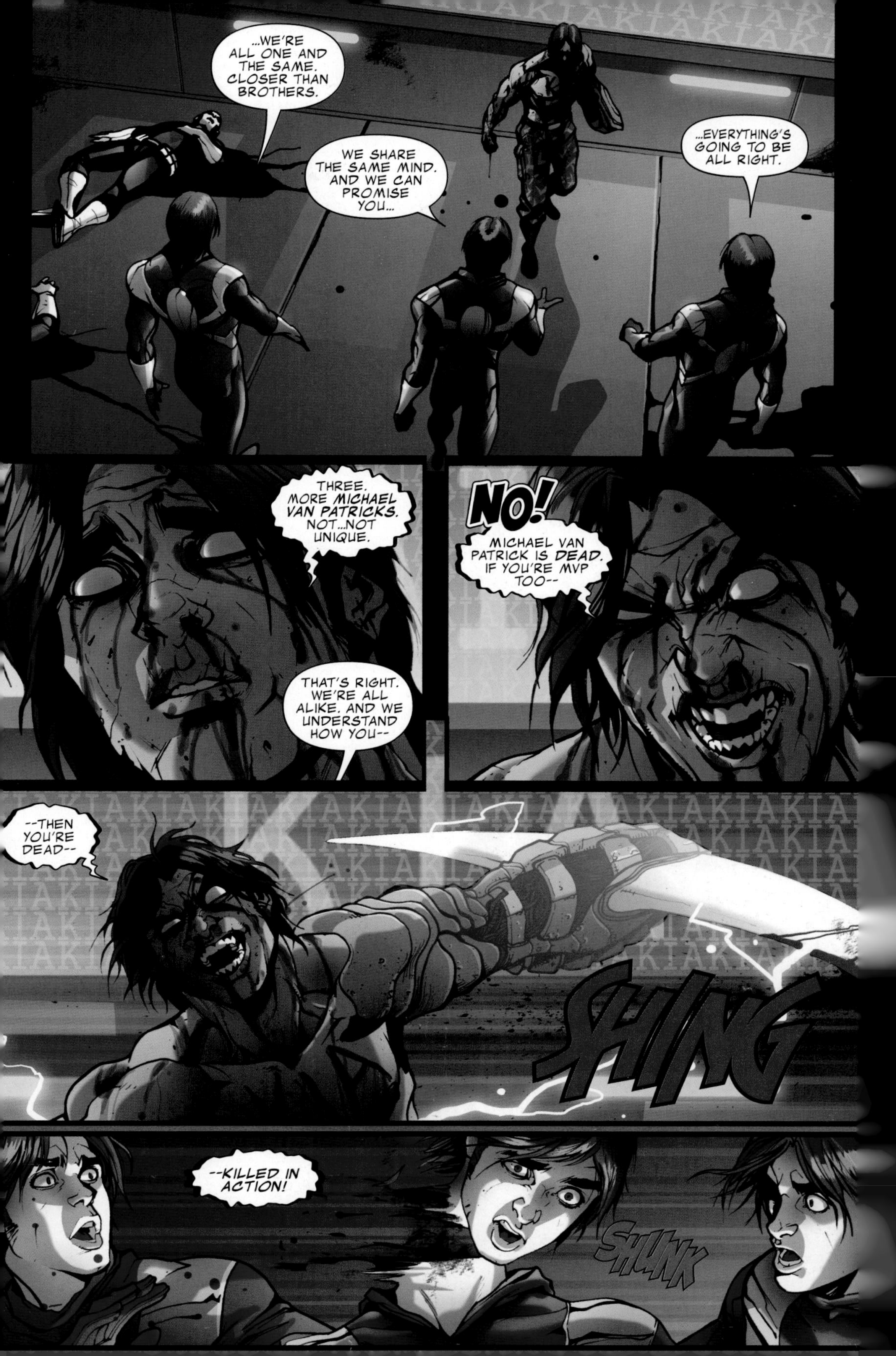
...WE'RE ALL ONE AND THE SAME. CLOSER THAN BROTHERS.
WE SHARE THE SAME MIND. AND WE CAN PROMISE YOU...
...EVERYTHING'S GOING TO BE ALL RIGHT.
THREE. MORE MICHAEL VAN PATRICKS. NOT...NOT UNIQUE.
THAT'S RIGHT. WE'RE ALL ALIKE. AND WE UNDERSTAND HOW YOU--
NO!
MICHAEL VAN PATRICK IS DEAD. IF YOU'RE MVP TOO--
--THEN YOU'RE DEAD--
SHING
--KILLED IN ACTION!
SHUNK

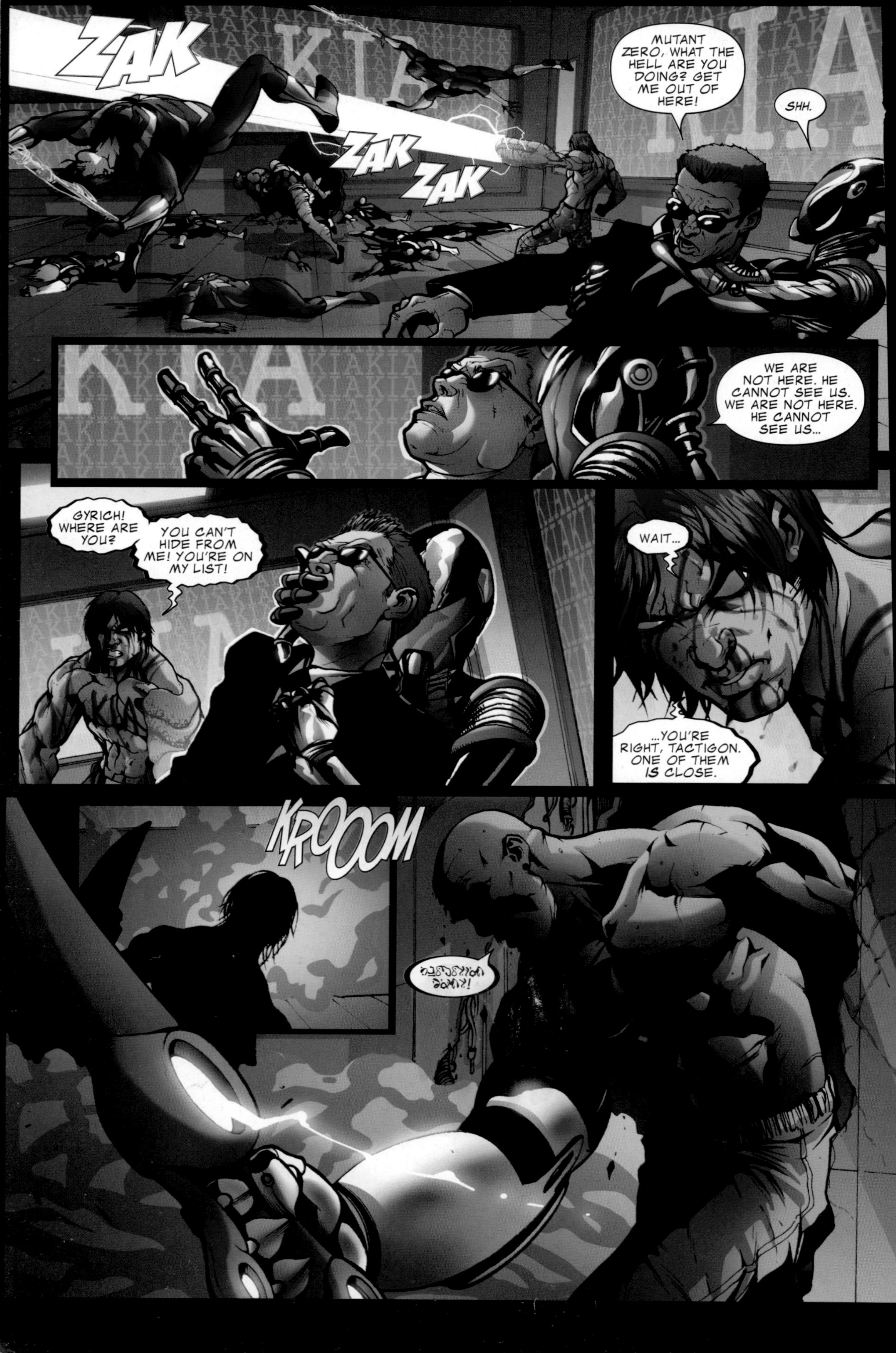
ZAK
ZAK
ZAK
MUTANT ZERO, WHAT THE HELL ARE YOU DOING? GET ME OUT OF HERE!
SHH.
WE ARE NOT HERE. HE CANNOT SEE US. WE ARE NOT HERE. HE CANNOT SEE US...
GYRICH! WHERE ARE YOU?
YOU CAN'T HIDE FROM ME! YOU'RE ON MY LIST!
WAIT...
...YOU'RE RIGHT, TACTIGON. ONE OF THEM IS CLOSE.
KROOOM

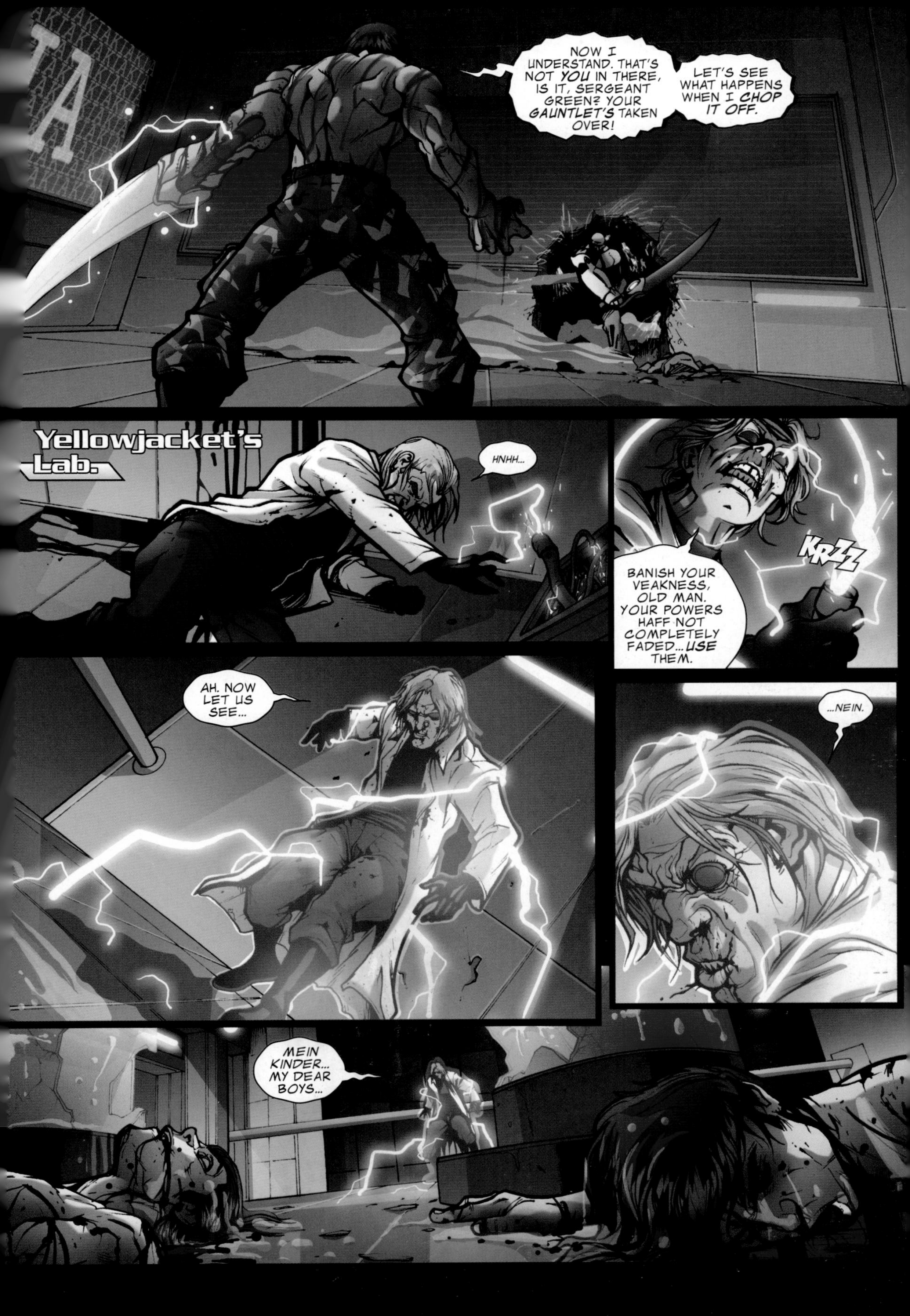
NOW I UNDERSTAND. THAT'S NOT YOU IN THERE, IS IT, SERGEANT GREEN? YOUR GAUNTLET'S TAKEN OVER!
LET'S SEE WHAT HAPPENS WHEN I CHOP IT OFF.
Yellowjacket's Lab.
HNHH...
KRZZZ
BANISH YOUR VEAKNESS, OLD MAN. YOUR POWERS HAFF NOT COMPLETELY FADED... USE THEM.
AH. NOW LET US SEE...
...NEIN.
MEIN KINDER... MY DEAR BOYS...

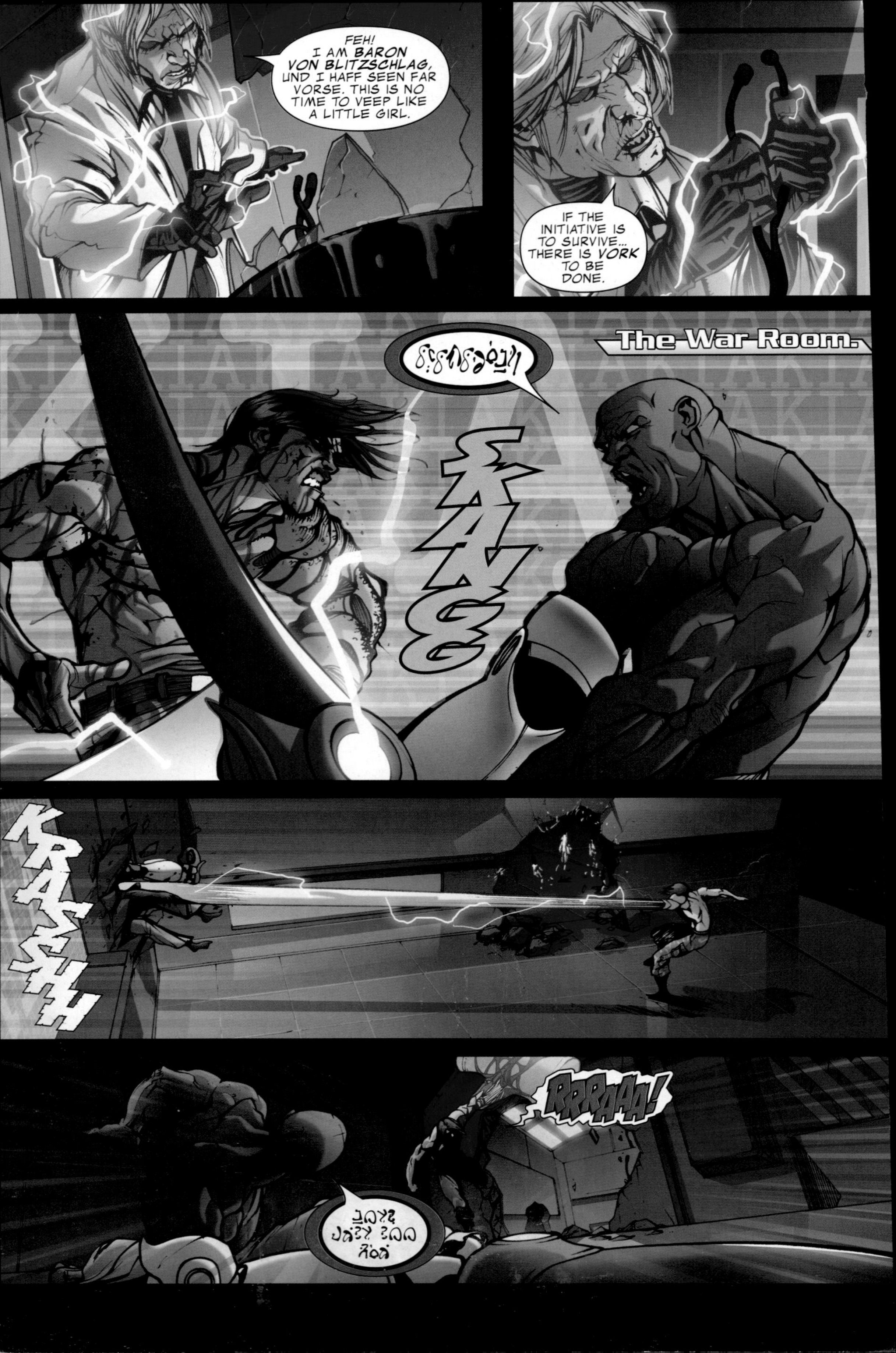
FEH! I AM BARON VON BLITZSCHLAG, UND I HAFF SEEN FAR VORSE. THIS IS NO TIME TO VEEP LIKE A LITTLE GIRL.
IF THE INITIATIVE IS TO SURVIVE... THERE IS VORK TO BE DONE.
The War Room.
KRANG
KRASHH
RRRAAA!

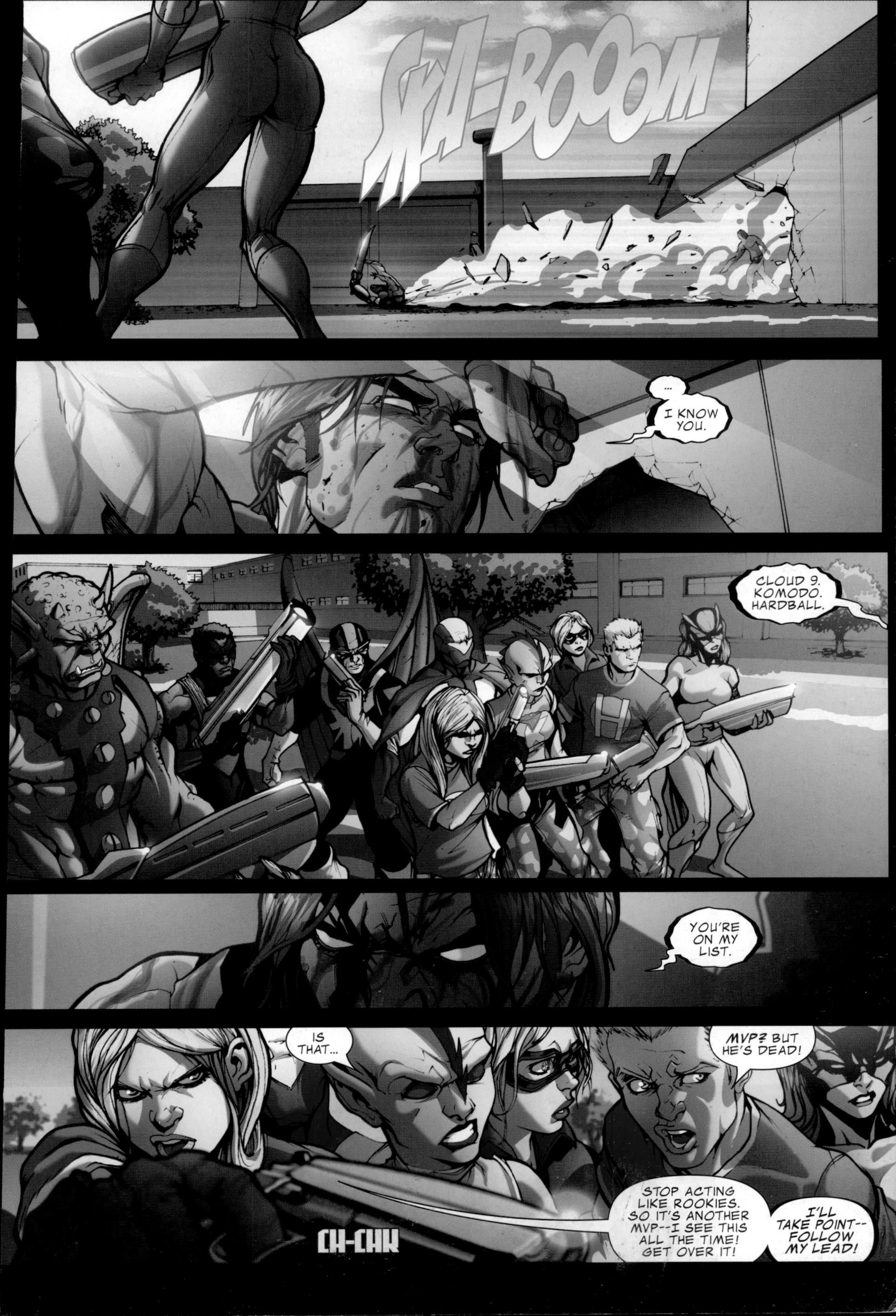
SKA-BOOOM
... I KNOW YOU.
CLOUD 9. KOMODO. HARDBALL.
YOU'RE ON MY LIST.
IS THAT...
MVP? BUT HE'S DEAD!
STOP ACTING LIKE ROOKIES. SO IT'S ANOTHER MVP--I SEE THIS ALL THE TIME! GET OVER IT!
I'LL TAKE POINT--FOLLOW MY LEAD!
CH-CHK

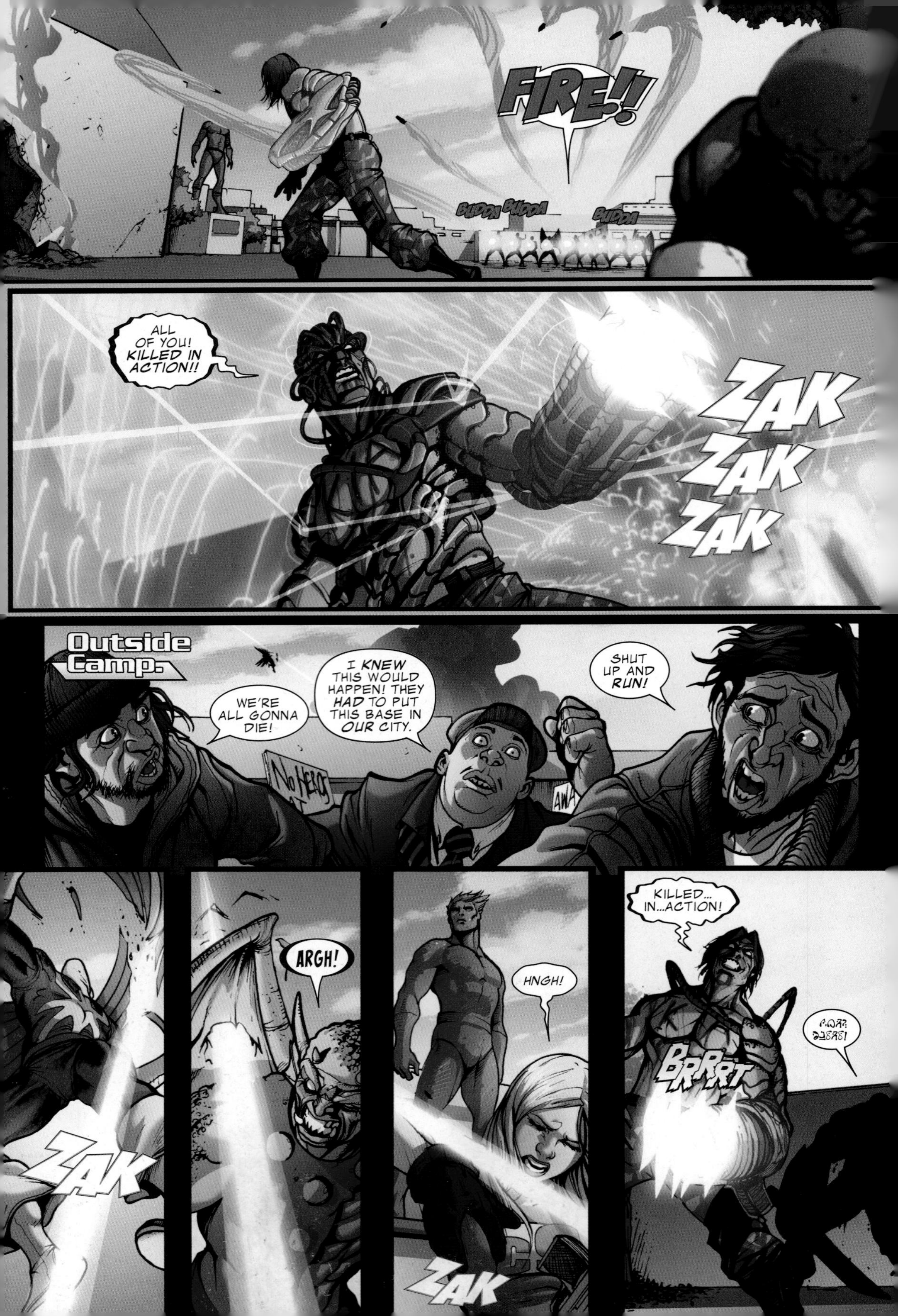
FIRE!!
BUDDA BUDDA
BUDDA
ALL OF YOU! KILLED IN ACTION!!
ZAK ZAK ZAK
Outside Camp.
WE'RE ALL GONNA DIE!
I KNEW THIS WOULD HAPPEN! THEY HAD TO PUT THIS BASE IN OUR CITY.
SHUT UP AND RUN!
ZAK
ARGH!
HNGH!
ZAK
KILLED... IN...ACTION!
BRRRT

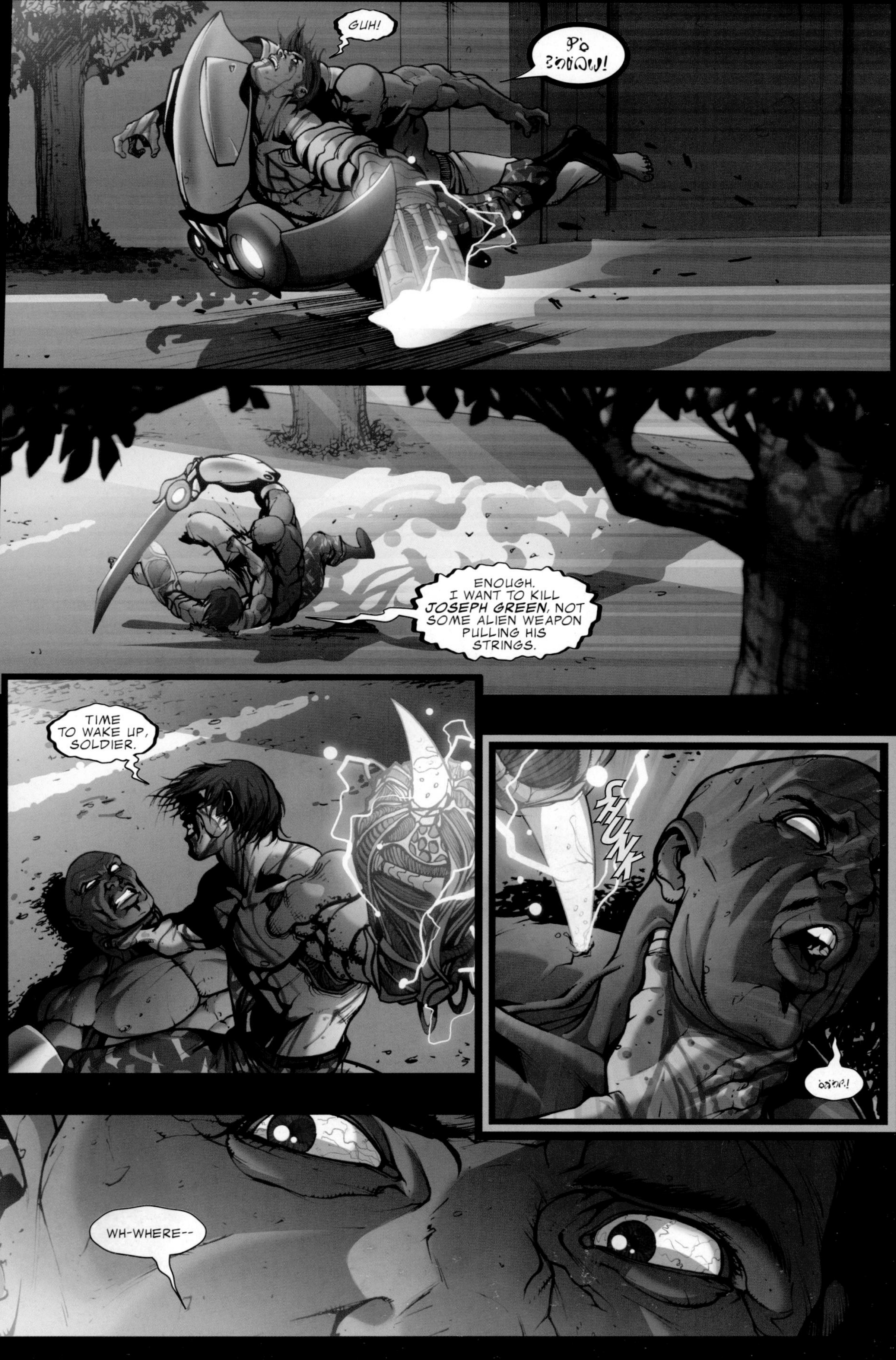
GUH!
ENOUGH. I WANT TO KILL JOSEPH GREEN, NOT SOME ALIEN WEAPON PULLING HIS STRINGS.
TIME TO WAKE UP, SOLDIER.
CHUNK
WH-WHERE--

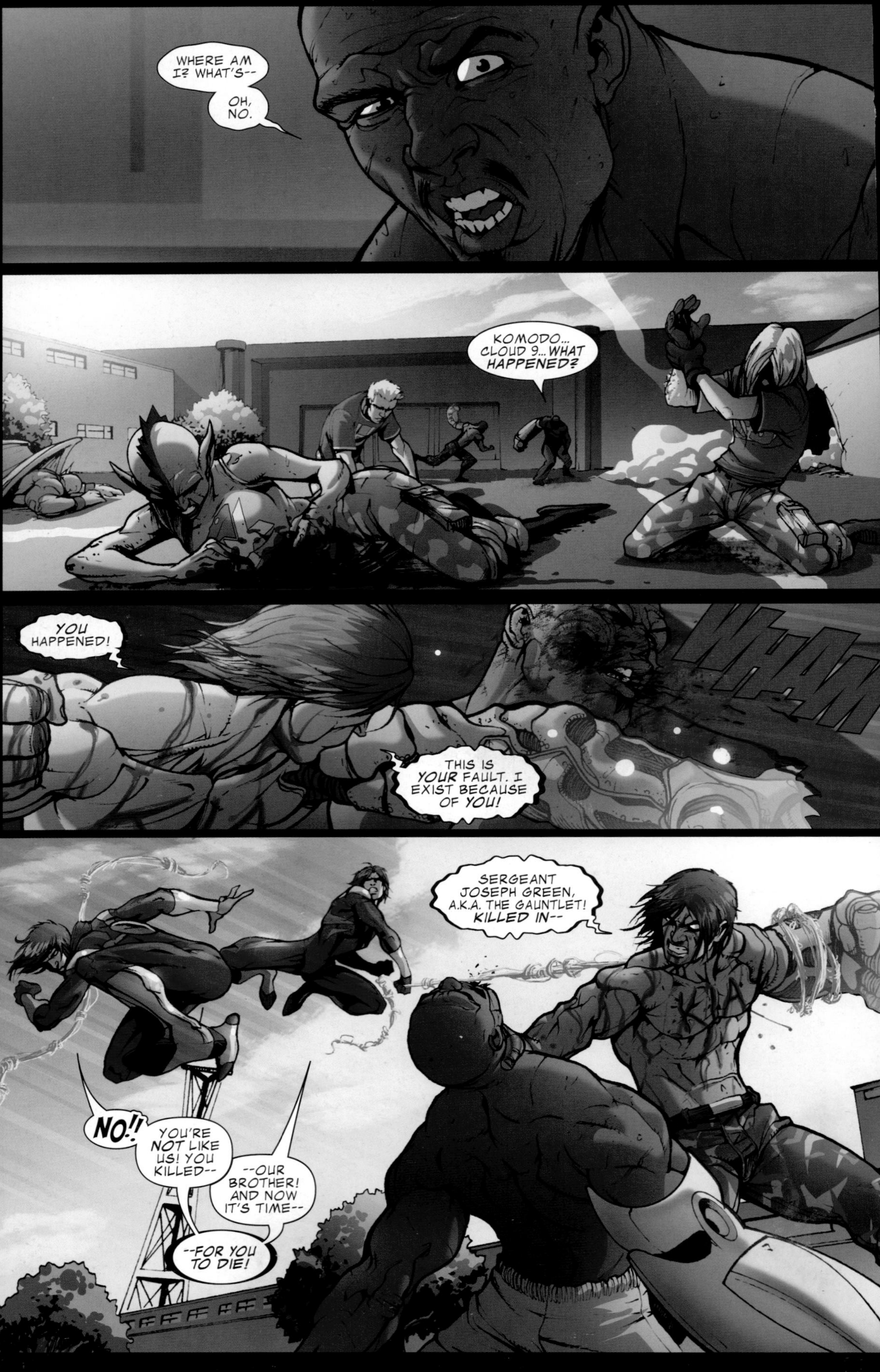

WHERE AM I? WHAT'S--
OH, NO.
KOMODO... CLOUD 9... WHAT HAPPENED?
YOU HAPPENED!
WHAM
THIS IS YOUR FAULT. I EXIST BECAUSE OF YOU!
SERGEANT JOSEPH GREEN, A.K.A. THE GAUNTLET! KILLED IN--
NO!!
YOU'RE NOT LIKE US! YOU KILLED--
--OUR BROTHER! AND NOW IT'S TIME--
--FOR YOU TO DIE!

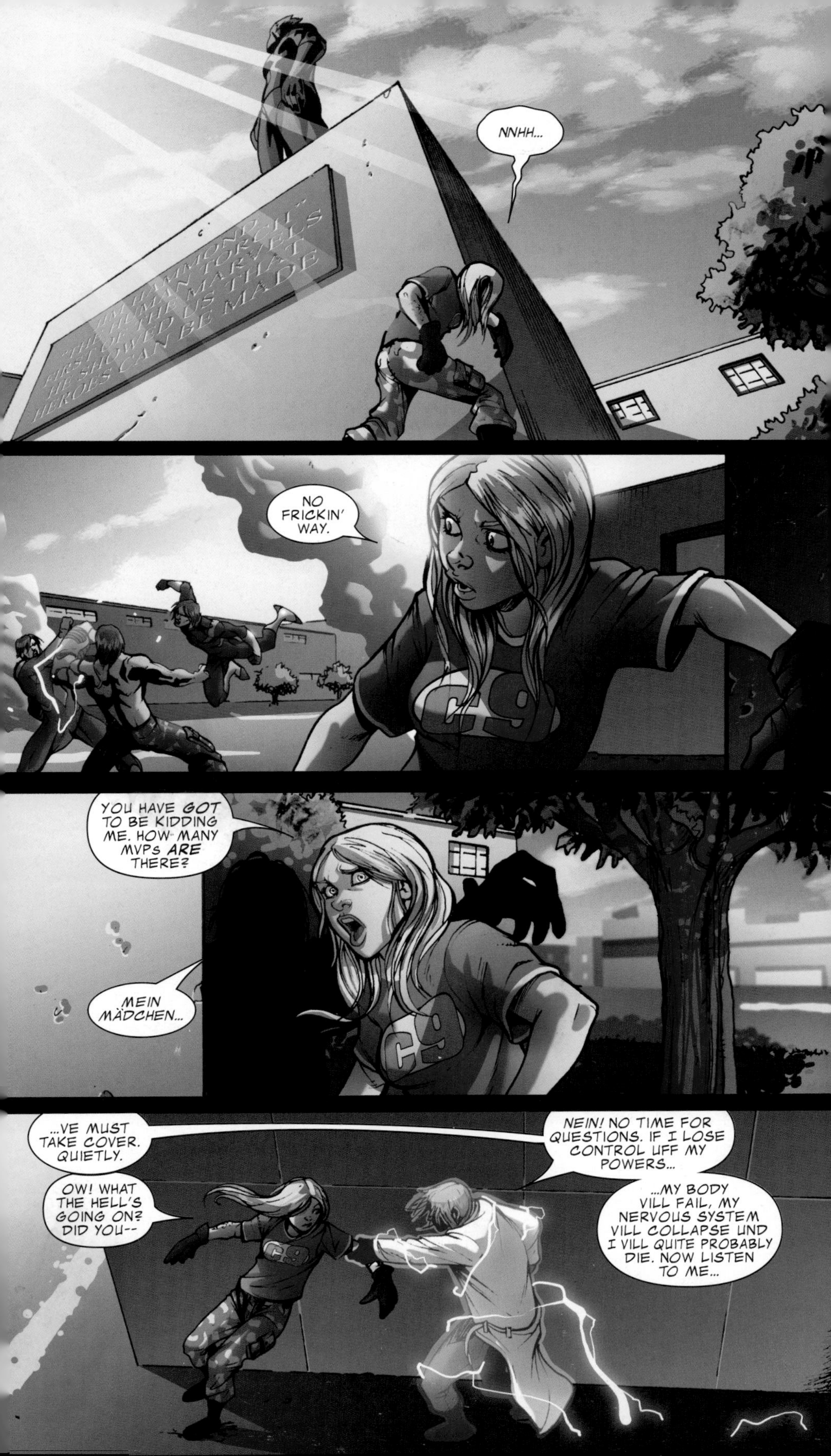
HE SHOWED US THAT
HEROES CAN BE MADE
NNHH...
NO FRICKIN' WAY.
YOU HAVE GOT TO BE KIDDING ME. HOW MANY MVPs ARE THERE?
MEIN MÄDCHEN...
...VE MUST TAKE COVER. QUIETLY.
OW! WHAT THE HELL'S GOING ON? DID YOU--
NEIN! NO TIME FOR QUESTIONS. IF I LOSE CONTROL UFF MY POWERS...
...MY BODY VILL FAIL, MY NERVOUS SYSTEM VILL COLLAPSE UND I VILL QUITE PROBABLY DIE. NOW LISTEN TO ME...

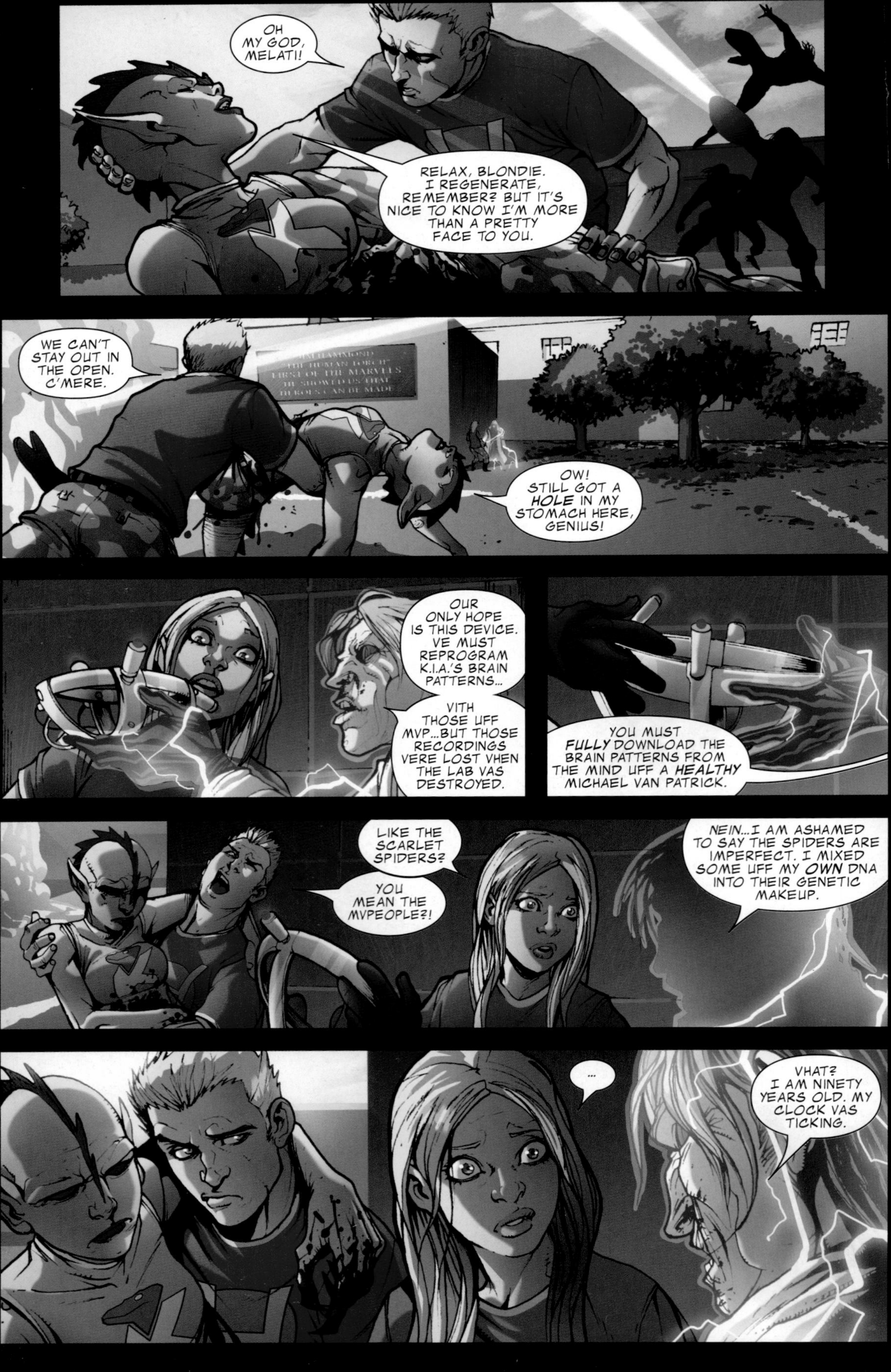

OH MY GOD, MELATI!
RELAX, BLONDIE. I REGENERATE, REMEMBER? BUT IT'S NICE TO KNOW I'M MORE THAN A PRETTY FACE TO YOU.
WE CAN'T STAY OUT IN THE OPEN. C'MERE.
OW! STILL GOT A **HOLE** IN MY STOMACH HERE, GENIUS!
OUR ONLY HOPE IS THIS DEVICE. VE MUST REPROGRAM K.I.A.'S BRAIN PATTERNS...
VITH THOSE UFF MVP...BUT THOSE RECORDINGS VERE LOST VHEN THE LAB VAS DESTROYED.
YOU MUST **FULLY** DOWNLOAD THE BRAIN PATTERNS FROM THE MIND UFF A **HEALTHY** MICHAEL VAN PATRICK.
LIKE THE SCARLET SPIDERS?
YOU MEAN THE MVPEOPLE?!
NEIN...I AM ASHAMED TO SAY THE SPIDERS ARE IMPERFECT. I MIXED SOME UFF MY **OWN** DNA INTO THEIR GENETIC MAKEUP.
...
VHAT? I AM NINETY YEARS OLD. MY CLOCK VAS TICKING.

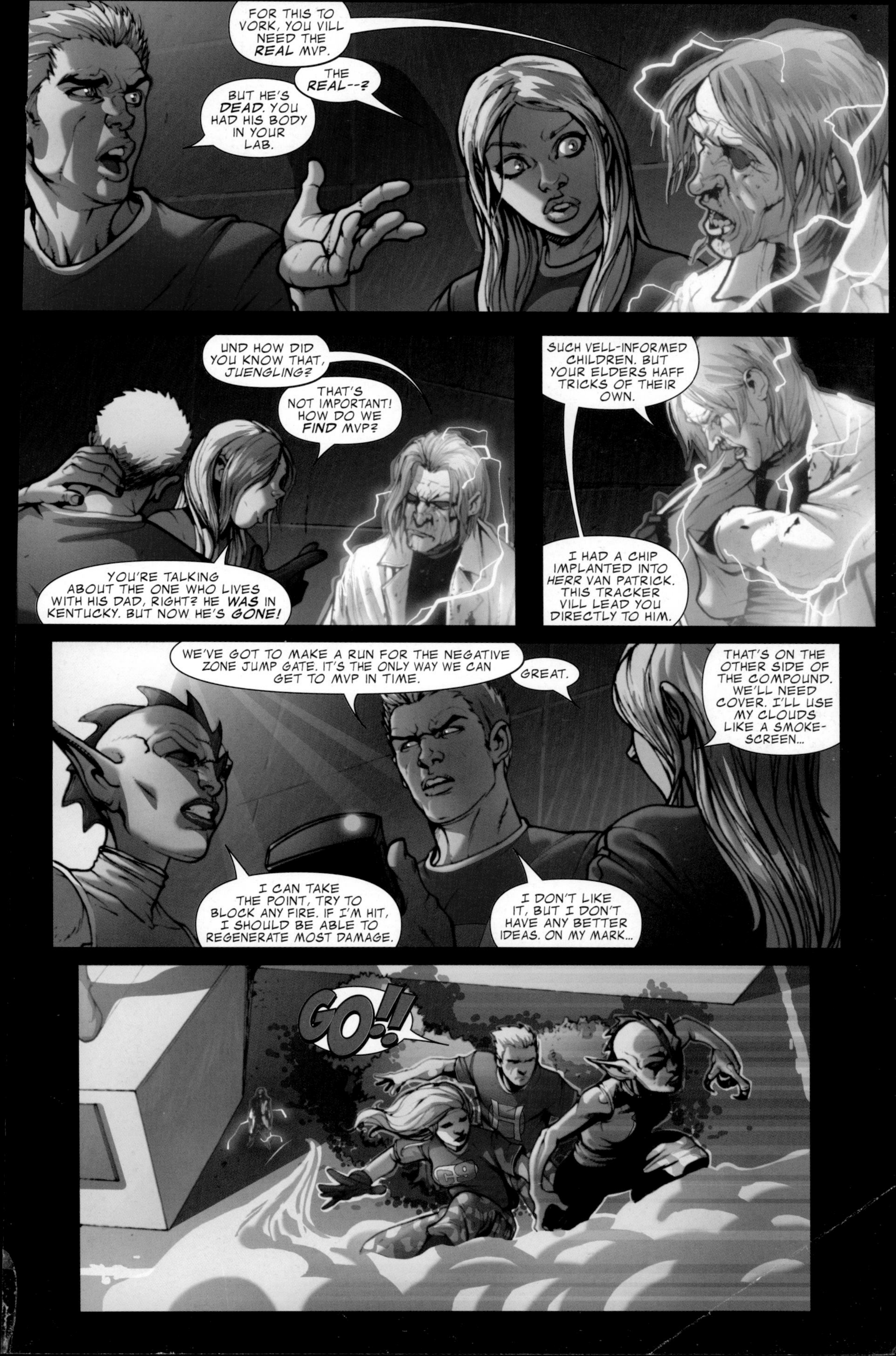
FOR THIS TO VORK, YOU VILL NEED THE REAL MVP.
THE REAL--?
BUT HE'S DEAD. YOU HAD HIS BODY IN YOUR LAB.
UND HOW DID YOU KNOW THAT, JUENGLING?
THAT'S NOT IMPORTANT! HOW DO WE FIND MVP?
YOU'RE TALKING ABOUT THE ONE WHO LIVES WITH HIS DAD, RIGHT? HE WAS IN KENTUCKY. BUT NOW HE'S GONE!
SUCH VELL-INFORMED CHILDREN. BUT YOUR ELDERS HAFF TRICKS OF THEIR OWN.
I HAD A CHIP IMPLANTED INTO HERR VAN PATRICK. THIS TRACKER VILL LEAD YOU DIRECTLY TO HIM.
WE'VE GOT TO MAKE A RUN FOR THE NEGATIVE ZONE JUMP GATE. IT'S THE ONLY WAY WE CAN GET TO MVP IN TIME.
GREAT.
THAT'S ON THE OTHER SIDE OF THE COMPOUND. WE'LL NEED COVER. I'LL USE MY CLOUDS LIKE A SMOKE-SCREEN...
I CAN TAKE THE POINT, TRY TO BLOCK ANY FIRE. IF I'M HIT, I SHOULD BE ABLE TO REGENERATE MOST DAMAGE.
I DON'T LIKE IT, BUT I DON'T HAVE ANY BETTER IDEAS. ON MY MARK...
GO!!

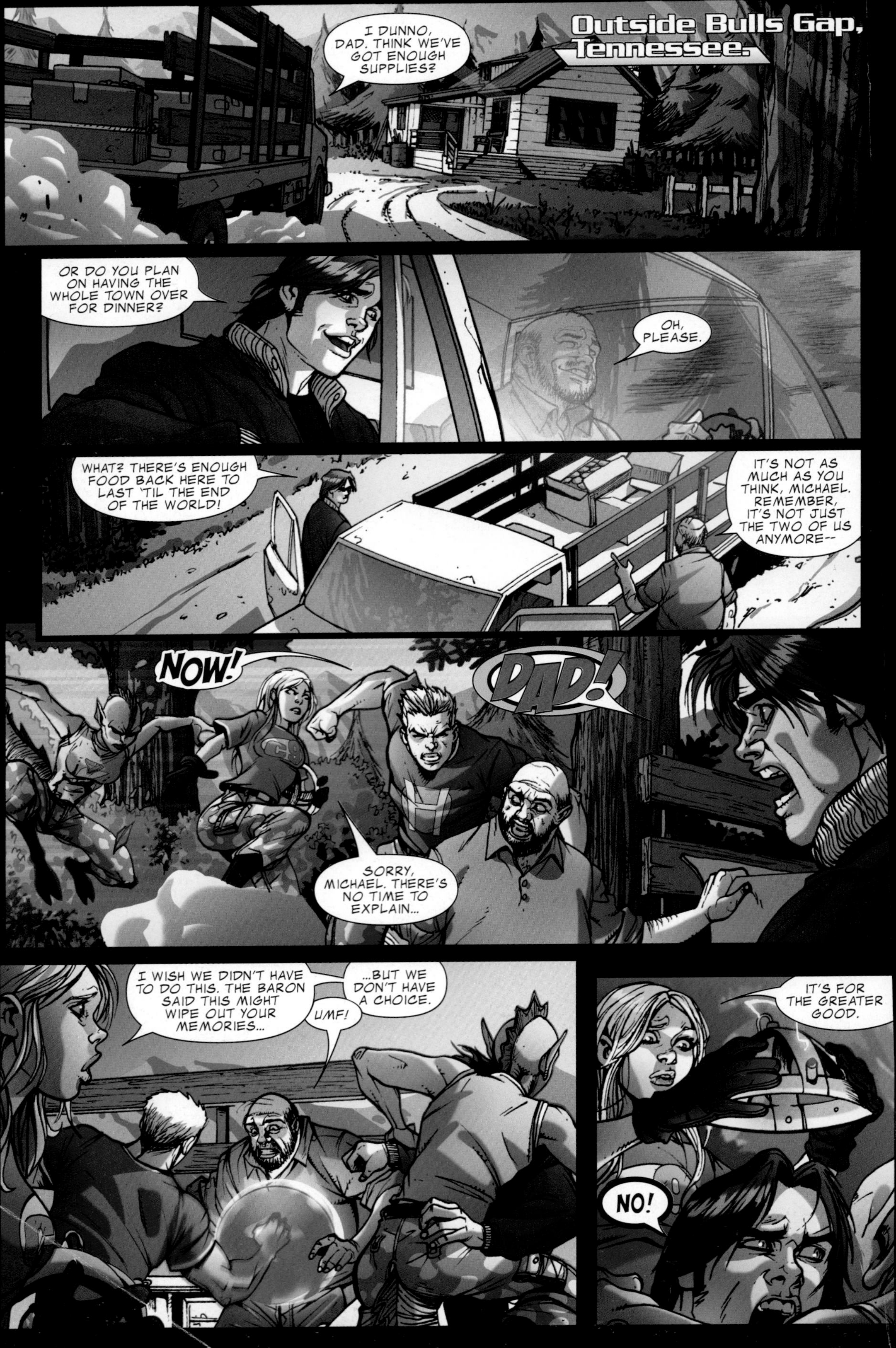
Outside Bulls Gap, Tennessee.
I DUNNO, DAD. THINK WE'VE GOT ENOUGH SUPPLIES?
OR DO YOU PLAN ON HAVING THE WHOLE TOWN OVER FOR DINNER?
OH, PLEASE.
WHAT? THERE'S ENOUGH FOOD BACK HERE TO LAST 'TIL THE END OF THE WORLD!
IT'S NOT AS MUCH AS YOU THINK, MICHAEL. REMEMBER, IT'S NOT JUST THE TWO OF US ANYMORE--
NOW!
DAD!
SORRY, MICHAEL. THERE'S NO TIME TO EXPLAIN...
I WISH WE DIDN'T HAVE TO DO THIS. THE BARON SAID THIS MIGHT WIPE OUT YOUR MEMORIES...
...BUT WE DON'T HAVE A CHOICE.
UMF!
IT'S FOR THE GREATER GOOD.
NO!

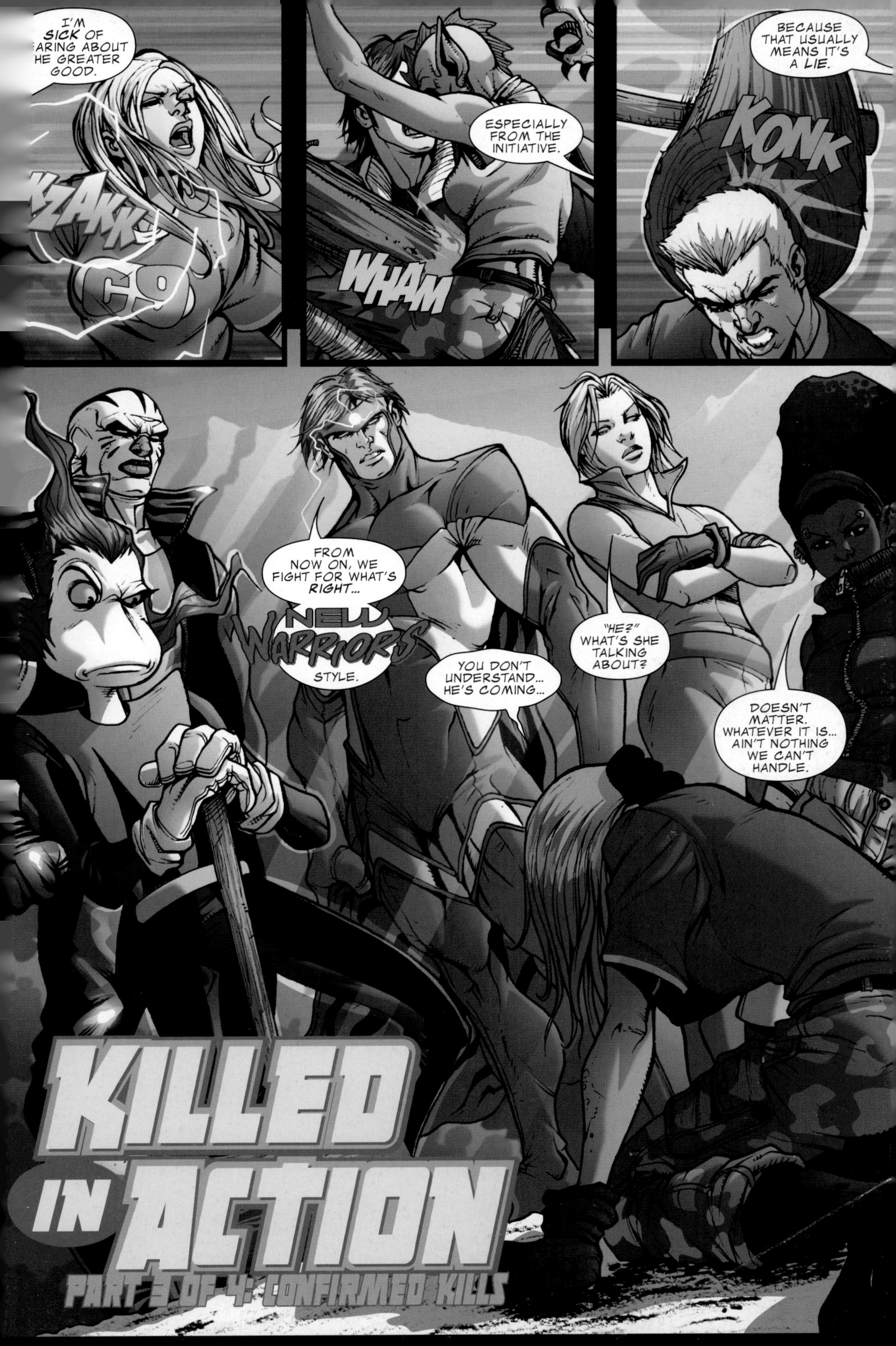
I'M SICK OF HEARING ABOUT THE GREATER GOOD.
KZAKK
ESPECIALLY FROM THE INITIATIVE.
WHAM
BECAUSE THAT USUALLY MEANS IT'S A LIE.
KONK
FROM NOW ON, WE FIGHT FOR WHAT'S RIGHT... NEW WARRIORS STYLE.
YOU DON'T UNDERSTAND... HE'S COMING...
"HE?" WHAT'S SHE TALKING ABOUT?
DOESN'T MATTER. WHATEVER IT IS... AIN'T NOTHING WE CAN'T HANDLE.
KILLED IN ACTION
PART 3 OF 4: CONFIRMED KILLS

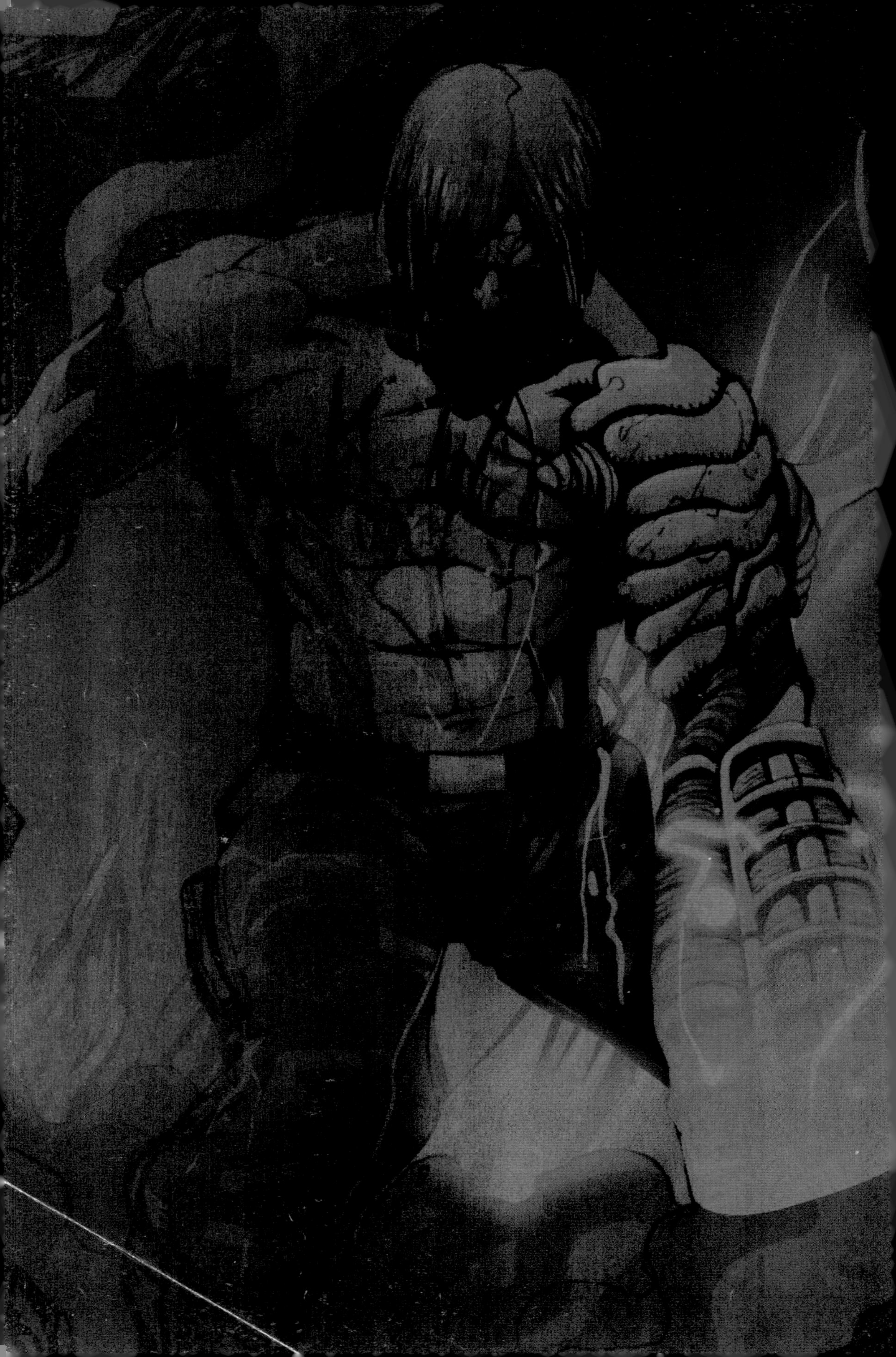

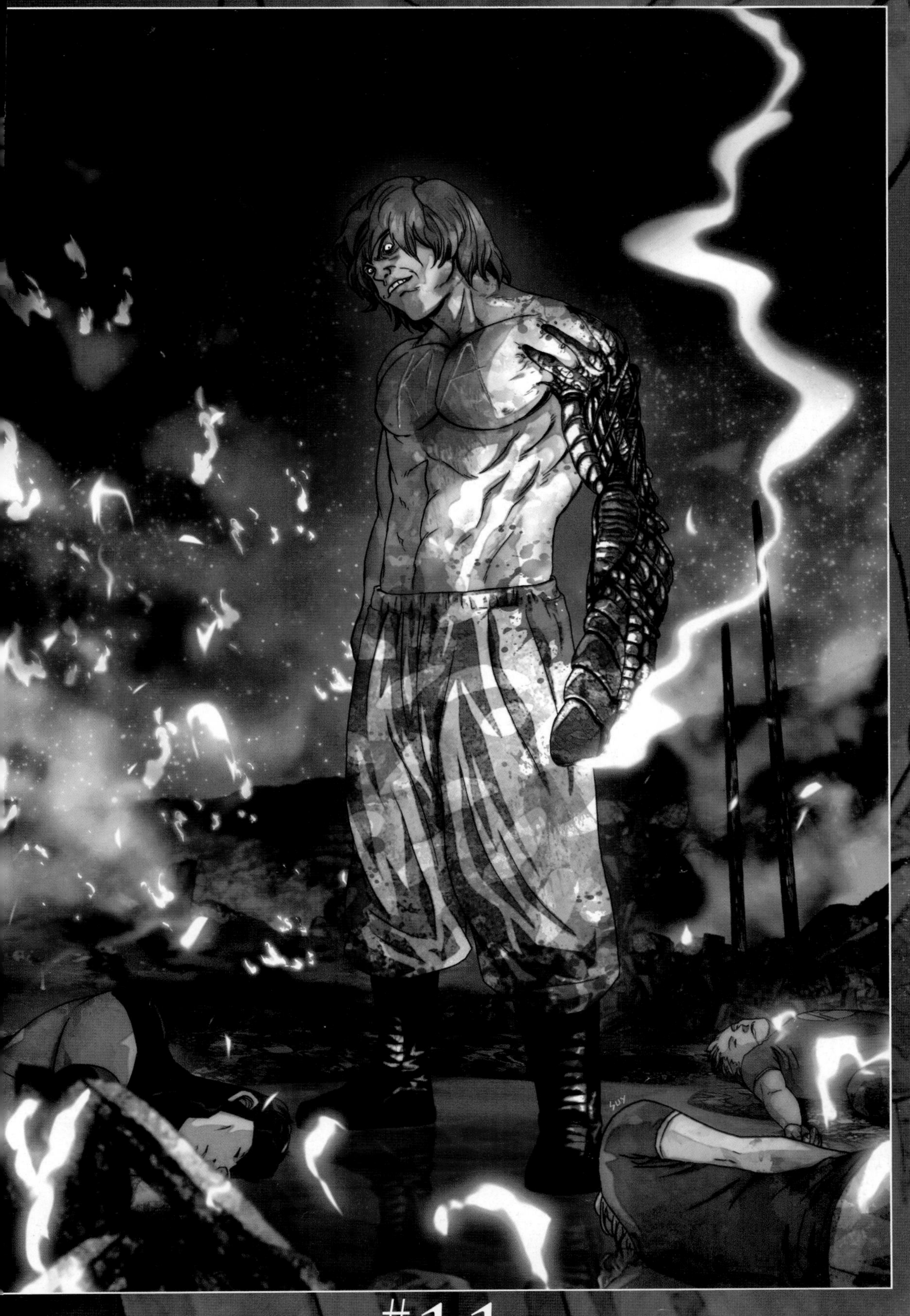

#11

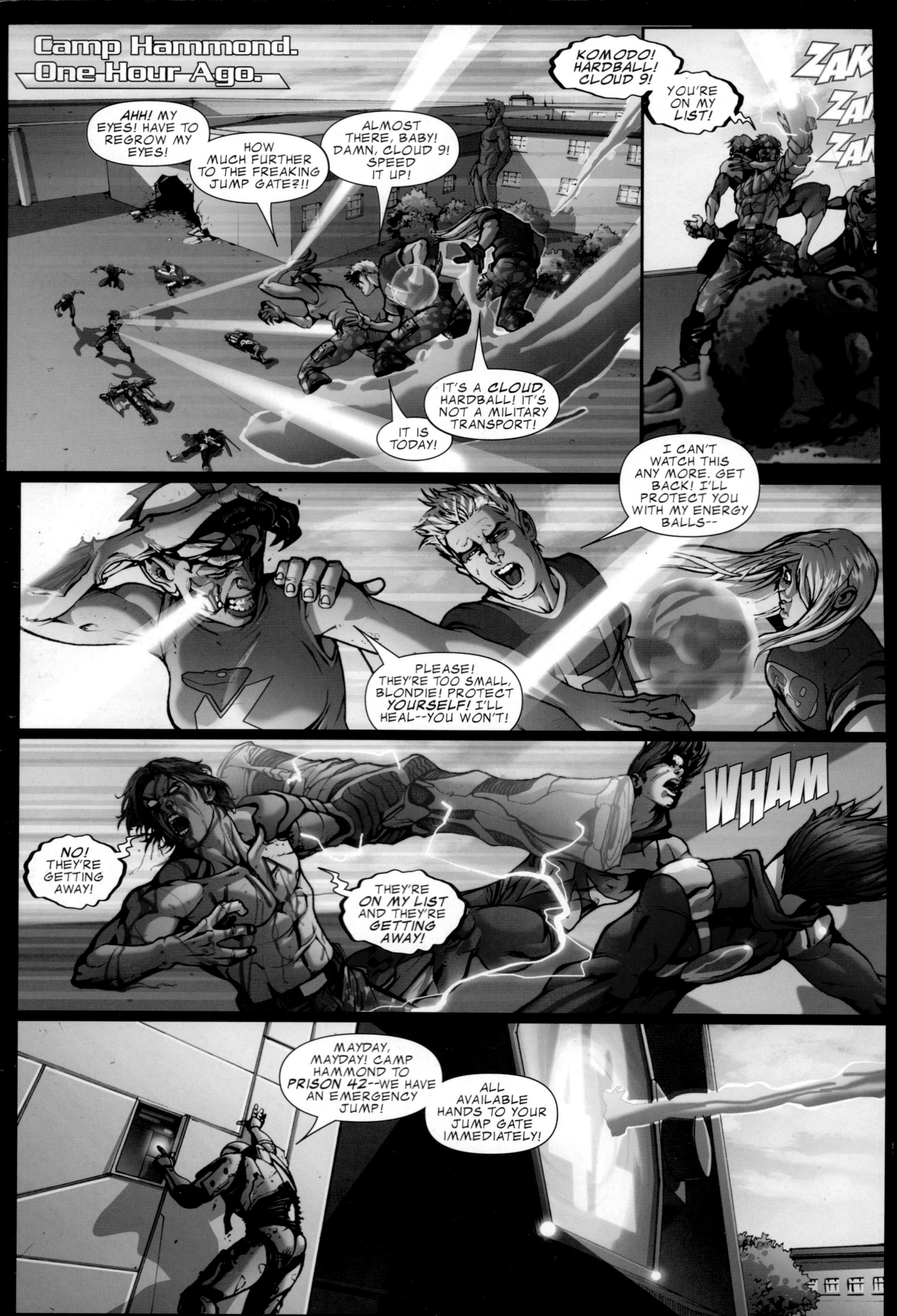
Camp Hammond. One Hour Ago.
AHH! MY EYES! HAVE TO REGROW MY EYES!
HOW MUCH FURTHER TO THE FREAKING JUMP GATE?!!
ALMOST THERE, BABY! DAMN, CLOUD 9! SPEED IT UP!
IT'S A CLOUD, HARDBALL! IT'S NOT A MILITARY TRANSPORT!
IT IS TODAY!
KOMODO! HARDBALL! CLOUD 9!
YOU'RE ON MY LIST!
ZAK
ZAK
ZAK
I CAN'T WATCH THIS ANY MORE. GET BACK! I'LL PROTECT YOU WITH MY ENERGY BALLS--
PLEASE! THEY'RE TOO SMALL, BLONDIE! PROTECT YOURSELF! I'LL HEAL--YOU WON'T!
WHAM
NO! THEY'RE GETTING AWAY!
THEY'RE ON MY LIST AND THEY'RE GETTING AWAY!
MAYDAY, MAYDAY! CAMP HAMMOND TO PRISON 42--WE HAVE AN EMERGENCY JUMP!
ALL AVAILABLE HANDS TO YOUR JUMP GATE IMMEDIATELY!

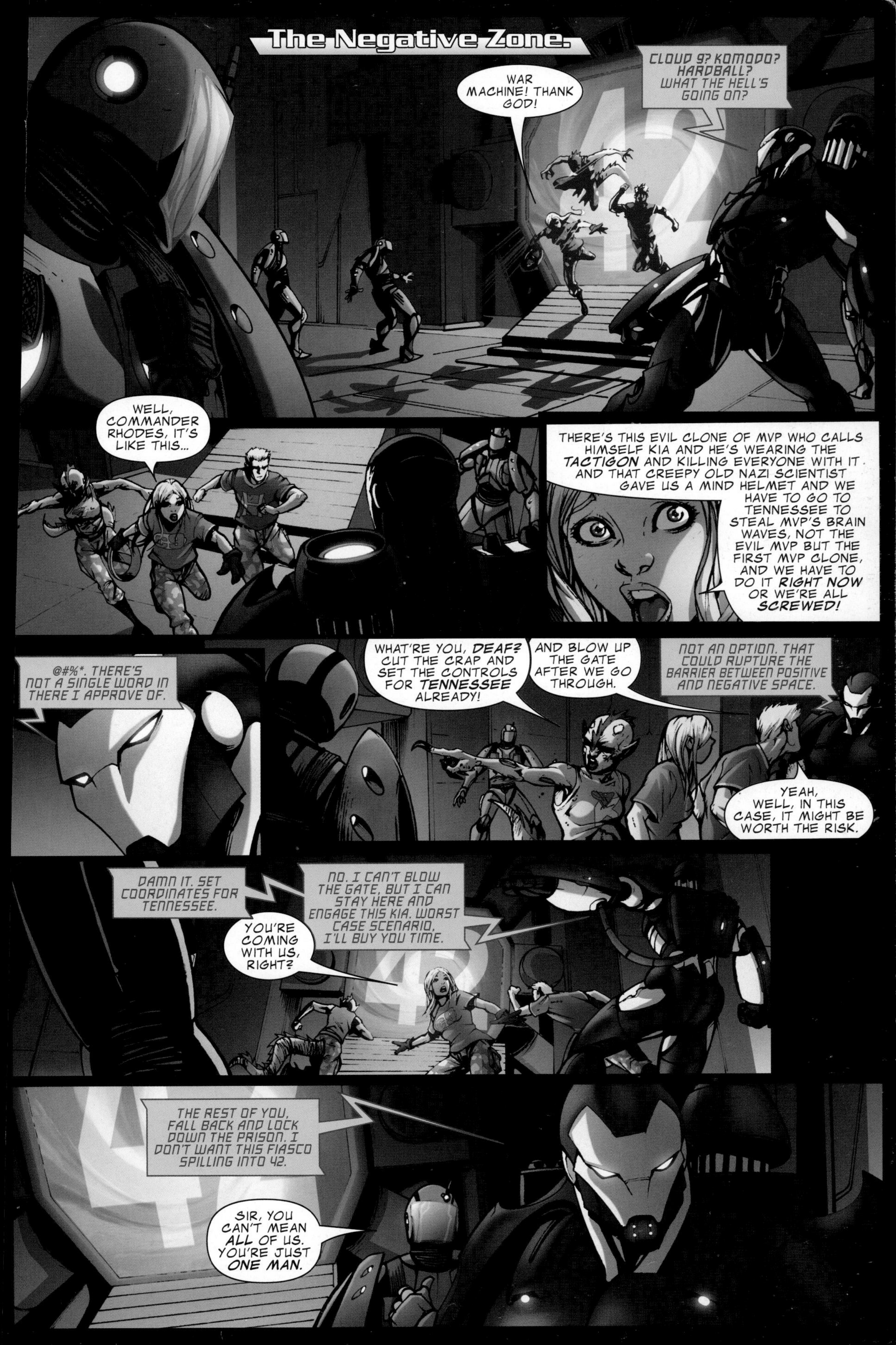
The Negative Zone.
WAR MACHINE! THANK GOD!
CLOUD 9? KOMODO? HARDBALL? WHAT THE HELL'S GOING ON?
WELL, COMMANDER RHODES, IT'S LIKE THIS...
THERE'S THIS EVIL CLONE OF MVP WHO CALLS HIMSELF KIA AND HE'S WEARING THE TACTIGON AND KILLING EVERYONE WITH IT AND THAT CREEPY OLD NAZI SCIENTIST GAVE US A MIND HELMET AND WE HAVE TO GO TO TENNESSEE TO STEAL MVP'S BRAIN WAVES, NOT THE EVIL MVP BUT THE FIRST MVP CLONE, AND WE HAVE TO DO IT RIGHT NOW OR WE'RE ALL SCREWED!
@#%*. THERE'S NOT A SINGLE WORD IN THERE I APPROVE OF.
WHAT'RE YOU, DEAF? CUT THE CRAP AND SET THE CONTROLS FOR TENNESSEE ALREADY!
AND BLOW UP THE GATE AFTER WE GO THROUGH.
NOT AN OPTION. THAT COULD RUPTURE THE BARRIER BETWEEN POSITIVE AND NEGATIVE SPACE.
YEAH, WELL, IN THIS CASE, IT MIGHT BE WORTH THE RISK.
DAMN IT. SET COORDINATES FOR TENNESSEE.
NO. I CAN'T BLOW THE GATE, BUT I CAN STAY HERE AND ENGAGE THIS KIA. WORST CASE SCENARIO, I'LL BUY YOU TIME.
YOU'RE COMING WITH US, RIGHT?
THE REST OF YOU, FALL BACK AND LOCK DOWN THE PRISON. I DON'T WANT THIS FIASCO SPILLING INTO 42.
SIR, YOU CAN'T MEAN ALL OF US. YOU'RE JUST ONE MAN.

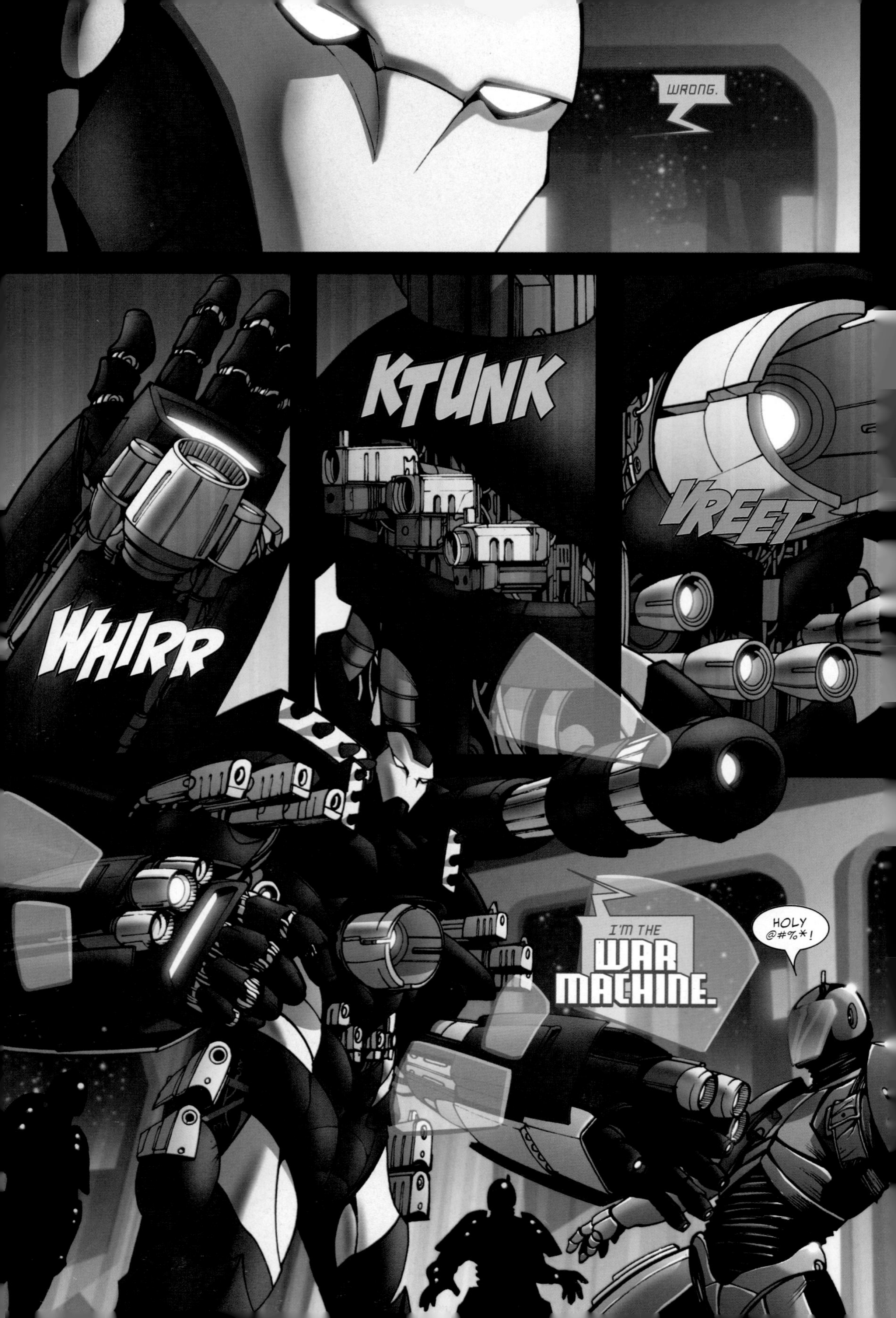
WRONG.
WHIRR
KTUNK
VREET
I'M THE WAR MACHINE.
HOLY @#%*!

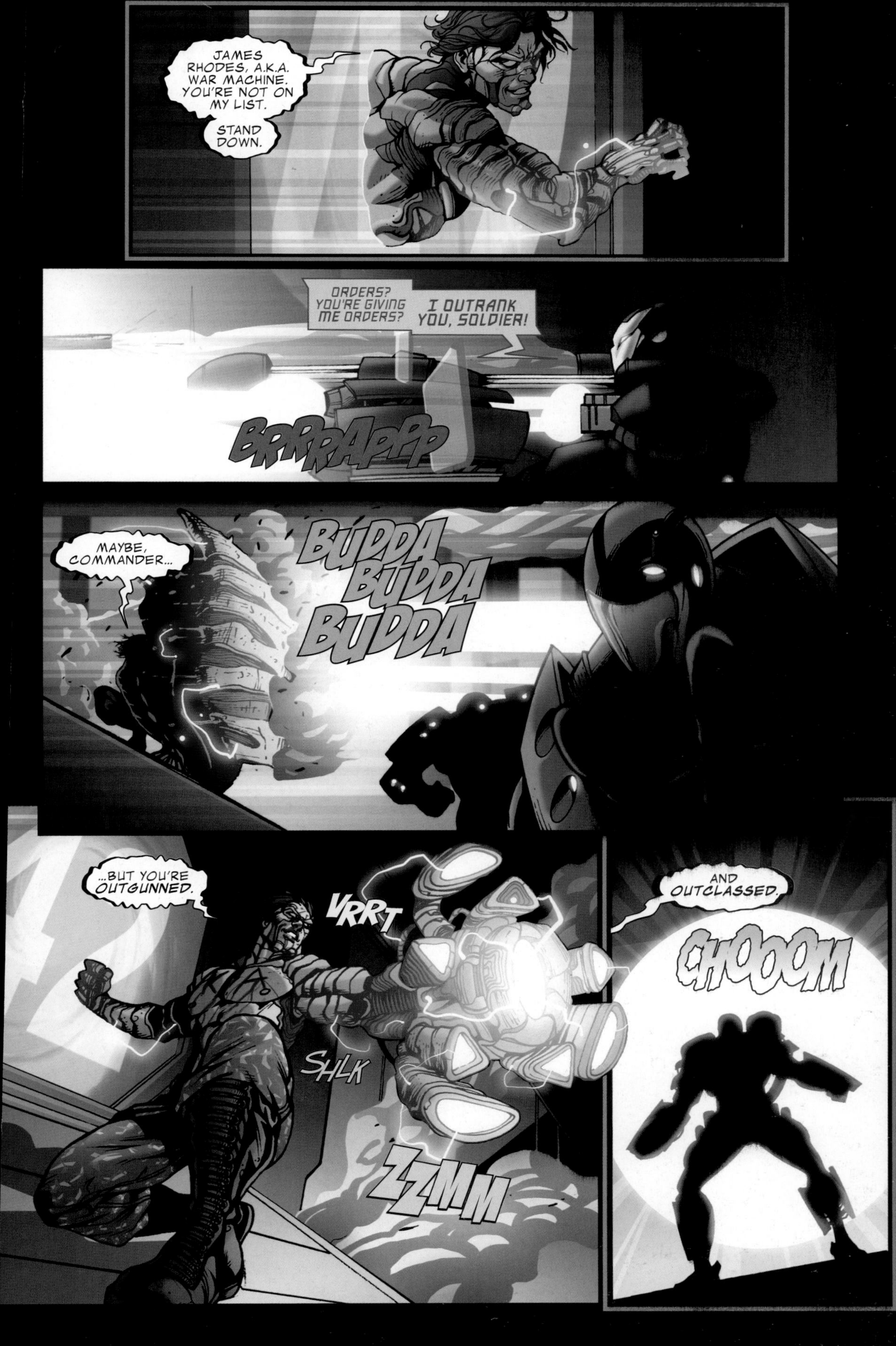
JAMES RHODES, A.K.A. WAR MACHINE. YOU'RE NOT ON MY LIST.
STAND DOWN.
ORDERS? YOU'RE GIVING ME ORDERS?
I OUTRANK YOU, SOLDIER!
BRRRAPPP
MAYBE, COMMANDER...
BUDDA BUDDA BUDDA
...BUT YOU'RE OUTGUNNED.
VRRT
SHLK
ZZMM
AND OUTCLASSED.
CHOOOM

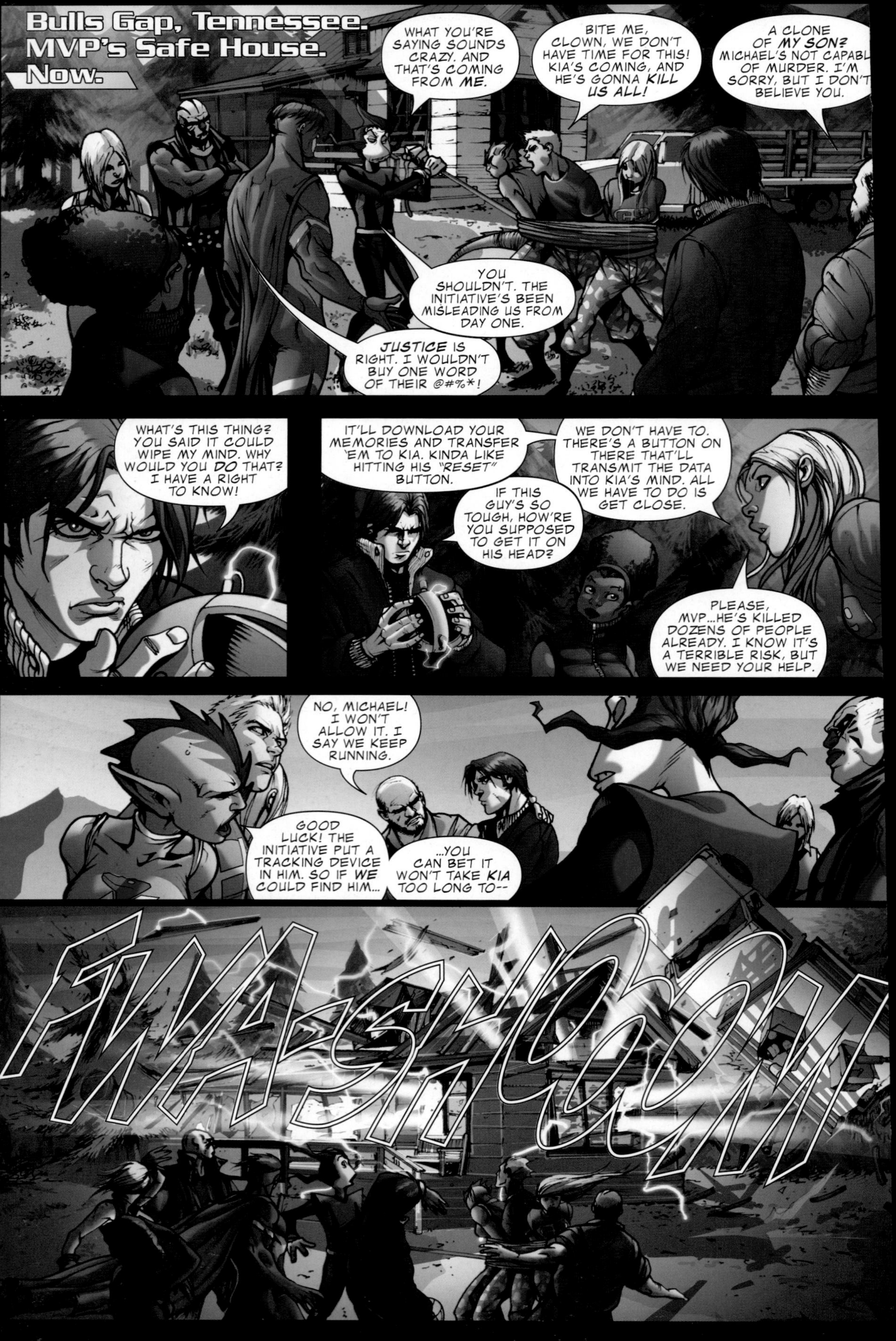

Bulls Gap, Tennessee.
MVP's Safe House.
Now.
WHAT YOU'RE SAYING SOUNDS CRAZY. AND THAT'S COMING FROM ME.
BITE ME, CLOWN, WE DON'T HAVE TIME FOR THIS! KIA'S COMING, AND HE'S GONNA KILL US ALL!
A CLONE OF MY SON? MICHAEL'S NOT CAPABL OF MURDER. I'M SORRY, BUT I DON'T BELIEVE YOU.
YOU SHOULDN'T. THE INITIATIVE'S BEEN MISLEADING US FROM DAY ONE.
JUSTICE IS RIGHT. I WOULDN'T BUY ONE WORD OF THEIR @#%*!
WHAT'S THIS THING? YOU SAID IT COULD WIPE MY MIND. WHY WOULD YOU DO THAT? I HAVE A RIGHT TO KNOW!
IT'LL DOWNLOAD YOUR MEMORIES AND TRANSFER 'EM TO KIA. KINDA LIKE HITTING HIS "RESET" BUTTON.
IF THIS GUY'S SO TOUGH, HOW'RE YOU SUPPOSED TO GET IT ON HIS HEAD?
WE DON'T HAVE TO. THERE'S A BUTTON ON THERE THAT'LL TRANSMIT THE DATA INTO KIA'S MIND. ALL WE HAVE TO DO IS GET CLOSE.
PLEASE, MVP...HE'S KILLED DOZENS OF PEOPLE ALREADY. I KNOW IT'S A TERRIBLE RISK, BUT WE NEED YOUR HELP.
NO, MICHAEL! I WON'T ALLOW IT. I SAY WE KEEP RUNNING.
GOOD LUCK! THE INITIATIVE PUT A TRACKING DEVICE IN HIM. SO IF WE COULD FIND HIM...
...YOU CAN BET IT WON'T TAKE KIA TOO LONG TO--
FWASHOOM

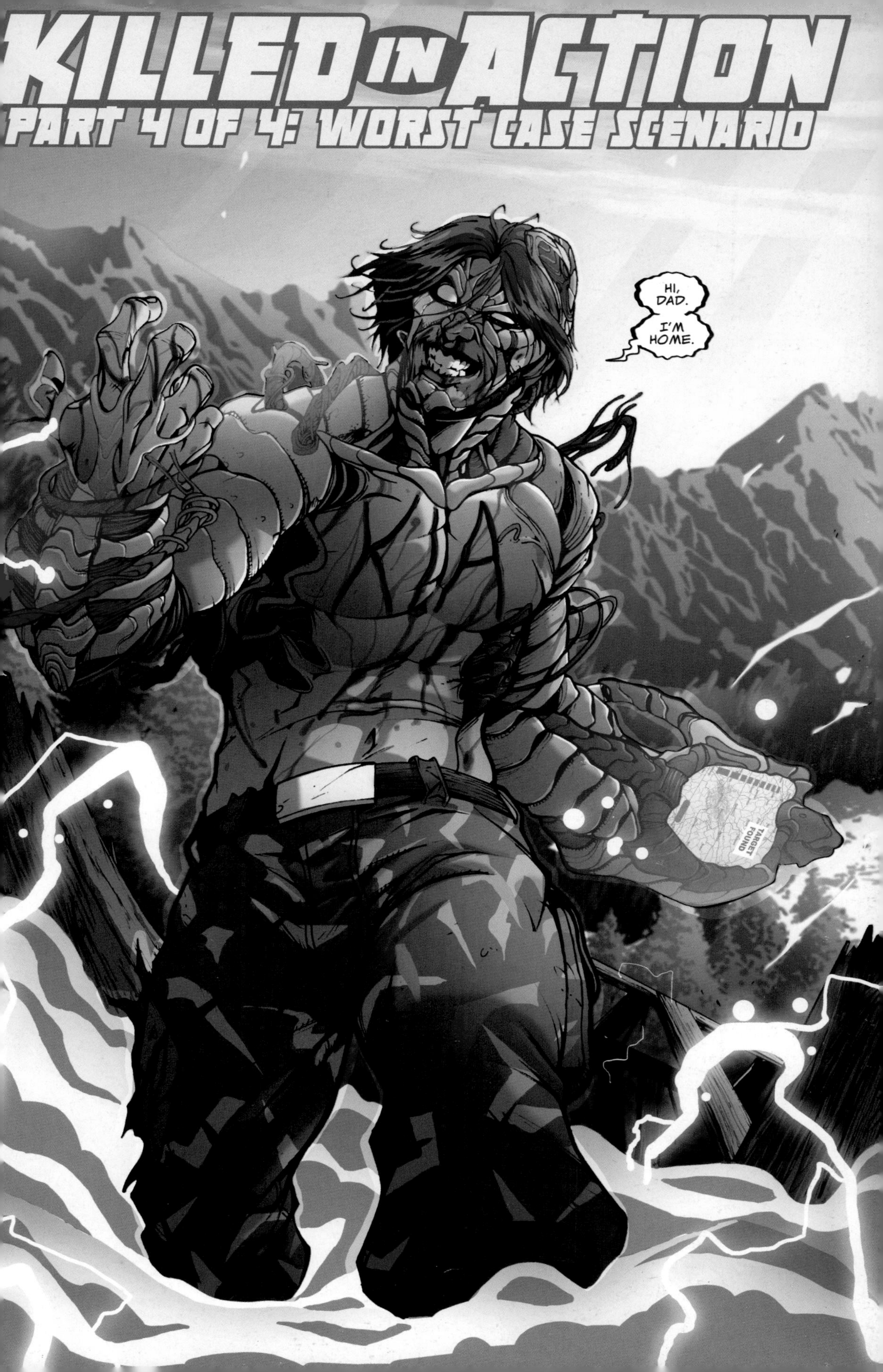
KILLED IN ACTION
PART 4 OF 4: WORST CASE SCENARIO
HI, DAD.
I'M HOME.
TARGET FOUND

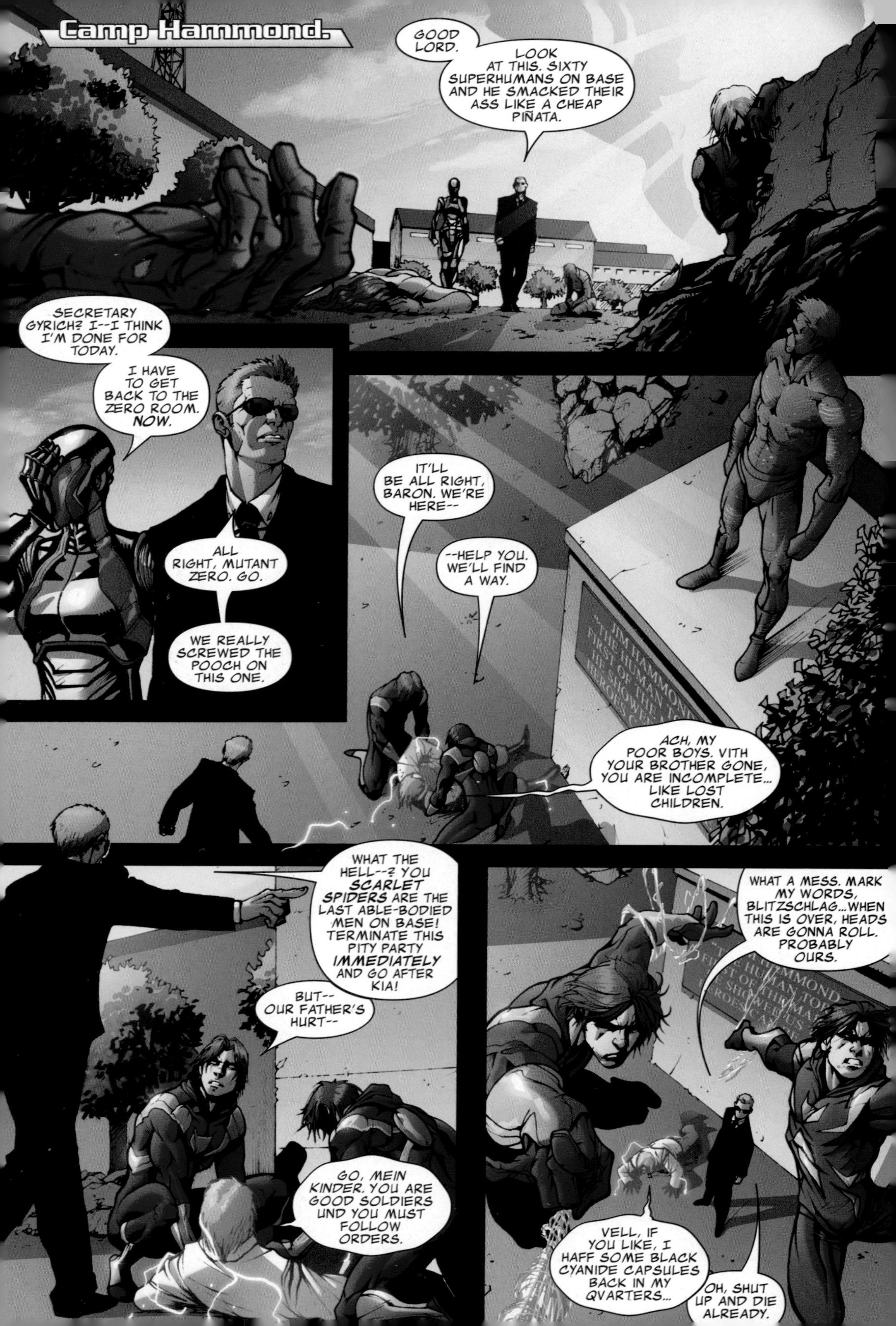
Camp Hammond.
GOOD LORD.
LOOK AT THIS. SIXTY SUPERHUMANS ON BASE AND HE SMACKED THEIR ASS LIKE A CHEAP PIÑATA.
SECRETARY GYRICH? I--I THINK I'M DONE FOR TODAY.
I HAVE TO GET BACK TO THE ZERO ROOM. NOW.
ALL RIGHT, MUTANT ZERO. GO.
WE REALLY SCREWED THE POOCH ON THIS ONE.
IT'LL BE ALL RIGHT, BARON. WE'RE HERE--
--HELP YOU. WE'LL FIND A WAY.
ACH, MY POOR BOYS. VITH YOUR BROTHER GONE, YOU ARE INCOMPLETE... LIKE LOST CHILDREN.
WHAT THE HELL--? YOU SCARLET SPIDERS ARE THE LAST ABLE-BODIED MEN ON BASE! TERMINATE THIS PITY PARTY IMMEDIATELY AND GO AFTER KIA!
BUT-- OUR FATHER'S HURT--
GO, MEIN KINDER. YOU ARE GOOD SOLDIERS UND YOU MUST FOLLOW ORDERS.
WHAT A MESS. MARK MY WORDS, BLITZSCHLAG...WHEN THIS IS OVER, HEADS ARE GONNA ROLL. PROBABLY OURS.
VELL, IF YOU LIKE, I HAFF SOME BLACK CYANIDE CAPSULES BACK IN MY QVARTERS...
OH, SHUT UP AND DIE ALREADY.

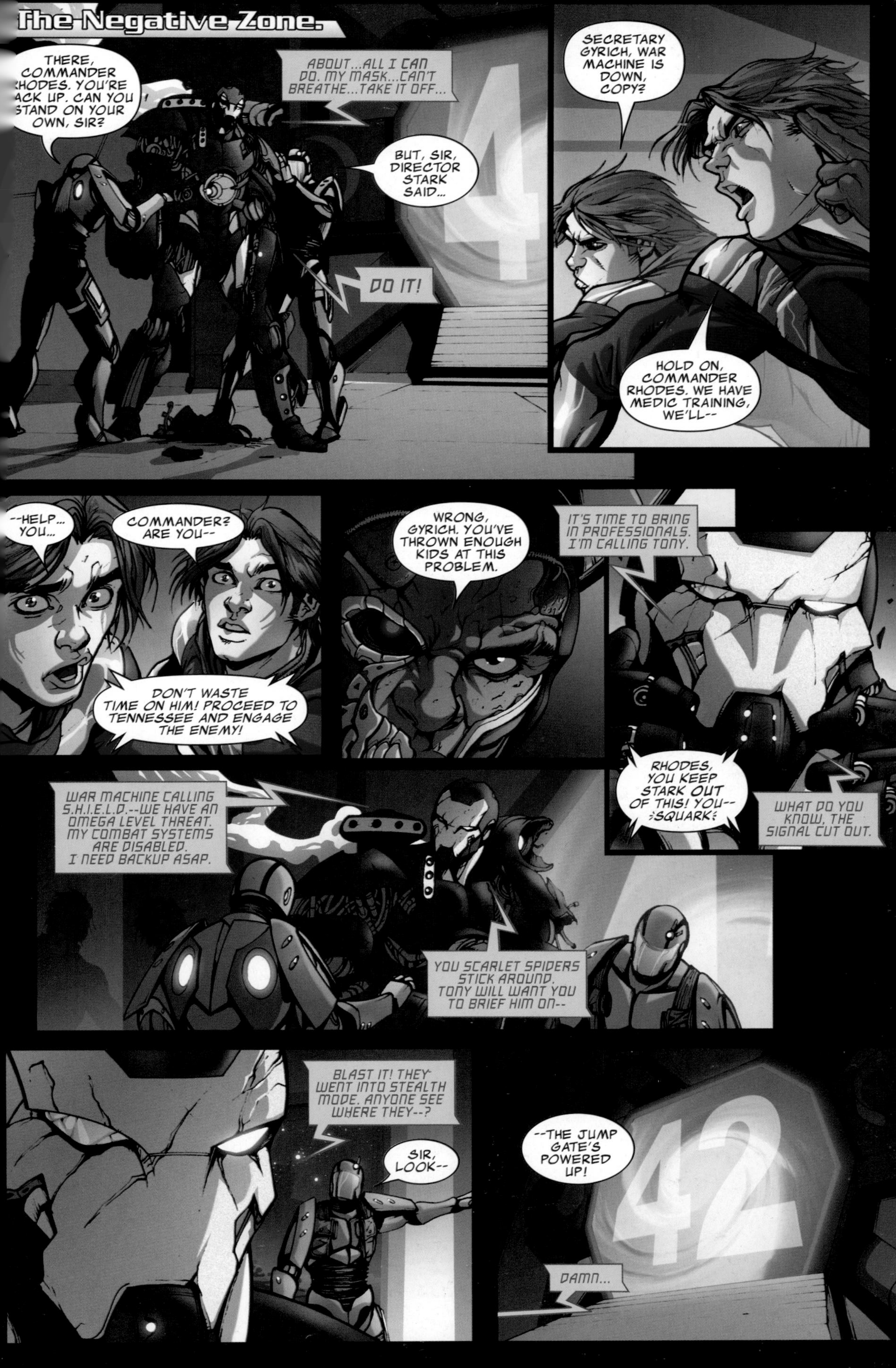
The Negative Zone.
THERE, COMMANDER RHODES. YOU'RE BACK UP. CAN YOU STAND ON YOUR OWN, SIR?
ABOUT...ALL I CAN DO. MY MASK...CAN'T BREATHE...TAKE IT OFF...
BUT, SIR, DIRECTOR STARK SAID...
DO IT!
SECRETARY GYRICH, WAR MACHINE IS DOWN, COPY?
HOLD ON, COMMANDER RHODES. WE HAVE MEDIC TRAINING, WE'LL--
--HELP... YOU...
COMMANDER? ARE YOU--
DON'T WASTE TIME ON HIM! PROCEED TO TENNESSEE AND ENGAGE THE ENEMY!
WRONG, GYRICH. YOU'VE THROWN ENOUGH KIDS AT THIS PROBLEM.
IT'S TIME TO BRING IN PROFESSIONALS. I'M CALLING TONY.
RHODES, YOU KEEP STARK OUT OF THIS! YOU-- *SQUARK*
WHAT DO YOU KNOW, THE SIGNAL CUT OUT.
WAR MACHINE CALLING S.H.I.E.L.D.--WE HAVE AN OMEGA LEVEL THREAT. MY COMBAT SYSTEMS ARE DISABLED. I NEED BACKUP ASAP.
YOU SCARLET SPIDERS STICK AROUND. TONY WILL WANT YOU TO BRIEF HIM ON--
BLAST IT! THEY WENT INTO STEALTH MODE. ANYONE SEE WHERE THEY--?
SIR, LOOK--
--THE JUMP GATE'S POWERED UP!
42
DAMN...

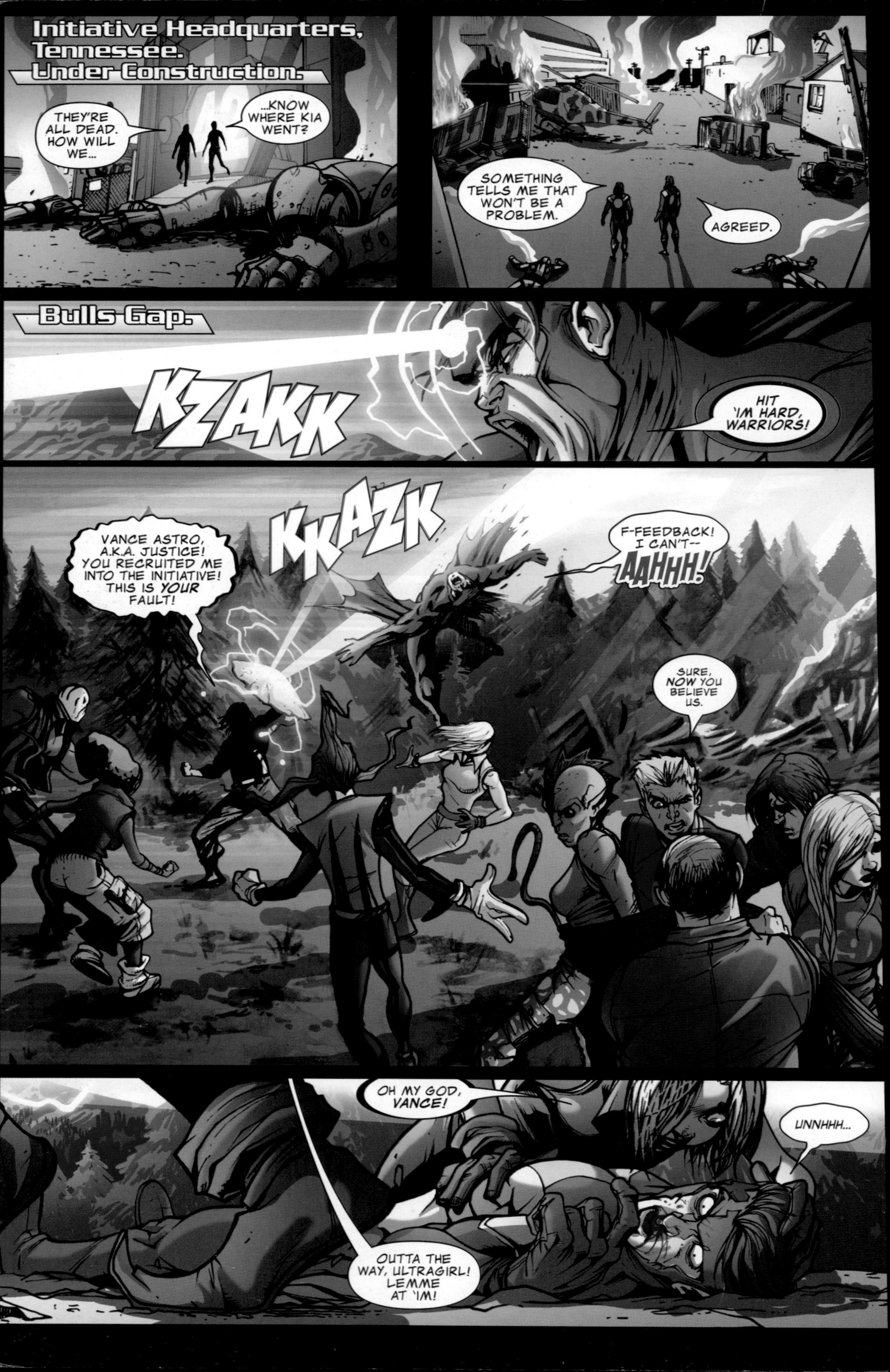

Initiative Headquarters, Tennessee. Under Construction.
THEY'RE ALL DEAD. HOW WILL WE...
...KNOW WHERE KIA WENT?
SOMETHING TELLS ME THAT WON'T BE A PROBLEM.
AGREED.
Bulls Gap.
KZAKK
HIT 'IM HARD, WARRIORS!
KKAZK
VANCE ASTRO, A.K.A. JUSTICE! YOU RECRUITED ME INTO THE INITIATIVE! THIS IS YOUR FAULT!
F-FEEDBACK! I CAN'T-- AAHHH!
SURE, NOW YOU BELIEVE US.
OH MY GOD, VANCE!
UNNHHH...
OUTTA THE WAY, ULTRAGIRL! LEMME AT 'IM!

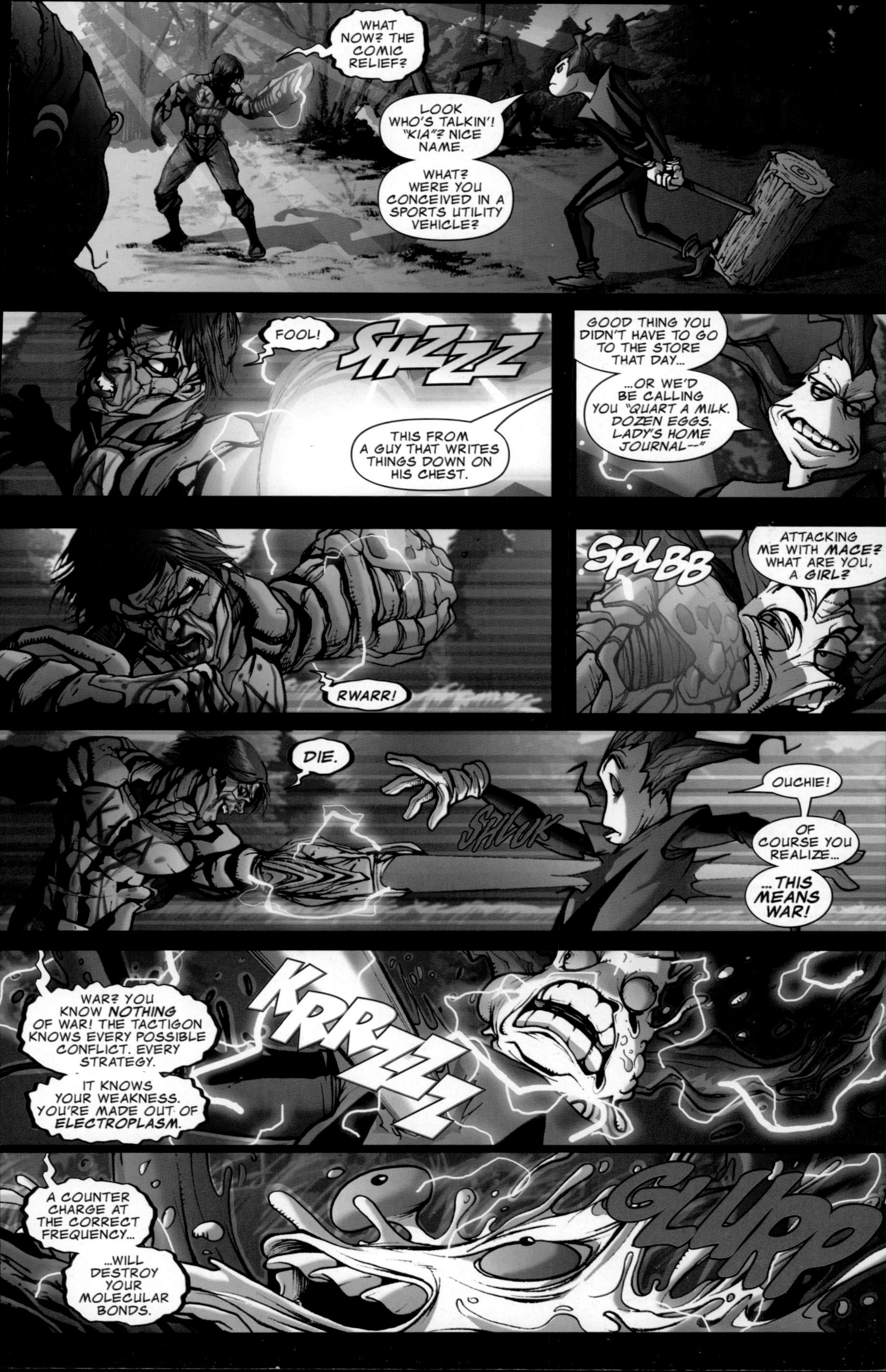
WHAT NOW? THE COMIC RELIEF?
LOOK WHO'S TALKIN'! "KIA"? NICE NAME.
WHAT? WERE YOU CONCEIVED IN A SPORTS UTILITY VEHICLE?
FOOL!
SHZZZ
THIS FROM A GUY THAT WRITES THINGS DOWN ON HIS CHEST.
GOOD THING YOU DIDN'T HAVE TO GO TO THE STORE THAT DAY...
...OR WE'D BE CALLING YOU "QUART A MILK. DOZEN EGGS. LADY'S HOME JOURNAL--"
RWARR!
SPLBB
ATTACKING ME WITH MACE? WHAT ARE YOU, A GIRL?
DIE.
SPLUK
OUCHIE!
OF COURSE YOU REALIZE...
...THIS MEANS WAR!
WAR? YOU KNOW NOTHING OF WAR! THE TACTIGON KNOWS EVERY POSSIBLE CONFLICT. EVERY STRATEGY.
IT KNOWS YOUR WEAKNESS. YOU'RE MADE OUT OF ELECTROPLASM.
KRRZZZ
A COUNTER CHARGE AT THE CORRECT FREQUENCY...
...WILL DESTROY YOUR MOLECULAR BONDS.
GLUPP

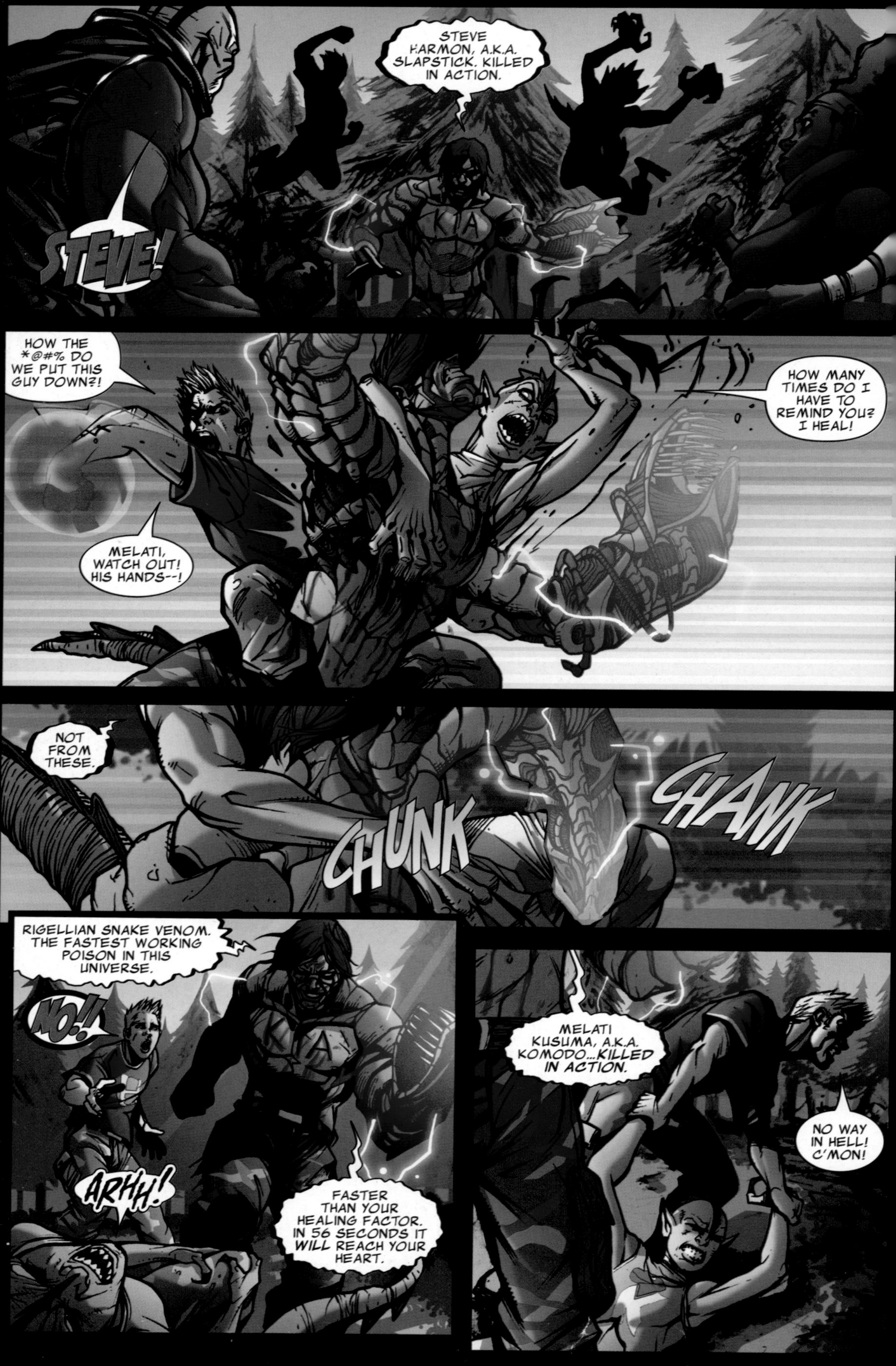
STEVE HARMON, A.K.A. SLAPSTICK. KILLED IN ACTION.
STEVE!
HOW THE *@#% DO WE PUT THIS GUY DOWN?!
HOW MANY TIMES DO I HAVE TO REMIND YOU? I HEAL!
MELATI, WATCH OUT! HIS HANDS--!
NOT FROM THESE.
CHUNK
CHANK
RIGELLIAN SNAKE VENOM. THE FASTEST WORKING POISON IN THIS UNIVERSE.
NO!!
ARHH!
FASTER THAN YOUR HEALING FACTOR. IN 56 SECONDS IT WILL REACH YOUR HEART.
MELATI KUSUMA, A.K.A. KOMODO...KILLED IN ACTION.
NO WAY IN HELL! C'MON!

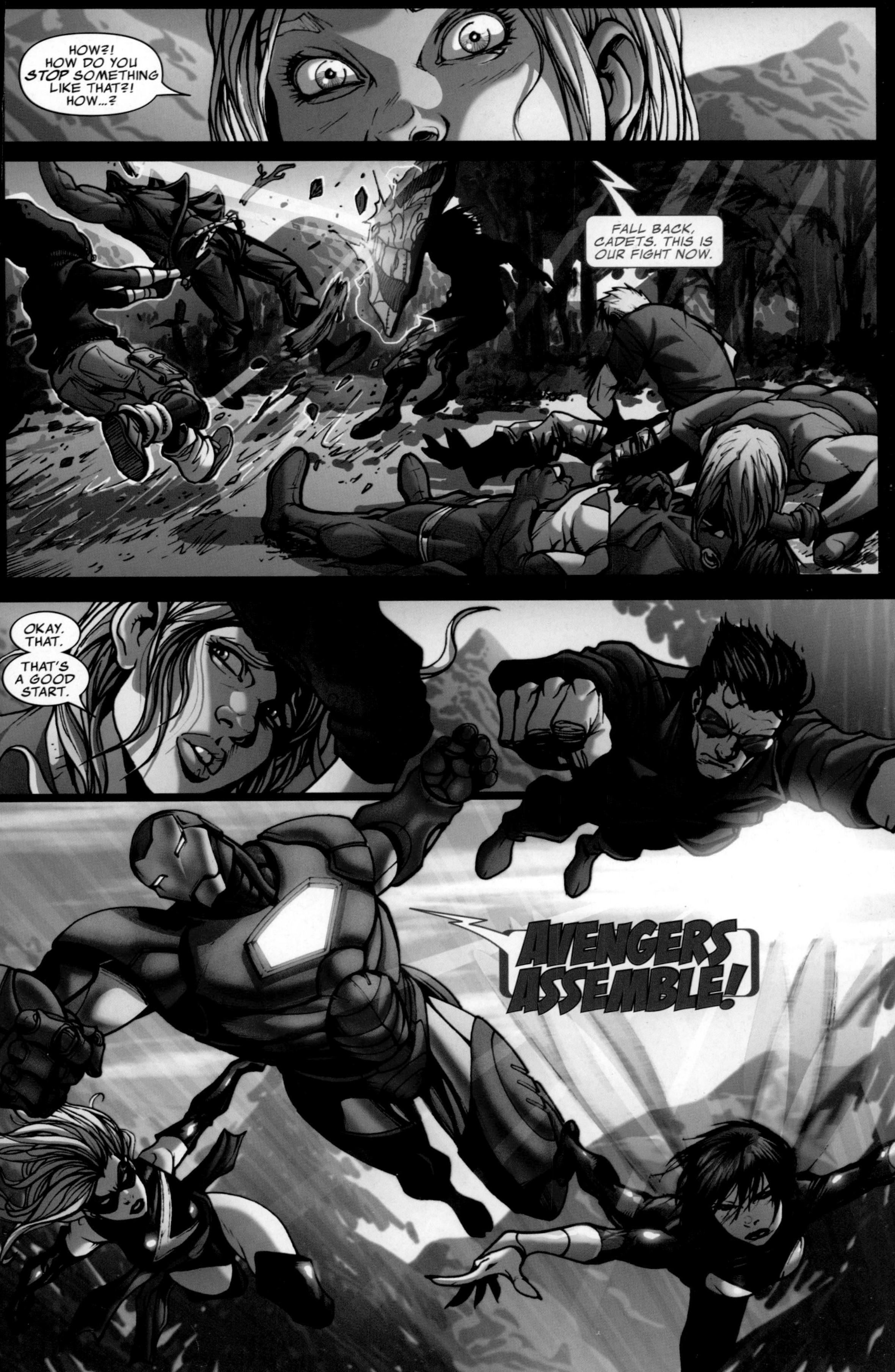
HOW?! HOW DO YOU STOP SOMETHING LIKE THAT?! HOW...?
FALL BACK, CADETS. THIS IS OUR FIGHT NOW.
OKAY. THAT.
THAT'S A GOOD START.
AVENGERS ASSEMBLE!

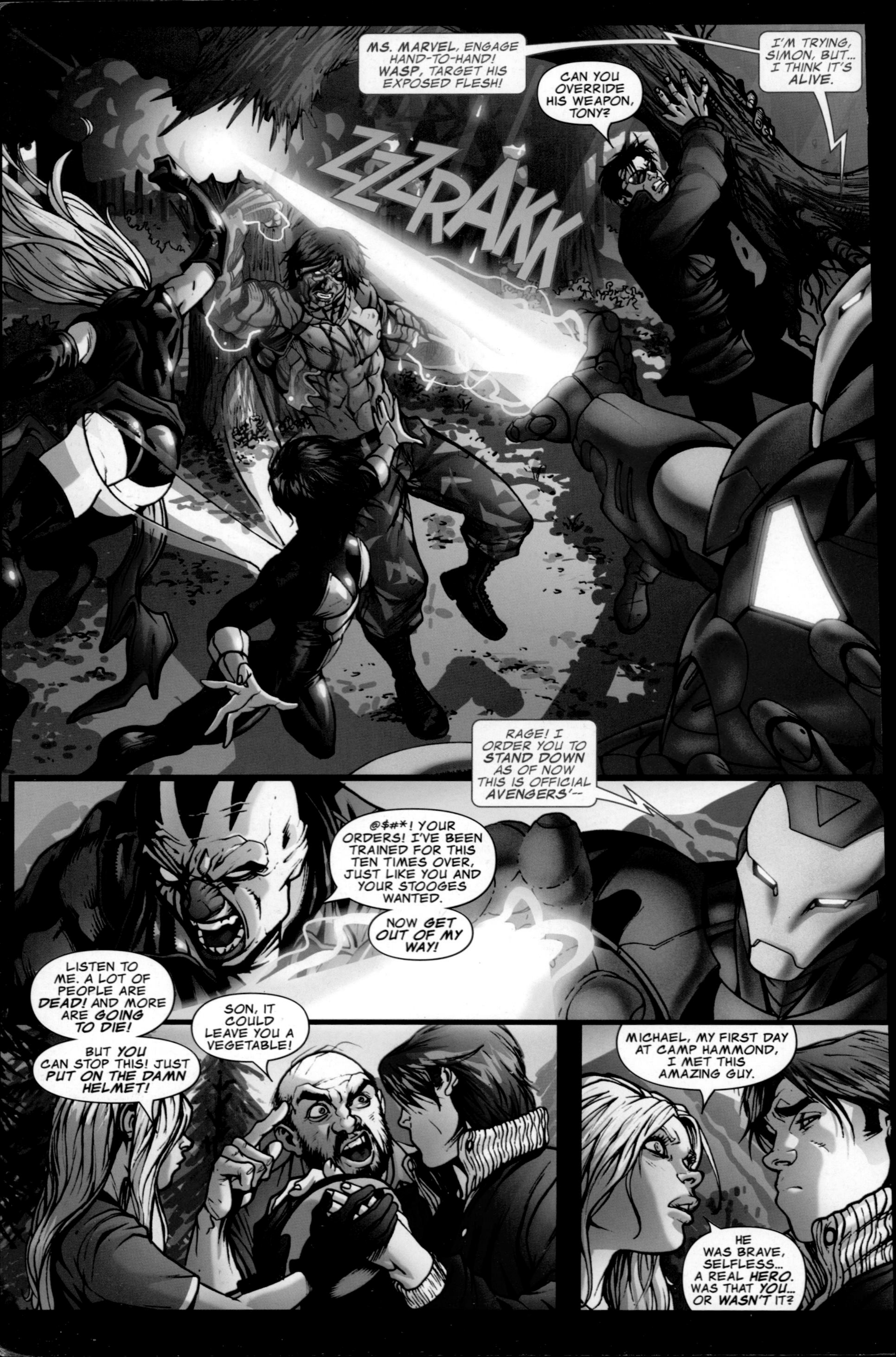

MS. MARVEL, ENGAGE HAND-TO-HAND! WASP, TARGET HIS EXPOSED FLESH!
CAN YOU OVERRIDE HIS WEAPON, TONY?
I'M TRYING, SIMON, BUT... I THINK IT'S ALIVE.
ZZZRAKK
RAGE! I ORDER YOU TO STAND DOWN AS OF NOW THIS IS OFFICIAL AVENGERS'--
@$#*! YOUR ORDERS! I'VE BEEN TRAINED FOR THIS TEN TIMES OVER, JUST LIKE YOU AND YOUR STOOGES WANTED.
NOW GET OUT OF MY WAY!
LISTEN TO ME. A LOT OF PEOPLE ARE DEAD! AND MORE ARE GOING TO DIE!
BUT YOU CAN STOP THIS! JUST PUT ON THE DAMN HELMET!
SON, IT COULD LEAVE YOU A VEGETABLE!
MICHAEL, MY FIRST DAY AT CAMP HAMMOND, I MET THIS AMAZING GUY.
HE WAS BRAVE, SELFLESS... A REAL HERO. WAS THAT YOU... OR WASN'T IT?

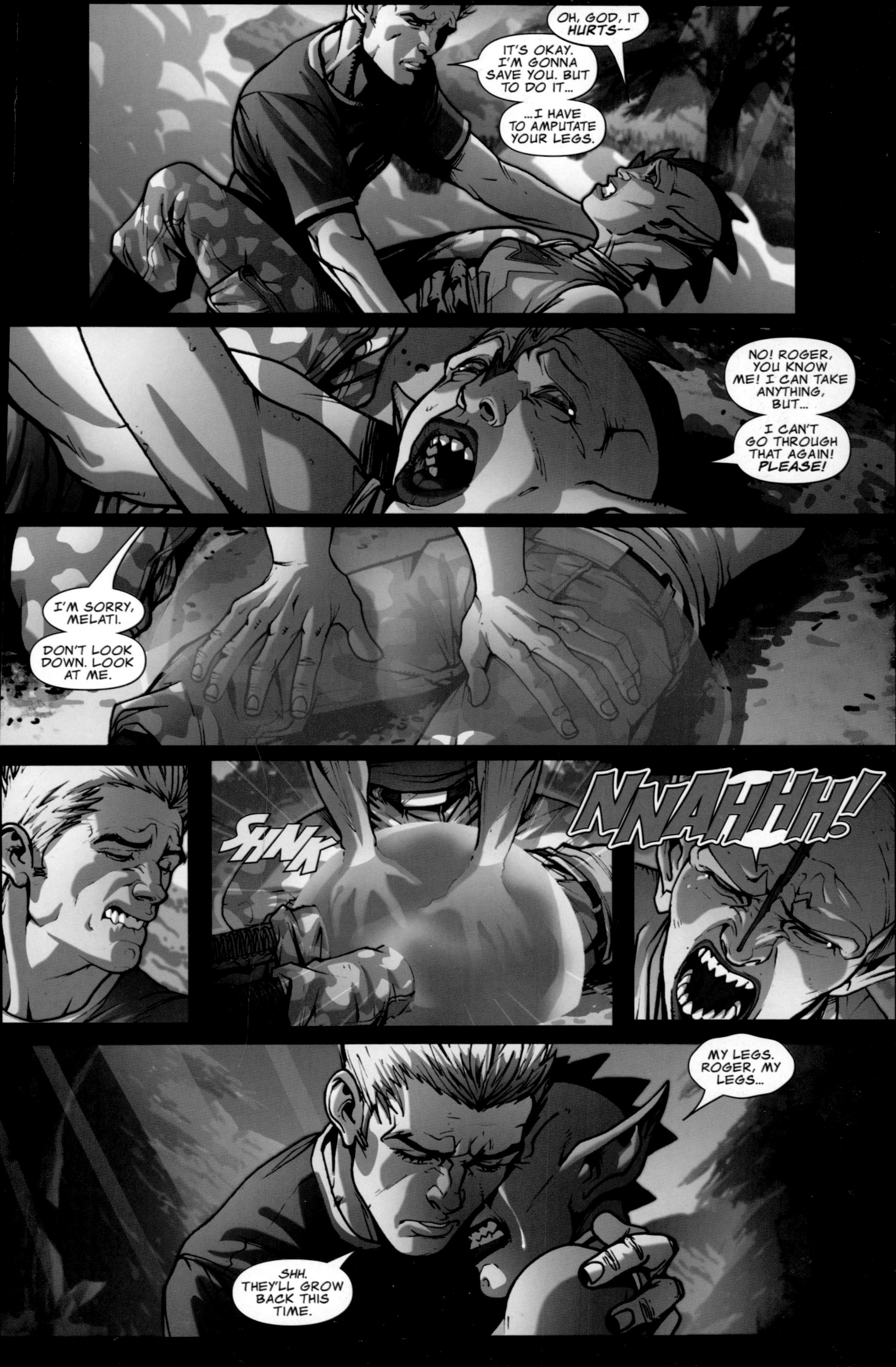
OH, GOD, IT HURTS--
IT'S OKAY. I'M GONNA SAVE YOU. BUT TO DO IT...
...I HAVE TO AMPUTATE YOUR LEGS.
NO! ROGER, YOU KNOW ME! I CAN TAKE ANYTHING, BUT...
I CAN'T GO THROUGH THAT AGAIN! PLEASE!
I'M SORRY, MELATI.
DON'T LOOK DOWN. LOOK AT ME.
SHNK
NNAHHH!
MY LEGS. ROGER, MY LEGS...
SHH. THEY'LL GROW BACK THIS TIME.

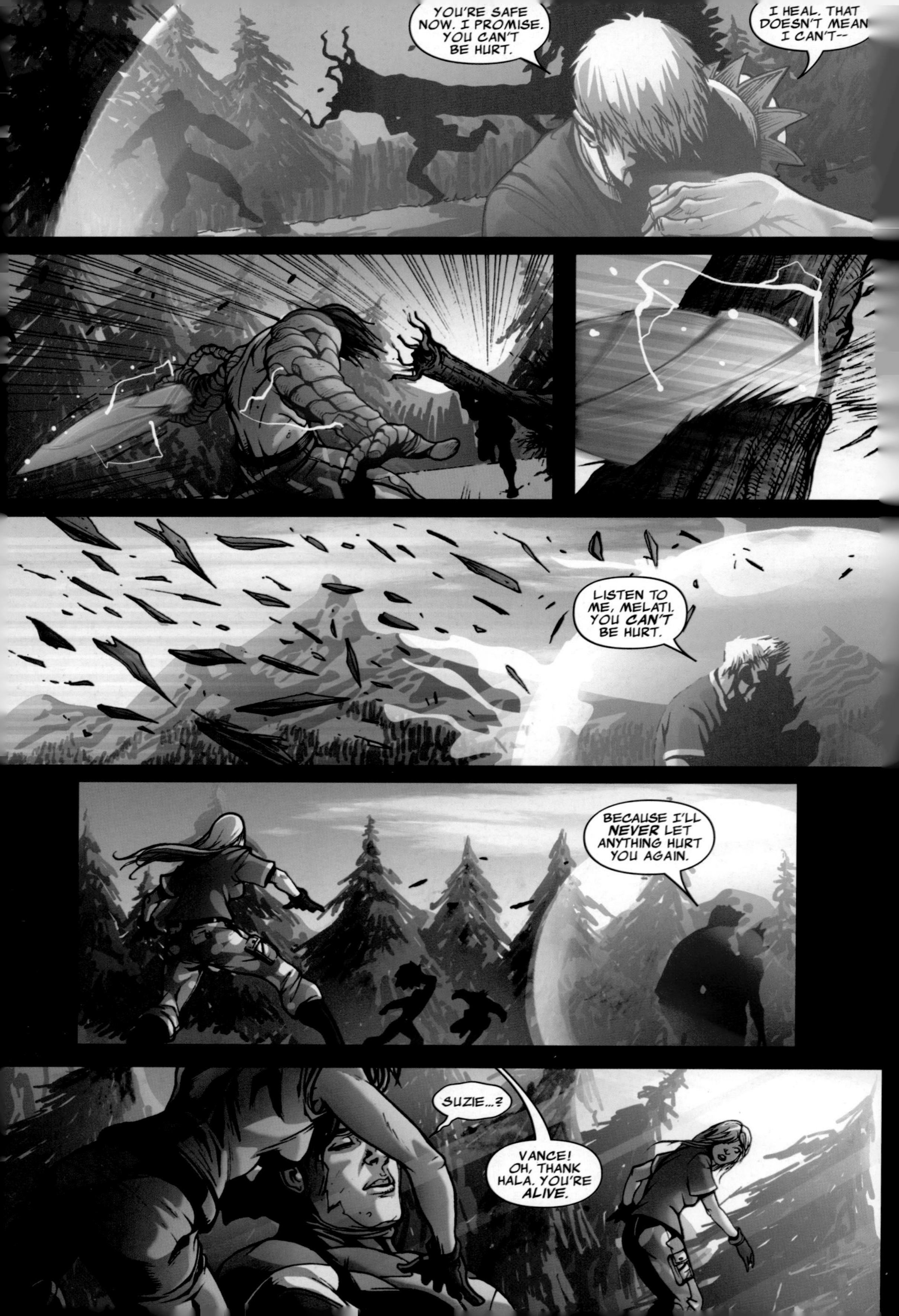
YOU'RE SAFE NOW. I PROMISE. YOU CAN'T BE HURT.
I HEAL. THAT DOESN'T MEAN I CAN'T--
LISTEN TO ME, MELATI. YOU **CAN'T** BE HURT.
BECAUSE I'LL **NEVER** LET ANYTHING HURT YOU AGAIN.
SUZIE...?
VANCE! OH, THANK HALA. YOU'RE **ALIVE**.

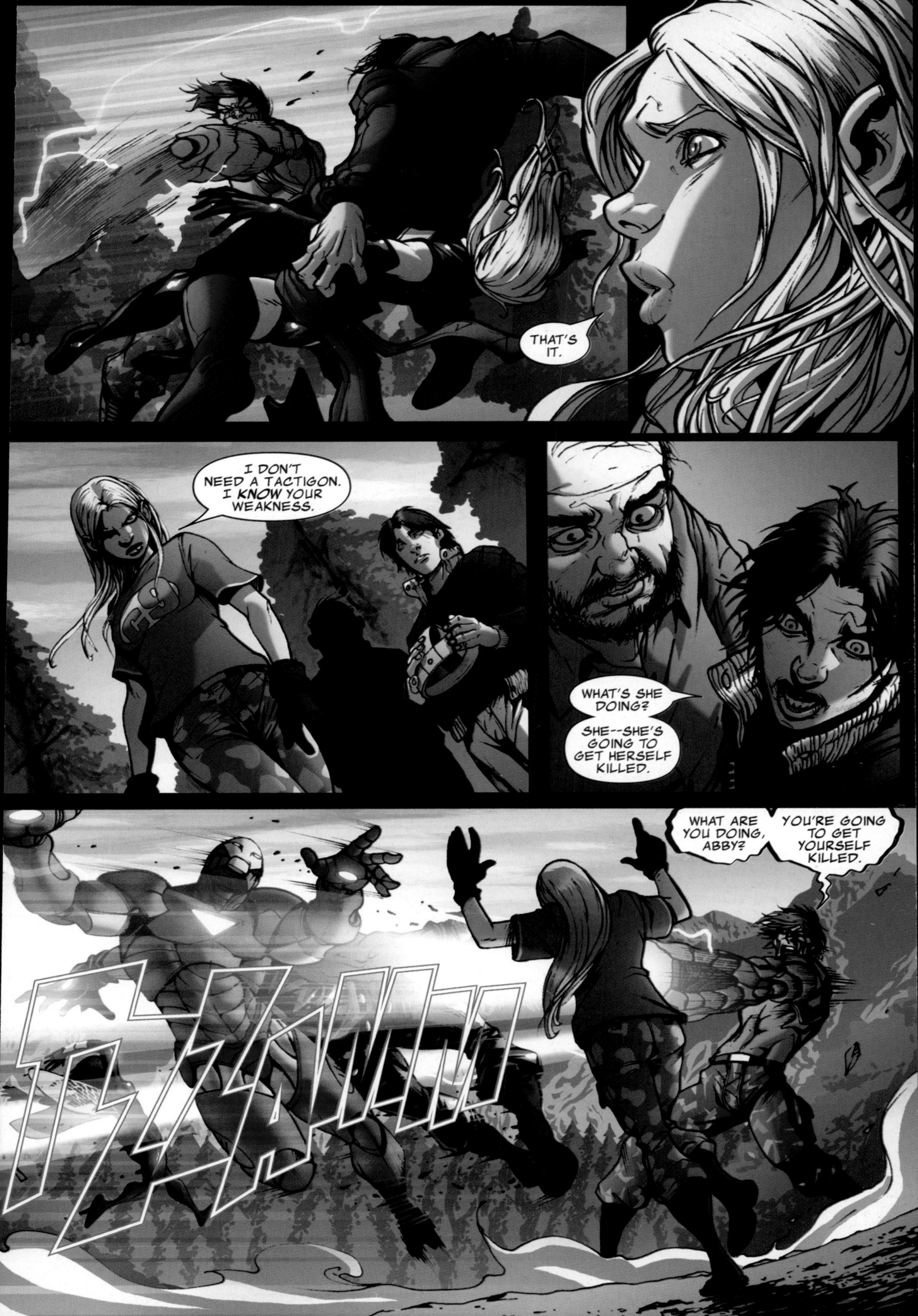
THAT'S IT.
I DON'T NEED A TACTIGON. I KNOW YOUR WEAKNESS.
WHAT'S SHE DOING?
SHE--SHE'S GOING TO GET HERSELF KILLED.
WHAT ARE YOU DOING, ABBY?
YOU'RE GOING TO GET YOURSELF KILLED.

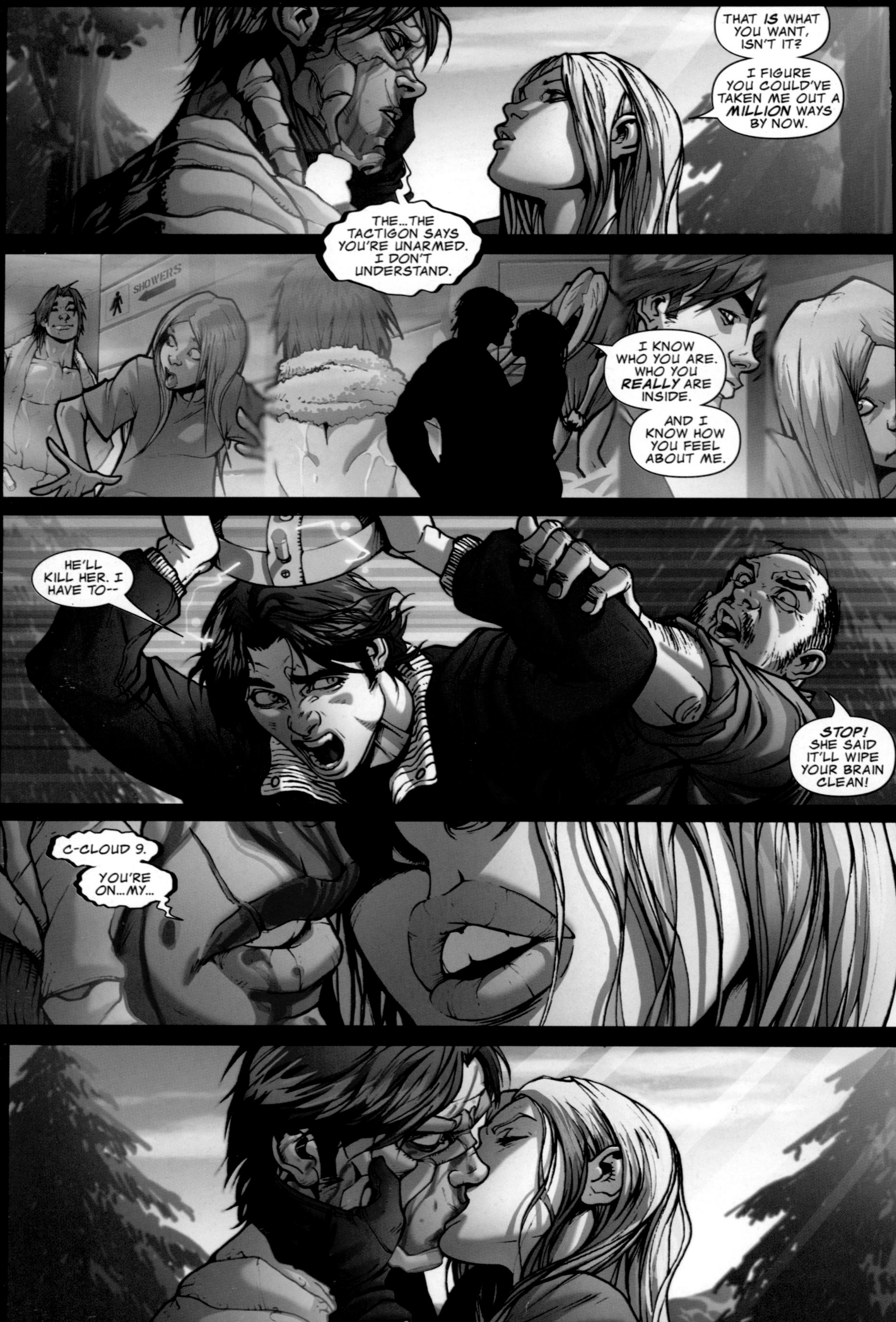

THAT IS WHAT YOU WANT, ISN'T IT?
I FIGURE YOU COULD'VE TAKEN ME OUT A MILLION WAYS BY NOW.
THE...THE TACTIGON SAYS YOU'RE UNARMED. I DON'T UNDERSTAND.
SHOWERS
I KNOW WHO YOU ARE. WHO YOU REALLY ARE INSIDE.
AND I KNOW HOW YOU FEEL ABOUT ME.
HE'LL KILL HER. I HAVE TO--
STOP! SHE SAID IT'LL WIPE YOUR BRAIN CLEAN!
C-CLOUD 9.
YOU'RE ON...MY...

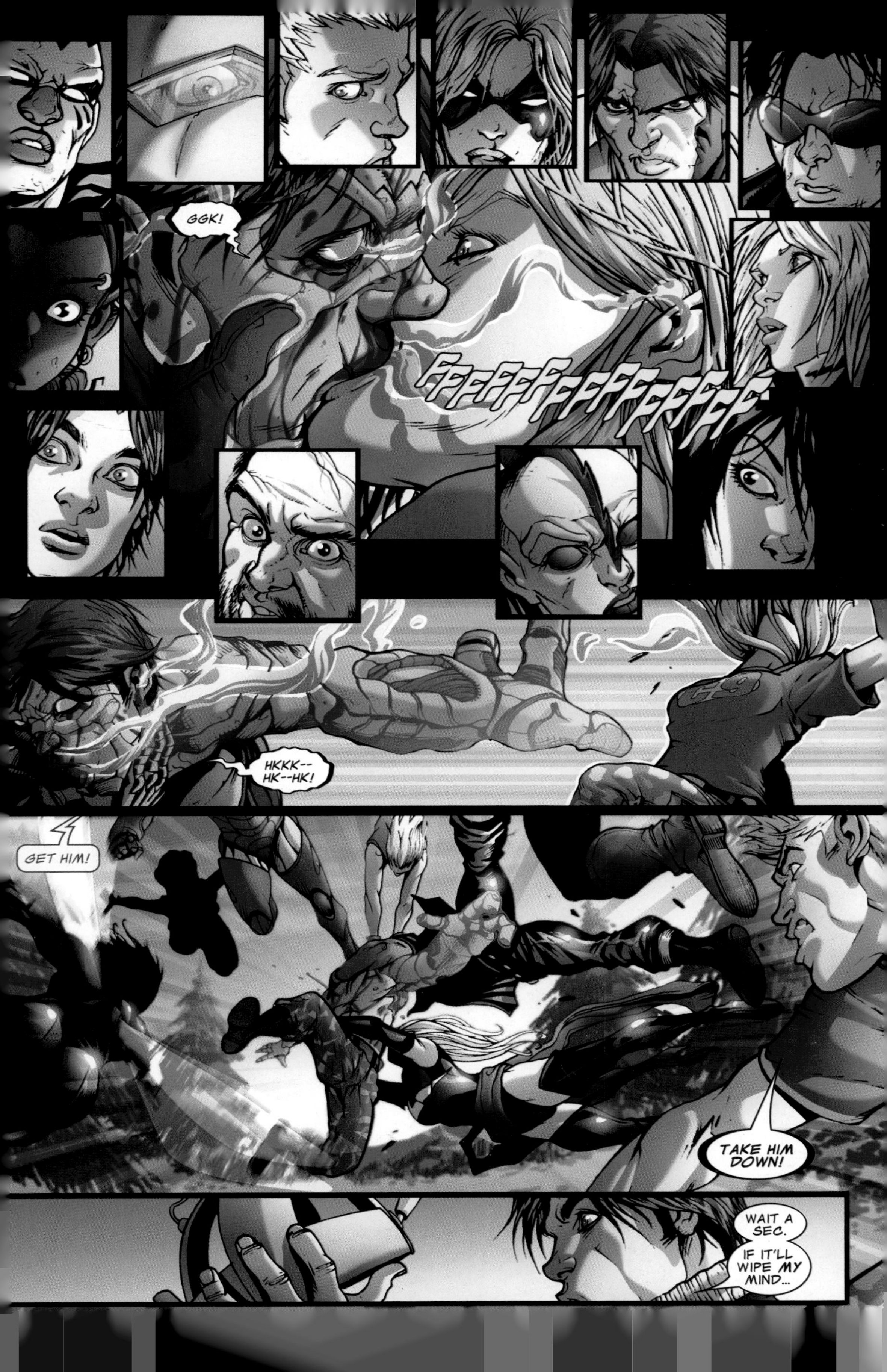
GGK!
FFFFFFFFFFFFFFFFF
HKKK-- HK--HK!
GET HIM!
TAKE HIM DOWN!
WAIT A SEC.
IF IT'LL WIPE MY MIND...

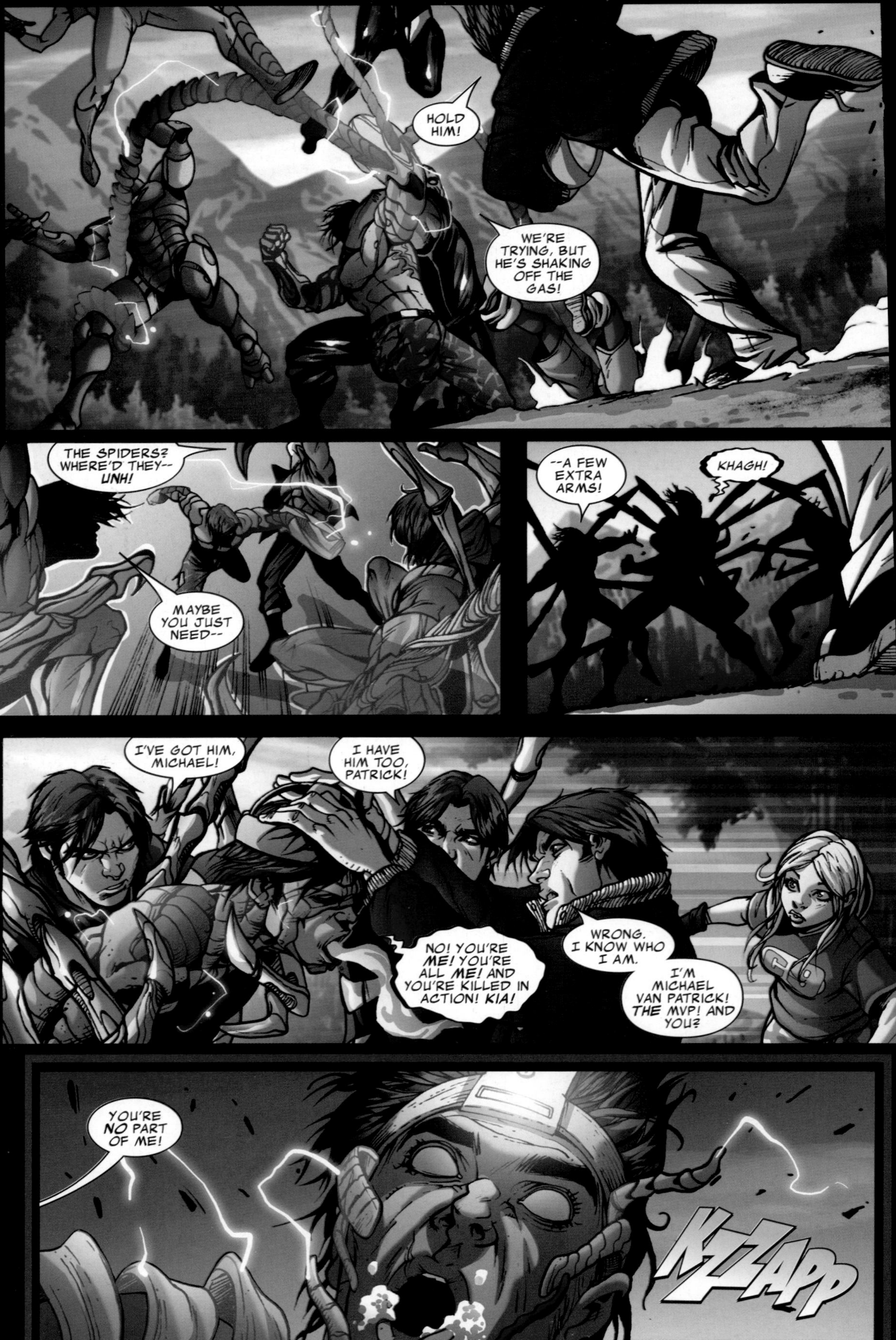
HOLD HIM!
WE'RE TRYING, BUT HE'S SHAKING OFF THE GAS!
THE SPIDERS? WHERE'D THEY-- UNH!
MAYBE YOU JUST NEED--
--A FEW EXTRA ARMS!
KHAGH!
I'VE GOT HIM, MICHAEL!
I HAVE HIM TOO, PATRICK!
NO! YOU'RE ME! YOU'RE ALL ME! AND YOU'RE KILLED IN ACTION! KIA!
WRONG. I KNOW WHO I AM.
I'M MICHAEL VAN PATRICK! THE MVP! AND YOU?
YOU'RE NO PART OF ME!
KZZAPP

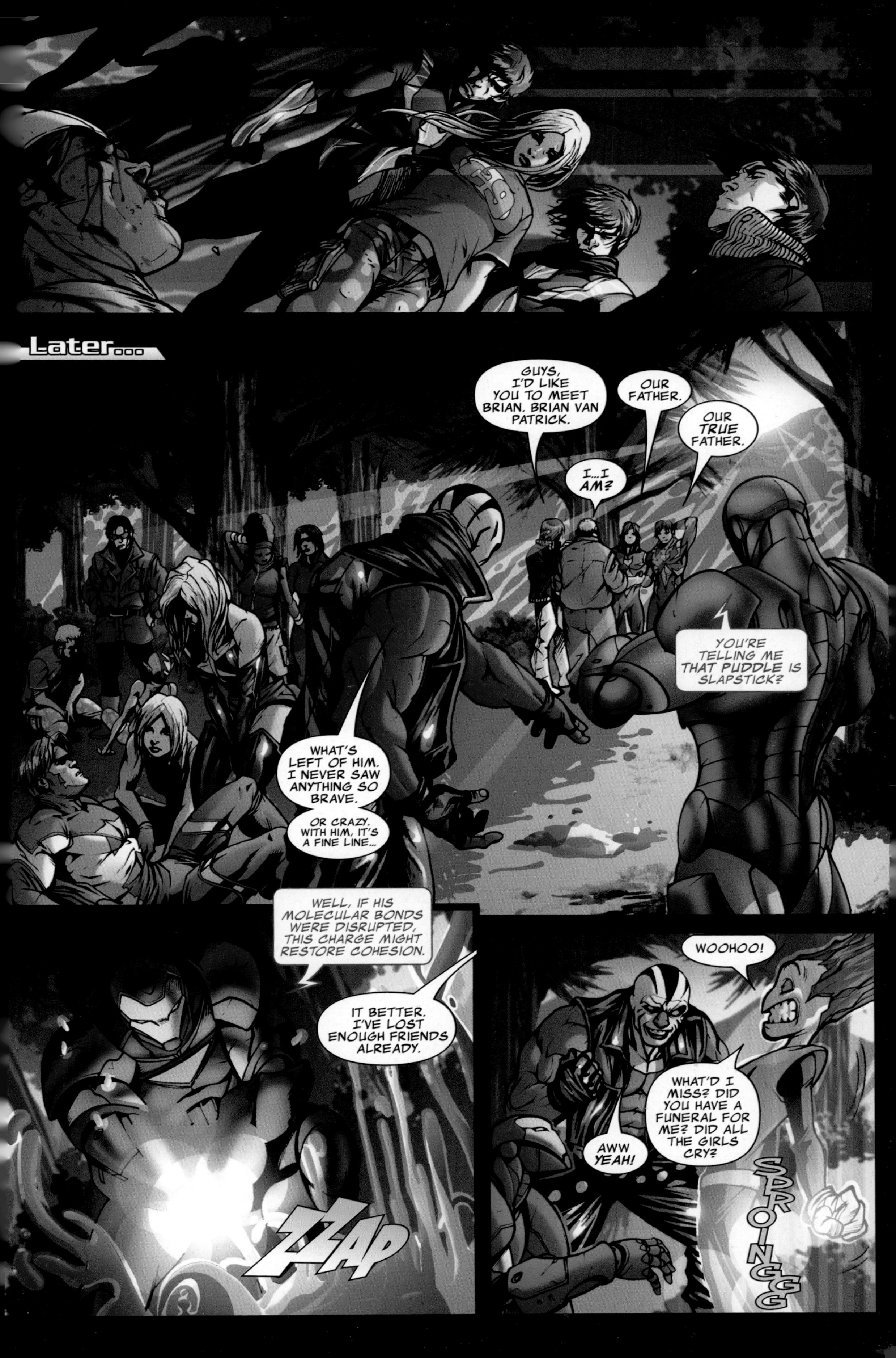

Later...
GUYS, I'D LIKE YOU TO MEET BRIAN. BRIAN VAN PATRICK.
OUR FATHER.
OUR TRUE FATHER.
I...I AM?
YOU'RE TELLING ME THAT PUDDLE IS SLAPSTICK?
WHAT'S LEFT OF HIM. I NEVER SAW ANYTHING SO BRAVE.
OR CRAZY. WITH HIM, IT'S A FINE LINE...
WELL, IF HIS MOLECULAR BONDS WERE DISRUPTED, THIS CHARGE MIGHT RESTORE COHESION.
IT BETTER. I'VE LOST ENOUGH FRIENDS ALREADY.
ZZAP
WOOHOO!
WHAT'D I MISS? DID YOU HAVE A FUNERAL FOR ME? DID ALL THE GIRLS CRY?
AWW YEAH!
SPROINGG

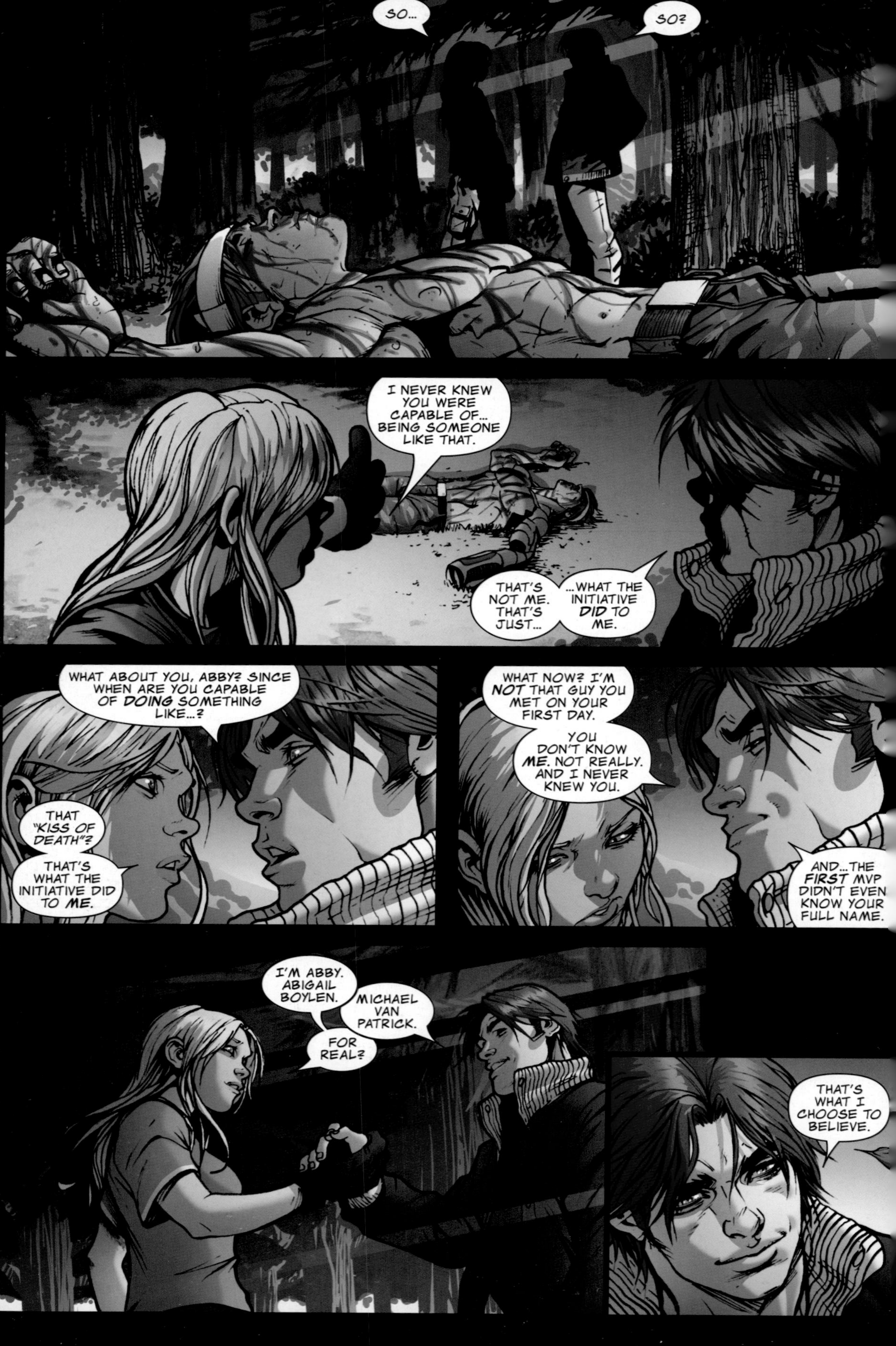
SO...
SO?
I NEVER KNEW YOU WERE CAPABLE OF... BEING SOMEONE LIKE THAT.
THAT'S NOT ME. THAT'S JUST...
...WHAT THE INITIATIVE DID TO ME.
WHAT ABOUT YOU, ABBY? SINCE WHEN ARE YOU CAPABLE OF DOING SOMETHING LIKE...?
THAT "KISS OF DEATH"?
THAT'S WHAT THE INITIATIVE DID TO ME.
WHAT NOW? I'M NOT THAT GUY YOU MET ON YOUR FIRST DAY.
YOU DON'T KNOW ME. NOT REALLY. AND I NEVER KNEW YOU.
AND...THE FIRST MVP DIDN'T EVEN KNOW YOUR FULL NAME.
I'M ABBY. ABIGAIL BOYLEN.
MICHAEL VAN PATRICK.
FOR REAL?
THAT'S WHAT I CHOOSE TO BELIEVE.

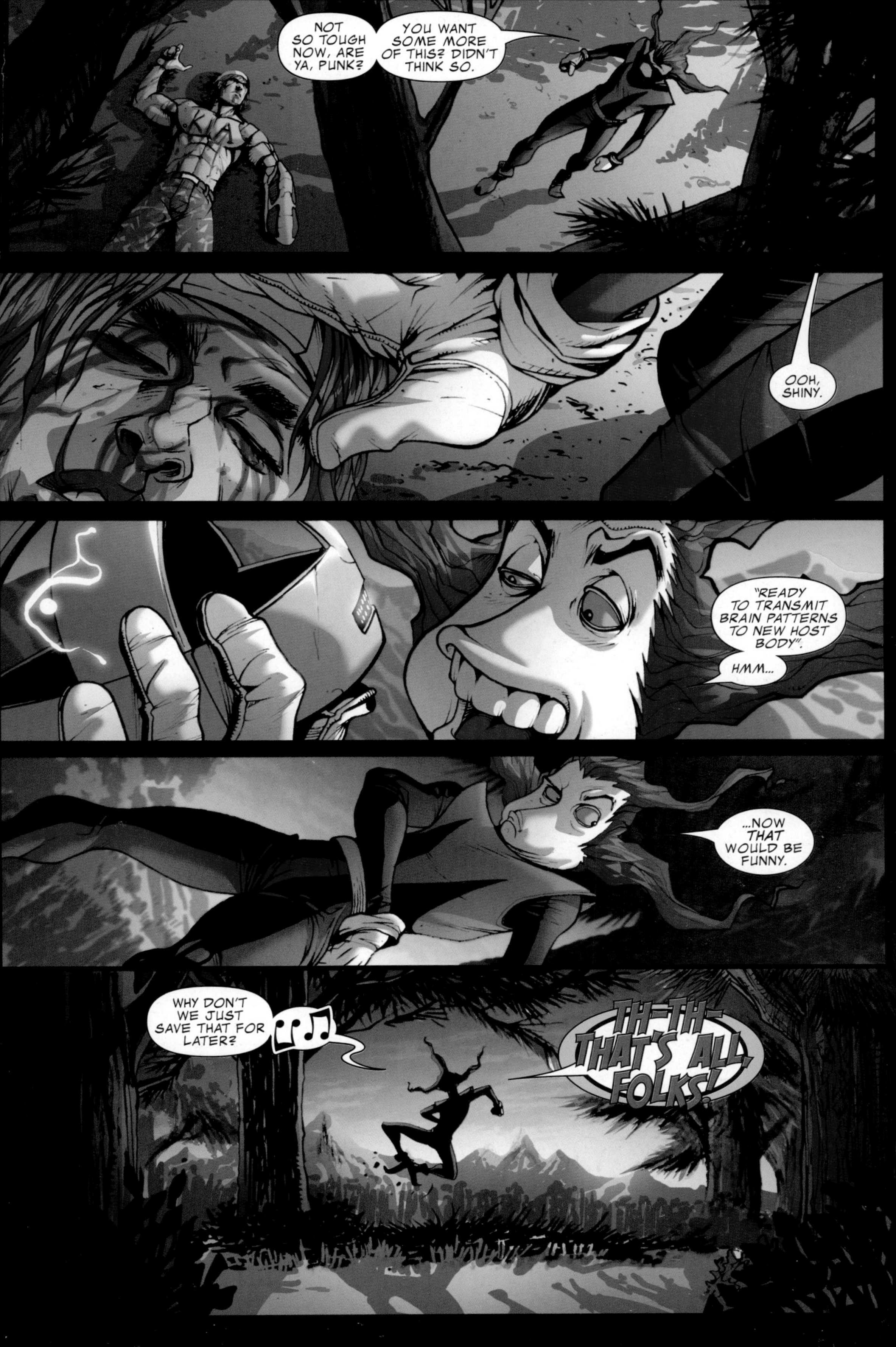
NOT SO TOUGH NOW, ARE YA, PUNK?
YOU WANT SOME MORE OF THIS? DIDN'T THINK SO.
OOH, SHINY.
"READY TO TRANSMIT BRAIN PATTERNS TO NEW HOST BODY".
HMM...
...NOW THAT WOULD BE FUNNY.
WHY DON'T WE JUST SAVE THAT FOR LATER?
TH-TH-THAT'S ALL, FOLKS!

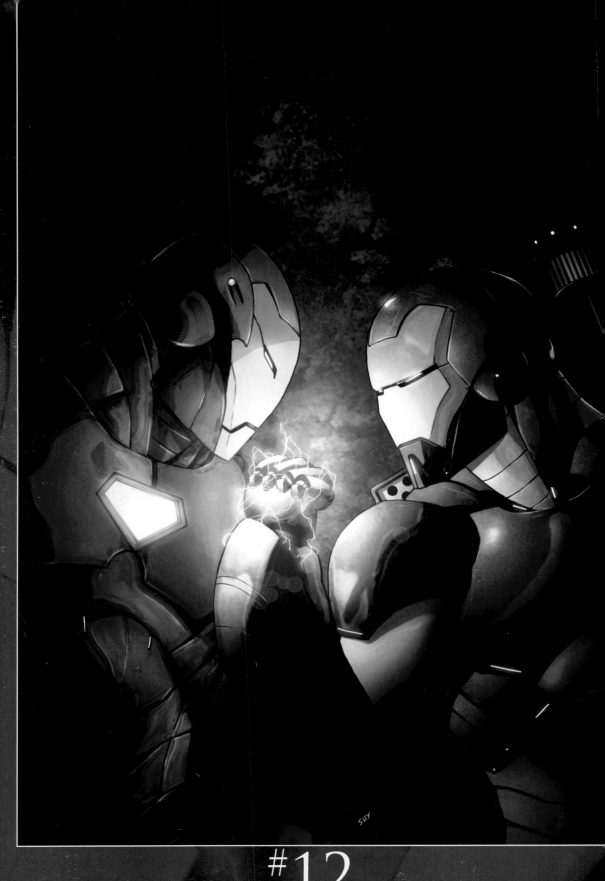

#12

Camp Hammond.
The Gauntlet

LOOK AT YOU, SO HANDSOME! WE SHOULD TAKE SOME FAMILY PICTURES. PUT THE KIDS IN THEIR SUNDAY CLOTHES...

I'M GLAD TO BE BACK WITH YOU TOO, BABY.

BUT THIS IS NO TIME TO BE CELEBRATING.

Cloud 9

Yellowjacket

Komodo

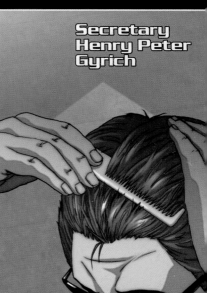

Secretary Henry Peter Gyrich

Hardball

War Machine

Trauma

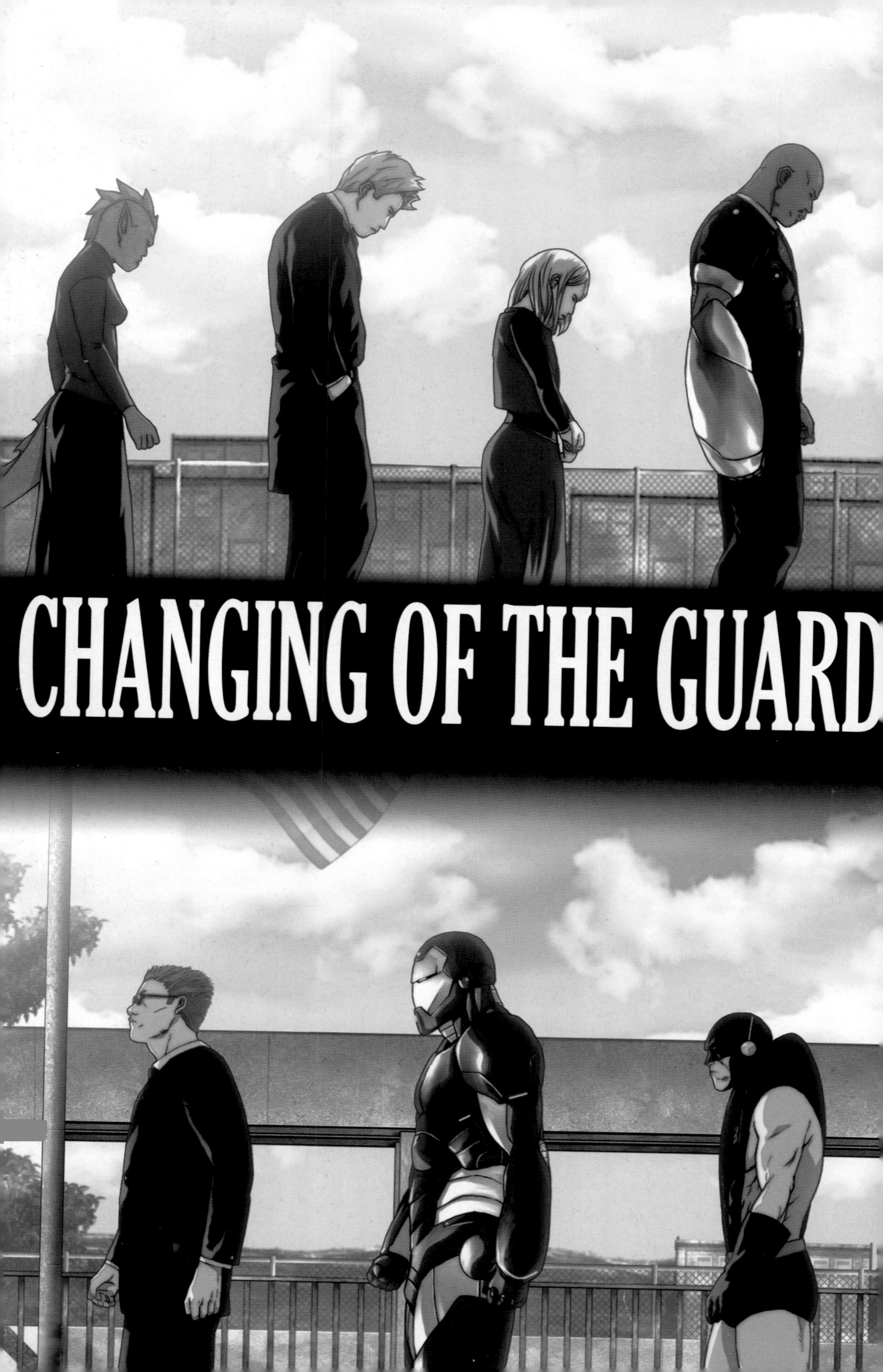
CHANGING OF THE GUARD

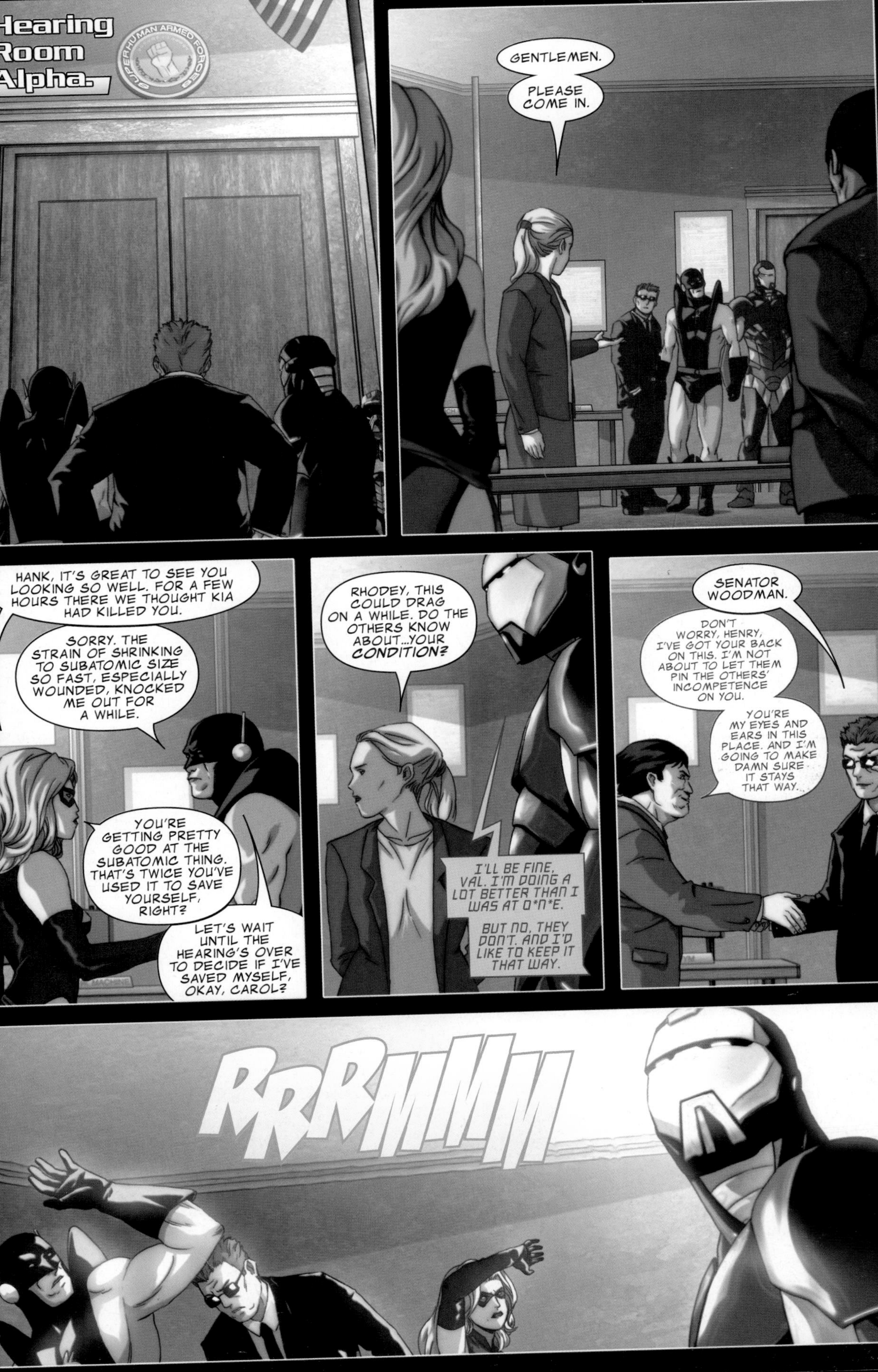
Hearing Room Alpha.
SUPERHUMAN ARMED FORCES
GENTLEMEN.
PLEASE COME IN.
HANK, IT'S GREAT TO SEE YOU LOOKING SO WELL. FOR A FEW HOURS THERE WE THOUGHT KIA HAD KILLED YOU.
SORRY. THE STRAIN OF SHRINKING TO SUBATOMIC SIZE SO FAST, ESPECIALLY WOUNDED, KNOCKED ME OUT FOR A WHILE.
YOU'RE GETTING PRETTY GOOD AT THE SUBATOMIC THING. THAT'S TWICE YOU'VE USED IT TO SAVE YOURSELF, RIGHT?
LET'S WAIT UNTIL THE HEARING'S OVER TO DECIDE IF I'VE SAVED MYSELF, OKAY, CAROL?
RHODEY, THIS COULD DRAG ON A WHILE. DO THE OTHERS KNOW ABOUT...YOUR CONDITION?
I'LL BE FINE, VAL. I'M DOING A LOT BETTER THAN I WAS AT O*N*E.
BUT NO, THEY DON'T. AND I'D LIKE TO KEEP IT THAT WAY.
SENATOR WOODMAN.
DON'T WORRY, HENRY, I'VE GOT YOUR BACK ON THIS. I'M NOT ABOUT TO LET THEM PIN THE OTHERS' INCOMPETENCE ON YOU.
YOU'RE MY EYES AND EARS IN THIS PLACE. AND I'M GOING TO MAKE DAMN SURE IT STAYS THAT WAY.
RRRMMM

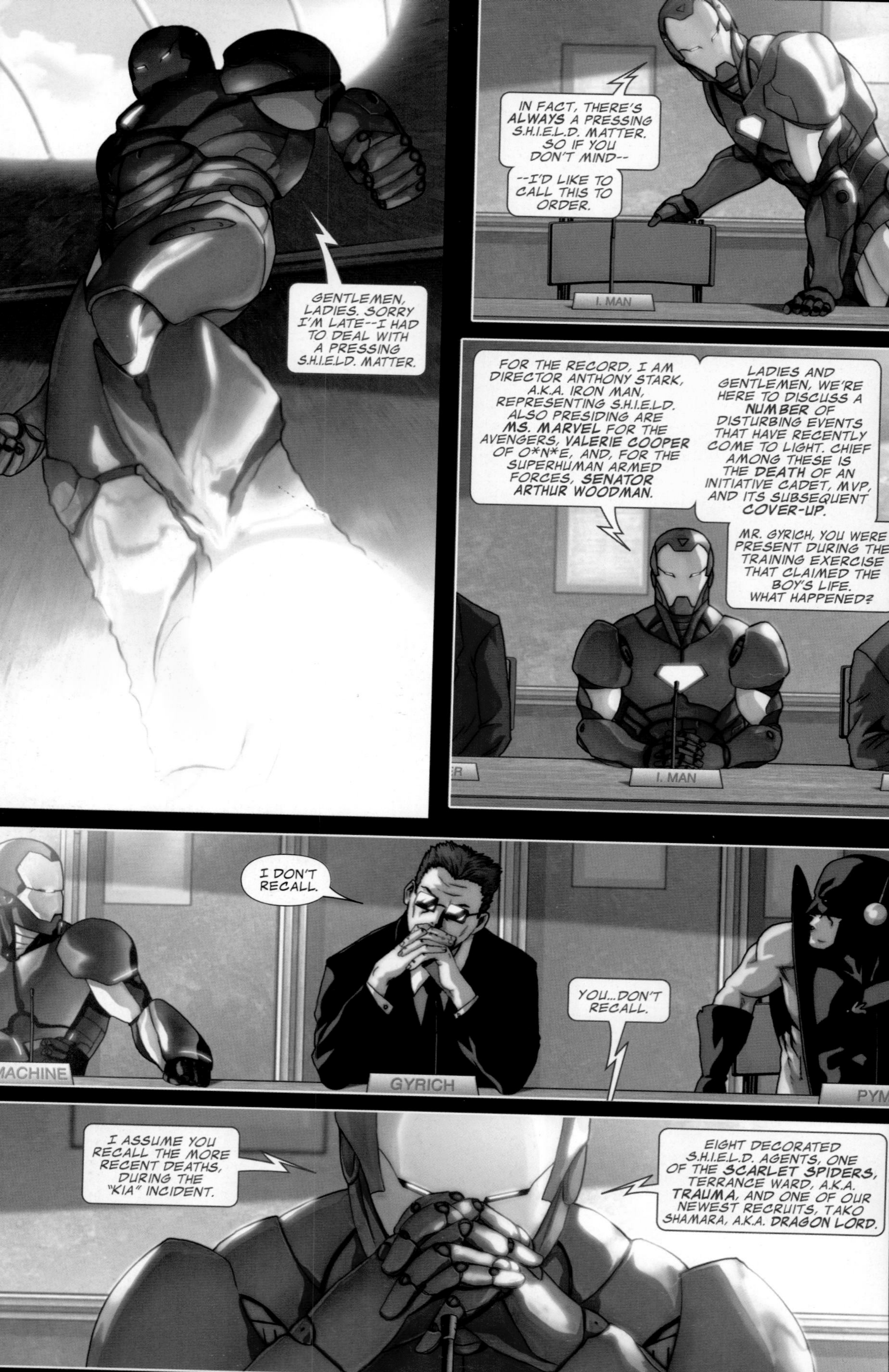
GENTLEMEN, LADIES. SORRY I'M LATE--I HAD TO DEAL WITH A PRESSING S.H.I.E.L.D. MATTER.
IN FACT, THERE'S ALWAYS A PRESSING S.H.I.E.L.D. MATTER. SO IF YOU DON'T MIND--
--I'D LIKE TO CALL THIS TO ORDER.
I. MAN
FOR THE RECORD, I AM DIRECTOR ANTHONY STARK, A.K.A. IRON MAN, REPRESENTING S.H.I.E.L.D. ALSO PRESIDING ARE MS. MARVEL FOR THE AVENGERS, VALERIE COOPER OF O*N*E, AND, FOR THE SUPERHUMAN ARMED FORCES, SENATOR ARTHUR WOODMAN.
LADIES AND GENTLEMEN, WE'RE HERE TO DISCUSS A NUMBER OF DISTURBING EVENTS THAT HAVE RECENTLY COME TO LIGHT. CHIEF AMONG THESE IS THE DEATH OF AN INITIATIVE CADET, MVP, AND ITS SUBSEQUENT COVER-UP.
MR. GYRICH, YOU WERE PRESENT DURING THE TRAINING EXERCISE THAT CLAIMED THE BOY'S LIFE. WHAT HAPPENED?
I. MAN
I DON'T RECALL.
YOU...DON'T RECALL.
MACHINE
GYRICH
PYM
I ASSUME YOU RECALL THE MORE RECENT DEATHS, DURING THE "KIA" INCIDENT.
EIGHT DECORATED S.H.I.E.L.D. AGENTS, ONE OF THE SCARLET SPIDERS, TERRANCE WARD, A.K.A. TRAUMA, AND ONE OF OUR NEWEST RECRUITS, TAKO SHAMARA, A.K.A. DRAGON LORD.

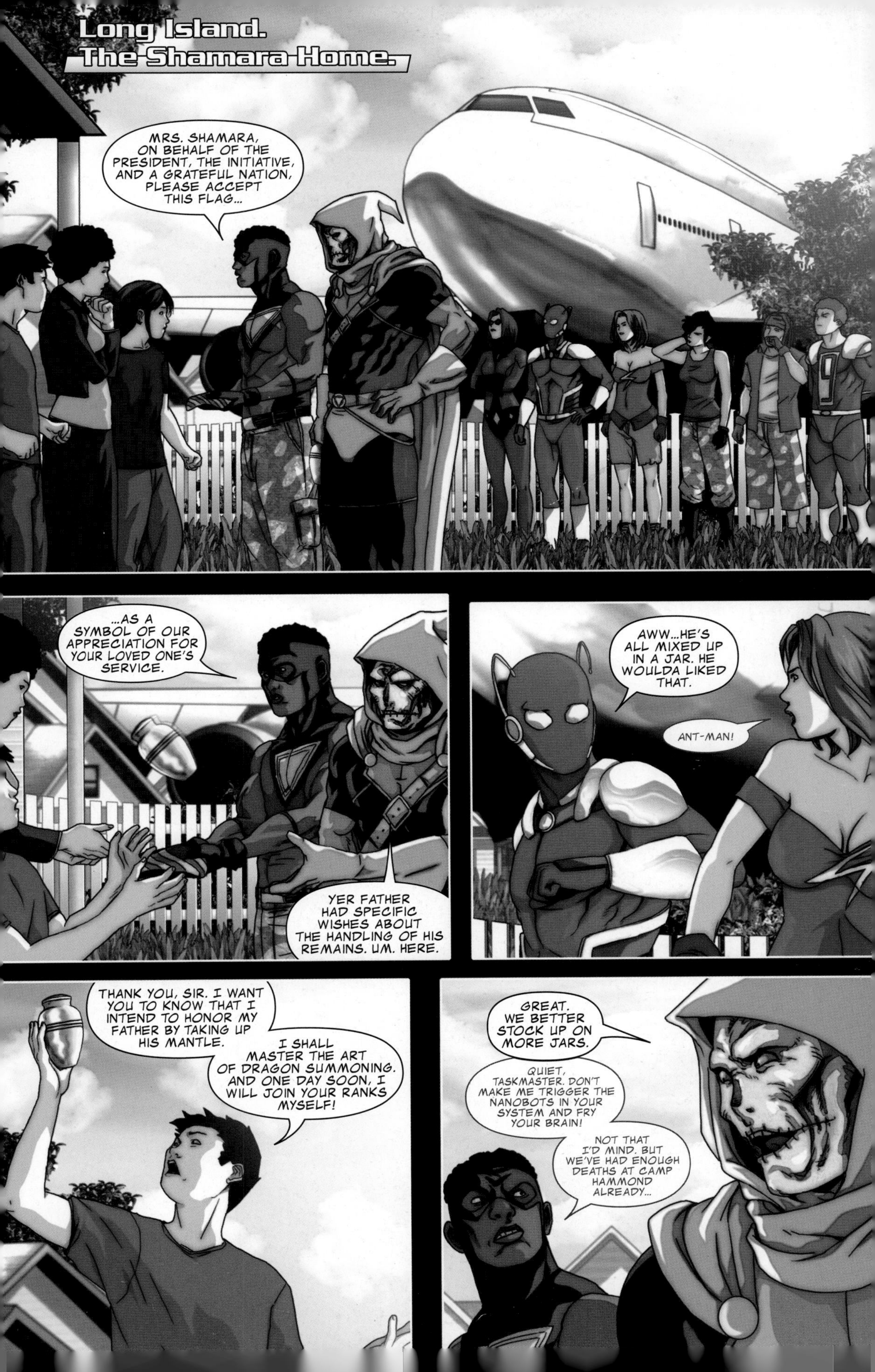
Long Island.
The Shamara Home.
MRS. SHAMARA, ON BEHALF OF THE PRESIDENT, THE INITIATIVE, AND A GRATEFUL NATION, PLEASE ACCEPT THIS FLAG...
...AS A SYMBOL OF OUR APPRECIATION FOR YOUR LOVED ONE'S SERVICE.
YER FATHER HAD SPECIFIC WISHES ABOUT THE HANDLING OF HIS REMAINS. UM. HERE.
AWW...HE'S ALL MIXED UP IN A JAR. HE WOULDA LIKED THAT.
ANT-MAN!
THANK YOU, SIR. I WANT YOU TO KNOW THAT I INTEND TO HONOR MY FATHER BY TAKING UP HIS MANTLE.
I SHALL MASTER THE ART OF DRAGON SUMMONING. AND ONE DAY SOON, I WILL JOIN YOUR RANKS MYSELF!
GREAT. WE BETTER STOCK UP ON MORE JARS.
QUIET, TASKMASTER. DON'T MAKE ME TRIGGER THE NANOBOTS IN YOUR SYSTEM AND FRY YOUR BRAIN!
NOT THAT I'D MIND. BUT WE'VE HAD ENOUGH DEATHS AT CAMP HAMMOND ALREADY...

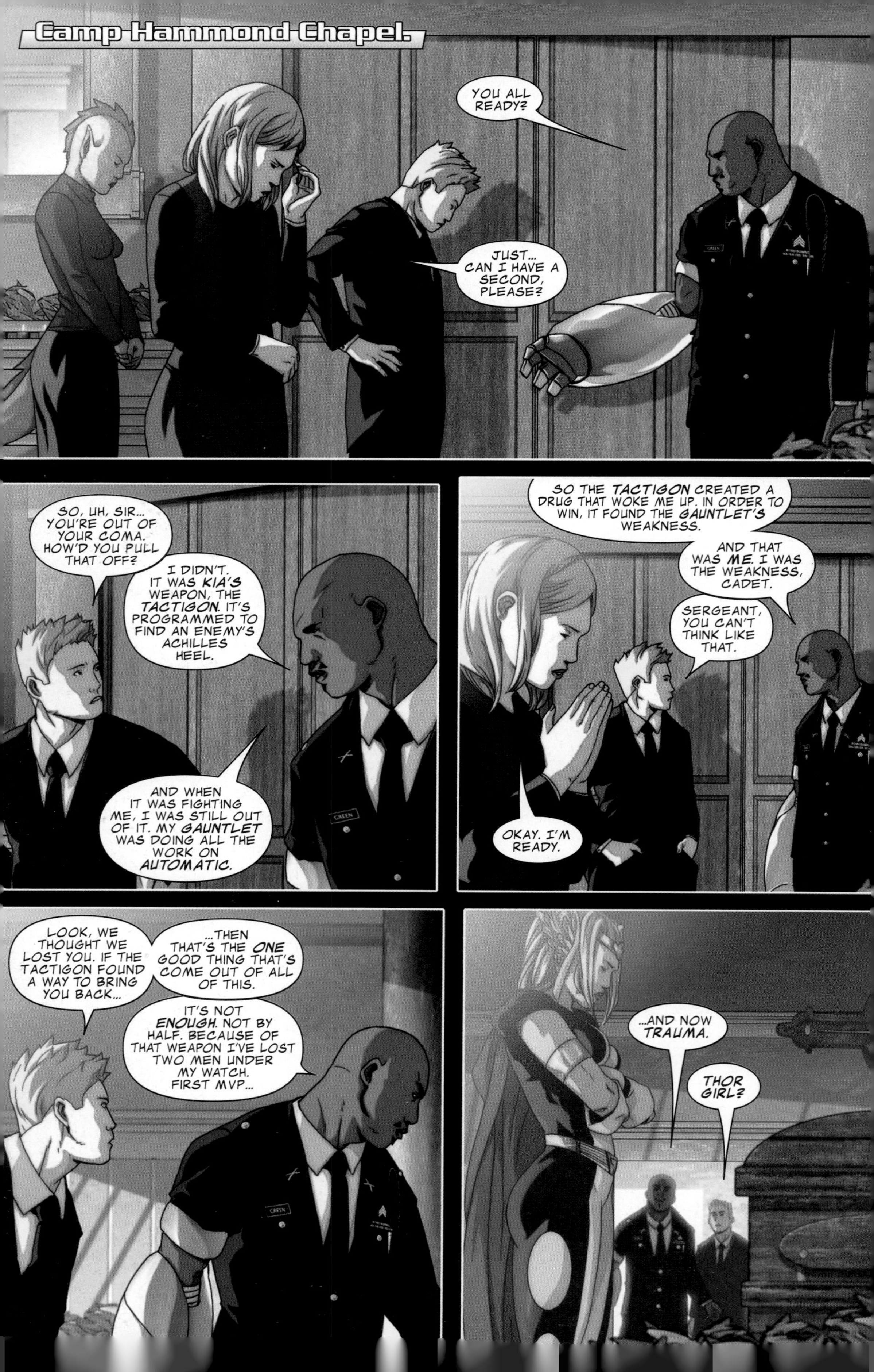
Camp Hammond Chapel.
YOU ALL READY?
JUST... CAN I HAVE A SECOND, PLEASE?
SO, UH, SIR... YOU'RE OUT OF YOUR COMA. HOW'D YOU PULL THAT OFF?
I DIDN'T. IT WAS KIA'S WEAPON, THE TACTIGON. IT'S PROGRAMMED TO FIND AN ENEMY'S ACHILLES HEEL.
AND WHEN IT WAS FIGHTING ME, I WAS STILL OUT OF IT. MY GAUNTLET WAS DOING ALL THE WORK ON AUTOMATIC.
SO THE TACTIGON CREATED A DRUG THAT WOKE ME UP. IN ORDER TO WIN, IT FOUND THE GAUNTLET'S WEAKNESS.
AND THAT WAS ME. I WAS THE WEAKNESS, CADET.
SERGEANT, YOU CAN'T THINK LIKE THAT.
OKAY. I'M READY.
LOOK, WE THOUGHT WE LOST YOU. IF THE TACTIGON FOUND A WAY TO BRING YOU BACK...
...THEN THAT'S THE ONE GOOD THING THAT'S COME OUT OF ALL OF THIS.
IT'S NOT ENOUGH. NOT BY HALF. BECAUSE OF THAT WEAPON I'VE LOST TWO MEN UNDER MY WATCH. FIRST MVP...
...AND NOW TRAUMA.
THOR GIRL?

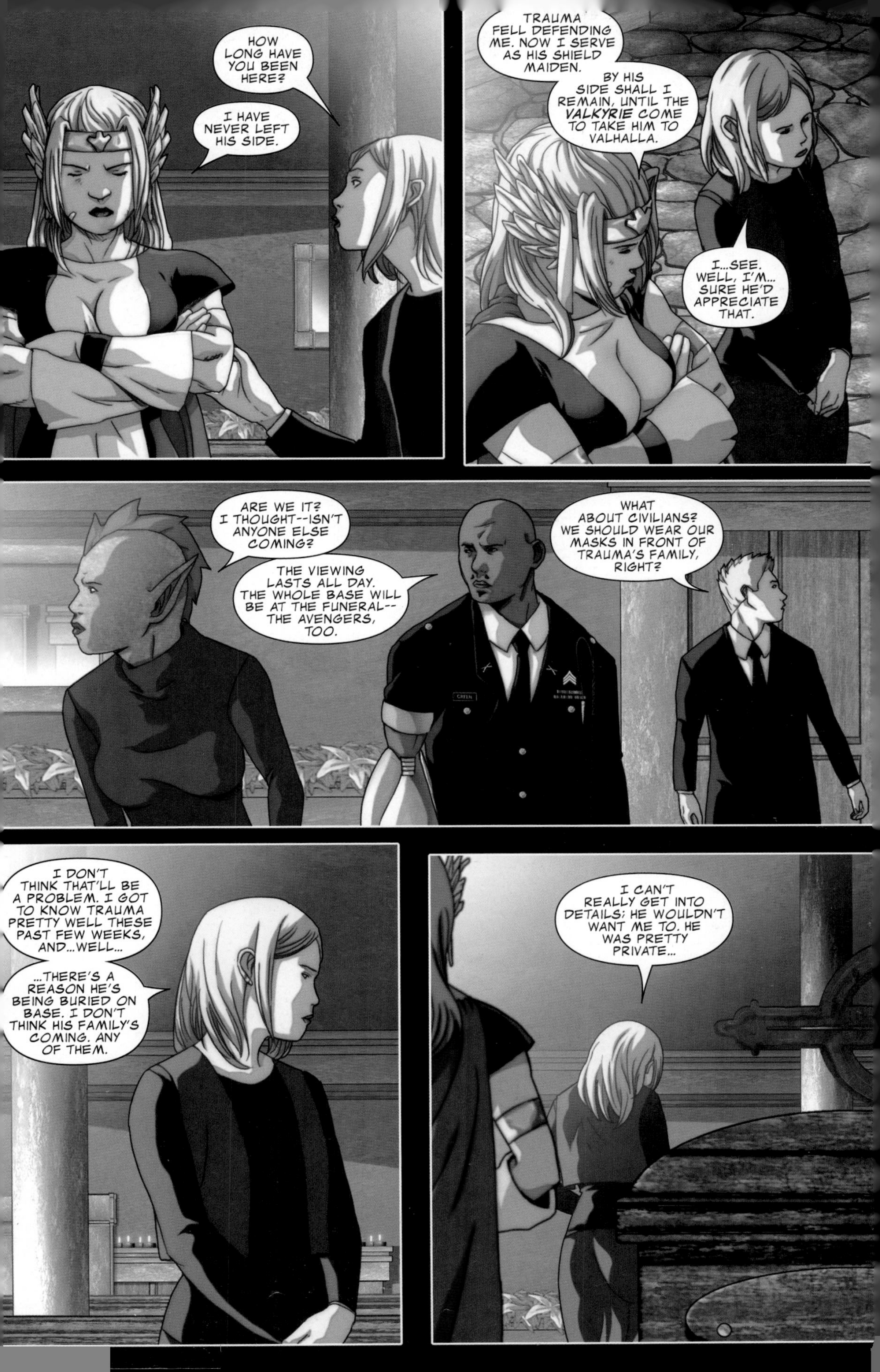
HOW LONG HAVE YOU BEEN HERE?
I HAVE NEVER LEFT HIS SIDE.
TRAUMA FELL DEFENDING ME. NOW I SERVE AS HIS SHIELD MAIDEN.
BY HIS SIDE SHALL I REMAIN, UNTIL THE VALKYRIE COME TO TAKE HIM TO VALHALLA.
I...SEE. WELL, I'M... SURE HE'D APPRECIATE THAT.
ARE WE IT? I THOUGHT--ISN'T ANYONE ELSE COMING?
THE VIEWING LASTS ALL DAY. THE WHOLE BASE WILL BE AT THE FUNERAL-- THE AVENGERS, TOO.
WHAT ABOUT CIVILIANS? WE SHOULD WEAR OUR MASKS IN FRONT OF TRAUMA'S FAMILY, RIGHT?
I DON'T THINK THAT'LL BE A PROBLEM. I GOT TO KNOW TRAUMA PRETTY WELL THESE PAST FEW WEEKS, AND...WELL...
...THERE'S A REASON HE'S BEING BURIED ON BASE. I DON'T THINK HIS FAMILY'S COMING. ANY OF THEM.
I CAN'T REALLY GET INTO DETAILS; HE WOULDN'T WANT ME TO. HE WAS PRETTY PRIVATE...

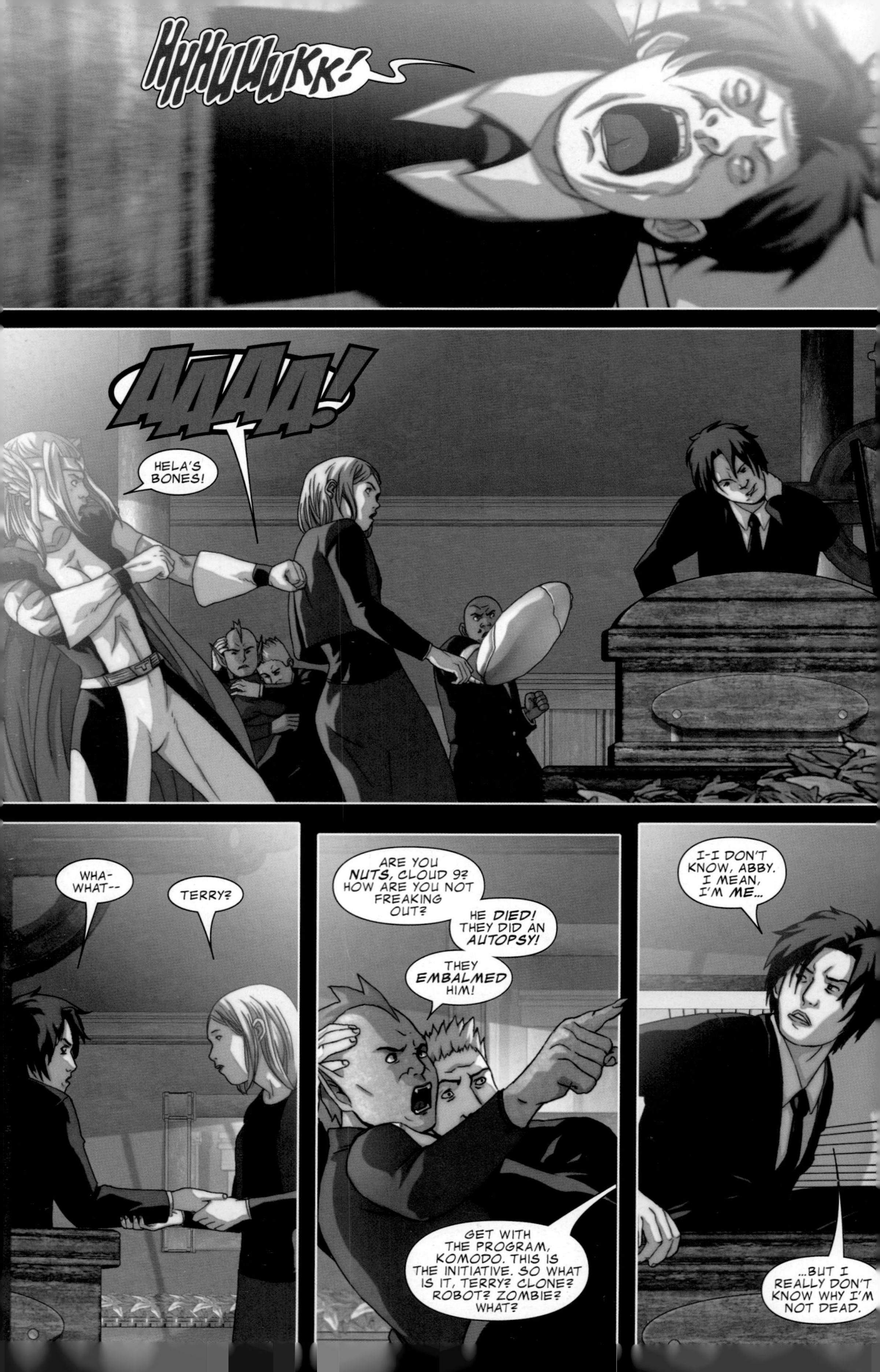
HHHUUUKK!
AAAAA!
HELA'S BONES!
WHA- WHAT--
TERRY?
ARE YOU NUTS, CLOUD 9? HOW ARE YOU NOT FREAKING OUT?
HE DIED! THEY DID AN AUTOPSY!
THEY EMBALMED HIM!
GET WITH THE PROGRAM, KOMODO. THIS IS THE INITIATIVE. SO WHAT IS IT, TERRY? CLONE? ROBOT? ZOMBIE? WHAT?
I-I DON'T KNOW, ABBY. I MEAN, I'M ME...
...BUT I REALLY DON'T KNOW WHY I'M NOT DEAD.

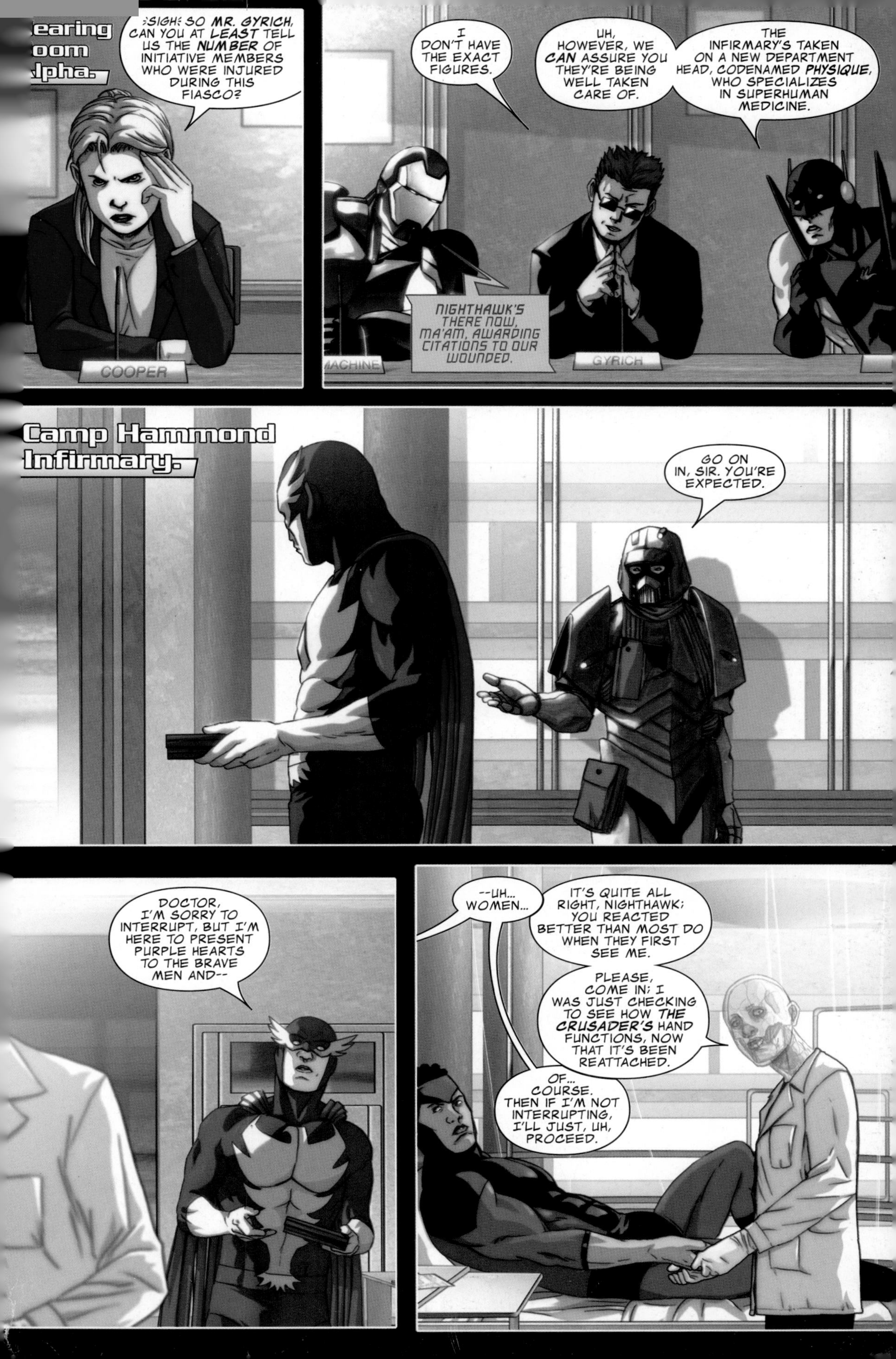

earing oom lpha.
:SIGH: SO MR. GYRICH, CAN YOU AT LEAST TELL US THE NUMBER OF INITIATIVE MEMBERS WHO WERE INJURED DURING THIS FIASCO?
COOPER
I DON'T HAVE THE EXACT FIGURES.
UH, HOWEVER, WE CAN ASSURE YOU THEY'RE BEING WELL TAKEN CARE OF.
THE INFIRMARY'S TAKEN ON A NEW DEPARTMENT HEAD, CODENAMED PHYSIQUE, WHO SPECIALIZES IN SUPERHUMAN MEDICINE.
NIGHTHAWK'S THERE NOW, MA'AM, AWARDING CITATIONS TO OUR WOUNDED.
MACHINE
GYRICH
Camp Hammond Infirmary.
GO ON IN, SIR. YOU'RE EXPECTED.
DOCTOR, I'M SORRY TO INTERRUPT, BUT I'M HERE TO PRESENT PURPLE HEARTS TO THE BRAVE MEN AND--
--UH... WOMEN...
IT'S QUITE ALL RIGHT, NIGHTHAWK; YOU REACTED BETTER THAN MOST DO WHEN THEY FIRST SEE ME.
PLEASE, COME IN; I WAS JUST CHECKING TO SEE HOW THE CRUSADER'S HAND FUNCTIONS, NOW THAT IT'S BEEN REATTACHED.
OF... COURSE. THEN IF I'M NOT INTERRUPTING, I'LL JUST, UH, PROCEED.

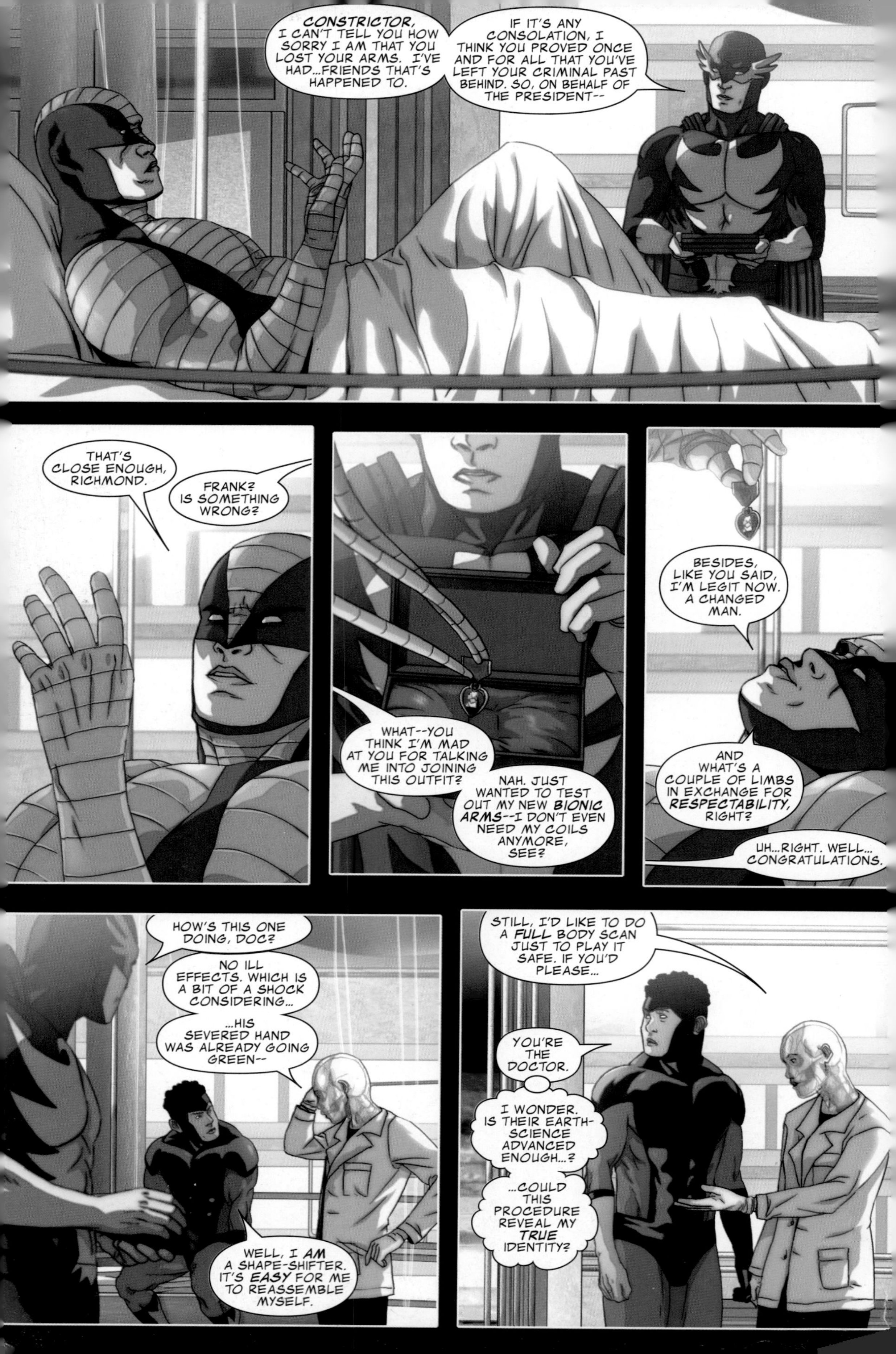
CONSTRICTOR, I CAN'T TELL YOU HOW SORRY I AM THAT YOU LOST YOUR ARMS. I'VE HAD...FRIENDS THAT'S HAPPENED TO.
IF IT'S ANY CONSOLATION, I THINK YOU PROVED ONCE AND FOR ALL THAT YOU'VE LEFT YOUR CRIMINAL PAST BEHIND. SO, ON BEHALF OF THE PRESIDENT--
THAT'S CLOSE ENOUGH, RICHMOND.
FRANK? IS SOMETHING WRONG?
WHAT--YOU THINK I'M MAD AT YOU FOR TALKING ME INTO JOINING THIS OUTFIT?
NAH. JUST WANTED TO TEST OUT MY NEW BIONIC ARMS--I DON'T EVEN NEED MY COILS ANYMORE, SEE?
BESIDES, LIKE YOU SAID, I'M LEGIT NOW. A CHANGED MAN.
AND WHAT'S A COUPLE OF LIMBS IN EXCHANGE FOR RESPECTABILITY, RIGHT?
UH...RIGHT. WELL... CONGRATULATIONS.
HOW'S THIS ONE DOING, DOC?
NO ILL EFFECTS. WHICH IS A BIT OF A SHOCK CONSIDERING...
...HIS SEVERED HAND WAS ALREADY GOING GREEN--
WELL, I AM A SHAPE-SHIFTER. IT'S EASY FOR ME TO REASSEMBLE MYSELF.
STILL, I'D LIKE TO DO A FULL BODY SCAN JUST TO PLAY IT SAFE. IF YOU'D PLEASE...
YOU'RE THE DOCTOR.
I WONDER. IS THEIR EARTH-SCIENCE ADVANCED ENOUGH...?
...COULD THIS PROCEDURE REVEAL MY TRUE IDENTITY?

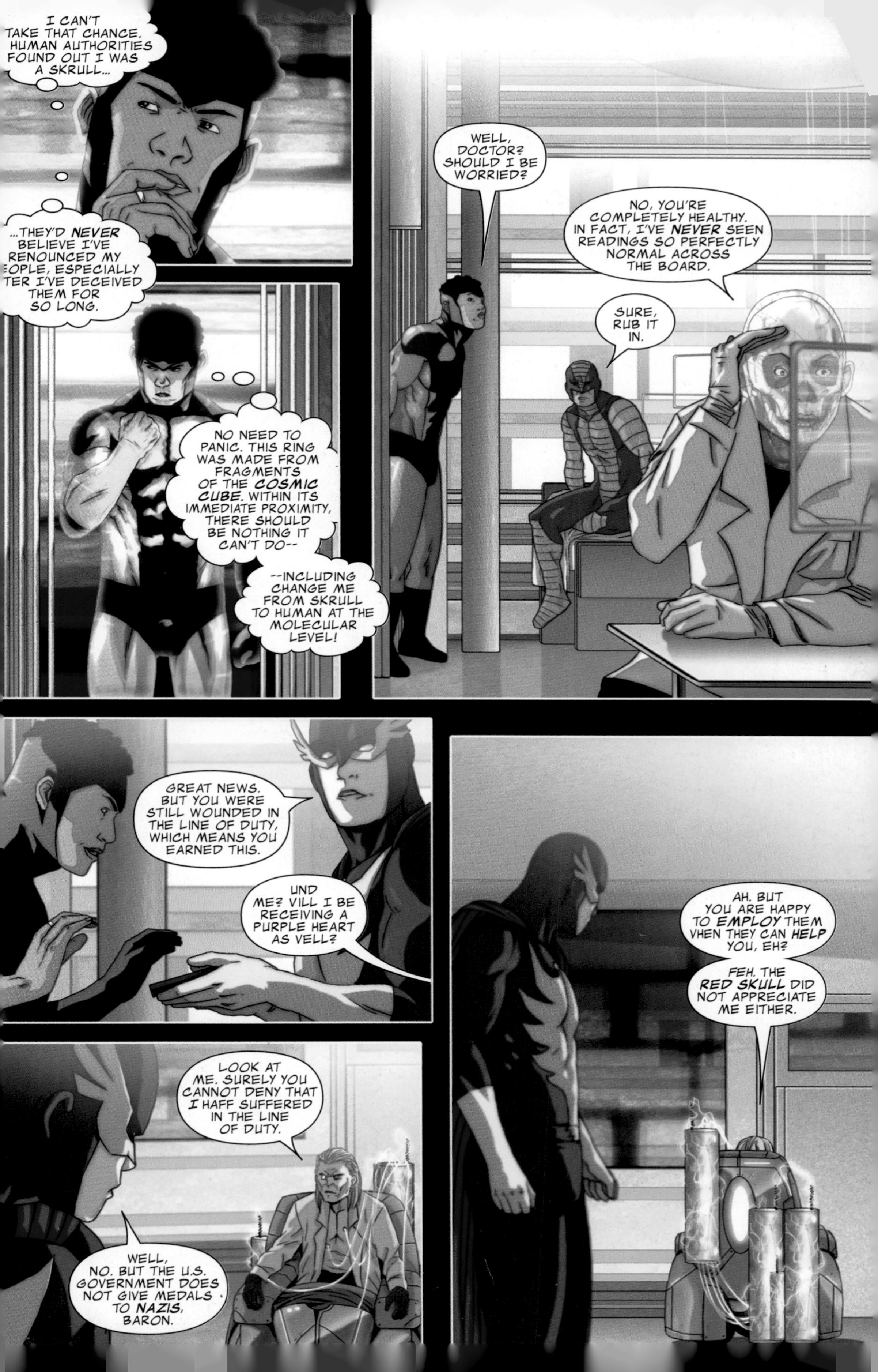
I CAN'T TAKE THAT CHANCE. HUMAN AUTHORITIES FOUND OUT I WAS A SKRULL...
...THEY'D NEVER BELIEVE I'VE RENOUNCED MY EOPLE, ESPECIALLY TER I'VE DECEIVED THEM FOR SO LONG.
NO NEED TO PANIC. THIS RING WAS MADE FROM FRAGMENTS OF THE COSMIC CUBE. WITHIN ITS IMMEDIATE PROXIMITY, THERE SHOULD BE NOTHING IT CAN'T DO--
--INCLUDING CHANGE ME FROM SKRULL TO HUMAN AT THE MOLECULAR LEVEL!
WELL, DOCTOR? SHOULD I BE WORRIED?
NO, YOU'RE COMPLETELY HEALTHY. IN FACT, I'VE NEVER SEEN READINGS SO PERFECTLY NORMAL ACROSS THE BOARD.
SURE, RUB IT IN.
GREAT NEWS. BUT YOU WERE STILL WOUNDED IN THE LINE OF DUTY, WHICH MEANS YOU EARNED THIS.
UND ME? VILL I BE RECEIVING A PURPLE HEART AS VELL?
LOOK AT ME. SURELY YOU CANNOT DENY THAT I HAFF SUFFERED IN THE LINE OF DUTY.
WELL, NO. BUT THE U.S. GOVERNMENT DOES NOT GIVE MEDALS TO NAZIS, BARON.
AH. BUT YOU ARE HAPPY TO EMPLOY THEM VHEN THEY CAN HELP YOU, EH?
FEH. THE RED SKULL DID NOT APPRECIATE ME EITHER.

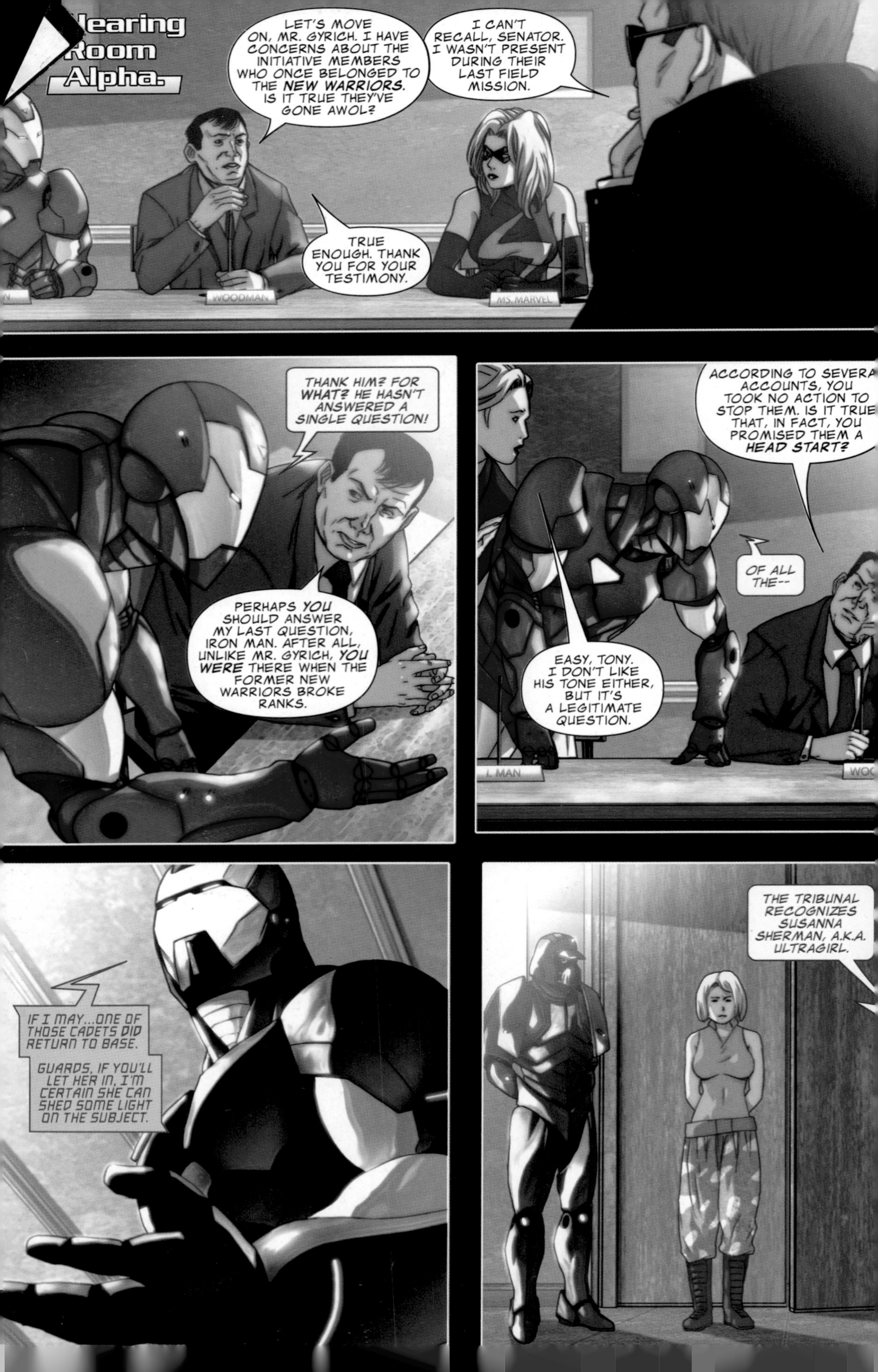
Hearing Room Alpha.
LET'S MOVE ON, MR. GYRICH. I HAVE CONCERNS ABOUT THE INITIATIVE MEMBERS WHO ONCE BELONGED TO THE NEW WARRIORS. IS IT TRUE THEY'VE GONE AWOL?
I CAN'T RECALL, SENATOR. I WASN'T PRESENT DURING THEIR LAST FIELD MISSION.
TRUE ENOUGH. THANK YOU FOR YOUR TESTIMONY.
WOODMAN
MS. MARVEL
THANK HIM? FOR WHAT? HE HASN'T ANSWERED A SINGLE QUESTION!
PERHAPS YOU SHOULD ANSWER MY LAST QUESTION, IRON MAN. AFTER ALL, UNLIKE MR. GYRICH, YOU WERE THERE WHEN THE FORMER NEW WARRIORS BROKE RANKS.
ACCORDING TO SEVERA ACCOUNTS, YOU TOOK NO ACTION TO STOP THEM. IS IT TRUE THAT, IN FACT, YOU PROMISED THEM A HEAD START?
OF ALL THE--
EASY, TONY. I DON'T LIKE HIS TONE EITHER, BUT IT'S A LEGITIMATE QUESTION.
I. MAN
IF I MAY...ONE OF THOSE CADETS DID RETURN TO BASE.
GUARDS, IF YOU'LL LET HER IN, I'M CERTAIN SHE CAN SHED SOME LIGHT ON THE SUBJECT.
THE TRIBUNAL RECOGNIZES SUSANNA SHERMAN, A.K.A. ULTRAGIRL.

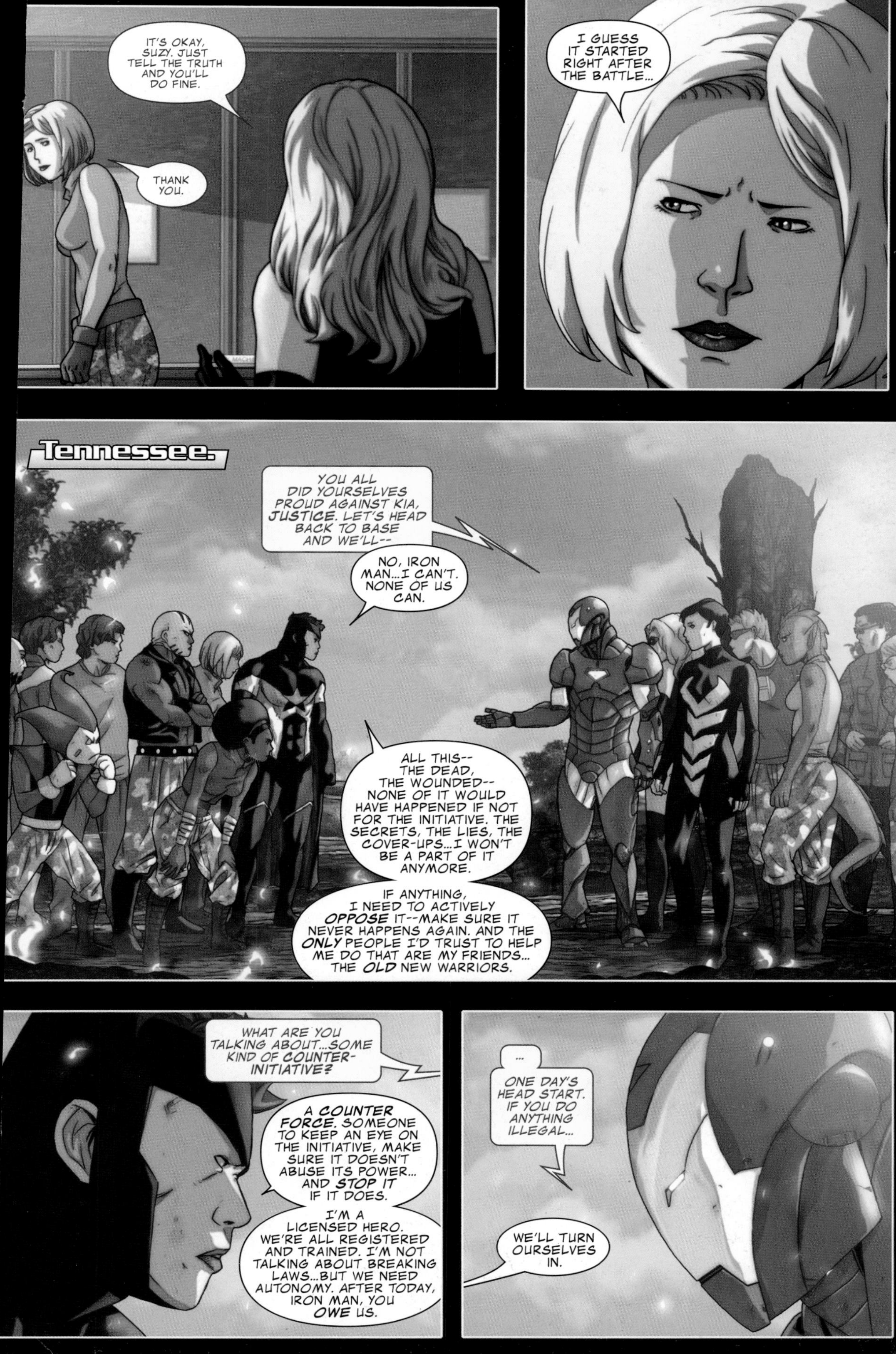
IT'S OKAY, SUZY. JUST TELL THE TRUTH AND YOU'LL DO FINE.
THANK YOU.
I GUESS IT STARTED RIGHT AFTER THE BATTLE...
Tennessee.
YOU ALL DID YOURSELVES PROUD AGAINST KIA, JUSTICE. LET'S HEAD BACK TO BASE AND WE'LL--
NO, IRON MAN...I CAN'T. NONE OF US CAN.
ALL THIS--THE DEAD, THE WOUNDED--NONE OF IT WOULD HAVE HAPPENED IF NOT FOR THE INITIATIVE. THE SECRETS, THE LIES, THE COVER-UPS...I WON'T BE A PART OF IT ANYMORE.
IF ANYTHING, I NEED TO ACTIVELY OPPOSE IT--MAKE SURE IT NEVER HAPPENS AGAIN. AND THE ONLY PEOPLE I'D TRUST TO HELP ME DO THAT ARE MY FRIENDS... THE OLD NEW WARRIORS.
WHAT ARE YOU TALKING ABOUT...SOME KIND OF COUNTER-INITIATIVE?
A COUNTER FORCE. SOMEONE TO KEEP AN EYE ON THE INITIATIVE, MAKE SURE IT DOESN'T ABUSE ITS POWER... AND STOP IT IF IT DOES.
I'M A LICENSED HERO. WE'RE ALL REGISTERED AND TRAINED. I'M NOT TALKING ABOUT BREAKING LAWS...BUT WE NEED AUTONOMY. AFTER TODAY, IRON MAN, YOU OWE US.
...
ONE DAY'S HEAD START. IF YOU DO ANYTHING ILLEGAL...
WE'LL TURN OURSELVES IN.

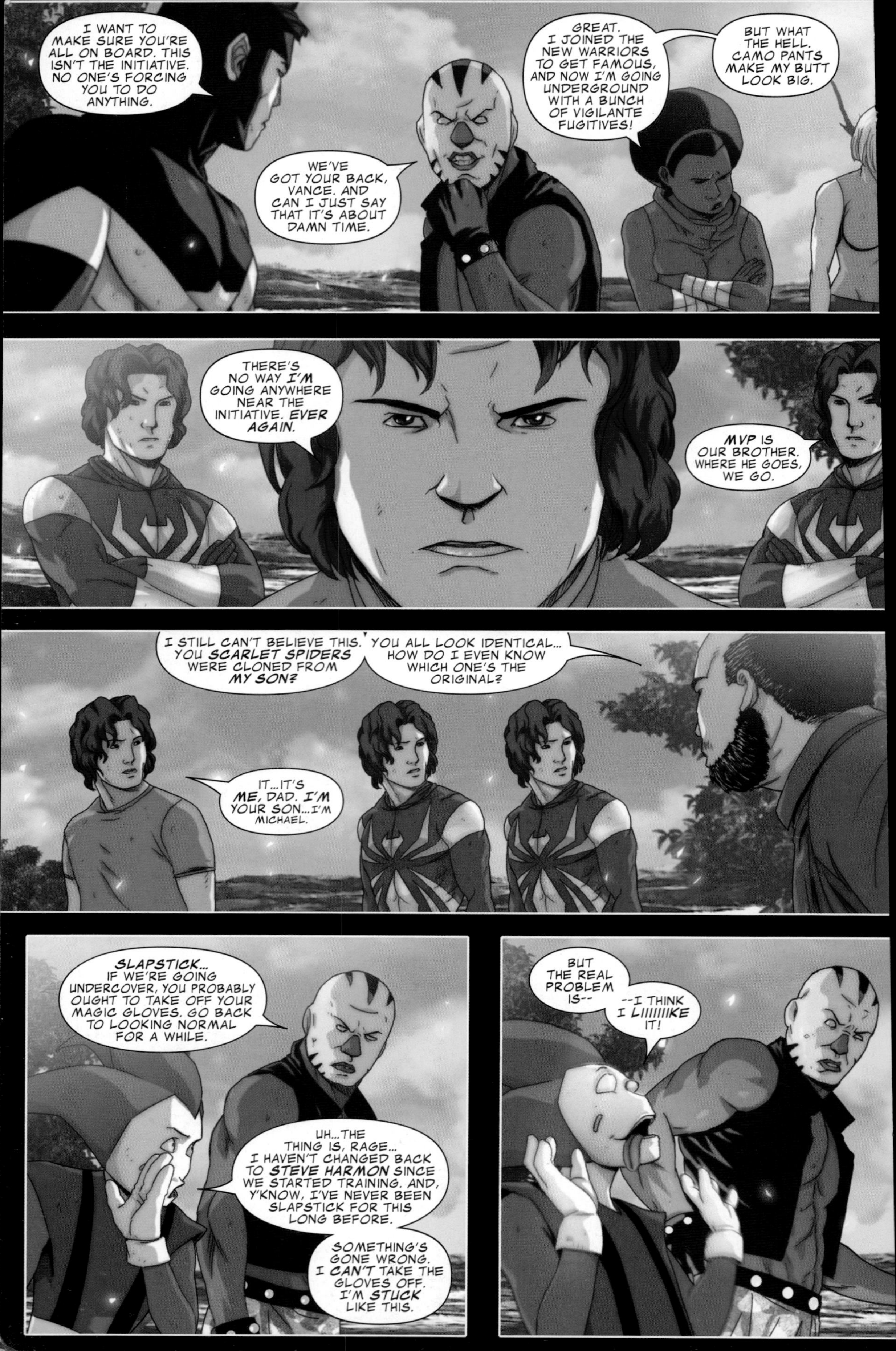
I WANT TO MAKE SURE YOU'RE ALL ON BOARD. THIS ISN'T THE INITIATIVE. NO ONE'S FORCING YOU TO DO ANYTHING.
WE'VE GOT YOUR BACK, VANCE. AND CAN I JUST SAY THAT IT'S ABOUT DAMN TIME.
GREAT. I JOINED THE NEW WARRIORS TO GET FAMOUS, AND NOW I'M GOING UNDERGROUND WITH A BUNCH OF VIGILANTE FUGITIVES!
BUT WHAT THE HELL. CAMO PANTS MAKE MY BUTT LOOK BIG.
THERE'S NO WAY I'M GOING ANYWHERE NEAR THE INITIATIVE. EVER AGAIN.
MVP IS OUR BROTHER. WHERE HE GOES, WE GO.
I STILL CAN'T BELIEVE THIS. YOU SCARLET SPIDERS WERE CLONED FROM MY SON?
YOU ALL LOOK IDENTICAL... HOW DO I EVEN KNOW WHICH ONE'S THE ORIGINAL?
IT...IT'S ME, DAD. I'M YOUR SON...I'M MICHAEL.
SLAPSTICK... IF WE'RE GOING UNDERCOVER, YOU PROBABLY OUGHT TO TAKE OFF YOUR MAGIC GLOVES. GO BACK TO LOOKING NORMAL FOR A WHILE.
UH...THE THING IS, RAGE... I HAVEN'T CHANGED BACK TO STEVE HARMON SINCE WE STARTED TRAINING. AND, Y'KNOW, I'VE NEVER BEEN SLAPSTICK FOR THIS LONG BEFORE.
SOMETHING'S GONE WRONG. I CAN'T TAKE THE GLOVES OFF. I'M STUCK LIKE THIS.
BUT THE REAL PROBLEM IS--
--I THINK I LIIIIIIIKE IT!

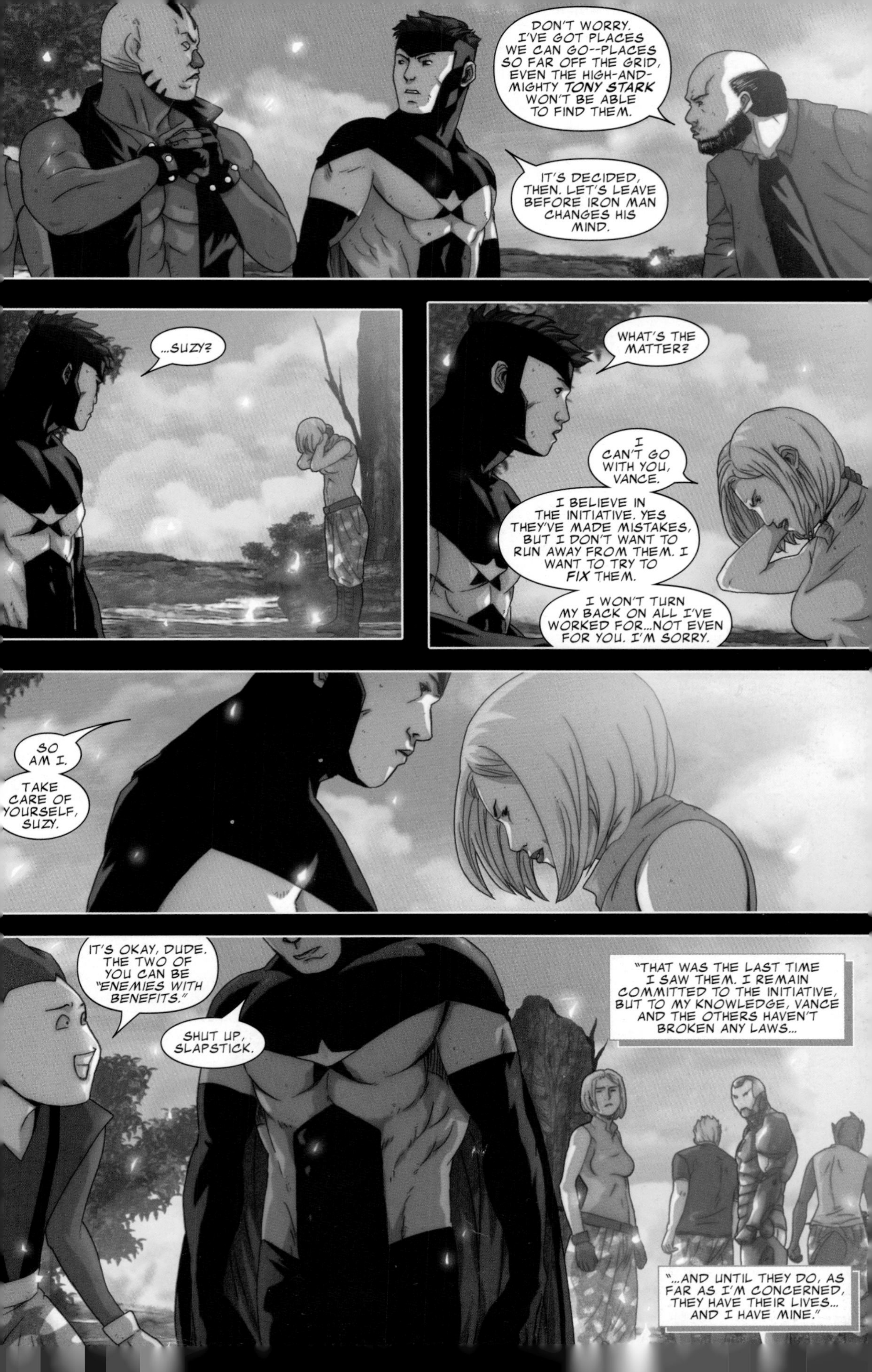
DON'T WORRY. I'VE GOT PLACES WE CAN GO--PLACES SO FAR OFF THE GRID, EVEN THE HIGH-AND-MIGHTY TONY STARK WON'T BE ABLE TO FIND THEM.
IT'S DECIDED, THEN. LET'S LEAVE BEFORE IRON MAN CHANGES HIS MIND.
...SUZY?
WHAT'S THE MATTER?
I CAN'T GO WITH YOU, VANCE.
I BELIEVE IN THE INITIATIVE. YES THEY'VE MADE MISTAKES, BUT I DON'T WANT TO RUN AWAY FROM THEM. I WANT TO TRY TO FIX THEM.
I WON'T TURN MY BACK ON ALL I'VE WORKED FOR...NOT EVEN FOR YOU. I'M SORRY.
SO AM I.
TAKE CARE OF YOURSELF, SUZY.
IT'S OKAY, DUDE. THE TWO OF YOU CAN BE "ENEMIES WITH BENEFITS."
SHUT UP, SLAPSTICK.
"THAT WAS THE LAST TIME I SAW THEM. I REMAIN COMMITTED TO THE INITIATIVE, BUT TO MY KNOWLEDGE, VANCE AND THE OTHERS HAVEN'T BROKEN ANY LAWS...
"...AND UNTIL THEY DO, AS FAR AS I'M CONCERNED, THEY HAVE THEIR LIVES... AND I HAVE MINE."

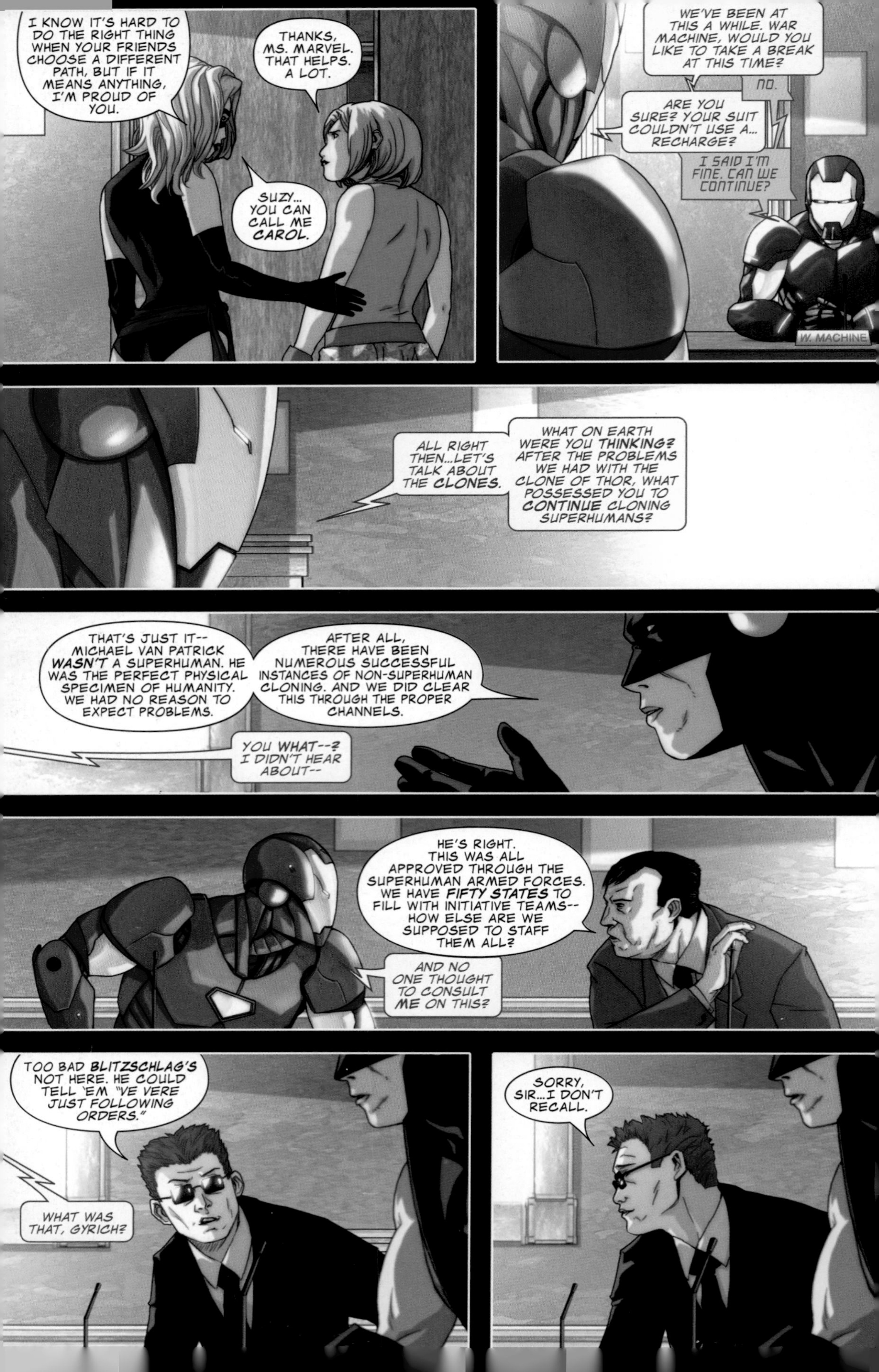
I KNOW IT'S HARD TO DO THE RIGHT THING WHEN YOUR FRIENDS CHOOSE A DIFFERENT PATH, BUT IF IT MEANS ANYTHING, I'M PROUD OF YOU.
THANKS, MS. MARVEL. THAT HELPS. A LOT.
SUZY... YOU CAN CALL ME CAROL.
WE'VE BEEN AT THIS A WHILE. WAR MACHINE, WOULD YOU LIKE TO TAKE A BREAK AT THIS TIME?
NO.
ARE YOU SURE? YOUR SUIT COULDN'T USE A... RECHARGE?
I SAID I'M FINE. CAN WE CONTINUE?
W. MACHINE
ALL RIGHT THEN...LET'S TALK ABOUT THE CLONES.
WHAT ON EARTH WERE YOU THINKING? AFTER THE PROBLEMS WE HAD WITH THE CLONE OF THOR, WHAT POSSESSED YOU TO CONTINUE CLONING SUPERHUMANS?
THAT'S JUST IT-- MICHAEL VAN PATRICK WASN'T A SUPERHUMAN. HE WAS THE PERFECT PHYSICAL SPECIMEN OF HUMANITY. WE HAD NO REASON TO EXPECT PROBLEMS.
AFTER ALL, THERE HAVE BEEN NUMEROUS SUCCESSFUL INSTANCES OF NON-SUPERHUMAN CLONING. AND WE DID CLEAR THIS THROUGH THE PROPER CHANNELS.
YOU WHAT--? I DIDN'T HEAR ABOUT--
HE'S RIGHT. THIS WAS ALL APPROVED THROUGH THE SUPERHUMAN ARMED FORCES. WE HAVE FIFTY STATES TO FILL WITH INITIATIVE TEAMS-- HOW ELSE ARE WE SUPPOSED TO STAFF THEM ALL?
AND NO ONE THOUGHT TO CONSULT ME ON THIS?
TOO BAD BLITZSCHLAG'S NOT HERE. HE COULD TELL 'EM "VE VERE JUST FOLLOWING ORDERS."
WHAT WAS THAT, GYRICH?
SORRY, SIR...I DON'T RECALL.

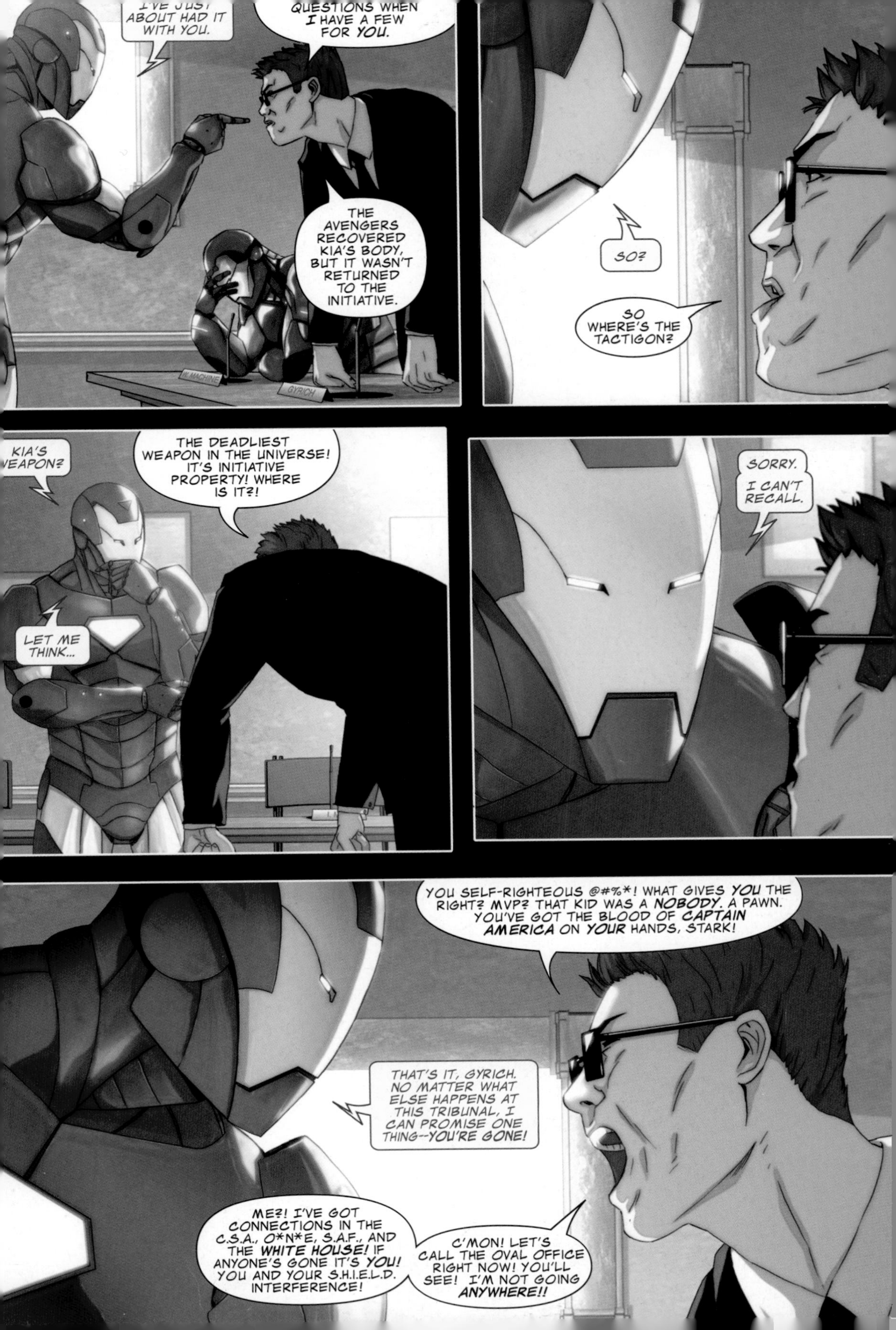
I'VE JUST ABOUT HAD IT WITH YOU.
QUESTIONS WHEN I HAVE A FEW FOR YOU.
THE AVENGERS RECOVERED KIA'S BODY, BUT IT WASN'T RETURNED TO THE INITIATIVE.
W. MACHINE
GYRICH
SO?
SO WHERE'S THE TACTIGON?
KIA'S WEAPON?
THE DEADLIEST WEAPON IN THE UNIVERSE! IT'S INITIATIVE PROPERTY! WHERE IS IT?!
LET ME THINK...
SORRY.
I CAN'T RECALL.
YOU SELF-RIGHTEOUS @#%*! WHAT GIVES YOU THE RIGHT? MVP? THAT KID WAS A NOBODY. A PAWN. YOU'VE GOT THE BLOOD OF CAPTAIN AMERICA ON YOUR HANDS, STARK!
THAT'S IT, GYRICH. NO MATTER WHAT ELSE HAPPENS AT THIS TRIBUNAL, I CAN PROMISE ONE THING--YOU'RE GONE!
ME?! I'VE GOT CONNECTIONS IN THE C.S.A., O*N*E, S.A.F., AND THE WHITE HOUSE! IF ANYONE'S GONE IT'S YOU! YOU AND YOUR S.H.I.E.L.D. INTERFERENCE!
C'MON! LET'S CALL THE OVAL OFFICE RIGHT NOW! YOU'LL SEE! I'M NOT GOING ANYWHERE!!

...AND SO, AFTER A GREAT DEAL OF THOUGHT AND SOUL-SEARCHING...

...I'VE DECIDED TO LEAVE THE INITIATIVE IN ORDER TO SPEND MORE TIME WITH MY FAMILY.

SUPER-HUMAN ARMED FORCES

SALLY FLOYD, *FRONT LINE.*

MR. GYRICH...YOU DON'T *HAVE* A FAMILY.

NO MORE QUESTIONS. THANK YOU.

GOD, I HATE THAT WOMAN.

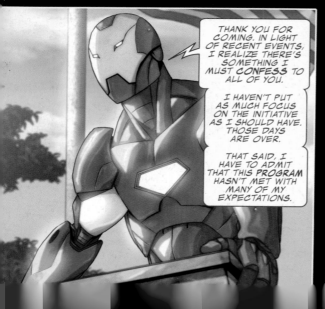

THANK YOU FOR COMING. IN LIGHT OF RECENT EVENTS, I REALIZE THERE'S SOMETHING I MUST **CONFESS** TO ALL OF YOU.

I HAVEN'T PUT AS MUCH FOCUS ON THE INITIATIVE AS I SHOULD HAVE. THOSE DAYS ARE OVER.

THAT SAID, I HAVE TO ADMIT THAT THIS **PROGRAM** HASN'T MET WITH MANY OF MY EXPECTATIONS.

HOWEVER, I CONSIDER MYSELF FORTUNATE--

--FORTUNATE THAT THIS GRADUATING **CLASS** HAS EXCEEDED THEM!

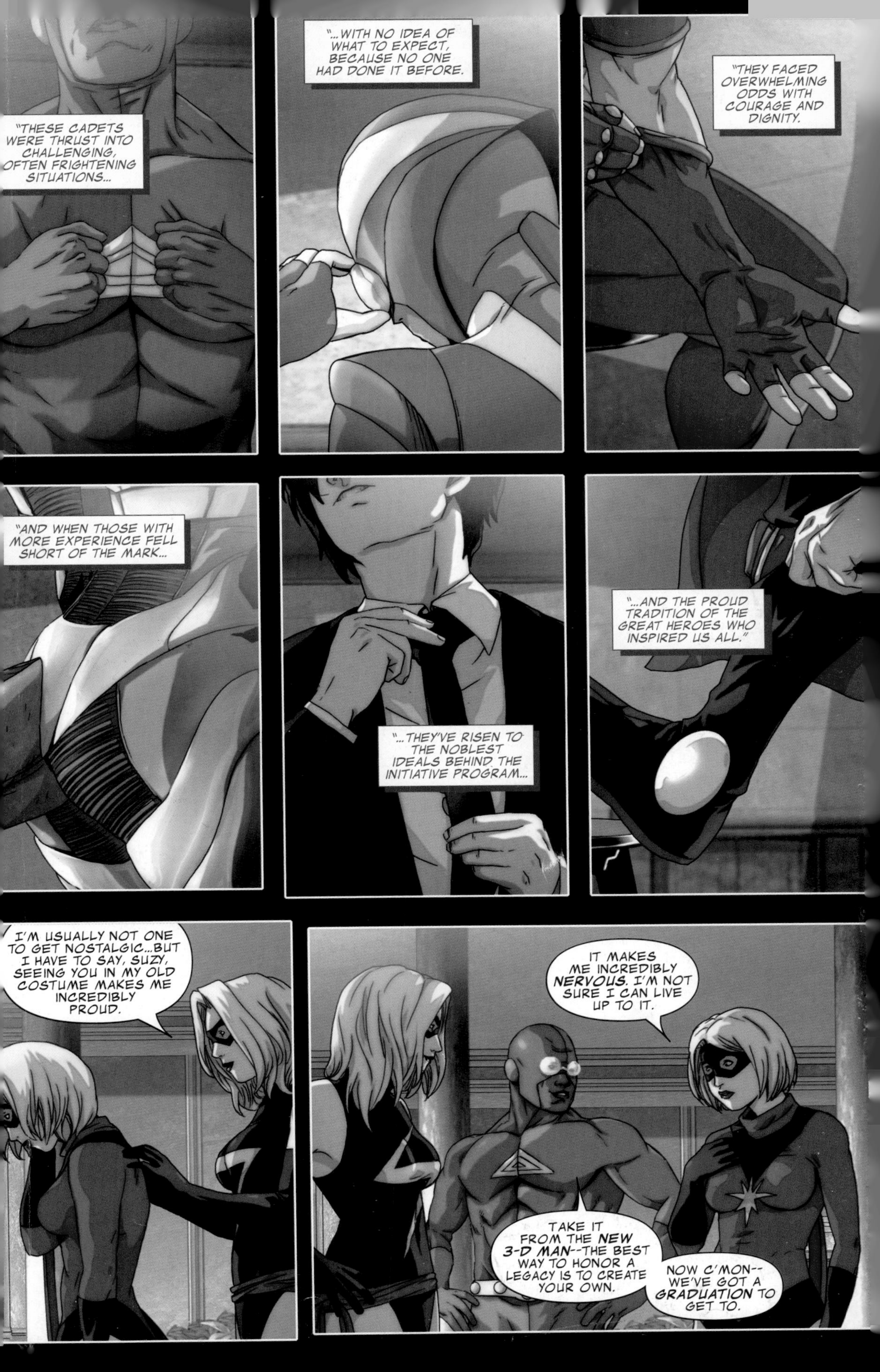
"THESE CADETS WERE THRUST INTO CHALLENGING, OFTEN FRIGHTENING SITUATIONS...
"...WITH NO IDEA OF WHAT TO EXPECT, BECAUSE NO ONE HAD DONE IT BEFORE.
"THEY FACED OVERWHELMING ODDS WITH COURAGE AND DIGNITY.
"AND WHEN THOSE WITH MORE EXPERIENCE FELL SHORT OF THE MARK...
"...THEY'VE RISEN TO THE NOBLEST IDEALS BEHIND THE INITIATIVE PROGRAM...
"...AND THE PROUD TRADITION OF THE GREAT HEROES WHO INSPIRED US ALL."
I'M USUALLY NOT ONE TO GET NOSTALGIC...BUT I HAVE TO SAY, SUZY, SEEING YOU IN MY OLD COSTUME MAKES ME INCREDIBLY PROUD.
IT MAKES ME INCREDIBLY NERVOUS. I'M NOT SURE I CAN LIVE UP TO IT.
TAKE IT FROM THE NEW 3-D MAN--THE BEST WAY TO HONOR A LEGACY IS TO CREATE YOUR OWN.
NOW C'MON--WE'VE GOT A GRADUATION TO GET TO.

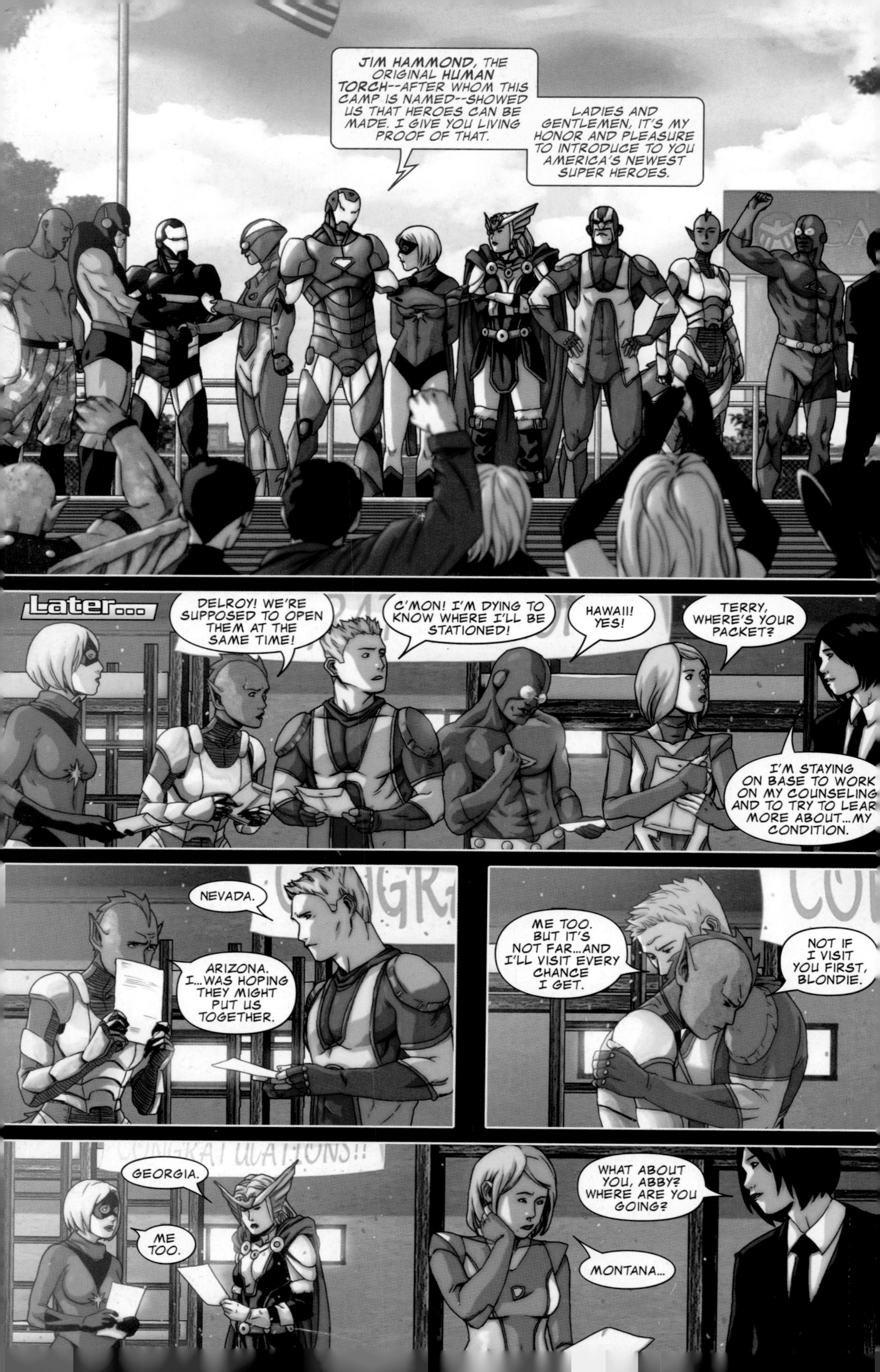

JIM HAMMOND, THE ORIGINAL HUMAN TORCH--AFTER WHOM THIS CAMP IS NAMED--SHOWED US THAT HEROES CAN BE MADE. I GIVE YOU LIVING PROOF OF THAT.
LADIES AND GENTLEMEN, IT'S MY HONOR AND PLEASURE TO INTRODUCE TO YOU AMERICA'S NEWEST SUPER HEROES.
Later...
DELROY! WE'RE SUPPOSED TO OPEN THEM AT THE SAME TIME!
C'MON! I'M DYING TO KNOW WHERE I'LL BE STATIONED!
HAWAII! YES!
TERRY, WHERE'S YOUR PACKET?
I'M STAYING ON BASE TO WORK ON MY COUNSELING AND TO TRY TO LEAR MORE ABOUT...MY CONDITION.
NEVADA.
ARIZONA. I...WAS HOPING THEY MIGHT PUT US TOGETHER.
ME TOO. BUT IT'S NOT FAR...AND I'LL VISIT EVERY CHANCE I GET.
NOT IF I VISIT YOU FIRST, BLONDIE.
CONGRATULATIONS!!
GEORGIA.
ME TOO.
WHAT ABOUT YOU, ABBY? WHERE ARE YOU GOING?
MONTANA...

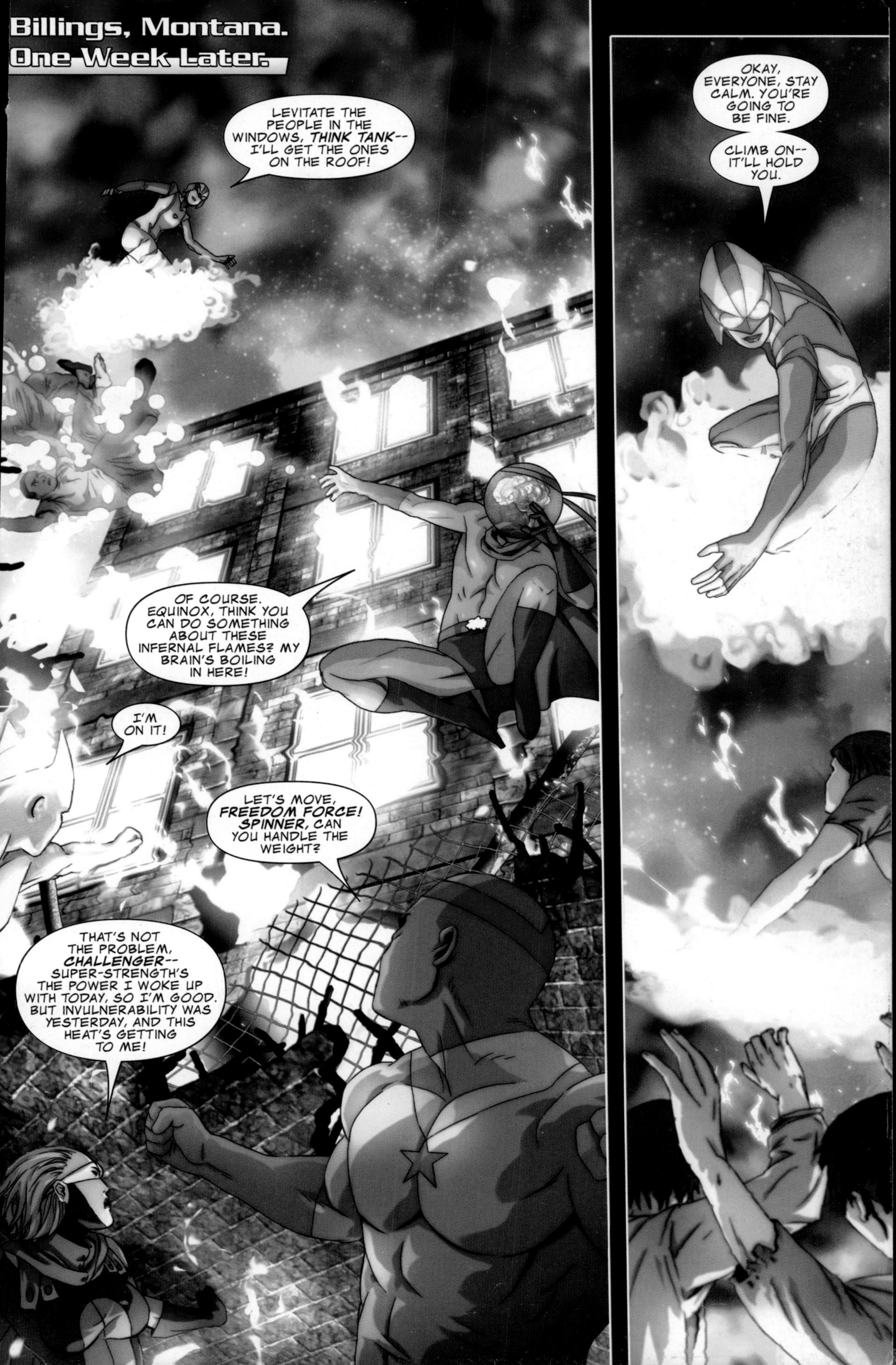
Billings, Montana. One Week Later.
LEVITATE THE PEOPLE IN THE WINDOWS, THINK TANK-- I'LL GET THE ONES ON THE ROOF!
OF COURSE. EQUINOX, THINK YOU CAN DO SOMETHING ABOUT THESE INFERNAL FLAMES? MY BRAIN'S BOILING IN HERE!
I'M ON IT!
LET'S MOVE, FREEDOM FORCE! SPINNER, CAN YOU HANDLE THE WEIGHT?
THAT'S NOT THE PROBLEM, CHALLENGER-- SUPER-STRENGTH'S THE POWER I WOKE UP WITH TODAY, SO I'M GOOD. BUT INVULNERABILITY WAS YESTERDAY, AND THIS HEAT'S GETTING TO ME!
OKAY, EVERYONE, STAY CALM. YOU'RE GOING TO BE FINE.
CLIMB ON-- IT'LL HOLD YOU.

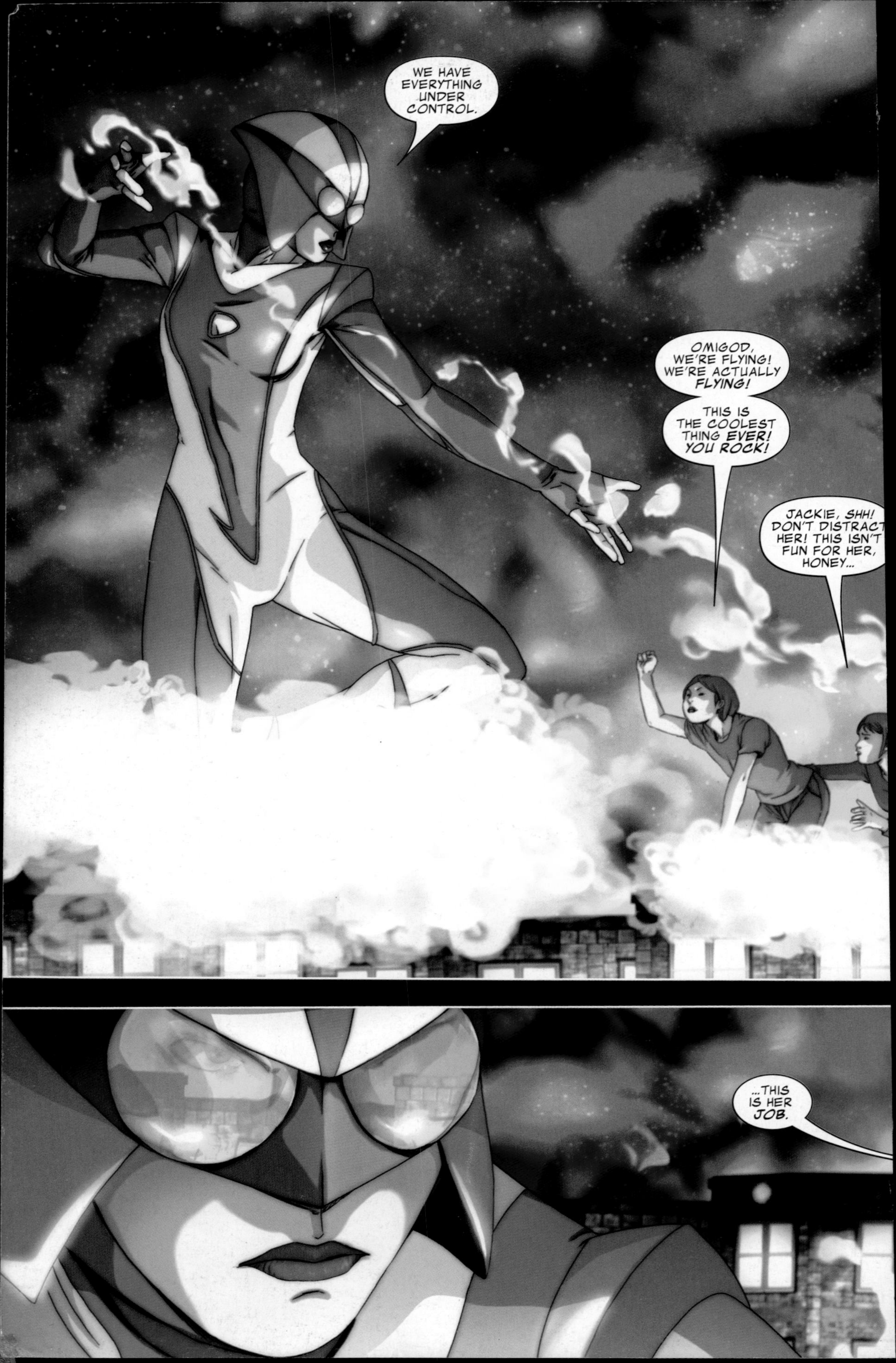
WE HAVE EVERYTHING UNDER CONTROL.
OMIGOD, WE'RE FLYING! WE'RE ACTUALLY FLYING!
THIS IS THE COOLEST THING EVER! YOU ROCK!
JACKIE, SHH! DON'T DISTRACT HER! THIS ISN'T FUN FOR HER, HONEY...
...THIS IS HER JOB.

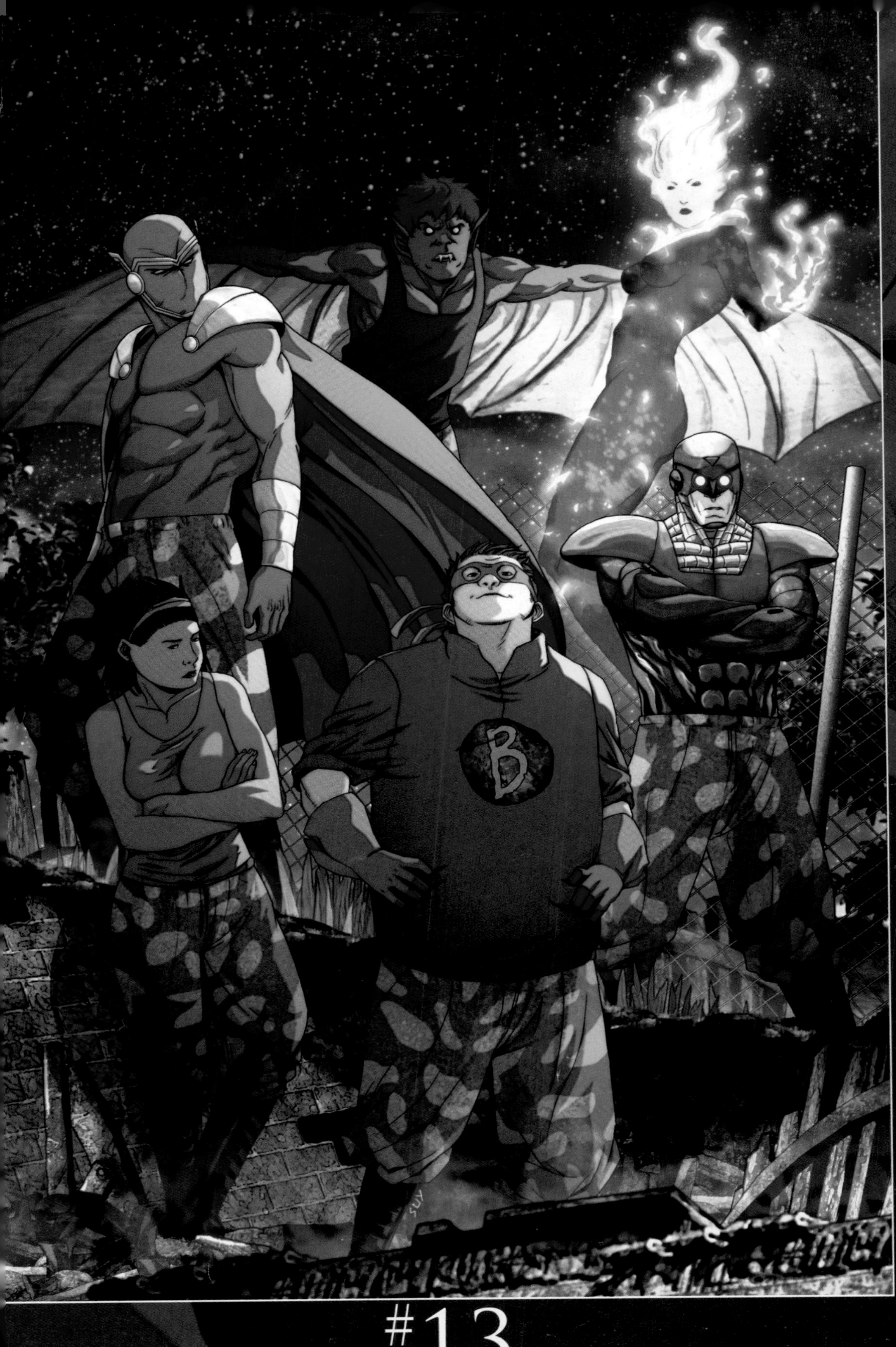
B

#13

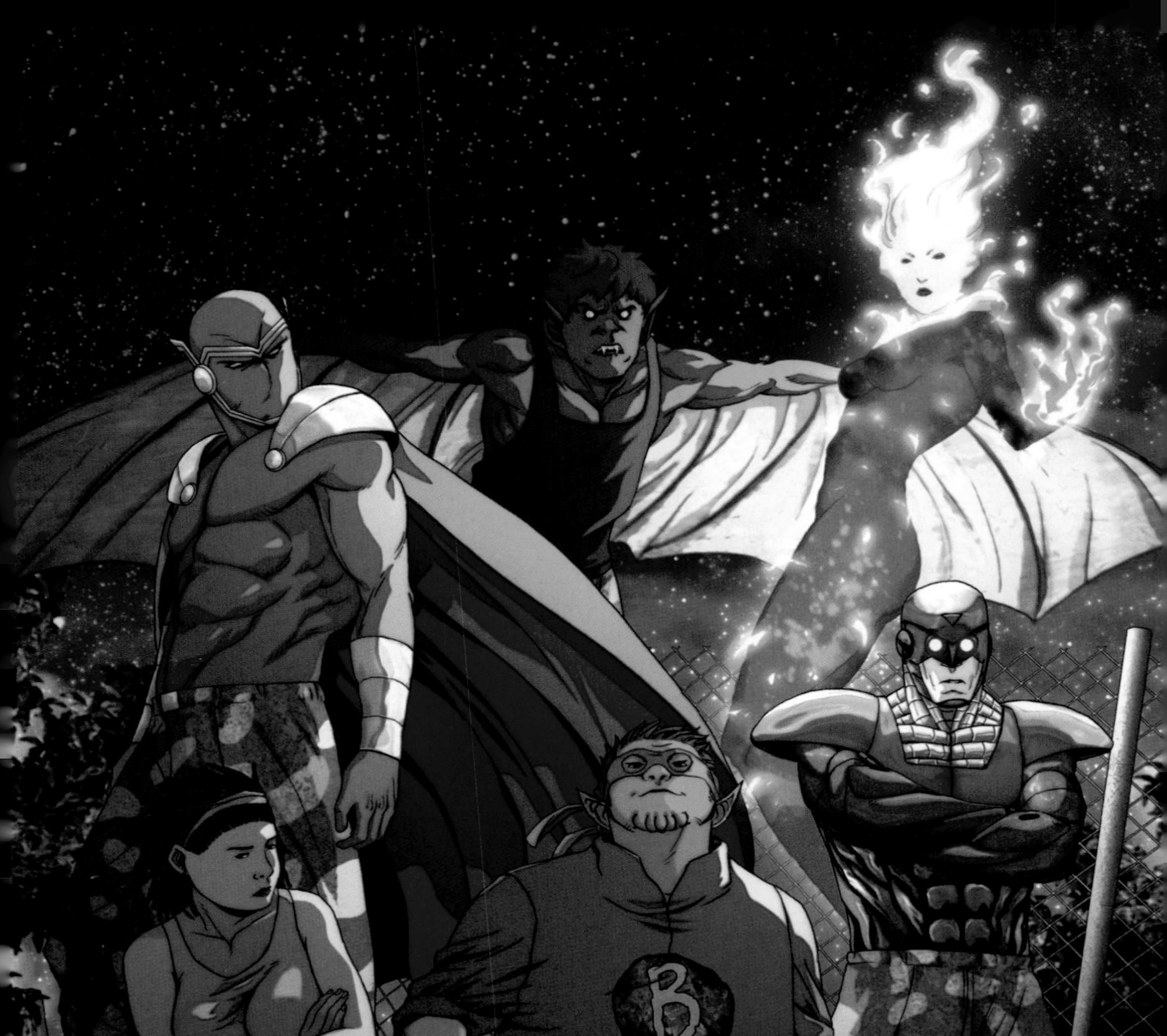

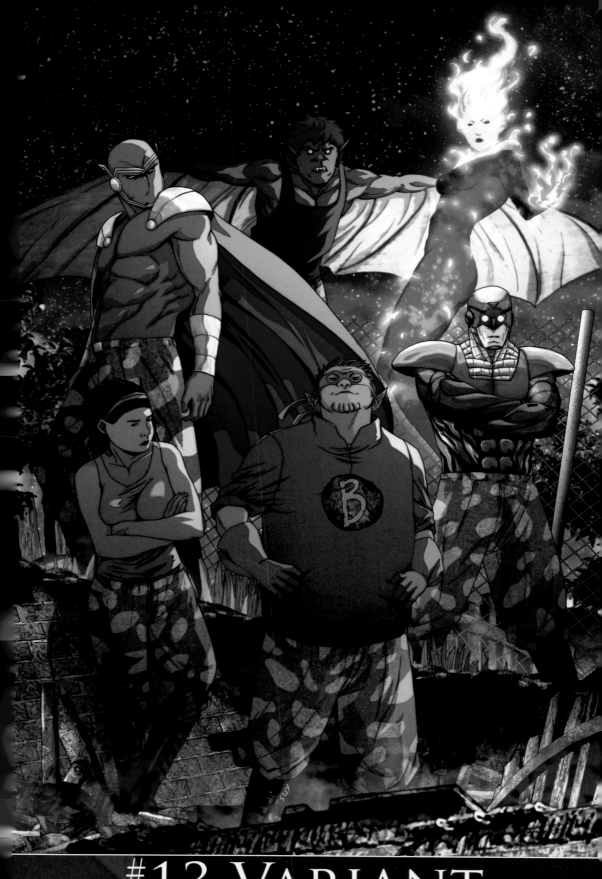

#13 VARIANT

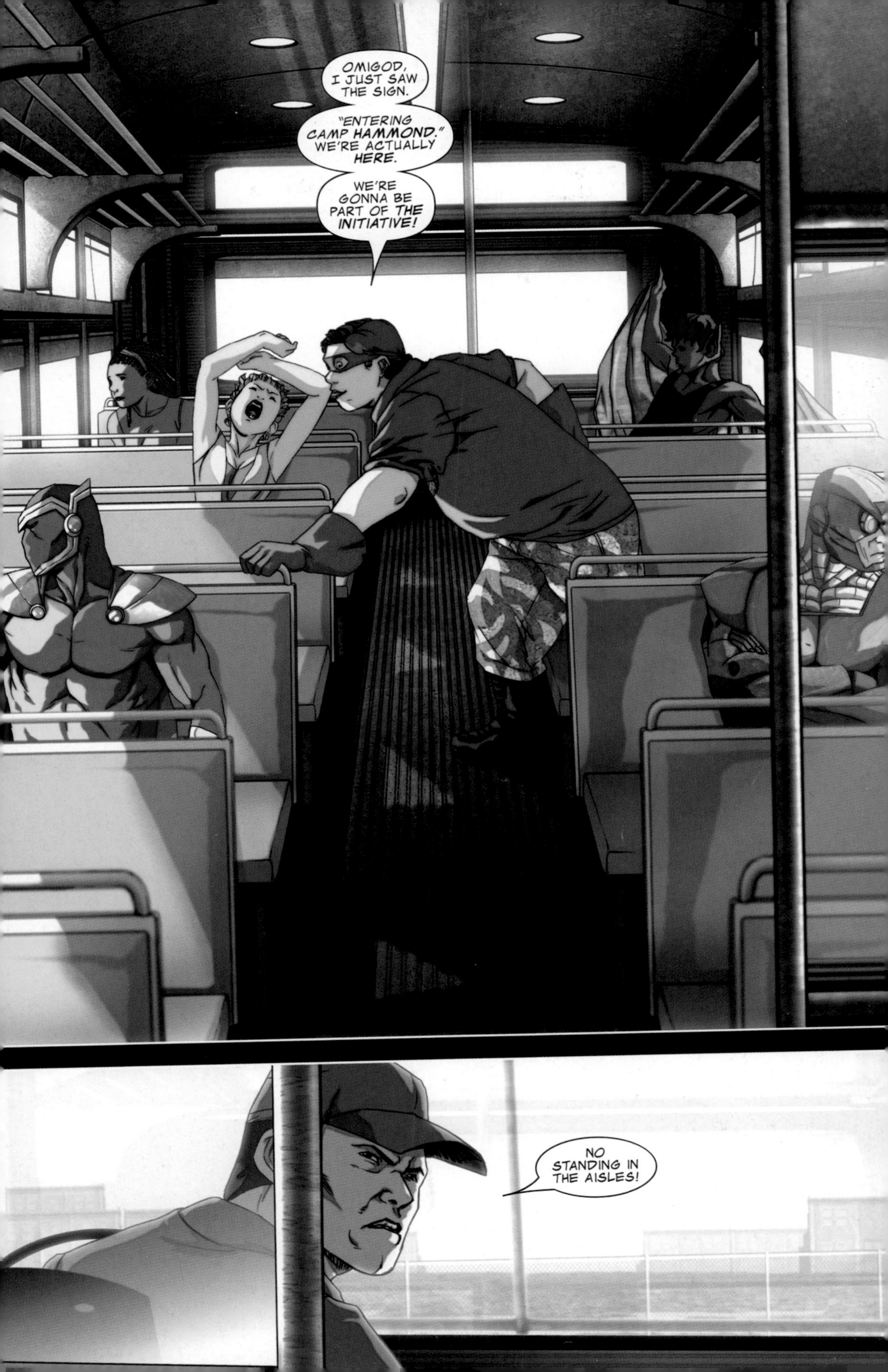
OMIGOD, I JUST SAW THE SIGN.
"ENTERING CAMP HAMMOND." WE'RE ACTUALLY HERE.
WE'RE GONNA BE PART OF THE INITIATIVE!
NO STANDING IN THE AISLES!

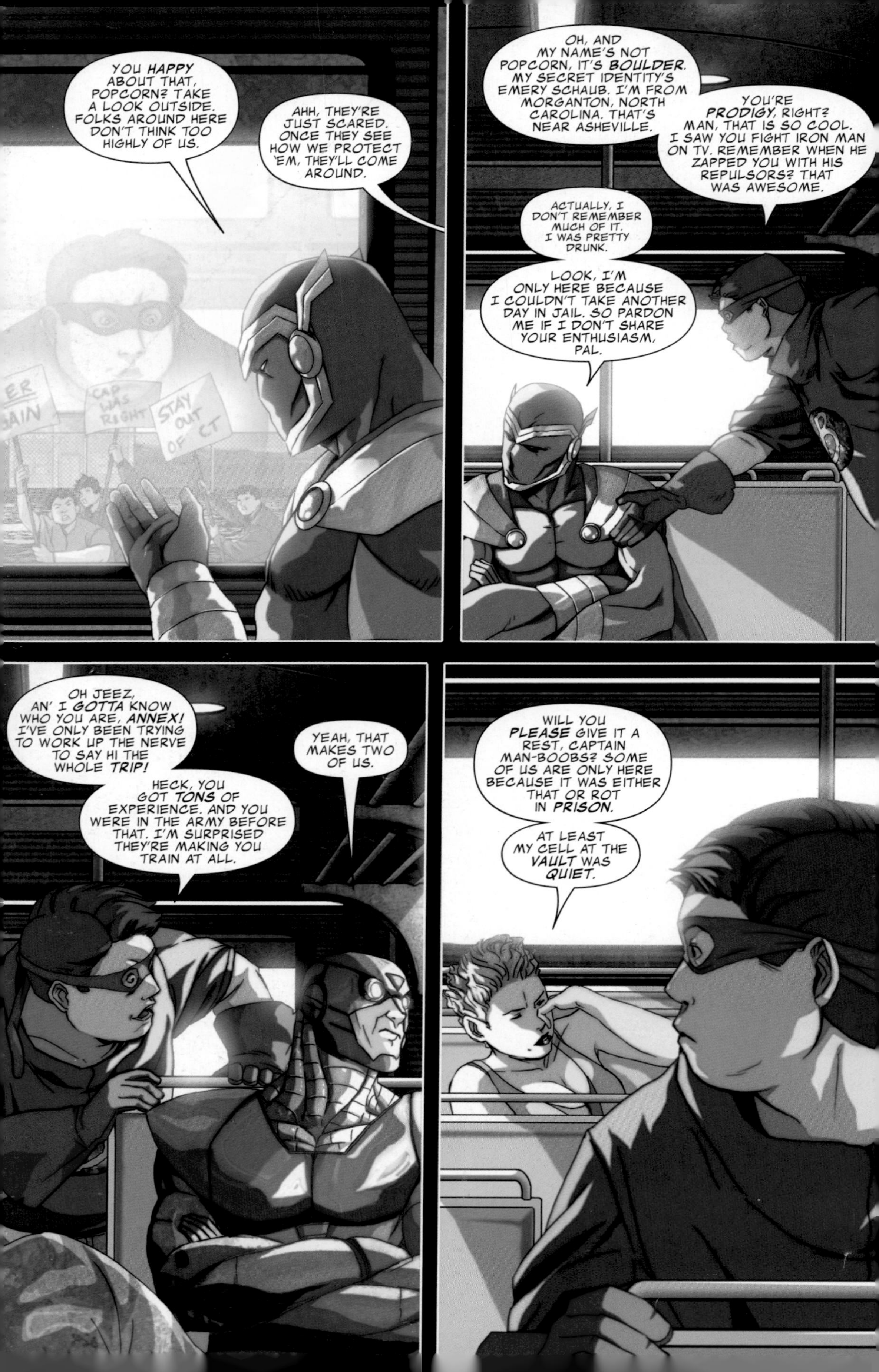
YOU HAPPY ABOUT THAT, POPCORN? TAKE A LOOK OUTSIDE. FOLKS AROUND HERE DON'T THINK TOO HIGHLY OF US.
AHH, THEY'RE JUST SCARED. ONCE THEY SEE HOW WE PROTECT 'EM, THEY'LL COME AROUND.
CAP WAS RIGHT
STAY OUT OF CT
OH, AND MY NAME'S NOT POPCORN, IT'S BOULDER. MY SECRET IDENTITY'S EMERY SCHAUB. I'M FROM MORGANTON, NORTH CAROLINA. THAT'S NEAR ASHEVILLE.
YOU'RE PRODIGY, RIGHT? MAN, THAT IS SO COOL. I SAW YOU FIGHT IRON MAN ON TV. REMEMBER WHEN HE ZAPPED YOU WITH HIS REPULSORS? THAT WAS AWESOME.
ACTUALLY, I DON'T REMEMBER MUCH OF IT. I WAS PRETTY DRUNK.
LOOK, I'M ONLY HERE BECAUSE I COULDN'T TAKE ANOTHER DAY IN JAIL. SO PARDON ME IF I DON'T SHARE YOUR ENTHUSIASM, PAL.
OH JEEZ, AN' I GOTTA KNOW WHO YOU ARE, ANNEX! I'VE ONLY BEEN TRYING TO WORK UP THE NERVE TO SAY HI THE WHOLE TRIP!
HECK, YOU GOT TONS OF EXPERIENCE. AND YOU WERE IN THE ARMY BEFORE THAT. I'M SURPRISED THEY'RE MAKING YOU TRAIN AT ALL.
YEAH, THAT MAKES TWO OF US.
WILL YOU PLEASE GIVE IT A REST, CAPTAIN MAN-BOOBS? SOME OF US ARE ONLY HERE BECAUSE IT WAS EITHER THAT OR ROT IN PRISON.
AT LEAST MY CELL AT THE VAULT WAS QUIET.

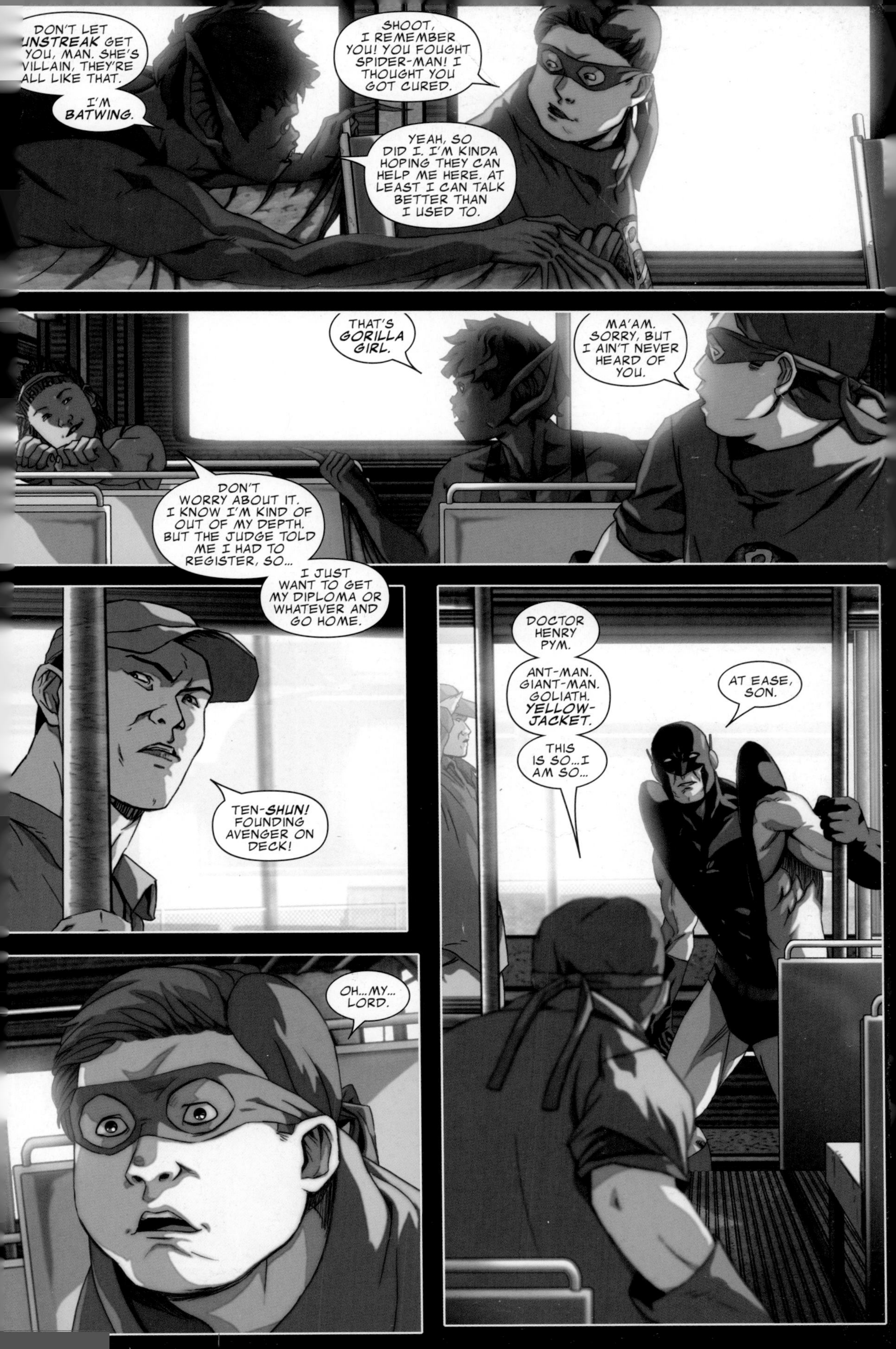
DON'T LET UNSTREAK GET YOU, MAN. SHE'S VILLAIN, THEY'RE ALL LIKE THAT.
I'M BATWING.
SHOOT, I REMEMBER YOU! YOU FOUGHT SPIDER-MAN! I THOUGHT YOU GOT CURED.
YEAH, SO DID I. I'M KINDA HOPING THEY CAN HELP ME HERE. AT LEAST I CAN TALK BETTER THAN I USED TO.
THAT'S GORILLA GIRL.
MA'AM. SORRY, BUT I AIN'T NEVER HEARD OF YOU.
DON'T WORRY ABOUT IT. I KNOW I'M KIND OF OUT OF MY DEPTH. BUT THE JUDGE TOLD ME I HAD TO REGISTER, SO...
I JUST WANT TO GET MY DIPLOMA OR WHATEVER AND GO HOME.
TEN-SHUN! FOUNDING AVENGER ON DECK!
DOCTOR HENRY PYM.
ANT-MAN. GIANT-MAN. GOLIATH. YELLOW-JACKET.
THIS IS SO...I AM SO...
AT EASE, SON.
OH...MY... LORD.

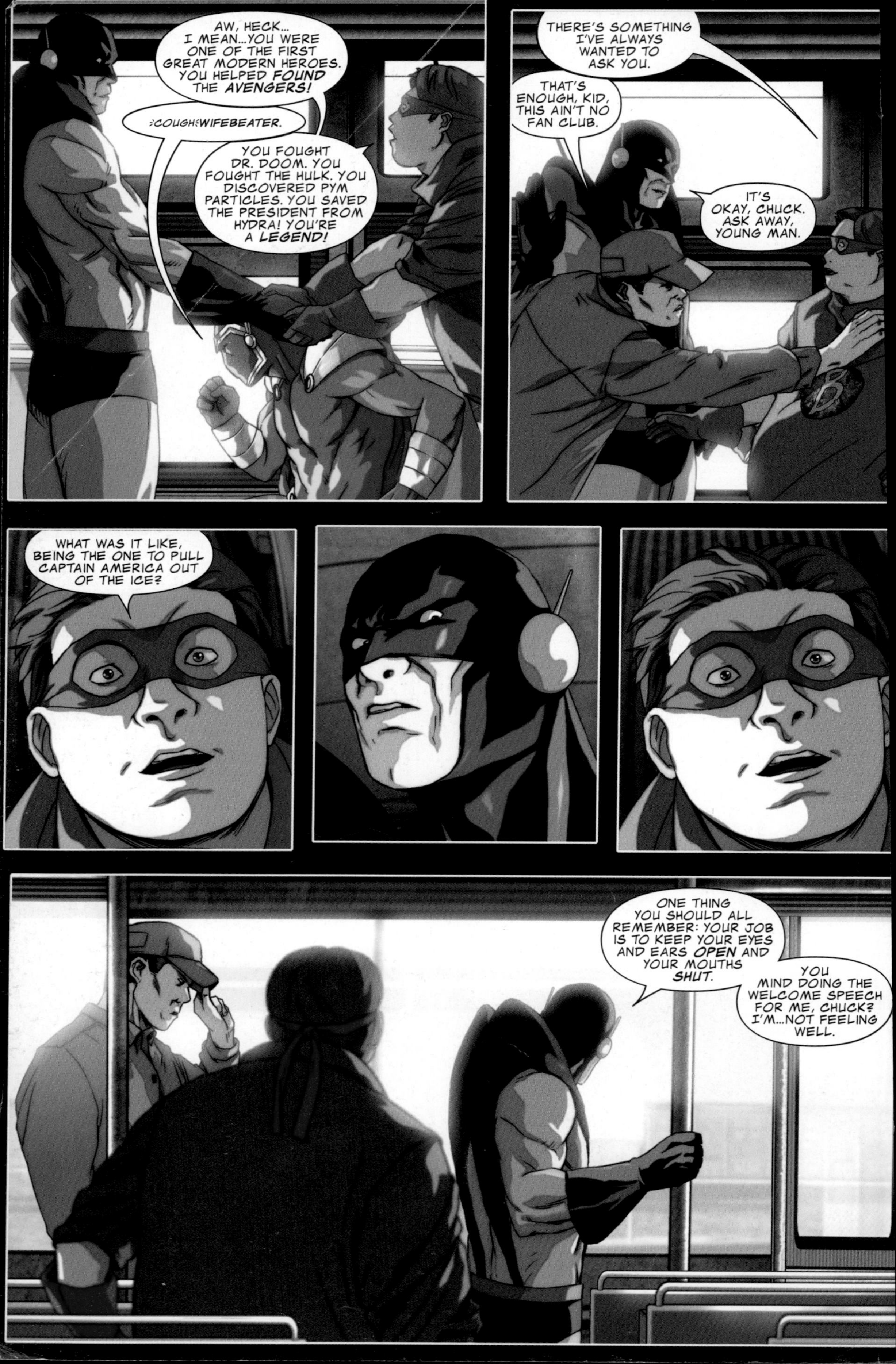
AW, HECK... I MEAN...YOU WERE ONE OF THE FIRST GREAT MODERN HEROES. YOU HELPED **FOUND** THE **AVENGERS!**
:COUGH: **WIFEBEATER.**
YOU FOUGHT DR. DOOM. YOU FOUGHT THE HULK. YOU DISCOVERED PYM PARTICLES. YOU SAVED THE PRESIDENT FROM HYDRA! YOU'RE A **LEGEND!**
THERE'S SOMETHING I'VE ALWAYS WANTED TO ASK YOU.
THAT'S ENOUGH, KID, THIS AIN'T NO FAN CLUB.
IT'S OKAY, CHUCK. ASK AWAY, YOUNG MAN.
WHAT WAS IT LIKE, BEING THE ONE TO PULL CAPTAIN AMERICA OUT OF THE ICE?
ONE THING YOU SHOULD ALL REMEMBER: YOUR JOB IS TO KEEP YOUR EYES AND EARS **OPEN** AND YOUR MOUTHS **SHUT**.
YOU MIND DOING THE WELCOME SPEECH FOR ME, CHUCK? I'M...NOT FEELING WELL.

WHAT'D I SAY?

DUDE, THINK ABOUT IT. OF ALL THE POSSIBLE TOUCHY SUBJECTS--

ALL RIGHT, YOU WALKING WASTES OF TAXPAYER DOLLARS... ...FALL IN!

I'M *THE TASKMASTER.* AND I WILL BE YOUR DRILL INSTRUCTOR.

OVER THE NEXT FEW WEEKS, YOU'LL GO FROM HATING ME TO DESPISING ME TO LOATHING ME. I'LL GO FROM NOT CARING TO NOT GIVING A DAMN TO *ENJOYING* IT.

THE LAST GUY WHO DID THIS JOB WAS STRAIGHT-UP MILITARY--THE YELLING AND THE SCREAMING AND THE WHOLE *"FULL METAL JACKET"* THING. THAT AIN'T ME.

HERE'S MY WAY: YOU DO *EXACTLY* WHAT I SAY EXACTLY *WHEN* I SAY OR I MAKE YOU *HURT* UNTIL YOU DO. IS THAT *UNDERSTOOD?*

SIR, YES SIR!

YOU. WHAT'S YOUR CODE NAME?

BO--

WRONG!

YOU HAVE TO *EARN* THE RIGHT TO CHOOSE YOUR CODE NAME. UNTIL THEN, *I* PICK IT.

LET'S SEE... WHAT'S A GOOD ONE FOR YOU... AHA! GOT IT.

WELCOME TO THE INITIATIVE, *BUTTERBALL.*

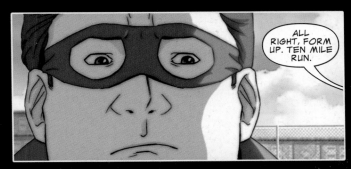

ALL RIGHT, FORM UP. TEN MILE RUN.

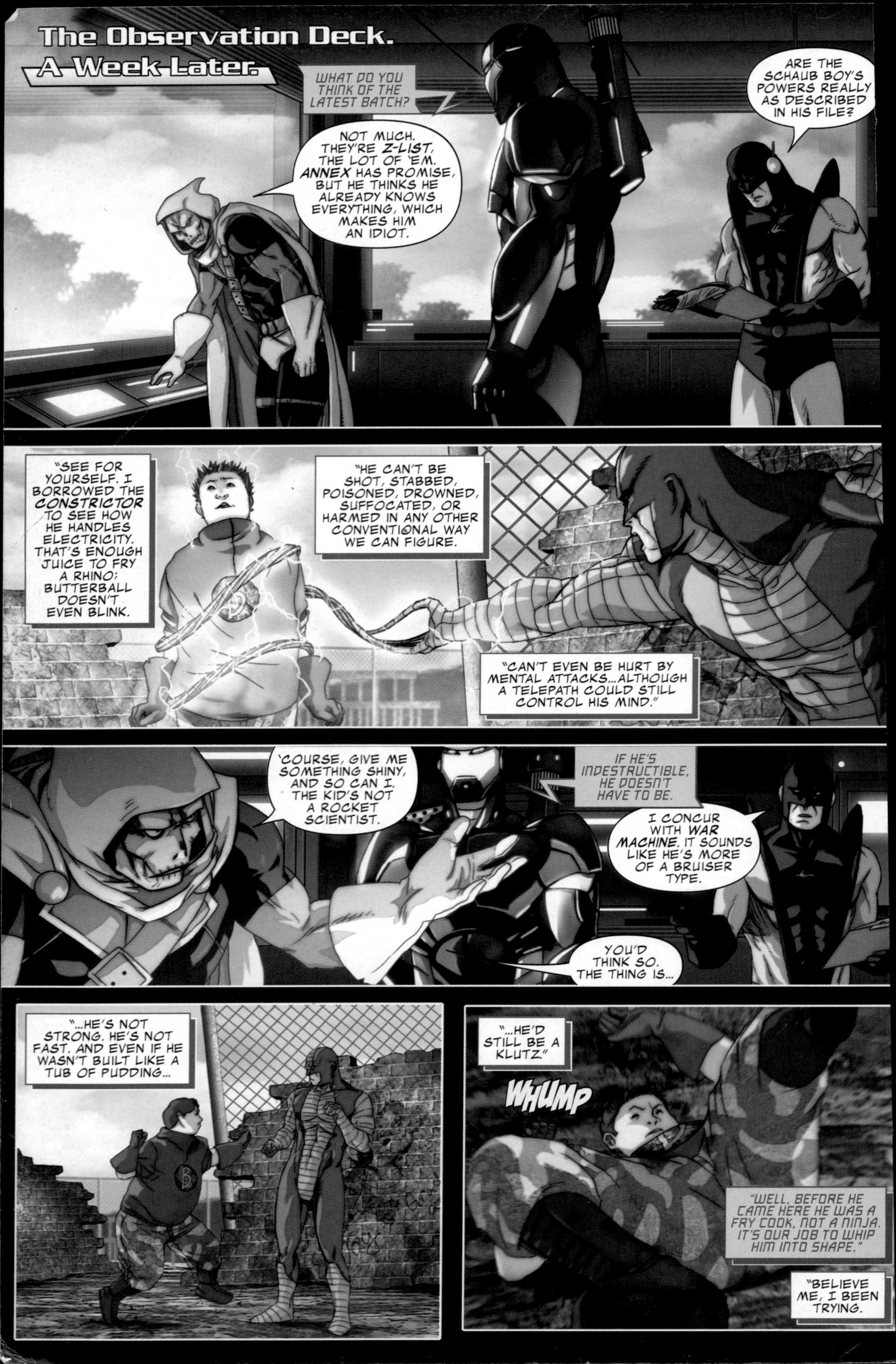
The Observation Deck.
A Week Later.
WHAT DO YOU THINK OF THE LATEST BATCH?
NOT MUCH. THEY'RE Z-LIST, THE LOT OF 'EM. ANNEX HAS PROMISE, BUT HE THINKS HE ALREADY KNOWS EVERYTHING, WHICH MAKES HIM AN IDIOT.
ARE THE SCHAUB BOY'S POWERS REALLY AS DESCRIBED IN HIS FILE?
"SEE FOR YOURSELF. I BORROWED THE CONSTRICTOR TO SEE HOW HE HANDLES ELECTRICITY. THAT'S ENOUGH JUICE TO FRY A RHINO; BUTTERBALL DOESN'T EVEN BLINK.
"HE CAN'T BE SHOT, STABBED, POISONED, DROWNED, SUFFOCATED, OR HARMED IN ANY OTHER CONVENTIONAL WAY WE CAN FIGURE.
"CAN'T EVEN BE HURT BY MENTAL ATTACKS...ALTHOUGH A TELEPATH COULD STILL CONTROL HIS MIND."
'COURSE, GIVE ME SOMETHING SHINY, AND SO CAN I. THE KID'S NOT A ROCKET SCIENTIST.
IF HE'S INDESTRUCTIBLE, HE DOESN'T HAVE TO BE.
I CONCUR WITH WAR MACHINE. IT SOUNDS LIKE HE'S MORE OF A BRUISER TYPE.
YOU'D THINK SO. THE THING IS...
"...HE'S NOT STRONG. HE'S NOT FAST. AND EVEN IF HE WASN'T BUILT LIKE A TUB OF PUDDING...
"...HE'D STILL BE A KLUTZ."
WHUMP
"WELL, BEFORE HE CAME HERE HE WAS A FRY COOK, NOT A NINJA. IT'S OUR JOB TO WHIP HIM INTO SHAPE."
"BELIEVE ME, I BEEN TRYING.

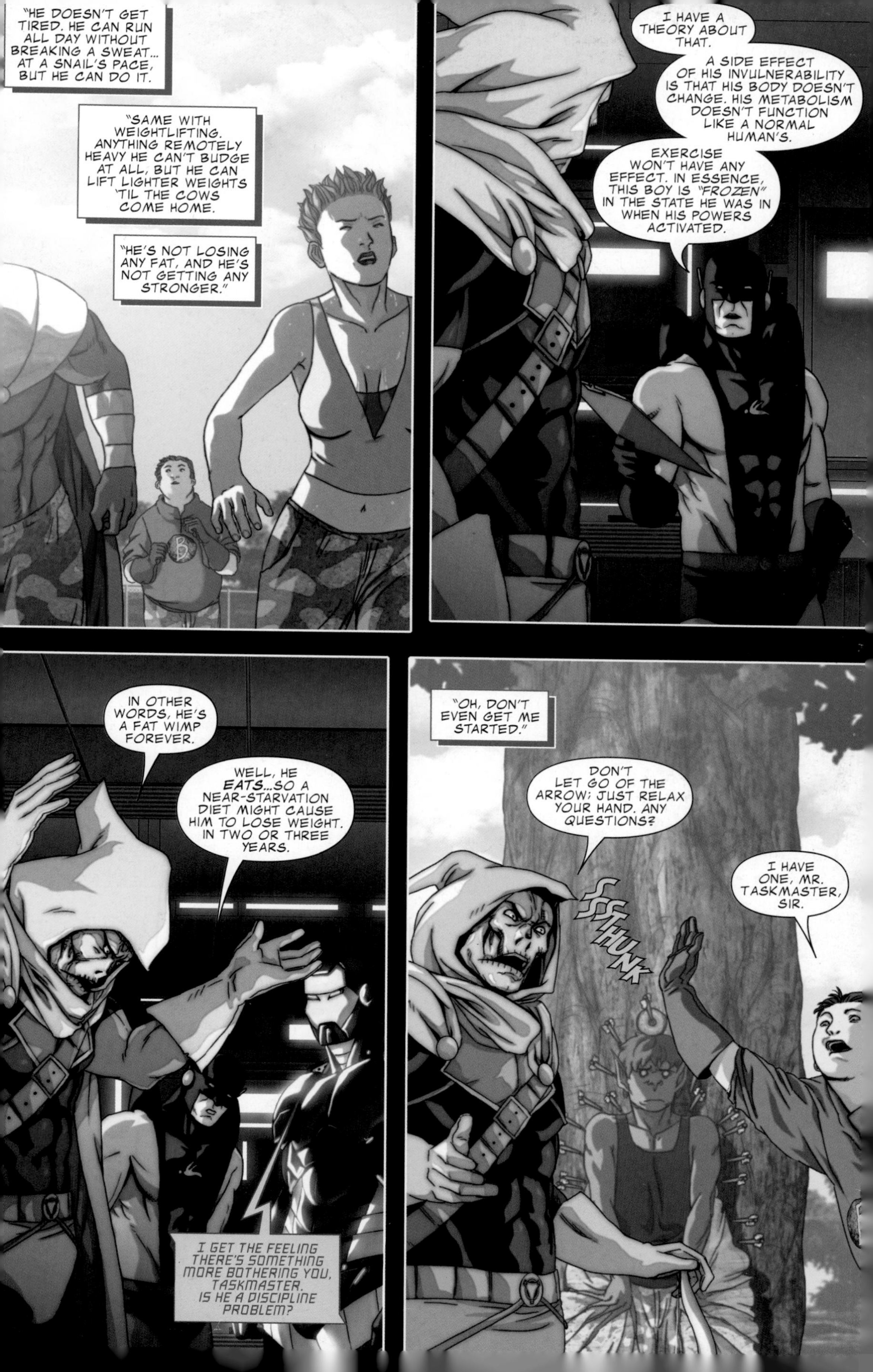
"HE DOESN'T GET TIRED. HE CAN RUN ALL DAY WITHOUT BREAKING A SWEAT... AT A SNAIL'S PACE, BUT HE CAN DO IT.
"SAME WITH WEIGHTLIFTING. ANYTHING REMOTELY HEAVY HE CAN'T BUDGE AT ALL, BUT HE CAN LIFT LIGHTER WEIGHTS 'TIL THE COWS COME HOME.
"HE'S NOT LOSING ANY FAT, AND HE'S NOT GETTING ANY STRONGER."
I HAVE A THEORY ABOUT THAT.
A SIDE EFFECT OF HIS INVULNERABILITY IS THAT HIS BODY DOESN'T CHANGE. HIS METABOLISM DOESN'T FUNCTION LIKE A NORMAL HUMAN'S.
EXERCISE WON'T HAVE ANY EFFECT. IN ESSENCE, THIS BOY IS "FROZEN" IN THE STATE HE WAS IN WHEN HIS POWERS ACTIVATED.
IN OTHER WORDS, HE'S A FAT WIMP FOREVER.
WELL, HE EATS...SO A NEAR-STARVATION DIET MIGHT CAUSE HIM TO LOSE WEIGHT. IN TWO OR THREE YEARS.
I GET THE FEELING THERE'S SOMETHING MORE BOTHERING YOU, TASKMASTER. IS HE A DISCIPLINE PROBLEM?
"OH, DON'T EVEN GET ME STARTED."
DON'T LET GO OF THE ARROW; JUST RELAX YOUR HAND. ANY QUESTIONS?
SSSTHUNK
I HAVE ONE, MR. TASKMASTER, SIR.

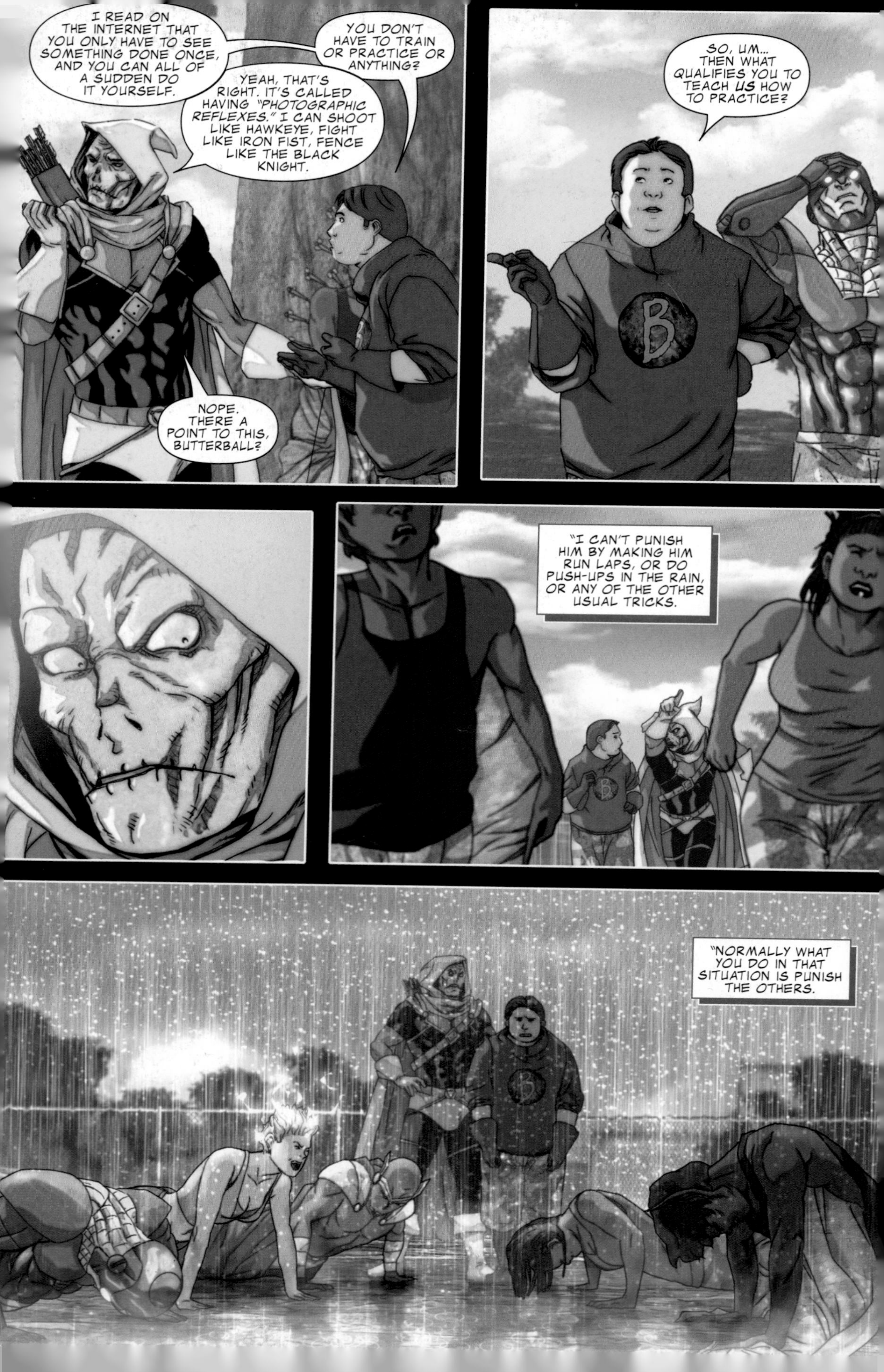
I READ ON THE INTERNET THAT YOU ONLY HAVE TO SEE SOMETHING DONE ONCE, AND YOU CAN ALL OF A SUDDEN DO IT YOURSELF.
YOU DON'T HAVE TO TRAIN OR PRACTICE OR ANYTHING?
YEAH, THAT'S RIGHT. IT'S CALLED HAVING "PHOTOGRAPHIC REFLEXES." I CAN SHOOT LIKE HAWKEYE, FIGHT LIKE IRON FIST, FENCE LIKE THE BLACK KNIGHT.
NOPE. THERE A POINT TO THIS, BUTTERBALL?
SO, UM... THEN WHAT QUALIFIES YOU TO TEACH US HOW TO PRACTICE?
"I CAN'T PUNISH HIM BY MAKING HIM RUN LAPS, OR DO PUSH-UPS IN THE RAIN, OR ANY OF THE OTHER USUAL TRICKS.
"NORMALLY WHAT YOU DO IN THAT SITUATION IS PUNISH THE OTHERS.

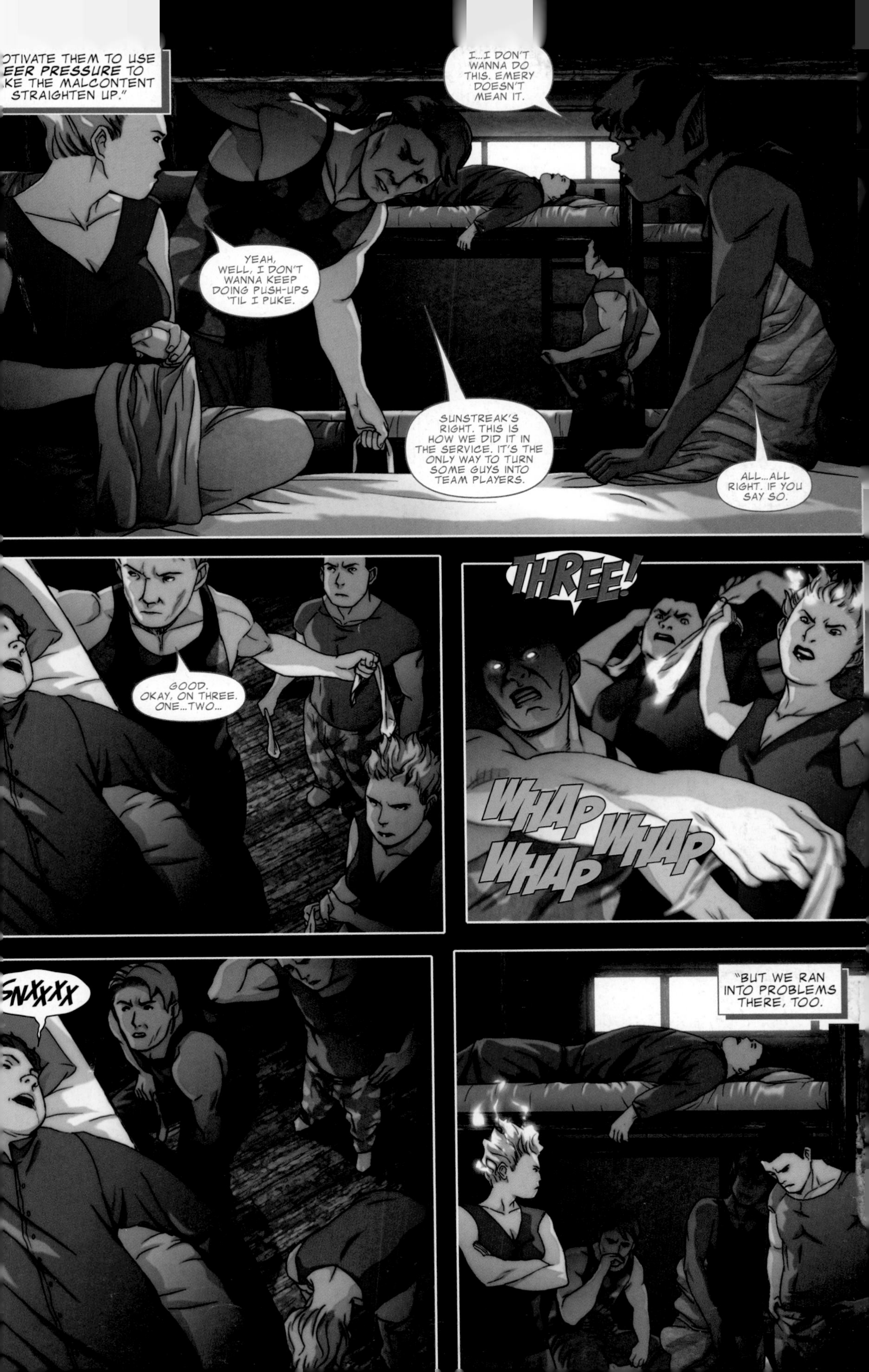
OTIVATE THEM TO USE
EER PRESSURE TO
KE THE MALCONTENT
STRAIGHTEN UP."
I...I DON'T WANNA DO THIS. EMERY DOESN'T MEAN IT.
YEAH, WELL, I DON'T WANNA KEEP DOING PUSH-UPS 'TIL I PUKE.
SUNSTREAK'S RIGHT. THIS IS HOW WE DID IT IN THE SERVICE. IT'S THE ONLY WAY TO TURN SOME GUYS INTO TEAM PLAYERS.
ALL...ALL RIGHT. IF YOU SAY SO.
GOOD. OKAY, ON THREE. ONE...TWO...
THREE!
WHAP WHAP WHAP
SNXXXX
"BUT WE RAN INTO PROBLEMS THERE, TOO.

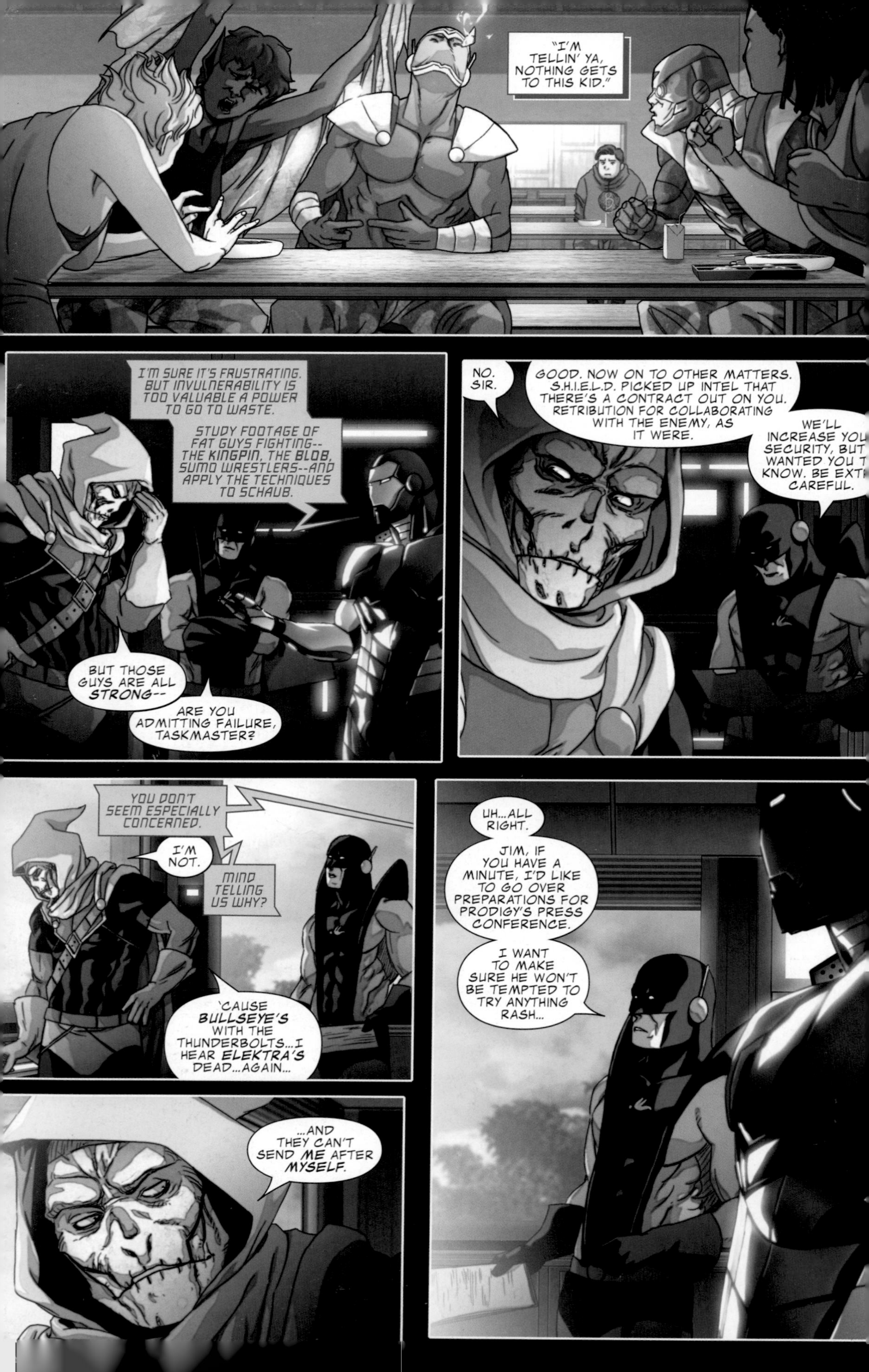
"I'M TELLIN' YA, NOTHING GETS TO THIS KID."
I'M SURE IT'S FRUSTRATING. BUT INVULNERABILITY IS TOO VALUABLE A POWER TO GO TO WASTE.
STUDY FOOTAGE OF FAT GUYS FIGHTING--THE KINGPIN, THE BLOB, SUMO WRESTLERS--AND APPLY THE TECHNIQUES TO SCHAUB.
BUT THOSE GUYS ARE ALL STRONG--
ARE YOU ADMITTING FAILURE, TASKMASTER?
NO. SIR.
GOOD. NOW ON TO OTHER MATTERS. S.H.I.E.L.D. PICKED UP INTEL THAT THERE'S A CONTRACT OUT ON YOU. RETRIBUTION FOR COLLABORATING WITH THE ENEMY, AS IT WERE.
YOU DON'T SEEM ESPECIALLY CONCERNED.
I'M NOT.
MIND TELLING US WHY?
'CAUSE BULLSEYE'S WITH THE THUNDERBOLTS...I HEAR ELEKTRA'S DEAD...AGAIN...
...AND THEY CAN'T SEND ME AFTER MYSELF.
UH...ALL RIGHT.
JIM, IF YOU HAVE A MINUTE, I'D LIKE TO GO OVER PREPARATIONS FOR PRODIGY'S PRESS CONFERENCE.
I WANT TO MAKE SURE HE WON'T BE TEMPTED TO TRY ANYTHING RASH...

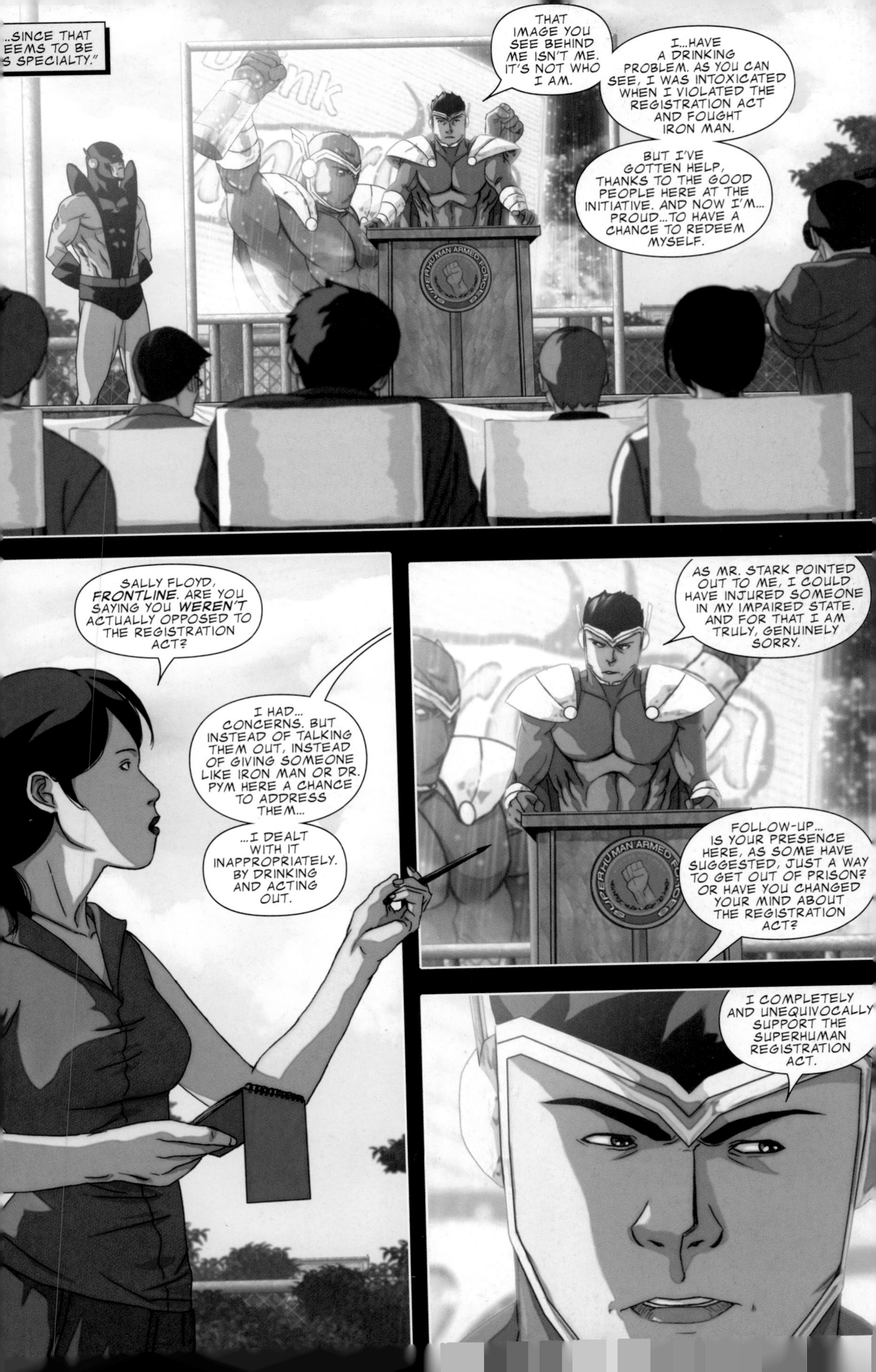

...SINCE THAT
EEMS TO BE
S SPECIALTY."
THAT IMAGE YOU SEE BEHIND ME ISN'T ME. IT'S NOT WHO I AM.
I...HAVE A DRINKING PROBLEM. AS YOU CAN SEE, I WAS INTOXICATED WHEN I VIOLATED THE REGISTRATION ACT AND FOUGHT IRON MAN.
BUT I'VE GOTTEN HELP, THANKS TO THE GOOD PEOPLE HERE AT THE INITIATIVE. AND NOW I'M... PROUD...TO HAVE A CHANCE TO REDEEM MYSELF.
SUPERHUMAN ARMED FORCES
SALLY FLOYD, FRONTLINE. ARE YOU SAYING YOU WEREN'T ACTUALLY OPPOSED TO THE REGISTRATION ACT?
I HAD... CONCERNS. BUT INSTEAD OF TALKING THEM OUT, INSTEAD OF GIVING SOMEONE LIKE IRON MAN OR DR. PYM HERE A CHANCE TO ADDRESS THEM...
...I DEALT WITH IT INAPPROPRIATELY. BY DRINKING AND ACTING OUT.
AS MR. STARK POINTED OUT TO ME, I COULD HAVE INJURED SOMEONE IN MY IMPAIRED STATE. AND FOR THAT I AM TRULY, GENUINELY SORRY.
FOLLOW-UP... IS YOUR PRESENCE HERE, AS SOME HAVE SUGGESTED, JUST A WAY TO GET OUT OF PRISON? OR HAVE YOU CHANGED YOUR MIND ABOUT THE REGISTRATION ACT?
SUPERHUMAN ARMED FORCES
I COMPLETELY AND UNEQUIVOCALLY SUPPORT THE SUPERHUMAN REGISTRATION ACT.

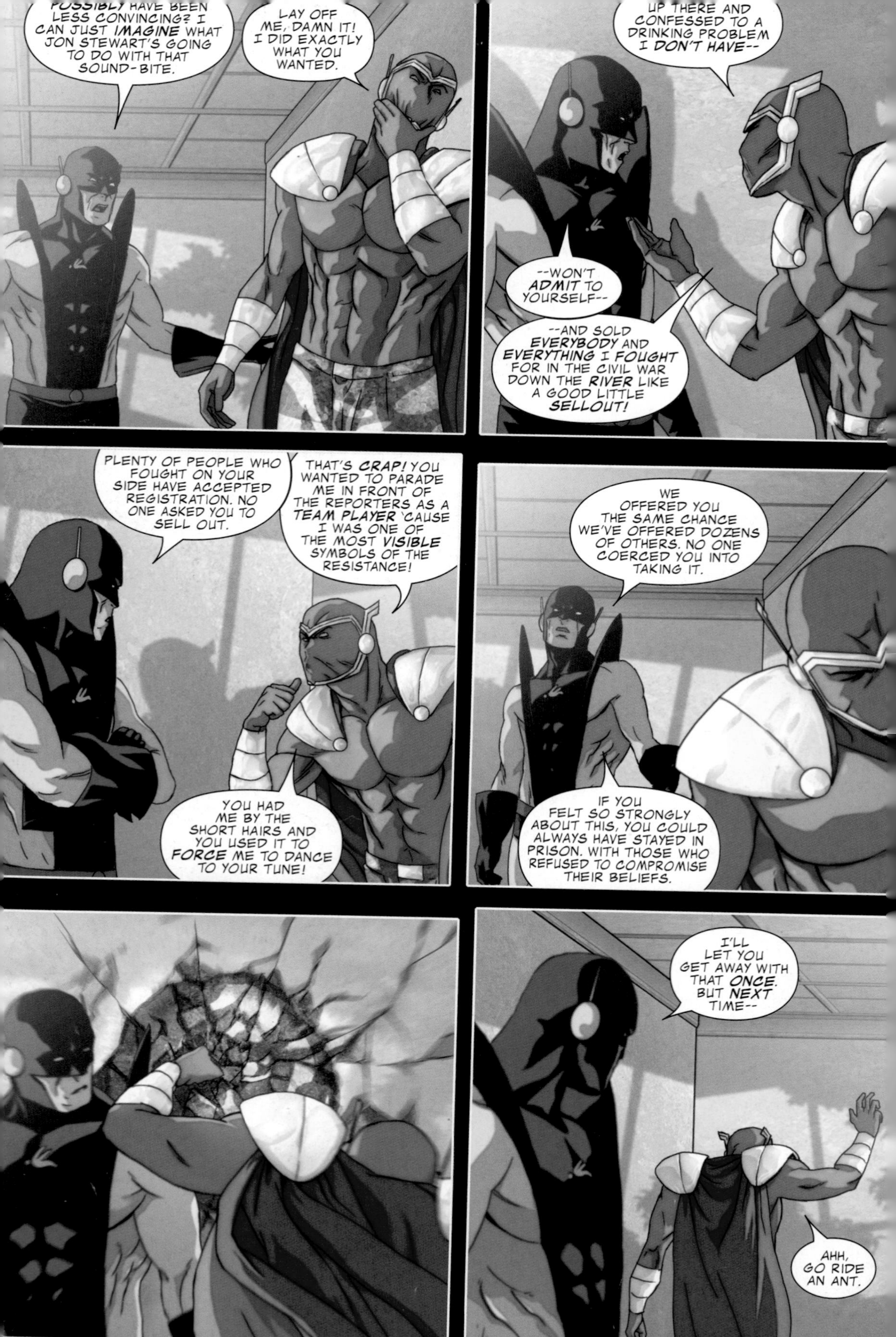
POSSIBLY HAVE BEEN LESS CONVINCING? I CAN JUST IMAGINE WHAT JON STEWART'S GOING TO DO WITH THAT SOUND-BITE.
LAY OFF ME, DAMN IT! I DID EXACTLY WHAT YOU WANTED.
UP THERE AND CONFESSED TO A DRINKING PROBLEM I DON'T HAVE--
--WON'T ADMIT TO YOURSELF--
--AND SOLD EVERYBODY AND EVERYTHING I FOUGHT FOR IN THE CIVIL WAR DOWN THE RIVER LIKE A GOOD LITTLE SELLOUT!
PLENTY OF PEOPLE WHO FOUGHT ON YOUR SIDE HAVE ACCEPTED REGISTRATION. NO ONE ASKED YOU TO SELL OUT.
THAT'S CRAP! YOU WANTED TO PARADE ME IN FRONT OF THE REPORTERS AS A TEAM PLAYER 'CAUSE I WAS ONE OF THE MOST VISIBLE SYMBOLS OF THE RESISTANCE!
YOU HAD ME BY THE SHORT HAIRS AND YOU USED IT TO FORCE ME TO DANCE TO YOUR TUNE!
WE OFFERED YOU THE SAME CHANCE WE'VE OFFERED DOZENS OF OTHERS. NO ONE COERCED YOU INTO TAKING IT.
IF YOU FELT SO STRONGLY ABOUT THIS, YOU COULD ALWAYS HAVE STAYED IN PRISON. WITH THOSE WHO REFUSED TO COMPROMISE THEIR BELIEFS.
I'LL LET YOU GET AWAY WITH THAT ONCE. BUT NEXT TIME--
AHH, GO RIDE AN ANT.

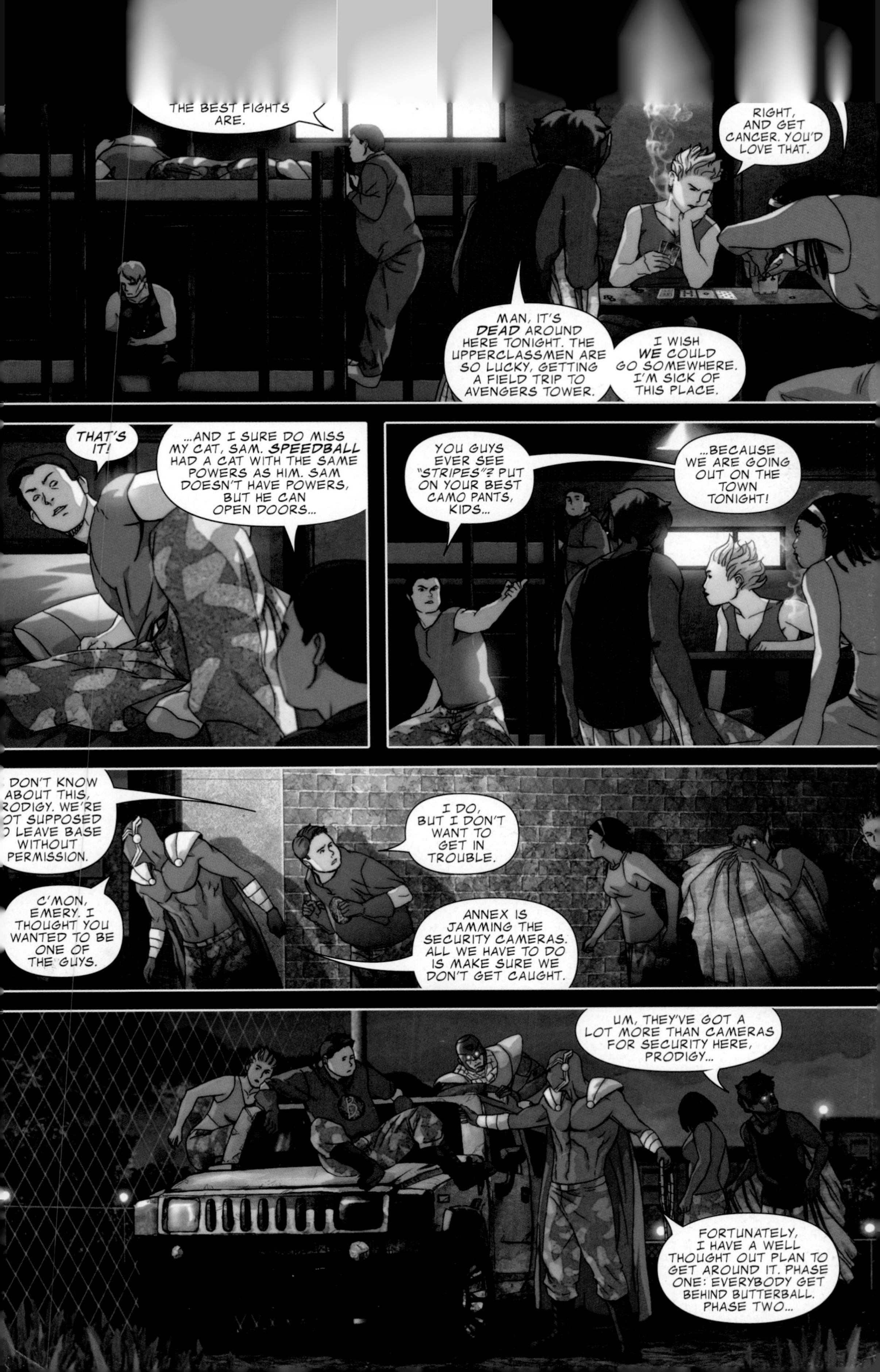

THE BEST FIGHTS ARE.
RIGHT, AND GET CANCER. YOU'D LOVE THAT.
MAN, IT'S DEAD AROUND HERE TONIGHT. THE UPPERCLASSMEN ARE SO LUCKY, GETTING A FIELD TRIP TO AVENGERS TOWER.
I WISH WE COULD GO SOMEWHERE. I'M SICK OF THIS PLACE.
THAT'S IT!
...AND I SURE DO MISS MY CAT, SAM. SPEEDBALL HAD A CAT WITH THE SAME POWERS AS HIM. SAM DOESN'T HAVE POWERS, BUT HE CAN OPEN DOORS...
YOU GUYS EVER SEE "STRIPES"? PUT ON YOUR BEST CAMO PANTS, KIDS...
...BECAUSE WE ARE GOING OUT ON THE TOWN TONIGHT!
DON'T KNOW ABOUT THIS, RODIGY. WE'RE OT SUPPOSED LEAVE BASE WITHOUT PERMISSION.
C'MON, EMERY. I THOUGHT YOU WANTED TO BE ONE OF THE GUYS.
I DO, BUT I DON'T WANT TO GET IN TROUBLE.
ANNEX IS JAMMING THE SECURITY CAMERAS. ALL WE HAVE TO DO IS MAKE SURE WE DON'T GET CAUGHT.
UM, THEY'VE GOT A LOT MORE THAN CAMERAS FOR SECURITY HERE, PRODIGY...
FORTUNATELY, I HAVE A WELL THOUGHT OUT PLAN TO GET AROUND IT. PHASE ONE: EVERYBODY GET BEHIND BUTTERBALL. PHASE TWO...

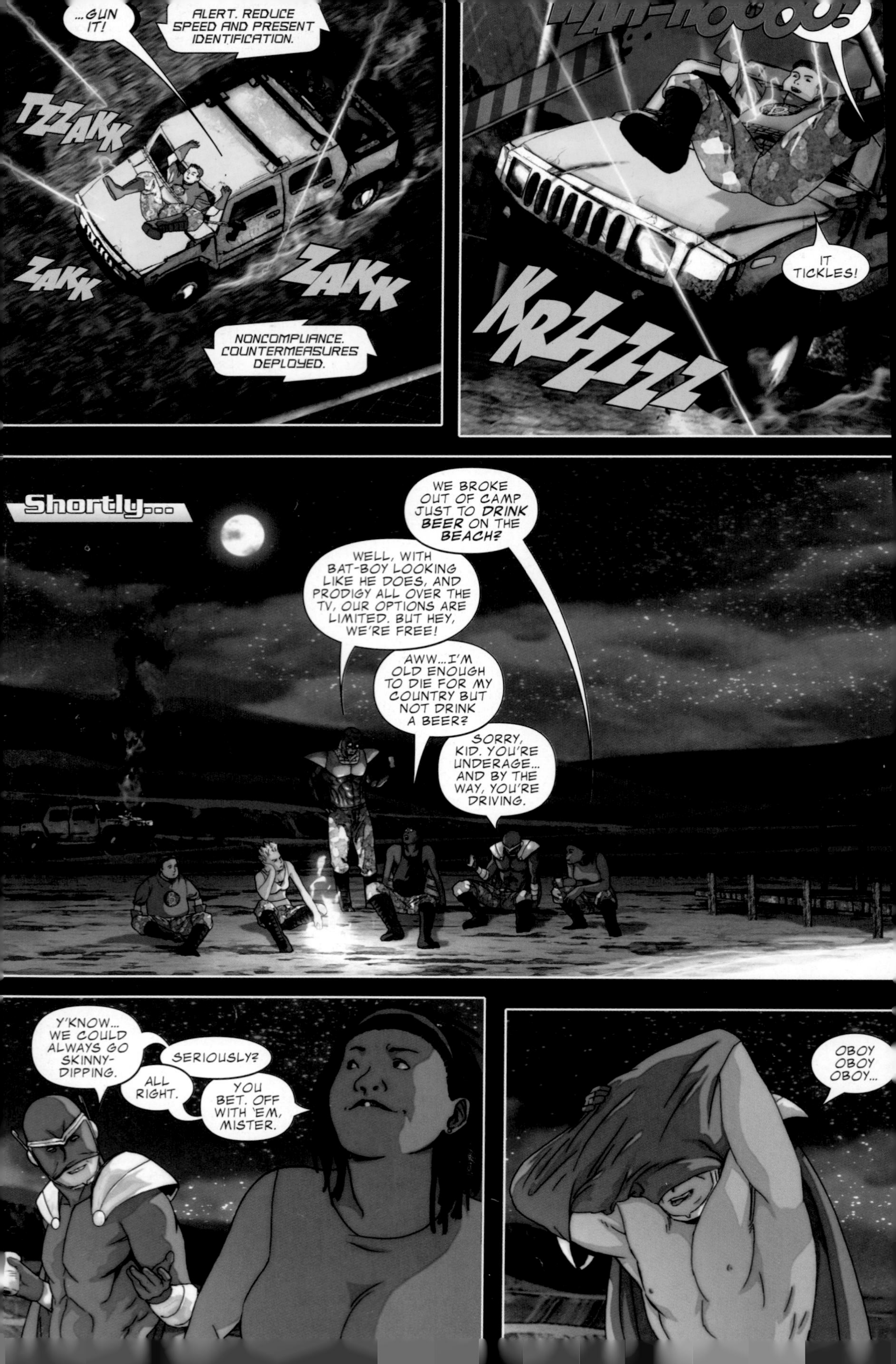
...GUN IT!
ALERT. REDUCE SPEED AND PRESENT IDENTIFICATION.
TZZAKK
ZAKK
ZAKK
NONCOMPLIANCE. COUNTERMEASURES DEPLOYED.
IT TICKLES!
KRZZZZZ
Shortly...
WE BROKE OUT OF CAMP JUST TO DRINK BEER ON THE BEACH?
WELL, WITH BAT-BOY LOOKING LIKE HE DOES, AND PRODIGY ALL OVER THE TV, OUR OPTIONS ARE LIMITED. BUT HEY, WE'RE FREE!
AWW...I'M OLD ENOUGH TO DIE FOR MY COUNTRY BUT NOT DRINK A BEER?
SORRY, KID. YOU'RE UNDERAGE... AND BY THE WAY, YOU'RE DRIVING.
Y'KNOW... WE COULD ALWAYS GO SKINNY-DIPPING.
SERIOUSLY?
ALL RIGHT.
YOU BET. OFF WITH 'EM, MISTER.
OBOY OBOY OBOY...

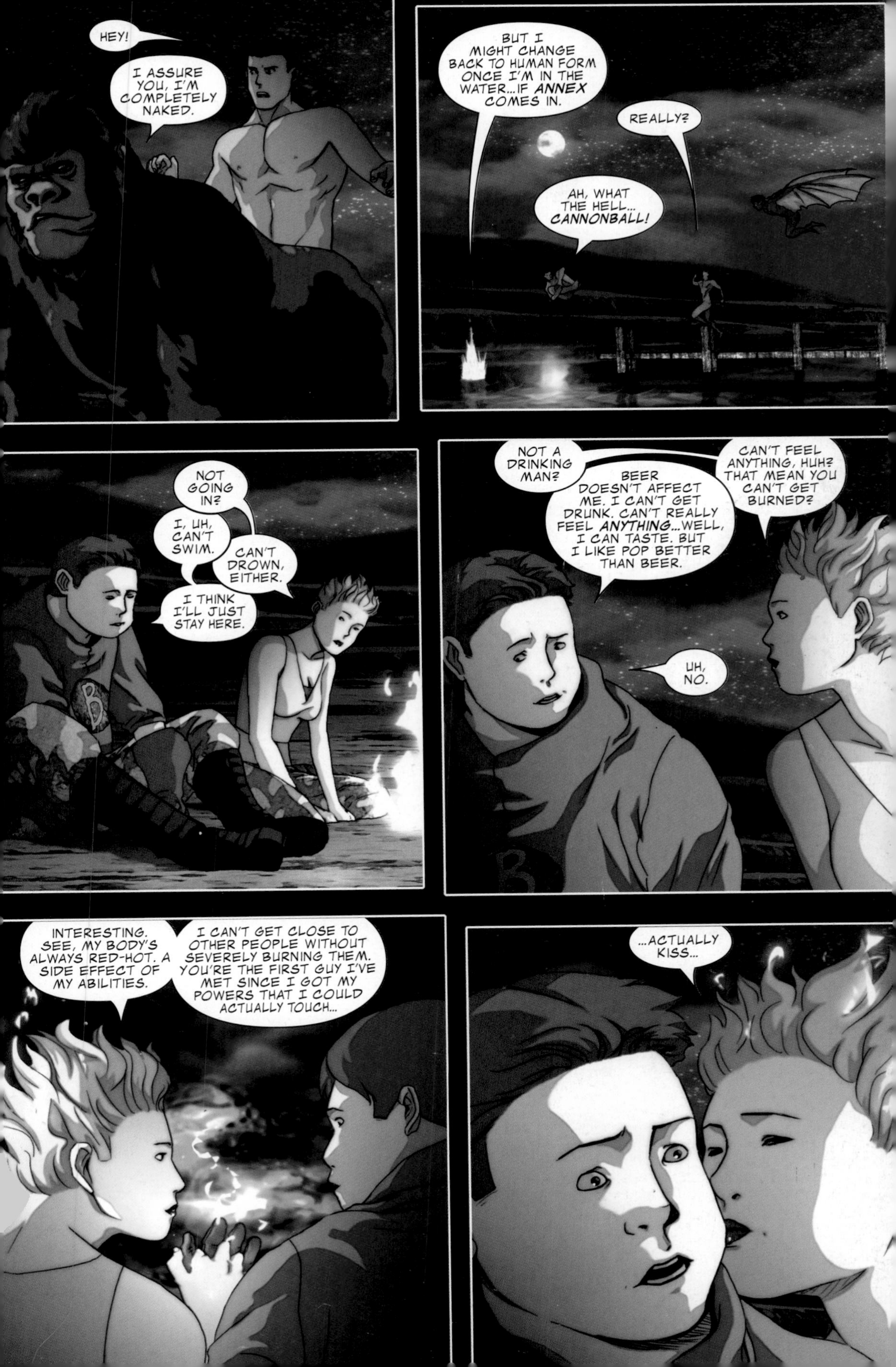
HEY!
I ASSURE YOU, I'M COMPLETELY NAKED.
BUT I MIGHT CHANGE BACK TO HUMAN FORM ONCE I'M IN THE WATER...IF ANNEX COMES IN.
REALLY?
AH, WHAT THE HELL... CANNONBALL!
NOT GOING IN?
I, UH, CAN'T SWIM.
CAN'T DROWN, EITHER.
I THINK I'LL JUST STAY HERE.
NOT A DRINKING MAN?
BEER DOESN'T AFFECT ME. I CAN'T GET DRUNK. CAN'T REALLY FEEL ANYTHING...WELL, I CAN TASTE. BUT I LIKE POP BETTER THAN BEER.
CAN'T FEEL ANYTHING, HUH? THAT MEAN YOU CAN'T GET BURNED?
UH, NO.
INTERESTING. SEE, MY BODY'S ALWAYS RED-HOT. A SIDE EFFECT OF MY ABILITIES.
I CAN'T GET CLOSE TO OTHER PEOPLE WITHOUT SEVERELY BURNING THEM. YOU'RE THE FIRST GUY I'VE MET SINCE I GOT MY POWERS THAT I COULD ACTUALLY TOUCH...
...ACTUALLY KISS...

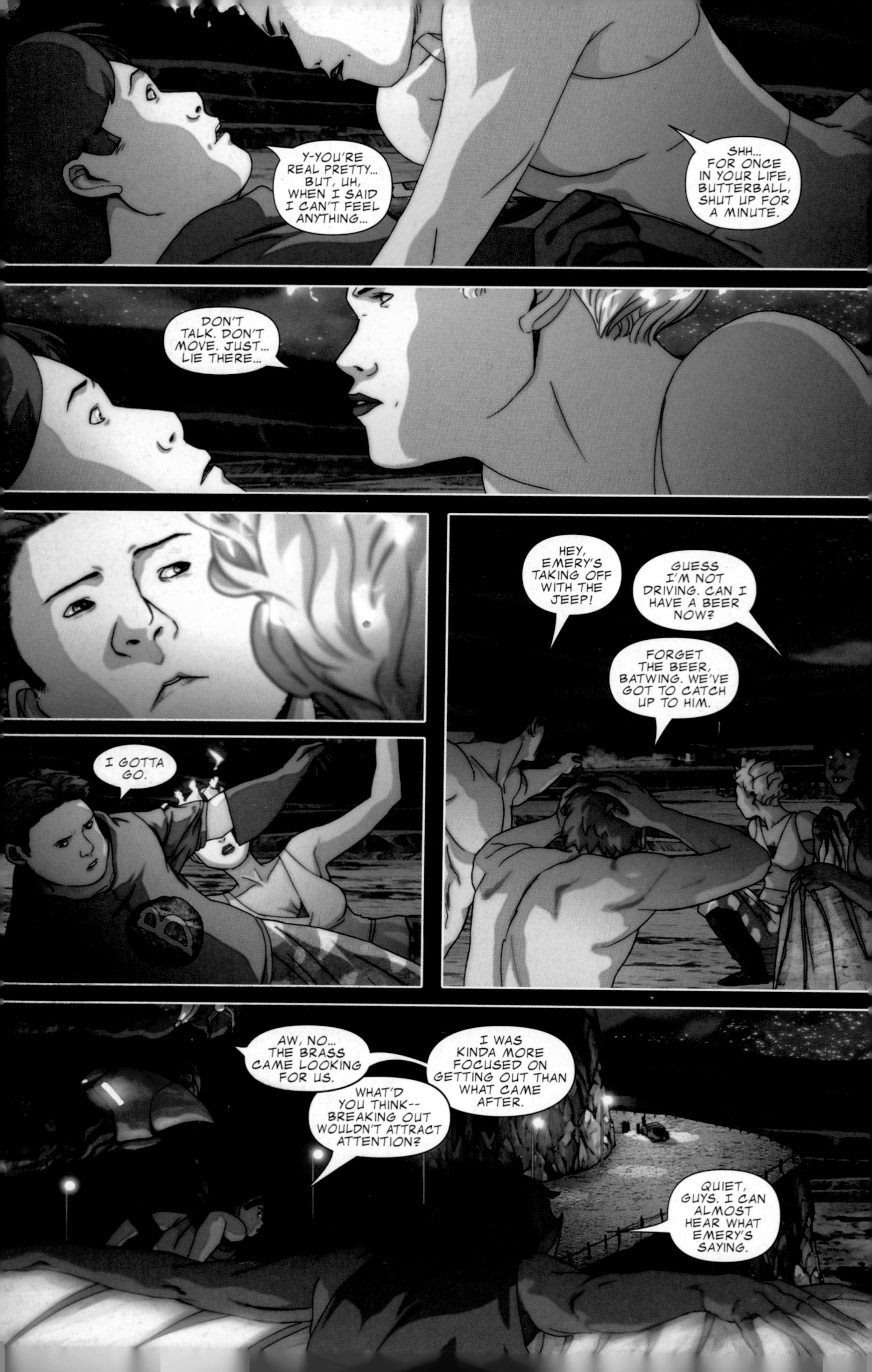
Y-YOU'RE REAL PRETTY... BUT, UH, WHEN I SAID I CAN'T FEEL ANYTHING...
SHH... FOR ONCE IN YOUR LIFE, BUTTERBALL, SHUT UP FOR A MINUTE.
DON'T TALK. DON'T MOVE. JUST... LIE THERE...
I GOTTA GO.
HEY, EMERY'S TAKING OFF WITH THE JEEP!
GUESS I'M NOT DRIVING. CAN I HAVE A BEER NOW?
FORGET THE BEER, BATWING. WE'VE GOT TO CATCH UP TO HIM.
AW, NO... THE BRASS CAME LOOKING FOR US.
I WAS KINDA MORE FOCUSED ON GETTING OUT THAN WHAT CAME AFTER.
WHAT'D YOU THINK-- BREAKING OUT WOULDN'T ATTRACT ATTENTION?
QUIET, GUYS. I CAN ALMOST HEAR WHAT EMERY'S SAYING.

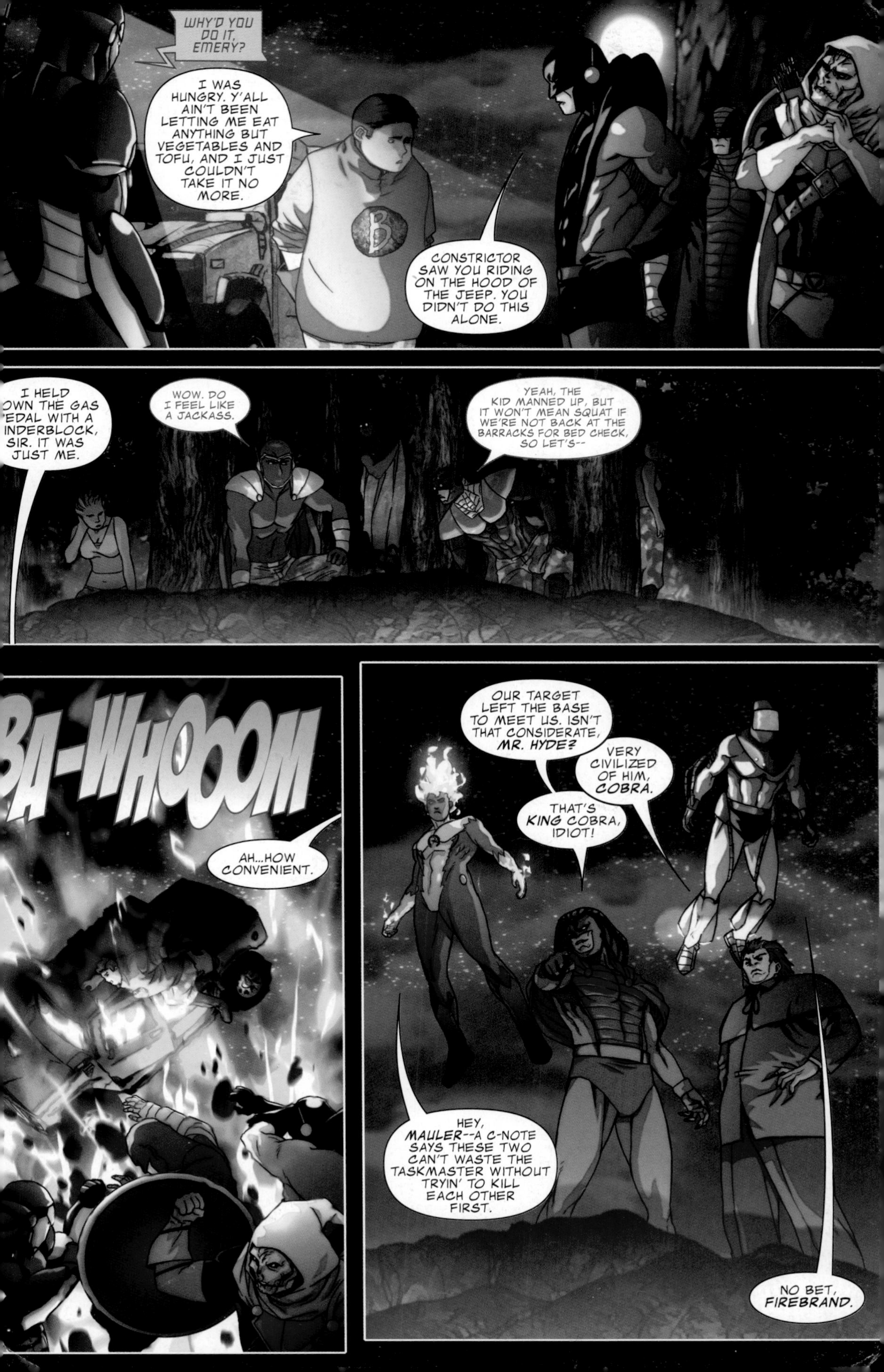
WHY'D YOU DO IT, EMERY?
I WAS HUNGRY. Y'ALL AIN'T BEEN LETTING ME EAT ANYTHING BUT VEGETABLES AND TOFU, AND I JUST COULDN'T TAKE IT NO MORE.
CONSTRICTOR SAW YOU RIDING ON THE HOOD OF THE JEEP. YOU DIDN'T DO THIS ALONE.
I HELD OWN THE GAS PEDAL WITH A INDERBLOCK, SIR. IT WAS JUST ME.
WOW. DO I FEEL LIKE A JACKASS.
YEAH, THE KID MANNED UP, BUT IT WON'T MEAN SQUAT IF WE'RE NOT BACK AT THE BARRACKS FOR BED CHECK, SO LET'S--
BA-WHOOOM
AH...HOW CONVENIENT.
OUR TARGET LEFT THE BASE TO MEET US. ISN'T THAT CONSIDERATE, MR. HYDE?
VERY CIVILIZED OF HIM, COBRA.
THAT'S KING COBRA, IDIOT!
HEY, MAULER--A C-NOTE SAYS THESE TWO CAN'T WASTE THE TASKMASTER WITHOUT TRYIN' TO KILL EACH OTHER FIRST.
NO BET, FIREBRAND.

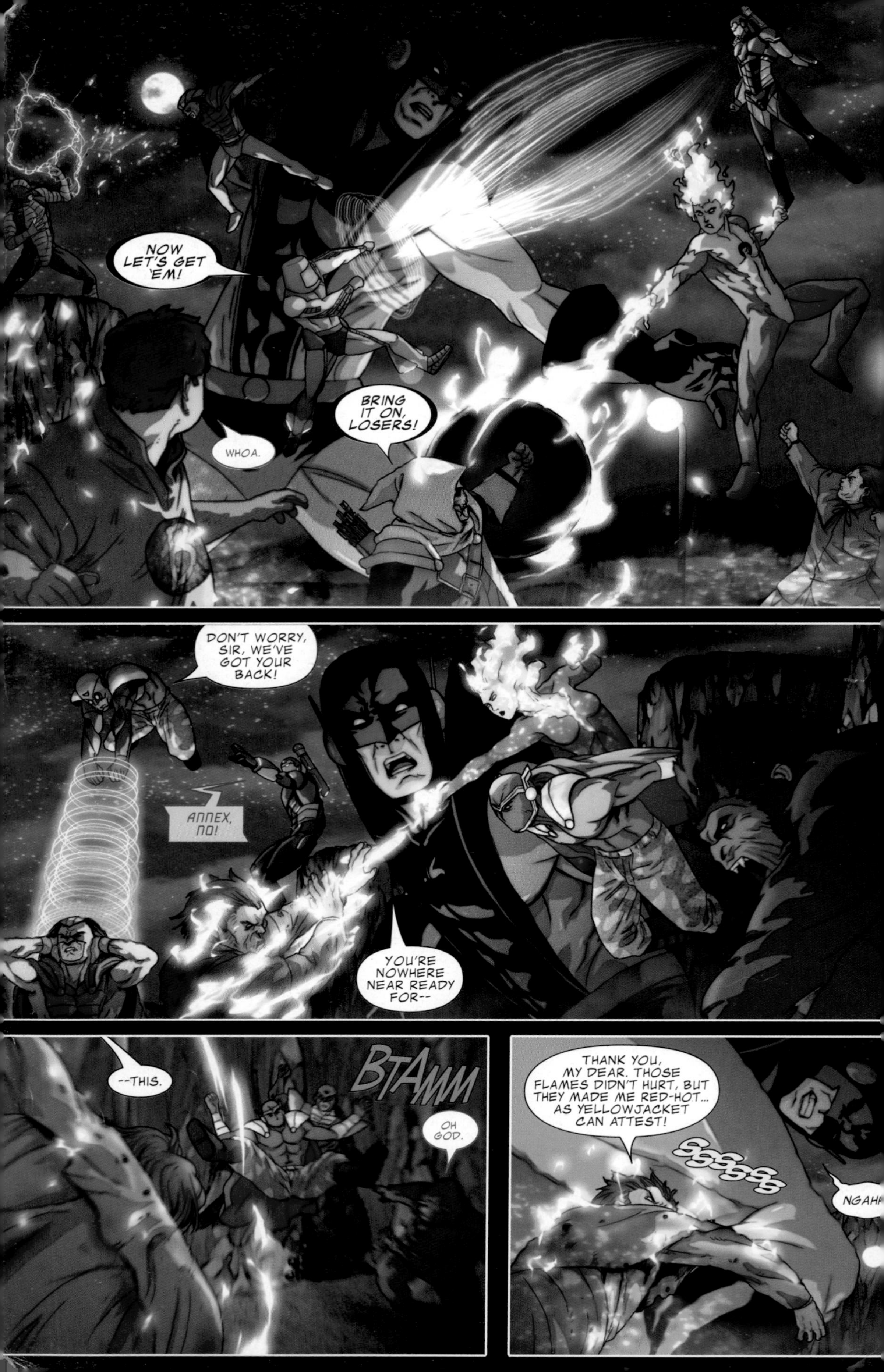
NOW LET'S GET 'EM!
BRING IT ON, LOSERS!
WHOA.
DON'T WORRY, SIR, WE'VE GOT YOUR BACK!
ANNEX, NO!
YOU'RE NOWHERE NEAR READY FOR--
--THIS.
BTAMM
OH GOD.
THANK YOU, MY DEAR. THOSE FLAMES DIDN'T HURT, BUT THEY MADE ME RED-HOT... AS YELLOWJACKET CAN ATTEST!
SSSSSS

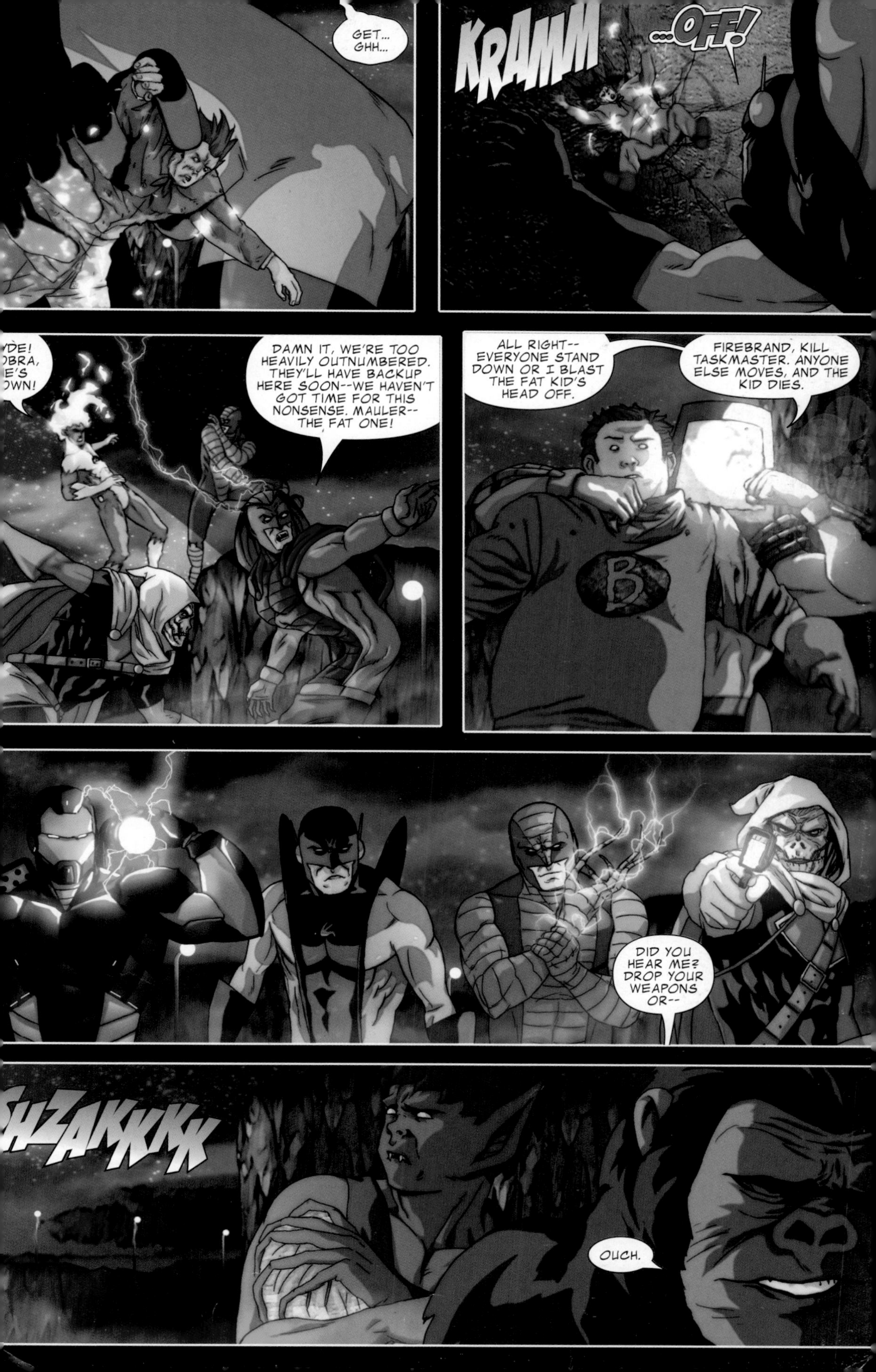
GET... GHH...
KRAMM
...OFF!
DAMN IT, WE'RE TOO HEAVILY OUTNUMBERED. THEY'LL HAVE BACKUP HERE SOON--WE HAVEN'T GOT TIME FOR THIS NONSENSE. MAULER-- THE FAT ONE!
ALL RIGHT-- EVERYONE STAND DOWN OR I BLAST THE FAT KID'S HEAD OFF.
FIREBRAND, KILL TASKMASTER. ANYONE ELSE MOVES, AND THE KID DIES.
DID YOU HEAR ME? DROP YOUR WEAPONS OR--
OUCH.

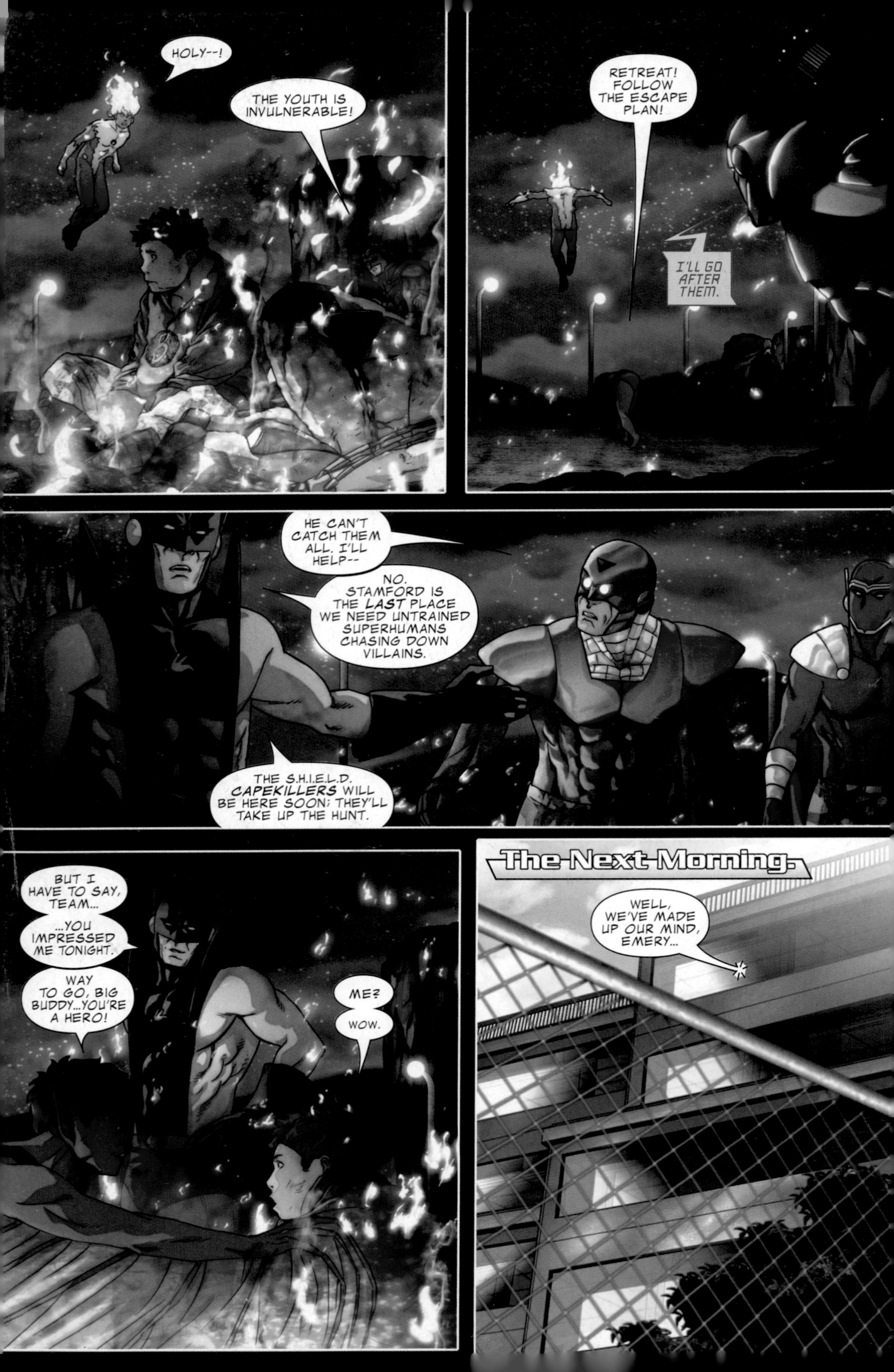
HOLY--!
THE YOUTH IS INVULNERABLE!
RETREAT! FOLLOW THE ESCAPE PLAN!
I'LL GO AFTER THEM.
HE CAN'T CATCH THEM ALL. I'LL HELP--
NO. STAMFORD IS THE LAST PLACE WE NEED UNTRAINED SUPERHUMANS CHASING DOWN VILLAINS.
THE S.H.I.E.L.D. CAPEKILLERS WILL BE HERE SOON; THEY'LL TAKE UP THE HUNT.
BUT I HAVE TO SAY, TEAM...
...YOU IMPRESSED ME TONIGHT.
WAY TO GO, BIG BUDDY...YOU'RE A HERO!
ME?
WOW.
The Next Morning
WELL, WE'VE MADE UP OUR MIND, EMERY...

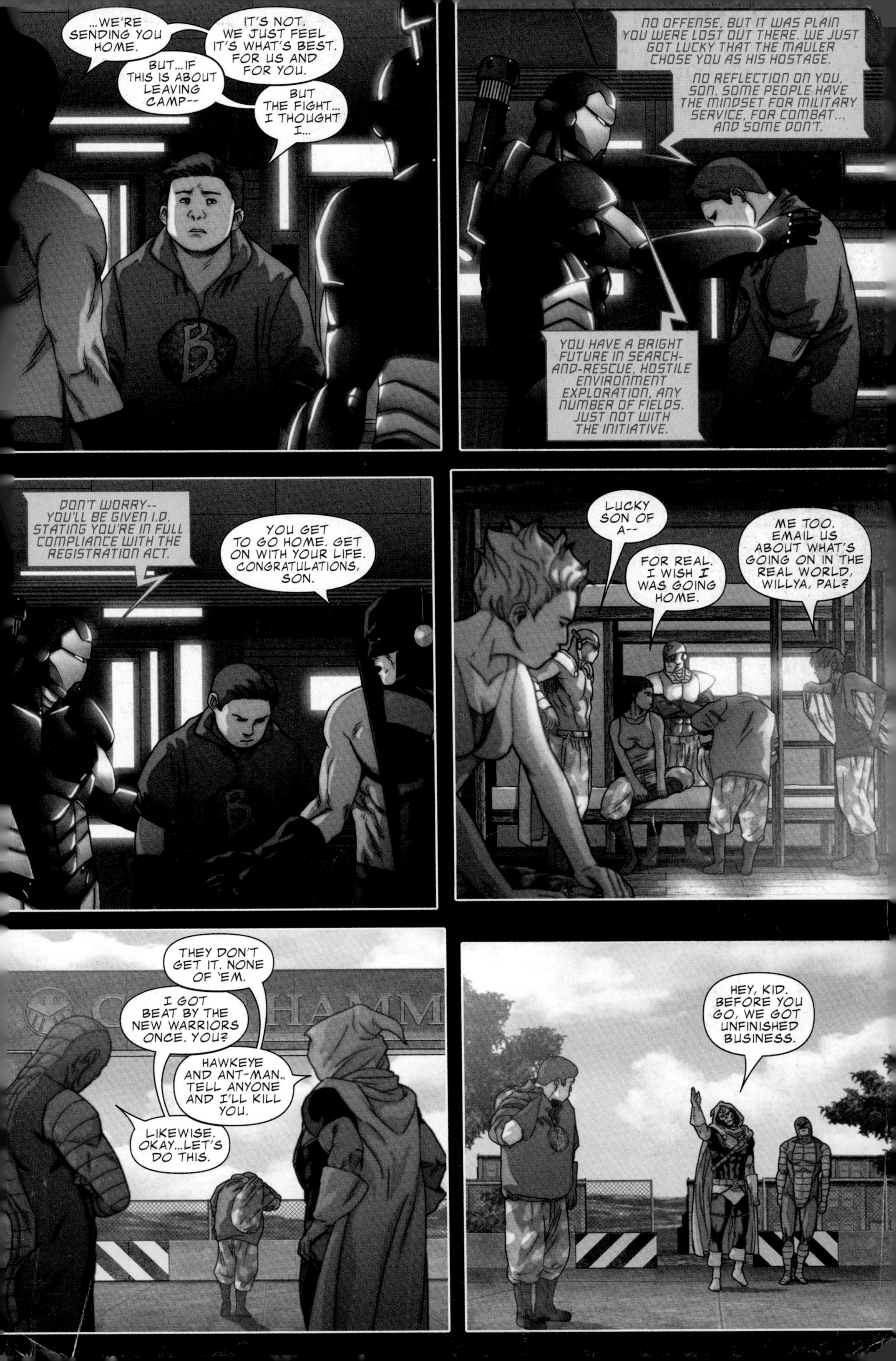
...WE'RE SENDING YOU HOME.
BUT...IF THIS IS ABOUT LEAVING CAMP--
IT'S NOT. WE JUST FEEL IT'S WHAT'S BEST. FOR US AND FOR YOU.
BUT THE FIGHT... I THOUGHT I...
NO OFFENSE, BUT IT WAS PLAIN YOU WERE LOST OUT THERE. WE JUST GOT LUCKY THAT THE MAULER CHOSE YOU AS HIS HOSTAGE.
NO REFLECTION ON YOU, SON. SOME PEOPLE HAVE THE MINDSET FOR MILITARY SERVICE, FOR COMBAT... AND SOME DON'T.
YOU HAVE A BRIGHT FUTURE IN SEARCH-AND-RESCUE, HOSTILE ENVIRONMENT EXPLORATION, ANY NUMBER OF FIELDS. JUST NOT WITH THE INITIATIVE.
DON'T WORRY-- YOU'LL BE GIVEN I.D. STATING YOU'RE IN FULL COMPLIANCE WITH THE REGISTRATION ACT.
YOU GET TO GO HOME. GET ON WITH YOUR LIFE. CONGRATULATIONS, SON.
LUCKY SON OF A--
FOR REAL. I WISH I WAS GOING HOME.
ME TOO. EMAIL US ABOUT WHAT'S GOING ON IN THE REAL WORLD, WILLYA, PAL?
THEY DON'T GET IT. NONE OF 'EM.
I GOT BEAT BY THE NEW WARRIORS ONCE. YOU?
HAWKEYE AND ANT-MAN. TELL ANYONE AND I'LL KILL YOU.
LIKEWISE. OKAY...LET'S DO THIS.
HEY, KID. BEFORE YOU GO, WE GOT UNFINISHED BUSINESS.

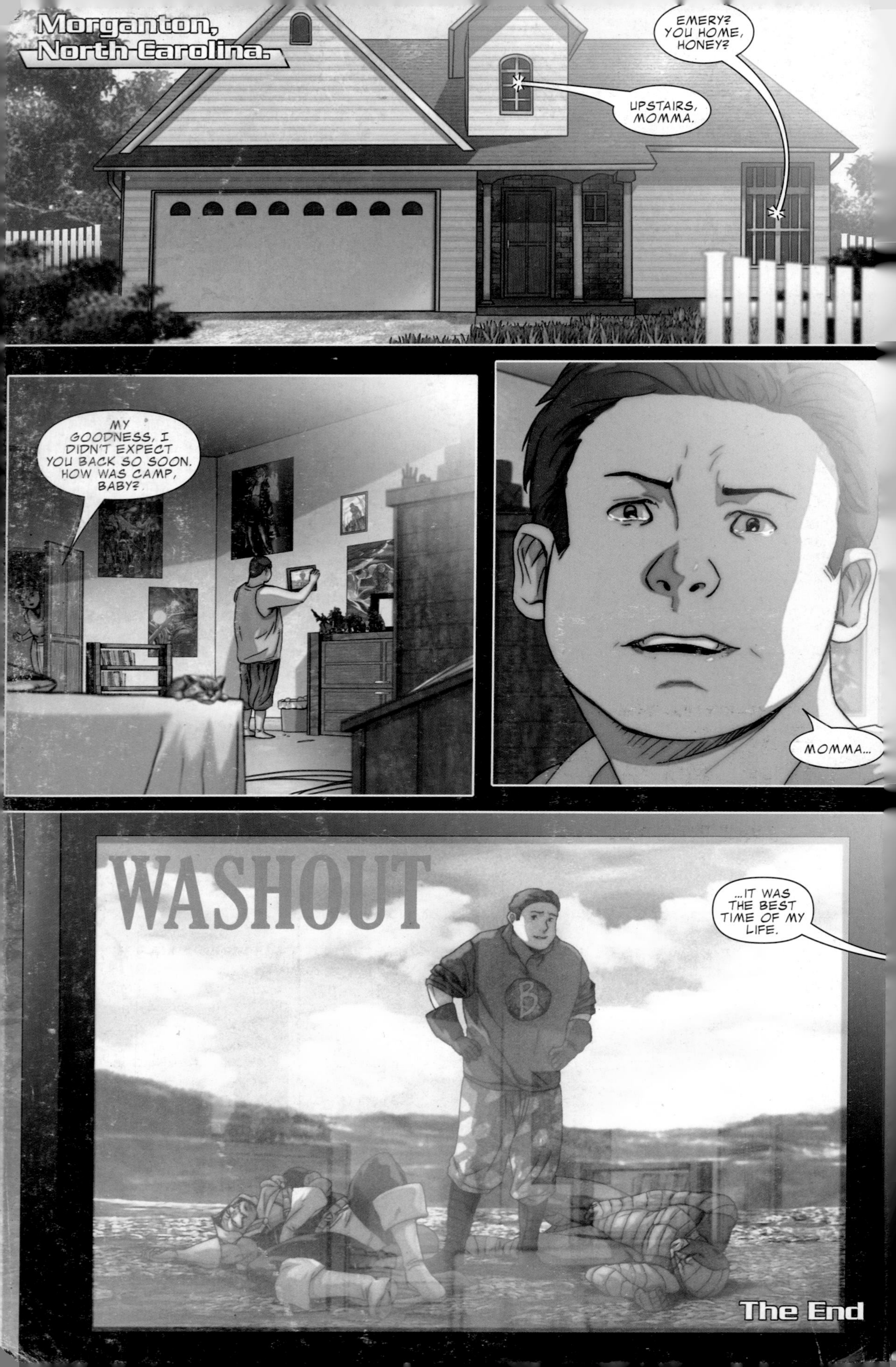
Morganton, North Carolina.
EMERY? YOU HOME, HONEY?
UPSTAIRS, MOMMA.
MY GOODNESS, I DIDN'T EXPECT YOU BACK SO SOON. HOW WAS CAMP, BABY?
MOMMA...
WASHOUT
...IT WAS THE BEST TIME OF MY LIFE.
The End